EARLY URBAN LIFE IN THE LAND OF ANSHAN: EXCAVATIONS AT TAL-E MALYAN IN THE HIGHLANDS OF IRAN

Aerial view of Malyan (Photograph by Georg Gerster, 1978).

University Museum Monograph 117

MALYAN EXCAVATION REPORTS
William M. Sumner, Series Editor
VOLUME III

EARLY URBAN LIFE IN THE LAND OF ANSHAN: EXCAVATIONS AT TAL-E MALYAN IN THE HIGHLANDS OF IRAN

William M. Sumner

With Contributions by John Alden, P. Nicholas Kardulias, Annette Ericksen, Samuel K. Nash, Vincent Pigott, Holly Pittman, David Reese, Harry C. Rogers, and Massimo Vidale

University of Pennsylvania Museum
of Archaeology and Anthropology
Philadelphia

Sumner, William M.
    Early urban life in the land of Anshan : excavations at Tal-e Malyan
in the highlands of Iran / William M. Sumner ; with contributions by
John Alden ... [et. al.]
        p. cm. – (Malyan excavation reports ; v. 3) (University Museum
monograph)
Includes bibliographical references and index.
    ISBN 1-931707-45-6
    1. Anshan (Extinct city) 2. Excavations (Archaeology)–Iran–Anshan
(Extinct city) I. Title. II. Series. III. Series: University Museum
monograph
DS262.A57 S86 2003
935–dc21
                                        2003002452

Printed in the United States of America on acid-free paper.

Published with the support of the Hagop Kevorkian Fund

Contents

Tables

Illustrations

Figures

Plates

Preface

Tal-e Malyan has been known as an archaeological site at least from the mid-nineteenth century. Ancient ruins at the village of Malyan are mentioned in the Fars Nameh Nasiri, published in 1896 based on a survey of Fars Province conducted by Hasan-e Fasa'i beginning in 1863 (Fasa'i 1896). The first archaeological excavations at the site, conducted by Feridun Tavallali in about 1960, have never been published.

My first visit to Malyan was on March 27, 1968 during the course of a regional survey of the Kur River Basin (hereafter KRB) carried out as a dissertation research project under the supervision of Robert H. Dyson, Jr. During that visit I was amazed by the sheer size of the site—at some 200 hectares, larger than any site I had visited in the valley. Sherds on the surface of the site indicated that it was occupied at least intermittently from Proto-Elamite times (Banesh Phase) until Islamic times. Surface finds discovered later pushed the earliest occupation back to Jari times in the 6th millennium. Early in 1970 I discussed the site with Dr. John Hansman who later published a convincing analysis of geographical and historical evidence identifying the site as Anshan, one of the two royal capital cities of the Elamite realm (Hansman 1972). Following discussions with Robert H. Dyson, Jr., then curator of the Near Eastern Section, I proposed trial excavations under University Museum sponsorship. This proposal was approved by the Expeditions Committee of the University Museum Board of Managers in December 1970 and the first season was planned for the following summer.

On March 5, 1971, while preparing for the first season of excavations, a second visit to the site was made in the company of Pierre and Battya de Miroschedji. At that time a fragmentary exemplar of the Hutélutush-Inshushinak brick (Lambert 1972) was discovered on the surface. This brick, along with other fragments collected later that year, allowed Erica Reiner (1973) to confirm the identification of Malyan with Anshan.

Excavations under the sponsorship of the University Museum were conducted in 1971, 1972, 1974, 1976, and 1978. This is the third volume in a projected series of monographic reports on the University Museum, University of Pennsylvania excavations at the site. The first volume, by Ilene Nicholas (1990), reports on the excavations in a small isolated mound in the northeastern corner of the site, which was occupied only in the Banesh period. The second volume, by Elizabeth Carter (1996) reports on the excavation of a large Middle Elamite building located on an elevation near the center of the west edge of the mound. Monographs are also available on some of the Middle Elamite texts (Stolper 1984) and on faunal and economic analysis (Zeder 1991). A monograph on glyptic is in preparation (Pittman n.d.). Finally, dissertations or theses are available on botanical remains, agriculture, and environment (Miller 1982), craft production in the Kaftari period (J. L. Nickerson 1983), human and animal figurines (J. W. Nickerson 1979), faunal analysis (Zeder 1985b), and Banesh settlement patterns (Alden 1979). The present work completes the publication of the major Banesh Period levels excavated at the site.

Acknowledgments

The excavations at Tal-e Malyan were sponsored by the University Museum of the University of Pennsylvania. I owe my first debt of gratitude to Robert H. Dyson, Jr., who, as curator of the Near Eastern Section of the museum, encouraged me to initiate the project and convinced the Expeditions Committee and Froelich G. Rainey, then Director of the Museum, to approve the project and to provide the essential initial funding for the 1971 season. It was an extraordinary act of faith on Dyson's part to entrust such a project to an untried Ph.D. candidate. Since then, as Curator, and later as Director of the Museum, he has been steadfast in his support for the project. He has provided valuable advice on everything from research design to practical matters of funding, staffing, and management. He supervised and encouraged students working on the project and he was a source of strength in moments of crisis.

I wish to acknowledge the encouragement and support provided throughout the project by Henry Wright. He supervised the dissertations of John Alden, Naomi Miller (paleoethnobotany) and Melinda Zeder (archaeozoology) who have made such valuable contributions to our understanding of the architecture, stratigraphy, subsistence economy and environment of Malyan. M. James Blackman (mineralogy, geology) has been with the project since 1975 and has made fundamental contributions to our understanding of materials, technology, production systems and trade.

I owe an additional debt of gratitude to John Alden, who completed the initial analysis of the Banesh Period levels in Operation ABC. He analyzed the basic stratigraphy and drafted the building plans that are published here in slightly modified form. The report in Chapter I relies heavily on his careful analysis and clear understanding; I am, of course, responsible for my modifications of his conclusions. He also prepared the final topographic map of the site.

Site supervisors who actually supervised and recorded the excavations in Operation ABC are listed in the Introduction. The value of this account is fundamentally a result of their talent and diligence.

The Malyan computer register, part of which is published here in Appendix A, was produced by Kathleen MacLean. She coded finds registered in the early seasons before the computer system was established and edited all entries for consistency. Without her attention to detail and keen eye for inconsistencies, none of the Malyan publications could have been as accurate and detailed as they are.

Other members of the staff who made essential contributions, directly or indirectly, to the work in Operation ABC, either in the field or in the laboratory were:

Jack Martin Balcer, The Ohio State University, Photographer, 1976
Carol Beeman, Field Registrar, 1974, 1976
Elizabeth Carter, University of California at Los Angeles, Asstistant Field Director, 1972-78
Romayne Downey, Artist, 1971
Peter Farries, Sherd Yard, 1971
Annette Ericksen, The Ohio State University, Research Assistant, 1988-90
Mary Virginia Harris, University of Pennsylvania, Field Registrar, 1972
Bari Hill, The Ohio State University, Sherd Yard and Ceramic Analysis, 1976
Aaron Keirns, The Ohio State University, Artist, Draftsman, 1975-1981
Betty Kole, The Ohio State University, Assistant Field Registrar, 1978
Renata Liggett, University of California at Los Angeles, Sherd Yard and Epigrapher, 1978
Brian MacDonald, Topographic Survey, 1972

Janet Nickerson, The Ohio State University, Artist, 1974–78
Peggy Sanders, The Oriental Institute, Artist, Computer Assisted Drafting, 1990–97
Frances Sumner, Field Registrar, 1971
Kathleen MacLean, The Ohio State University, Registrar and Research Asstistant 1976–81
Susan Wolkow, The Ohio State University, Artist and Sherd Yard, 1972

In addition, many work study students and volunteers at The Ohio State University worked diligently to assist with many details as this report was written.

Our work was facilitated in many ways by Dr. Firouz Bagherzadeh, Director of the Iranian Centre for Archaeological Research and the representatives of the Centre who shared our work in the field:

Haydeh Eqbal, 1978
Mohammed Mavedat, 1976
Jaffar Nikkah, 1974
Aschar Mir Fattah, 1971, 1972

Funding for excavation, analysis, and publication of the Malyan project was provided by grants or gifts from the following institutions: The American Council of Learned Societies, The Boston Museum of Fine Arts, The Ford Foundation Travel Grant Program, The National Geographic Society, The National Science Foundation (SOC75-01483, BNS76-0645, BNS79-05860), The National Endowment for the Humanities (RO-21677-88), The University of California at Los Angeles, Harvard University, The Metropolitan Museum of Art, New York, The University of Michigan, The Ohio State University, The University of Oregon, The University Museum Excavation Fund, University of Pennsylvania, The Oriental Institute of the University of Chicago, The Hagop Kevorkian Fund, and private donors. In addition, analysis has been performed using the staff and resources of The Smithsonian Institution, The National Institute of Standards and Technology, and MASCA at The University of Pennsylvania Museum of Archaeology and Anthropology.

I am grateful for the many constructive comments made by John Alden and Henry Wright who both read the completed manuscript. I wish to thank Walda Metcalf, Director of Publications, for guiding this book into print. I am most grateful to Matthew J. Manieri, Production Editor, for his forebearance with my request for many changes, for his careful attention to detail, and his creative solutions to a number of formatting and production problems. I alone accept responsibility for all errors, omissions, or mistaken analysis and interpretation.

The work at Malyan could never have been accomplished without the support of the many institutions and individuals mentioned here and others whose contributions are difficult to enumerate. To all of them I offer my gratitude and the hope that this report will serve as some measure of compensation for their participation in this attempt to reach a new understanding of our shared cultural heritage from ancient Iran.

Introduction

Until very recently the primacy of Sumerian civilization over its neighbors to the east has been taken for granted, at least in part because excavations in southern Babylonia during the early decades of the twentieth century provided such a wealth of detail on Sumer, in contrast to our meager knowledge of Elam and Anshan. The *oikumene*, the great culture region, of archaic Near Eastern civilization extended far to the west along the upper reaches of the Euphrates and beyond Anshan to the east. Within this vast territory the urbanizing polities, the farmers, and the pastoralists not only shared a joint history, but were also inextricably entangled in a single network of ecological and evolutionary processes that form the context and much of the motivating force behind their history. From this perspective the notion of historical priority has little meaning and the task of scholarship is to make comprehensible a history composed of intricate social relationships set in an environmental mosaic composed of both unifying and fragmenting elements.

The great city-states of Sumer—well known from excavations at Ur, Warka, and other sites in southern Babylonia—stand as fundamental exemplars of archaic civilization for archaeologists, ancient historians, and in the popular imagination. Excavations in Sumerian cities revealed temples, ordinary houses, and a rich variety of objects ranging from spectacular works of art wrought in precious materials to prosaic utilitarian objects of stone and clay. Archaic Sumerian economic texts and lexical lists, together with literary texts preserved in later copies, add detail and texture to our vision of Sumerian history, culture, and economic life. The literary texts also document Sumerian contacts with its nearest neighbors to the east—among them, Elam and Anshan, located in the foothills and highland valleys of the Zagros mountains. Although these early references are in the form of heroic myths of uncertain historicity, they nevertheless forcefully introduce in vivid detail the characteristic forms of interaction between Sumer and Elam/Anshan. These stories tell of trade to supply rare materials for Sumerian craftsmen, diplomacy to assure the flow of trade and to adjust the balance of power and, when all else fails—warfare.

The earliest history of Elamite civilization has long been overshadowed by Sumer because, with the notable exception of Susa, almost no Elamite sites were known until recently. The past decades have witnessed an era of flourishing archaeological research in Persia that has at last provided evidence of the high cultural accomplishments of the people of Anshan in particular, and of highland Elamites in general. This new perspective, the recognition of a flourishing Elamite civilization in the Zagros mountains, and the view of Sumer from the mountains, demands a reconsideration of the historical trajectory and evolutionary forces that formed early Near Eastern civilizations. The hint of intense interaction on a grand geographical scale, found in such poetic tales as "Enmerkar and the Lord of Aratta" and "Lugalbanda and the Thunderbird" (Jacobsen 1987) is given substance by archaeological discoveries at Malyan and contemporary sites in the Zagros mountains and on the Iranian plateau.

The earliest marker of Elamite civilization is an assortment of administrative artifacts that includes Proto-Elamite (hereafter P-E) tablets, cylinder seals, and clay sealings found in association at sites within a large geographical territory from Susa in the west to Shahr-i Sokhta in the east. Although P-E tablets and Archaic Sumerian texts share a number of attributes, they are differentiated by many specific details, which support the conclusion that they do indeed represent two different languages (Stolper 1985).

It has been shown that the development of Near Eastern writing was preceded by a long evolutionary phase in which small clay tokens, often enclosed in clay envelopes bearing seal impressions, were used to record local transactions. The last refinements of the token system in the Elamite world occurred at Susa and other sites in Khuzistan at a time when the archaeological record indicates that Susa was under Sumerian political domination. In addition to identical ceramics, the complex tokens from Sumer (Uruk) and Susa were practically indistinguishable (Schmandt-Besserat 1986, 1992). This period was followed by a complete change in the cultural assemblage at Susa; new ceramic and glyptic styles appeared and Proto-Elamite writing was introduced. At first the tablets bore only numerical impressions, but soon pictographs and abstract signs were added and a form of logographic writing evolved. Although the P-E texts are not entirely decipherable, it is clear that they record transactions related to local distribution and storage of commodities under the control of kinship, state, or temple administrative units (Amiet 1966, Damerow and Englund 1989, Lamberg-Karlovsky 1986, Vallat 1986). This administrative recording system best indicates the unity of the otherwise culturally diverse Proto-Elamite world, now uniting Susa, no longer under Sumerian domination, with Anshan and the other centers in the Zagros mountains and on the Iranian plateau. These centers represent the earliest stage in the development of those Elamite polities: Anshan, Awan, Marhashi, and Shimashki (Steinkeller 1982, Stolper 1982, Vallat 1980), that soon contended with one another and with Mesopotamian states and empires in the ancient Near Eastern geopolitical arena.

At this critical juncture in Elamite history, Anshan (Malyan) was the largest urban center with a population of at least 4,000, perhaps as great as 16,000, dwelling in a city of at least 40 hectares, perhaps twice that area. The city was a craft production center, a center of trade, and an administrative center mediating local exchange among craftsman, farmers specializing in field crops, and pastoral nomads herding flocks of sheep and goats. This monograph, which provides a description of an elite quarter in the city of Anshan, set in the regional and international context of the times, constitutes a novel perspective on ancient Near Eastern civilization.

Excavations at Tal-e Malyan

Tal-e Malyan, located 46 km north of Shiraz in Fars Province, Iran (Figs. 1 and 2), is the site of Anshan, a major Elamite city, comparable to Susa in size and importance. The ancient city wall embankment encloses more than 200 hectares, and the habitation mound within the wall occupies 130 hectares (Figs. 3, 4, and Frontispiece). Although first occupied in the Jari Period (ca. 5500 B.C.) or earlier, Malyan flourished during four great eras: the Banesh Period, when P-E texts were present (ca. 3500-2800 B.C.), the Kaftari Period (ca. 2200-1600 B.C.), The Middle Elamite Period (ca. 1300-1000 B.C.), and the Sasanian Period.

The objectives of the initial excavation season in 1971 were threefold: 1) to excavate a stratified chronological sequence, 2) to conduct a systematic surface survey of the site designed to locate areas where deposits of various periods could be efficiently explored, and 3) to conduct trial excavations to identify the sub-surface characteristics of various topographic features of the site. Although we did not conduct a topographic survey of the site until 1972, it was already apparent from aerial photographs and surface reconnaissance that a traditional step trench down the side of the site would not serve our chronological purpose because the city wall along the edge of the mound, representing discrete construction and reconstruction events, would not have provided the more continuous and detailed stratigraphic record required to establish a ceramic chronology for the site. Therefore we decided to excavate several soundings in different topographic features of the site with the expectation that these separate soundings could be linked by stylistic analysis of ceramics and other artifacts to produce a general stylistic chronology based on stratified deposits. In 1971 two adjacent 10x10 m Operations, A and B, and a narrow step trench, Test Trench D, were opened to explore stratigraphy in the central plateau area of the site. In subsequent seasons the upper strata of the site were excavated in Operations EDD, GHI, GGX98, FX106 and several less productive operations. Operation TUV was opened to explore Banesh levels in a small isolated mound within the NE corner of the city wall.

By the end of the 1978 season 3300 m^2 (0.25% of the site area) had been excavated in operations ranging in depth from 1 to 8 m and in area from small soundings to extensive openings consisting of 10 adjacent 10x10 m squares. The stratigraphic and chronological results of excavations in Operation ABC are presented in Chapters I and III.

Excavation of Operation ABC

Operation ABC at Malyan produced the largest exposure of Banesh or contemporary high status residences or public buildings excavated in Iran to date.

Building Level 2 (hereafter BL 2), with a storeroom containing 12 huge polychrome storage jars, was constructed on a monumental scale extending beyond the limits of excavation (26x16 m) in all directions. BL 3 is a sumptuous 17 room structure, also extending beyond the limits of excavation (25x15 m), with elaborately painted walls (J. W. Nickerson 1977), and other indications of high status. BL 4 (20x10 m) and BL 5 (13x10 m) produced substantial, well-built structures that provided considerable evidence of domestic activities and craft production.

Finds from these buildings include Proto-Elamite texts (Stolper 1985), cylinder seals, a large collection of sealings (Pittman infra and n. d.), elaborate relief-decorated jars and a variety of utilitarian ceramics, stone vessels, many small objects, including semi-precious stones, gold ornaments, copper artifacts, and other indicators of elite status. Subsistence and craft production activities are well represented by botanical remains (Miller 1984a), animal bones (Zeder 1984, 1985a, 1991), imported and local mineral raw materials (Blackman 1984), and cupriferous slag (Pigott, Rogers, and Nash, Chapter IV). These finds constitute a unique source of information on activities conducted in an elite quarter of a city founded in the earliest stages of Elamite history. Banesh finds from contemporary levels at other operations provide important information on an isolated domestic and craft production center (Operation TUV, Nicholas 1990), the city wall (Operation BY8, Sumner 1985), and Banesh stratigraphy (Operation H5). These excavations, a systematic surface survey, and isolated finds in other excavations (Operations EE16, F26, Z46, and XX) provide information on the spatial organization of other quarters in the Banesh Period city.

Operation ABC is the general designation for a group of 6 adjacent 10x10 m squares: Operations A, A1, B, B1, C, C1, and 3 operations established to excavate the lower levels: ABCN, ABCS, and ABC. The location of Operation ABC on the site is shown in Figure 4 and the plan of the individual operations and the limit of excavations in each season are indicated in Figure 5. The datum point for the 10x10 m site grid was established at the SW corner of Operation A in the flat plateau area of the site. This flat area was characterized by a dense surface concentration of Kaftari sherds. Test Trench D was located on a gentle slope just to the south of Operation A; a relatively high density of Partho-Sasanian sherds were found on the surface at the top of this slope. The year of excavation and the site supervisor for each of the ABC operations are as follows:

A	1971	Michael Nimtz, University of Pennsylvania
B	1971	Vincent Pigott, University of Pennsylvania
B	1971	Margery Weishaar, University of Pennsylvania
C	1972	Margery Weishaar, University of Pennsylvania
A1	1972	Michael Nimtz, University of Pennsylvania
B1	1972	Vincent Pigott, University of Pennsylvania
C1	1972	Edward Hale, Ohio State University
ABCN	1974	John Nickerson, Ohio State University
ABCS	1974	John Alden, University of Michigan
ABCS	1974	Vesta Sarkosh, Institute of Archaeology, University of London
ABC	1976	John Alden, The University of Michigan
ABC	1978	Rita Wright, Harvard University

A Kaftari trash deposit with interspersed fragmentary buildings was encountered in the upper strata of all 6 adjacent 10x10 m ABC (A, A1, B, B1, C, C1) operations. Soundings were excavated into Banesh strata in all 6 of these operations but the main horizontal exposure of Banesh levels was accomplished in the reduced area of Operations ABCN and ABCS in 1974, and Operation ABC in 1976. Operation ABC in 1978 was restricted to a sounding below Banesh levels. The reduction in the area excavated in the lower strata provided platforms to facilitate the removal of excavated earth and a margin of safety if the scarp should collapse.

The excavation and recording procedure followed at Malyan was a modified version of the practices developed by Robert Dyson, Jr., at Hasanlu and T. Cuyler Young, Jr., at Godin Tepe. The basic unit of excavation was the *Lot*, defined in the Malyan *Instructions for Excavation and Recording* as "an arbitrary or natural subdivision of any natural or cultural stratum or feature." Since lots could always be combined in analysis, but could never be divided, site supervisors were encouraged to keep lots small and to change lot numbers frequently as a means of minimizing the damage caused by missing a stratigraphic or feature boundary. Despite the best of intentions, the economizing property of human nature would sometimes prevail, and huge lots would be excavated. On one occasion a site supervisor complained of "being forced to use up too many numbers."

The standard recording practice, tersely outlined in the 1971 instructions to site supervisors, evolved with experience, and by 1974 the information to be recorded for each lot included the exact boundaries in three dimensions, the provisional field stratum number to which the lot was assigned, the feature number in which the lot was located, and the deposit code assigned to the lot. This information was recorded in the site supervisor's narrative notes and in a columnar *Lot Index* designed to facilitate the transfer of information to a computer data base. In the 1976 and 1978 editions of the *Instructions for Excavation and Recording,* several new codes were added: a period code, a code to identify the type of feature in which each lot was located, and a code to indicate mixed lots.

The concept of a *Deposit Code,* intended to indicate the nature of each deposit, and related to the notion that artifacts or other items found in different types of deposit should be interpreted in terms of what we now call site formation processes (Schiffer 1972, 1976), was certainly not invented at Malyan. Although it is possible that we were influenced by Schiffer's seminal publications, the most important influence on the evolving Malyan recording system was simply the experience we shared in attempting to interpret the relationship between finds in the excavated archaeological context and the antecedent human activities that resulted in the initial formation of the archaeological record.

The term *"find"* as used here and throughout this report includes all items removed from archaeological deposits and entered in the register of finds (Appendix A). Finds are not restricted to artifacts, but also include possible raw materials, incomplete or broken artifacts, production by-products, and certain types of samples (see Appendix A for further discussion). Each registered find has a unique "Malyan find number" that is identified by the prefix "mf" in lower case. Some finds are also assigned a "Malyan object number" that is identified by the prefix "M" in upper case. The purpose of "M" numbers, which are not used in this report, is described in Appendix A. Ceramic sherds and animal bones, recovered in considerable quantity, were recorded in bulk by lot number and were not entered in the register of finds except under special circumstances.

As we considered the problem of deposit types we recognized that the initial patterns created by human activity were subject to ongoing alteration— "transformations" in Schiffer's (1976) terminology—by further human activity as well as natural processes. There was no attempt to make a close analysis of these processes, although in retrospect I believe such analysis would be of great value. Thus, the deposit codes, discussed in Chapter I, represent a broad classification of deposits into three categories with several sub-types in each category. In the final analysis only 15 deposit codes were used in the ABC Banesh excavations: no primary deposits, 5 secondary deposit types (21, 22, 23, 28, 29), and 10 tertiary codes (31, 34, 35, 36, 37, 39, 40, 41, 49, and 50). The analytical implications of deposit code classifications are discussed by Nicholas (1980: 107-126; 1990: 15-20) and in Chapters I, and IV below.

I

Stratigraphy and Architecture

The purpose of this chapter is to describe the stratigraphic sequence and the architectural features of the Banesh building levels excavated in Operation ABC. The stratigraphic and spatial units identified in this analysis will, in turn, serve as the framework for analysis of artifacts, raw materials, production by-products, trash, animal bone, botanical remains, and pottery presented in Chapters II and IV. The stratigraphy section, organized from the surface down, is intended to present an analysis and description of the superimposed stratigraphic units within and between building levels as they were excavated. The emphasis in this section is on the composition or nature of each deposit and the depositional processes that created the observed stratigraphic sequence. Thus, stratigraphic deposits are conceptualized as solid units composed of clay, bricky rubble, or trash along with the embedded finds (Register of Finds, Appendix A), bones, and sherds that were removed in the course of excavation (Lot Inventory, Appendix B).

The architecture section, presented from the earliest to the latest building level, is intended to recover the sequence of construction and occupation events and to provide a description of excavated architectural units: area, court, corridor, or room, and features: door, bench, hearth, oven, pit, platform, trash pile, or wall (Feature Inventory, Appendix C). Although there is some redundancy between the stratigraphic analysis and the presentation of building levels, the focus in this section is on empty spaces such as rooms, defined along the vertical dimension by surfaces and floors and along the horizontal dimension by walls. The descrip-

tion also includes small features such as hearths that are located within rooms or other spaces. A brief description is provided of the types of finds from each area, court, corridor, and room. Each find mentioned in the text is identified with a registration number, such as "mf 000" as defined in the Register of Finds (Appendix A). An analysis of finds and production and consumption activities is provided in Chapter IV.

Excavation Recording

Deposit Codes

The basic excavation and recording unit at Malyan was the *lot*, assigned a sequential number within each operation. Each lot is assigned a *deposit code*, abbreviated "DC", which identifies a type of deposit identified and classified on the basis of color, texture, hardness, and other properties such as chunkiness or lamination. Deposit codes are classified in three broad categories: 1) primary deposits (DC 11-17) such as undisturbed finds on the floor of an abandoned room or the contents of an intact burial, 2) secondary deposits (DC 21-29) such as trash on surfaces or in pits, or primary deposits disturbed in antiquity, and 3) tertiary deposits (DC 31-50) such as purposeful construction fill or natural deposits resulting from destruction of buildings by erosion. All deposit codes used at Malyan are shown in Table 1, as listed in *Instructions for Excavation and Recording, Malyan 1978*. Deposit codes used in ABC Banesh strata are indicated by an

Table 1. MALYAN DEPOSIT CODES

Primary Deposits

11	Undisturbed floor deposit; artifacts abandoned on the floor where they were last used. Plan and photograph all finds *in situ*.
12	Undisturbed surface deposit, courtyard, open area. Plan and photograph all finds *in situ*.
13	Burial deposit (each burial deposit should have a separate lot number). Plan and photograph all finds *in situ*.
14	Cache. Plan and photograph all finds *in situ*.
15	Cluster: a group of objects apparently deposited together, not on a surface or floor.
16	Collapsed second-story floor deposit.
17	Artificially deposited pebble/cobble layer (added for Operation TUV, Stratum 2).

Secondary Deposits

21*	Trash deposits on a floor or surface; unlike DC 11, this is the result of bad housekeeping, not sudden abandonment. Trash accumulation occurred before the room was abandoned as a habitation. Deposit is probably compacted and relatively level. Not sloping much at the sides. Use careful judgment on whether or not to plan and photograph *in situ*.
22*	Trash in a pit or well; boundaries of the pit or well must be clearly defined.
23*	Amorphous trashy deposit, boundaries must be difficult to establish.
24	Disturbed burial.
25	Disturbed floor or surface deposit. Use this code only if deposit is extensively disturbed, otherwise use DC 11.
26	Trash deposit which accumulated on a surface within a room after that room was abandoned as a habitation. Difficult to identify; probably sloping against walls. See definition of DC 21.
27	Ceiling collapse.
28*	Contents of kiln, hearth, or container.
29*	Removal of floor surface. Actual material floor is made of.

Tertiary Deposits

31*	Surface pickup.
32	Disturbed top soil.
33	Rodent burrow.
34*	Amorphous bricky fill, associated wall not identified.
35*	Bricky fill below tops of identified walls.
36*	Feature removal; this refers to the actual material a feature is made of, the bricks in a wall, the clay of a hearth.
37*	Arbitrary floor cleaning lot composed of bricky or other fill which cannot be identified as having a trash component.
38	Balk removal code. Not to be used in the future.
39*	Dump.
40*	Unknown.
41*	Clean-up.
42	Non bricky fill within identified walls.
43	Rocky-trash fill not associated with mud brick walls.
44	Surface wash.
45	Sandy fill probably water laid product of erosion.
46	Sample.
47	Mixed fill with some brick components not within identified walls.
48	Mixed fill with some brick components within identified walls.
49*	Redeposited material.
50*	Sterile natural soil deposit.

* Deposit codes used in ABC Banesh levels

asterisk and are described and analyzed in the following paragraphs.

This system of deposit codes was a pragmatic development that took place during the course of field work. The initial list of deposit codes was expanded, mostly in the tertiary range (DC 42-49), at the request of site supervisors who were working in deposits that did not seem to fit into the system. In addition, several codes do not indicate deposit types at all (DC 31, 38, 39, 41, 46), but rather conditions created in the course of excavation. These conditions should have been covered by a coding system designed to deal with excavation and recording errors or problems as discussed below in the section on mixed lots. The codes were first used for analytical purposes and published by Nicholas (1990:16-20, Figs. 8, 9 and 10).

Deposit codes serve two functions: 1) as a broad classification of deposits in terms of site formation processes, which facilitates discussion of the sequence of construction, occupation, maintenance, and destruction events by which the observed stratigraphy was created and, 2) to facilitate the interpretation of finds, sherds, and bones embedded in excavated deposits. Thus, deposit codes are one indication of the level of relevance that finds bear to cultural activities in the vicinity of each building level, and in some instances even within particular buildings or rooms. Deposit codes (DC) are listed in the Register (Appendix A) and in the Lot Inventory (Appendix B). Finds, bones, and sherds are usually assigned the deposit code of the lot in which they were found. In some cases different parts of a lot or individual finds from a given lot may be assigned different deposit codes on the basis of information in the field notes. All such instances are indicated in the Lot Inventory (Appendix B) by multiple entries when more than one DC is assigned to items from a single lot.

No primary deposits were identified in the ABC building levels reported here. Although some individual finds and clusters of finds were found on floors, they all appear to be the result of gradual trash accumulation before abandonment. Clearly identifiable secondary trashy deposits are present, but relatively rare in these levels. Tertiary deposits are the most common type of deposit identified at ABC. The characteristics of

Table 2. NUMBER OF FINDS BY DEPOSIT CODE AND LOT INDICATOR

DC	G	H	M	B	K	SUM
21	902	0	0	0	0	902
22	74	0	0	0	0	74
23	287	0	0	0	0	287
28	27	0	0	0	0	27
29	225	32	13	1	0	271
31	0	0	0	3	0	3
34	26	0	19	0	0	45
35	80	46	114	5	2	247
36	153	0	58	0	0	211
37	267	17	39	0	0	323
39	0	0	1	3	0	4
40	0	0	0	8	0	8
41	0	0	32	46	0	78
49	11	0	0	0	0	11
50	46	0	0	0	0	46
SUM	2098	95	276	66	2	2537

DC = deposit code, G = unmixed lot; H = horizontally mixed lot found in more than one feature, M = vertically mixed lot found in more than one stratum, B = Banesh and K = Kaftari, assigned to finds from mixed lots on stylistic criteria

the various deposit types are discussed below in the section on deposit code analysis.

In addition to deposit codes, each lot was assigned a lot indicator code (column LI in Appendixes A and B) that indicates the status of each lot or find in terms of recovery and recording. Lot indicator (LI) G is assigned to lots that are not stratigraphically mixed and come from only one bounded feature (Room, Area, Corridor, Pit); LI H is assigned to lots that are not stratigraphically mixed, but come from several bounded features. Lot indicator M is assigned to lots that come from more than one stratum. Lot indicators B (Banesh) and K (Kaftari) are assigned on the basis of stylistic criteria to finds from mixed lots (LI M) or other lots in which the context is indeterminate (DC 31, 39, 40, 41). Lot indicators are discussed in the sections below on deposit code and mixed lot analysis.

Each deposit code has a characteristic signature based on the mean values and ranges for several variables: mean find density (finds/m^3), mean sherd density (sherds/m^3), mean bone density (bones/m^3), mean bone weight (gm/bone) and mean sherd weight (gm/sherd). The analysis that produced these signatures, based on data presented in the Lot Inventory (Appendix B), is summarized in Tables 3-8. The signatures are presented in the following discussion of each deposit code used in the ABC Banesh excavations.

Trash Deposits on Floors (Deposit Code 21)

DC 21 is assigned to trash that accumulated on floors or surfaces during occupation or soon after abandonment of a building or outside area. It is assumed that finds from DC 21 deposits are generally related to nearby activities contemporary with the occupation during which the trash accumulated. These trash deposits, usually darker in color and softer than bricky rubble deposits, typically contain high concentrations of finds, sherds, and animal bones. Deposit code 21 lots excavated in ABC produced 902 finds, all from good context (LI G) (Table 2). The DC 21 deposit density signature, based on the contents of lots with estimated volume (Tables 3-6), has the following characteristics: 98.32 finds/m^3, 151 sherds/m^3, and 2299 bones/m^3. The mean weight of animal bones (Table 7) found in all DC 21 lots is 1.72 gm/bone, but the mean weight of bones in different DC 21 lots varies from 1.63 to 7.36 gm/bone (Appendix B. I). The mean weight of straw tempered rim sherds (Table 8) from DC 21 lots is 9.48 gm/sherd but varies in different lots from 9.44 to 17.5 gm/sherd (Appendix B. II).

Trash in Pits or Wells (Deposit Code 22)

DC 22 is assigned to trash that had been dumped into pits or wells. The 6 DC 22 lots excavated at ABC, all from Pit 236 in Room 64 of BL 4, produced 74 finds. The DC 22 deposit signature has the following characteristics: 304.17 finds/m^3, 408 sherds/m^3, 5554 bones/m^3. The mean weight of animal bones (Table 7) found in DC 22 lots is 2.23 gm/bone, but the mean weight of bones in different DC 22 lots varies from 1.45 to 3.35 gm/bone (Appendix B. I). The mean weight of straw tempered rim sherds (Table 8) from DC 22 lots is 13.21 gm/sherd but varies in different lots from 9.4 to 24.89 gm/sherd (Appendix B. II).

Amorphous Trash Deposits (Deposit Code 23)

DC 23 is assigned to amorphous trash deposits in Stratum 9 (ABCS Lot 46) and Stratum 10A (ABCS Lot 36) that are associated with leveling operations in preparation for the construction of BL 2. The 2 DC 23 lots excavated in ABC produced 287 finds. The DC 23 deposit signature has the following characteristics: densities are 52.14 finds/m^3, 10 sherds/m^3. Bone density and fragmentation data are not available for DC 23. Observation during excavations suggest low sherd fragmentation. The finds from these deposits, including a large collection of sealings, are likely to be related to activities contemporary with the occupation of BL 3A.

Trash in Hearths or Ovens (Deposit Code 28)

DC 28 is assigned to trash found on the surface of hearths or inside ovens. In some cases DC 28 deposits are similar to DC 21 and in other cases they resemble DC 22 deposits. The 8 DC 28 lots excavated in ABC produced 27 finds, 6 sherds, and no bones; volume estimates are not available for these lots.

Clay or Plaster Floors (Deposit Code 29)

DC 29 is assigned to the clay or plaster material of floors or surfaces. These deposits range from 2 to 10 cm in thickness, generally depending on the number of resurfacings. DC 29 lots excavated in ABC produced 269 finds. The DC 29 deposit signature has the following characteristics: densities are 8.16 finds/m^3, 20 sherds/m^3, 229 bones/m^3. The mean weight of animal bones (Table 7) found in all DC 29 lots is 1.24 gm/bone, but varies in different DC 29 lots from 0.46 to 1.81 gm/bone (Appendix B. I). The mean weight of straw tempered rim sherds (Table 8) from DC 29 lots is 10.06 gm/sherd but varies in different lots from 6.5 to 21 gm/sherd (Appendix B. II).

Although some finds from DC 29 deposits may have been brought in with clay used to resurface floors, it is also likely that many of these finds were embedded in floors or surfaces by trampling during the time the floor was in use.

Surface Finds (Deposit Code 31)

DC 31, which does not represent a deposit type, is used for 3 finds recovered from the mound surface in the vicinity of ABC and assigned to the Banesh (LI B) period on stylistic grounds.

Rubble Between Building Levels (Deposit Code 34)

DC 34 is assigned to intermediate strata (Strata 9 and 12) below the earliest floor of a later building level, but above the standing wall stubs of the preceding building level. These deposits are composed of blocky mud brick rubble of a yellow or tan color that is generally lighter in color than trashy deposits. DC 34 lots excavated in ABC produced 45 finds. The DC 34 deposit signature has the following characteristics: densities are 0.43 finds/m^3, 4 sherds/m^3, and 41 bones/m^3. The mean weight of animal bones (Table 7) from two DC 34 lots is 1.72 gm/bone (Appendix B. I). The mean weight of straw tempered rim sherds (Table 8) from DC 34 lots is 10.34 gm/sherd but varies in different lots from 7.88 to 13 gm/sherd (Appendix B. II).

Finds from DC 34 deposits are assumed to derive mainly from the bricks, mortar, and plaster of the walls razed in the construction leveling process. However, dense coherent trash deposits—coded DC 23—may be encapsulated within DC 34 deposits during ancient construction leveling activities. Finds from DC 34 deposits are assumed to be broadly related to local activities at some indeterminate time before the bricks forming the rubble were made.

Rubble Within a Building Level (Deposit Code 35)

DC 35 is assigned to bricky rubble deposits, sometimes including purposely laid bricks, above the floor of a building level but below the top of standing wall stubs of that level. DC 35 lots excavated in ABC produced 247 finds. The DC 35 deposit signature has the following characteristics: densities are 1.08 finds/m3, 11 sherds/m3, 27 bones/m3. The mean weight of animal bones (Table 7) found in one DC 35 lot is 1.03 gm/bone and varies from 0.56 to 3.4 gm/bone (Appendix B. I). The mean weight of sherds (Table 8) from one DC 35 lot is 12.5 gm/sherd (Appendix B. II).

Since BLs 5, 4, and 3 were razed, each in its turn, to make way for construction of the next building, DC 35 deposits in these levels result from construction activity similar to that responsible for DC 34 deposits. BL 2 was not razed and the DC 35 deposits are interpreted as the result of natural deterioration of the abandoned building—roof and wall collapse. There is usually little observable distinction in the character of DC 35 and DC 34 deposits and finds from these deposit types are considered to relate to activities in the general vicinity at some earlier time.

Wall and Feature Removal (Deposit Code 36)

DC 36 is assigned to feature removal lots composed of the actual bricks, mortar, plaster, and other material of which walls and other features were made. DC 36 lots excavated in ABC produced 211 finds. The DC 36 deposit signature has the following characteris-

tics: densities are 1.00 finds/m^3, 7 sherds/m^3. It is probably not coincidental that the highest density DC 36 deposit for both finds and sherds was a small lot (0.03 m^3) used to remove Doorblocking 191 in BL 2. This lot produced only 1 find and 6 sherds, suggesting the possibility that high density in this case and in other similar cases is an artifact of the ordinal nature of find counts as opposed to the continuous nature of volume measurements. The mean weight of straw tempered rim sherds (Table 8) from two DC 36 lots is 9.95 gm/sherd (Appendix B. II).

Finds from DC 36 lots are treated the same as finds from DC 34 and 35 lots. ABC produced no foundation deposits or other cases of items purposely incorporated in walls or features except for the use of sherds in the construction of hearths.

Rubble on Floors or Surfaces (Deposit Code 37)

DC 37 is assigned to bricky rubble deposits, apparently similar in composition to DC 34 and 35 deposits, but resting directly on the floor or surface of a building level. DC 37 lots excavated in ABC produced 323 finds. The DC 37 deposit signature has the following characteristics: densities are 3.11 finds/m^3, 15 sherds/m^3, 99 bones/m^3. The mean weight of animal bones (Table 7) found in DC 37 lots is 1.29 gm/bone, but the mean weight of bones in different DC 37 lots varies from 0.57 to 7 gm/bone (Appendix B. I). The mean weight of straw tempered rim sherds (Table 8) from DC 37 lots is 6.81 gm/sherd but varies in different lots from 5.68 to 14.6 gm/sherd (Appendix B. II).

It was recognized early in the analysis of Operation TUV (Nicholas 1990:15-19) that some DC 35 lots contained unusually high concentrations of sherds, bones, and finds. This finding was not a surprise—several site supervisors had commented in the field and in their notes on the difficulty often encountered in distinguishing between "bricky" and "trashy" deposits. The assignment of DC 37 to bricky floor lots allows a comparison of the find, bone, and sherd density signature of these problematic deposits with the signature of trash deposits (DC 21-29) and probable (DC 34, 35) or known (DC 36) tertiary construction material deposits. This matter is discussed below in the section on deposit code analysis.

Excavation Dump (Deposit Code 39)

DC 39, which does not represent a deposit type, is used for 4 finds recovered from the ABC excavation dump and assigned to the Banesh period on stylistic grounds (LI B).

Unknown Deposit Type (Deposit Code 40)

DC 40 is assigned to 8 finds from lots of unknown deposit type that are classified as Banesh on stylistic grounds (LI B).

Cleaning Operations (Deposit Code 41)

DC 41, which does not truly designate a deposit type, is assigned to lots used during cleaning operations at the beginning of a season or in other circumstances in which a correct provenance can not be assigned to finds. DC 41 lots are by definition mixed and the significance of DC 41 finds is problematic. There are 78 finds from DC 41 lots of which 46 are stylistically identified as Banesh (LI B). Volume estimates are not available for DC 41 lots.

Foundation Trench (Deposit Code 49)

DC 49 is assigned to the fill from the foundation trench for Wall 240 in BL 4A. The 2 DC 49 lots produced 11 finds. The DC 49 deposit signature has the following characteristics: densities are 0.96 find/m^3 and 8 sherds/m^3. No bones were recorded in these lots. This deposit is considered to be equivalent to tertiary construction fill.

Pre-construction Strata (Deposit Code 50)

DC 50 is assigned to 11 lots excavated in the sounding below BL 5, which produced 46 finds, 1 sherd and no bones; density estimates are not available for DC 50 lots. This usage constitutes a modification of the definition of DC 50, which was originally intended for natural deposits—"virgin soil."

Analysis of Deposit Codes

The deposit code system was initiated in the 1974 season. Deposit codes were assigned in the field by site supervisors in 1974, 1976, and 1978 and were retrospectively assigned to lots excavated in 1971 and 1972 on the basis of field note descriptions of deposits. Some deposit codes assigned in the field were changed in the course of analysis on the basis of field descriptions. In general this change involved assigning DC 37

to floor lots previously coded DC 35. The purpose of this change was to allow the analysis presented below to determine whether or not these lots, resting on floors or surfaces, contained significant trashy components that were not recognized in the field. A few tertiary lots were reclassified as secondary lots based on field descriptions. The most notable example of such a change is ABCS Lots 36 and 46, used to excavate dense concentrations of sealings encapsulated within the DC 34 fill of Stratum 9 (Lot 46) or the DC 35 fill of Stratum 10A (Lot 36).

The following analysis and discussion of deposit codes is based on many discussions, sometimes heated, with members of the Malyan staff, but most particularly it draws on the published work of Ilene Nicholas (1980, 1981, 1990) and correspondence between us while she was conducting her analysis. In her initial analysis of deposit codes Nicholas (1980:107-126) developed the concept of "lot content profile" in an effort to identify the characteristics of different types of deposit. Her subsequent analysis (1990:10, 15-20) was based on the concept of deposit "density signatures" in a way that is very similar to the discussion and analysis presented here. The results of her analysis of the deposits excavated at TUV are compared with the results of similar analysis for the ABC deposits in the following discussion.

Our present understanding of site formation processes, at Malyan and elsewhere, is that secondary deposits should be distinguished from tertiary deposits by differences in the density (number per cubic meter) of finds, sherds, and animal bones and by differences in the extent of fragmentation as indicated by the average weight of bones or sherds (grams/bone or sherd). It is assumed that brick-making, plastering, surface preparation, and other construction activities involved the selection of suitable material and probably also the removal of some inclusions, particularly large items. Water and wind erosion, cleaning, dumping, and trampling are additional examples of processes that may alter the density or fragmentation signature of deposits.

Ideally, the volume of all lots should be calculated on the basis of accurate field measurements at the time of excavation. At Malyan the requirement to calculate lot volume in the field was not initiated until the final season in 1978 and even then such measurements were not consistently recorded. Consequently the following density analysis is based only on those lots measured in 1978 and those lots excavated in earlier seasons for which volume could be estimated from the

Table 3. DENSITY OF FINDS BY DEPOSIT CODE

DC	NO. LOTS	NO. FINDS	VOLUME M³	DENSITY FINDS/M³
21	12	878	8.93	98.32
22	5	73	0.24	304.17
23	1	73	1.40	52.14
29	24	214	26.23	8.16
21-29	42	1238	36.80	33.64
37	71	276	88.86	3.11
34-36	79	225	228.45	0.98
34	4	10	23.44	0.4
35	52	141	130.82	1.08
36	23	74	74.19	1.00
49	1	9	9.4	0.96
	193	1748	363.11	4.81

plans, sections and field notes (Appendix B). The dimensions of the selected lots are not always easily established, and the resulting volume estimates should be considered approximate. Likewise the collection of finds was not uniform. Only selected lots, usually in secondary deposits, were screened and differences among crews, time of day, and other variables affect the recovery of finds (Appendix A and Appendix B).

The density of finds, including artifacts, raw materials, production by-products, and analytical samples, in lots for which volume estimates are available is presented by deposit code in Table 3. Lots with estimated volume, but no registered finds, are included in this analysis. Density of sherds and bones from lots for which volume estimates are available is presented in Tables 5 and 6. The bones counted in Table 6 (Appendix B) include both diagnostic and non-diagnostic bones from lots selected for analysis by Zeder (1985, Volume II:470 and personal communication). Sherd counts are based in part on counts made in the field and in part on counts made later. Sherd and bone counts were not completed for lots left in storage at Malyan or in Tehran. Therefore, lots with estimated volume, but no recorded sherds, are not used in Table 5 and lots with estimated volume, but no recorded bones, are not used in Table 6.

The following discussion compares secondary deposits (DC 21-29) with tertiary deposits (DC 34-36) excavated at ABC in terms of density (count or weight divided by m³) and fragmentation (weight in grams divided by count). In addition the density and fragmentation signatures of DC 37 deposits are compared with the same characteristics of secondary deposits on the one hand, and tertiary deposits on the other hand, to help determine how DC 37 lots should be interpreted in the analysis of finds presented in Chapter IV.

Density Patterns

Find Density Signatures

The mean find density of secondary deposit lots (DC 21-29) is 33.64 finds/m³ and the mean density for tertiary (DC 34-36) lots is 0.93 finds/m³. The find density signature of DC 37 lots, at 3.11 finds/m³, falls between the patterns observed for secondary and tertiary lots as shown in Table 3. However, lots assigned to different deposit codes present a wide range of variation in find density signatures, as summarized in Table 4.

The following discussion is based on the assumption, suggested by Tables 3 and 4, that any DC 37 lot with a find density signature greater than 8 finds/m³ is likely to contain a trash component. High density secondary lots (DC 21-23), with a signature of 8 finds/m³ or greater, account for 1197 (96.7%) of all finds from secondary lots for which volume estimates are available. This pattern for secondary deposit lots stands in sharp contrast to the pattern for tertiary lots (DC 34-36). The 5 tertiary lots with density signatures above 8 finds/m³ account for only 15 finds (7.1%). Furthermore, 1 of these lots (ABCN 112) is the removal lot (DC 36) for a door blockage with a volume of only

Table 4. DISTRIBUTION OF FIND DENSITY SIGNATURES BY DC GROUPS

DC	DENSITY RANGE	0-7	8-37	50-120	150-950	ALL
DC 21-29	LOTS	18	12	7	5	42
	FINDS	41	132	249	816	1238
DC 37	LOTS	54	14	1	2	71
	FINDS	129	54	12	81	276
DC 34-36	LOTS	74	5	0	0	79
	FINDS	210	15	0	0	225
ALL	LOTS	146	31	8	7	192
	FINDS	380	201	261	897	1739

There are 18 lots with densities betweeen 0 and 7 finds per m³; these lots contain 41 finds. DC 49 is omitted from this table and the following discussion.

0.03 m^3, an anomaly caused by the difference between ordinal and continuous scales of measurement. When this case is eliminated, the highest density for any tertiary lot (DC 34-36) is 14.29 finds/m³.

When we compare the find density signature pattern of DC 37 lots with the patterns for secondary and tertiary lots it is clear that some finds from DC 37 lots for which volume measurements are available derive from trashy floor components that were not recognized as such during excavation. The 17 DC 37 lots with a density signature of 8 or greater produced 147 finds. Following the logic noted above in the discussion of lot ABCN 112, we should eliminate 4 DC 37 lots (ABCN 69, ABCN 76, ABCN 137, and ABC 13), with estimated volume of less than 0.1 m³, which produced only 6 finds, reducing the count to 141 finds that may be from DC 37 trashy context. Within this group there are 91 finds from very high density (≥ 50 finds/m³) DC 37 lots that are most likely to derive from trashy deposits not recognized during excavation. Find densities this high are not known for other types of tertiary lots (DC 34-36). The conclusion from this examination of find density signatures is that the distinction between secondary trash deposits and tertiary bricky deposits was generally recognized during excavation. However, trashy components within bricky deposits resting on floors or surfaces clearly were not recognized in a few instances. The remaining DC 37 lots, those for which volume estimates are not available, account for only 46 finds, which may or may not be from trashy deposits.

These results are similar to the find density patterns recorded for TUV (Nicholas 1990:20, Table 4).

Finds from secondary deposits (DC 21-26) at TUV have an average density of 15 finds/m3, tertiary deposits (DC 34-36) have an average density of 2.5 finds/m3, and DC 37 lots have an average density of 3 finds/m³. However, TUV produced a richer assemblage of different types of secondary deposits, which enabled Nicholas to track a wider range in average density signatures[*]. Unscreened trash pits (DC 22B, 2 lots), produced an average find density of 20/m³, while unscreened trash piles (DC 23, 2 lots) produced only 2 finds/m³. Nicholas also demonstrated a considerable difference between some sets of screened and unscreened lots; for example, DC 37 screened lots (26 lots) produced 12 finds/m³, but only 3/m³ were recovered from unscreened lots (10 lots).

Sherd Density Signatures

Sherd density signatures occur in patterns (Table 5) similar to the patterns for find density signatures (Table 4), but are less useful because of the very wide range of density variation. This wide range of density variation may be accounted for in part by variation in the frequency of screening and in the intensity of sherd collecting by hand. The mean sherd density of secondary deposit lots (DC 21-29) is 52 sherds/m³, and varies from a low of 1.25 to a high of 4,516/m³. The mean sherd density of tertiary deposit lots (DC 34-36) is 8 sherds/m³ with a range of 0.45 to 433/m³. Mean sherd density for DC 37 lots, is 15 sherds/m³ (range 1.43 to 592/m³). These patterns provide only minimal evidence for unrecognized trashy deposits among DC 37 lots.

---

[*] The entry in Table 4 (Nicholas 1990) should read 0.250 in the Total Volume column instead of 0.025.

Table 5. DENSITY OF STRAW TEMPERED SHERDS BY DEPOSIT CODE

DC	NO. LOTS	NO. SHERDS	VOLUME M³	DENSITY SHERDS/M³
21	11	1060	7.03	151
22	5	98	0.24	408
23	1	14	1.40	10
29	18	436	22.01	202
21-29	35	1608	30.68	52
37	43	785	51.70	15
34-36	64	1811	220.54	8
34	4	81	23.44	4
35	38	1232	114.41	11
36	22	498	73.29	7
49	1	73	9.40	8
ALL	143	4277	302.92	14

Several high sherd density lots (ABCN 14, ABCN 143, ABCN 146, and ABC 13) also produced high find densities, but there are also high sherd density lots with low find density.

Grit tempered sherd densities at TUV show an interesting pattern in which tertiary lots have greater variation in density than secondary lots and the highest densities—over 200 sherds/ m³—were recorded for tertiary lots (Nicholas 1990, Fig. 8). A similar pattern characterizes densities of straw tempered sherds, although the highest densities—>800/m³—are found in two secondary lots[*].

Animal Bone Density Signatures

The mean bone density of secondary deposit lots (DC 21-29) is 1069 bones/m³ and ranges from 31 to 20,178/m³. The mean bone density of tertiary deposit lots (DC 34-35) is 31 bones/m³ with a range of 4 to 155/m³. As with find and sherd density patterns,

bone density for DC 37 lots falls between the secondary and tertiary patterns. Mean bone density for DC 37 lots is 99 bones/m³ (range 3 to 426/m³). Three of the 5 high bone density DC 37 lots (bone density ≥200/m³) coincide with lots that also have high find and sherd densities (ABCN 30, ABCN 143, and ABCN 146), supporting the proposition that these lots contained a trash component that was not recognized during excavation.

Bone density patterns at TUV (Nicholas 1990, Fig. 10)[†] are quite similar to the ABC patterns with the highest densities—>400 gm/m³ and >300 bone fragments/m³—recorded only for secondary deposits.

Summary of Density Patterns

The density of finds, sherds, and animal bones (items /cubic meter) all support the conclusion that different types of deposit have characteristic density patterns. These patterns have theoretical implications

[*] The caption in Nicholas 1990, Fig. 9, should read "...two secondary (DC2x) lots with chaff-ware densities over 800 cubic meters..."

[†] The captions for Fig. 10A and 10B (Nicholas 1990) are correct but should be reversed.

Table 6. DENSITY OF ANIMAL BONES BY DEPOSIT CODE

DC	NO. LOTS	NO. BONES	VOLUME M³	DENSITY BONES/M³
21	4	3748	1.63	2299
22	5	1333	0.24	5554
29	5	841	3.67	229
21-29	14	5922	5.54	1069
37	20	1657	16.74	99
34-35	5	449	14.27	31
34	1	177	4.34	41
35	4	272	9.93	27
ALL	39	8028	36.55	220

Table 7. FRAGMENTATION OF ANIMAL BONES BY DC

DC	NO. LOTS	BONE GRAMS	BONE COUNT	MEAN WEIGHT GRAMS/BONE
21	4	6441	3748	1.72
22	5	2976	1333	2.23
29	5	1044	841	1.24
37	22	2241	1743	1.29
34	2	267	278	0.96
35	4	279	272	1.03
41	2	386	107	3.61

for our attempt to understand site formation processes and methodological implications relevant to the design of data recovery systems. These patterns also have fundamental substantive implications that are essential elements in the interpretation of finds from different types of deposit. This conclusion, apparent despite the far from ideal quality of the data from ABC, makes a strong case for more careful design and execution of data recovery methods to facilitate the study of site formation processes, including the paths by which finds, sherds, and animal bones are incorporated in different deposits.

Fragmentation Patterns

Site formation processes can be expected to involve mechanical action such as trampling, moving and dumping, and sorting that would produce deposits with distinctive patterns of fragmentation of such fragile materials as ceramics (Alden 2003) and animal bones. It might be expected that sherds and bones from DC 21 and DC 29 lots on or embedded in floors would be subject to trampling and would be more highly fragmented than sherds and bones from DC 22 lots dumped into pits. Furthermore, fragmentation in DC 21 deposits should vary depending on traffic patterns—sherds and bones on a surface in a cul de sac or other out of the way location should be less fragmented than sherds and bones in a heavy traffic area. Sherds and bones from tertiary deposits (DC 34-36) are expected to be more fragmented than those from secondary deposits because they are likely to have been subjected to a succession of fragmentation processes: dumping, trampling, transport during construction activities or hand sorting to remove large items in the course of making bricks and mortar. Since we expect relatively high fragmentation in both floor deposits (DC 21) and tertiary deposits (DC 34-36), high fragmentation is not likely to be useful in evaluating the status of DC 37 lots. However, low fragmentation, on

the order of the pattern for DC 22 lots, would imply a trash component in a DC 37 lot.

Animal bone and sherd fragmentation patterns for different deposit types are summarized in Tables 7 and 8 from data recorded in Appendix B. The bones included in Table 7 include both diagnostic and nondiagnostic bones from lots (Appendix B, Part I) selected for analysis by Zeder (1985, Volume II:470 and personal communication). The sherds included in Table 6 are straw tempered pedestal base goblet rim sherds (Fig. 21) from contexts described below in Chapter II and recorded in Appendix B, Part II.

The greatest mean bone weight, 7.36 grams/bone, is found in Area 307 in BL 4A (ABCS 87, DC 21), but another lot from Area 307 produced much more fragmented bones with a mean weight of only 1.62 grams/bone (ABCN 139, DC 21). This pattern highlights the considerable variability found even within similar deposits, even within the same feature. The highest fragmentation, with mean bone weight of only 0.46 grams/bone, is found in a DC 29 floor removal lot (ABCN 60). DC 37 lots, with a mean bone weight of 1.29 grams/bone, are often less fragmented than tertiary lots (DC 34, 35). However, DC 37 mean bone weight is more variable than any other type of deposit, has a range (0.57 to 7 grams/bone) that almost exactly matches the range of all lots analyzed (0.46-7.36 grams/bone).

There are several possible explanations for these disappointing results including bias against recovery of smaller bones and underlying patterns in bone size that are not related to either site formation processes or recovery and recording biases.

It is apparent from Table 8 that mean sherd fragmentation differs very little among deposit types, sherds from trash pits (DC 22) being on average somewhat heavier than sherds from other deposits and sherds from DC 37 lots being somewhat lighter. However, just as in the case of bones, the range of mean sherd weight is considerable from 28.89 grams/sherd

Table 8. MEAN WEIGHT OF STRAW TEMPERED RIM SHERDS BY DC

DC	LOTS	SHERDS WEIGHT	SHERDS NUMBER	MEAN WEIGHT GRAMS/SHERD
21	4	4465	471	9.48
22	5	819	62	13.21
29	7	503	50	10.06
37	6	708	104	6.81
34	5	796	77	10.34
35	1	200	16	12.50
36	2	189	104	9.95

(ABCN 148, DC22) to less than 6 grams/sherd (ABCN 99, DC 37). Also matching the bone pattern, considerable variation in mean sherd weight occurs within each deposit type.

Summary of Fragmentation Patterns

In general the data available from ABC has not revealed reliable fragmentation signatures for different deposit types. This disappointing result is in part an artifact of inadequate data recovery. However, the highly variable fragmentation, which is observed even within a single deposit type in the same feature, implies the existence of a variety of fragmentation processes in all deposit types.

Alden (2003) recently studied sherd fragmentation using the data presented here (Table 8 and Appendix B, Part II) and his surface survey data from two Banesh ceramic production dumps (Alden 1979). He identifies a number of processes that may be responsible for variation in sherd fragmentation and presents a comparison of the production dump sherds with sherds from the Malyan ABC deposits. He notes that large sherds (13-18 grams/sherd), characteristic of the ceramic production dumps, are similar in size to sherds from trash pits (ABCN 148 and 162; DC 22) and floor removal lots (B 49, DC 29) (16-24 grams/sherd). He also shows that trampling in areas of heavy foot traffic probably account for the smallest sherds (5.7-6.9 grams/sherd) in the ABC collection (ABC 65 and ABCN 99). These processes and the patterns they produce are worthy of further study with recovery methods designed to reliably retrieve relevant data.

Mixed Lots

Lots are small sub-units established to control excavation within larger natural or cultural units. Thus, many lots may be used to excavate a room or a stratum, but no lot should contain material derived from more than one room or stratum. Mixed lots are identified with the code M in the Lot Indicator (LI) column of the Lot Inventory (Appendix B); finds from mixed lots are coded M in the LI column of the Register of Finds (Appendix A). Other codes that appear in the LI column of the Lot Inventory and the Register of Finds are "B" for surface finds, items from mixed lots, or the dump that are assigned to the Banesh period on stylistic grounds, "H" for lots that contain material from more than one feature, but are not stratigraphically mixed, "G" for lots and finds from unmixed contexts, and "K" for finds assigned to the Kaftari period on stylistic grounds. In a few cases specific finds from lots coded M are listed in the register with code G when the correct context of that specific find is shown on plans, section drawings, or described in the field notes.

The concept "mixed lot" as used here refers exclusively to mixing caused by improper excavation or recording. The mixture of deposits from different periods—with different chronological marker types or other distinctive characteristics—in antiquity as a consequence of ancient earth-moving activities is not within the definition of mixed lot used here, although failure to recognize such deposits will result in misunderstanding of the significance of finds from such deposits. A lot excavated from a deposit mixed in antiquity would be classified as a tertiary lot in the deposit coding (DC) system, but if properly excavated and recorded would not be considered a mixed lot in the lot indicator (LI) system.

There are many processes that may mix deposits of different origin or that may transport items from one deposit to another. Examples include rodent or other animal burrows. A collapsed fox or porcupine burrow has the potential for creating a tertiary mixture of considerable volume. Both fox and porcupine burrows were observed on the mound at Malyan but only small rodent burrows were encountered in the ABC excavations. The decision on whether or not to code a lot as mixed was made at the analytical stage using all evidence from the field records including notes, sections, plans, and photographs.

It is the task of the excavator to recognize, excavate, and record different deposits separately. Either a failure of *recognition* or a failure of *execution* can cause the excavation of mixed lots. Under the actual conditions of field work the constant interplay between recognition and execution often makes it difficult to sort out the true nature of apparently mixed deposits or the causes of excavation errors. In some instances site supervisors at ABC recognized mixed lots during excavation, but often the only evidence of mixing was the recovery of both Banesh and Kaftari sherds in the same lot, as shown in the Lot Inventory (Appendix B). However, this criteria for identifying mixed lots only applies to the major stratigraphic, chronological, and cultural distinction between the huge Kaftari trash deposit resting on the erosion surface designated Stratum 7 and the Banesh strata below that surface that are the subject of this report. Several mixed lots were identified on ceramic criteria in Stratum 8A, immediately below the Kaftari-Banesh interface at Stratum 7. Some mixed lots in lower strata were also identified by the presence of Kaftari sherds. The most likely explanation for this latter group of mixed lots is incomplete cleaning of Kaftari pits or wells.

More subtle mixing among the various Banesh strata is not easy to detect because reliable ceramic markers are not available at this level of chronological precision. The major stratigraphic units—building levels—defined by the construction surfaces and earliest floors of each building level, Strata (STR) 8D, 11B, and 14B, appear to have been generally, although not invariably, excavated with minimal mixing. The recognition of mixing between strata within a given building level, for example between STR 10A and 10B, is still more difficult and some mixed lots may be erroneously coded as unmixed lots (LI G). Finally, the interface between STR 9 (DC 34) and STR 10A (DC 35) and the interface between STR 12 and STR 13A, basically defined by the height of standing wall stubs in BL 3A and in BL 4A respectively, is not sharply defined and mixing between these strata is not considered to be significant.

In ABC Banesh deposits 261 unmixed lots (LI G) produced 2098 finds; 66 finds from mixed lots are classified as Banesh (LI B), and 95 finds are coded H (Table 2). Within the restraints imposed by deposit types, this group of 2259 finds may be considered the most reliable for the study of activities in the ABC buildings and neighborhood.

There are 57 mixed lots, which produced 276 finds: 13 from DC 29 deposits and 39 from DC 37 lots. The remaining 224 finds from mixed lots are from tertiary (DC 34-36) deposits or DC 39 and DC 41 lots. Thus, 97% of all finds from secondary deposits (DC 21-29) are from unmixed lots (LI G) and 83% of finds from DC 37 deposits are also from unmixed lots, while only 53% of finds from tertiary deposits (DC 34-36, 49) are from unmixed lots.

Stratigraphy

The stratigraphy of the Banesh building levels excavated in Operation ABC is the result of a relatively uncomplicated sequence of construction, occupation, modification, and reconstruction events. BL 5 was constructed on the plain in an area with no evidence of earlier architecture although hearths and flints were found below the BL 5 construction surface. Each successive building level was constructed on a surface prepared by leveling the preceding building. The walls of BLs 4, 3, and 2 were built of mud brick directly on the leveled bricky rubble of the preceding building without foundation trenches or stone footings except for three walls in BL 4. As a result, floors and surfaces are relatively level, and with few exceptions are found at approximately the same elevation within each building level. The latest P-E building in this area (BL 2) was abandoned and gradually destroyed by weathering and erosion, leaving a distinctive pebbly erosion surface (STR 7) on which the later Kaftari trash deposit accumulated.

The following stratigraphic summary provides a description of each stratum as illustrated in Figure 6, which is an east-west schematic cross-section located one meter south of the boundary between Operations B and C (Fig. 5). The exaggerated vertical dimension in Figure 6 is not drawn to scale. The section drawing (Fig. 7) documents stratigraphy at the south scarp. The stratigraphic relationship of the four building levels at the north end of the operation is shown in Pl. 3. Except as specified below, floors and surfaces are referred to by the same number as the deposit resting directly on them; thus, Floor 8B is the floor on which Stratum 8B rests. Because there are additional strata in the western parts of BLs 3 and 4, the earliest surfaces of these buildings, Floors 11B and 14B, are assigned separate stratum numbers. For purposes of this stratigraphic description horizontally mixed lots (LI H) are counted with unmixed lots (LI G). A summary account of finds, sherds, and animal bones from stratigraphically unmixed lots (LI G, H) is provided only as a rough indication of the productivity of each stratum.

Intermediate Surface 7

The stratigraphically complex ABC Kaftari trash deposit, incorporating BL 1, is divided into six broad stratigraphic units (J. L. Nickerson 1983). This trash deposit rests on a pebbly clay surface, designated Stratum 7, resulting from an erosional event of unknown duration following the abandonment of BL 2. The Stratum 7 surface, which is more or less level from east to west, slopes down slightly to the north and more steeply to the south from a point at about the center of the ABC operation. Stratum 7, illustrated at the south end of Operation A in Plate 4, was quite distinctive and easy to follow. Nevertheless it was breached by no less than 40 pits and wells that originated at various levels in the Kaftari trash. The wells are identifiable by their regular cylindrical structure, often including hard plaster linings and toe-holds, and by the presence of Kaftari sherds. Otherwise the integrity of the surfaces separating building levels was rarely breached in antiquity.

Pithos 165, located in BL 2, Room 71 (Pl. 13), protruded through Surface 7, which leaves the stratigraphic context of 3 finds in doubt. These finds include a human figurine (mf 656; Pl. 21a), a bull figurine (mf 655; Pl. 21b; compare Le Brun 1971, Fig. 69:20), and a radiocarbon sample (mf 2343, P-2186). The figurines are stylistically quite unlike Kaftari figurines and, if properly assigned to the Banesh assemblage, are the only known Banesh figurines from Malyan. Other figurines found in ABC Banesh levels are from mixed lots and are identical to Kaftari figurines (Nickerson, Janet W. 1979). The radiocarbon sample produced a date of 2185-1950 BC (CRD 1 SD), which is clearly not a Banesh date. The field notes are silent on the question of the relative location of the figurines and the charcoal within the pithos. Although they are included in the register for the Banesh levels the figurines may well be Kaftari.

Building Level 2 Strata

Stratum 8A

Stratum 8A is composed of a yellow clay bricky rubble deposit (DC 35) within BL 2 rooms. This stratum results from the collapse of the roof and upper walls of BL 2. All evidence of the roof structure such as beams, brush, or matting was removed by erosion in antiquity. A number of baked clay tiles (Type 48, Appendix A), possibly from the ceiling or upper walls, were embedded in Stratum 8A, mostly in Room 71 and Corridor 118 (see discussion of BL 2 below). There are 89 finds and 325 sherds from unmixed (LI G, H) Stratum 8A lots (DC 35) that are assumed to relate to activities in the general vicinity of BL 2 at some indeterminate time before BL 2 was constructed.

Stratum 8B

Stratum 8B is composed of deposits resting on the upper floor, designated Floor 8B, in BL 2 including trashy deposits (DC 21) and bricky rubble (DC 37) resting on Floor 8B, or on the surface of Platforms 27, 13, or 32 (Fig. 20), and the clay material of Floor 8B (DC 29). Finds from the surface of Hearth 310 are included in this stratum. The chronological context of finds from inside Pithoi 163 and 165 (DC 28) is problematic, but they are counted here. There are 1070 finds, 286 Banesh sherds, and 149 animal bones from (LI G, H) lots in this stratum.

Stratum 8B was formed by activities during the final phase of occupation and by natural deterioration and erosion after BL 2 was abandoned; there is no sign of fire or other catastrophic destruction. The distinction between Strata 8A and 8B is arbitrary; it was not observed in section and is intended to isolate the lots closest to Floor 8B, particularly in Operations B and B1 where the walls stand to a considerable height (1.3-1.6 m).

Stratum 8C

Stratum 8C includes floor repairs and resurfacings (DC 29) between Floor 8B and the next BL 2 floor, designated Floor 8C, together with removal lots (DC 36) for features built on Floor 8C. The Stratum 8C deposit between floors is relatively clean clay with only 3 finds, 42 animal bones, and 3 Banesh sherds from a DC 29 lot and 2 from a DC 37 lot. These finds are assumed to represent activities during the occupation of BL 2. The platforms and walls dividing rooms or blocking doorways (Feature Inventory, Appendix C), added after BL 2 was completed, were removed using DC 36 lots assigned to Stratum 8C. These lots produced 31 finds and 231 Banesh sherds, all from unmixed lots, which relate to earlier activities, probably before BL 2 was founded.

Stratum 8D

Stratum 8D is composed of the original floor or construction surface of BL 2, designated Floor 8D (DC 29), and the removal lots (DC 36) for all walls, platforms and other original features built on Floor 8D. Features with removal lots (DC 36) assigned to Stratum 8D are indicated in the Feature Inventory (Appendix C). Stratum 8D unmixed (LI G, H) floor removal lots (DC 29) produced 193 finds, 174 sherds, and 428 animal bones. These finds are assumed to relate to activities during or after the foundation of BL 2. The 5 mixed wall removal lots (DC 36) in this stratum, which produced 50 finds and 112 Banesh sherds, and 19 Kaftari sherds, are difficult to understand. All of the walls were cleaned, the plaster was followed, and bricks were articulated (Pls. 4, 13, and 14), but still there were wall removal lots with Kaftari sherds.

Intermediate Stratum 9

Stratum 9 is a deposit of bricky rubble (DC 34) resulting from the destruction of BL 3 and the preparation of a level surface (Floor 8D) on which BL 2 was constructed. Stratum 9 is thin or absent below the north-eastern rooms of BL 2 where the red painted plaster surface of BL 3 walls appeared as a red line immediately below Floor 8D (Pl. 4). The deposit is deeper along the west side of the operation where a large trash dump (DC 23) was incorporated in the bricky rubble matrix. The base of Stratum 9, not readily distinguishable from Stratum 10A, is defined by the tops of BL 3 wall stubs and fragments of painted wall plaster found in the fill on top of wall stubs or at that level in the bricky fill (Pls. 8 and 9).

There are 16 finds, 106 sherds, and 101 animal bones from unmixed (LI G) DC 34 lots in Stratum 9, that are assumed to be related to activities before BL 3 was constructed. However, the 214 finds, including 208 sealing and 3 tablet fragments from the compact trash dump (ABCS Lot 46, DC 23), are the result of short-term trash disposal and are almost certainly related to nearby activities during the BL 3A occupation (see Chapter IV, Class 21).

Building Level 3A Strata

Stratum 10A

Stratum 10A is composed of purposely laid brick fill and rubble (DC 35) below the tops of BL 3A wall stubs, bricky rubble on Floor 10A (DC 37), a trash deposit on Floor 10A (DC 21), and a compact trash deposit within bricky fill (DC 23). There are 7 finds and 75 Banesh sherds from unmixed (LI G, H) secondary deposits (DC 21, 29). In addition there are 73 finds, including 1 tablet and 70 sealing fragments, from the compact trash deposit (ABCS Lot 36, DC 23) embedded in Stratum 10A (see Chapter IV, Class 21). Lot 36 shares some sealing designs with ABCS Lot 46 (DC 23) in Stratum 9 and is also very probably related to nearby activities during the occupation of BL 3. There are also 30 finds, 134 sherds, and 150 animal bones from good (LI G, H) DC 37 lots, and 15 finds, 83 sherds and 148 animal bones from DC 35 lots.

Stratum 10B

Stratum 10B is composed of a clay surface deposit (DC 29) and bricky fill (DC 37) resting on Surface 10B in Area 260. There are 9 finds, 146 sherds, and 292 animal bones from this stratum, all from unmixed lots. The 5 DC 29 finds are assumed to result from activities in BL 3A.

Building Level 3B Strata

Stratum 11A

Stratum 11A is a sterile purposeful clay deposit (DC 29), resting on Surface 11B in BL 3B, Rooms 228, 229, 230, and 232. There are no finds from this deposit, but there are finds from Floor 11B in these rooms.

Stratum 11B

Stratum 11B is the foundation surface and earliest floor (DC 29) and the removal lots (DC 36) for BL 3A and 3B walls and features. There are 26 finds, 214 sherds, and 277 bones from unmixed (LI G, H) DC 29 lots. There are 74 finds and 130 sherds from wall removal lots (DC 36).

Intermediate Stratum 12

Stratum 12 is a thin (less than 10 cm thick) deposit (DC 34) composed of patches of laid bricks, bricky rubble, with a mud plaster surface below BL 3 Floor 11B, but above the stubs of BL 4 walls. Stratum 12 is the result of the destruction of BL 4 and the preparation of the surface on which BL 3 was constructed. There are 10 finds and 49 sherds from unmixed (LI G) DC 34 lots from this stratum, which, together with finds from mixed (LI M) lots, relate to activities during or before the occupation of BL 4.

Building Level 4A Strata

Stratum 13A

Stratum 13A is the deposit resting on the upper floors and surfaces, designated Floor 13A, but below the tops of the BL 4A wall stubs. This deposit includes bricky rubble above the floor (DC 35), bricky rubble resting on the floor (DC 37), trashy floor deposits (DC 21), a find from a hearth (DC 28), floor removal (DC 29), and trash from Pit 236 (DC 22), which was excavated in antiquity from Floor 13A. There are 98 finds, 1103 Banesh sherds, and 5081 bones from unmixed (LI G) secondary (DC 21-29) lots in this stratum. Unmixed DC 37 lots produced 39 finds, 147 sherds, and 503 bones; 3 of these lots (ABCN 146, B 57, and B 62) have a relatively high find density and may be from trashy deposits. The unmixed DC 35 lots produced 17 finds, 220 sherds and 22 bones.

Stratum 13B

Stratum 13B is a series of floor repairs (DC 29) in Corridor 241 and finds on Floor 14B (DC 21) in Room 64 of BL 4A. There are 13 finds and 68 sherds from unmixed secondary lots in this stratum that relate to activities contemporary with BL 4A.

Stratum 13C

Stratum 13C is the cobble, gravel, and bricky rubble fill (DC 49) in Feature 334 , which is the foundation for Wall 240. Stratum 13C also includes the removal of Wall 240 (DC 36). There are 13 finds and 111 sherds in this stratum, all from unmixed tertiary lots that relate to pre-BL 4 activities in the neighborhood.

Building Level 4B Strata

Stratum 14A

Stratum 14A is the rubble (DC 37) on Floor 14B in Areas 331, 332, and 333, which produced 9 finds and 91 Banesh sherds, all from unmixed lots. Only 1 of these DC 37 lots has a moderately high find density

(ABC 13, density 17 finds/m3). Three finds came from inside a bowl (mf 3770, Fig. 26c, DC 28) on the floor.

Stratum 14B

Stratum 14B is removal of the earliest floor or surface (DC 29) in BL 4, which produced 8 finds and 5 sherds; Hearth 345 produced 1 find (DC 28). Removal lots (DC 36) for BL 4B walls constructed on Floor 14B east of Wall 240 produced 9 finds.

Building Level 5 Strata

Stratum 15A

Stratum 15A is composed of bricky rubble (DC 35) below the top of the BL 5 wall stubs, but not resting on Floor 15A and bricky rubble that is resting on the floor (DC 37). No intermediate stratum was identified between BLs 4 and 5. There are 10 finds, 92 shreds, and 101 animal bones from unmixed (LI G, H) lots in this stratum. The 4 DC 35 finds are assumed to relate to activities before the construction of BL 5 and the 6 DC 37 finds may relate to activities during or before BL 5.

Stratum 15B

Stratum 15B is composed of trashy debris (DC 21) and a bricky deposit (DC 37) below Floor 15A and resting on Floor 15B. Also included are lots used to remove some of Floor 15B (DC 29) and parts of Walls 244, 254, and 258 (DC 36) to open the sounding (Area 367) below BL 5. Material from Oven 363 (DC 28), excavated from Floor 15B, is also included. There are 28 finds and 46 sherds in this stratum, all from unmixed (LI G) lots. The 26 finds from secondary or DC 37 deposits are assumed to relate to BL 5 activities.

Sounding Below BL 5

In 1976 a small (230x150 cm) sounding, designated Area 367 was excavated below the earliest BL 5 building surface in the south end of Rooms 246 and 247 and below Wall 244. This sounding was reopened in 1978 and expanded to the north for a total area of 320x250 cm. The datum for all depth measurements reported here for Strata 16-20 is the BL 5 construction surface composed of a smooth clay layer.

Stratum 16

A few Banesh sherds, 3 flints, and a burned area, designated Hearth 366, were found in the first 15 cm below the BL 5 building surface in a relatively silty deposit.

Stratum 17

No finds were recovered in this clean silty deposit between 15 and 50 cm below the BL 5 building surface.

Stratum 18A

A lens of fist sized and smaller river pebbles, designated Area 369, produced several fragments of charcoal, 13 flints, 1 hammer stone, and a scatter of bones between ca. 50-60 cm below BL 5. A flotation sample produced barley grains and some unidentifiable cereal grains, but no other carbonized material (Miller 1982; Table B.2., ABC Lot 48). The clay matrix of Feature 369 was darker than the surrounding deposit. About 80% of the stones were burned or fire-cracked. One Banesh sherd appeared in the sherd yard with the pebbles from this feature but John Alden, who removed the pebbles one-by-one, believes this sherd was not from Feature 369 or anywhere else in Stratum 18A.

Stratum 18B

Just below Feature 369, between 60 and 70 cm below BL 5, more pebbles, flints, and bones were found in a slightly flattened circular concentration about 1 m in maximum diameter, designated Feature 370. One red slipped grit tempered sherd (mf 9277), probably Banesh, came from this deposit. The soil was dark brown, hard, and broke into chunky pieces.

Stratum 19

Stratum 19 was generally sterile brown clay between 70 and 180 cm. One chert blade with use nibble (mf 9278) was found in this deposit at the 107 cm level.

Stratum 20

Stratum 20 was a sterile layer of heavy dark brown clay between 180 and 207 cm below BL 5. This is the only sounding at Malyan that reached a stratum interpreted as virgin soil.

Architecture

The purpose of this section is to provide an account of the construction, occupation and abandonment sequence of the 4 Banesh building levels, beginning with the earliest level, BL 5, and working up to BL 2. The focus is on an architectural description of walls, floors, rooms, courtyards, corridors, and areas, in addition to other features such as doors, hearths, ovens, niches, and the permanently installed pithoi. Walls, floors, and door frames in these buildings are often colored white, yellow, black, or red, or less commonly left the natural tan color of mud plaster. Although some technical analysis has been done on the wall paintings of BL 3 (infra, page 28, 71), the following descriptions indicate the color of features without any technical implication regarding the method of application (i.e. "plastered" or "painted"). A summary count and description of finds, sherds, and animal bones from each room or other space is provided as a general indication of activities that might have taken place there. A more detailed description and analysis of finds is reserved for Chapter IV.

Building Level 5

Construction Sequence

Building Level 5 (BL 5) (Fig. 8; Pl. 5) was constructed on a prepared clay surface (Stratum 15B) above Stratum 16, a 15 cm clay deposit that incorporates Hearth 366, a roughly circular burned area (47x42 cm), 8-10 cm below the floor of Room 247. No finds were associated with Hearth 366.

BL 5 is composed of a group of rectangular rooms and courts constructed as a single unit, as evidenced by the regularity of the plan and the bonding of all walls except Wall 356, which, although partly destroyed by a BL 4 foundation trench, was probably bonded to Wall 326. The N-S walls of BL 5 are oriented 7.5 degrees west of magnetic north. The walls, constructed directly on a prepared surface, were made of standard mud bricks (37x17x7 cm) laid in courses composed of one row of stringers and one row of headers. There are some departures from this brick-laying pattern, notably in Wall 326 just south of Hearth 327, where there are 2 rows of 3 headers. But in general the masonry work is very regular. All walls were finished with 3-5 cm of plaster on each face and bonded with mud mortar (1 cm) for a total average wall thickness of 63 cm.

The evidence suggests that this building extended beyond the excavated area in all directions. There are partially excavated interior spaces with well preserved white, or red and white, walls and white floors on 3 sides: Rooms 342 and 347 to the south, Room 252 and the splinter of space east of Wall 250 in the NE corner, and Rooms 249 and 253 to the north. The status of Areas 358 and 359 is not clear, but Court 353, with a blocked door converted into Hearth 344 and Door 341 giving access to Room 342, appears to be well integrated into the original building, with the implication that Areas 358 and 359 were also part of the original plan. The upper deposit in Areas 358 and 359, and Court 353, above the stubs of Walls 356 and 254, but below the top of Wall 326, was excavated as a single unit designated Area 336, which may represent either a late occupation phase west of Wall 326 or an artifact of the leveling of BL 5 and the construction of BL 4.

Because the plan was only partly revealed by excavation it is not possible to identify the entrance to BL 5, although it is seems likely to have been the extra wide doorway (349) with a central pillar (364). All of the rooms east of Wall 326/368, as well as Court 353, are interconnected except for Room 252, which must have been entered through a door in the unexcavated extension of Wall 250. The alignment of Doors 325, 337, 338, and the western part of 349 along Wall 326/368 in Rooms 325-347 stands in distinct contrast to the staggered layout of doors in a comparable group of rooms in BL 3 (Fig. 12). Rooms and features are described in the following section, beginning with Room 347 and working north through the rooms east of Wall 326/368 and then south through the rooms east of Wall 244; the courts and rooms west of Wall 326/368 are described last.

Description of Features

Room 347

Only a small area (2.4 m²) of this room was excavated. The walls are white plaster; the floor, resurfaced at least once, is also white. Door 351 was blocked by a single row of 3 header bricks, forming the back of Hearth 360, in Court 348. There were no finds in this room except for a broken pedestal base goblet embedded in the NE corner of the floor and 6 Banesh sherds in the fill (DC 35). Door 349, leading north into Room 346, was originally 215 cm wide; both door jambs and the sill were plastered white. Later a brick support was constructed at about the center of the

door, leaving an opening on either side. The lower course of this support is composed of two rows of stretchers, the next course is a single row of headers; it has unpainted plaster on the east and west faces. Plaster on the south face curved over the south edge of the door sill and plaster on the north face, protruding slightly into Room 346, was probably cut off during excavation.

Room 346

This small (291x143 cm) room has plastered floor and walls that were originally white, then red, and finally white again. Door 350 leads east into Court 348 and Door 338 leads north into Room 251. The only find from this room is charcoal from Stratum 15A (DC 37).

Room 251

This room (285x200 cm) has white walls and floor. Feature 344, badly damaged by BL 4 Foundation Trench 334, was originally a door leading to Court 353. Soon after construction the door was blocked and feature 344, which may have been either a niche or a hearth, was added to Court 353. The plaster face of this door blocking in Room 251 shows traces of white paint but the plaster on the other side, in Court 353, it is not painted. No finds came from this room except for a sample of azurite (mf 3735) and Banesh sherds from Stratum 15A (DC 35). Door 337 leads north into Room 247.

Room 247

This room (465x285 cm) was excavated only to the upper white floor but a second white floor 10 cm lower was identified in the section of the sounding in Area 367. The walls were originally red but later painted white; fragments of wall plaster with black paint were found in the fill but not on the walls. A copper pin (mf 1916, Fig. 36h) and a red pigment sample (mf 3738), as well as animal bones and Banesh sherds, are recorded from Stratum 15A (DC 37) in this room. Hearth 327, located in the center of the room against Wall 326, was constructed of a single layer of standard BL 5 bricks (37x17x7 cm); the plaster on the hearth was poorly preserved except for a patch of burned plaster on top. Door 325 leads north into Room 249.

Room 249

Only a small area (290x95 cm) of this room was excavated. The floor is white; the walls were originally red, then white. Animal bones were found in Stratum

15A (DC 37) but no finds or sherds were recovered. Door 245 leads east into Room 253.

Room 253

Only a small area (1.38 m²) of this room was excavated; walls and floor are white. No finds, animal bones, sherds, or features are recorded. Door 324, destroyed by Kaftari Well 76, was reconstructed from evidence of a plaster corner in Wall 257. This door leads south into Room 246.

Room 246

This room (465x240 cm) has white walls with evidence of a red painted design. There is an unpainted upper surface, associated with preparation for construction of BL 4, and a lower white plaster floor. The only finds from this room are a chert blade segment (mf 6659), a slag sample (mf 6790), and animal bones from fill, Stratum 15A (DC 35).

Room 252

The entrance to Room 252 (295x245 cm) must have been from the east. The walls and floor are white. Hearth 259 is located in the center of the room against Wall 258. No finds are recorded from this room except Banesh sherds from the fill (DC 35).

Court 348

Only a small area (2.52 m²) of this court was excavated. The designation of this space as an unroofed court is based on the walls, which are finished with unpainted plaster, and the rough, unfinished character of the floor. Fragments of red, white, and yellow (limonite) wall plaster were recovered from the fill (DC 37) in this court. Feature 360 is an enigmatic bench or platform made of poorly laid bricks built against Wall 244 and blocking Door 351. The top surface of the bench is 20-25 cm above the lower floor of Court 348, but the actual ground plan is conjectural since no clear vertical plaster face was discovered and it is possible the bench extended into the south scarp at the same level as a small burned area (Hearth 365), which may have been a part of the same structure. The surface of the bench was covered with ash but not burned; there are 4 post holes of variable diameter (8-15 cm) in the top of the bench, arranged as shown on the plan. The entire feature may be part of an outdoor cooking facility shaded by an awning or other light weight roof supported by wooden posts. Banesh sherds and a sample of earthy limonite (mf 3941) were found in a mixed Stratum 15B (DC 37) lot, possibly resting on Hearth 360.

Room 342

Only a small corner (152x85 cm) of this room was excavated. The walls and floor are white. Banesh sherds and charcoal (mf 4020) were found in Stratum 15A (DC 37). Door 341 leads north into Court 353.

Court 353

The excavated area (460x ca. 200 cm) represents a little over half the total area of the court if Hearth 355 is located in the center of the north wall. The walls are poorly preserved unpainted plaster. There are two floor surfaces in the court, both are rough, composed of flaking laminated water-laid lenses. The lower surface, cleaned only in the north half, is 5-15 cm below the upper surface. Hollows in the fill that accumulated on the lower surface were partly filled with brick rubble and leveled with an application of *cagel* (clay, water and straw mixture) to create the upper floor, which then deteriorated as a result of erosion. Both surfaces were better preserved in a strip about 50 cm wide along the walls, which may have been protected by roof overhang. A curb on the inside edge of Door 341 was built to prevent water from the court flooding Room 342. The upper surface in Courtyard 353 produced a concentration of sheep/goat knuckle bones and a cluster of coarse ware potsherds. A jasper blade (mf 3926), a banded travertine bowl rim (mf 3746, Fig. 41a), compact hematite (mf 5081), specular hematite (mf 3736), and charcoal (mf 3772) were recovered from Stratum 15B (DC 21).

Hearth 355 (55x55 cm), built against Wall 254, has a burned plaster surface (35x30 cm) at the level of the upper floor and raised 12 cm above the lower floor. The plaster faces were badly preserved and difficult to define accurately. Hearth 344, built into a blocked door, is of unusual design suggesting an unknown specialized function.

Area 359

The undulating rough floor surface and the badly preserved unpainted wall plaster indicate either a court or an exterior space (230x190 cm) between buildings. The favored interpretation as a court would be reinforced if it could be shown that Wall 356 was bonded to Wall 326. However, the BL 4 foundation trench has destroyed the evidence and the fact that Wall 356 is not quite perpendicular to Wall 326 or parallel to Wall 254 suggests the possibility that Wall 356 was a late addition. Banesh sherds, 2 chert blades (mf 3918), an unimpressed sealing (mf 3768), and a conical jar stopper (mf 3769) were found in Stratum 15B (DC 37) of this room. Hearth 357 was built against Wall 356.

Area 358

This area (380x245 cm) may also be either a court or exterior space between buildings. The floor surface is badly preserved and the wall plaster is unpainted. Hearths 361 and 362 are burned areas on the floor. Oven 363 is a subterranean feature in Stratum 15B. It has a diameter of 36 cm at the opening and 39 cm at 3 cm above the slightly concave bottom, which is 19-20 cm below the surface. This oven was burned and contained ash, 2 bricks (17x15 and 17x12 cm), a radiocarbon sample (mf 3774 and mf 4055=P-3060) and several Banesh sherds. Oven 363 also yielded several enigmatic clay finds with smooth surfaces and triangular cross-section that may have been unimpressed sealings (mf 3947 and 3948).

Area 336

This area includes all of Areas 358, 359 and part of Court 353 above the stubs of Walls 254 and 356. No features or floors were discovered in Area 336, which is interpreted as an artifact of building activity at the time BL 5 was razed to make way for BL 4. Banesh sherds and charcoal (mf 3766) were found in this area.

Building Level 4

Construction Sequence

Building Level 5 was razed to make way for the construction of BL 4 (Fig. 9; Pls. 3, 6, 7). In some instances BL 5 rooms were partly filled with more or less regularly laid bricks and in other instances rooms were simply filled with the rubble from the destruction of the BL 5 walls, as indicated by the presence of angular chunks of broken brick and fragments of plaster with traces of wall painting in the fill below and immediately above the top of BL 5 wall stubs.

The first stage of construction, BL 4B, is the NE building and isolated walls to the south and west (Figs. 9 and 10). The N-S walls of the NE building in BL 4 are oriented exactly as in BL 5—7.5 degrees west of magnetic north. The NE building, composed of Rooms 64-67, was constructed directly on the leveled rubble of BL 5 using 42x21 cm bricks and some 21x21 cm half bricks laid in courses of 1 stringer and 1 header for an average wall thickness of 80-85 cm, depending on the thickness of mortar and plaster. The only departure from this pattern is Wall 62, an interior curtain wall, which has two rows of stringers. Wall 329, made of 42x21 cm bricks like those used in the NE building,

was probably constructed at the same time or soon after the construction of the NE building; Wall 330, with larger bricks (46x23 cm) was probably added later.

South of the NE building, BL 4 walls are made of either large (47x22 cm) or small (37x16 cm bricks). The small bricks are comparable in size to standard BL 5 bricks (37x17x7 cm), suggesting the possibility that the small brick walls of BL 4 (Fig. 9) may antedate the construction of the NE building. The scarp section (Fig. 7) at the south edge of Court 348 (BL 5) shows that BL 4 Wall 284 is later than BL 5 Wall 244, and while it is impossible to reconstruct an exact sequence of events, it is clear that the small brick walls (Walls 292, 295, 294, 284, 285, and 298) were standing before the additions and modifications of BL 4A were constructed, and are properly assigned to BL 4B (Figs. 9, 10).

The brick laying pattern in the small brick walls was irregular, half-bricks are common, and several patterns may appear in a single course. Walls 284, 285, and 298 have courses of a single header or 2 stretchers; the other walls are heavier, with either 1 stretcher and 1 header or 2 stretchers and 1 header. A tentative reconstruction of parallel small brick E-W walls perpendicular to Walls 292 and 295 is suggested by the apparent alignment with Walls 294 and 296. Such a reconstruction is given some support by what appears to be an earlier rounded outside corner below the later corner of Walls 295 and 286.

The next construction stage, leading to the final BL 4A plan (Figs. 9, 11), was initiated when foundation trenches were excavated for Walls 240 and 242, cutting through Walls 329 and 330 of BL 4B. These foundations, excavated to a depth of 35-40 cm, with a smooth flat bottom, were filled with fair sized cobbles (25-50 cm in diameter), gravel, and bricky clay (Pl. 7a). A number of new walls were then constructed, defining Corridor 241 to the west and the spaces to the south of the NE building. Wall 240 was built against the NE building after an additional layer of plaster was applied to Wall 239. Walls 240 and 241 are bonded to Wall 291 and Bench 290. Walls 286, 287, and 289 were roughly attached to the earlier small brick walls (295 and 296) to form Corridor 288 and the irregular spaces to the south. Oven 300 and Hearth 299 were constructed and the opening between the north end of Wall 284 and Wall 323 of the NE building was blocked, completing the final plan of BL 4A. The 4 rooms of the NE building, associated Court 281, and then the remaining spaces, first to the west and then to the south are described in the following section.

Description of Features

Room 64

This small (290x255 cm) room has white plaster on all 4 walls. Brick Platform 61 (minimum 140x140 cm), preserved to a maximum height of 50-60 cm (minimum, 15 cm), stands near the center of the room. The platform, partly destroyed by erosion and slump between the time it was first encountered in 1971 and final excavation in 1974, was constructed of bricks almost identical in dimensions (43x20 cm) to the standard bricks used in the NE building (42x21 cm); the difference may be measurement variation rather than a real difference in brick size. A relatively thin (ca. 2 cm) coating of wall plaster was definitely identified on the west and south faces and possibly on the north and east faces, suggesting the platform was a free-standing structure. This tentative conclusion is supported by the brick pattern (Fig. 9), by the presence of wall plaster on all 4 walls of the room, by the trashy nature of deposits north and east of the platform, and by the fact that Door 72 would be partly blocked if the platform abutted Wall 59. The function of Platform 61 is unclear. Since it slopes up steeply from the SE corner, it may have been a stairway but no indication of actual steps or signs of wear were evident.

Access to Room 64 from Court 281 was through Door 322, which has a sill 60 cm above the lower floor of the room and 2-4 cm above the latest surface of Court 281. The reason for this unusual arrangement is discussed below in connection with Court 281. Access to Room 64 from Room 65 is by white plastered Door 72, sill height unrecorded.

Finds from Stratum 13B, resting on Floor 14B (DC 21), include 6 flakes of jasper, chalcedony and chert (mf 2204, 6560, 6561), an animal tooth (mf 2206), Banesh sherds, and charcoal (mf 2196). BL 4A finds, resting on Floor 13A (DC 21) include a weathered orange stone bead (mf 220), a white marble cylindrical bead (mf 223), fragments of clinoptilolite (mf 2201, Fig. 37k) and charcoal (C14 mf 2195.1=P-2187 and mf 2195.2=TUNC-31). Stratum 13A DC 37 lots produced 2 bitumen beads (mf 6739, 6740; Fig. 38m, n), 2 unfinished clinoptilolite beads (mf 9789; Fig. 37i), and a carved fish vertebra bead (mf 6795; Fig. 38c). There are also chert and jasper blade segments (mf 6656, Fig. 33d; 6657, Fig. 34d), a limestone polishing tool (mf 7306) and 5 sealing fragments (mf 1976, 1979.2), one impressed with design 4J (mf 1979.1). Several finds in this group, including radiocarbon sample mf 9930 = P-2334, come from a high density (92 finds/m³) DC 37

lot (ABCN 143) that is classified as mixed on the basis of one possible Kaftari sherd in a collection of 76 Banesh sherds. It is very likely that these finds are in good context from a trashy deposit on Floor 13A. Unmixed DC 37 lots on this floor produced a collection of Banesh sherds and animal bones.

Pit 236, excavated from Floor 13A of BL 4A, produced 42 unbaked clay balls (mf 2012, 7282-91), 3 conical jar stoppers (mf 1978; 7281, Fig. 42b; 7293), 2 steatite beads (mf 7425.1 and 7425.2, Fig. 37u, v), a *Dentalium* shell bead (mf 7425.3, Fig. 38k), ground stone tools (mf 2633-35), a fired clay tube (*tuyère?*) (mf 6810, Fig. 42d), a copper* bar (mf 9814), bitumen (mf 7467), fresh water *Unio* shell (mf 6831), and several charcoal and plaster samples. This pit also produced a large collection of Banesh straw tempered sherds and animal bones. Miller (1982:364; discussed under the original field number: Pit 84) suggested that Pit 236 may have been "...an ad hoc kiln, in which pistachio and oak wood and straw/dung were used as fuel to make..." straw tempered pottery. This suggestion is certainly possible, but the presence of large quantities of animal bone implies that the final use of the pit was as a trash pit.

Room 65

Only partly excavated (300x>220 cm), Room 65 has white plastered walls and door jambs and a series of 10 plaster floors (total thickness, 12 cm). Access was through Door 72 from Room 64 or Door 69, with a sill 8 cm above the upper floor, leading to Room 67. A *Conus* shell bead (mf 222) and a calcite bowl fragment prepared for some kind of reuse (mf 2192, Fig. 40c) were found during removal of the lower floor (Floor 14B, DC 29), while a prase flake (mf 6556, Fig. 32f), jasper flakes (mf 2184, Fig. 30g; mf 6555), bitumen (mf 2186), and a fresh water *Melanopsis* shell (mf 2187) were recovered from Stratum 13A (DC 37).

Room 67

This partially excavated room (610x>380 cm) has white plastered walls and doors and a series of 9 white plaster floors (total thickness, 13 cm). Hearth 238, built in the center against Wall 59, is rectangular (67x53 cm) and has a burned plaster surface (re-plastered twice) raised 26 cm above the floor. Door 234, with a sill 4 cm above the upper floor, leads into an unexcavated room to the north. Door 70, with a sill 4 cm above the upper floor, gives access to Room 66 to the west. A chert flake (mf 6642), a plaster sample (mf

---

* Copper is used throughout to refer to copper-base metals, which in Banesh contexts are usually arsenical coppers; see Chapter IV.

9871), animal bones and Banesh sherds come from a mixed DC 37 lot; an unmixed DC 37 lot produced only Banesh sherds.

Room 66

This long, narrow partially excavated room (>660x205 cm) has white plastered walls but with 3 superimposed (total thickness 17 cm) charcoal flecked plain clay floors. Floor 14B (DC 29) produced an unusual grit tempered button base sherd (mf 6811) that had been pierced and a copper pin (mf 1918, Fig. 36g) found in a horizontally mixed lot (LI H) but probably from this room. Stratum 13A (DC 37) produced a *Conus* shell bead (mf 209), steatite bead (mf 6649), bitumen (mf 2185), and fresh water *Unio* shells (mf 2183, 2197). The DC 37 lots (B 57, ABCN 137) that produced these finds both have high find densities (12 finds/m^3 and 200 finds/m^3). This deposit also produced animal bones and Banesh sherds.

Court 281

Unlike the walls of inside rooms, the walls of this small court (ca. 7.7 m^2) were finished with plain clay plaster. The floor is rough, weathered, and includes an area of water laminated clay in the NW corner. There are 2 floor surfaces; the lower one seals the deposit in the foundation trench (Feature 334) for Wall 240, indicating that the lower floor was in use after Wall 240 was constructed. The sill of Door 322, originally 25 cm above the lowest floor, was raised 35 cm to a position 60 cm above the lower floor (50 cm above the latest floor) in Room 64 and 2-4 cm above the latest floor in Court 281, apparently to prevent water from Court 281 draining into Room 64. The brick blocking placed inside Door 322 to raise the sill rested against the unplastered bricks of the door jamb, implying the brick blocking was in place before plaster was applied to the door jamb. After the door sill was raised, Wall 323 inside Room 64 was plastered, including the door blocking and the door jambs. Three rows of bricks were laid along Wall 323 in the NW corner of Court 281, apparently to reinforce the closure of Door 322. All of these events occurred after Wall 240 was constructed.

The upper surface of Hearth 299, constructed on the lower floor of Court 281, was composed of a layer of sherds covered with burned plaster.

Floor 14B (DC 29), partly excavated, produced only charcoal (mf 3765) and a plaster sample (mf 3730). Two gold beads (mf 5082.1, Fig. 43c) and a frit bead (mf 5082.2) were found on Floor 13A (DC 21). A jasper flake (mf 7017), 3 sealings (mf 1932, 2023), plaster samples (mf 9852, 6801) and Banesh sherds were found in Stratum 13A (DC 37).

Area 331

The condition of the floor, the trashy deposit on the floor and the lack of white pigment in the Wall 330 plaster suggest this is an outside area (>460x>320 cm). The nature of the articulation between Area 331 and the NE building is unknown due to the excavation of a foundation trench (Feature 334; Pl. 7A) for Wall 240. There are several ephemeral surfaces but no floor could be followed over the entire area. Stratum 14 A (DC 37) resting on these fragmented surfaces produced 3 copper prills (mf 3742, 3743) and charcoal (mf 3777, 3779, 4007). Hearth 339 is a small oval hollow (28x24x4.5 cm) with signs of burning, which contained ashes and sherds of an unusual pottery bowl (mf 3770, Fig. 26c) with an incised cross on the base. Hearth 343 is a narrow oval hollow (30x12x3.5 cm) burned white and red, which produced charcoal (mf 4016) and was full of ashes that were also scattered to the west and north.

Area 332

Area 332 (600x>380cm) is bounded on the north by Wall 330 (bricks, 46x23 cm) and on the south by Wall 329 (bricks 42x21cm), with the possible implication that Area 332 is open space between two buildings. The poor condition of walls and floor surfaces reinforces the conclusion that Area 332 was not roofed. As with Area 331, the articulation of Area 332 with the NE building was destroyed by the Wall 240 foundation trench (Feature 334). The floor deposit in Area 332 included a number of black and white wall painting fragments. Hearth 328 is a rectangular hearth (67x53 cm) with a burned surface 26 cm above the lowest surface identified along Wall 329. The burned hearth surface was renewed with 3 cm of plaster. An obsidian blade (mf 3753; Pl. 19) from Nimrut Dağ I (Blackman 1984; Appendix B, MAO-022) a jasper flake (mf 3755; Pl. 19), Banesh sherds, and charcoal (mf 3778) were found in Stratum 14A (DC 37).

Area 333

Area 333 (ca. 3.9 m^2) is apparently an outside area, perhaps a court associated with an unexcavated building to the south. Wall 329 was built over Hearth 345, which is a roughly oval hollow (90x80 cm). Several Banesh sherds were found, but no finds are recorded for this area.

Corridor 241

Soon after the NE building was constructed Areas 331, 332, and 333 to the west were abandoned and Corridor 241 (ca. 15 m long; 210-170 cm wide) was created when Walls 240, 242, and 291 were built. These walls are made of 42x21 cm bricks, like those used in the NE building, but unlike the bricks used to build Walls 329 and 330. Although the walls of the corridor may have been plastered white, the plaster is so worn that the presence of white pigment is not certain, and it is probable that the corridor was not roofed. The floor surface is uneven, with several areas of laminated water-laid clay, some patches of yellow pigment, a cluster of pebbles in the SW corner, and a scatter of pebbles along Wall 240. The only known entrance to Corridor 241 is through Door 384 from open Area 307 to the west. The unusual pattern of brick-laying in the center of Wall 291 suggests the possibility that a doorway may have originally allowed access to the corridor from the south, but this possibility was not confirmed since Wall 291 and Bench 290 were not dismantled.

Fragments of limestone (mf 3750), a copper prill (mf 3741), plaster (mf 3739) and charcoal (mf 3775, 3776) were found embedded in Floor 13B (DC 29). A copper nail (mf 6772), 4 unimpressed sealing fragments (mf 1934), red ochre (mf 6689), and a fresh water gastropod shell (mf 6828) were found in Stratum 13A (DC 37). A cylinder seal (mf 1903, Fig. 44b) came from Stratum 13A (DC 35). The corridor also produced animal bones, Banesh pottery and one possible Kaftari sherd.

The foundation trench for Wall 240 (Feature 334, Pl. 7A) produced 11 finds, including a unique triangular unfired clay object (mf 3731), an exhausted obsidian bladelet core (mf 3752), an obsidian blade (mf 3756; Pl. 19) from Nimrut Dağ I (Blackman 1984; Appendix B, MAO-021), a flake and 4 chert blades (mf 3749, 3751, 3754, 3758, 3759; Pl. 19), slag (mf 3762), an *Ancilla* shell (mf 3733), and a quantity of pottery and bone. Although this deposit is all considered to be a tertiary context (DC 49), these finds may relate to BL 4B activities.

Area 307

A narrow strip (13.66 m²) excavated west of Walls 242 and 292 in BL 4A is designated Area 307. This area is characterized by a trashy deposit composed of dense sherd and animal bone concentrations, fire cracked rocks, and pebbles. Hearth 308 is a small (30x15 cm) roughly rectangular burned area with a scatter of ash and fragments of a rectangular Banesh tray nearby. Finds from the trashy deposit, Stratum 13 A (DC 21), in Area 307 include fragments of yellow pigment (mf 11235), a chert blade segment (mf 7027, Fig. 33h) and flake (mf 7029), slag (mf 6789), a chunk of dolomite (mf 9792), charcoal (mf 7423), and a sealed tablet (mf 1690) resting on rough ephemeral surfaces that generally slope down to the west. The exact stratigraphic context of an early style cylinder seal with a suspension loop (mf 1901, Fig. 44a, Pl. 22b) found in Area 307 is in doubt. It could be as late as the BL 3 construction surface, Stratum 11B, but John Alden, the supervisor of ABCS when the seal was found, concluded that it was more likely to come from below Stratum 12 with the implication that it dates to the time of BL 4 or earlier. Area 307 is interpreted as an open space, on the westward sloping edge of a small hill created by the accumulation of debris from the BL 5 occupation.

Corridor 288

This short, narrow corridor (ca. 8.48 m²) runs SW from Room 282 and then turns south. The walls are coated with white plaster but it is unclear whether the corridor was roofed or open. There are 2 clay floors; the upper floor, which turns up against the wall plaster of all adjacent walls, is badly worn. The lower floor, 4-6 cm below the upper floor, has a shallow depression 5-10 cm deep in the center and traces of white plaster, particularly along the walls. A white stone ball (mf 6741) and 2 fresh water gastropod shells (mf 6835) came from Stratum 13A (DC 37), which also produced Banesh sherds and animal bones. The DC 35 bricky fill produced 6 flint flakes and slag.

Bench 290 is built against Wall 291 in a niche formed by the south end of Wall 242 to the west and Wall 240 to the east. The bench (area 2.1 m²), which stands 40 cm above the upper floor of Corridor 288, is built on a stone footing. A charred bone bead (mf 11262), a fresh water *Unio* shell (mf 7330.1), 2 smooth chert cobbles, a fragment of red conglomerate grindstone, charcoal (mf 7330.2, 7395), Banesh sherds, and animal bones were on the surface of the bench.

Room 282

Room 282 (ca. 3.36 m²) is a trapezoidal space at the east end of Corridor 288 with white plastered walls. Door 321 gives access to Room (or corridor) 293 to the east. Banesh sherds and bitumen (mf 6695) were found in the fill, Stratum 13A (DC 35), in this room.

Room 293

The walls of Room 293 (110x>120 cm), which may have been a corridor, were plastered in white with evidence of black stripes higher up. Three layers of fallen black and white painted wall plaster on the floor of this room were not removed (Pl. 7b). No finds, sherds, or bones are recorded for this room.

Room 297

This white plastered room was explored only in a narrow strip (1.4 m²) to define the east face of Walls 285 and 284. Access to Oven 300 was from Room 297. The oven was damaged in antiquity during the construction of BL 3, but the preserved section of burned plaster floor (120x40 cm), the configuration of the space created by Wall 306, and the curvature of the interior plaster, suggest a large domed oven, probably for baking bread. Banesh sherds were found in the fill (DC 35) but no finds are recorded.

Area 301

This small area (ca. 0.48 m²) is known only to the extent that the faces of the enclosing white walls (Wall 298, Wall 284, the brick Door Blocking 383, and Wall 323) were traced. The bricks used in Doorblocking 383 are the same size as those used in the NE building and in the construction of Walls 240 and 242. No finds, sherds, or bones were found.

Area 283

This area (>340x190 cm) has unpigmented plaster walls and a well worn floor without evidence of water-laid clay. The triangular areas to the east, between Walls 287 and 296, and to the west, between Walls 289 and 295, were not excavated below the level necessary to define the walls. Jasper (mf 7020), prase (mf 7018), and chert (mf 7019, Fig. 31b) flakes, and Banesh sherds were found in the fill (DC 35) of Area 283.

Building Level 3

Construction Sequence

Building Level 4 was razed to prepare the surface on which BL 3 (Fig. 12; Pls. 8, 9) was constructed. BL 3, which extends beyond the excavated limits of the ABC operation in all directions, was constructed on a thin (5-10 cm) layer of smoothed mud plaster over bricky rubble, designated Stratum 12, just above the BL 4 wall stubs and on bricky rubble or roughly laid bricks

within BL 4 rooms and spaces. The N-S walls of BL 3 are oriented 1 degree west of magnetic north, which represents a 6.5 degree clock-wise rotation from the orientation of BL 5 and the NE building of BL 4. The first construction phase of BL 3B (Fig. 13) included all of the walls defining the central row of rooms (Rooms 211, 220, 222, 267, and 268), the eastern row (Rooms 373, 63, 35, and 34), and the SW group (Rooms 269, 270, and 271), which are bonded together (Figs. 12, 13). Soon after these central, eastern, and southwestern rooms were completed the area north of Wall 275 and west of Wall 210 was divided into 4 rooms (Rooms 228, 229, 230, and 232) by the addition of Walls 225, 226, and 227, which are not bonded to Wall 210. Although it cannot be conclusively demonstrated, it is probable that all 3 walls were constructed at about the same time, which completed the plan designated BL 3B (Fig. 13). At a later date this group of added rooms were abandoned and replaced by an outdoor space designated Area 260 (Fig. 14). At about this time the west end of Wall 275 was removed and the BL 3B Room 304 also became a part of Area 260. The creation of Area 260 resulted in the plan designated BL 3A (Fig. 14).

The standard brick used in BL 3 measures 40(±2)x20x8 cm. The observed variation is probably a result of the difficulty of obtaining accurate measurements on excavated bricks rather than the use of several brick sizes. In BL 3 walls a variety of brick-laying patterns were used in alternating courses, including: HHH, SHHS, HSHS, HH, SHS, HSS, HS, SS, and H, where H stands for "header" and S stands for "stretcher" (Fig. 12; Pls. 8, 9).

Wall Paintings

Fragments of Banesh period wall paintings were found in Operation TUV and in other levels at ABC, but the largest number, clearly derived from ABC BL 3, were recovered from Strata 9 and 11A. These paintings were studied by Janet W. Nickerson (1977) and much of the following discussion is based on her work and the analysis of plasters and pigments by M. James Blackman (1982). The larger fragments are catalogued in Table 9 and illustrated in Figures 15-19 and Plates 11 and 12; the location of these fragments is shown in Figure 14 and Plates 8 and 9.

The 9 small fragments (Table 9, 12 and 13a-h) found in Room 304 are from BL 3B, Stratum 11A. The others, which were found in the Stratum 9 bricky rubble, are generally at the level of the top of BL 3 wall stubs, about 40 cm above Floor 10A. Two large fragments (numbers 14 and 15) were found resting partly on top of the stub of Wall 210 and 2 others (numbers 28 and 29) were found on top of Wall 17. All of the fragments recovered were found face up and appear to have been preserved when sealed beneath the final mud surface on which BL 2 was constructed.

Direct evidence that these paintings were installed on the walls in BL 3 comes from Room 268, where the border of a panel stretching the length of the room is preserved on the painted eastern face of Wall 210. This border is composed of a series of black, white, red, and yellow horizontal stripes on the red painted surface of the wall beginning 18 cm above the floor. The stripes turn to form a vertical border at the NW corner of the room, defining a central white panel. This pattern matches the pattern on a large fragment (Table 9, number 14) found on Wall 210, which has stripes defining opposing red and white fields. A second fragment, with a step pattern (Table 9, number 15), found below number 14, may have been from the center of the white panel.

In other places, however, the find spot of fragments does not appear to be a reliable indication of the room in which they were installed. In particular, the fragments from the fill in Area 260 (Table 9, numbers 1-9) are unlikely to have come from the west face of Wall 210, which has only unpainted mud plaster above Floor 10B. In general the distribution pattern of fragments, forming a gentle curve from the north end of Area 260 through rooms 222, 267 and into Room 34, suggests that the leveling process involved a westward movement of material to build up a level surface in the large open space of Area 260. Only fragments 16 and 17 were found to the north east. There are other lines of evidence indicating that the western rooms of these buildings were founded on unstable sloping ground. Alden originally interpreted Wall 242 in BL 4 as a local defensive wall founded on trashy rubble sloping to the west and he recorded in his field notes a suggestion by R. H. Dyson, Jr. that subsidence of these trashy deposits on the surface sloping to the west might explain the abandonment of rooms along the western margin in both BL 4 and BL 3. It is even possible that the deliberate brick fill in the western rooms of BL 2 may also be related to the same problem. Although not unequivocal, it is probable that the paintings described here were originally on the walls of the central and eastern rooms of BL 3A and 3B.

Blackman's analysis has shown that a small amount of slaked lime was probably added to the mud wall plaster used to finish the BL 3 walls, producing a relatively hard smooth surface that is less likely to shrink and crack than mud plaster alone:

> The general procedure for preparation and decoration of walls, based on examination of several fragments of polychrome wall plaster, seems to be as follows. The exposed mud brick, bonded with mud and straw mortar, was first covered with up to several centimeters of tan to brown "plaster." Next a thin coat (1 mm or less) of white unpigmented or pigmented "plaster" was added. In the monochrome-decorated rooms this was the finishing coat. In the polychrome-decorated rooms the white coat formed the base and was incorporated into the multicolored design. Over the white coat, additional thin coats of red, yellow, black, and gray pigmented material were applied to create the desired motif. Microscopic examination of the interface between the various layers of material indicated that each layer was allowed to dry before the next was added. (Blackman 1982: 111)

The white plaster "appears to be a finely ground, incompletely calcined lime plaster to which no material other than pigment has been added." The pigments have been identified as "hematite, geothite, and probably organic carbon to produce the red, yellow, and black coloration respectively" (Blackman 1982:111).

Aside from the striped borders, 3 distinct motifs are represented: step patterns (Figs. 15, 16), swirl patterns (Fig. 19) and rosettes (Figs. 17, 18). The polychrome step motif is composed of thin (1.7 cm), medium (2.5 cm) or broad (3.8 cm) stepped bands in various patterns that also incorporate crosses, four-petaled rosettes or isolated petals, and acute triangles. Several step motif fragments (Fig. 16d) also have broad curved elements. Bands of different width are not found together on the same fragment. The swirl motif consists of rows of sloping "S" or reversed "S" polychrome patterns with or without black "Z" elements in the center (Fig. 19).

Swirl motifs do not occur on the same fragment with any other motif. The isolated rosettes may be part of large step motif patterns but the only 2 examples are quite different from the leaf rosettes found on known step motif fragments. Two fragments (Fig. 16c and 17a) have low relief lines indicating that some central panels were set back 1-2 cm from the surrounding wall surface. Partial reconstruction of decorated panels, based on symmetry, are shown in Figures 17-19 (J. W.

Table 9. INVENTORY OF WALL PAINTINGS FROM BL 3

LOC	FIELD NO.	STR	FEAT	MOTIF	DIMEN
1	ABCN-246	9	260	RST	10X5
2	ABCN-230	9	260	MSC	16X10
3	ABCN-229	9	260	BND/MSC	44X34
4	ABCN-228	9	260	STP	14X13
5	ABCN-188	9	260	STP/RLF	58X47
6	ABCN-082	9	260	CRV	75X58
7	ABCN-083	9	260	STP	40X40
8	ABCN-123	9	260	STP/PTL	42X40
9	ABCN-124	9	260	BND	74X34
10	ABCS-119	9	304	STP/RST	55X36
11	ABCS-144	9	271	STP	29X25
12	ABCS-145	11A	304	STP/RST	15X15
13A	ABCS-154	11A	304	MSC	18X12
13B	ABCS-153	11A	204	—	SMALL
13C	ABCS-152	11A	304	STP	12X8
13D	ABCS-151	11A	304	STP/CRV/PTL	17X14
13E	ABCS-150	11A	304	BND	14X11
13F	ABCS-149	11A	304	—	SMALL
13G	ABCS-148	11A	304	STP	8X8
13H	ABCS-147	11A	304	BND?	SMALL
14A	ABCS-143	9	269	BND	56X40
14B	ABCS-143	9	269	BND	36X31
15	ABCS-156	9	269	STP	40X36
16	ABCN-227	9	373	STP	35X12
17	ABCN-231	9	373	BND	42X22
18	ABCN-144	9	222	STP/TRI	50X48
19	ABCN-145	11A	222	CRV	47X36
20	ABCN-146	9	222	STP/TRI/PTL	56X48
21	ABCS-040	9	267	STP/TRI/RST	42X32
22	ABCS-39	9	267	CRV	64X60
23	ABCS-38	9	267	CRV	50X44
24	ABCS-38	9	267	CRV	65X65
25	ABCS-15	9	268	RST	21X15
26	ABCS-37	9	268	STP/PTL	58X47
27A	A-	9	34	CRV	SMALL
27B	A-	9	34	CRV	SMALL
28	A-	9	34	STP/RST	—
29	A-110	9	34	STP	35x28
30	A-	9	34	CRV	SMALL

LOC- location number on Fig. 21; FIELD NUMBER- operation find number;   STR- stratum number; FEAT- found in the fill in this feature; MOTIF- BND= band, CRV= curved or swirl, MSC= miscellaneous, PTL= petal, RLF= part of the surface is set back 1-2 cm, RST= rosette, STP= step pattern, TRI= triangular pattern; DIMEN- dimensions in cm

Nickerson 1977). Although various step, swirl, and rosette motifs are found on pottery and glyptic from the eastern Mediterranean to central Asia, no stylistically comparable contemporaneous wall paintings are known.

Description of Features

BL 3 rooms are described below beginning with the north central Room 211 and moving south through the central group to Room 268, followed by the eastern group of rooms (Rooms 373, 63, 35, and

34), also from north to south. The SW group of rooms (Rooms 269, 270, 271, and Room 304) are described next, followed by outside Area 260 and the NW group of BL 3B rooms (Rooms 228, 229, 230, and 232).

Room 211

Room 211 is a long narrow room (>670x310 cm), probably about 700 cm long if a reconstruction based on symmetry around Hearth 213 is correct. The walls are coated with red painted plaster 6-8 cm thick. The floor is white and shows evidence of five replasterings within 7 cm above Floor 11B. Hearth 213 is a low rectangular plastered platform one brick (about 8 cm) high built against Wall 210. It was constructed on Surface 11B; the later replastered surfaces abut the face of the hearth. Doors 212, leading to Room 63; 216, leading to Room 373; and 217, leading to Room 220, are all plastered white and have sills 6-10 cm above Floor 11B.

A sealing (mf 1973), tablet fragments (mf 1693), and a retouched chert blade (mf 6643, Fig 34g) were found in a mixed, but clearly Banesh context in Floor 11B (DC 29). Finds in lots above Floor 10A (DC 37, LI G) include a chert blade (mf 1221, Fig. 34c) and specular hematite (mf 6703).

Alden (2003) notes that this deposit (ABCN 99, DC 37) produced exceptionally small straw tempered goblet rims (mean weight 5.7 grams/sherd). The only other ABC lot that produced a relatively large collection of similar light weight sherds is ABCS 65, a floor removal lot (DC 29) in Room 304, which has the only identified entrance to BL 3. Alden suggests that heavy foot traffic tramping through Room 304 was responsible for the fragmented sherds on the floor, which in turn may imply that Room 211 was also an area of heavy traffic, possibly near another doorway into the building.

Other DC 37 finds at this level that may be either from this room or from Room 220 (LI H) include a chert blade with sickle sheen (mf 6624, Fig. 34i), a pierced bitumen disk (mf 6737, Fig. 38h), chert and flint flakes (mf 11230, 6625, Fig. 32b), nacre inlay (mf 6820), a fragment of plaster vessel rim (mf 9790), a rare strainer sherd (mf 11232), calcite (mf 11231), and slag with copper prills (mf 1515). This deposit also produced Banesh sherds and animal bones.

Room 220

Room 220 is a small square (320x320 cm) room with white plastered walls, floors and doors. The unique feature of Room 220 is the small (160x120 cm) "closet" formed by Wall 219 to the north, Wall 33 to the east and Wall 387, built against the plaster face of Wall 223 to the south. The east end of Wall 223 was not discovered in excavation, leaving the nature of bonding between Walls 33 and 223 in doubt. However, the reconstruction is supported by the fact that all other walls extending to the west from Wall 33 are bonded to Wall 33. The reconstruction of the bond between Wall 33 and the row of bricks along Wall 223 is modeled on the bonding of Wall 219 with Wall 33. Wall plaster is absent from the row of bricks, and plaster on Wall 33 inside the "closet" is only 2-3 cm thick while it is 5-6 cm thick north of Wall 219. The BL 3 construction surface, Floor 11B, is 10 cm below the upper surface of Floor 10A, which had been replastered once. Door 221, with a sill 6 cm above Floor 10A, leads into Room 222.

Charcoal (mf 7326) was found on Floor 10A (DC 21) and a chert blade (mf 6612, Fig. 34e) was found above (DC 37) the floor; a relief decorated sherd (mf 1192, Fig. 27e) came from the Stratum 10A fill (DC 35), but certainly belongs in the BL 3 assemblage. Stratum 10A (DC 21, 29, 37) also produced Banesh sherds and animal bones.

Room 222

Room 222 is a small (315x290 cm) room, almost square, with white floors and doors and red walls. All three replasterings of Floor 10A (total thickness 4 cm) abut the final coat of wall plaster. Door 215, leading to Room 63, has a sill 7-8 cm above Floor 10A. Door 224, sill height not recorded, leads to Room 267. A stone sample (mf 5979), charcoal (mf 7329, 7402), Banesh sherds and animal bones were found in Stratum 10A (DC 37). Floor 11B (DC 29) produced a seal impressed tablet (mf 1692, Fig. 44c).

Room 267

This small room (310x300 cm), with white plaster doors and floor, and red plaster walls, stands in a pivotal position in the plan of BL 3 because it is the only room in the central group that can be entered from the west. Door 38, sill height 9 cm, leads to Room 35; Door 316, sill height 4-7 cm, leads to Room 271; Door 315, sill height 7 cm, leads to Room 268. Stratum 10A (DC 37) produced 2 chert flakes (mf 7004, 7005) and animal bones.

Room 268

This long narrow room (>630x385 cm) is very similar to Room 211 in plan and dimensions. The base of Hearth 277, built against Wall 210, is constructed of bricks covered with plaster but the upper surface of the hearth was apparently destroyed during the construction of BL 2. There is a small (20x20 cm) red plastered niche (Niche 379) in Wall 279, 28 cm above the floor and 18 cm west of Wall 17. A large fragment of striped wall painting was found on top of the stub of Wall 210 near the NW corner of Room 268. This fragment, together with the discovery of horizontal stripes on Wall 210 18 cm above the floor, suggest the reconstruction of a white panel surrounded by black, white, red, and yellow stripes on the east face of Wall 210. Floor 11B consists of 3 superimposed white plaster surfaces (total thickness 4 cm) with traces of red and yellow pigment splattered on the middle surface, which suggest that the walls were first painted soon after the initial occupation of BL 3B. Doors 37 and 374 lead to Room 34. The existence of Door 374 is not absolutely secure although the evidence of some type of feature in Wall 17 at this point is clear. Just in front of Door 374 there is a flat stone (30x20x2 cm) (Misc. 382) set into the floor, perhaps part of a narrow step (70x20 cm) or other feature associated with Door 374.

Stratum 10A (DC 37) produced a relief decorated sherd (mf 1049, Fig. 27c) a limestone ball (mf 1204), and Banesh sherds. Stratum 11B (DC 29) produced a backed jasper blade (mf 7021, Fig. 34f) with no micro wear, Banesh sherds, and charcoal (mf 7334).

Room 373

Room 373 (>650x>210) was only excavated enough to define the wall faces, which are red plastered, and to confirm that no door into Room 63 exists along the excavated stretch of Wall 214. No finds, sherds, or animal bones are recorded for this room.

Room 63

This is the largest room (1070x>630 cm) in BL 3. It is comparable to Room 71 (1580x420 cm) and 2 other possible large rooms with only one dimension defined by excavation (Rooms 31 and 130), all in BL 2. Under the assumption that the east wall of Rooms 373, 63 and 35 is a long north-south wall, similar to Walls 210 and 33, and assuming that Hearth 36 is symmetrically centered along Wall 16, the dimensions of Room 63 would be 1070x700 cm. The excellent condition of the red plaster walls and the white plastered floors indicates that Room 63 was roofed, but the minimum E-W roof beam span, about 700 cm wall-center-to-wall-center, is exceptional. The absence of stone column bases or disturbed areas where such stones could have been installed, implies that the roofing system spanned

Room 63 without internal support. In present day building practice roof span is seldom greater than 480 cm, and generally no more than 380 cm, when poplar or willow beams are used. In Banesh buildings only Room 71 in BL 2 and Room 63 are known to exceed these dimensions. Carbonized wood from BL 3 flotation samples includes poplar, maple, elm, oak, pistachio, and almond (Miller 1982, Table C1). It is unlikely that any of these samples are from roof beams because the roof beams would have been removed when BL 3 was razed to construct BL 2. There is no evidence at Malyan for sturdier beams that would have spanned distances greater than 3-5 m.

Wall 33 along the western side of Rooms 63 and 373, but not along the western side of Room 35, is thicker than any other wall in BL 3 and is only equaled in ABC Banesh buildings by Wall 106 (including Walls 156, 190) in BL 2. The exceptionally sturdy construction of Wall 33 may be related to structural requirements for roofing Rooms 63 and 373. The only other evidence bearing on this problem is the representation of two building facades on the pithoi from BL 2. These two motifs appear to represent light weight structures with reed mat walls and pitched roofs. One of them (Fig. 28e) appears to have a stream of smoke rising from one corner and the pitched roof is supported by a truss system. The notion of a truss supported pitched roof is unexpected in a Banesh context and is only tentatively proposed here as a solution to the problem of roofing Room 63 and other large rooms in these buildings. The absence of any roofing tiles in BL 3 implies that such a roof would have been thatch, boards, or shingles. The clay tiles discovered in BL 2 are not well designed for roofing, are rather heavy, and were not recovered in sufficient quantity to suggest that they were used on a pitched roof. Given the light weight of thatch or wooden roofs in comparison with traditional beam, mat, brush, and clay flat roofs, it might have been possible to span the area of Room 63 with a truss supported pitched roof. The only evidence that I know of concerning truss structures in ancient Iran is the interpretation of a Susa sealing as representing a truss support to elevate granaries above ground (Farshad and Isfahanian 1977).

There are 6 white plaster floors (total thickness 11 cm) laid on a prepared clay surface 8 cm thick on which the walls were constructed; because there are no intervening deposits, Surface 11B cannot be distinguished from Floor 10B. Hearth 53 is constructed of several courses of bricks and has a plastered surface measuring 115x90 cm. The plaster does not cover the row of bricks along the north and south sides, leaving open the possibility that Hearth 53 was enclosed with higher wing walls or perhaps even roofed.

Stratum 10A (DC 37, LI M) produced Banesh sherds, a jasper tranchet point (mf 2108, Fig. 35f) with no microwear, a prase flake core (mf 9907), a chert blade segment (mf 6541, Fig. 34j) a microlithic crescent (mf 2113), several chert flakes (mf 6615), *Ancilla* (mf 7278) and *Pinctada* shells (mf 6815), and a piece of rose quartz (mf 6718, Fig. 37e). Stratum 11B (DC 29) produced Banesh sherds, chert flakes (mf 9908, 9899), a jasper flake (mf 6640, Fig. 31e), slag (mf 2147), plaster (vessel fragment?, mf 2148), pyrite (mf 2149), a fragment of nacre (mf 9898), and a calcite sample (mf 9793). The removal of Hearth 53 (Stratum 11B, DC 36) produced 60 bitumen beads (mf 6698, Fig. 38p, q), a bitumen sample (mf 9808), 2 nacre inlay pieces (mf 6826), and a piece of clinoptilolite (mf 9788, Fig. 37h), a mineral used to produce beads and cylinder seals. It seems unlikely that these finds were part of the hearth building material; they may belong to the BL 3 assemblage.

Room 35

Room 35 (>420x310 cm) has red plastered walls and a series of 3 white plastered floors without intervening deposits. Hearth 36 (Pl. 10A) is a domed hearth (75x40 cm). The flat surface and back wall, preserved to a height of 20 cm above the hearth floor, show signs of multiple plaster layers. The lower sill of plastered Niche 378 (85 cm long, 15-18 cm deep) in Wall 16 is preserved near the SW corner of the room (Pl. 10B). A jasper drill (mf 7013) was found in Stratum 11B (DC 29).

Room 34

Room 34 (>660x290 cm) has red plaster walls and 3 superimposed white plaster floors resting on a clay surface (total thickness 6 cm) with no intervening deposits. No features were found in this room. The width of Wall 15 was established in two small cuts which also showed that the east face is coated with white plaster. Stratum 10A (DC 21) produced a handsome incised plaster bowl rim with red and black painted design (mf 189, Fig. 41e; Pl. 21d). Stratum 10A (DC 37) produced Banesh sherds, a copper bar (mf 874), a shell bead (mf 224), and a wooden or bone knob (mf 228). A relief decorated sherd (mf 1733, Fig. 27g) and a turquoise (?) bead (mf 6743, Fig. 37q) came from Surface 11B (DC 29).

Room 269

Room 269 (560x290 cm) has white plastered walls and a series of three thin white plaster floors on a 6 cm thick clay layer above a fourth white plaster floor. The floor slopes so that the SW corner of the room is 30 cm lower than the SE and NE corners, additional evidence that the western edge of this building is founded on unstable deposits. Hearth 278 (87x>20x27 cm high), was built on the earliest floor. This is the only ABC Banesh indoor hearth that is unquestionably not located in the center of one side of the room. Door 375, leading into a room to the south, is painted with white plaster and has an 8 cm sill. Door 320, leading into Room 270, has a white plastered jamb and a 6 cm sill.

Stratum 10A (DC 21) produced nacre inlay pieces (mf 1262) while DC 37 (LI G) lots in the same stratum produced Banesh sherds, animal bones, chert flakes (mf 1217, 7003), a heat treated jasper pointed tool (mf 9833), and calcite (mf 9840). A Stratum 10A lot (DC 37) classified as mixed (LI M) on the basis of a single possible Kaftari sherd also produced a relief sherd (mf 1187, Fig. 27h) slag (mf 1499), a chert flake (mf 7001.1), a chert blade (mf 7002, Fig. 33a), and a chert drill with microwear indicative of use on hard material (mf 7001.2, Fig. 35j), specular hematite (mf 9830), and a *Pinctada* shell. The relief sherd and the nacre inlay certainly belong to the Banesh assemblage and the other DC 37 finds may well belong to the BL 3A assemblage. Charcoal (mf 7331) and Banesh sherds came from Surface 11B (DC 29).

Room 270

Room 270 (285x185 cm) has white plaster walls and a series of four white plaster floors (total thickness, 4 cm) without intervening deposits. There are splatters of yellow pigment on the earliest floor. Door 319 leads into Room 271. Banesh sherds and charcoal were found in Stratum 10A (DC 37).

Room 271

This small room (280x180 cm) is a passageway or vestibule between Room 304 and rooms to the south and east. The walls are white plaster and there are three white plaster floors on an 8 cm clay layer resting on a layer of bricks. The door jamb plaster of Door 317 was worn away and the sill, between 3 and 6 cm high was badly worn. Door 316, leading to Room 267, is in better state of repair; white plaster on the jamb is intact, but the doorsill (4-7 cm high) is also badly worn.

During BL 3A, when Area 304 was no longer an enclosed room, a single row of bricks was placed just inside Door 317 to act as a windbreak or privacy screen for Rooms 271 and 267. No sherds or finds were found on the floor of this room in deposits derived from the occupation of the room (DC 21, 29, or 37), and the concentration of trash (Stratum 10A, DC 23) extending below the tops of walls 273, 275, and 276 and sloping down to a point on the floor in the southwest corner of the room is a result of leveling activities during the preparation for construction of BL 2. Although the finds from this trash deposit, mostly sealings and tablets, probably relate to activities during the existence of BL 3, they do not relate to activities within Room 271.

Room 304

In BL 3A, the final occupation of BL 3, Room 304, along with Rooms 228, 229, 230, 230, and 232, was part of the outside space designated Area 260. Room 304 was added to Area 260 by removing Door 318, Hearth 311, and the west end of Wall 275. The following discussion is focused only on Room 304 as it existed during BL 3B (Fig. 13). Only a small corner (>210x>130 cm) of the room was excavated, revealing red painted walls and nine small wall painting fragments on Surface 11B, sealed below Floor 10B. Below BL 3A Floor 10B there was a 9 cm clean clay layer (Stratum 11 A) resting on 2 superimposed badly worn white plaster floors. Door 318 gave access to Room 228. Stratum 11A produced a copper pin (mf 1496, Fig. 36j; Pl. 20c) and a limestone bowl rim (mf 9844) The exceptional small size (6.9 grams per sherd) of sherds from the floor (ABCS 65, DC 29) of this room supports the identification of Room 304 as an entrance area subject to heavy foot traffic (Alden 2003)

Room 228

Room 228 (>490x410 cm), which only existed in BL 3B, was sealed by Floor 10B consisting of a clay deposit 5 cm thick laid at the same level as the top of Wall 227. Below Floor 10B there are two plastered floors (total thickness 7 cm) resting on a 5 cm gravel deposit on a prepared clay surface designated Floor 11B. The use of gravel to level the floor, unusual in these buildings, may be an attempt to solve the problem of subsidence west of Wall 210. A fragment of black and white wall plaster was found on the surface above the gravel deposit on Floor 11B. Platform 380 is a red plastered feature (23 cm wide) built against Wall 210. Although Wall 227 may have been articulated with this feature, both the wall and all floors in Room 228 abut the plaster of Wall 210, demonstrating that they were constructed after Wall 210 was in place. Hearth 311, originally constructed on Floor 11B, was rebuilt after the gravel deposit floor repairs. The poorly preserved first version of Hearth 311 was at least 25 cm wide along Wall 275, extending out 30 cm; the later version of the hearth was 70 cm along the wall by 25 cm. Door 318 gives access to Room 304. A polished *Dentalium* shell (mf 6824), probably used as a bead, was found in Stratum 11B (DC 29).

Room 229

Room 229 (>490x240 cm) has a floor sequence similar to Room 228 except there is only one plaster surface between the Surface 11B gravel deposit and Floor 10B. Wall 226, like Wall 227 abuts the plaster face of Wall 210 and is sealed by Floor 10B. Door 231 leads into Room 230. A fragment of red wall paint was found still in place on the south face of Wall 226 between Door 231 and the west scarp. The possibility of a blocked door in Wall 226 1 m west of Wall 210 is indicated by a line of plaster that may define the door jamb.

Stratum 11B produced Banesh sherds, animal bones, and a group of finds from either this room or Room 228 (DC 29, LI H). These finds include a copper prill (mf 1508), a chert end scraper with microwear evidence of use on hide (mf 6628, Fig. 35d), flint and jasper blades (mf 6629, Fig. 33i; 6630, Fig. 34k), and a fresh water *Unio* shell (mf 6822).

Room 230

Rooms 230 and 232 are separated by Wall 225, which is not quite parallel to other BL 3 E-W walls, makes a right angle turn to the north 310 cm west of Wall 210 and then turns west again after 120 cm. Thus, the east-west length of Room 230 is >480 cm and the width is 320 cm in the east end and 510 cm in the west end. Wall 225 abuts the plaster face of Wall 210. The floor sequence is the same as in Room 229. No door was found leading north into Room 232. No finds are recorded from this room.

Room 232

Room 232 (>500x>210 cm) was only excavated in small soundings to establish the north face of Wall 225. Niche 385 (90x40 cm) on the north side of Wall 225 is associated with a stone door socket. The exact relationship of the socket to the niche could not be established and the socket may belong to blocked Door 136 in BL 2. The floor sequence in Room 232 is not known and no finds are recorded.

Area 260

Area 260 is an outside area west of Wall 210 (>1870x>500 cm) that includes the space formerly occupied by BL 3B Rooms 304, 228-230 and 232. When these rooms were abandoned Walls 225-227 and the part of Wall 275 west of Wall 276 were razed to within 20 cm of Surface 11B. A thin deposit of gravel was spread in the area of Room 230 and then a clay layer about 5 cm thick, designated Floor 10B, was laid down over the whole of Area 260. The west face of Wall 210 and the north face of Wall 275 have only plain tan plaster; no features are in Area 260 and the only access to rooms to the east is through Doors 317 and 316.

Stratum 10B (DC 29) produced Banesh sherds, animal bones, a retouched jasper flake (mf 1231, Fig. 31a), charcoal (mf 7321), and several unidentified stones (mf 8733, 9819, 9827). Finds from Stratum 10B (DC 37) include a jasper flake (mf 6613), a copper pin (mf 1504), a red marble spindle whorl or bead (mf 1289, Fig. 43d), a limestone bowl rim with tool marks still visible (mf 6055, Fig. 40i), Banesh sherds, and animal bones. Stratum 10A (DC 29) produced charcoal (mf 1161) and 2 relief sherds (mf 1186 and 1193; Fig. 27i, o).

Building Level 2

Construction Sequence

BL 2 (Fig. 20; Pls. 13, 14) was constructed on a surface prepared by razing BL 3 down to within 40 cm of Floor 10B and leveling the rubble from the walls. This leveling process produced a bricky rubble deposit, designated Stratum 9, above the stubs of some BL 3 Walls, particularly to the west, but less evident to the east where BL 3 wall stubs are immediately below Floor 8D, the earliest BL 2 floor (Pl. 4). The distribution of BL 3 wall painting fragments in Stratum 9, previously discussed, suggests that rubble was moved in a westerly direction to counter subsidence along trashy sloping ground to the west of the excavated area so that BL 2 could be extended further to the west than BL 3A. The N-S walls of BL 2 are oriented 3.5° east of magnetic north, which represents a 4.5° clockwise rotation of the N-S axis from that of BL 3.

The first phase of BL 2 construction involved all of the rooms west of Wall 28 and south of Wall 104. The construction of Walls 105 and 103 to form Corridors 117 and 118 no doubt occurred at the same time. The creation of Rooms 30 and 31 must have been later since Walls 56 and 12 are not articulated with Wall 28. The later addition of brick platforms, curtain walls, and door blockings is described below for each room.

BL 2 walls were built directly on a smooth clay surface laid over BL 3 rubble. There is some evidence, not conclusive, that Wall 125 was constructed on a lower surface or in a shallow foundation trench. The majority of bricks used in the original walls are 42x22x8 cm, but there are a few examples of bricks with other dimensions: 46x23, 40x22, 37x19, and 25x10 cm. Brick laying patterns in the thickest walls such as Wall 190/156/106 include courses of 2 headers (H) and 1 stretcher (S): HHS, HSH. Medium walls, such as Walls 28 and 104, have either SSSS, HH or combinations: SHS, SSH. Lighter walls, such as Wall 103, have SH patterns. Walls are typically finished with 4-8 cm of unpainted tan plaster although poorly preserved traces of white plaster can be discerned on the west face of Wall 28. Floors are tan plaster except for the remains of bitumen on the plaster floor in Room 129.

Tiles

A unique characteristic of BL 2 is the presence of over 100 fragments of fired clay tiles in the rubble fill of BL 2 rooms (Stratum 8A) and in the lower strata of the Kaftari trash deposit. These tiles range from 39-42 cm long, 20-23 cm wide, and 16-36 mm thick. They have either 4 holes, one in each corner, or 6 holes, adding a pair mid-way along the length (mf 643, Pl. 14c); one example has a fifth central hole and another example has no holes. The holes, which are not precisely positioned, are usually tapered, 6-14 mm in diameter and located at 24-90 mm from the end and 15-77 mm from the side.

Frequency distributions of tile thickness, hole diameter, and hole distances from end and side are basically unimodal, approximately normal or skewed curves, suggesting the tiles were produced following a general pattern that did not require a high level of uniformity. The sides and ends of the tiles are not ruler straight and the surfaces are not precisely level. These observations indicate that the tiles were made of clay slabs formed by hand, probably using a roller, and then cut to size. The holes were punched, the surface and corners were smoothed by hand, and in some cases a slip was added. The well fired, fully oxidized, heavy clay body is generally red or buff and is tempered with coarse black, brown, or red grit, with straw also present in some cases. The smoothed or slipped surface is usually red or reddish buff, but there are also some yellow or greenish yellow fragments. One example has a black painted target motif in the center and another has a deep groove in the surface. Many examples have a thin coating of bitumen on 1, 2, or—in a few cases—3 edges. Only one example has a bitumen coating thick enough to have formed a good seal between the uneven edges of adjacent tiles, but this is probably an artifact of preservation and it is likely that the bitumen was used as a sealant.

The aggregate area of all tiles recovered is 3 m^2. The fact that some tiles have bitumen on 3 edges implies that they were arranged in at least 3 rows, side-to-side, for a minimum panel width of 60-70 cm, allowing for a length of about 460 cm. Most of the tiles were concentrated in the north end of Room 71 and in Corridor 117, but they were also found in other rooms and it is certainly possible they were installed in several places. It is also possible that a few tiles were not recorded during excavation and that others from the same installation were outside the limits excavated. No evidence of mounting, such as bitumen lines or peg holes, was found in the walls or floors of BL 2. It is possible, but unlikely, that these tiles were used as roofing tiles. Among other possible functions, they may have been used to protect a surface from moisture, to provide a smooth hard surface, or for ornamental purposes.

Description of Features

The description of features begins with the rooms south and west of Walls 104 and 28: first Rooms 129 and 130, then 128, 131, 154, 185, and 188, followed by Rooms 71 and 186. After that Corridors 117 and 118 are described, followed by a description of the partially excavated rooms along the eastern and northern edge of the operation.

Room 129

This small room (>285x225 cm) has unpainted tan plaster walls and no features (Pl. 14b). There are 2 tan plaster floors, Floors 8C and 8D separated by a 20 cm deposit. Door 136, originally leading to Room 128, was blocked at a later date by a packed clay (*chineh*) wall.

An odd shaped stone object (mf 1907, Fig. 43e), a perforated bitumen(?) disc (mf 1921.1, Fig. 38f) with a bead in the perforation (mf 1921.2, Fig. 38l), metallic slag (mf 6788), 12 nacre inlay pieces (mf 6813), a grinding or polishing hand tool (mf 10220), and Banesh sherds were found in Stratum 8D (DC 29). Stratum 8B (DC 29) produced an irregular nacre inlay (mf 6456) and an unidentified shell (mf 2574).

Room 130

Room 130 (1240x>330 cm) has unpainted tan plastered walls standing to a height of 150 cm (Pl. 14b). There is a coating of bitumen 2-3 cm thick covering Floor 8B in the north half of the room. Brick Platform 155, preserved to a height of 120 cm, was made of 15 courses of roughly laid half-bricks (22x22x8 cm) resting on a thin pebble layer on Floor 8C in the south half of Room 130. The north face of Platform 155 is smooth and was probably roughly plastered. The function of Platform 155 is not known, but the fact that Floor 8C slopes down to the west suggests that the platform may be related to the continuing problem of subsidence in the west rooms of these buildings. The badly preserved remains of Hearth 310 were found below Platform 155 beside the west scarp just north of Wall 159. Bitumen coating was also found on the floor near Hearth 310.

Stratum 8C (DC 29) produced Banesh sherds, animal bones, a chert flake (mf 7011), calcite (mf 9847), and charcoal (mf 7362); 2 nacre inlay pieces (mf 756.1, Fig. 39s; 756.2; Fig. 39c) are from a DC 37 lot in this stratum. Stratum 8B (DC 29) produced an obsidian flake (mf 2557) from the Renfrew 3A source (Blackman 1984; Appendix B, MAO-016), a *Dentalium* bead (mf 6427), and Banesh sherds. Also in Stratum 8B (DC 21): a charred wooden bead (mf 644), *Conus* shell beads (mf 645, 9963), a *Monodonta* shell bead (mf 9964), an obsidian flake (mf 2572) from Nimrut Dağ I (Blackman 1984; Appendix B, MAO-017), 10 rock crystals (mf 2570, 2571), a relief decorated sherd (mf 11288), and 71 *Dentalia* shells (mf 2568, 2569). DC 37 lots in Stratum 8B produced a stone bead (mf 6429), 15 *Dentalium* beads (mf 600, 601), a *Conus* shell bead (mf 629), 3 nacre inlays (mf 751.1, 751.2, 751.3; Fig. 39g, h), and fragments of fresh water *Unio* shell (mf 2554, 2575). Although these are not high find density DC 37 lots, the nacre inlays and possibly the other finds belong in the BL 2 assemblage.

Room 128

Room 128 (410x320 cm) has tan plaster walls and two tan plaster floors, 8C and 8D, separated by 3-5 cm (Pl. 14a). Room 128 is separated from room 129 by blocked Door 136, which originally had a door sill one brick high. The *chineh* blocking in Door 136 was preserved to over a meter in height. Room 128 is separated from Room 71 by blocked Door 26, composed of a *chineh* and brick extension of Wall 106 for 120 cm to the north and finished by a closure wall one brick wide at the north side of the door, all preserved to over a meter in height. Rooms 128 and 131 are separated by Wall 127, which is only 190 cm long, leaving a 220 cm wide opening that does not have a sill or a door jamb extension from Wall 106.

Stratum 8B (DC 29) produced a flint blade (mf 639), a copper bar (mf 763.2) and wire hook (mf 763.1), a tablet (mf 632), and 2 lead fragments (mf 9967). The DC 37 lots of this stratum produced Banesh sherds, a denticulated chert sickle blade with gloss and grass cutting microwear (mf 2573, Fig. 34a), a clay sealing (mf 623, motif 37, Fig. 44g), possible tablet fragments (mf 761), and an odd clay object that may be a plug for a vessel with an oval neck (mf 604, Fig. 43g).

Room 131

Rooms 131 (460x410 cm) and 154 were created by the construction of *chineh* Wall 160, which was built after Door 371 was blocked by a narrow *chineh* wall over 1 meter in height. The surface on which Wall 160 was constructed, presumed to be Floor 8C, was nor identified.

Stratum 8B (DC 29) produced a bone (?) 4 hole spacer bead (mf 599) and charcoal (mf 2566). The floor deposit (DC 21) contained a carved *Conus* shell bead (mf 590), 7 pieces of nacre inlay (mf 749, Fig 39i, j), 10 *Dentalium* shell segments (mf 2316), and Banesh sherds. The DC 37 lots produced fragments of specular hematite (mf 2310), unworked lapis lazuli (mf 2318), a copper bar (mf 2307), a clay knob (mf 753), a land snail shell (mf 2309), and charcoal (mf 2322).

Room 154

Room 154 (600x410 cm) is separated from Room 185 by a *chineh* wall, preserved to a height of 1 m, blocking Door 157. Access to Room 71 is through Door 170, which has no sill. Bin 146 is a shallow plaster hollow partly destroyed by Kaftari Pit 152. Feature 147 is a badly preserved small (25x25x10 cm high) flat topped plastered structure that may be a hearth.

Ostrich egg shell fragments (mf 2326) were found in Stratum 8B (DC 29). Stratum 8B DC 37 lots produced a calcite ball (mf 2580), 1 white (mf 758.1) and 2 black (mf 758.2) stone disc beads, a chert flake core (mf 2313), 5 pieces of nacre inlay (mf 745, Fig. 39q; 6421, Fig 39e, f), a clay loop (mf 752), a biconical unfired clay spindle whorl (mf 742), fragments of specular hematite (mf 2317), unworked pyrophyllite (mf 2308), unworked weathered quartz (mf 2321), lead fragments (mf 2315, Fig. 36m; mf 2325), 1 possibly silver fragment (mf 2314, Fig. 36o), and copper fragments (mf 760, mf 6435, Fig. 36p, q; mf 2324).

Room 185 and Area 187

Room 185 (E-W >800x420 cm) has an extension to the south designated Area 187 (ca. >200x>100 cm). Room 185 is isolated from all other excavated BL 2 rooms by *chineh*-blocked Doors 157, 193, and 191. After BL 2 was constructed, Platform 189 was built against the plaster of Wall 159. The platform, which has plaster on the east and part of the south face, stands to a height of 1 meter where it abuts Wall 159 but slopes down sharply to the south because of erosion after BL 2 was abandoned. The remains of a large storage jar (Pythos 198) rest on the floor near the SE corner of Platform 189. A blob of slaked lime plaster (mf 931), a pyrite crystal (mf 932), 2 fragments of lead (mf 933), fragments of specular hematite (mf 934), 2 unfired clay sealings (mf 1956) without impressions, and an obsidian flake from Nimrut Dağ (mf 930) were found in Stratum 8B (DC 37). These finds are from a horizontally mixed (LI H) lot, but probably from this room.

Room 188

Only a small part of Room 188 (420x>70 cm) was excavated to define the east and south faces of Wall 192 and the chineh blocking in Door 191. No sherds or finds are recorded for this room.

Room 71

Room 71 is an exceptionally long narrow room (1590x520 cm) created from an even larger space by the construction of brick Wall 14. Room 71 is connected to Room 154 by Door 170. The existence of blocked Door 376 was not positively established during excavation. The first indication of this door through Wall 28 from Room 71 was noted during the removal of the balk between Operations A and B in 1971. The difficulty at this point in tracing the plaster on Wall 28, which was well preserved elsewhere and easy to clean on both sides, suggested the presence of a door. When the bricks that were purposely laid in the doorway were removed, a smooth but apparently unplastered door frame was revealed. The door sill, which was also smooth, was at the approximate level of the floor in Room 31 and the surface of Platform 27 in Room 71. The existence of a false door, created by the fortuitous presence of mortar joins between bricks from top to bottom of the wall, is unlikely in view of the use of alternate courses of stretchers and headers in the construction of Wall 28. Whether or not Door 376 provided access to Room 71 at some time, it is clear that it was not open at the end of the BL 2 occupation. If Door 376 did not exist, it is evident that Rooms 71 and 154, sealed by the construction of Walls 14 and 157, were never reopened.

Room 71 is distinguished by the presence of Platform 27 and at least 11, but probably 13 large painted pithoi (Pl. 13). The pithoi, described in Chapter II, are 1-2 m in maximum diameter and over 1 m in height (Fig. 28). They have narrow mouths, ca. 10-20 cm, and relatively small flat bases; at least one had a hole (diameter ca. 25 mm) near the base. Several of the pithoi, still in an upright position close to Wall 106 or blocked Door 26, were partly supported by mud plaster around the base. A number of the fired clay tiles discussed in the introduction to BL 2 were found in the Stratum 8A fill, on Floor 8B, or on Platform 27 near the pithoi. Several fragments of bitumen coated matting were also found on Floor 8B (Pl. 14d). Platform 27 is not bonded to Wall 28 but was constructed before the wall was plastered and before Wall 14 was added. The platform, apparently never more than a single course of bricks high, is 120 cm wide, with a finished mud plaster surface preserved on the west face but none on the top surface.

A number of finds came from the clay layer, designated Stratum 8D, below Floor 8C; although several surfaces were followed in different parts of Room 71, none of them could be followed over the whole room and none could be clearly identified as Floor 8C. These Stratum 8D (DC 29) finds include an obsidian blade from Renfrew Source 3A (mf 1303), 2 chert flake cores (mf 7263.1, 7300), chert and flint flakes (mf 6605, 7263.2, 6608), including one used to incise hard material (mf 6606), a chert tranchet point (mf 6607, Fig. 35e), a jasper pointed tool (mf 1224), 7 nacre inlay pieces (mf 1272), a fragment of *Pinctada* shell (mf 7280), a plaster vessel fragment (mf 1436), specular hematite (mf 6706), and copper fragments (mf 1131). Finds found either on the platform surface at the north end of Platform 27 (DC 21) or on Floor 8B (DC 21) between the platform and Wall 104 include 6 P-E

tablets (mf 624-27, 634, 635), 5 sealings (motifs 33, 34, 35, 36, 38) (mf 633, 636, 637) 2 lead fragments (mf 2333), and a pile of intrusive seeds (mf 2452). DC 37 lots in Stratum 8B produced a bone awl (mf 748), a clay bead (mf 1019, Fig. 37j), and worked fragments of *Pinctada* shell (mf 2146). Banesh sherds were found throughout the fill in Room 71 but animal bones are not recorded.

Room 186

Room 186 (>600x290 cm) is separated from Room 71 by Wall 14, which is not bonded to either Wall 28 or Wall 156. Wall 14 was built over Platform 27, which continues along Wall 28 in this room. No features were found except for a concentration of large pithoi sherds (Pythos 197) just north of the south scarp of the excavation. Door 29, leading to Room 31, was apparently cut through Wall 28 after BL 2 was constructed and then at some later time filled with bricks measuring 46x23x5 cm, a brick size not found elsewhere in ABC, although 23x23x8 cm half-bricks are found in Wall 28. After Door 29 was blocked the west face was finished with 45 mm of plaster but the east face was left unplastered. Only Floor 8B was well preserved in this room; it produced only a wall tile (mf 643, Pl. 14c) in a DC 37 context.

Corridor 118

Corridor 118 (>1720x160 cm) runs the entire width of operation ABC between Wall 104 to the south and Wall 105 to the north (Pl. 14). There are several doors leading north beyond the excavated area and an opening between Walls 104 and 103 leading to Corridor 117 (Pl. 14a, b). The walls and Floor 8B are finished with well preserved tan plaster and, although the floor is rather rough, it is not clear whether or not the corridor was roofed. A large (>100 cm in length), rough unworked stone (Misc. 386) was found on Floor 8B about 100 cm west of the entrance to Corridor 117. Several small wall painting fragments, found in the fill (Stratum 8A) well above Floor 8B, cannot be associated with any excavated room in BL 2. A trashy gravel deposit, designated Stratum 8D, composed of many finds, animal bones, and stones ranging from pea to fist size, extended the length of Corridor 118. There were scattered pebbles and gravel below BL 2 floors in a few spots south of Wall 104, but there is no evidence for other dense gravel deposits similar to Corridor 118, Stratum 8D. It is not known whether the gravel deposit extended under Wall 105 but it does not appear in section below the south face of Wall 104. Fragments of white painted plaster found at the base of Stratum 8D are probably from BL 3A, but could represent remains of an earlier floor in Corridor 118.

Finds from Stratum 8D (DC 29) include Banesh sherds, animal bones, 2 hollow clay balls, 1 from an Operation TUV clay source (mf 2013.2) and 1 from an ABC clay source (mf 2013.1) (Blackman p.c.; Blackman and Zeder 2003), *Conus* shell beads (mf 6817), 2 *Dentalium* segments (mf 7276, 7277), 69 pieces of nacre inlay (mf 6816), fresh water *Unio* fragments (mf 7275), 3 chert blade segments (mf 6660, 6661, Fig. 34b; 6662, Fig. 33g), a chert notched tool (mf 6663, Fig. 31c), 3 jasper flakes (mf 6616, Fig. 31d; 6617), a prase flake (mf 6618), 2 obsidian flakes (mf 7307, 10239)—both from Nimrut Dağ 1 (Blackman 1984, Appendix B), 42 sealings or fragments (motifs 9, 10, 31) (mf 1949, 1969, 1970, 1974, 1975, 1980), a P-E tablet (mf 1685), a stone vessel fragment (mf 9786), specular hematite (mf 6715), a relief decorated sherd from BL 3 (mf 1731, Fig. 27a), a copper prill (mf 1512), 15 lead fragments (mf 1510, 9807), and a radiocarbon sample (mf 1388, P-2335).

A tiny white frit or stone bead (mf 1306) was found during the cleaning of Floor 8B. Other finds from Stratum 8B come from a DC 21 and DC 37 lots. From DC 21: a perforated wooden disc (mf 764, Fig. 38g), 733 pieces of nacre inlay (mf 1276, 2448, Fig. 39a, k-m, u-dd), a P-E tablet (mf 628), many specular hematite crystals (mf 2447, 9924, 2564), 2 lead fragments (mf 2455, Fig. 36k), carbonate rock (mf 2450), quartz (mf 2451), charcoal (mf 2453), unidentified shell (mf 2456), 3 *Dentalium* segments (mf 2449, 2454), and a red pigment sample (mf 2458). From DC 37: a bitumen 2 hole spacer bead (mf 1305, Fig. 38i), 75 pieces of nacre inlay (mf 1093), specular hematite (mf 6704, 7266), *Engina* shell (mf 1107), an unidentified mineral sample (mf 9787), and charcoal (mf 7311). All of these DC 37 finds except the charcoal and *Engina* shell come from a high density DC 37 lot (ABCN 17; 188 finds/m^3) and probably belong to the BL 2 secondary trashy floor deposit.

Corridor 117

Corridor 117 runs south from Corridor 118 between two pairs of opposing piers that form niches in Walls 28 and 103 (150x500 cm). The corridor continues south into an open area (180x>290 cm), still designated Corridor 117, that is defined by Wall 103 to the north, Wall 56 to the south, and Wall 28 to the west. Before the construction of Walls 56 and 12, which are

not bonded to Wall 28, this could have been a very large courtyard or open space. Several base sherds from a pythos, similar to those found in Room 71, were found in the fill leaning against Wall 103 between the north and south piers. A thin sterile clay deposit, designated Stratum 8D, was excavated on the level of the gravel deposit in Corridor 118 but the gravel does not extend into Corridor 117.

Stratum 8B (DC 37) produced Banesh sherds, a carnelian bead (mf 9797), 2 lapis lazuli beads (mf 9798), and a white stone bead (mf 10244), specular hematite (mf 6686), charcoal (mf 7310.1), and *Conus* (mf 1112), *Engina* (mf 7268), *Pinctada* (mf 1113), *Dentalium* (mf 7310.2), and land snail shells (mf 7269, 7310.3). One of these DC 37 lots had high find density (ABCN 14; 22 finds/m^3) and the other (ABCN 16) was a flotation sample taken from ABCN 14; it is probable that these finds belong to the BL 2 trashy floor deposit.

Room 207

Only a small area (>500x>150 cm) of Room 207, north of Wall 105, was excavated down to Floor 8B. Descriptions of the floors and walls are not available and no features were found.

Stratum 8B (DC 37) produced 2 shark or ray vertebrae beads with traces of yellow and black pigment (mf 6664, 6793, Fig. 38e, d), an unfinished bead (mf 1294, Fig. 38j), a chert blade (mf 8851), a jasper flake core (mf 1069), chert (mf 6602, Fig. 30f) and flint (mf 6601) flakes, a nacre inlay (mf 1089), a small copper ring (mf 1135, Fig. 36b), a ceramic wheel (intrusive?) (mf 1913, Fig. 42a), zeolite (mf 9828), specular hematite (mf 6714), charcoal (mf 7315), and *Dentalium* shell (mf 1117). These DC 37 finds come from 2 high density lots (ABCN 42; 10 finds/m^3 and ABCN 30; 28 finds/m3); it is probable that these finds belong to the BL 2 trashy floor deposit.

Room 265

Room 265 (>70x290 cm) was excavated to Floor 8B. Descriptions of the floors and walls are not available and no features were found. Only Banesh sherds and animal bones were found in Stratum 8B (DC 37).

Room 31

Room 31 (>160x1010 cm) was excavated to Floor 8B; no features were found although dense bricky material found against the south face of Wall 56 may have been a platform similar to Platforms 27, 13, and 32. Banesh sherds, nacre inlay and a variety of unworked exotic minerals—turquoise, bitumen, calcite and rock crystal—were recovered in a mixed Stratum 8A (DC 35) context. No finds were recorded from Stratum 8B.

Room 30

Platforms 32, against the east face of Wall 28, and 13, against the south face of Wall 12 were the only features in Room 30 (>300x>210 cm). No additional information is available on the platforms, walls, or floors; no sherds, animal bones, or finds were recorded.

Summary

The stratigraphy described in this chapter represents a simple sequence of construction, occupation, alteration, and reconstruction activities in a series of 4 superimposed mud brick buildings. With the notable exception of BL 4, all of these buildings are designed on a regular rectangular plan and constructed with a fair degree of precision. Even in BL 4 the NE building has a regular rectangular plan. The more irregular rooms and corridors to the south and west of the NE building may relate to some combination of topography such as sloping ground to the west and south, defensive requirements, or adjustments required as infill construction closed the space between the NE building and unexcavated buildings to the SE, which may have had a different orientation. In some instances walls that were added to the original plan are not exactly perpendicular to the earlier wall they abut, for example Wall 356 in BL 5 and Wall 225 in BL 3B. Walls generally range in width from 90-110 cm, but narrower walls in the 50-70 cm range are not uncommon. Wall 33 in BL 3, at 140 cm, is the widest wall, but does not appear to be an exterior wall as might be expected.

Brick Dimensions

The standard BL 5 brick is 37x17x7 cm. Bricks from the NE building in BL 4B and the later additions in BL 4A are generally 47x22x8 cm or 43x20-21x8 cm, while bricks in the earlier walls of BL 4B are 37±1x17±1x7-8 cm. The most common brick size in BL 3 is 40±2x19±1x8 cm, but slightly smaller bricks 36x17-19 are reported. Brick specifications at TUV BL

3, which is contemporary with ABC BL 3, are 40x20x8 cm. Bricks of similar size (40x20x10 cm) are found in the Banesh city wall (Sumner 1985). The common brick size in ABC BL 2 is 44x22x8 cm, but smaller bricks are recorded: 29-40x18-19 and 23x23, which may be a half brick. Half bricks (22x22x8 cm) are common but are probably over reported in the field notes because the inexperienced workers from Malyan village tended to articulate 44x22 bricks as 22x22, which is close to the common 20x20 cm brick size made in the village at that time (Jacobs 1979:179). The brick dimensions reported here are as recorded in the ABC field notes and it is likely that some of the variation reported is due to imprecise measurement.

TUV BLs 1 and 2 have a brick size, 36x36x8.5 cm, not encountered in ABC (Nicholas 1990:21). The standard brick used in the Yahya IVC building is 48x24x8 cm (Beale and Carter 1983:82). The closest matches at Malyan are the 47x22x8 cm bricks found in ABC BL 4 and 50x25 cm bricks found in late additions to the Banesh city wall (Sumner 1985). It does not appear that the ABC buildings were designed using the Yahya Large Kuš (Beale and Carter 1983) as a standard of measurement.

Roof Beams

The maximum roof beam length required to span all but three ABC rooms, wall center to wall center, ranges between 310 and 480 cm, barely within the limits generally observed in contemporary vernacular buildings with flat roofs. The exceptions, Room 63 in BL 3, and possibly Rooms 67 and 332 in BL 4, exceed the limits imposed by poplar or willow beams used in the region today. The possibility of a truss roofing structure is discussed above in the section on Room 63. Maximum roof span in the Yahya IVC building does not exceed 380 cm (Beale and Carter 1983, Fig. 3) and neither Godin V (Young 1986, Fig. 1), nor Susa, Acropole I:17-14A (Le Brun 1971, Figs. 33 and 34; 1978b, Tab. 1, Figs. 14 and 17) appear to have spans exceeding 400 cm, although it is possible that some of the incompletely excavated rooms at Susa are larger.

The notion that the use of poplar or willow roof beams imposes a limitation on the width that can be spanned (wall center-to-wall center) is supported by the ethnoarchaeological literature on Iran. Watson (1979: 294) reports average room widths of 305 cm at Hasanabad, with the implication that some rooms were over 400 cm in width. The poplar beams used at

Hasanabad are 12-14 cm in diameter. Jacobs (1979:179) states that room widths are limited by the capacity of beams and are generally between 2 and 3 meters in a village in Fars.

Banesh levels at both TUV and ABC have produced charcoal from several other species of tree—oak, elm, ash, pistachio, almond, and maple—that might have provided timber for roof beams (Miller 1982, Tables C.1, C.2, D.1, D.2), but the samples are small in diameter and none appear to be from beams. Further, there were no stone bases or other evidence that beams were supported by columns at either ABC or TUV.

Hearths and Ovens

Hearths and ovens, which are the most notable features in these buildings, occur in several varieties. There are ephemeral burned areas in BL 5 (Area 358), BL 4B (Area 331) and BL 2 (Room 154), but they are not as common as the "casual hearths" at TUV (Nicholas 1990:42, 43). There are also 16 built hearths, usually rectangular in plan, in BLs 5-3. These hearths are all built against walls; 4 are centered along the wall and 5 others may have been centered. However, this possibility cannot be established because the walls were not completely excavated and the relevant room dimensions were not established. Only 2 hearths—Hearths 278 in BL 3 Room 269 and 299 in BL 4 Court 281—are definitely not centered along a wall. The built hearths are raised 1 to 3 bricks above the floor (ca. 8-27 cm) and usually measure 150-60 cm along the wall and extend out 110-60 cm from the wall. The surfaces are a rosy brick red, often badly worn, and show signs of previous repairs and resurfacing. Hearth 36, BL 3, (Pl. 10a) is domed and Hearth 238 in BL 4, which shows signs of side walls, may also have been domed; Hearth 327 in BL 5 also shows signs of raised brick side walls. Poorly preserved Oven 300 in BL 4A is a rectangular brick structure opening through Wall 285/299. The firing or baking chamber was only 80x70 cm in area; height undetermined. Hearth 344 (BL 5) is an enigmatic feature built into and adjacent to a blocked doorway leading into Court 353. There is evidence of a flue in the doorway and 2 separate burned surfaces, 1 in the doorway and 1 on the floor of the courtyard.

The rectangular built hearths in ABC are not closely paralleled by hearths at TUV, where cobbles and sherds are much more commonly used in hearth structures. However, there is evidence for flues within walls (Nicholas 1990, Pl. 7a) and domed hearths (Nicholas 1990, Pl. 7b) at TUV as well as ABC. The simple raised hearths found at ABC, with or without side walls or

dome, are similar to hearths at Susa, Acropole I:17B (Le Brun 1978b:64, Fig. 14 and Pl. XII, feature 819 in room 770) and Godin (Weiss and Young 1975, Pl. IIa) The distinctive raised box hearth found at TUV (Nicholas 1990, Pl. 7a), Godin (Weiss and Young 1975, Pl. IIb), and Susa, Acropole I:16C (Le Brun 1971, Pl. XIX:2) is not present at ABC.

Comment on Building Levels

The Banesh levels at ABC produced only 2524 finds from all contexts, although a concerted effort was made to collect and record a very broad range of objects, raw materials, production by-products, and a variety of samples for analysis. The low frequency of finds limits the extent to which purpose or usage of different buildings or rooms can be established on the basis of their contents. The fact that so few finds were present appears to be a consequence of good housekeeping and also quite likely a purposeful decision by the ancient builders to remove materials from BLs 5, 4, and 3 before they were razed and from BL 2 before it was sealed and left unoccupied. The limitations imposed by the small number of finds in good secondary context is ameliorated to some extent by the high density signature of some DC 37 lots, which allows the assumption that finds from such lots are in secondary context. Here we can describe the function of these buildings only in the most general terms. A more analytical approach to the assemblage is presented in Chapter IV.

BL 5 was a well designed and constructed building with no fewer than 13 rooms or courtyards, 6 of which were equipped with hearths. The building, excavated within a 115 m² area, extends beyond the limits of excavation in every direction. The interior walls and floors were generally finished with painted white or red plaster and several fragments of wall plaster with black paint suggest the possibility that some walls had wall paintings similar to those found in BL 3. BL 5 produced very few finds: several flints, a stone bowl, pigment samples, mineral samples, and several unimpressed jar stoppers and sealings. The ceramic assemblage is typical Banesh with at least one early type (Fig. 26b). Nothing about the plan or contents of BL 5 provides a strong clue to the function of the building, which is tentatively classified as a fine domestic house.

BL 4 also appears to have had a domestic function, with evidence for food preparation, small scale craft production, and administrative activity. The northeast structure of BL 4B had a carefully designed regular plan. This building appears to have been associated with several adjacent buildings that were modified to arrive at the final irregular plan of BL 4A, with its curved Corridor 241 and enigmatic structures to the south. It has been suggested that Malyan grew from a cluster of small settlements similar to Tal-e Qarib (Alden 1982a, Sumner 1986) and the curving double wall (Walls 240 and 242) along the western edge of BL 4A may enclose one such small settlement. There is also evidence of an enclosure wall around the TUV mound (Alden 1979: 200, 201). Later these small settlements were all protected by the main city wall constructed in Late Banesh times (Sumner 1985).

The ABC builders appear to have faced a serious construction problem along the western side of the excavated area. The western limit of BL 5 is not known and there is no evidence that the western part of the building was unstable. The earliest rooms (Rooms 331-333) along the western side of BL 4B were replaced by 2 wide walls (Walls 240 and 242) built on stone footings in BL 4A. This radical reconstruction, which occurred soon after the founding of BL 4B, may have been motivated either by problems of stability of the northwestern rooms of BL 4B or by the decision to build an enclosing wall, possibly defensive in nature, along the western edge of the ABC quarter. The notion that the western side of the ABC quarter was unstable, possibly due to sloping ground below BL 4B, was first suggested by Robert Dyson, Jr. This idea may also explain the unusual construction sequence in BL 3. BL 3B was originally laid out with an open space west of Wall 210 and north of Wall 275. This space was divided almost immediately into 4 rooms (Rooms 228-230 and 232) by the construction of Walls 225-227, which were not bonded with Wall 210. Very soon afterwards these rooms were abandoned, resulting in the BL 3A configuration. When BL 3 was razed to make way for the construction of BL 2 the general distribution of BL 3 wall painting fragments along a curve from northwest to southeast suggests that bricky debris, and even piles of discarded sealings, was dumped along the western edge of BL 3A. Sometime after BL 2 was constructed the south half of Room 130 and the west part of Room 185 were filled with carefully laid bricks (Platforms 155 and 189) that were intact up to the top level of the standing walls at the time of excavation. Although this discussion is by no means conclusive, it appears that the evidence of subsidence along the western edge of the ABC quarter and the presence of an enclosing wall in BL 4A suggest that the ABC excavations were near the western edge of a small settlement, one of the cluster of settlements, like Tal-e Qarib, that later grew into the city of Malyan.

In BL 3 the striking wall paintings, the exceptionally fine relief decorated pottery, a painted plaster vessel sherd, personal ornaments, sealings, and tablets all suggest an elite status for the occupants of this building. However, there were also a number of more mundane finds indicative of ordinary domestic activities—flints, minerals, animal bones, and ordinary straw tempered pottery. Thus BL 3 may have been part of an elite domestic complex or it may have served an institutional or administrative function; a combination of these functions is certainly possible.

A recent effort (Wasilewska 1991) to demonstrate that BLs 4, 3, and 2 served a religious function is provocative but not entirely convincing. Certainly the traditional continuity in the location of temples in Mesopotamia would suggest that if BL 4 was a temple, then it would not be unexpected to find the same function for the succeeding buildings. However, the argument for a religious function in BL 4 is speculative at best and the argument for BL 2 is even less convincing. Only in BL 3 does the discussion of color symbolism, patterns of circulation, and the nature of finds hint at a possible religious function.

Although the original purpose of BL 2 is unknown, its final function appears to have been primarily as a warehouse, with evidence of administrative activities. The warehouse could have been under the control of a religious or a secular institution—either public or private. In addition to P-E tablets and sealings, flint blades and flakes, mother-of-pearl inlay pieces, *Dentalium* and other shells, beads, scrap metal, lead, semi-precious stones, obsidian, and hematite crystals were found in the main building and in Corridor 118. These finds are related to long distance trade and the production of personal ornaments and other decorated objects. It is assumed that liquids were kept in the pithoi, although we were unable to demonstrate that all of them had holes near the base for removing liquids.

The blocked doors and packed mud curtain walls, added to the building during a late phase of occupation may have been temporary features designed to control storage activities by creating sealed rooms. However, when the building was abandoned these makeshift temporary walls were left in place, but the sealed rooms were virtually empty, and even the pithoi in room 71 appear to have been empty, which seems to be an anomaly if the walls were meant to control storage. An alternate interpretation might be that this building was closed and sealed before it was abandoned, but this too raises the logical question —why seal an empty building?

II

Banesh Ceramics

The Banesh ceramic assemblage was initially defined on the basis of sherds found in small survey collections (Sumner 1972:42-44) representing types not described by Vanden Berghe (1952, 1954) in his original formulation of the KRB ceramic sequence. Since then Alden (1979, 1982a) has published an important collection of Banesh sherds from an intensive surface survey of a number of sites and from excavated strata at Tal-e Kureh (this volume, Appendix D), the type site near the village of Banesh. Banesh ceramics from Malyan have been published in preliminary reports (Sumner 1974, 1976, 1985) and in the final report of excavations in Operation TUV (Nicholas 1990).

Stylistic parallels for Middle Banesh ceramics are found at Susa in Acropole I, levels 17–14A (Le Brun 1971 and 1978b; de Miroschedji 1976). Similar ceramics are also found in the Bakhtiari mountains (Zagarell 1982: 43-51), at Yahya, Period IVC (Lamberg-Karlovsky 1973: 30-34), and possibly at other sites in Fars (Stein, Sir Aurel 1936: 208-210).

General Description

The ABC Banesh ceramic assemblage includes coarse straw or grit tempered wares in a relatively limited number of forms. The interpretation of stylistic change through time (BL 5 through BL 2) and the interpretation of functional variation of sherds from different features is complicated by the fact that 72% of the ceramic assemblage that is available for analysis came from tertiary (DC 34-37) deposits that are related to

activities of an indeterminate earlier date and different context. Almost all sherds—95%—from secondary lots are from Area 307 (DC 21) and Pit 236 (DC 22), both in BL 4A (STR. 13A). The following discussion of Banesh straw tempered ware (ST Ware) is focused on these two contexts but sherd counts from tertiary bricky fill lots (DC 34-37) are also reported. Due to the relatively small number of sherds, all lots are included in the discussion of Banesh grit tempered ware (GT Ware). The general configuration of the assemblage, based on sherds available for study (Appendix B), is presented in Table 10.

The assemblage summarized in Table 10 is dominated by Banesh straw tempered ware (86% of all sherds), which is a coarse low-fired utility ware that occurs in 3 predominant forms. The most common form, represented by the straw tempered goblet rim (Rim: 73%; Fig. 21) and the straw tempered goblet pedestal base (Ped: 8%; Fig. 22r-ac), is a relatively tall flaring pedestal based goblet (Pl 15). The only other form that occurs with any frequency is the straw tempered tray (Tray: 17%; Fig. 23). Bevel rim bowls are relatively rare (BRB: 2%; Fig 22i-n) and just over half of the 44 sherds, counting rims and bases, derive from secondary deposits (DC 21-29, 37), which implies that the BRB was infrequently used in these buildings. The remaining straw tempered sherds (ST Misc.: 2%; Fig. 22a-h, o-q) represent conical or open channel spouted bottles or small pots, small vessels with holes pierced below the rim, and a few unclassified rims and bases. The remainder of the assemblage consists of Banesh grit tempered ware (GT: 12%) or miscellaneous (Misc.: 2%) sherds including Bakun, some stray Kaftari, and a few unclassified sherds.

Table 10. CERAMIC ASSEMBLAGE BY BUILDING LEVEL AND DEPOSIT TYPE

BL/DC	ST Rim	ST Ped	ST Tray	ST BRB	ST Misc.	ST Sum	GT Sum	Misc. Sum	ST+GT Sum
BL 2									
DC 21-29	142	10	28	4	1	185	51	6	242
DC 37	48	7	14	1	1	71	26	1	98
DC 35-36	153	14	47	5	3	222	82	18	322
Subtotal	343	31	89	10	5	478	159	25	662
Stratum 9									
DC 34	85	6	22	1	0	114	10	6	130
BL 3									
DC 21-29	244	5	32	6	0	287	27	6	320
DC 37	182	7	14	3	1	207	23	1	231
DC 35-36	230	14	24	4	2	274	60	26	360
Subtotal	656	26	70	13	3	768	110	33	911
Stratum 12									
DC 34	89	8	5	0	2	104	3	0	107
BL 4									
DC 21-29	580	119	196	2	15	912	55	0	967
DC 37	144	7	47	6	13	217	30	2	249
DC 35-36	195	20	33	10	3	261	43	1	305
Subtotal	919	146	276	18	31	1390	128	3	1521
BL 5									
DC 21-28	8	7	4	0	1	20	2	0	22
DC 37	21	2	8	1	7	39	3	3	45
DC 35	31	3	18	1	2	55	2	0	57
Subtotal	60	12	30	2	10	114	7	3	124
TOTAL	2152	229	492	44	51	2968	417	70	3455
%	(73)	(8)	(17)	(2)	(2)	86	12	2	100

Note: In the % row values in parentheses are % of ST Ware only, which totals 86% of the entire assemblage.

Banesh Straw Tempered Ware

The description of straw tempered forms presented here is based on sherds from unmixed secondary deposits (DC 21-23), mainly the outdoor trash deposit in Area 307, BL 4A and the contents of Pit 236 in Room 64, also in BL 4A. The sample of sherds available for study from other secondary contexts is too small to be reliable and the sherds from tertiary deposits are difficult to interpret, although they are included in Table 10.

Pedestral-Based Goblet

The pedestal based goblet (Fig. 21, 22; Pl. 15) is a large open conical vessel made of straw (chaff) tempered alluvial clay from the valley floor fired to a temperature between 600°-725° centigrade (Blackman 1981), frequently with an unoxidized black core in the thickest sherds. The surface of these vessels is roughly smoothed, often showing pits where the temper burned out. The color is a light tan or buff (Munsell 7.5 YR 7/4, 7/6, 6/4). String cut bases and deep spiral fin-

Table 11. PEDESTAL BASED GOBLET RIM FORMS BY STRATUM AND DEPOSIT TYPE

BL/DC	A	B	C	D	E	Sum
BL 2						
DC 21-29	6	1	0	2	6	15
DC 35-36	15	0	6	3	1	25
Subtotal	21	1	6	5	7	40
BL 3						
DC 21-29	38	5	0	2	3	48
DC 37	74	0	4	0	0	78
DC 35	5	1	0	0	1	7
Subtotal	117	6	4	2	4	133
Stratum 12						
DC 34	22	4	7	2	0	35
BL 4						
DC 21-22	462	29	7	8	8	514
DC 37	17	2	3	4	0	26
DC 36	1	0	8	1	0	10
Subtotal	480	31	18	13	8	550
BL 5						
DC 35	1	0	7	3	8	19
TOTAL	641	42	42	25	27	777
%	82.5	5.4	5.4	3.2	3.5	

ger impressions inside near the base provide evidence that these vessels were wheel thrown. When straw tempered sherds from Pit 236 in BL 4A were washed some of them dissolved releasing a number of carbonized seeds. A selection of these sherds were purposely dissolved in the flotation tank and produced a relatively large collection of wheat, barley, and weed seeds (Miller 1982:364, where Pit 236 is identified as Pit 84, the original field number).

There are five pedestal base goblet rim forms (Table 11), representing the same range of forms known from surface assemblages at other sites in the valley and from soundings at the Banesh type site (Alden 1979:218 and infra Appendix D). There are gradations (Fig. 21:l-r) in form between Type A (Fig. 21:a-k) and Type B (Fig. 21:s-ac), and there are also variations that do not fit into the typology (Fig. 21:ax-bd).

The rim counts reported in Table 11 include all sherds from unmixed lots available for study.

Measurements of rim diameter, rim thickness and rim angle prepared for an earlier study (Keirns n.d.), are used in this description, in addition to measurements of sherds not available during the earlier study.

Rim Type A

Rim Type A (Fig. 21:a-k), designated the "concave rim" by Alden (1979: 218, Figure 31:1-16), is a rounded, sometimes slightly flaring rim with at least one shallow concavity inside below the lip that appears to have been made by the thumb or forefinger as the rim was formed. Type A is found at TUV (Nicholas 1990, Pl. 13:m, o, p, r, t).

Rim Type B

Rim Type B (Fig. 21:s-ac) has an interior thickening just below the lip; there is a slope but no concavity between the lip and the thickest point. This type is found in surface collections and at TUV (Alden 1979, Fig. 31:27, 28; Nicholas 1990, Pl. 13:p).

Rim Type C

Rim Type C (Fig. 21:ad-ai) is a variant of Type B in which the thickest point is at the lip and is relatively flat. Type C, which is the same as the "thickened rim" defined by Alden (1979: 218, Fig. 31:17-30), is not illustrated from TUV (Nicholas 1990, Pl. 13).

Rim Type D

Rim Type D (Fig. 21:aj-aq) is characterized by a groove and ridge on the outer surface below the lip. Type D is quite variable, particularly in the morphology of the groove, which may be gently concave or sharply incised. This type is the same as the "pinched rim" defined by Alden (1979:218, Fig. 31:31-47). Type D is not illustrated from TUV (Nicholas 1990, Pl. 13).

Rim Type E

Rim Type E (Fig. 21:ar-aw), equivalent to the "round rim" defined by Alden (1979:218, Fig. 31:48-55), is a simple rounded rim, sometimes slightly everted. Some small examples of Type A, where the characteristic groove is not preserved, may be classified as Type E. Type E is not illustrated from TUV (Nicholas 1990, Pl. 13).

Rim Measurements

The diameters of 115 goblet rim sherds of all types as measured Keirns (n.d., Fig. 3) yielded a mean of 19.9 cm, with a range of 11-27 cm. This result is comparable to the diameters of 434 sherds (all rim types) measured by Alden (1979:219): mean 19.1 cm, range 12-32 cm, with a single exceptionally large example at 40 cm not counted. As apparent from Table 11, Rim Type A predominates in the ABC assemblage, most notably in the secondary deposits of BL 4 (Strata 13-14) and the BL 3 tertiary deposits (Strata 9-11). A group of Type A rims from BL 4A trash in Area 307, Stratum 13A (ABCN Lot 139) has a mean diameter (N=64) of 18.8 cm, range 13-27 cm, somewhat smaller than the collection (N=21) of Type A rims from other sites (Alden 1979: 219), which has a mean diameter of 19.2 cm, range 14-30 cm. Rim thickness and rim angle were also measured for Type A sherds from Area 307. The mean

thickness (N=113) is 0.8 cm, range 0.6-1.1 cm. Mean rim angle (N=50) is 64 degrees, range 45-78 degrees.

Pedestal Bases

Two types of goblet bases have been recognized in the Banesh assemblage: an early straight sided type and a later constricted or necked type (Alden 1979:218, Fig. 32; Nicholas 1990, Pl. 13). In the ABC assemblage only 31 of the 229 Pedestal Bases can be securely classified: 20 (65%) are straight sided (Fig. 22:r, u, y) and 11 (35%) are constricted (Fig. 22:s, t, v, w, x-ac). The mean diameter of bases (N=83) from Area 307, BL 4, is 7.3 cm (range 5.2-9 cm) excluding 1 exceptionally small (3.5 cm) and 1 unusually large (ca. 14 cm) example. Constricted pedestal goblet bases, which range in diameter from 4.5 to 8.25 cm, are dominant at TUV (Nicholas 1990:57, Pl. 13:w-bb).

Flat Tray

The Banesh tray (Fig. 23) is a hand-formed flat bottomed tray, up to 60 cm along its longest axis, with low sides, ca. 5 cm high, and simple straight or slightly flaring rims formed by pulling up the sides of a flat plaque of straw tempered clay; some rims are folded over to make them thicker. These trays may be round, oval, tear-drop or sub-rectangular in plan and the base retains the rough surface of the ground on which the tray was resting when it was formed. Some trays have a pouring lip. Surface treatment, color range, and firing conditions are the same as for the straw tempered pedestal based goblets. Trays are found in Banesh period surface assemblages throughout the Kur River Basin (Alden 1979:215, Fig. 33) and at TUV, where they make up 43-56% of the Banesh straw tempered assemblage (Nicholas 1990, Pl. 13:a-j and Plate 14:c, d).

Beveled Rim Bowls

Only 12 of the 44 BRB sherds (Fig. 22:i-n) in the ABC assemblage come from secondary trash deposits (DC 21-29), with an additional 11 from DC 37 lots, suggesting that the BRB was seldom used in the ABC buildings. The BRB sherds are small, making it difficult to establish the correct rim angle and diameter. BRBs are a much more common form at TUV, where they constitute 38-41% of straw tempered rim sherds from trash deposits in BL 3A-B and 12-14 % in BLs 1 and 2

(Nicholas 1990:54). The BRB is also found in many of Alden's surface collections (Alden 1979:325-327; Table 47).

Miscellaneous Forms

Other straw tempered forms, representing less than 2% of the ABC assemblage, include small pots and bottles with simple or folded rims and conical or open channel spouts and flat bases, larger restricted vessels with plain or folded rims, with or without holes below the rim (Fig. 22:a-h), bases (Fig. 22, o-q) and possibly several flat plaques. These forms are not represented in the TUV assemblage, but all of them are found at other sites in the valley (Alden 1979:220–21, Fig. 35; infra Appendix D).

Functional Classification

The increasing frequency of goblets and the decreasing frequency of BRBs after the Early Banesh Phase, postulated by Alden (1979:52, 349-55), and observed by Nicholas (Nicholas 1990:57) suggests the possibility that goblets may be a functional replacement for BRBs. Attempts to determine the function of BRBs have a long history, most recently reviewed by Chazan and Lehner (1990, with references), who present a strong argument in favor of BRBs as molds for baking bread. They also take note of the possible evolution of BRBs into a variety of conical vessels or "flower pots" found in Mesopotamian Early Dynastic sites. This explanation stands in contrast to earlier suggestions that BRBs were ration bowls (Nissen 1970; Johnson 1973), vessels for votive food offerings to a temple or in a domestic context (Beale 1978) or contributions (taxes?) to a secular authority Nicholas (1987). Nicholas and others recognize that these bowls may serve multiple functions and that their function in Mesopotamia may well be quite different from their uses in the Iranian highlands. Although Nicholas offers a systematic analysis that examines several functional, technological, and contextual variables, her conclusions remain tentative.

The goblets differ from BRBs in form, volume, and means of production. Knowledge of the function of BRBs, which still eludes us, would not automatically translate into an understanding of the function of the goblets. Moreover, the chronological picture is more complex than the simple goblets-replace-BRBs model.

Glyptic evidence suggests that ABC BL 4 is earlier than TUV BL 3. In TUV BL 3 BRBs predominate, but ABC BL 4 produced 126 goblet bases in secondary contexts (DC 21-29 and DC37) and only 8 BRB sherds from the same contexts. Most of the goblets came from a dense trash deposit west of Wall 242 (Area 307), which is probably derived from BL 4A buildings, and from Pit 236 in Room 64 of the NE building (Fig. 9). This demonstrates with some clarity that the chronological variable alone will not explain the relative frequency of BRBs and goblets in different contexts. Furthermore, ABC BL 4A is more closely comparable to TUV BL 3 than any other ABC level in terms of the *ad hoc* character of the architecture and evidence for domestic activities, which forces us to acknowledge that similar contexts may have very different frequencies of these two enigmatic ceramic types.

Aside from the fact that goblets were found in large numbers in trash deposits associated with domestic quarters in ABC BL 4A, only the morphology and volume of goblets may be useful in the quest for the function of these vessels. Although it isn't possible to estimate the volume of goblets with great accuracy, a rough estimate is possible. Assuming that the form of the goblets approximates a cone, one of the intact examples (Fig. 22:r; Plate 15a, b) has a volume of about 2100 cm^3. The mean diameter (18.8 cm) and mean rim angle (64°) of goblets from Area 307, BL 4A, would indicate an average volume of about 1600 cm^3. Some two thirds of the measured examples have a diameter between 17 and 21 cm and a rim angle between 59° and 71°. These dimensions would produce cones that range in volume from 1300-2600 cm^3. Thus goblets hold about twice as much as BRBs.

It seems most likely that goblets, trays, and other straw tempered forms are all functionally associated with food preparation and consumption, but a more specific statement does not appear to be warranted by the ABC evidence.

Chronological Implications

From the data presented in Table 11, the evidence of chronological changes in the ABC straw tempered assemblage is not strong. However, the sherds from secondary deposits in BL 4A, taken to represent an Early Middle Banesh assemblage, have 3 notable characteristics: 1) 90% of the goblet rims are Type A, 2) 89% of the goblet bases are straight sided, and 3) BRB sherds are rare (3 sherds: DC 21-29; 4 sherds DC37).

Sherds from all tertiary deposits, exclusive of the small BL 5 assemblage, may represent an hypothetical earlier assemblage because they are derived from deposits laid down at some indeterminate earlier date. The characteristics of such an hypothetical earlier assemblage stand in contrast to the BL 4A assemblage as follows: 1) 77% of the goblet rims are Type A, 2) 47% of the goblet bases are straight sided, and 3) 40% (17 sherds) of the BRB sherds found at ABC are in these deposits. On the basis of associations observable in surface collections Alden (1979, appendix E) proposed that the straight base was present in all sub-phases, but the necked goblet was present only in the Late Middle and Late Phases. The unexpected high frequency of constricted bases in this hypothetical early assemblage may be viewed as a challenge to the assignment of a relatively late date to necked goblets.

Banesh Grit Tempered Ware

Grit tempered sherds form a very small proportion (12%) of the ABC assemblage and an even smaller proportion of these sherds come from good secondary contexts (large storage jars, Fig. 28, and fine relief decorated sherds Fig. 27, are excluded from Table 10). All grit tempered vessels and sherds, including the large storage jars (pithoi) and relief decorated sherds, from all deposits (DC 21-37) are described here, with details on provenience provided in the captions for Figures 24-28.

Banesh grit tempered ware is quite variable; the temper includes fine, but more frequently medium to coarse, black, red, or white grit. Slips or partial slips above the shoulder in a variety of colors, but usually a thin white wash, are found on vessels with smooth to slightly abrasive surfaces. Painted decoration, usually restricted to bands, is commonly confined to the area above the carination on bowls or above the shoulder on pots and jars. Examples of incised or impressed decoration are rare in these levels but relief decoration on large storage vessels is well represented in BL 3 (Fig. 27).

It has been argued that at least some Banesh grit tempered forms were produced on the wheel by craft specialists using alluvial and better quality clay from deposits probably found near production villages located at the valley's edge (Alden 1979, 1982a, infra Appendix D). These clays fall into 3 chemically defined groups (Blackman 1981). Only 4% of the grit tempered vessels are made from the local high carbonate alluvial clay (chemical group I), probably because grit tem-

pered vessels were fired above the temperature of calcination, with the associated destructive gas discharge and volume changes. Most grit tempered ware was made of chemical group II clay (65%) or group III clay (31%). Blackman (1981) has argued convincingly that group II and III clays were in use from the earliest to the latest levels of Operation TUV and they were probably also in use during the entire occupation of ABC. The significance of a few samples that do not belong to any of the defined groups is not yet understood. Alden (1982a:83-100) has advanced a convincing argument to the effect that certain Early Banesh grit tempered forms were transported to a centrally located market for further distribution and it is likely that other forms were distributed in similar fashion.

Open Forms

Small Bowls

Carinated bowls are the most common grit tempered form (Fig. 24). They are typically between 12 and 20 cm in diameter and from 5 to 8 cm in depth, but larger examples, up to 30 cm diameter and 15 cm deep also occur. The carination, turning an angle of 120-130°, is usually located 1-3 cm below the rim and is generally quite distinctive (Fig. 24:a-d, h, i, m, p, t-z). The carination in some cases is ambiguous because the curve is gradual (Fig. 24:f, g, p). Other small bowls are not carinated (Fig. 24:k, n, o). Simple rounded rims predominate but there are a few slightly thickened examples (Fig. 24:b-d, f) and several examples with flattened club or expanded rims (Fig. 24:s, aa, ab, ac). These bowls must have round bases since no suitable ring or flat disk bases are present in this assemblage. Decoration is confined to brown or black bands. The bowls with more elaborate designs (Fig. 24:e, q, r) are stylistically Late Banesh. Their presence in the ABC Kaftari deposit and in Stratum 8A imply that Middle Banesh to Late Banesh transitional levels, not evident at ABC, were nearby, probably in the H5 deep sounding (see Chapter III). Similar small bowls are present in surface assemblages at other Banesh sites (Alden 1979, Fig. 38-40) and at TUV (Nicholas 1990:58-61, Pl. 20, 21).

Flaring Open Forms

These forms, more like beakers or vases than bowls, are characterized by a concave profile and a beveled or slightly thickened carinated rim (Fig. 26:b, d-f)). They are plain or decorated with black or brown painted bands on a smooth red or tan slipped surface. These forms resemble the plaster vessel from a Banesh grave in TUV (Nicholas 1990 Pl. 33) and a similar plaster vessel from ABC, BL 3 (mf 189, Fig. 41:e; Pl. 21d). Alden's surface collections include some similar flaring forms that he classified as terminal Lapui or Initial Banesh (Alden 1979, Fig. 52).

Burnished Plates

These large plates, up to 40 cm in diameter, have a dark red-brown roughly burnished surface, simple round or flattened rims, and unburnished rough flat bases (Fig. 24:i, j). The paste, relatively crumbly, is probably not fired to a high temperature, leaving a black unoxidized core. The temper includes coarse white grit and specular hematite. On the basis of one analyzed sample, it appears that the clay used to produce burnished plates does not fall into any of the chemical groups defined by Blackman (1981 and personal communication). These plates are also found in the TUV assemblage (Nicholas 1990, Pl. 15:c) but appear to be rare or absent from surface assemblages (Alden 1979, Fig. 40:12).

Closed Forms

Small Storage or Utility Pots

These vessels, with rim diameters up to 20 cm, have a great variety of neck and rim forms. There are hole mouth forms with rounded rims (Fig. 25:m, n), low necks with everted round or slightly thickened rims (Fig. 25:a, g, h), and a variety of expanded rims (Fig. 25:o-r). Some examples have nose lugs on the shoulder (Pl. 18c). Bases are flat with a straight or concave flaring profile above the bottom (Fig. 25:w-z). Some sherds have incised lines, impressed relief bands (Fig. 25:i) or painted bands (Fig. 25:a, g-i). Sherds with shoulder ridges (Fig. 25:j), carinations (Fig. 26:g, h), nose lugs, open channel spouts (Fig. 26:i, j) or closed conical spouts are present in extremely low frequency. Vessels of comparable form are common in Alden's surface collections (Alden 1979, Figs. 43-46) and at TUV (Nicholas 1990 Pls. 16-19).

Relief Decorated Jars

The large relief decorated vessels from BL 3 (Fig. 27:a-j; Pls. 16a, b, 17a-e) are perhaps too elaborate to be classified as simple storage jars. These vessels are made of brown paste with black and red grit temper; some sherds also have straw temper. The density of temper is variable, with some sherds, notably mf 1731 (Fig. 27:a), appearing to be almost untempered. The interior surface, slipped in brown or red-brown, is sometimes burnished. The exterior surface shows worn traces of brown slip on the background surface. The relief animals are carved from slabs of clay applied to the vessel surface, as indicated by a crack between the cow and the background surface of mf 1049 (Fig. 27:c). It is not certain, but likely, that the rope and floral designs are also carved from applied slabs. The carving is beautifully executed and highly expressive. Traces of black paint are preserved in the cracks of the rope decoration on mf 1187 (Fig. 27:h) and on the flank of the bull on mf 1043 (Fig. 27:d). The ropes and leaves: mf 1192, mf 1732, and mf 1187 (Fig. 27:e, b, h) and one example of an animal had a fugitive white paste on the surface.

Miscellaneous Relief Decorated Sherds

Other relief decorated sherds include two rosette plaques or flat tiles (Fig. 27:l,m). The rosette plaque from a Kaftari context (Fig. 27:m) is stylistically different from the Banesh rosette and may belong to the Kaftari assemblage, although almost no relief decoration was found in Kaftari contexts. There is a flat plaque, not a relief, in the shape of a parapet (Fig. 27:p). The parapet motif, in relief and painted black, also occurs on a sherd (Fig. 27:n) and from Stratum 6 at TUV (Nicholas 1990, Pl. 23:a). Similar step motifs, reminiscent of to the BL 3A wall paintings (Fig. 16), are found on a BL 3A storage jar (Pl. 18d, e). A small sherd with wheat or barley seeds (Fig. 27:k), reminds us of the sheaf of wheat shown on a sherd at TUV (Nicholas 1990, Pl. 23:h). One leaf motif sherd (Fig. 27:f), which came from a Kaftari lot, but no doubt belongs to the Banesh assemblage, appears to be a flat plaque. There is a relief sherd from TUV that appears to be the body of a snake with rows of scales (Nicholas 1990, Pl. 23:j), perhaps comparable to the snakes that appear in relief at Susa (Steve and Gasche 1971, Pl. 20:22-23) and Yahya IVC (Lamberg-Karlovsky 1973:32).

Large Storage Pithoi

Thirteen large pithoi were found in a row in BL 2, Room 71. These jars were all broken, toppled over, and several were crushed into relatively small pieces (Pl. 13). However, several were held in place by the BL 2 bricky fill. The following description is based entirely on rough measurements, sketches, and notes made by Susan Wolkow, the excavation artist, before they were removed from Room 71 during the 1972 season. Each jar was removed and reburied along the south wall of the excavation compound to preserve them for future reconstruction; unfortunately the planned study season never took place. Concentrations of pithos sherds were found in Room 185 (Fig. 20, Pithos 198) and Room 186 (Fig. 20, Pithos 197) and a pithos base was found in Corridor 117, all in BL 2.

These pithoi are biconical in form with some (Pithos 115) more sharply carinated than the illustrated form (Fig. 28:a). All of the jars for which approximate measurements were possible have similar dimensions: over a meter tall (ca. 100-200 cm) and about the same diameter at the widest point (ca. 100-260 cm). The opening of these vessels is restricted, in some cases less than 20 cm, but at least one isolated rim sherd has an outside diameter of 58 cm and an opening of about 34 cm (Fig. 28:g, Pl. 18a). All bases are flat, with a relatively small diameter (ca. 20-40 cm). At least 1 jar (Fig. 28:a) has a small, ca. 25 mm diameter, hole located 20 cm above the base, suggesting liquid storage.

These vessels have a well fired hard brick red body, sometimes with a dark grey core, tempered with black grit and some straw. Painted decoration, generally but not invariably confined to the area at or above the shoulder, consists of a variety of diaper patterns featuring diamonds, reversing triangles and checkerboard squares in panels defined by single or multiple horizontal and vertical bands. In one case the band forms a festoon below a checkerboard pattern. These patterns are painted in black directly on the smooth brick red surface or on a thin white slip that is confined to the painted panel. Two examples resemble houses with pitched roofs and reed mat walls. One of these has a curl of smoke rising from the roof and clear indications of a truss supported roof (Fig. 28:e); in the other the roof does not appear to span the entire building (Fig. 28:b). One vessel, Pythos 164, has several narrow (11-15 mm) black bands defining a broad empty panel with a brown slip. Above each black band there appears to be a broader (ca. 27 mm) band of fugitive blue pigment (mf 2337). Two potter's marks are recorded from the BL 2 pithoi. A common Proto-Elamite sign (Brice 1962-3, Fig. 1) is incised on the rim (Fig. 28:g; Pl. 18a) of one jar and an inverted U near the base of another (Pl. 18b).

Several sherds of a similar, but smaller, storage jar were recovered from BL 3A, Room 211, Stratum 10A, DC 37. These sherds are decorated with black painted step motifs on a thin white slip that resemble some of the wall painting step motifs (Pl. 18c-e).

Summary

The ABC ceramic assemblage is quite coherent in form, style and production technique. The narrow range of common forms—goblets, trays, small bowls, and large storage jars—suggests a relatively restricted range of activities requiring the use of pottery for food preparation and consumption and for large scale storage of liquids and solids. The elaborate relief decorated vessels, mostly from BL 3A, suggest a context in which the representation of floral and animal images has some symbolic significance, perhaps religious. The chronological implications of the ABC Banesh ceramic assemblage are discussed in Chapter III. In general parallels for forms in the ABC assemblage are found as early as Susa II (Acropole I:17), and continue through Susa III (Acropole I:16-14A).

III

Chronology

The ceramic chronological sequence of the Kur River Basin, first established by Vanden Berghe (1952, 1954), has been expanded and revised as a result of subsequent surveys and excavations. The sequence was summarized by Carter (1984), and has recently been presented in detail by Voigt and Dyson (1992). The Kur River Basin sequence and chronological periods represented at Malyan are summarized in Table 12.

The buildings and strata reported in this monograph all belong to the Banesh Period. However, the following discussion also includes a summary of the preceding Lapui Period (Sumner 1972, 1988b; Alden 1979 and infra, Appendix D; Alizadeh n.d.) and the following Kaftari Period (Nickerson, J. L. 1991; Sumner 1972, 1989a) to provide a chronological context for the Banesh Period. The final section of this chapter is a discussion of the radiocarbon chronology for the Banesh Period based on the calibrated determinations presented in Table 13.

The Lapui Period

The Lapui Period, named for a large village located on the talus slope in the Zargan District, is best known from the disturbed upper levels at Tall-i-Bakun A. Lapui ware has traditionally been called Bakun A, Level V, red ware (McCown 1942:48). As a result of more recent survey and excavation (Sumner 1988b; Alden 1979 and infra, Appendix D; Alizadeh n.d.) it is clear that Bakun A V red ware, distinct from the red slipped pottery found in Kaftari assemblages, defines a period between the Bakun and Banesh Phases in the local chronology.

Lapui plain red ware occurs in both fine and common varieties. The fine ware has a hard dense buff or red body, with frequent lime inclusions and a smooth or burnished surface. Lapui common ware has a coarse body tempered with black grit. An unoxidized grey core is characteristic of many common ware sherds and breaks leave a rough crumbly edge, as compared to the sharp smooth edge of breaks in fine ware. The surface is usually slipped, roughly burnished, and is often crazed or pitted. Both fine and common Lapui wares occur in a limited number of simple forms: bell shaped or cylindrical beakers, open bowls, and restricted hole mouth or low necked jars with simple rounded rims and flat, disk, or ring bases. Pierced lugs are present in late Lapui assemblages.

Strong parallels for Lapui wares can be found in plain red wares from Susa as early as Susa I in Acropole I:25, when Susa A painted ware was still dominant and in level 24 when painted buff ware was radically reduced in frequency. Later parallels for Lapui Ware are not found at Susa, probably because of the intrusive appearance of Uruk plain wares in level 22 (Le Brun 1971:175-76, 1978a). Lapui parallels have also been noted in assemblages from Godin VII, surface collections from the Bakhtiari mountains, Iblis I-II, and Yahya VI-VA2 (Beale 1986a, Voigt and Dyson 1992:140). Alden (Appendix D) identified a late variant of Lapui ware in the lower levels at Tal-e Kureh in association with a distinctive transitional ware that combined Lapui and Banesh attributes, which suggests a gradual transition from Terminal Lapui through Initial Banesh and into Early Banesh.

Table 12. THE KUR RIVER BASIN SEQUENCE

Date/Period	Malyan Operations
Islamic	surface—NE corner, city wall embankment
A.D. 600 Sasanian	TUV—coin in burial
	EDD—coin, possibly BL 1
	X65—kiln
Sasanian/	A63—disturbed architecture
Parthian	Surface—many sherds in SW
	quarter of site
	Test Trench D—upper building
50 B.C. Parthian	Z46—coin in burial
	GHI—coin in burial
300 B.C. Achaemenid	surface—7 sherds
600 B.C. Hiatus?	
900 B.C. Qale/Middle	EDD—BLs 3 & 4
Elamite	BB33—Qale Kilns
	XX—BL 1
	GHI—BL 1;
	ABC—upper wells
	Test Trench D—middle strata
Shogha	a few surface sherds
1600 B.C.	
	ABC—upper strata
	GHI—BLs 2-4
	GGX98—all strata;
Kaftari	FX106—all strata
	BY8—upper strata
	F26—upper strata;
	Test Trench D—lower strata
2200 B.C. Depopulation	possible continuity only at Malyan,
	H5 sounding—upper strata
2600 B.C. Late Banesh	BY8—lower strata
	H5 sounding—lower strata
	TUV—BL 1
2900 B.C. Late Middle	ABC—BLs 2-4A
	TUV—BLs 2-3A
3300 B.C. Early Middle	ABC—BLs 4B-5
	TUV—BL 3B
3400 B.C Early Banesh	not known at Malyan
3500 B.C. Lapui	surface—a few sherds
4000 B.C. Bakun	surface—12 sherds
	EE16 and Z46—a considerable number
	of sherds in disturbed contexts
5000 B.C. Jari	surface—a few sherds
5800 B.C. Mushki	not identified at Malyan

The Banesh Period

Initial and Early Banesh

Alden divided the Banesh Period into five subphases on the basis of excavations at Malyan, his sounding at Tal-e Kureh, and the stylistic seriation of his very large surface collections. The Initial and Early Banesh Phases, which have not been discovered at Malyan, are discussed here by Alden in the Tal-e Kureh report (Appendix D).

Stylistic parallels for Early Banesh are found in Susa II, Acropole I, level 17 (Alden 1979; Le Brun 1971 and 1978b; Dittmann 1986b and 1987; Voigt and Dyson 1992:141). However, many of the vessel forms found in Early Banesh levels continue to be found in Middle Banesh assemblages (Alden 1979, Fig. 59).

Middle Banesh

Early Middle Banesh

Early Middle Banesh, defined by Alden on the basis of the sounding at Tal-e Kureh, is difficult to distinguish from the Late Middle Banesh on ceramic criteria (Alden 1979:52, and Table 59). However, ABC BLs 4B and 5 are assigned to this period on the basis of glyptic evidence from BL 4A (Pittman, infra Chapter IV) and a number of ceramic \ (Le Brun 1971, 1978a, 1978b).

Late Middle Banesh

Late Middle Banesh is defined by the ceramic and glyptic corpus from Malyan, Operation TUV, BLs 2 and 3A, and ABC, BLs 2, 3, and 4A. Strong parallels are found in Susa III A and B (Acropole I:16-13), but there are also many parallels as early as Susa II (Acropole I:17) as indicated in Chapter II (Voigt and Dyson 1992:141, Pittman infra Chapter IV).

Late Banesh

The Late Banesh ceramic assemblage is defined by material from excavations in the city wall, Operation BY8 (Sumner 1985), but TUV, BL 1, also appears to represent an early manifestation of Late Banesh. Alden's (1979) surface collection confirms the presence of a significant Late Banesh occupation on the TUV mound.

The Late Banesh assemblage includes Middle Banesh ST wares in large numbers accompanied by an increasingly popular repertoire of small painted grit tempered carinated bowls and pots. These vessels have a smooth surface often with a thin white wash above the carination that bears simple maroon or black painted geometric designs (Sumner 1985 Figs. 3 and 4).

Stylistic parallels for Late Banesh ceramics are found in Susa IIIA-C (Ville Royale I:18-13; Acropole I:13-15) and Susa IVA (Ville Royale I:9-12) (Carter 1980). The presence of a Godin IV sherd (see Young 1969, Fig. 11) in the disturbed upper strata of BL 1 at TUV (Nicholas 1990, Plate 23:d) implies that late Banesh began before Godin III6.

Late Banesh-Kaftari Transition

Banesh levels in Operation ABC were separated from the later Kaftari strata by an erosional episode of unknown, but apparently centuries-long, duration. Similar erosion surfaces may also be present between Late Banesh and Kaftari strata in the trench across the city wall (Operation BY8). The TUV mound was not occupied after the Banesh Phase, which leaves the deep sounding in NE corner of Operation GHI (Fig. 4), at present unpublished, as the only source of information on the question of continuity between Banesh and Kaftari.

The earliest deposit in this sounding, Stratum 26, produced a small assemblage of Banesh straw tempered ware—3 BRBs, 7 trays, 18 goblet rims and one constricted goblet base. Stratum 25 produced an assemblage of standard straw tempered Banesh types as well as grit tempered sherds with Late Banesh attributes—black and maroon paint applied over a thin white slip. The diagnostic ceramics from Stratum 25 also include a carinated pot with a flame motif, which has close parallels in Susa IVA (Ville Royale I:12-10), but is perhaps better known from the Godin III6 assemblage (Carter 1980, Fig. 28: 2 and 7; Henrickson, R. 1986, Fig. 4:1-4).

Stratum 24 was assigned to a burial in and above a large vessel embedded in the north face of the sounding. Stratum 23 produced standard Banesh straw tempered forms, a number of Late Banesh painted sherds and other painted sherds that could be either Banesh or Kaftari. None of these latter forms are typical of either the Banesh or the Kaftari assemblage, but in a general way they are more like Kaftari than Banesh. There are few Susa parallels for these forms although several can be found in Susa IVA and V (Carter 1980).

Stratum 22 produced several sherds of Banesh straw tempered ware and several grit tempered Banesh sherds including a nose lug and a sherd with maroon paint applied over a thin white wash. However, Stratum 22 also produced typical early Kaftari red slipped ware and a unique variant of the Kaftari left facing bird motif. The Stratum 22 sherd depicts 3 birds swimming to the left in association with several floral motifs. Like Kaftari birds, these birds are fat, but the general shape of the body is different, the rendering of the head and beak is different, and the tails turn up, unlike other Kaftari birds (Sumner 1999 Fig. 4b). Birds facing left that are comparable in style to Kaftari birds occur in very low frequency only in Susa IVA (Ville Royale I:9) (Carter 1980, fig. 28: 14; 29: 9) and first appear in the Godin sequence in Level III5 (Henrickson R. 1986, Fig. 8: 2, 3).

The H5 sounding, which was small—300x160 cm, stepped down to 70x50 cm, produced relatively few sherds and other finds. Several pebbly surfaces were detected in the sounding that could represent erosional episodes similar to the interface between Banesh and Kaftari strata in ABC. However, the stylistic progression between H5 Stratum 26 and Stratum 22 implies at least some degree of continuity of occupation at Malyan through the third millennium.

The Third Millennium Hiatus

In the past I have argued for a mid-third millennium hiatus—from about 2800 to 2200—in the sedentary occupation of central Fars (Sumner 1986, 1989a). It seems possible now that the earliest stages in the evolution of the Kaftari ceramic style are seen in the H5 sounding, Strata 23 and 22, and there is no reason to believe that this development did not continue through the third millennium until the fully articulated Kaftari style was established in the Shimashki period, c. 2200-1900 B.C. Nevertheless, the evidence for a radical decline in the sedentary population of the valley at the end of the Late Banesh Phase is compelling. Consider the following points:

1) There is evidence of possible continuity between Late Banesh and Kaftari only at Malyan and two other sites. In Alden's survey, ceramic phase markers for Late Banesh are extremely rare. In the 36 sites for which he provides phase marker counts, only 40 sherds from 11 sites are exclusively late Banesh types. Thirty of these sherds come from just 3 sites, including 10 Late Banesh

sherds from the TUV mound at Malyan (Alden 1979, Tables 38 and 47). Put another way, Alden collected over 53,000 Banesh sherds, including 32,361 grit tempered sherds, from 172 surface collection units at 15 sites. All exclusively Late Banesh sherd types are grit tempered and the fact that only 40 Late Banesh types could be identified in a collection of over 32,000 sherds is a clear indication of the rarity of surface assemblages with Late Banesh markers.

These collections yielded only 3 Kaftari sherds, all from the TUV mound at Malyan, which must indicate a radical discontinuity between Banesh and Kaftari settlements. Even the TUV mound does not represent settlement continuity between Banesh and Kaftari. The presence of Banesh strata just below the surface in Operation TUV and Test Trench F nearby, and the very low density of Kaftari sherds in the TUV mound surface assemblage demonstrate that the TUV mound was not occupied in the Kaftari period.

2) In his survey of the Marv Dasht Vanden Berghe (1952, 1954, 1959) recorded 57 previously unreported Achaemenid and earlier sites. He also excavated soundings in at least 25 mounds. He did not report finding any ceramic assemblages that would fill the third millennium hiatus—no Banesh, no distinctive early Kaftari. These results support the claim that settled occupation in the Kur River Basin during the period between Banesh and Kaftari was exceedingly limited.

3) No assemblage remotely resembling the mid 3rd millennium Jalyan (Fig. 1) cemetery ceramic assemblage (Miroschedji 1971, 1973, 1974) or the similar elaborate painted wares from Susa IVA, Ville Royale I:12-7 (Carter 1980, Figs. 28 and 29) and the Acropole, couche 3 and 4 (Steve and Gasche 1971, Pl. 16-18, 21, 22) has been reported from any site in Fars except Jalyan itself. The small assemblage from Strata 23-22 in Operation H5 at Malyan barely hints at the stylistic elaboration found at Jalyan.

4) The plain wares characteristic of Susa IVB and V (Carter 1980, Figs. 41-51) are missing or rare in excavated and surface assemblages in Fars.

5) A considerable chronological gap between Late Banesh levels and the fully developed Kaftari ceramic style at Malyan is indicated by the radiocarbon chronology. The latest date for Late Banesh from the Malyan city wall falls in the 3090-2620 B.C range at the 95.4% confidence level (P-2982, Table 13). The date for the Banesh-Kaftari transition in H5 (burial 149 between Stratum 22 and

Stratum 25), is not useful because of a high SD (P-3072, Table 13). The lower limit for a cluster of 10 Kaftari dates from the University of Pennsylvania Laboratory with low SD is 2200 B.C. or later.[*] Three Kaftari dates with SD over 200, which have lower limits between 3200 and 2900 B.C., are not helpful. That leaves only one early Kaftari radiocarbon date (P-3068), which has a lower limit of 2900 B.C. (95.4% confidence level), but this date is contradicted by another sample (P-3347) from the same stratum that falls in the interval 1960-1680 B.C (95.4% confidence interval). It is this chronological gap between about 2800 and 2200 B.C. that can only be filled by a transitional assemblage such as the one dimly discerned in the small H5 sounding, but is invisible in all other excavated or surface assemblages in Fars with the exception of the Jalyan cemetery assemblage.

This line of reasoning may not constitute absolute proof but is certainly a strong argument for the existence of a major population collapse in Fars between about 2800 and 2200 B.C. During this period Malyan and perhaps several other sites may have been occupied by a small sedentary population with a ceramic tradition that eventually evolved into the mature Kaftari style found at Malyan and 73 other sites in the valley late in the third millennium. Although there is no evidence for anything but a very small sedentary population in the Kur River Basin during this time, ca. 2800-2200 B.C., the presence of a pastoral nomadic population is possible. The Jalyan cemetery provides circumstantial evidence in support of this notion.

The Kaftari Period

The sedentary village population of the valley increased rapidly during the Kaftari Period beginning late in the third millennium B.C. By the early second millennium a four level settlement hierarchy was in place and the inhabited area within the reconstructed Malyan city wall reached 130 ha. By the mid-second millennium both the population of Malyan and the village population in the valley were again in decline (Sumner 1989a; Nickerson, John L. 1983, 1991).

Kaftari glyptic will ultimately provide a link to the Elamite historic chronology (Pittman n.d.), but the present chronology relies mainly on radiocarbon dates,

which are consistent with other evidence that the Kaftari occupation of the Kur River Basin, identified by the Kaftari ceramic style in surface assemblages, spans the period from 2200-1600 B.C.

Banesh Radiocarbon Chronology

Radiocarbon determinations for the Banesh and Early Kaftari Periods are presented in Table 13. Eight of these determinations with large margins of error (one standard deviation greater than ± 260 years) are not helpful. The remaining 17 determinations have smaller margins of error, less than ± 90 years, but one of them (P-2981), possibly juniper, elm or poplar beam wood, is rejected as too early, leaving 16 determinations: 3 from Early Kaftari contexts, 1 from a Late Banesh context, and 12 from Middle Banesh Contexts.

Two of the dated samples from ABC were recovered from Room 64 in BL 4A. The first sample (P-2334 = mf 9930) came from Operation ABCN Lot 143 (LI M; DC 37), a high-density lot that was almost certainly in good secondary context on the upper floor of BL 4A. The second sample from Room 64 (P-2187 = mf 2195) came from Operation B, Lot 63 (LI G; DC 21), a trash deposit on an earlier floor. The third ABC sample (P-2335 = mf 1388) came from a trash deposit between lower and upper floors (ABCN Lot 90; LI G; DC 29) in Corridor 118, BL 2 (see Chapter 2 for details).

Two of the TUV samples (P-3266 and P-3050) came from trash deposits on the floor of Room 258 in the west architectural unit. Two others came from a vacant area north of the BL 3A buildings (Operation V168)—one (P-2985) from an amorphous trash deposit and the other (P-3269) from a bricky fill associated with an earlier brick platform. Sample P-3061 came from a small open space (Area 338) at the NW corner of the BL 3A structures where 5 P-E tablets, sealings, and other finds were recovered from a dense trash deposit (Nicholas 1990:110). Finally, P-3268 came from a dead-end alley (Area 307) along the west edge of BL 3A. The lot that produced this sample (Operation V166 Lot 45) is coded DC 51, "brick packing," but the description of this context (Nicholas 1990:108) clearly indicates a trash deposit. It is probable that all of these samples, possibly excepting only P-3268, P-3269, or P-2986, are from well documented trash deposits that were contemporary with the occupation of ABC BL 2, ABC BL 4A, and TUV BL 3A. It is likely that the three possible exceptions were also contemporary with TUV BL 3A, but they could be from the earlier phase, BL 3B.

---

[*] Kaftari Period C14 determinations discussed here are CRD 1 B.C. as reported in Voigt and Dyson 1992 Table 2 and the Addenda to Table 2.

Table 13. CALIBRATED RADIOCARBON DATES

Lab#	14C Yrs bp	BC Range (95.4%)	BC Range (68.2%)	mf #	STR	BL	DC
GGX98 Early Kaftari Dates:							
P-3068	3980±80	2900–2200	2620–2340	9717	7	—	22
P-3347	3510±50	1960–1680	1890–1740	9730A	7	—	22
ABC Early Kaftari Date:							
P-2186	3670±60	2210–1880	2140–1950	2343	7	—	28
GHI Test Trench Banesh-Kaftari Transition Date:							
P-3072	4170±260	3600–1900	3100–2300	9706	24	—	—
BY8 Late Banesh Dates:							
P-2984	4770±290	4300–2700	3950–3100	9711	10B	—	—
P-2981	4780±60	3660–3370	3650–3510	9713	10D	—	37
P-2982	4260±70	3090–2620	3010–2690	9712	11B	—	23
TUV Middle Banesh Dates:							
P-2333	4150±250	3500–1900	3100–2300	9931	10	3	—
P-3266	4410±60	3340–2900	3270–2910	5323B	10	3	37
P-3063	4430±70	3350–2910	3310–2920	6214	10	3	26
P-2985	4450±60	3350–2920	3340–3010	6207	10	3	23
P-3269	4480±50	3360–2930	3340–3040	3898	10	3	35
P-3061	4490±70	3370–2920	3350–3090	6060B	10	3	42
P-3050	4500±60	3370–2920	3350–3090	3874	10	3	26
P-3268	4520±70	3500–2900	3360–3100	5398	10	3	51
P-2986	4590±70	3650–3000	3510–3100	3837	10	3	51
ABC Middle Banesh Dates:							
P-2335	4390±90	3350–2880	3310–2890	1388	8D	2	29
P-2334	4460±70	3350–2920	3340–3020	9930	13A	4	37
P-2187	4370±60	3330–2880	3090–2900	2195.1	13B	4	21
P-2336	4630±260	4000–2600	3650–3000	9929	13B	4	22
TUNC31	4671±88	3650–3100	3630–3350	2195.2	13B	4	21
P-3060	5040±270	4500–3100	4250–3500	3774*	15B	5	28
Tal-e Kureh Early Banesh Dates:							
P-2626	4550±280	4000–2400	3650–2900	Lot 8	5	—	—
P-2627	4360±230	3700–2300	3400–2650	Lot 9	5	—	—
Tal-e Kureh Terminal Lapui Phase Date:							
P-2624	5000±290	4500–3000	4250–3350	Lot 10	7	—	—

* combined with mf 4055. Sources- Meulengracht *et al* 1981:232; Fishman and Lawn 1978: 225-26; Bovington *et al* 1973:594; Unpublished University of Pennsylvania Laboratory Reports dated March 30, 1982 and July 1, 1985. Calibrated using OxCal v. 3.3 Bronk Ramsey 1999.

All of these samples are carbonized wood, but in no case was the species of the carbonized wood determined before the sample was submitted for dating. However, several determinations from TUV (P-2985, P-3050, P-3063) used split samples. Charcoal in the part of these split samples not used for dating was juniper, almond, poplar, and pistachio. The frequency of carbonized wood species from all Banesh contexts (300 samples) is almond (31%), juniper (24%), pistachio (14%), poplar (14%), elm (7%), oak (7%) and maple (3%) (Miller 1982:217, Table 6.5). Ubiquity, that is, the percentage of samples that contained each species, is almond (26%), juniper (22%), pistachio (17%), poplar (11%), elm (10%), and oak (9%) (Miller 1982:224, Table 6.9). The largest pieces of carbonized wood from any Banesh context were collected by hand in Room 258 at TUV (Lot 133 and Lot 138, which produced P-3050). These two samples consisted of 73 pieces with a total weight of 114.13 gm for an average weight of 1.56 gm (Miller 1982 Appendix D).

There is no evidence that any Banesh building excavated at TUV or ABC was destroyed by fire or even had small uncontrolled fires that might have damaged roofs or walls. The frequency and ubiquity of the wood species found together and the small size of most pieces of carbonized wood—less than 0.5 gm—support the interpretation of the Banesh wood samples as the residue of small controlled fires using brushwood fuel (Miller 1982:221). If this interpretation is correct, and the archaeological contexts have been accurately recorded, we would expect the radiocarbon determinations from these samples to date the death of growth rings that occurred no more than a decade or so before the use of the brush wood as fuel.

The date of the Banesh Period was reviewed by Voigt and Dyson, who concluded that ..."the radiocarbon evidence for Banesh firmly dates this period to the late fourth millennium, but does not provide good evidence for its precise duration." (1992: 142; Table 2 and Addenda to Table 2 and Dyson 1987:650; Table 2) A more recent study of the radiocarbon chronology of Uruk and related assemblages (Wright and Rupley 2001) includes an analysis of 11 Middle Banesh determinations with standard deviations less than ±100 years, all from the University of Pennsylvania Laboratory (Table 13, calibrated by OxCal v.3.3; Bronk Ramsey 1995).[*]

Wright and Rupley base their analysis on the 95.4% confidence interval of the calibrated dates. They present several models for combining the 11 dates—the "summed range," which emphasizes the maximum range of the probability distributions, is 3370-2900 B.C. The "combined range," which emphasizes the overlap among the dates, is 3330–3030 B.C. Finally, using a date from a Late Banesh context (P-2982, 95.4 % confidence level, Table 13) to constrain the end of Middle Banesh Period, they arrive at a time interval of 3450-2920 B.C. for the events represented by these 11 Middle Banesh dates. In view of this result, combined with the conclusions presented above regarding the nature of the charcoal samples and the contexts in which they were found, we can say that ABC BL 4A, BL 2, and TUV BL 3A were all inhabited during this time interval. We are unable to date the beginning of the Middle Banesh Period or to say when the earlier levels, ABC BL 4B, ABC BL 5, and TUV BL 3B were inhabited. Likewise the end of Late Banesh remains in doubt, but is unlikely to have been later than 2600 B.C.

---

[*]The calibrations were performed by E.A. Rupley (Wright and Rupley 2001).

IV

Functional Classes and Activity Patterns

This chapter presents a description and analysis of small finds assigned to the Banesh levels excavated in Operation ABC. The term "find" refers to any item removed during the course of excavations and entered in the Malyan Find Register, including artifacts, raw materials, production by-products, and analytical samples. Complete ceramic profiles and unusual sherds are registered, but the bulk of sherds are only recorded by lot number. Flotation samples and carbonized materials are registered but the seeds and other organic materials extracted from flotation samples are not registered. Small finds such as beads found in the heavy fraction of flotation samples are given separate registration numbers. With the exception of a few flints from problematic context, all registered finds included in this study are listed in Appendix A, Part I, which provides coded information on provenience, type, material, dimensions, functional class, status code, quantity, illustrations, notes, and present location. Additional descriptive and analytical results for metals and shells are presented in Appendix A, Part II.

The Chapter begins with a description of the functional class model and a summary tabulation of the number of finds assigned to each functional class at ABC and TUV (Nicholas 1990, Table 22). Each functional class identified in the ABC assemblage is described, followed by more technical contributions on various groups of finds: flint (Kardulias), metal (Pigott, Rogers, and Nash), shell (Reese), beads and stone bowls (Vidale), and seals and sealings (Pittman).

The stratigraphic and architectural context of ABC finds is discussed in Chapter I. Here it is sufficient to state that different contexts are classified by Deposit

Codes (DC) identifying secondary trashy deposits (DC 21-29), tertiary deposits of bricky debris on floors or surfaces that may include trashy components (DC 37), and tertiary deposits that are less likely to include trash components (DC 34-36, 49). The degree of precision in excavating and recording different deposits is indicated by the Lot Indicator code, also discussed in Chapter I. These elements of archaeological context provide a basis for evaluating the scope and significance of the production and consumption processes that are the principle focus of attention in this chapter.

THE FUNCTIONAL CLASS MODEL

Annette Ericksen and William M. Sumner

The Functional Class model used here is based on the model designed by Nicholas (1990) for her study of the Banesh settlement at TUV. The basic design of the model follows that proposed by South (1977) in that activities are inferred and finds are assigned to these activities on an intuitive basis. In the present study functional classes are divided into 3 categories: 1) production classes identified by the presence of raw materials and recycled materials, production by-products, finished preforms or components, items broken in production, and unfinished items, 2) use and consumption classes, including storage of finished products or commodities, identified by the presence of containers, weapons and tools, personal ornaments, decorated items, evidence of food preparation and consumption, and 3) an information processing class identified by

Table 14. FUNCTIONAL CLASSES AT ABC AND TUV

FUNCTIONAL CLASS	TUV	ABC
CLASS 1- FLINT KNAPPING	270	141
Raw Material	14	1
Cores	18	10
Debitage	114	89
Larger Flakes	124	42
CLASS 2- METALLURGY	225	92
Slag	93	10
Iron-rich copper slag	3	1
Crucible or furnace fragments	39	—
Sheet stock	16	3
Bar stock	4	19
Molds	4	—
Ingots	2	—
Ores	5	7
Prills and scraps of metal	59	19
Lead scraps	—	32
Unidentified	—	1
CLASS 3- STONE BEAD PRODUCTION	25	69
Raw material	24	58
Unfinished beads	1	11
CLASS 4- SHELL WORKING	104	1106
Mother-of-pearl inlay pieces	4	987
Bivalve/Mother-of-pearl	47	84
Unidentified shell	12	12
Cone shells	13	9
Other shells	15	14
Dentalium shells (see Class 16, Beads)	8	—
Cowrie shells	2	—
Olive shells	3	—
CLASS 5- PLASTERS/PIGMENTS CRAFT	60	7
CLASS 6- CLOTH INDUSTRY	8	1
CLASS 7- FOOD PREPARATION	214	62
CLASS 8- POTTERY PRODUCTION	13	5
CLASS 9- OTHER CRAFT ACTIVITIES	21	88
Carbonate rock	10	15
Specular hematite	5	32
Bitumen	1	14
Misc.	5	27
CLASS 10- STORAGE	304	370
Sealings without impressions	79	176
Jar stoppers without impressions	6	6
Sealings with impressions	219	188
CLASS 11- BASKETRY/MATTING	5	3
CLASS 12- SPECIAL CONTAINERS	64	48
Stone vessels	58	24
Plaster vessels	1	8
Other	5	16
CLASS 13- CUTTING TOOLS	116	62
CLASS 14- VARIOUS TOOLS	83	33
CLASS 15- PIERCING/BORING	3	10
CLASS 16- PERSONAL ORNAMENTS	41	257
Beads (metal, stone, and shell)	31	249
Copper-base metal pins	9	4
Rings	1	3
Gold leopard ornament	—	1
CLASS 17- ARCHITECTURAL ELEMENTS	22	49
CLASS 18- FOOD CONSUMPTION	12	NA

Table 14 (continued)

CLASS 19- CARPENTRY	1	1
CLASS 20- DECORATED ITEMS	17	25
Relief sherds	7	13
Painted pottery	10	NA
Decorated stone vessels	—	8
Figurines; Spout	—	3
Gold leopard ornament	—	1
CLASS 21- INFORMATION PROCESSING	278	329
Cylinder seals	4	2
Seal impressions	219	244
Tablets	18	28
Bullae	11	-
Counters	17	51
Potter's marks	5	4
CLASS 22- POINTS	—	6
SUB-TOTAL	1886	2744
CLASS 00- FINDS NOT ASSIGNED	125	28
TOTAL	2011	2792

the presence of Proto-Elamite tablets, seals, seal impressions, bullae, counters and potter's marks. Some types of finds that could be used for several purposes are assigned to more than one functional class.

One potential problem with this methodology is that the definition of a functional class may be faulty or the finds assigned to the class may not be appropriate. However, if a class is properly defined and the finds are assigned appropriately, then the frequency of finds assigned to a particular class would be expected to indicate the intensity of the activity represented by that functional class.

The location of a specific activity or group of activities can be identified by the clustering or association of finds that share functional attributes in good stratigraphic context. In the case of finds from tertiary lots, the clustering of finds within the ABC operation indicates no more than the condition of deposits that were the source of building materials for the ABC buildings.

Certainly South's work in the American Carolinas was not considered to be of universal applicability, and Nicholas chose functional categories that are relevant to a late fourth millennium settlement in the Near East. The preliminary study of the ABC assemblage indicated that the same set of functional classes used by Nicholas at TUV would work for finds from ABC with minimal adjustment. Still, the assignment of specific finds to a particular functional classes is often problematic. The functional interpretation of a find

type may not be correct in some instances and the assumption that functions are static and do not change during the useful life of an item is sometimes unrealistic. This problem is addressed here in part by the introduction of a parallel model representing the position of each find within a hypothetical sequence of procurement, production, storage, consumption, recycle, and discard.

The significance of functional classes is more or less difficult to interpret depending on the nature of the activity that created each particular functional class. For example, the assignment of finds to the Architectural Functional Class (Class 17) is unlikely to be ambiguous, but the analytical implications of the whole class are problematic. Clearly site formation processes that produce many of the individual finds of Class 17 are quite different from the processes responsible for the presence of such finds as clusters of flint debitage (Class 1) and the meaning of the 2 classes is different in character. In addition, the selective process by which architectural items are recorded is far more arbitrary than it is for other classes. For example, the decision to remove, save, and record a single brick from all the bricks in a building has very different implications from the decision to collect and record all flint debitage. Furthermore, the logical coherence of different functional classes may reside in entirely different principles of association. Compare, for example, the rationale for a class such as flint production (Class 1) based on evidence assumed to represent a single type of activity—flint knapping—with a class such as information processing (Class 21), which may represent a variety of activities (Nicholas 1990, Fig. 20). These problems are, however, inherent in any classificatory scheme in which artifact function is a central issue. With these points in mind the Functional Class Model will serve as the basic framework within which to evaluate the assemblage of finds recovered at ABC and to identify and understand the activities of the human inhabitants of the buildings excavated at ABC.

Methods

All initial functional classifications were made by Ericksen on the basis of information contained in the Malyan Register, specifically the Class, Type, Material, and Variety codes, as defined in Appendix A. The Malyan Register consists of registration forms originally prepared in the field by the field registrars and later edited for consistency and correctness by Kathleen MacLean, Malyan Research Assistant. Additional registration information on material and material variety coding was provided by M. James Blackman and John Nickerson. The photographs and drawings of finds were also consulted as well as those objects available in the collection of the University of Pennsylvania Museum (Location Code P in Appendix A). Subsequently these classifications were modified and supplemented on the basis of additional information provided by the technical studies reported in the later sections of this chapter.

The Malyan Register Database was down-loaded from the Ohio State University mainframe computer and imported into a Macintosh computer using the Borland Reflex+ database program. The register was later converted to Microsoft Excel for editing and entering new data. The functional classification of each find was added, using three columns (FA, FB, FC) because the functional classes are not mutually exclusive. The coding of finds in the production-consumption model, described below, were added in a single column (Stat). The resulting database is published in its entirety in Appendix A.

Functional Classes

All of the 21 functional classes identified at TUV by Nicholas (1990), plus Class 22, Projectile Points, were identified in the ABC assemblage. Nicholas' classification scheme, together with the frequency of finds in the TUV and ABC assemblages, is outlined in Table 14. It should be noted that the ABC and TUV counts listed in Table 14 are not exactly comparable for several classes and for that reason the table gives only a general indication of the relative importance of different classes at ABC and TUV. It should also be emphasized that many finds are counted more than once because they are assigned to more than one functional class.

In Nicholas' model, functional Classes 1-9 are considered to represent production and processing activities, Class 10-12 represent holding and storage activities, Classes 13-20 represent consumption and use activities and Class 21 represents information recording or processing that may be related to any of the other classes (Nicholas 1990, Fig. 20).

In the model used by Nicholas some specialized tools were assigned to production classes, for example crucible fragments and metal casting molds to Class 2, Metal Working, spindle whorls and needles to Class 6, Spinning and Weaving, and grinding or pounding stones to Class 7, Food Production. Other tools, less clearly associated with a particular production activity, were assigned to Class 13, Cutting Tools, Class 14, Various Tools, and Class 15, Piercing Tools. In the present study all finished tools are assigned to consumption or use Classes 13, 14, or 15. Unfinished tools are assigned to a production class associated with the production of tools. For example, large flint flakes that show no signs of use or retouch are considered to be unfinished tools in storage, assigned to Functional Class 1. The implications of this departure from Nicholas' method are discussed below for individual functional classes and in the summary comparison of the functional characteristics of ABC and TUV.

The functional model used by Nicholas at TUV is supplemented here by an experimental production-consumption model that views the status of each find in a slightly different way (Fig. 29). Locally procured or imported raw materials and recycled materials enter the production-consumption cycle and are then modified to produce artifacts for use or consumption. At any point in the ongoing cycle of production, use, recycle, and consumption, material items, defined here as finds, may enter the archaeological record. This occurs when they are abandoned in place, stored, lost, or discarded. The subsequent fate of finds, determined by the action of cultural and natural site transformation processes (Schiffer 1972, 1976), as well as archaeological recovery processes, produces the archaeological record that forms the basis for archaeological analysis and interpretation.

The analytical model of this cycle (Fig. 29) is used to determine the final state of each find as it entered the archaeological record and must be interpreted in terms of subsequent natural or cultural processes, monitored here by deposit codes (DC) and archaeological recovery processes, monitored here by lot indicator codes (LI).

Each diamond in Fig. 29 represents a decision point in the classification process. The criteria for making decisions at each stage of the cycle vary with types of finds and materials. Each sub-rectangular label represents a point of entry into the archaeological record—discarded, lost, or stored and never retrieved.

The first step in the classification process it to determine the quality of unaltered finds classified as raw materials or as recycled materials (the first diamond in Fig. 29). If the quality of such finds is judged to be poor, they are classified as unsuitable raw material when they entered the archaeological record, Status Code P 1.2. If it is not possible to determine the quality of presumed raw material finds, they are classified as P 1.0.

Raw materials that are of good quality, including recycled materials, are then examined for evidence of alterations (the second diamond in Fig. 29). If there is no evidence of alteration, good raw materials (P 2.x) and recycled materials (R 2.x) are classified as lost or in storage when they entered the archaeological record, P 2.2 or R 2.2 . If there is evidence of alteration but the material is identified as waste material or a by-product of production, the find is classified as production waste, P 2.1. If a find cannot be identified as production waste and the evidence of alteration is unclear, the find is classified as possibly lost or stored raw material, P 2.0 or R 2.0.

Raw materials that show evidence of alteration, but are not classified as production waste are then examined for evidence of completeness (the third diamond in Fig. 29). At this point the distinction between new raw materials and recycled materials is dropped. Incomplete altered materials are classified as unfinished products lost or discarded during production, P 3.2. Finds that are partially completed in a recognizable multi-step production process are classified as finished components or preforms ready to be completed, placed in storage or lost, P 3.1. Preforms might include flint flakes of a size suitable for use to make retouched tools. Examples of finished components in the ABC assemblage are the mother of pearl inlay pieces that do not appear to have been used to make an inlay decorated object.

Finds that show evidence of having been completed are then examined for evidence of breakage (the fourth diamond in Fig. 29). If it is not clear whether or not a completed find is broken, it is classified as in an indeterminate consumption status, C 4.0). Finds that are broken are then examined for evidence of use (the fifth diamond in Fig. 29). Broken finds with evidence of use are classified as broken and lost or discarded while in use, C 5.1. Broken finds that do not show evidence of use are classified as broken and discarded before use, C 5.2. If it cannot be determined whether or not a broken find was used, it is classified as broken during or before use, C 5.0.

Completed finds that show no evidence of breakage are examined for evidence of use (the sixth diamond in Fig. 29). Unbroken finds that show slight evidence of use are classified as lost in use, C 6.1. Unbroken finds that show evidence of heavy use are classified as worn out and discarded after use, C 6.3. Unbroken finds that show no evidence of use are classified as in storage, C 6.2. If the question regarding evidence of use cannot be answered, unbroken finished finds are classified as lost, discarded, or stored, C 6.0.

The status of finds in each functional class serves as an indicator of the stages in the production-consumption cycle that are represented at ABC. Status coding distinguishes activities that include the complete production cycle from activities only represented by early or late stages in the production cycle, or only by evidence for the use or consumption of finds produced elsewhere.

ANALYSIS OF FUNCTIONAL CLASSES

William M. Sumner

In the following description and discussion of functional classes individual finds are characterized using the following register codes, as defined in Appendix A: 1) type of find—Type, 2) find sub-type—Stp, 3) material a find is made of—Mat, 4) variety of material—V, 5) status of a find in the production-consumption model—Stat. The Functional Class assignment of finds, listed in the register in columns FA, FB, and FC, is identified in the following discussion by the designation "Class" followed by the functional class number. Individual finds are identified by Malyan registration numbers preceded by the abbreviation "mf."

Functional Class 1. Flint Knapping

This discussion of flint knapping is based on the analysis of flint technology by Kardulias presented in

Table 15. FREQUENCY OF FLINT REDUCTION SEQUENCE SUB-TYPES

SUB-TYPE	N	%
Primary Decortication Flakes (PDF)	6	6.5
Secondary Decortication Flakes (2DF)	26	28.0
Secondary Non-cortical Flakes (2NDF)	36	38.7
Tertiary Non-cortical Flakes (3NDF)	10	10.8
Debris (DBS)	14	15.1
Platform Preparation Flake (PPF)	1	1.1
SUM	93	

this chapter, the descriptions of flint finds prepared by Annette Ericksen while she was a research associate on the Malyan project, information from the register of finds, and my own examination of some of the flints. The 141 finds assigned to this class include 10 cores (Type 12), one chunk of chert raw material (Mat 102, V 2), and 130 flakes (Type 20) (Figs. 30-32, Pl. 19). There are 8 flake cores and 2 cores that are probably exhausted blade cores. From the flint knapping perspective all 10 cores are classified as production by-products (Stat P 2.1), but 2 of the cores (mf 2313, 7300) have properties that make them desirable recycled raw material for bead making (Class 3, Stat R 2.2). There are 34 cryptocrystalline quartz (Mat 102) flakes with a preserved length or width of 2.5 cm or more that are classified as modified but unfinished material that could be used to produce tools or could be used as tools without further modification (Stat P 3.1), but 2 of these flakes (mf 6601, 7263.2) are also classified as bead-making recycled raw material (Stat R 2.2). All 8 obsidian flakes are classified as Stat P 3.1 on the assumption that obsidian is valuable material suitable for making very small tools. The remaining 88 flakes are classified as production by-products (Stat P 2.1).

Without microwear analysis the classification of flakes as either discarded debitage, flakes suitable for further use, or flakes that have been used, is problematic. In an experiment conducted by Young and Bamforth (1990) 9 archaeologists were successful in distinguishing used or modified flake edges from unused or unmodified flake edges in only 25% of the cases. However, a comparison of the results of Kardulias' microwear analysis of 24 flakes from ABC with three previously recorded classifications, first by the excavation registrar in the field, second by Ericksen in the early stages of analysis for this study, and finally by Kardulias before selecting samples for microwear analysis, produces more encouraging results. Among the 54 attempts to classify flakes that showed no

microscopic evidence of use wear, 65% of all previous classifications indicated no use wear or retouch, with different individuals achieving success rates ranging from 56-78%. Among the 18 attempts to classify flakes that showed microscopic evidence of use wear, 61% of the previous classifications noted use damage or retouch; success rates of different individuals ranged from 50-83%. These results suggest that classification of flakes without microwear analysis is not very reliable, but the margin of error is acceptable for purposes of the present analysis, which is only intended to give a general indication of the level and type of flint knapping activity in the ABC area.

All flakes that show evidence of purposeful retouch, use wear or other edge damage, all blades or blade segments (Type 4) and all tools (Type 49) are assigned to functional classes assumed to be for cutting tools (Class 13), various tools (Class 14), or piercing tools (Class 15). One hammerstone (mf 9843) that could have been used in flint knapping is also assigned to Class 14, various tools.

Ninety-two flakes have been classified according to Kardulias' reduction sequence typology as shown in Table 15, and it is assumed that the remainder of the assemblage, not available for study, would conform to a similar frequency pattern. The low frequency of primary decortication flakes and debris is interpreted by Kardulias as evidence that the early stages of core reduction are underrepresented in the vicinity of ABC, with the implication that much of this work was done elsewhere. The virtual absence of raw material, which was systematically collected during excavation, and the presence of only one hammerstone, reinforce this interpretation. The small number of possible blade cores (2), compared to the relatively high frequency of blades and blade segments (55) also suggests that flint knapping was not an important specialized craft activity around ABC.

There are almost twice as many finds in Class 1 at TUV (270) than at ABC (141). However, the proportion of cores to flakes (TUV: 18/238=0.076; ABC 10/129=0.078) is practically identical, which may indicate similar flint knapping activities at ABC and TUV.

The average unbroken length of 39 flakes is 2.25 cm (variation 1.2). The average unbroken width of 63 flakes is 1.79 cm (variation 0.54) and the average thickness of all 75 measured flakes is 0.5 cm (variation 0.1). These average dimensions provide only a general indication of flake size because the distinction between whole flakes and broken flakes is often problematic.

Material

Cryptocrystalline quartz (Mat 102) accounts for 94% of the flint knapping debris (Class 1) and 96% of the tool assemblage. The most common type of cryptocrystalline material is chert (Mat 102, V 2), which accounts for 57% of the flint knapping debris and 72% of the tools (Classes 13, 14, 15, 22). The cherts are quite variable in color ranging from dark reddish brown (5YR 3/2), dark reddish grey (5YR 4/2), to grey (5YR 5/1) and various shades of pale grey and light brown (10YR 6/3 and 6/3).

Jasper (Mat 102, V 3), ranging from dusky red (10R 3/3), red (10R 5/6), to pale red (10R 6/3), is the second most common material, accounting for 22% of the knapping debris and 14% of the tools. The remainder of the collection is made of prase (Mat 102, V 5), 5% and 3%, chalcedony (Mat 102, V 7), 2% and 0%, flint (Mat 102, V 1) 4% of the debris and 1% of tools, cryptocrystalline quartz without further identification (Mat 102) 4% and 6%. There are 8 obsidian (Mat 105) flakes and 1 exhausted obsidian blade core, which account for 6% of debris and 4% of tools. Eleven of the obsidian pieces that have been subjected to trace element analysis using neutron activation (Blackman 1984) were from Nemrut Dağ I source at Lake Van (Fig. 1) in eastern Anatolia; 1 was from Group C (Renfrew and Dixon 1976).

There is no striking difference between materials assigned to Class 1, flint knapping debris, and the materials finished tools are made of, with the implication that tools could have been produced locally even though it is likely that the early stage of core reduction took place elsewhere.

Four of the chert finds (Mat 102 V 2), 3 of the chalcedony finds (Mat 102 V 7), and 1 flint find (Mat 102 V 1) are classified as possible raw material for bead making (Class 3, Stat R 2.2) on the basis of color or color bands. Two of the chert decortication flakes and 1 non-cortical flake show signs of heat treatment, but none of the flake cores appear to have been heat treated.

Context

There is no strong evidence suggesting the concentration of flint knapping in any particular location in any building level. Some flints may have been stored in BL 2, which produced a total of 62 finds, 35 from good context (LI G or H). There are 16 finds from secondary deposits, 5 from DC 37 deposits and 14 from tertiary deposits. BL 3 produced a total of 18 finds, 13 from good context. There are 5 finds from secondary deposits, 6 from DC 37 deposits and 2 from tertiary deposits. BL 4 produced a total of 23 finds, 20 from good context. There are 7 finds from secondary deposits, 4 from DC 37 deposits, and 9 from tertiary deposits. There is no evidence of flint knapping in BL 5, although there are 4 blades or blade segments, with the implication that few of the finds from tertiary contexts in BLs 2-4 were derived from production activities in the excavated area of BL 5. There are 4 finds from tertiary contexts in intermediate Strata 9 and 12, and 21 finds from Strata 16-19 (DC 50), below BL 5.

The virtual absence of raw materials and hammerstones, and the small number of primary decortication flakes suggests that flint cores and preforms were produced elsewhere and brought to the vicinity of ABC by local craftsmen who then produced tools as evidenced by the presence of exhausted cores, waste flakes (Stat P 2.1) and larger flakes (Stat P 3.1).

Functional Class 2. Metal Working

Class 2 includes evidence for smelting or working copper based metals and lead. The following discussion is based on the technical review of metallurgical evidence from both ABC and TUV by Pigott, Rogers, and Nash, which is presented in this chapter and in Appendix A, Section IIA. There are 92 finds from ABC Banesh levels assigned to Class 2. Metal finds assigned to Classes 2, 16, and 20, including 2 items made of gold, are illustrated in Figs. 36 and 43; Pls. 20, 21 and 25-40.

Evidence for lead working is limited to 32 scraps of lead (Mat 203) interpreted as recycled material in storage (Stat R 2.2), including one possible casting. There are no finished lead artifacts in the ABC corpus and the function of lead in Banesh technology is poorly understood. However, a lead bowl containing 2 lead discs was found in TUV BL 3 (Nicholas 1990:76, Plate

28:D), a context otherwise associated with copper working.

Although the evidence for smelting or working copper based metals is much less common in the ABC assemblage than it is at TUV (Table 14), several stages in the production process are represented. There are several samples of copper ore (Stat P 2.2; mf 9834), including azurite (Mat 125; mf 3735, 9837) and minerals that may be associated with copper ores (Stat P 1.0; mf 2102). Some possible ore samples are distinguished by a high iron content (mf 2300) and evidence of roasting (mf 2288, 2324). By-products of metallurgical industry (Stat P 2.1) are represented by 14 copper prills (mf 1145.1, 1508, 1509, 1512, 1516.1, 2104, 2120, 2156, 2283, 3741, 3742, 3743), some associated with ceramic material or slag (mf 1515), and 11 samples of slag (Mat 800; i.e. mf 9850), some with adhering ceramic material (mf 1147).

The PIXE analysis (Pigott et al., inf., Tables 27, A 3 and A 4) demonstrates that the Banesh copper base metal from ABC and TUV is an arsenical copper with traces of nickel. An interesting, and possibly significant, difference between ABC and TUV is that 10 out of 16 samples from TUV have arsenic content greater than 2% (range 0.98-7.15%) while only 1 out of 14 samples from ABC fall above 2% (range 0.14-3.06%). Arsenic content in the 2-6% range (Pigott et al., inf.) provides added hardness to the metal with the implication that the TUV metalsmiths may have known about the properties of arsenical copper and were purposely seeking to produce a harder material. Although Pigott and his collaborators are cautious in their interpretation, it seem most likely that Banesh copper was derived from the ore bodies at Talmessi or Meskani in the Anarak district (Fig. 1). The ores were most likely smelted by one of several simple methods that would produce arsenical copper at relatively low temperatures without producing masses of slag. In the words of Pigott and his collaborators (inf.), "The presence of small amounts of slag, prills, and industrial ceramics indicates some on-site ore and metal processing took place at Malyan."

Metallographic analysis demonstrates that many of the samples studied are "the scraps and discards of simple mechanical metal working" (Pigott et al., inf.). There is evidence for casting, annealing, and hot and cold hammering. In some cases broken or discarded objects were recycled and in other instances the metalsmiths used previously prepared sheet or bar stock.

The only tools that might be related to the production of metal are a ceramic tube (mf 6810, Fig. 42d),

and a copper tube (mf 607, Fig. 36f), both assigned to Class 14, various tools. The ceramic tube may have been used as a *tuyère* and the metal tube may perhaps have been used as a spout for a bellows.

Corroded scraps of metal—ring fragments (Type 42; i.e. mf 1148, Fig. 36c), bits of sheet metal (Type 62; i.e. mf 1143), 19 fragments of bar stock (Type 63, i.e. mf 1136, Fig. 36n), and 2 corroded copper samples—are interpreted as scrap metal collected to be recycled (Stat R 2.2). However, the distinction between these items and other copper finds assigned to Class 16, Personal Ornaments, or other consumption-use functional classes is problematic. In general the less damaged and corroded finds that have a specific functional identity such as "awl" or "pin" are assigned to consumption-use functional classes (Classes 13-22) while badly corroded finds or those with a less specific functional identity such as "sheet metal" or "bar stock" were assigned to the metal production functional class (Class 2).

Context

There are 62 Class 2 finds from BL 2, 48 from good context (LI G or H). The evidence that lead was stored in BL 2 is strong: there are 21 fragments (Mat 203, Stat R 2.2) from secondary deposits and 6 from DC 37 deposits. These 27 fragments represent 84% of all lead finds recovered at ABC. The evidence for copper metallurgy in BL 2 is less strong than the evidence found at TUV, but not to be ignored. Secondary deposits produced 4 scraps classified as recycled material (Stat R 2.2) a prill (Stat 2.1) and a sample of corroded slag (Mat 800, Stat 2.1). There are 2 bits of recycled material (Mat 201, Stat R 2.2) and a roasted iron-rich nodule from DC 37 lots in BL 2.

BL 3 produced only 7 Class 2 finds, 6 from good context. There is a prill (Stat P 2.1) and a slag sample from floor removal lots (DC 29). DC 37 lots produced a slag sample with prills (Stat P 2.1) and a recycled piece of bar stock (Stat R 2.2).

BL 4 produced 8 Class 2 finds, all from good context. There is a prill from a DC 29 lot and 3 prills from DC 37. A bit of recycled bar stock and a slag sample came from secondary deposits.

BL 5 produced only an azurite sample (Stat P 2.2) and a slag sample (Stat P 2.1) from tertiary deposits (DC 35).

The use of the BL 2 to store lead for some unknown use seems clear. It also seems likely that copper or bronze was smelted and worked in the vicinity of ABC, but not in the buildings excavated.

Table 16. STONE BEAD PRODUCTION MATERIAL BY STATUS CODE

Material	Mat	V	P 2.2	R 2.2	P 3.2	C
Stone	100	—	1•	—	2	7
Quartz	101	—	2	—	—	1
Rock crystal	101	1	11	—	1	—
Flint	102	1	—	1	—	—
Chert	102	2	—	4	1	—
Chalcedony	102	7	—	3	—	—
Carbonate	103	—	1		—	—
White Marble	103	3	—	1	—	3
Calcite	103	4	8	—	1*	—
Turquoise	106	—	1	—	—	1
Lapis Lazuli	107	—	2	—	2**	—
Carnelian	108	—	1	—	2	1
Talc Rock	110	—	—	—	—	1
Green Talc Rock	110	5	1	—	—	—
Steatite	110	2	—	—	—	4
Bitumen	116	—	13	—	—	64
Azurite	125	—	2	—	—	—
Zeolite	127	—	1	—	—	—
Clinoptilolite	127	2	2	—	2	—
Barite	129	1	1	—	—	—
SUM			47	9	11	82

Stat. P 2.2 = altered raw materials (except • = P 2.0, possible raw material). Stat. R 2.2 = recycled materials. Stat. P 3.2 = unfinished products (except * = R 3.2 and ** = P 3.0). C = finished beads (Stat. C 5.0–6.2)

Functional Class 3. Stone Bead Production

This discussion is based on the contribution by Vidale presented in this chapter. There are 67 finds assigned to Class 3 including 47 examples of possible raw materials (Stat P 2.0, P 2.2), 9 possible recycled materials (Stat R 2.2), and 11 partly worked or unfinished beads (Stat P 3.2, R 3.2, or P 3.0)(Fig. 37). In addition to these finds 82 finished beads, classified as personal ornaments (Class 16), were recovered in the ABC excavations. A number of Class 3 finds are also classified as possible raw materials or products in other functional classes (Classes 1, 2, 9, 12). All-purpose tools that may have been used in bead production are assigned to use consumption classes (Class 13, 14, 15). Microwear analysis (Kardulias, inf., Tables 24, 25) identified one drill point (mf 7001.2, Fig. 35j) that was used to drill hard material and one blade segment (mf 7026, Fig. 33e) that was used to shave soft stone. The reconstruction of the technique used to produce clinoptilolite (Mat 127 V 2) beads at TUV (Blackman and Vidale n.d.) requires the use of flint

blades to score tabular plaques of clinoptilolite to produce small squares from which the beads were fashioned. No doubt similar techniques were in general use by bead makers working in or around the buildings excavated in ABC.

Material

Raw materials were assigned to Class 3 on the basis of color, a general understanding of the types of material used to make stone or mineral beads, and the presence of beads in the ABC assemblage made from the same material. Materials assigned to Class 3 are summarized in Table 16.

Table 16 shows that raw materials were available at ABC to make all of the finished beads recovered except for talc rock and steatite. In addition there are bead rough-outs, unfinished beads, or beads broken in production made of white stone, rock crystal, carnelian, chert, and clinoptilolite. Bitumen, which technically should not be included in Class 3 because it is not a stone, is also a raw material for bead production in addition to its utility in other craft production activities.

Table 17. CONTEXT OF CLASS 3 FINDS BY BL AND DC

	BL 2	BL 3	BL 4	BL 5	SUM
Secondary	7	1	5	—	13
DC 37	8	3	5	—	16
Tertiary	25	6	3	1	35
SUM	40	10	13	1	64

Context

As shown in Table 17, more than half (35) of the finds assigned to Class 3, excluding 3 finds from Stratum 9 (DC 34) and DC 41, occur in tertiary deposits (DC 35, 36). It is assumed that these small and unobtrusive finds were likely to have been accidentally incorporated in bricks used to construct the ABC buildings. The fact that more than half of these finds are from BL 2 tertiary deposits may be expected because the volume of bricky fill excavated in BL 2 is relatively large. If the bricks were made nearby, as is often the custom, they also probably incorporated a greater density of finds because trash had been accumulating in the neighborhood for several hundred years at the time BL 2 was constructed. In contrast, BLs 3 and 4, razed and leveled in the process of constructing later buildings, contained a smaller volume of bricky fill and were built earlier in the occupation of the site, with the implication that there was less accumulated trash available to be incorporated in the clay used for brick making.

At both TUV and ABC the evidence of bead production, particularly in the form of unfinished beads, is unequivocal, but the frequency of bead production debris is quite low. If bead production is an important activity, even a specialized craft, we might expect to find more plentiful evidence. One explanation for the low frequency of finds is the miniature scale of the evidence. Although selected secondary deposits were screened, the screen used was coarse (ca. 1x1 cm) and few samples were put through a finer screen. The heavy fraction of flotation samples produced 24% of the finished or partly finished beads recovered at ABC, which implies a low recovery rate by handpicking.

It is also possible that the presence of Class 3 finds in ABC is largely accidental. If dispersal of trash was an ongoing process in the Banesh town at Malyan then debris from any localized activity would eventually be distributed widely, but at a density and frequency inversely proportional to distance from the original location of the activity. Low recovery rate and a frequency decline over distance are not mutually exclusive processes and it seems likely that both were at work in this instance, leading to the conclusion that a bead production quarter of the town may have been near ABC, perhaps within several hundred meters, but not in the immediate vicinity.

Functional Class 4. Shell Working

This section is based on the field identification of shells, indicated by the material code (Mat), and the subsequent study of the shells by David Reese (inf.) including his scientific identifications, indicated by the variety code (V) in the Register of Finds(Appendix A) and Table 18. Additional descriptive information from the study conducted by Reese for shells from both ABC and TUV is reported in Section IIB of Appendix A.

Shell provided raw material for two crafts at ABC—bead making and the production of mother of pearl inlay. Both of these crafts present difficulties when we attempt to separate unfinished objects associated with production from the finished products in the distribution, storage, and consumption cycle. All mother of pearl (nacre or *Pinctada*) inlay pieces, raw materials and by-products associated with inlay production are assigned to Class 4, Shell Working. All shells that have been made into beads or that could be used as beads, whether or not they have been worked, are assigned to Class 16, Personal Ornaments. This category includes all dentalia and a number of other shells that have holes, either natural or drilled. Shells or fragments that do not fall into either of these two categories are assigned to Class 4, Shell Working. There are 1106 shells in Class 4 and 149 shell items in Class 16.[*]

---

[*] There are minor differences in the counts discussed here (Table 18) and those presented by Reese below and in Appendix A. Section IIB. These differences are the result of differences in the criteria for inclusion in the study and in difficulties encountered in counting samples composed of many fragments. None of these differences alter the basic conclusions reached by me or by Reese.

Table 18. IDENTIFICATION OF SHELLS BY CLASS

NAME	Mat	V	Cl. 4	Cl. 16	SUM
Unidentified	500	—	12	1	13
Ancilla	500	1	—	2	2
Land Snail	500	6	14	—	14
Monodonta	500	8	—	1	1
Bivalve shell	501	—	24	—	24
Nacre, mother of pearl	501	9	961	—	961
Pinctada , mollusk	501	10	38	—	38
Unio, fresh water mussel	501	11	48	—	48
Dentalium, tusk shaped	502	—	—	14	14
Dentalium, tusk shaped	502	3	—	116	116
Conus, cone shaped	504	—	2	4	6
Conus, cone shaped	504	2	—	5	5
Engina	504	4	1	4	5
Gastropod, fresh water	504	5	3	1	4
Melanopsis, fresh water	504	7	3	1	4
SUM			1106	149	1255

Specific name, Variety (V) is as determined by David Reese; generic name is as assigned in the field register; Material (Mat)—coded by field registrars. In a few cases the Mat coding follows corrections made by Reese.

Shell Beads

A variety of shells can be used as beads with minimal modification. The most common bead shell in the ABC collection (130 examples) is *Dentalium*, which naturally has apertures at both the anterior and posterior ends connected by a continuous cavity, so no drilling is necessary for these shells to be strung either whole or broken into segments. The exterior of the *Dentalium* shell has natural fluting (i.e., mf 7425.3, Fig. 38k) that is ornamental without being worked. Five of the *Dentalium* finds that are classified as beads (Type 3, Class 16, Personal Ornament) show signs of polishing or other modifications including one elaborately carved example (mf 590, Fig. 43a). However, all of the other unmodified *Dentalium* shells may have been used or intended for use as beads or for other personal ornamentation such as arm bands, head bands or to decorate clothing and are assigned to Class 16. It is assumed that some of these may have been raw materials for the shell carving craft.

Less frequent (19 examples) in the ABC collection are beads made of a diverse group of cone or spiral shaped shells, some of them multi-colored. Thirteen of the shells in this group have one or more holes, usually in the apex, which could have been used to hang these shells as beads. However it is not clear whether or not these holes were already present as the result of predation before the shells were collected or were drilled by human bead makers. All holed shells and finished shell beads are classified as beads (Type 3, Class 16, Personal Ornaments). There are 21 shells in Class 4 that could have been raw materials for beads of this type. Flint drills and abrading or polishing stones assigned to Class 14, Tools, could have been used in shell bead production.

Mother of Pearl Inlay

The ABC collection contains 1023 finds related to the production of mother of pearl inlay. There are 986 finds classified as finished or partly finished pieces of inlay, (Types 15, 25, or 88; Stat 3.1) (Fig. 39); 955 are made of nacre (Mat 501 V 9), some of which are specifically identified as *Pinctada* (Mat 501 V 10). There are also 24 finds classified as production waste (Type 88, Stat P 2.1); 4 of these are made of unspecified bivalve shell (Mat 501), 6 of nacre (Mat 501 V 9), and 14 of *Pinctada* (Mat 501 V 10). There are 13 finds (Mat 501 or Mat 501 V 10) classified as raw material (Type 88, Stat P 2.2). Altogether 38 finds are identified as *Pinctada* (*Meleagarina*)(Mat 501 V 10), the famous pearl mollusk of the Persian Gulf, also valued as a source of mother of pearl.

In addition, there are 48 examples of fresh water mussels (*Unio*, Mat 501, V 11), mostly fragmentary, that may have been used for inlay work. At least 1 example

Table 19. BL 2 SHELL FINDS BY STATUS CODE AND DC

	DC 21-29	DC 37	DC 35-36	SUM
CLASS 4				
Stat P 1.0	—	5	5	10
Stat P 2.1	5	5	32	42
Stat P 2.2	2	5	19	26
Stat P 3.1	829	87	24	940
CLASS 16				
Stat C 6.0	92	23	13	124
SUM	928	125	93	1142
%	81	11	8	100

from TUV was worked into a rectangle, possibly for use as an inlay. However, the ABC mussels are not classified as inlay raw material or debris because no *Unio* inlays have been positively identified in the ABC assemblage. Mussels are edible and some varieties are known to produce pearls. A number of the mussel shells at TUV and ABC are burned.

Production

The inlay pieces occur in a great variety of rectangular shapes (Fig.39a-j) and a variety of less common shapes: curved (Fig. 39s, t), triangular (Fig. 39r, cc, dd), circular (Fig. 39p), zig-zag (Fig. 39n), teardrop (Fig. 39bb), and diamond shapes with concave and convex sides (Fig. 39u–z). Some pieces have incised lines, usually parallel to one or more edges (Fig. 39g–j). Many pieces are lightly scored on one side, possibly to make them adhere better to the objects they are meant to decorate (Appendix A. Part II). The edges are generally beveled in one direction, which may be a feature to facilitate fitting the pieces together to form designs. Bitumen was found adhering to no more than three or four pieces in the collection and no evidence of any other adhesive was detected. No inlay pieces were found adhering to any object and no wooden or other flat surfaces were found that the inlays might have been intended to decorate.

Context

BL 2 produced 1142 shell finds, representing 91% of all shells found at ABC—1018 finds in Class 4, and 124 finds in Class 16. As shown in Table 19, 1053 of the shell finds (92%) from BL 2, including both Class 4 and Class 16, come from floors or just above floors (DC 21-29 or 37) with the implication that shell objects were made, stored, or used in BL 2.

The largest concentration of shell within BL 2 is from Corridor 118, which produced 883 finds, 877 of which are inlay pieces. The largest cluster of inlay pieces was split into two samples, one of which went to the museum in Tehran. We were unable to study the sample in Tehran and no exact count is available, but it should be very similar to the sample recorded here as mf 2448, which contained 669 pieces of inlay. The relatively low frequency of raw material (Stat P 2.2) or production debris (Stat P 2.1) in comparison to the high frequency of finished inlay pieces, indicates that inlay production was not located in BL 2 and certainly not in Corridor 118, which was a busy passageway with a considerable amount of trash trampled into the floor. It is assumed the inlays were lost in the corridor, perhaps as they were being brought to or from storage in one of the BL 2 rooms, although it is not clear from the area excavated if the rooms to the south of Corridor 118 could have been entered from the corridor. A few inlays were found inside the building on floors (DC 21 or 29) or in DC 37 deposits in Rooms 71 (7 inlays), 129 (14 inlays), 130 (5), 131 (7), 154 (5), and Room 207 (2), but none of these rooms have any significant quantity of raw material or production waste. Room 130 also contained 88 *Dentalium* shells or segments, assigned to Class 16, and it is assumed that unworked shell, finished beads and finished inlay components were stored in BL 2.

The shell industry is minimally represented in BL 3 (15 finds) and BL 4 (23 finds). Only 7 of the BL 3 finds, all related to inlay production (Stat P 3.1 or P 2.1), come from secondary or DC 37 lots. There are 16 finds from secondary or DC 37 lots in BL 4, related to inlay or bead production (Stat 2.1 or 2.2).

Summary

The evidence suggests that shell ornaments played a small role in the lives of the inhabitants of ABC before the construction of the BL 2 warehouse. The small number of shell finds in ABC BLs 3 and 4 suggest there was very little shell working in the vicinity of ABC and the use of only a few shell beads by the inhabitants of those levels. The majority of shells from ABC BL 2 appear to have been lost in the final stages of production (Stat P 3.1, 3.2) in connection with the storage of craft materials in the BL 2 warehouse. These products, including *Dentalia*, which require little or no modification, and inlay components were kept in the warehouse. Tablets and sealings found in BL 2 suggest a system of administrative control over storage spaces or commodities, perhaps including the shell finds. The presence of a considerable quantity of sea shell, as well as ray or shark vertebrae used to make beads, indicates some form of trade with the Persian Gulf coastal region. The easiest route to the gulf, via Firuzabad, is a distance of some 350 km that would require 12 days or more by donkey caravan. The distance and hazards of transport would have considerably increased the value of shells, some of which were available for the gathering on the gulf beaches.

Functional Class 5. Plasters and Pigments

Blackman (1982) has published a technical analysis of burned lime plaster used to produce plaster vessels and plaster wall paintings in the Banesh levels at Malyan, together with a discussion of the implications of this production technology. He makes a strong case for lime burning as a summer seasonal activity that required the mobilization of a considerable labor force, particularly in those years when large buildings with wall decorations, such as ABC BL 3, were under construction. This work would very likely have been under administrative control, responsive to demand, and may have been supervised by potters, who would have the necessary pyrotechnical skills, as a part-time specialization. Lumps of unused plaster, as well as evidence of white or colored plaster walls and plaster vessels were found in small quantities in all building levels at ABC.

In the same paper Blackman also reported on his examination of the pigments used in the BL 3 wall paintings. He concludes that hematite, goethite, and probably organic carbon were used. Small quantities of compact and earthy red hematite (mf 3940 and 5081) and yellow limonite (mf 3941) were found on BL 5 floors (DC 21 and 37). Earthy hematite was also found in a DC 37 context in BL 4A. Charcoal to produce black and grey was plentiful. Several of the plaster ves-

sel fragments are decorated with red and black panels divided by incised lines (Fig. 40j, k and 41e), also probably using carbon and red ochre (earthy hematite). Pigments used on painted pottery have not been identified but are likely to include the same group of minerals with the addition of some mineral to produce the characteristic white wash slip on some Banesh vessels. The presence of a wide band (27 mm), apparently fugitive blue, on Pithos 164 in BL 2 presents the intriguing possibility that turquoise was used as a pigment.

Functional Class 6. Spinning and Weaving

A large number of sealings from BLs 2 and 3 show the impression of cloth used to cover jars, but there is no evidence of textile production or other uses in the ABC assemblage. Two finds, one (mf 742) from BL 2 (DC 37) and the other (mf 1289, Fig. 43d) from BL 3A (DC 37) are classified as spindle whorls and assigned to Class 14, Tools. However, these objects are quite small and light weight (wt ca. 10-20 grams; dia. 2.2-2.5 cm) for whorls and may have served some other function. One copper needle (mf 1132, Fig. 36i) was recorded during excavations in Banesh levels in 1974, but its context is not recorded and it may not belong to the Banesh assemblage. In any event it can be said that the evidence for spinning, weaving, and sewing is practically absent from ABC, and as shown in Table 14, from TUV as well.

Functional Class 7. Food Preparation

One of the principal reasons for adopting the functional class model in this report is to facilitate the comparison of the Banesh levels excavated in ABC with those excavated in TUV. In the case of food production this comparison relies more on an analysis of architecture and features than the frequency of finds assigned to this class. An examination of the character of the buildings and features at ABC suggests that food preparation was not a major activity within any building level.

Evidence of Features

In BL 2 there are several burned areas on the earlier floor, but only one constructed hearth (Hearth 147), which is consistent with the functional interpretation of the excavated rooms as part of a warehouse. However, it is entirely possible that unexcavated rooms in this building could have served other functions, including a kitchen for food preparation on a domestic or institutional scale.

The decorated walls and fine objects from BL 3 suggest this building was devoted to some important institutional function, but certainly do not rule out the possibility that it could have been a dwelling for members of a local elite class. There are six well-constructed hearths in BL 3, one of which (Hearth 36 in Room 35, Pl. 10a) was domed. However, no other facilities for food preparation, such as grinding stones or domestic storage jars were found in BL 3 and it seems probable that any kitchen associated with this building was located beyond the limits of our excavation.

BL 4 produced two well-constructed hearths and a feature that is interpreted as an oven (Oven 300), probably for baking bread. Although grinding stones are rare, it seems likely that food was prepared in this building.

There are six hearths and one small oven in BL 5. Four of these are well-constructed hearths similar to those in the other buildings. One hearth (360, in Area 348) was equipped with two large vertical posts on either side of the burnt area and two smaller posts in front and to one side. This hearth appears to be located in an open court and the posts may have suspended an awning, but could also have functioned to hold a roasting spit. The small underground oven (363) in Area 358, probably an open court, is enigmatic but may have been used for cooking. It seems probable that some food was prepared in BL 5.

Two pieces of pyrite that may have been used as strike-a-lights are recorded for ABC; 1 (mf 2149) from BL 3A (DC 29) and another (mf 932) from BL 2 (DC 37).

Pounding and Grinding Tools

Pounding and grinding tools are represented at ABC by only three finds (mf 2633, 2634, 2235) all from Pit 236 in BL 4A.

Botanical Evidence

Botanical evidence from ABC includes wood charcoal and a variety of carbonized seeds of cereals (wheat and barley), field weeds, grape, and fig (Miller 1982, Tables B1, 2, 3) from floor deposits in all four building levels and from Hearth 345 in BL 4A. Seeds were also recovered from friable Banesh straw tempered pottery (mf 7467). It is notable that Pit 236 in BL 4A, which produced a large quantity of wood charcoal, produced only a few carbonized seeds. Miller (1984a and 1984b) has demonstrated that many seeds recovered at Malyan entered the archaeological record as a result of using animal dung for fuel, and therefore represent the diet of animals rather than the human inhabitants of the city. The relatively low ratio of seeds to wood charcoal at ABC probably means that dung cake fuel was not used extensively in these buildings. Based on a change in the seed/wood charcoal ratio Miller (1985; 1990) argues that land clearing intensified only after the Banesh period, with the implication that firewood would have been available nearby in Banesh times. The presence of a few sickle blade segments (Kardulias, this volume, inf.) implies that some residents in the neighborhood of ABC may have been involved in farming, but it is not clear how this relates to the location of food preparation activities.

Faunal Evidence

The discussion of faunal evidence summarized here is based on the analysis published by Zeder (1984, 1985, 1986, 1988, 1991). In her analysis Zeder (1991:129) combined the animal bones from all Banesh levels at ABC because of small sample size. The diagnostic sheep, goat, and cattle bones from ABC, excluding 22 bones from clean-up lots (DC 41), are summarized by deposit code and building level in Table 20. Other mammals present in low frequency are equid (BL 2, Corridor 118, DC 29) and gazelle (BL 3, Area 260, DC 37). The equids are probably domestic asses used for transport although the presence of hunted equids cannot be ruled out (Zeder 1986, 1991:138). The only bird present is a chukar partridge (BL 4, Area 307, DC 21). There are also fragments of ostrich egg shell, fresh water mussel shells, and several ray or shark vertebrae, used to make beads but possibly derived from imported preserved (smoked or salted) fish (Reese, this volume, inf.). Zeder's analysis is a reliable indication of conditions prevalent in BL 4, which comprises 79% by weight and 71 % by count of all diagnostic bones from ABC, but interpretation of the small samples from BLs 2, 3, and 5 is problematic. A total of 8,313 animal bones were recovered at ABC, of which 781 were analyzed in detail (Zeder 1991, Tables 24, 25), with the remainder classified by mammal size. The assemblage of identified bones is dominated by sheep/goat, which constitute 99% of the analyzed sample by count and 96% by weight. This picture is reinforced by the high frequency of medium-sized mam-

Table 20. WEIGHT AND NUMBER OF SHEEP, GOAT, AND CATTLE BONES BY BL and DC

BL	DC	SG wt	SG #	S wt	S #	G wt	G #	C wt	C #	SUM wt	SUM #
2	29	224	41	55	5	26	5	—	—	305	51
2	37	86	30	—	—	30	3	—	—	116	33
2	35	9	6	—	—	2	1	—	—	11	7
SUB.		319	77	55	5	58	9	—	—	432	91
9	34	56	22	5	1	—	—	—	—	61	23
3	29	43	19	—	—	10	2	—	—	53	21
3	37	187	66	13	3	70	15	71	2	341	86
3	35	35	5	—	—	7	1	—	—	42	6
SUB.		265	90	13	3	87	18	71	2	436	113
4	21/2	1960	353	206	18	547	47	—	—	2713	418
4	37	335	67	52	8	56	8	—	—	443	83
4	35	13	4	14	1	—	—	—	—	27	5
SUB.		2308	424	272	27	603	55	—	—	3183	506
5	37	23	8	5	1	5	1	—	—	33	10
5	35	10	2	20	3	—	—	18	1	48	6
SUB.		33	10	25	4	5	1	18	1	81	16
SUM		2981	623	370	40	753	83	89	3	4193	747

SG = sheep or goat, S = sheep, G = goat, C = cattle; 9 in the BL column is Stratum 9

mals in the combined assemblage of identified and unidentified bones, in which they constitute 99% by count and 98% by weight.(Zeder 1991:136-137).

For the Banesh levels at ABC, as compared to TUV, Zeder (1991:130) expected that "The combined faunal assemblage from all four building levels at ABC would show the strongest indications of the receipt of meat resources through an indirect system of distribution." By an indirect system of distribution she means a system in which consumers procure at least some meat from a middleman, perhaps a butcher, rather that dealing directly with the individuals who own and manage flocks, with the further implication that the consumers in such an indirect system are not themselves owners of animals raised for meat. The analysis designed to test this expectation relies on three aspects of animal utilization: "(1) the types of animals selected for distribution, (2) the ages of animals selected, and (3) the butchery and meat preparation techniques employed" (Zeder 1991:42-43, 135-136). The contrasting requirements of optimal herd management on the one hand and efficient provisioning management on the other hand should be expressed by these variables. If meat is procured directly from herders het-

erogeneity is expected for all variables: more species, a wider range of ages at butchering, and less uniformity in butchering practices. This stands in contrast to the homogeneity expected in an indirect procurement system in which a middle man—"the butcher shop"—stands between the herder and urban consumers. In this case the requirements of efficient provisioning imply a focus on the best meat producing species butchered at a relatively young age, and more uniform butchering practices. This brief summary does not do justice to the model developed by Zeder, which is fully presented elsewhere (Zeder 1991:23-44 and 75-118).

Zeder interprets the sharp focus on sheep/goat as an indication of indirect meat procurement at ABC. However, the goat/sheep ratio in BLs 3 and 4 is 2:1 by weight, which is unexpected in view of the fact that sheep generally provide more meat than goats. As expected for an indirect distribution system, there is a strong focus on animals in the 2-3 year age range, as determined by analysis of both long bone fusion and mandibular tooth eruption and wear (Zeder 1991:141-148).

It has been alleged that "parts is parts" but Zeder (1991:41-42) argues convincingly that an uneven distribution of skeletal parts should be expected when meat is distributed through an indirect system—there will be a higher or lower frequency of certain skeletal elements as compared to the frequency of parts in a "standard bovid skeleton". Although all skeletal parts are represented in the ABC assemblage, there is a slightly elevated frequency of "meatier cuts from the hindlimb haunch region". However, Zeder (1991:151-153) notes some reservation concerning this observation due to possible sampling bias.

The pattern of butchery marks is more highly standardized at ABC, compared with TUV, which may be due to more skillful butchering, and is interpreted by Zeder as further evidence that at least some meat at ABC was procured through an indirect distribution system (Zeder 1991:153). Zeder's conclusions are best summarized in her own words:

As predicted, evidence for indirect modes of meat distribution is strongest in the assemblage from ABC (in comparison to TUV). Meat distribution to high status occupants of the residential/public buildings at ABC focused tightly on resources drawn from caprid herds, with goats outnumbering sheep by 2 to 1. Little utilization of noncaprid domesticates or of supplementary hunted game is indicated. Caprid meat was derived almost exclusively from animals between two and three years of age.

Some of the caprids came to ABC as whole animals, butchered in the ABC area. Given the strong indications of indirect provisioning in other lines of faunal data, these animals were probably not raised by residents of ABC or obtained through direct contacts with herders. At least a portion of caprid meat was received as selected parts—with cuts from the axial portion of the skeleton and especially from the limbs. Limb cuts from the hindquarter haunch region were frequently utilized; nonmeat-bearing portions of limbs were often removed before distribution. Butchery of the animals left relatively infrequent scars, consistently located at the same place on the joint—a pattern expected when butchery technique is standardized. The location of specialized butchers or kitchens that prepared meat for ABC is uncertain. (Zeder 1991:159)

Although this assemblage is not large in comparison to TUV, which produced about three times as many animal bones, it nevertheless provides evidence that meat may have been prepared within the excavated rooms of BL 4, but more likely in the vicinity. Meat was probably not prepared within the excavated limits of the other building levels at ABC.

Ceramic Evidence

Because of the relatively small number of sherds from good trash contexts at ABC, no attempt is made here to duplicate Nicholas' (1990) analysis of bulk sherds. However the distribution of sherds by level and deposit code is presented in Chapter 2 (Table 10). The ABC ceramic assemblage from secondary contexts (DC 21-29, 37) is dominated by straw tempered ware in a very narrow range of forms. The most common form is a solid footed conical goblet with a capacity of 1300-2600 cubic centimeters (Figs. 21, 22; Pl. 15). The second most common form is the flat Banesh tray (Fig. 23). As noted in Chapter II, there have been several suggestions regarding the function of these forms, generally in connection with food preparation and more specifically with food service. A significant number of these forms come from good secondary deposits, particularly in BL 4 (Table 10), which reinforces the other lines of evidence presented above. The only unusual find in this class is a strainer sherd (mf 11232) from BL 3A.

Summary

This review of the data suggests that food was prepared in BL 4, although not on the large scale identified at TUV. The evidence is less convincing for the other levels but is sufficient to suggest that food was prepared on occasion in or near all the other ABC buildings.

Functional Class 8. Pottery Production

There is no convincing evidence for the production of pottery in the vicinity of ABC. Four pieces of possible ceramic slag—that is, slag not obviously a by-product of metal working—were recovered from tertiary contexts in BL 2 (mf 2170 and 2296), from a DC 37 lot in BL 3A (mf 1499), and in Stratum 9 (DC 34)(mf 8725), and in Stratum 10A (DC 23) (mf 1500). Neither TUV nor any other operation at Malyan has produced significant evidence for Banesh pottery production. A number of sites in the valley produced evidence for the production and distribution of either grit tempered or straw tempered Banesh pottery (Alden 1979:85-118; 1982a; 1988; and this volume, Appendix D). Analysis of Banesh ceramics by x-ray diffraction and thin section techniques (Blackman 1981) indicates that straw tempered ceramics were all made of local clayey alluvial soils (Blackman's Group I) and grit tempered ceramics were made of two distinct clays (Groups II and III). Blackman concludes:

> This study has demonstrated that three chemically distinct clays were used to make the vast majority of ceramics of Banesh age found at Tal-e Malyan, and that these chemically distinct clays are probably due to geochemical differences in the clay sources utilized by the Banesh potters. The origin of the clays can only be inferred at this point, however the frequency of occurrence of the various ceramic forms included in this study argues for local manufacture at sites within the Kur River Basin. Importation of ceramics from outside the basin, except on a very small scale, seems unlikely during the Banesh period.
> The chaff tempered ceramics seem to have been produced from alluvial clays available over a wide area within the basin. The producers of grit tempered ceramics seem to have avoided the use of alluvial clays for the most part, possibly because of their high carbonate content. They favored the use of two other chemically distinct clays, whose sources are probably located in the folded mountains that rim the Kur River Basin. The use of the two clays seems to proceed simultaneously at one or more sites, with Group II clays favored over Group III clays for a wider variety of vessels. This usage pattern seems to be traditionally or spatially motivated rather than the result of physical differences in the workability or esthetics of the clays (Blackman 1981:19).

Functional Class 9. Other Crafts

Functional Class 9 includes a variety of materials that may have been used in stone work and other items of unknown function.

The evidence for the production of carbonate stone (calcite, limestone and dolomite) bowls (inf., Vidale) includes 8 unworked (Stat P 2.2) carbonate rocks and 2 waste products (Stat 2.1) of the same materials. The later production stages (Stat P 3.0, 3.2) are represented by a vessel preform (mf 2334, Fig. 40e), 3 unfinished vessels (mf 6055, Fig. 40i; mf 6056, 2450) and one that may be unfinished (mf 2284). There are several stone grinding or polishing tools assigned to Class 14 that may have been used in stone bowl production. Vidale (inf.) suggests that an unusual piece of ground stone (mf 7304, Fig. 42i) is probably a specialized tool used to smooth the inside of stone or plaster vessels.

Unlike the stone bead, metal, and shell working crafts, all of which seem to have used the storage facility in BL 2 at some stage in the production cycle, stone bowl production or storage is not concentrated in BL 2. Seven finds associated with this craft come from tertiary deposits (DC 35 or 36) in BL 2. There is one find (Stat P 2.2) from a good floor deposit in Corridor 118 (mf 2450) and another (Stat P 2.1) from the floor (DC 29) in Room 130 (mf 9847).

Stratum 9 and BL 3 together produced 4 finds in secondary (DC 29 or 23) or DC 37 context. BL 4A produced 2 unworked finds (Stat P 2.2) and the smoothing tool (mf 7304, Fig. 42i) in a DC 37 context.

These finds indicate that calcite and limestone vessels were produced in the vicinity of ABC, but the evidence does not imply large scale production. Fifteen vessels made of carbonate stones are assigned to Class 12, Special Vessels.

Some of the stones assigned to this class are also listed in Class 3, Bead Production, because there are both beads and stone vessels made of these materials. In addition, a number of finds that are probably raw materials for unidentified production activities, are assigned to this class. There is a calcite cylinder, probably a cylinder seal blank (mf 10222) (Stat P 3.2). Several pieces of ostrich egg shell (mf 2295, 2326, 2071, 9868, Fig. 38a, b) are possibly material for bead making (Stat P 2.2). Bitumen, the all-purpose adhesive and sealant is plentiful. There are also cleaned clay samples, probably for making sealings or tablets, unworked specular hematite crystals, and a miscellaneous group of stones and minerals of unknown utility.

Functional Class 10. Storage

Class 10 is represented by 370 finds: 188 clay sealing fragments with clear or probable impressions, 176 sealing fragments without impressions, and 5 conical clay jar stoppers without impressions (mf 604, Fig. 43g; 1978, 3769, 7281, Fig. 42b; 7292), and one made of plaster (mf 7293). Virtually all of the sealings, which had been used to seal jar openings covered with cloth or animal skin and tied with cord, were discarded when the jars were opened (Stat C 5.1), although several may be tags and at least one may be a door sealing. Sealing design and analysis of clays used for sealings is discussed in the section on Class 21, Information Processing.

Context

The identification of the central rooms in the excavated area of BL 2 as a warehouse is clearly established by the presence of 13 large storage pithoi in Room 71 and 1 each in Rooms 186 and 185, all in BL 2 (Fig. 28, Pl. 13). There are also 52 clay sealings, 11 impressed, and one jar stopper from BL 2. Secondary deposits in Room 71 produced 6 sealings, all but one impressed. There are 42 sealings, 5 with impressions, from Corridor 118 (DC 29), 2 from Room 128 (DC 37), and 2 from Room 185. The evidence shows that BL 2 was used to store bulk commodities, probably liquid, and a variety of materials and worked craft products, particularly stone beads, shell inlay pieces, shell beads, and copper pins and rings. These storage functions appear to be related to an administrative system involving both inscribed tablets (Class 21) and sealings.

The storage function of BL 3 is less clear. There are sealing fragments (mf 1693) from a mixed floor deposit (DC 29) in BL 3B, and (mf 2598) from a mixed DC 35 lot in BL 3A. Fragments of several smaller storage jars and sherds and one jar with nose lugs on the shoulder (Pl. 18c-e) were recovered from BL 3 in addition to the elaborate relief decorated vessels (Fig. 27, Pls. 16, 17), which seem exceptionally fine for such a prosaic purpose, but could have been used for storage. There appear to be at least 2 of these jars with well made lids (mf 1192, Fig. 27e) and holes in the rope ornament on the shoulder that made it possible to tie the lids down (mf 1731, Fig. 27a). No sealing was recognized in any context that might have been used to seal these jars and it seems likely they were used to store something for ready use in one of the rather elegant BL 3A rooms. Although this evidence implies a different type of storage in the excavated rooms of BL 3, the presence of 2 dense concentrations (DC 23) of sealings (278 sealings; 169 with impressions) within Stratum 9 below BL 2 floors and in Stratum 10A, the bricky filling of BL 3A, implies the presence nearby of rooms equipped with storage jars like those found in BL 2.

There are 18 sealings or jar stoppers from BL 4A. Pit 236 produced 1 impressed sealing (mf 1971) and 4 conical jar stoppers. There are 4 impressed sealings (mf 1932.1, 1932.2, 1979.1, 2023), and 9 unimpressed sealings from DC 37 deposits in Court 281, Room 64, and Corridor 241. These finds indicate relatively modest domestic storage activities in BL 4.

BL 5 produced 14 sealing fragments (DC 28 and 37) without impressions and one unimpressed jar stopper in good context, (DC 37) which suggest a modest level of domestic storage activity within the excavated rooms of BL 5.

The evidence for relatively large scale non-domestic storage activities in BL 2 and somewhere in the neighborhood of the excavated rooms of BL 3 is unequivocal. The evidence for domestic storage in BLs 4 and 5 is less impressive, but it is likely that some storage activities were associated with both of these buildings.

Functional Class 11. Baskets and Matting

This functional class is interpreted by Nicholas as associated with storage activities at TUV. At ABC bitumen impregnated reed matting (mf 2344; Pl. 14d) was found on the floor in association with the large pithoi in BL 2, Room 71. Reed mat impressions in clay were also found in Room 71 (mf 1092) and in BL 3A (mf 7234). Although these finds are assigned to Class 11, the relationship of reed mats to storage activities is at best ambiguous. There is no evidence for the production of baskets or mats in or near ABC and the place where mats were produced remains unknown.

Functional Class 12. Special Containers

There are 48 finds assigned to this class: 24 stone vessel fragments (Figs. 40, 41), 8 pieces of plaster vessels (Figs. 40, 41; Pl. 21d), 13 relief sherds (Fig. 27; Pls. 16, 17), a miniature pot (mf 531), a humped bull vessel spout (mf 1737, Fig. 42e) and a crenellated tray (mf 746).

Material

The stone vessels are made of travertine, green marble, white marble, calcite, limestone, talc rock, and chlorite. Evidence presented under Class 9 suggests that some of these vessels were produced in the ABC neighborhood. Three of the plaster or limestone vessels have incised and painted decoration in red and black (mf 7305, 9849, and 189; Figs. 40j, k; 41e; Pl. 21d). The relief sherds, also assigned to Class 20, Decorated Items, are described in Chapter II. The miniature vessel is unlike miniature vessels found at TUV and may be an intrusive Kaftari object. The bull head vessel spout, found on the surface, is assigned to the Banesh period on rather limited stylistic grounds and may belong to another period.

Context

Five of these finds come from secondary or DC 37 deposits in BL 2, 4 from secondary and 3 from DC 37 deposits in BL 3A, 2 from floors in BL 3B, one from a floor in BL 4B, and one from a floor in BL 5. The other 30 come from tertiary deposits or undetermined context (DC 31, 39, 40, or 41). The presence of 12 stone or plaster vessels in DC 35 or 36 deposits in BL 2 implies that stone bowls discarded at some earlier time were incorporated in the bricks used to construct BL 2. Unfortunately 9 of these vessels are from mixed lots and may belong to the Kaftari assemblage. All of these finds are broken, but it is not known whether or not they were in use when they were lost of discarded (Stat C 5.0).

Functional Class 13. Cutting Tools

There are 54 flint or obsidian blades or blade segments, 5 utilized flakes, and 2 microlithic crescents assigned to this class.

Material

These finds are made of chert, jasper, agate, flint, and obsidian. There are backed blades, blades with denticulated or nibbled edges, and blades with glossy edges (sickle sheen). The mean length of 50 measured blades or blade segments, excluding one microblade, is 27 mm. One blade retains bitumen hafting material (mf 1236, Fig. 33c, Pl. 20b) and two are classified as microlithic (mf 2113, 2158). Four of the blades subjected to use wear analysis were probably used to cut grass (Table 25; Fig. 34a, e, h. i) and one was used to shave soft stone (mf 7026, Fig. 33e).

The majority of these tools (32) show only moderate evidence of wear and are assigned to Stat C 6.1, lost during use, but 2 have signs of heavy wear and are classified as worn out and discarded (Stat C 6.3). There are 10 that show no evidence of use and are classified

as in storage (Stat C 6.2) and 17 which can only be classified as discarded, lost or stored (Stat C 6.0). It would also have been reasonable to classify unused blade segments as stored components (Stat P 3.1); this alternative was rejected because blade segments can be viewed as finished tools whether or not they are hafted as part of a composite tool. It is notable that the multi-purpose cutting tools in Class 13 are all made of stone, despite the considerable evidence of the use of copper or bronze for other purposes.

Context

Twenty-six of these finds were recovered from secondary or DC 37 deposits: 8 in BL 2, 6 in BL 3A, 4 in BL 3B, 4 in BL 4A, 1 in BL 4B, and 3 in BL 5. In addition, 7 were recovered from Stratum 18 (DC 50), below BL 5, 5 of them classified as lost in use (Stat C 6.1).

Functional Class 14. Various Tools

There are 33 tools assigned to this class. The largest group is composed of a variety of flint tools: pointed or notched flakes, retouched flakes, and a scraper. There are two small whorls (mf 742 and 1289, Fig. 43d), 2 disc sherds (mf 11285 and 11287), a variety of small limestone grinding or polishing stones (mf 2635, 3946, 5981, 7304, Fig. 42i; 7306), a limestone hammer stone (mf 9843), and a copper chisel (mf 760, Fig. 36p) and hook (mf 1134, Fig. 36a). There is also a copper tapering tube (mf 607, Fig. 36f) and a ceramic tube (mf 6810, Fig. 42d) that may have functioned as parts of a *tuyère* or bellows in the metal industry. Three of these tools were subjected to microwear analysis (Table 25): a pointed flake (mf 2119.3, Fig. 35b) was used to scrape bone, an end scraper (mf 6628, Fig. 35d) was used to scrape hide. A retouched notched flake (mf 6663, Fig. 31c) and a pointed flake (mf 1065, Fig. 35a) showed no evidence of wear. Eleven of these tools were discarded after breakage (Stat C 5.0-5.3) and the others were stored, discarded or lost before they were broken or worn out (Stat C 6.0-6.2). The tools in Class 14 represent a variety of production and maintenance activities similar to the activities evidenced for TUV.

Context

Only 13 of these tools were recovered from secondary or DC 37 deposits: 5 in BL 2, 3 in BL 3A, one in BL 3B, and 4 in BL 4A. There are also 3 tools from Stratum 18A, below BL 5.

Table 21. PERSONAL ORNAMENTS BY BL AND DC

Material Deposit Code	Sum	BL 2		BL 3		BL 4		Other
		2x	37	2x	37	2x	37	3x
Dentalium	130	88	17	1	—	4	2	18
Other shell	19	4	6	—	2	1	2	4
Stone	19	2	6	1	—	4	1	5
Bitumen	66	1	2	*	—	—	2	61
Gold	2	—	—	—	—	2	—	—
Bone/ivory	2	1	—	—	—	—	1	—
Wooden	2	1	1	—	—	—	—	—
Frit (?)	6	1	—	—	—	1	—	4
Shark or ray	3	—	2	—	—	—	1	—
Gold leopard	1	—	—	—	—	—	—	1
Copper pins	4	—	—	1	1	1	1	1°
Copper rings	3	—	1	—	—	—	—	2
SUM	257	98	35	3	3	13	9	96

All items are beads except the gold leopard, copper pins, and copper rings. DC 2x = DC 21—29; DC 3x = DC 34–36. *60 bitumen beads found with hearth 53 may be from a secondary context; °found in BL 5

Functional Class 15. Piercing/Boring Tools

The 10 finds assigned to this class are bone (mf 748) and copper (mf 1514) awls, a crude slate boring tool (mf 576, Fig. 42h), and a group of flint drill heads (mf 1082, Fig. 35i; mf 1210, 3939, 6595.1, 7008.2, 7013) including one example that preserves traces of bitumen hafting material and has micro wear indicative of use in drilling hard material (mf 7001.2, Table 25, Fig. 35j). Only three of these finds come from secondary or DC 37 deposits: the bone awl from BL 2 and two drill heads (mf 7001.2, 7013) from BL 3. Three of these tools are complete and broken, but it is not clear whether or not they were used (Stat C 5.0). Two are classified as broken in use (Stat C 5.1). Five are not broken and are classified as lost during use (Stat C 6.1) or stored awaiting use (Stat 6.2). These tools may have been used in leather or wood working, bead making, or other sorts of production and maintenance activities.

Functional Class 16. Personal Ornaments

With 257 finds, this is one of the largest and most diverse classes at ABC. The types of finds and materials are summarized by BL and DC in Table 21.

Context

A number of unusual finds in Class 16 appear in unmixed secondary (DC 21-29) or DC 37 contexts:

mf 6664, 6793—beads made of shark or ray verte brae with traces of yellow paint (Fig. 38e, d)
mf 6795—carved fish vertebrae bead (Fig. 38c)
mf 644 and 764—charred wooden disc beads (Fig. 38g)
mf 5082.1—2 gold foil beads (Fig. 43c)
mf 5082.2—blue and white frit bead
mf 590—carved *Dentalium* bead (Fig. 43a)
mf 599—ivory or bone 4 hole spacer bead
mf 1305—bitumen 2 hole spacer bead (Fig. 38i)

The gold foil leopard (mf 1030, Fig. 43b, Pl. 21c) was found on the Operation ABCS dump early in the 1974 season during the removal of BL 2 walls and the initial excavations in BL 3A. No Kaftari lots were under excavation in ABCS at the same time, but it is still possible that the leopard does not belong to the Banesh assemblage. Stylistically it is reminiscent of felines seen on P-E sealings.

Unusual finds in tertiary contexts include two frit (?) beads (mf 598.1, 598.2) from BL 2 and one from BL 3 (mf 1287). A group of 60 bitumen beads (mf 6698, Fig. 38p, q) was found when Hearth 53 was being dismantled in BL 3. The context is problematic and may actually be a secondary context (DC 28).

It cannot be determined how many of these finds were actually being used as personal ornaments and how many were in storage or being held by craftsmen when they entered the archaeological record. Many beads are unbroken and were stored, discarded, or lost while in use when they entered the archaeological record (Stat C 6.0), but some were broken and are classified as Status 5.0 or 5.1. The evidence for production of beads and other personal ornaments within the excavated area of ABC is not strong and it is likely that most of these finds from BL 3, 4, and 5 were either in storage or were lost personal property. The high frequency of beads and other personal ornaments at ABC stands in sharp contrast to the low frequency of such finds at TUV (Table 14). This fact is not entirely unexpected in view of the more formal, elaborate, and carefully constructed buildings in ABC as well as the probable role of BL 2 as a storage depot for craft items. However, the rather poor showing of BL 3 is unexpected in view of its sumptuous wall paintings, elaborate relief ceramics, and elegant stone and plaster vessels, which might suggest that the occupants of this building would also have many high quality personal ornaments. Beads and other small ornaments may be under represented in the BL 3 assemblage because the floors were kept clean, unlike the messy condition of Corridor 118 in BL 2, for example (suggested by John Alden, p.c.).

Functional Class 17. Architecture

Among the 49 finds assigned to this class are 2 wall cones (mf 11291, 11293) and 7 fired ceramic tiles (see description in Chapter 2, Plate 14c) from tertiary deposits in BL 2. The other items are analytical samples of wall painting pigments and bricks. Some of the plaster and pigments assigned to Class 5 may also relate to architectural activities at ABC.

The buildings are the best indication of architectural activity at both TUV and ABC. The specialized storerooms and long corridors of BL 2 and the elegant decorations and formal arrangement of BL 3 in ABC have no parallels at TUV. Although TUV BLs 1 and 2 are well planned and carefully constructed neither building is comparable in scale or function to BL 2 or BL 3 at ABC. The domestic character of BLs 1 and 2 at TUV is unmistakable. TUV BL 3 is more cramped, shows less planning, and is not as well built as its successor structures, but it too is clearly domestic in character with the addition of areas or rooms devoted to craft production. At ABC the most nearly comparable domestic buildings are BLs 4 and 5. It is notable that P-E tablets, excluding uninscibed fragments, are more prevalent at TUV (18 finds) than at ABC (14 finds)(Stolper 1985, Table 1) despite the fact that the excavated area of TUV possesses no warehouse comparable to ABC BL 2. Wall cones and tiles are found at both TUV and ABC, but nothing is known of their exact function in Banesh levels at Malyan. Only one problematic door socket, possibly associated with Niche 385 in BL 3 (Fig. 12), is known from ABC, while 4 door sockets were recovered at TUV. No ceramic roof drains like those found at TUV (Nicholas 1990:81) were discovered at ABC.

Functional Class 18. Food Consumption

ABC produced sherds of small bowls and restricted pots similar to forms assigned to Class 18 at TUV (Nicholas 1990:82) in all levels and evidence for food consumption is similar in both places. However, the limited ABC ceramic assemblage available for study makes it difficult to arrive at a more specific quantified comparison.

Functional Class 19. Carpentry

The only find assigned to this class is a cu/bronze nail (mf 6772) from Corridor 241 in BL 4.

Functional Class 20. Decorated Objects

This class, which matches the functional structure established for TUV, is only intended to provide a general indication of the relative importance of decoration at ABC and TUV. There are 25 finds in this class; all are also assigned to other functional classes except for 2 figurines. There are 8 decorated plaster or stone vessels (Fig. 40f, j, k; 41d, e), 13 relief decorated sherds (Fig. 27, Pls. 16, 17), a gold foil leopard (mf 1030, Fig. 43b; Pl. 22c), and a bull head spout (mf 1737, Fig. 42e).

The unfired clay bull figurine (mf 655, Fig. 42f; Pl. 21b) and an unfired human figurine (mf 656, Fig. 42g; Pl. 21a) were recovered from near the top of the fill in Pithos 165, BL 2. The broken top of this pithos protruded above the erosion surface (Stratum 7) that defines the base of the Kaftari trash deposit in ABC.

Therefore, it is possible that these figurines belong to the Kaftari period although they are entirely different from the painted, red slipped, fired figurines found in abundance in the ABC Kaftari trash (J.W. Nickerson 1977).

The painted pithoi from BL 2 (Fig. 28) and the wall painting fragments from BL 3 (Table 9, Figs. 15-19) are not assigned to Class 20 although they are indicators of the importance of ornamentation in the ABC buildings. Ordinary painted pottery was not registered at ABC and is not assigned to this class, but unregistered painted pottery at ABC (Figs. 24-26) is comparable to some of the registered forms from TUV. Seals and sealing impressions are not assigned to this class (Fig. 44).

The greater number and variety of decorated items found at ABC in comparison with TUV reinforces the impression gained from other evidence—architecture, ceramic decoration, personal ornaments—that ABC is a more sumptuous quarter of the city than TUV.

Functional Class 21. Information Processing

The following account of information processing is based on the classification of sealings by Pittman (1997 and n.d.) and her discussion presented in this chapter. The discussion of the Proto-Elamite texts relies on Stolper (1976, 1985). The discussion of clays is based on analysis conducted by Blackman (Zeder and Blackman 2003). The 329 finds assigned to this class include 50 clay or stone balls (Type 2) and 1 disk (Type 15) only tentatively classified as accounting tokens, 244 sealing fragments (Type 43), two cylinder seals (Type 14), 28 Proto-Elamite tablets or tablet fragments (Type 47), and 4 potter's marks (Type 71). All sealings are also assigned to Class 10, Storage.

The classification of balls (Type 2) and the disk (Type 15) as accounting tokens is doubtful in view of the limited frequency, small number of forms, and the rough morphology of the clay balls. Although the use of tokens as administrative devices has been clearly documented in earlier times, their use diminished significantly as written tablets, plentiful at P-E Malyan, became the main tool for recording information (Schmandt-Besserat 1992, Vol. I:198).

The 5 stone balls range in diameter from 1.5 to 3.7 cm (mean 2.3 cm), the 45 clay balls range from 2.7 to 4 cm in diameter, and the clay disk is 1 cm in diam-

eter. The stone balls are well formed, with a smooth or polished surface. The clay balls are roughly formed, often rather egg shaped, of unfired clay. Broken examples show a laminar interior and several appear to be hollow with a smaller ball inside. Both the stone and clay balls discussed here fit into the less common "large subtypes" of tokens studied by Schmandt-Besserat (1996:16). The rarity of smaller balls and the virtual absence of other common token shapes—cones, discs, and cylinders—may be an artifact of recovery in ABC where very few lots were screened with a mesh small enough to capture small tokens. These balls may be sling projectiles rather than tokens (see Class 22).

There are two cylinder seals in Class 21, one intact with a loop handle (mf 1901 Fig. 44a, Pl. 22b), made of white stone and one broken in half (mf 1903, Fig. 44b) made of soft white stone. Some 140 of the 244 sealings have designs that have been identified and classified by Pittman (Stp, Appendix A). There are 38 designs in the ABC sealing catalog including the 2 cylinders (Pittman n.d.). The most common design, Stp 21 (Fig. 44h; Pl. 22c) is represented by 43 impressions, followed by Stp 14 (Pl. 22e), with 32 impressions, and Stp 13 with 11 impressions. There are multiple impressions (2 to 6) of at least 7 other designs and the remaining 25 designs occur only once each. It should be emphasized that these counts are have only a generalized significance because of the fragmentary condition of many sealings.

The seal designs from BL 4A fall into the early Proto-Elamite style (Fig. 44a, b). Seal designs from BL 2 belong to the classic Proto-Elamite style type (Fig 44c, e-h) with rare exceptions (Fig. 44d) (Pittman, this chapter). Seal designs from the compact trash deposit (DC 23) embedded within Stratum 9 construction fill (DC 34) and the similar deposit (DC 23) from construction fill (DC 35) in BL 3A Room 271 are in the same classic style as the designs found in BL 2, although only one design (Stp 13) found in these deposits is also found in BL 2.

There are 16 entries in the register (Appendix A) for tablets (Type 47) and several additional items among the sealing samples (Type 43) that may be tablet fragments (mf 633, 2015.1, and 637.3). Three of the registered tablets have no inscribed numbers or signs (mf 624, 635, and 1690) and some of the small fragments registered as a group (mf 1693) may also be uninscribed. One tablet (mf 1692) has a seal impression on the reverse and a damaged inscription on the obverse. The remaining 11 tablets include 5 that are essentially intact (mf 628, 1685, PL. 21e; 1686, 1687, 1688) and several others that are relatively well preserved (mf 632 and 1689) and have at least some preserved signs. None of the fragments without signs are complete enough to be classified as blank tablets, nor can it be established that the broken tablets with only preserved number signs did not originally have pictographic signs (Stolper 1985).

There are 4 potter's marks in the ABC Banesh collection. The earliest is a cross incised on the base of an atypical open bowl (mf 3770, Fig. 26c) from BL 4B. A large pithos rim from Room 71, BL 2 is inscribed with a common P-E sign (Brice 1962, Fig. 1, Number 1, DUB) (Fig. 28g; Pl. 18a). An inverted U is incised near the base of another pithos (Plate 18b), also from Room 71 in BL 2. Neither of these potter's marks appear as signs on tablets from Malyan or Yahya. A double c mirror image mark incised or stamped into the rim of a large jar (mf 6057) from a mixed clean-up lot (DC 41), is probably from Kaftari levels.

Clay Sources

Blackman used instrumental neutron activation analysis to study the chemical composition of sealings and other unfired clay samples from TUV and ABC as part of a larger project involving Yahya and several sites in Khuzistan (Zeder and Blackman 2003). Sixty-eight Banesh clay samples were analyzed: 31 from ABC and 37 from TUV. The ABC samples include many impressed jar sealings, unimpressed sealing clay found in close association with impressed sealings, 2 fragments that may be from P-E tablets (mf 637.3 and 2015.1), an unimpressed conical jar stopper (mf 1978), and clay balls (mf 2014 and 2013.1).

All but 4 of the samples fall into one of 2 clusters: 27 in a cluster found only at ABC (the ABC Clay Group) and 37 in a cluster identified as the TUV Clay Group because 35 samples in this group were found at TUV. Two jar sealings from TUV are from clay sources that do not fit into either the ABC or TUV clay group and likewise 2 from ABC are from unidentified sources. The ABC samples from unidentified sources include an example (mf 2614) of a common ABC sealing design, Stp 14, illustrated by mf 1472 in Pl. 22e. This design is also made of ABC clay in 7 instances (mf 1563, 1566, 1569, 1571, 1642, 1657, and 1714) from Stratum 9 (DC 23). The other ABC sample of unidentified clay is an unsealed conical jar stopper (mf 1978) from Pit 236 in BL 4A. There are 2 samples from ABC made of TUV clay. One is a clay ball (mf 2013.2) from Corridor 118 in BL

2. The other is possibly a tablet fragment (mf 637.3) found at the north end of Platform 27 in Room 71, BL 2, in a cluster of sealings and P-E tablets. These results provide striking evidence for the essentially localized nature of the P-E administrative system at Malyan.

Context and Pattern

Building Level 2

There are 52 Class 21 finds from good secondary deposits (DC 21 and 29) and 2 from DC 37 deposits in BL 2. Room 71 produced a group of 5 jar sealings with designs not found elsewhere, including 2 known to be made of ABC clay (Stp 35, mf 637.1; Stp 34, mf 637.2) and one, possibly a tablet fragment, made of TUV clay (Stp 33, mf 637.3). There are also 4 tablets with numbers or signs preserved (mf 625, 626, 627, 634) and several fragments without signs (mf 624 and 635). These sealings and tablets were found at the north end of Platform 27 on the surface of the platform (Stratum 8B, DC 21). The 2 potter's marks on pithoi also were in Room 71. These finds must be related to activities during the final occupation of BL 2.

A second group of Class 21 finds, from Corridor 118, includes 35 sealing fragments, but only 3 with recognizable designs Two of these designs (Stp 10, mf 1949; Stp 9, mf 1969, 1970.1, 1970.2), are known only in this context but the third (Stp 13, mf 1975) is also found in the large Stratum 9 cluster (DC 23). There are also 2 tablets from Corridor 118, 1 found in association with the sealings (mf 1685) and the other (mf 628) found just east of the large stone (Misc. Feat. 386) near the entrance to Corridor 117 (Fig. 20). The sealings and associated tablet (mf 1685) were in a pebble deposit (Stratum 8D, DC 29) resting on the construction surface and may be related to activities during the construction of BL 2. The other tablet (mf 628) was resting on or just above the latest floor in BL 2 (Stratum 8B, DC 21) and must relate to activities contemporary with BL 2.

The pebble deposit in Corridor 118 is not found in any other area of BL 2 and the corridor floor was quite rough, suggesting heavy traffic. It seems likely that Wall 104 defines the north side of the excavated building and that Corridor 118 is a passageway between this building and the unexcavated buildings to the north, beyond Wall 105. Many finds in the corridor mirror finds in the excavated building: mother of pearl inlay, bitumen, and specular hematite, in addition to tablets and sealings. The isolation of Room 71 and the other excavated rooms south of Corridor 118 is consistent with the use of these rooms for storage, but access to these rooms and circulation patterns can not be reconstructed on the basis of the excavated plan. Although it seems likely that the sealings relate to activities in the excavated building, it is possible they relate to activities in unexcavated buildings to the north or even to the east or west.

A tablet (mf 632) and a seal impression, probably on a tablet fragment (Stp 37, mf 623, Fig. 44g; Pl. 22a), found on or just above the latest floor (stratum 8B, DC 29, 37) in Room 128 both relate to activities late in the occupation of BL 2.

Stratum 9 and Building Level 3

The 2 clusters (DC 23) of sealings and tablets found in Strata 9 and 10A are considered as a single contemporaneous group associated with storage activities in the vicinity of BL 3A but not in any of the excavated rooms. Four tablets and 23 sealing designs have been recognized in these 2 clusters, and 7 sealing designs were found in both clusters. The conclusion that the clusters are the residue of a single administrative locus is reinforced by the 4 tablets: 1 (mf 1689) from Stratum 10A (DC 23) and 3 (mf 1686-1688) from Stratum 9 (DC 23). As noted by Stolper (1985:10), these tablets are made of a distinctive pink clay, have identical form and dimensions, and appear to record similar transactions, perhaps related to lumber. A tablet (mf 1858) from TUV BL IIIB (DC 37), made of similar clay, appears to record a summary of several transactions like the ones recorded on the 4 ABC tablets. Other than the presence of a sealing (Stp 33, mf 637.3) that may be on a tablet fragment made of TUV clay in BL 2, Room 71, this is the only evidence for a connection between the TUV and ABC administrative systems (Stolper 1985:10-11).

The 124 sealings with identified designs in this group include all examples of the 2 most common designs (Stp 14 and 21), which account for 60% of the sealings from this context. However, even if the assumption that these sealings are all from a single administrative unit is correct, it cannot be assumed that the relative frequency of different designs is a proxy for the relative frequency of transactions by the holders of different seals. It is entirely possible that the relative frequency of different seals in the collection is simply an artifact of sampling. Even if sampling error is not involved, it is even less likely that the observed frequency pattern is related to some hierarchy of impor-

tance, particularly in view of Pittman's observation that there is very little difference in relative complexity among these classic Proto-Elamite designs. The most unusual characteristic of the ABC corpus, including the group from Strata 9 and 10A, is that practically every design belongs to the classic P-E style type, in contrast to the TUV corpus, which has seals of all 4 P-E style types. As Pittman (inf.) puts it, "This is a feature that is certainly a reflection of the special character..." of sealing activity at ABC, which reinforces her idea that style types are specialized within the P-E administrative system. Many of these sealings were used to seal large jars similar to those found in BL 2 Room 71.

Building Level 3B

BL3B produced one seal impression that may be on a tablet fragment (Stp 7, mf 1692, Fig. 44c) from a good floor deposit (DC 29). Several fragments of sealings or possibly tablets (mf 1973 and 1693), design not identified, come from a mixed floor deposit (DC 29), leaving open the possibility that they belong with the slightly later Stratum 9-10A (DC 23) cluster.

Building Level 4A

BL 4A produced 2 cylinder seals. The first (mf 1901; Fig. 44a) is from a deposit in Area 307 that was interpreted by the excavator as bricky fill (DC 35). However, Area 307 also produced a dense trash deposit (DC 21) and it is possible the seal came from that deposit. In any event it is safe to say this cylinder is no later than BL 4A. The second cylinder (mf 1903; Fig. 44b) is from bricky fill (DC 35) in Corridor 241. Both of these seals probably were used during the occupation of BL 4B or earlier. The other finds from BL 4A are the debris of administrative activities located in or near Room 64. Pit 236 in Room 64 produced one sealing (Stp 2, mf 1971) and 42 clay balls. Two sealings (Stp 4, mf 1979.1 and an unidentified design on mf 1979.2) came from a mixed DC 37 lot in Room 64. Three sealings (Stp 6, mf 1932.1, Stp 13, mf 1932.2, and Stp 5, mf 2023) came from above the floor (DC 37) in Courtyard 281, just outside Room 64. The last find from BL 4A is a tablet (mf 1690), with no preserved inscription or sealing, from the trash (DC 21) in Area 307.

Functional Class 22. Projectile Points

Six flint projectile points, three stemmed points (mf 577, Pl. 20a; mf 579, Fig. 35c, PL 20a; mf 1908) and three tranchet points (mf 2108, 2176, 6607, Fig. 35e-g)

Table 22. CRAFT PRODUCTION AT ABC AND TUV

CLASS	TUV		ABC			
	N	%	Na	Nb	%a	%b
1 Flint Knapping	270	42	141	141	9	28
2 Metallurgy	225	35	92	92	6	18
3 Stone Bead Production	25	4	67	67	5	13
4 Shell Working	104	16	1106	116	74	23
9 Other Crafts	21	3	88	88	6	18
SUM	645	100	1494	504	100	100

Na and %a include all 5 crafts at ABC; Nb and %b omit mother-of-pearl inlay from ABC count.

were recovered from Banesh levels at ABC. Two of the tranchet points are from secondary or DC 37 deposits in BL 2 and BL 3A and one is from Stratum 12 (DC 34). Two of the stemmed points were in tertiary context (DC 35) in BL 2 and one was from a clean-up lot (DC 41). All of these points were made from secondary non-cortical flakes or blades (Stp 2NCF) and, not unexpectedly, the 4 points examined by Kardulias showed no microscopic evidence of use wear. Stone points were not recovered at TUV.

Functional Class 23 Unspecified

Class 23, as defined here, is comparable to the residual group of finds listed by Nicholas at TUV under Class 00. This class includes several unusual objects of indeterminate use: a thin tapering fired clay rod (mf 11234), two fired clay wheels (mf 530, 1913, Fig. 42a, c), 11 small fired clay loops, and a finely made angular stone object (mf 1907, Fig. 43e) from various contexts in BL 2. BL 4 produced an unfired triangular clay cake (mf 3731) comparable to those found in quantity at Indus valley drains. Similar cakes were not found in the Kaftari wells that were converted to use as toilets and this isolated example is a mystery. This find also resembles the "spoons" from Kureh (Appendix D, Fig. D8:29, 30).

Summary—ABC and TUV

The relative frequency of various production and consumption activities at ABC and TUV, presented in summary form in Table 14, provides a rough picture of differences in these two neighborhoods located 800 m apart on separate mounds (Fig. 4). The most important craft production classes (Nicholas 1990, Fig. 20; Classes 1-9) are recapitulated in Table 22.

At TUV flint knapping and metallurgy are the leading craft production activities identified by the functional class analysis. Shell working is also a well represented activity and the production of stone beads, particularly from the mineral clinoptilolite, was present.

At ABC, by comparison, shell working, particularly the production and storage of mother of pearl inlay, was the dominant craft. Even when the large number of inlay pieces are excluded from the ABC shell industry count, the shell industry at ABC is still more important that it is at TUV. Flint knapping, metallurgy and stone bead production are also well documented for the general neighborhood of ABC. The importance of other crafts (Class 9) at ABC is indicated by numerous finds of specular hematite and bitumen and diverse evidence for the production of stone and plaster vessels, a craft activity that is only marginally represented at TUV. However, the low frequency of relevant finds implies that all these craft activities took place in the vicinity of ABC, but none of them were very important within the excavated Banesh buildings at ABC.

Other activities in the functional model (Classes 6 and 8) concerned with cloth and pottery production are only marginally represented at ABC and TUV. The find counts for plasters and pigments (Class 5) are not reliable indicators of relative importance because they are the consequence of different sampling strategies rather than different frequencies in the two assemblages.

At both ABC and TUV the dominant storage or holding class (Nicholas 1990, Fig. 20; Classes 10-12) is Class 10, consisting of sealings designed to control access to stored materials. The existence of the ABC BL 2 warehouse and the likelihood that a similar warehouse existed near BL 3 may account for the slightly greater number of sealings at ABC. However, the level of control exercised over storage at TUV is striking, particularly in the absence of evidence for a storage facility like ABC BL 2. The majority of sealings in both neighborhoods came from a few large clusters; thus the raw counts may be misleading, but the fact that at least some sealings were found in all building levels is a clear indication of the importance of sealing activities at both ABC and TUV.

The contrast between TUV and ABC in Class 12, Special Containers, seems to be related to the presence of more utilitarian stone vessels at TUV while ABC has more sumptuary vessels—decorated plaster bowls and fine relief decorated jars.

The considerable evidence of food preparation at TUV (Class 7), perhaps on an institutional rather than household level, is not matched at ABC although it is likely that food was prepared in BLs 4 and 5 and in the vicinity of BLs 2 and 3.

Among the multi-purpose tool classes (Nicholas 1990, Fig. 20; Classes 13-15), TUV has a greater number of cutting tools (Class 13), drills and pointed tools (Class 15), and other specialized tools such as scrapers and notched tools (Class 14). These differences are not great and may only be an indication that the inhabitants at TUV were more heavily engaged in agriculture and animal husbandry, which would require a variety of stone tools.

The presence of 2 types of projectile points only at ABC my be due to sampling error, but the large excavations at both ABC and TUV mitigates against this explanation. The presence of gazelle and chuckar partridge bones at ABC, both desirable game, suggests that the points were used for hunting. The only hunted animal at TUV was wild boar, not usually hunted with light projectiles.

The evidence from both TUV and ABC suggests a city populated by craftsmen engaged in the production of personal ornaments and decorated items made of a variety of materials, many imported from a considerable distance. The ubiquity and the intensity of craft activities and the focus on personal ornaments indicates production for trade or local distribution beyond the inhabitants of the city. The urban population could have been provisioned at least in part by farmers and herdsmen resident in the city. Miller's (1990a, 1990b) analysis of seeds and wood charcoal provides evidence that field crops were cultivated near Malyan. Weed seeds common to irrigated fields, stubble fields, and nearby natural pastures were present in quantity, but seeds from more distant pastures were rare. These seeds were probably derived from animal dung cakes used for fuel with the implication that field crops were cultivated and animals were pastured nearby.

However, Zeder's (1991) analysis of the faunal assemblage implies that some meat was procured through a middle man, perhaps from non-resident or even nomadic herdsmen.

The use of P-E tablets to record information and the use of seals and sealings to control access to commodities stored in large jars or behind sealed doors implies some form of administrative structure. This administrative system may have served kinship units involved in domestic production or institutions organized on political or religious principles. Our present understanding of the P-E texts (Damerow and Englund 1989; Stolper 1985) indicates that most of the texts deal with agricultural products in small quantities, suggesting a relatively small scale administrative unit. Nothing about the texts from Malyan can be interpreted as related to long range trade in those commodities we know were imported from distant sources—obsidian, semi-precious stones, shell, and copper or copper ores. However, the fact that this administrative technology, including the P-E writing system and the use of stylistically related cylinder seals for similar functions, is found at sites scattered across Iran from Susa in the west to Shahr-i Sokhta in the east; from Hissar in the north to Yahya in the south represents a shared administrative technology unknown in earlier times. Further discussion of the enigmatic "Proto-Elamite phenomenon" is reserved for Chapter V.

LITHICS: REDUCTION SEQUENCE AND MICROWEAR ANALYSIS

P. Nicholas Kardulias

With some notable exceptions, Old World archaeologists who work in areas where complex societies (states) emerged often assume that the development of metallurgy spelled the demise of flaked stone tool industries, as metal implements replaced lithic ones. Although in general this outline is correct, the replacement was neither immediate, uniform, nor complete. In the Mediterranean region, for example, Runnels (1982) has demonstrated the survival of flaked stone tool technology from the Bronze Age through the subsequent Dark Age (Geometric Period in Greece), and then into the Iron Age and the Classical Period. The production of threshing sledge flints has persisted into the twentieth century (Bordaz 1969; Fox and Perlman 1985). Associated with the concern over the persistence of such technology as a functional alternative to the use of metals is the degree to which lithic production reflects craft specialization. Evidence for the function of stone tools and for the organization of lithic production includes the following factors:

1) Quantity of lithic debris
2) Patterns of intra and intersite distribution of lithic materials
3) The relative proportion of mistakes in the reduction sequence.
4) Patterns of control and exploitation of particular sources or quarries.
5) Microwear analysis to demonstrate tool functions.

The present study is concentrated on factors 1), 2), and 5).

Consideration of craft specialization is particularly important for sites or components that relate to the emergence of civilization. Although craft specialization can occur in pre-state conditions, Childe (1950) was certainly correct in characterizing this phenomenon as a key criterion of civilization. The Proto-Elamite (Banesh) levels at Malyan date to a period of such development. The lithics from the ABC and other operations with Banesh levels, therefore, may supplement data from other evidence (architecture, ceramics, tablets, sealings and other finds) or stand as an independent indicator of increasing societal complexity.

There are 231 finds assigned to the ABC Banesh flaked stone assemblage. The number of these finds available for analysis (N=151) is small and conclusions drawn from the study are necessarily tentative. An additional 60 pieces from the excavation are in Iran and contribute to the study only in the form of specimens in particular categories, such as type of blank; no metrical attributes of this second group are considered here. There are also 33 finds included in the study that were later determined to be from mixed strata and are not included in the ABC Banesh assemblage as presented in Table 15 and discussed above in the Functional Class sections of this chapter.

All tables and statistics below include 151 finds assigned to the Banesh assemblage, and the 33 finds later removed from the assemblage, for a total of 184 finds in the study. The 60 finds still in Iran are not included in the following tables and statistics although reference is made to some of them to indicate the range of variation. Despite the small sample size, it is possible to draw several important inferences from the flaked stone assemblage. In short, the evidence indicates possible specialization in the production of blades, the abundance of which on the site reflects purposeful manipulation of cores. The small number of cores and the lack of crested blades in the ABC Banesh assemblage suggests preliminary reduction occurred at specialized activity loci some distance from the ABC quarter. Only tool blanks or finished blades were brought to the ABC area. Functional analysis of the material reveals little evidence for anything other than prosaic activities. Rather than specialization, the functional analysis suggests generalized activities associated with harvesting and processing of several types of material (hide, wood, and bone). The evidence thus suggests the possible specialized production of tool blanks that were brought to the ABC area for use in the unspecialized activities of daily life.

Methods of Analysis

Typological Classification

Each piece in the ABC lithic assemblage was assigned to one of eight possible reduction sequence types: a. core or core fragment, b. platform preparation flake (PPF), c. primary decortication flake (PDF), d. secondary decortication flake (2DF), e. secondary non-cortical flake (2NCF), f. tertiary non-cortical flake (3NCF), g. blade or blade segment (PBS, MBS, DBS), and h. debris. The characteristics of each category are described below. Subsequently, each specimen was examined with a 10x hand lens to determine the extent and nature of any retouch, which is defined as the purposeful modification of the edges in order to produce a desired shape. Minimally, retouch requires three adjacent flake scars oriented in the same direction. Knappers at Malyan used both percussion and pressure techniques to retouch flakes and blades. Retouched specimens received labels (e.g., scraper) which, although functional in nature, carry no particular use implication; the terms are archaeological conventions which do not necessarily indicate actual past usage. The basic terminology in this typology (both for blanks and retouched pieces) derives from several standard texts on lithic analysis (Crabtree 1972; Movius et al. 1968; Brezillon 1968; Bordaz 1970). Finally, each artifact was measured and weighed to provide a metrical base of comparison. The typological metrical analysis took place in the archaeology laboratory at Kenyon College. All information from the data sheets was transposed into a numeric code for analysis by SPSS on the VAX mainframe computer at Kenyon College.

Table 23. MODIFIED AND UNMODIFIED FLINTS BY REDUCTION SEQUENCE TYPE

Type	U	R	Sum, N	Sum, %
Core	8	0	8	4.3
PPF	1	0	1	0.5
Debris	7	1	8	4.3
Flakes	105	23	128	69.6
PDF	11	0	11	6.0
2DF	29	3	32	17.4
2NCF	50	19	69	37.5
3NCF	15	1	16	8.7
Blades-Blade Segments	22	17	39	21.3
Blades	2	0	2	1.1
PBS	7	4	11	6.0
MBS	7	13	20	10.9
DBS	6	0	6	3.3
SUM	143	41	184	100.0

The Flakes row and the Blades-Blade Segments row list the sub-total of all types of flakes and blades. The heading "U" = unretouched; the heading "R" = retouched.

Microwear Analysis

Semenov (1964) pioneered the determination of lithic tool function through the use of low-power microscopy. Although this method has proved to be effective with many types of wear (see Tringham et al. 1974; Odell and Odell-Vereecken 1980), some subtle traces evade detection. The high power technique (lens strength 50x-500x) uses incident light to discern such less distinct evidence, which includes a variety of polishes, striations, and micro-damage or alteration of edges which are peculiar to particular tool use functions (Keeley 1980; Vaughan 1985). The present study employed the high-power technique. Recognition of the minute traces created by various activities requires thorough cleaning of each specimen to aid in identification. The cleaning procedure used in this study involved soaking each piece in three successive baths: a) an ammonia-based cleanser (Top Job), b) a 10% solution of HCl, and c) 10% KOH. The artifacts were immersed for 10 minutes in each solution and thoroughly rinsed with water between each bath. To loosen soil and other extraneous particles without abrading the surface, the plastic containers containing the artifacts in the solutions were placed in an ultrasonic cleaner during the 10-minute baths. The cleaned pieces were examined with an Olympus binocular metallurgical incident light microscope. Sample selection and results of the micro-wear study are discussed below.

Reduction Sequence Analysis

The presentation of data reflects the technology of the reduction sequence. The various types of blanks—cores, debris, flakes, blades, and blade segments—are listed and described in the order in which they would appear during production. The finished tools receive separate and more detailed treatment because these items, along with blades, represent the ultimate products towards which the knappers worked. The various categories of blanks, debris, and tool types reflect production decisions made and procedures followed by the stone workers.

The ABC lithic assemblage, including the 33 finds from problematic contexts, is summarized in Table 23. With the exception of 11 obsidian artifacts that are not included in the study, the material in the assemblage consists of cryptocrystalline silicates (flint, chert, and jasper) of varying quality (Appendix A: Material and Variety).

Unretouched Lithics, N=143, 77.7%

Cores and Core Fragments, N=8, 4.3% (Fig. 30a)

All specimens are percussion flake cores or core fragments with angular outlines that represent irregular, unsystematic working. Flake scars indicate several directions of removal, and platform preparation is minimal. Three are complete, five are fragmentary, but all are small (maximum dimension 4.86 cm, weight 40.49 g). Seven are pebble cores, which may indicate a local source.

Core Rejuvenation or Platform Preparation Flake (PPF), N=1, 0.5%

This piece exhibits several flake scars perpendicular to the axis of force. It was probably detached to create a fresh platform for further flake removals.

Debris, N=8, 4.3%

Any blocky, irregular piece without a platform, bulb of percussion, or force lines falls into this category. Initial blows that shatter a core often produce such asymmetrical pieces, which rarely receive any secondary treatment.

Primary Decortication Flakes (PDF), N=11, 6.0% (Fig. 30b)

This category includes any flake with cortex covering more than 50% of the dorsal surface. In addition to the smooth, rounded pebble rind, a number of these flakes exhibit a chalky cortex.

Secondary Decortication Flakes (2DF), N=29, 15.8%. (Fig. 30c-g)

Any flake with cortex over less than 50% of the dorsal surface fits into this category. These flakes are generally smaller than primary ones.

Secondary Non-Cortical Flakes (2NCF), N=50, 27.2% (Fig. 31a-e, 32a-e)

Flakes in this group lack cortex and have a maximum dimension of at least 1.75 cm. These flakes represent secondary trimming of a core.

Tertiary Non-Cortical Flakes (3NCF), N=15, 8.2% (Fig. 32f)

This group is comprised of any flake devoid of cortex and with a maximum dimension less than 1.75 cm. These pieces represent both final core reduction and trimming of larger flakes in tool production.

Blades and Blade Segments N=22, 12.0% (Fig. 33a-i, 34a-k)

A blade is defined as an elongated flake with a length at least twice its width, parallel lateral margins, and one or more dorsal ridges parallel to those margins. Blade production requires the preparation of a specialized tabular or prismatic core which can be used to produce highly symmetrical, regular blanks. Blades can be used without further modification or can be retouched to make a variety of tools. The production of blades is a consistent feature of flaked stone technology in the Bronze Age throughout the Mediterranean region and the Near East. Blade segments are classified as proximal (PBS), medial (MBS), or distal (DBS).

Retouched Lithics, N=41, 22.3%

Any piece that receives secondary treatment after its removal from a core in order to shape the outline or change the profile of the working edge is defined here as a retouched lithic except for segmented blades. The retouch modifies the natural edge(s) and lends the piece a distinct morphology, which has traditionally been the basis for classifying tools. Although some of the category labels—projectile point, scraper, burin, drill—imply specific functions, various studies (e.g., Yerkes 1987; Young and Bamforth 1990; Bamforth et al. 1990) demonstrate that the uses implied by these morphological classifications often do not stand up to rigorous micro-wear examination. Therefore, the types listed below must be viewed as categories based exclusively on morphological attributes; these artifacts may or may not have been used for the implied purpose and some of them may not have been used at all. Nevertheless, they differ from the unmodified blanks described above. Most of the category labels are familiar to archaeologists and as such are important as heuristic devices.

Denticulated Sickle Elements, N=3 (Fig. 33c, Pl. 20b; Fig. 34a)

These types represent 1.6% of total assemblage and 7.3% of retouched items (mf 2573, 657, 6597). One specimen is made on a secondary decortication flake and two on blades. One lateral margin has a series of teeth; the serrated edge is formed by small, inverse (towards the dorsal surface) and direct (towards the ventral surface) retouch. In addition, the proximal and distal ends are roughly truncated. Bright polish (sickle sheen) is evident on both surfaces of the denticulated edge. One specimen has on both faces extensive patches of bitumen which was used as a hafting adhesive. Eleven denticulated or use nibbled blades, some with sickle gloss are also a part of the assemblage that was not available for study.

Undenticulated Sickle Elements, N=6 (Fig. 34e, h, i; Pl. 23a)

These types represent 3.3%, of total assemblage and 14.6% of retouched flints (mf 1085, 6612, 6624, 6648, 6684, 7035). All specimens are medial (MBS) or distal (DBS) blade segments. Except for the lack of denticulation, they share all characteristics with the denticulated sickle elements. Only one piece preserves any bitumen on the surfaces.

Tranchet Projectile Points, N=4 (Fig. 35e-g)

Tranchet points represent 2.2% of the assemblage and 9.8 % of retouched specimens (mf 2108, 2176, 6607, 9903). All four specimens are made on blades or secondary non-cortical flakes. All specimens are small (maximum length 1.95 cm), thin, and well made. Outline is an elongated trapezoid. Retouch is medium to large in size and invasive to covering on both surfaces. On two specimens a naturally sharp edge was not retouched.

Contracting Stem Projectile Point, N=1, 0.5%, 2.4% (Fig. 35c, Pl. 20a)

This complete piece (mf 579) is made on a large secondary non-cortical flake. There is fine covering retouch on the dorsal surface, but the naturally flat ventral face required minimal working along the base and stem edges and near the tip to provide the final shape. Edges are straight with distinct shoulders 1.0 cm from the base; the stem, also with straight edges, contracts to a narrow, slightly concave base. The workmanship is excellent.

Notch, N=1, 0.5%, 2.4%

This small secondary non-cortical flake (mf 6641) has a shallow concavity at the left distal end formed by a series of large, irregular, inverse flakes.

Pointed Pieces, N=9, 4.9%, 22.0% (Fig. 35a, b, h)

Six specimens (mf 1065, 1224, 2119.3, 6542.5, 6570, 6685, 7007, 9833, 9986.2) are formed on secondary non-cortical flakes, and one each on a secondary

decortication flake, a blade, and a piece of debris. Each piece has a distinct tip or point formed by small, marginal, converging direct and inverse retouch. The point, which may appear on a lateral, distal, or proximal margin, typically exhibits some rounding, presumably from use.

Backed Pieces, N=4, 2.2%, 9.8% (Figs. 33g, 34f)

Four blade segments, two proximal (PBS) and two medial (MBS) segments (mf 1210, 6662, 7021, 7033), have on one lateral margin steep, irregular, marginal, direct retouch which blunts that edge.

End Scraper, N=1, 0.5%, 2.4% (Fig. 35d)

The distal end of this round secondary non-cortical flake (2NCF, mf 6628) has a series of large, direct flake scars that create a very steep, thick working facet. The distal edge is also slightly curved.

Drills, N=3, 1.6%, 7.3% (Fig. 35j)

Two specimens are made on secondary non-cortical flakes (2NCF, mf 6595.1, 7008.2) and one on a tertiary non-cortical flake (3NCF, mf 7001.2). The latter is a short, thick piece with considerable bitumen on one end and a slightly rounded bit at the other formed by large irregular steep direct retouch. The other specimens have blunt distal tips, evidently rounded from use, formed by converging retouch.

Truncated Piece, N=3, 1.6%, 7.3%

Two secondary non-cortical flakes (2NCF) have proximal truncations that removed the platforms (mf 1014.7, 6668.2). One medial blade segment (MBS, mf 6660) has a single truncation formed by steep irregular direct retouch that purposefully abbreviates the length of the blank, perhaps so that the piece could be used in a composite tool, but no wear or mounting residue is visible macroscopically.

Retouched Pieces, N=6, 3.3%, 14.6

There are three secondary non-cortical flakes (2NCF) and three blades that exhibit some retouch, but which do not fit any of the previous classes. One specimen has rough retouch around the entire perimeter, another has distal retouch, a third has opposed retouch (direct on one lateral margin, and inverse on the other), and the other three have more limited direct retouch along one margin only (mf 1078, 1231, 6643, 6663, 6683, 7261).

Table 24. MICROWEAR ANALYSIS BY REDUCTION SEQUENCE TYPE

Type	Microwear Pattern					Sum
	G	M	H	Hd	No	
Core (N=8)	—	—	—	—	1	1
Platform Preparation Flake (N=1)	—	—	—	—	—	—
Debris (N=8)	—	—	—	—	—	—
Primary Decortication Flakes (PDF):						
Unretouched (N=11)	—	1	—	—	—	1
Secondary Decortication Flakes (2DF):						
Unretouched (N=29)	—	—	—	—	6	6
Retouched (N=3)	—	—	—	—	—	—
Secondary Non—Cortical Flakes (2NCF):						
Unretouched (N=50)	—	1	—	1	6	8
Retouched (N=14)	—	—	1	1	4	6
Tertiary Non-cortical Flakes (3NCF):						
Unretouched (N=15)	—	—	—	—	—	2
Retouched (N=1)	—	—	—	1	—	1
Blades and Blade Segments:						
Unretouched (N=22)	2	—	—	1	1	4
Retouched (N=17)	6	—	—	—	1	7
Points (N=5)	—	—	—	—	5	5
Sum (N=184)	8	2	1	4	26	41

Heading G = grass, M = meat. H = hide, Hd = hard material, No = none

Microwear Analysis

The sample for micro-wear analysis included 41 specimens (22.3% of total assemblage in the study). Sample selection occurred in two stages. Initially, 20 pieces with retouch were examined. Eleven specimens of this biased sample exhibited some form of microwear. The second sample of 21 specimens was randomly selected by choosing every eighth piece from the assemblage so as to determine the function of unmodified blanks which may have served as ad hoc tools. Four of the specimens in the second sample possessed microwear traces. The purpose of this sampling procedure was to insure that an adequate number of both retouched and unretouched pieces was analyzed. Together, the biased and random samples provide a good cross section of the assemblage.

The cleaned specimens were scanned at 50x on the Olympus microscope to discern any major wear traces. More detailed examination at 100x and 200x brought out the detail of the wear patterns. The wear was recorded on special forms with drawings of the artifacts and also on the SPSS coding sheets. Of the 41 pieces studied, 15 exhibit various types of wear (see Tables 23-25. In Figures 30-35 the edges that showed traces of wear are indicated by a line parallel to the worn edge and the direction of movement in tool use is indicated by arrows. In several cases, the highly crystalline structure of the lithic material precluded any determination of wear; therefore, the discussion of wear traces is based on a conservative estimate.

The most distinct, and most common (N=8), type of traces are those associated with the cutting of grass or grain stems (34a, e, h, i; Pl. 23a-c). A highly lus-

Table 25. MICROWEAR ANALYSIS BY REDUCTION SEQUENCE TYPE, FIND AND CONTEXT

mf	Type	Wear	BL/STR/DC
Core			
2313	flake core	none	2/8B/37
Primary Decortication Flake (PDF)			
6564	unretouched	cutting meat	2/8D/36
Secondary Decortication Flakes (2DCF)			
1014.5	unretouched	none	problematic
1084	unretouched	none	problematic
2184	unretouched	none	4A/13A/37
6598	unretouched	none	3A/10A/41
6600	unretouched	none	2/8A/35
6609	unretouched	none	3A/10A/35
Secondary Non-Cortical Flakes (2NCF)			
1014.6	retouched	none	problematic
1065	retouched (pointed)	none	2/8A/35
1237	unretouched	cutting meat	3A/10A/35
2119.3	retouched (pointed)	scraping bone	2/8A/35
6606	unretouched	incise w/b*	2/8D/29
6628	end scraper	scrape hide	3B/11A/29
6663	retouched	none	2/8D/29
6668.2	truncated	none	problematic
7001.1	unretouched	none	3A/10A/37
7006	unretouched	none	-/9/34
7012	unretouched	none	2/8B/28
7019	unretouched	none	4A/13A/35
7028	unretouched	none	4A/13A/35
7030	unretouched	none	problematic
Tertiary Non-Cortical Flakes (3NCF)			
6618	unretouched	none	2/8D/29
7001.2	drill tip	drill hard matl.	3A/10A/37
11229	unretouched	none	3A/10A/35
Blades and Blade Segments			
1078	retouched	cutting grass	problematic
1085	backed	cutting grass	problematic
2573	denticulated, gloss	cutting grass	2/8B/37
6541	unretouched	none	3A/10A/37
6571	denticulated	cutting grass	problematic
6612	backed	cutting grass	3A/10A/37
6619	unretouched, gloss	cutting grass	3A/10A/35
6624	backed, gloss	cutting grass	3A/10A/37
6648	unretouched, gloss	cutting grass	problematic
7021	backed	none	3B/11B/29
7026	unretouched	shave soft stone	-/12/34
Points			
0579	contracting stem	none	2/8A/35
2108	tranchet	none	3A/10A/37
2176	tranchet	none	-/12/34
6607	tranchet	none	2/8D/29
9903	tranchet	none	problematic

*w/b = wood or bone. The finds with context listed as "problematic" are from mixed lots not otherwise included in this volume.

trous polish with some comet-shaped pits covers the dorsal and ventral working edge and goes back as far as 3 mm from the margin (Fig. 34a, Pl. 23b). With extensive use, as is evident on six of the specimens, the polish works its way into small depressions on the surface of the implement (Fig. 34a, Pl. 23c). Although the linearity of the polish clearly indicates reciprocal motion parallel to a long edge, tiny striations are observable at oblique angles as well as parallel to that margin. Edge damage in the form of flake scars is minimal on these tools. The precise factors that create sickle sheen have been investigated for some time (Meeks et al. 1982; Unger-Hamilton 1984, 1985). Scholarly opinion is divided on whether the sheen is simply polishing of the stone surface or a layer added *onto* the surface.

The five projectile points exhibit no wear. One specimen has a metallic scratch but this may be from an excavator's tool.

The end scraper (mf 6628, Fig. 35d; Pl. 23d) has weakly developed hide-working wear. The traces consist of a greasy-looking polish on the ventral surface near the distal end, which is slightly rounded. It is not possible to determine if wet or dry hide was worked.

The one small drill bit (mf 7001.2, Fig. 35j) with bitumen lacks any polish that would indicate the material worked, but several striations indicate that it was used with a rotary motion.

One unretouched secondary non-cortical flake (mf 6606) with a blunt projection has a very small patch of bone or wood polish in an early stage of formation. It is not clear whether the wear is the result of incising or drilling action.

Three other artifacts have small patches of indistinct polish. Two specimens (mf 6564, Fig. 30b; mf 1237, Fig. 32a) are unretouched but have tiny edge damage that probably is the result of utilization. Polish on these pieces may be from meat cutting. One retouched piece (mf 2119.3, Fig. 35b) has a spot of bright polish caused by working a hard material, probably bone.

Finally, one blade (mf 7026, Fig. 33e, Pl. 24) has a narrow band of polish parallel to and striations perpendicular to the snapped distal end. This wear may have been produced by shaving a soft stone, such as serpentine or chlorite.

Discussion

Flaked stone tool technology has a long history and is the focus of much prehistoric research in many parts of the world. This long history has contributed to both appropriate and unjustified statements concerning the role of lithics in society. The durability of stone leads to higher differential preservation than most other materials humans use, and may thus provide a distorted view of a site's material record and, consequently, its functions. This problem can be overcome through careful assessment of residues from perishable materials and the judicious use of ethnographic analogies. In order not to overreach the interpretive ability of the data, the conclusions from the analysis of the ABC lithics presented below are tentative.

Beyond the purely technological traits of tool production, lithics can also reveal aspects of economic organization. Many scholars look to lithics to extract elements of craft specialization. Especially for the Banesh levels, which date to the period of the emergent Proto-Elamite state, it is important to investigate the data for evidence of the complex division of labor, with specialization of tasks, that is symptomatic of civilization. The present discussion stresses the difference between production and use or function in determining the existence of craft specialization. The evidence of this study suggests that flaked stone was produced by specialists, perhaps part-time, but the products were used for a wide range of agricultural and domestic activities. This seems to be a case of specialized production of artifacts which were not in turn used in other "industrial" activities, except perhaps for the drills. We have here an example of specialization which produces implements for an agricultural economy; one can interpret this as specialization for self-sufficiency.

Although some of the analyzed lithics were found on the surface or during cleaning (listed as problematic in Table 25), it is clear that many lithics are directly associated with the excavated ABC buildings (DC 21-29, 37) and others (DC 34-36) are probably associated with earlier activities in the neighborhood of ABC. The ABC lithics fit into a complex socio-economic mosaic and even though they are only one part of that fabric, the flaked stones add important detail to the total picture.

The typological analysis indicates that the ABC lithics do not represent the full range of activities in the reduction sequence. Cores (N=8) form a small part of the assemblage, and these pieces are all irregularly worked and not indicative of great skill. In addition, the small number of primary decortication flakes (N=11) and debris (N=8) indicates initial core preparation took place elsewhere, either at a quarry or in

Table 26. COMPARISON OF BLADE DIMENSIONS: MALYAN AND HISSAR

	Width					Thickness				
	N	X	SD	Max.	Min.	N	X	SD	Max.	Min.
Malyan	39	1.34	0.34	2.17	0.72	39	0.37	0.13	0.73	0.19
Hissar	18	1.89	NA	2.20	1.30	18	0.56	NA	0.70	0.40

another part of the settlement. The presence of rounded pebble and chalky rinds on the decortication flakes indicates procurement from at least two types of sources, stream beds with rounded nodules and tabular beds. The paucity of evidence precludes any further statement on procurement strategy.

If one assumes that the desired end product of the flint core reduction operation was to produce relatively large non-cortical blanks, that is secondary non-cortical flakes and blades, then the frequency of such blanks relative to the frequency of indicators of the initial stages in the reduction sequence should make it possible to distinguish primary production workshops producing blanks from the contexts where such blanks were modified and used. At ABC blanks—secondary non-cortical flakes (N=69) and blades (N=39)—constitute 58.7% of the assemblage. This stands in contrast to the low frequency of indicators of the initial stages of the reduction sequence—cores, debris, platform preparation flakes, and decortication flakes (N=60), which constitute only 32.6% of the assemblage. It is clear that the initial stages in the reduction sequence are entirely inadequate for the production of the number of blanks present. Tertiary non-decortation flakes (N=16), assumed to be the by-products of shaping, retouch, or sharpening blanks, make up the other 8.7% of the assemblage. This pattern suggests the majority of the blanks were brought to ABC from another part of the city where a primary production workshop was located. It has also been noted that primary lithic production sites are characterized by very large quantities of debris. For example, Rosenberg (1989:116; see also Deaver 1996) notes that the courtyard of a Middle Elamite building at Malyan yielded 170 kgs of flaked stone. By contrast, the ABC lithics total 0.77 kg, an amount which is more likely to indicate a zone of secondary production, use, or abandonment.

Many lithic analysts concentrate on the manufacture of blades as one indicator of specialization. The evidence here is inconclusive. On the one hand, the presence of only one blade core (in Iran and not available for study) and the lack of any crested blades

(formed in the process of making a prismatic blade core) again suggest the blades were produced elsewhere and transported to the ABC area. For Malyan as a whole, Rosenberg (1989:117) notes that chipping debris forms perhaps the major part of the lithic collection, but this is not true for the ABC assemblage in which blades constitute 21.2% of the total; in addition blades comprise 41.5% (17 of 41) of the retouched lithics. By comparison, secondary non-cortical flakes (37.5% of the blanks) form 46.3% (N=19) of the retouched lithics, but many of these are indistinct artifacts with only slight modification.

On the other hand, the ABC blades exhibit less uniformity in dimensions than those from Tepe Hissar (Table 26). Rosenberg (1989:115) argues that blades from Hissar were produced by hard hammer percussion but those from Malyan by a variety of techniques, which to him suggests more individualized production for the latter site (1989:116). Although I do not preclude the possibility that knappers used pressure or punch techniques in blade production at the two sites, I concur with Rosenberg's conclusion that the evidence for specialization in flaked stone tool production is stronger for Hissar than for Malyan. There is, however, evidence in the spatial separation of primary work areas from final resting place of the blades that discrete activity zones existed at Malyan. In addition, despite differences in blade dimensions between the two sites (Table 26), the Malyan blades do exhibit uniformity in style, e.g. in cross-section (30 trapezoidal, 6 triangular) and platform. Furthermore, the discrepancy between the measurements may be due in part to Rosenberg's concentration on what he calls diagnostic blades, i.e., proximal segments with platforms, while in the present study all blades (proximal, medial, distal segments and complete specimens) are considered.

Another major point in Rosenberg's discussion of the Hissar blades is the unspecialized use of the finished products. He notes:"...the Hissar blades were put to variable uses none of which were apparently related to the specialized crafts known to have been practiced at the site" (1989:117). This is precisely the case at

Malyan. The microwear component of the present study confirms this impression. Eight of the nine blades with micro-wear were used for cutting grasses, so while consistent, the use pattern does not reflect craft specialization. The other pieces with micro-wear exhibit a similar lack of craft activity, with the exception of the one drill, the one flake used for drilling or incising, and one blade used to scrape or shave soft stone. Microwear analysis reveals evidence for scraping bone or wood (N=1), scraping hide (N=1), and scraping or cutting a soft material (perhaps cutting meat, N=2). All of these activities, except for the drilling and stone shaving, fit into a category of generalized subsistence activities. One would expect some drilling, as in the manufacture of stone beads (cf. Fig. 37i, j). Bulgarelli (1979) has demonstrated the extensive drilling of lapis lazuli beads at Hissar, but the Malyan ABC lithics bear only limited evidence of such work.

While the evidence for craft specialization in the production of certain materials (e.g., metal objects) at Malyan is considerable, the inferences drawn from the ABC flaked stone are circumstantial. I believe the production techniques suggest some level of specialization: a) Core debris, found in very low frequency, is largely discrete and separate from usable blanks, and b) blades demonstrate good technical control in the production of reasonably uniform blanks. The quantity of material, however, is not sufficient to indicate the presence of full-time specialists. Sheets and Muto (1972) in an experiment required 2.5 hours to produce 83 blades from a polyhedral core. All of the ABC blades (N=39, and an additional 22 in Iran) could, thus, have been produced in one work episode. The fact that there are five different materials represented suggests that the maximum time for blade production was 12.5 hours. At best, one can postulate the existence of part-time specialists who produced the flaked stone. Examples of such activity abound in the ethnographic literature of state-level societies. For example, *metateros* produce *manos* and *metates* in Mesoamerica on a seasonal basis (Cook 1982), and carpenters often double as specialists in the production of threshing sledges on Cyprus (Fox 1984).

A key question concerns the relationship between lithics and metal artifacts. It is clear that flaked stone tools survived the advent of metallurgy, but what is still ambiguous is the way in which people correlated these technologies. Metal implements are often more "expensive" than stone tools because the former require high procurement and production costs, and specialized knowledge for efficient production. The high durability of metal tools is a major advantages over stone tools. If Gilman (1981) and others are correct and metal tools served primarily as high status objects in early complex societies, then the proportion of metal to stone implements should be more than just a measure of increasing technological efficiency. One would expect the ratio of stone to metal objects would be higher in low status sectors of the community and lower in elite sections. The fact that metal tools are frequently recycled, which reduces their presence in many archaeological contexts, and the problem of specifying comparable measures of frequency for stone and metal tools make any test of this hypothesis problematic at present.

The primary goal of the present analysis has been to elicit evidence for craft specialization from the flaked stone in the ABC excavations. The presence or absence of such specialization, in turn, speaks directly to the issue of complex society. While the ABC lithic assemblage is small, it does provide evidence for these phenomena. Flaked stone production at Malyan was spatially discrete, skewed towards the manufacture and use of blades and secondary non-cortical flakes, and controlled by part-time specialists. The micro-wear analysis supplements the typological study and suggests that although the production of blades was at least somewhat specialized, the use of the implements was not. Residents of the site used modified and unmodified blanks for a variety of agricultural and processing activities (scraping hide, bone, and wood). The only evidence for the use of stone tools by other specialists (assuming that wood, hide, and bone work were generalized tasks) are traces on a drill. The evidence reminds us of the overwhelmingly agrarian nature of early states. As with Hissar, the flaked stone from Malyan offers some tentative links to craft specialization in an early state context.

Acknowledgment

Richard W. Yerkes provided invaluable aid in conducting the microwear analysis. He granted permission to use his laboratory space and equipment at The Ohio State University, and offered expert advice on the identification of the wear traces.

ARCHAEOMETALLURGICAL INVESTIGATIONS AT TAL-E MALYAN: BANESH PERIOD FINDS FROM ABC AND TUV

Vincent C. Pigott, Harry C. Rogers, and Samuel K. Nash

Introduction

While evidence indicates that the earliest manipulations of metal—native copper—occurred during the Southwest Asian Neolithic in the highlands of Anatolia and Iran (Stech 1990), archaeological evidence for the actual smelting of metal from ores appears somewhat later, during the Chalcolithic. Some of the earliest and best evidence for smelting was excavated at the site of Tepe Ghabristan in Iran dating to the late 5th-early 4th millennium BC (Majidzadeh 1979). At this site, twenty kilograms of crushed, easy to smelt, copper carbonate ore (malachite) were found in a workshop along with crucibles, a hearth, a tuyère, molds and copper artifacts. By the 4th millennium the smelting of copper ores, commonly yielding arsenical copper, occurred regularly across Southwest Asia. In the same period the earliest occurrences of artifacts in tin-bronze at sites such as Mundigak, Susa, and Sialk are recorded (Stech and Pigott 1986).

The archaeometallurgical remains from Banesh contexts at Malyan are important because they comprise a well excavated late 4th/early 3rd millennium assemblage from the Iranian Plateau. The excavation of the Banesh TUV Mound at Malyan, published by Ilene M. Nicholas (1990), includes her functional analysis of the contexts from which the metalworking debris derives. In the following discussion, we present for the first time, the laboratory analysis of the Banesh metallurgical assemblages from both ABC and TUV. We begin with an overview of the context in which copper-base metallurgy developed in ancient Iran.

The Archaeometallurgical Background

Metal production assemblages roughly contemporaneous with Banesh Malyan that subsequently extend into the Bronze Age are known from a number of sites including Susa (Tallon 1987), Tal-i Iblis (Caldwell 1967), Tepe Hissar (Schmidt 1937; Dyson and Howard 1989; Pigott 1989a; Pigott *et al.* 1982), Shahr-i

Sokhta (Hauptmann 1980; Helmig 1986); Tepe Yahya (Heskel 1982; Heskel and Lamberg-Karlovsky 1980) and Shahdad (Hakemi 1992; Vatandoost-Haghighi 1978). Up to and during the early centuries of the Bronze Age the common use of arsenical copper characterizes the technology of this group of settlements. A number of traits, including the use of the Proto-Elamite script, defines the populations at these sites as a cultural group. Indeed, with the advent of the third millennium B.C. we can speak of the Iranian Plateau as a 'metallurgical province' using the term first proposed by Chernykh (1980; see Pigott 1999). Tin-bronze does not appear in any quantity at most Iranian Bronze Age settlements, with the exception of Susa in lowland Khuzistan, until the second millennium. During the second millennium, it becomes common in the Kaftari levels at Malyan. In some instances, not until the Iron Age in Iran does tin-bronze become truly established as the dominant alloy (Pigott 1989b).

In archaeological excavations in Southwest Asia it has been uncommon to find smelting installations *in situ*. Spanning the entire time from the prehistoric through the protohistoric period on the Iranian Plateau, that is, through the Iron Age, the only excavated examples of smelting installations are the aforementioned (crucible?) smelting installation at Ghabristan, and those found in the excavation of the 'metalworkers quarter' at Shahdad (Hakemi 1992). Concentrations of crucibles at Tal-i Iblis (Caldwell 1967) and of slag and furnace(?) fragments at Tepe Hissar (Schmidt 1937; Pigott et al. 1982; Dyson and Howard 1989; Pigott 1989a) also comprise the debris of production, but none was found *in situ*. At this point in the research, it is not well understood just how copper was being produced. At Malyan the contexts in which the metallurgical materials were excavated have yielded little useful data toward the reconstruction of the production process. Nicholas' (1990) discussion of TUV contexts indicate the types of Banesh period deposits in which metal was encountered and discussions elsewhere in this ABC volume treat the contexts which yielded the artifacts analyzed here. An effort to address in broad terms the question of how arsenical copper might have been produced during the Banesh period at Malyan follows.

The Smelting of Arsenical Copper Ores

Only a small number of finds that might arguably be called slag were made in Banesh contexts anywhere at Malyan. Furthermore, only very few copper ore samples were found. The corpus of fragments of industrial ceramics from the site do not suggest large scale production; however, the simple presence of slag and industrial ceramics indicates some on-site processing activities on a small scale. While the analysis of these materials has not been undertaken, it is difficult to imagine that such analysis would change our current view of the scale of metallurgical activity at the site in any substantial way. Unless the melting and smelting of metal during this period was going on elsewhere at Malyan, it does not appear that people at Malyan were involved in metal production on any significant scale. Therefore, the discussion to follow treats, in only the broadest terms, the possible scenarios by which arsenical copper might have been manufactured at Malyan, or perhaps elsewhere on the Iranian Plateau.

Budd et al. (1992:679ff), in their study of metallurgical developments during the Bronze Age in the British Isles, argue that there are three primary methods by which arsenical copper was produced. Their discussion has relevance here because these three methods could have been practiced in Bronze Age Iran as well. These methods are first discussed in general terms and then as they relate specifically to the study of the Malyan ABC and TUV metallurgical assemblages.

The First Method

The first method involves the addition of native arsenic to molten copper. The simple melting of arsenic-rich native copper can also be subsumed under this method as can the addition of the copper arsenides algodonite and domeykite, as well as realgar and orpiment to native copper.[*] Deposits of native arsenic do exist and are associated with silver, cobalt, or nickel ores in hydrothermal veins (Palache et al. 1944; Budd et al. 1992:679). While native arsenic may have been present in the complex polymetallic geology of Iran, we have little indication of exact deposit

locations or that it was exploited in prehistory anywhere on the Plateau. However, with regard to the availability and ancient exploitation of arsenic-bearing copper minerals in Iran the picture is clearer.

The single largest source for arsenical copper minerals on the Plateau are two ore bodies—Talmessi and Meskani—located in the 20,000 sq. km of the Anarak (Fig. 1) mining district of north central Iran. Archaeometallurgists (e.g., Heskel 1982; Heskel and Lamberg-Karlovsky 1980; Berthoud 1979; cf. Moorey 1982), have argued that Chalcolithic/Bronze Age sites on the Iranian Plateau used, almost exclusively, the copper deposits of Talmessi and Meskani (Bazin and Hübner 1969; Schürenberg 1963). From Talmessi, native copper is frequently bound up with the rare copper arsenides, algodonite ($Cu_{5.8}As$, 80-87% Cu by weight) and domeykite (Cu_3As, 72% Cu by weight). As late as 1935, native copper was being mined in the amounts of 300 kg/cubic meter at Talmessi (Maczek et. al. 1952:65). What is unusual about the two copper arsenides just mentioned, which are geologically very rare on a world-wide basis but common at Talmessi, is that they will dissolve 'like sugar in water' in molten copper (Rostoker, personal communication; see also Lechtman 1980:303). Reducing conditions also should be maintained in the crucible so that the highly volatile arsenic is not readily lost. The proper processing of a naturally occurring mixture of native copper and copper arsenides could be accomplished in a ceramic crucible buried in a bed of charcoal. Thus, if early metalworkers on the plateau had learned to melt these materials at a temperature of $1000°C$, they would have produced an alloy with an arsenic content comparable to that of the materials charged in the crucible (Budd 1993:36). In fact, Budd (1993:36) has indicated that

> "at lower temperatures, the forming alloy remained solid, limiting the rate of diffusion. ....In practice, smelting....at any temperature less than about 900°C, about the highest temperature achievable in an open fire without a hearth or furnace, always resulted in an alloy with a few percent arsenic, but never more than 5 percent—regardless of the arsenic content of the ore." (See also Method Three below)

This would hold true if melting native copper and copper arsenides together. The arsenic content of the analyzed Malyan Banesh samples measures consistently below five percent. Indeed, only two examples have more than 5% arsenic, suggesting copper produc-

---

[*] It is interesting to note that the arsenic sulfides (AsS), realgar and orpiment, are formed in association with hot springs, locations which would have been easily noticed by local peoples. Furthermore they are commonly associated with each other and with antimony, silver, lead and tin minerals and as mentioned in the text with cobalt and nickel, two elements critical to an understanding of Iranian Plateau metallurgy. Realgar and orpiment when heated both give off a fumes with a strong garlic smell. Some of the largest known masses of orpiment are known from Turkish Kurdistan and from Iran (Prinz et al. 1978).

the artifacts suggested ore sources in the Bardsir mining region from the Kashan zone, or the Sheikh Ali Valley near Tepe Yahya (Berthoud and Cleuziou 1983:243). However, we know little else about the nature of these potential sources. Moreover, at Hissar the quantity of smelting slag, the large number of arsenical copper artifacts found, and their elemental profiles also could be used to argue for the use of *fahlerz*, perhaps from the Taknar source mentioned earlier (Pigott *et al.* 1982; Pigott 1989a). Only further analysis of the Hissar metalworking assemblage will shed light on this question.

If such *fahlerz* was among those ores being exploited at Malyan, then the metalworkers were faced, whether or not they were aware of it, with having to cope with the presence of sulfur in the ore. In simple terms, despite Budd and colleagues' (1992:679) arguments to the contrary, the smelting of sulfide ores of copper, including *fahlerz*, will *not* produce copper directly in a single smelting operation (Koucky and Steinberg 1982:165, Fig. 19). The smelting of *fahlerz* results in the production of 'matte', a copper sulfide or copper iron sulfide mixture. Matte must itself be re-smelted in order for copper to result. Before one-step smelting can proceed, the common historical and technological perception has been that the sulfur must first be driven off by roasting the ores in an oxidizing fire. By roasting the ore, substantially less of the intermediate product matte would be formed and more copper metal would result. Ore roasting might have been practiced if and when the metalworkers somehow recognized the need to do so.

However, an alternative approach to roasting may have been practiced, i.e., a second method, not that proposed by Budd et al., but by Rostoker and colleagues. This other 'second method' inadvertently dealt with sulfur and, at the same time, gave sulfur a positive role in the smelting process. This technique is known as 'co-smelting' (Rostoker et al. 1989; Rostoker and Dvorak 1991), a direct one-step copper production involving the co-smelting of a mixed charge of an oxidic ore (e.g., malachite, azurite, or chrysocolla) and a sulfide ore (e.g., chalcopyrite, bornite, or *arsenic-bearing fahlerz*). Temperatures in the range of ca. 1250°C or higher are necessary for co-smelting to proceed. In addition, Budd (1993:36) points out, based on the work of Craddock and Meeks (1987), that smelting at high temperatures which yields a slag "...resulted in higher levels of iron in the copper." At Banesh Malyan not only do samples show no appreciable iron contents, but slag was generally not in evidence.

Regarding evidence for smelting temperature, at Hissar, for example, where slag is abundant, the refiring experiments conducted on a fragment of furnace lining indicated it had reached a temperature slightly above ca. 1220°C and below ca. 1250°C— within reach of the co-smelting temperature range (Pigott et al. 1982:225). No other such analyses are published for sites on the Iranian Plateau. Co-smelting may have been practiced on a far more widespread basis in ancient Iran and elsewhere in Southwest Asia than we currently understand. However, only future programs of analysis of production debris and metal are going to give us any clue as to just how widespread the practice may have been. Moreover, the evidence presented below offers another viable means by which arsenical copper could have produced in antiquity.

The Third Method

This third method comprises a low temperature, *non-slagging*, smelting process which yields an arsenical copper with a *low iron content* (Budd et al. 1992:680; Budd 1993). Such smelting can be conducted under the most rudimentary circumstances involving the use of a bonfire or simple bowl furnace. The ores used could be any "arsenic- and antimony-bearing secondary minerals from the oxidized zones of cupriferous base metal orebodies" (Budd et al. 1992:681). These minerals are commonly known as arsenates and they strongly resemble the more common oxidic copper minerals. By this method, arsenates can be reduced to copper at temperatures as low as 700°C and yield no slag. The presence of nickel in the final product necessitates temperatures around 1000°C. As stated in the discussion of Method One, at temperatures of ca. 900°C and below, the resulting arsenical copper will have an arsenic content of less than 5% (Budd 1993:36).[*]

---

[*] Method Three is process which involves the solid state reduction of the copper arsenate to arsenical copper (Budd 1993:36). This process need not have proceeded to a molten state. However, indications are that if Method Three was in fact used at Malyan, the metal appeared to have reached the molten state. Metallographic analysis suggest that all artifacts analyzed were made from arsenical copper which at one time was molten. It is also possible to suggest that arsenical copper reduced in the solid state could have been melted for casting as some point after it was smelted. Copper arsenates (and arsenides) are rich in arsenic, yet none of the Malyan artifacts appear to reflect this richness. The choice of technique as explained in the text will influence how much arsenic is retained in the smelted metal. The Malyan results suggest that significant arsenic was being volatilized and passing off as a gas—a gas which, as many have suggested, was decidedly unhealthy to those working in and around it.

tion could have proceeded regularly at temperatures around 900°C and below. This is an important clue as we proceed in the discussion.

Through the above mentioned process, an arsenic-copper alloy could have been obtained without the more difficult and time consuming process of smelting arsenical copper ores. Therefore, ease of production could have provided considerable incentive to travel hundreds of kilometers from Malyan (and from other sites as well) to procure ore from Talmessi-Meskani, by-passing copper ore deposits that may have been closer to the settlement.

Further support for this argument may come from the major Geological Survey of Iran (GSI) report on copper deposits in Iran, which indicates that arsenical copper ore deposits are known only from three locations in Iran. These locations are Talmessi and Meskani in the Anarak district and the deposit at Taknar, which is located some 300 km east of the Anarak district (Bazin and Hübner 1969: plate XVI, 65-7). Heskel and Lamberg-Karlovsky (1980:232) reaffirm the point that apparent copper sulfarsenides are scarce on the plateau. Of course it must be recognized that we are relying on a single report from 1969 and, moreover, that all potential deposits are not known today. Early metalworkers may have used deposits of which we remain unaware or that were mined away in antiquity. The GSI report, at a minimum, suggests that arsenical copper ores were not widely available on the Iranian Plateau. Dependence on the Anarak sources could help to explain the technological conservatism, part of a long tradition of arsenical copper metallurgy, which seems to characterize Chalcolithic and Bronze Age metalworking traditions across ancient Iran. (Pigott 1989b; Pigott 1999).[*]

---

[*] One could argue that a certain level of technological conservatism could have been promoted also by the relative ease of relying on only coldworked native copper for the production of small and simply shaped implements. A single annual mining expedition traveling several hundred kilometers or more could return with enough native copper nodules to last quite some time. The manufacture of more sophisticated and/or larger shapes would have necessitated heat treating the native copper so that it could be worked repeatedly. Heat treating could have led to the discovery of melting. Arsenic imparts its useful properties only after mixing with molten copper so the useful properties which derive from the combination of copper and arsenic minerals together is a pyrotechnological phenomenon. However, if during the process of geological formation the native copper had arsenic in solution then the beneficial properties of that arsenic conveys e.g. hardness and ease of working hot or cold could have been imparted to the metal which was being 'mined' provided that amounts above ca. 2 wt.% As were present in the metal.

The Second Method

A second method of smelting arsenical copper to be considered for Bronze Age Iran, despite the apparent lack of identified major deposits of copper sulfarsenide ore, depends on the presence of weathered copper sulfide ore bodies. These deposits contain the so-called *fahlerz* or gray copper ore. These deposits comprise the base metal sulfides with a high incidence of arsenic and/or antimony in a sulfur-rich matrix which are found deeper lying in the zone of secondary enrichment, e.g., enargite (Cu_3AsS_4), and ores in the tetrahedrite-to-tennantite series $[(Cu,Fe)_{12}Sb_4S_{13}$—$(Cu,Fe)_{12}As_4S_{13}]$—copper-iron sulfides. To a limited extent, weathered copper sulfide ore deposits do exist on the Iranian Plateau. Talmessi and Meskani are just such ore bodies, but at Talmessi "during mineralization the content of the sulfur diminished while the concentration of the arsenic increased so that parts of the copper sulfides were displaced by algodonite and domeykite" (Schürenberg 1963 cited in Heskel and Lamberg-Karlovsky 1980:259). Elsewhere on the Plateau *fahlerz*-bearing copper sulfide ore deposits may not have been readily detected by modern economic geological survey or we may not have access to the most current geological data or they may have been mined out in antiquity.

In the second method, according to Budd et al. 1992:679 (citing McKerrel and Tylecote 1972 and Zwicker 1980), the sulfarsenides or *fahlerz can be reduced to arsenical copper in a one-step process* at temperatures greater than 1300° C. This assertion is challenged below. In this process the loss of arsenic due to volatilization is minimal and "...[t]he rate of dissolution of arsenic into molten copper is such that objects produced from such smelted metal have almost the same ratio of arsenic to copper as in the ore charge" (Budd et al. 1992:679).

The exploitation of sulfarsenides merits some discussion in the context of early Iranian metallurgy. The presence of substantial quantities of *fahlerz* on the Iranian Plateau cannot be confirmed given the current state of published information on Iranian economic geology, so discussions of this second method are necessarily mostly speculative. However, according to Berthoud and Françaix (1980) cited in Malfoy and Menu (1987:364-5), copper-base artifacts in the later 4th millennium at Susa in southwestern Iran, off the Plateau, show a more heterogeneous composition containing quantities of arsenic, silver, antimony and bismuth. They argue that this cluster of elements suggests the exploitation of *fahlerz* and that the composition of

Table 27. COMPOSITION OF COPPER-BASE FINDS FROM ABC AND TUV

mf #	Cu	As	Sn	Pb	Fe	Ni	Sb	Ag	Zn	Cl	S
0874	97.0	1.60	≤0.070	0.042	0.006	0.10	0.12	0.048	≤0.57	≤0.002	≤0.010
1137	95.1	1.77	≤0.055	0.61	0.059	≤0.022	0.20	0.72	≤0.57	0.38	0.083
1143	95.8	0.96	≤0.025	≤0.058	0.077	≤0.022	0.24	≤0.018	≤0.57	0.97	0.048
1145.2	92.2	3.06	≤0.070	3.34	0.29	0.12	≤0.030	0.047	≤0.57	≤0.012	0.041
1490	96.6	2.06	≤0.070	0.32	0.045	0.092	0.12	0.12	≤0.57	≤0.009	0.044
1498	96.9	0.14	≤0.070	0.044	0.11	0.64	0.026	0.014	≤0.57	0.35	0.19
1504	96.7	1.55	≤0.027	≤0.044	0.052	0.55	0.075	0.037	≤0.57	0.071	≤0.008
1514	97.1	1.14	≤0.070	0.047	0.15	0.36	≤0.032	0.16	≤0.57	≤0.012	0.103
1515	97.8	0.22	≤0.028	≤0.044	0.18	≤0.022	0.14	0.067	≤0.57	0.41	0.026
2120	96.8	1.00	≤0.070	0.51	0.34	0.082	≤0.036	0.45	≤0.57	≤0.003	0.10
3569	94.7	3.73	≤0.070	0.16	0.33	0.095	0.12	0.28	≤0.57	≤0.007	0.037
3678	65.4	1.50	≤0.070	0.33	0.11	0.070	28.2	2.8	≤0.57	≤0.013	0.86
3742	96.0	1.78	≤0.034	0.24	0.13	0.22	≤0.73	0.051	≤0.57	0.39	0.079
3858	87.7	7.15	≤0.070	0.11	0.30	0.095	1.00	2.4	≤0.57	0.47	0.054
3973.1	96.3	2.52	≤0.070	0.16	0.054	0.13	≤0.024	0.15	≤0.57	≤0.011	0.072
3973.2	93.6	3.33	≤0.070	0.88	0.82	0.14	≤0.035	0.34	≤0.57	0.10	0.15
5041	85.5	5.60	≤0.070	5.8	0.27	0.081	0.80	1.0	≤0.57	0.19	≤0.010
5438	94.4	1.70	≤0.070	1.8	0.052	0.15	0.57	0.58	≤0.57	0.12	0.15
5439.1	94.2	0.98	≤0.070	3.3	0.25	0.12	0.41	0.10	≤0.57	≤0.011	≤0.012
5440	95.5	2.26	≤0.070	0.13	1.1	0.078	0.064	0.034	≤0.57	0.092	0.044
5441	96.2	1.57	≤0.070	0.46	0.14	0.10	0.51	0.20	≤0.57	0.017	≤0.017
6086.1	92.9	4.74	≤0.070	0.34	0.51	0.081	≤0.026	0.10	≤0.57	0.45	0.10
6086.2	94.0	4.38	≤0.070	0.11	0.26	0.092	0.091	0.27	≤0.57	0.052	0.066
6749	97.6	1.05	≤0.070	0.039	0.18	0.096	≤0.025	0.013	≤0.57	≤0.009	0.069
6772	96.9	1.00	≤0.043	0.53	0.061	≤0.020	≤0.033	0.36	≤0.57	0.033	0.15
6774	96.5	0.77	≤0.036	1.11	0.036	0.21	≤0.034	0.26	≤0.57	0.018	0.21
6936.1	94.1	2.04	≤0.070	0.29	1.2	0.050	0.13	0.21	≤0.57	1.00	0.17
6937	95.0	1.92	≤0.070	0.070	0.054	0.089	≤0.017	0.39	≤0.57	0.20	0.98
7109	95.7	1.29	≤0.070	0.061	0.18	0.47	0.035	0.047	≤0.57	0.14	0.33
9956	97.1	0.37	≤0.024	≤0.049	0.18	0.29	≤0.033	0.043	≤0.57	0.53	0.13

Elemental composition, determined by PIXE analysis is expressed as percentage by weight.

Such a technique could have characterized ancient Iranian metallurgy if judged by the sparseness of archaeometallurgical remains and the nature of available mineralizations. Once again Talmessi-Meskani comes into the picture. J. A. Charles (1980:168) has pointed out "the oxidation of copper arsenides produces an astonishingly wide range of green basic copper arsenates... many of which... closely resemble malachite." J.W. Barnes, cited in Charles (1980:169), "prefers the use of the arsenate-containing materials rather than the primary sulfarsenides as marking the discovery of selected copper minerals to produce alloys of improved properties," i.e., arsenical copper. (These arsenical minerals give off a garlic smell when hammered—a guide to arsenic-richness.) Budd and colleagues (1992:680 citing also Charles 1985; Gale et al. 1985; and Rapp 1988) indicate that the arsenic composition of the metal resulting from this low temperature operation (temperature must remain below that at which the copper arsenic alloy becomes molten) is independent of the ratio of the arsenic to copper in the ore charged in the 'furnace'. This eliminates the need to postulate that prehistoric metalworkers were carefully controlling the ore content of the smelting charge. It should be noted that nickel, present in trace amounts in the Malyan copper, according to Budd (1993:36), occurs in secondary copper ore deposits in minerals easily mistaken for malachite. Furthermore, the low levels of iron found in the Banesh copper-base artifacts suggests the low temperatures of Method Three could have prevailed during smelting.

Analysis of the Banesh Metallurgical Assemblage

The analysis of the Banesh metallurgical materials is part of continuing, long term program of archaeometallurgical investigation of metalworking traditions in Southwest Asia underway at the Museum Applied Science Center for Archaeology (MASCA) at the University of Pennsylvania Museum. In this program special emphasis has been placed on excavated evidence of metalworking from the Iranian Plateau.

As stated, the small group of slag samples and industrial ceramic debris excavated from ABC and TUV have yet to be studied. Their presence does suggest that some primary metal production occurred at Malyan, but the small area of the site that has been excavated makes it difficult to estimate the extent of such production. A number of lead artifacts (mostly amorphous lumps) have been submitted to Pb-isotope analysis at the National Institute of Standards and Technology, but the results are not yet published (M. James Blackman, personal communication). We know very little about the archaeometallurgy of lead on the plateau.

The elemental analyses of Malyan copper-base artifacts by PIXE (Proton Induced X-ray Emission Spectroscopy) was undertaken under MASCA's auspices by Stuart J. Fleming, Scientific Director, and Charles P. Swann of the Bartol Research Institute at the University of Delaware. It is this PIXE data in concert with the optical metallography of uncorroded copper-base artifacts, conducted by the authors and detailed at the end of this report, that permits the following observations to be made on the technology represented by the Malyan Banesh finds.

The Pixe Analysis

The elemental analysis by PIXE sheds light on the dominant alloy technology. Analysis indicates that the metal artifacts under study are composed primarily of an arsenical copper alloy with trace amounts of elements including nickel and antimony (Table 27). Individual PIXE tables for the ABC and TUV finds may be found in Appendix A, Part II.

On the Production and Working of Copper-base Metal as Practiced at Banesh Malyan

It is generally the case that, with the exception of the Talmessi-Anarak deposits, prehistoric Iran has provided little evidence for the presence of arsenic-bearing minerals and/or their mining. Budd (1993:35) noted a similar situation in the British Isles and this observation was pertinent to their presentation of the three methods of smelting arsenical copper under discussion here. The results of the metallographic analyses of Malyan metal presented below provide little indication that the enhanced properties of arsenical copper were necessarily being exploited in the process of manufacturing artifacts in this alloy.

If we return to the discussion of the three methods by which arsenical copper might have been produced, the first method has a number of points in its favor as the possible technique of choice at Banesh Malyan. The impurity pattern as revealed by PIXE is such that native copper and associated copper nickel arsenide minerals from deposits at Talmessi and Meskani could have been used. This suggestion is based on the incidence of arsenic and nickel in the metal, both of which are contributed to the smelted metal from the ore. In the ABC Banesh metal arsenic is not present in amounts that would improve its hardness as amounts in the range of 2–6 % are considered optimum for that purpose. Whereas, 8 out of 16 TUV Banesh artifacts have arsenic contents above 2.06%, with nickel contents somewhat higher than those seen in the ABC metal. These higher TUV arsenic levels do not necessarily reflect intentional arsenical copper production as the variations could have resulted from, for example, differing smelting techniques (e.g., higher temperatures) and/or a higher arsenic content of the ore utilized at TUV versus ABC.

Broadly speaking, the generally low but somewhat consistent amounts of arsenic and nickel in the Banesh artifacts suggest the utilization of raw materials with little knowledge of the properties these elements could impart to the final product. Budd (1993:36) noted that similar circumstances prevailed in the British Isles. Thus, one potential source for such metal is melted native copper that just happened to contain arsenical minerals as at Talmessi/Meskani. Such production would have proceeded under conditions tending towards reducing, which would have impeded volatilization of the arsenic. The mixture of arsenic and copper could also result from the fact that, in the weathered state, native copper and the two arsenides (algodonite and domeykite) are very similar in appearance. If lumps of both materials were melted together in a crucible under a bed of charcoal, a process which would require temperatures near that necessary to melt copper (1084°C), the result would be arsenical copper with an arsenic content consistent with the arsenic contained in the materials charged in the crucible. Therefore, if the native copper/copper arsenides were being melted to produce this metal one would expect appreciably higher arsenic contents in the TUV artifacts, given the fact that the arsenides are quite rich in arsenic. Oxidizing circumstances during melting as well as annealing the metal during working could reduce overall arsenic content to some extent. To what extent, however, we have no way of knowing. The low (below 2%) arsenic content of the ABC metal, for example, definitely does not appear to reflect the practice of melting native copper/copper arsenides together.

The attractiveness of this process lies, in part, in its simplicity. The process would have involved relatively easy surface collecting or 'grubbing' of lumps of copper arsenides and native copper which were then placed in a crucible under a bed of charcoal and melted. The melted metal could either have been cast into simple molds (no evidence from Banesh Malyan) or allowed to cool into an 'ingot' from which small pieces could have been removed for shaping or casting. However, the question as to whether the arsenic contents of the finished artifacts from Banesh contexts reflect the arsenic content of source material remains unanswered.

With regard to Method Two which involves the smelting of sulfur bearing ores, the PIXE analyses of the Malyan samples, which detects all elements present even in minute trace amounts, did not register the appreciable amounts of sulfur. Significant matte content (copper sulfides or copper iron sulfides) is characteristic of metals produced by the co-smelting process. In addition, the co-smelting process tends to generate masses of slag (Rostoker et al. 1989). Thus, given the lack of sulfur and appreciable slag it is difficult to suggest that the Malyan Banesh arsenical copper was a product of the co-smelting of oxides and sulfides generally or of co-smelting of oxides with *fahlerz* specifically.

Finally, the third method, involving the use of copper arsenates to produce arsenical copper, merits attention. This process is interesting because of its technical simplicity and ease of operation. These points, when combined with the fact that this process generates only ephemeral material remains, suit well our generalized view of how Chalcolithic (and perhaps even later) copper smelting may have been proceeding at sites like Malyan. Smelting in shallow bowl furnaces (or perhaps crucibles) under beds of charcoal is not as archaeologically permanent as fixed furnace installations. Moreover, the process is non-slagging. Slag is not at all common in the Banesh levels at Malyan and this must say something about the type of production practiced during this period at the site.

With regard to this third and final method, if most arsenates are the geologically derived by-products of the decomposition of copper sulfarsenide ores like enargite and tennantite, then the lack of the sulfarsenides in Iran would mean a lack of arsenates at most ore bodies on the plateau[*] *with the exception once again of Talmessi-Meskani.* Thus Method Three is perhaps the most likely candidate for arsenical copper production at Malyan for the following reasons: (1) the apparent rarity of sulfarsenide/*fahlerz* deposits tend to make Talmessi-Meskani likely sources for copper-bearing materials that contained arsenic, sulfur and nickel (as well as other impurities which appear in quantity in certain Banesh artifacts, e.g., antimony, lead, and silver). Ore bodies, like those at Talmessi-Meskani, which contained this mix of minerals, could easily have had arsenates present. (2) Arsenates are easily smelted at low temperatures and produce little slag. Arsenates smelted below ca. 900°C tend to yield copper with an arsenic content of less than 5%, which is generally the case at Banesh Malyan. Budd (1993:37) makes a very interesting observation directly relevant here, that if metalworkers lacked the technical capability to work at high temperatures, i.e., those adequate for co-smelt-

_____

[*] Prof. Reinhard Bernbeck and Prof. Susan Pollock (both at SUNY-Binghamton) reported in a presentation at the University of Pennsylvania Museum about their trip to Iran and participation in the conference entitled, 'The Archaeometallurgy of Central and Western Asia', April 18-25, 1997. The conference was organized by Dr. H.R. Vatandoost at the Musee Melli in Tehran. In the post-conference tour the participants visited a site not far from Tepe Sialk near Kashan known as Tepe Arismand. The surface of the site was dotted with slag heaps apparently from copper smelting and ceramics from the 4th millennium were found in association with these slags. This is but one intriguing example of what awaits the next generation of archaeologists who will be privileged to work once again Iran.

ing (1250°C and up), then "...it may be that only ore deposits with favorable mineralogies could be easily exploited." This could explain, at Malyan as well as any number of metal-producing settlements on the plateau, a reliance over time on the easily extracted and processed materials at Talmessi-Anarak, namely native copper, arsenides and arsenates.

Regrettably, in terms of our understanding of the technologies at work, once the native copper/arsenide mix from Talmessi/Meskani was melted it would not be possible to readily discriminate melted metal from smelted metal. Therefore, we cannot readily discriminate arsenical copper from Banesh Malyan, which might have been produced by Method One, from metal produced by Method Three on the basis of microstructure. However, the arsenic and iron contents metal allow us to suggest that Method Three, low temperature arsenate smelting, may have been practiced at Banesh Malyan at ABC, if not at TUV as well. Moreover, reasonably strong arguments presented above suggest the continuing exploitation of the Talmessi-Meskani deposits by metalworkers from Banesh Malyan.

In the end, laboratory based studies such as this one are beginning to assist in characterizing the remarkable technological achievement of reducing metal from ores. What will be required in the future are additional excavations in the critical regions, field research on ore deposits, and associated programs of archaeometallurgical analysis to determine just what deposits and ores were being processed at what time by what method and perhaps even by whom.

The Metallographic Analysis

Several metal artifact assemblages from sites elsewhere in Iran namely Susa, Yahya, Hissar, and Shahr-i Sokhta were the focus of an analytical program which included metallography in combination with elemental analysis undertaken by Dennis Heskel as part of Ph.D. dissertation research in the Dept. of Anthropology at Harvard University (Heskel 1982; Heskel and Lamberg-Karlovsky 1980). Heskel's work is the largest published metallographic study of metal artifacts from Iran, followed by the present study of Malyan finds. The details of the metallographic analysis, which support the following general observations, for each find are presented below in Appendix A. IIA.

The collection of artifacts from Malyan examined in this study provides sufficient evidence to suggest that workshops for one or more metalsmiths existed for an extended time during the Banesh Period. The presence of small amounts of slag, prills, and industrial ceramics indicates some on-site ore and metal processing occurred at Malyan. The Banesh period is distinguished metallurgically primarily by the predominance of arsenical copper while the Kaftari period is typified by the primacy of tin-bronze. Though a number of artifacts were investigated metallographically, the numbers are statistically small for an attempt to discern the 'workshop' patterns or 'technological styles' characteristic of Malyan metal products. As can be seen in the discussion to follow, those observations that can be made are minimal and little in the way of technique distinguishes the Banesh metalworking style as revealed by the excavated remains. This is due, in part, to the fact that most of the artifacts we have for analysis are the scraps and discards of simple mechanical metalworking.

The majority of the artifacts examined are copper or copper-base alloys that appear to have been subjected to considerable prior deformation, generally hot deformation. There are also several artifacts that are prills, some remaining entrapped in slag. Such prills could have resulted from either on-site melting and casting or smelting operations.

The worked artifacts for the most part do not appear to be the finished product of the metal smiths but rather scrap or trimmings from finished products or else unsatisfactory attempts at forming a particular shape or article. For example, two artifacts from TUV (mf 3569 and 6772) have severely mushroomed heads, probably the result of having been pounded into a mold or 'die' of some type, while hot. In the case of artifact mf 3569, the artifact that was being formed has been cut off; only the pounded head remains. On the other hand, mf 6772 is intact with the mushroomed head as well as the artifact being formed. It has a pointed shape with a quadrilateral cross-section and could have been the tip of a small point in the process of manufacture.

Several of the artifacts appear to be attempts at secondary shaping operations utilizing stock from more standard primary metalworking operations such as sheet or bar stock. Metallographic indications are that these primary metalworking operations were done hot using simple hammering implements.

The most significant differences between the artifacts from ABC and those from TUV are the following: a larger fraction of the artifacts from TUV are in the as-cast condition, that is, the majority of what we have termed amorphous prills or metal processing debris. This debris suggests the smelting of arsenical copper at TUV in small bowl furnaces (or perhaps crucibles) which were most probably quite friable. However, little in the way of structures, vessels, or tools related to metal processing was revealed in the excavation at TUV. It is possible that the debris is simply from metal casting, but in that case the presence of melting crucible sherds would be anticipated. More importantly, the inclusions in the artifacts from TUV either fragmented during mechanical deformation of the metal or retained their shape. Whereas, the worked metal artifacts from ABC generally contained inclusions that had been plastically deformed under mechanical working conditions. The implication of this observation is that there may be a general difference in composition in terms of minor elements present between the ABC and TUV groups of metal artifacts. However, the role of the temperature at which the metal was being worked could also have influenced the nature of inclusion deformation and should not be discounted. This could reflect a difference in the methods of working metal at the two Malyan loci.

Concluding Remarks

We will have to resist further argument concerning the production processes and sources of raw material for the Malyan artifacts at this stage in the analysis. Additional analysis would involve the use of the scanning electron microscope and electron microprobe in order to determine, at the microstructural level, the composition of phases and inclusions. This would assist in reconstructing the thermodynamics responsible for the metallurgical assemblages at Malyan.

With the completion of such work, which would necessarily include the analysis of the small group of 'slags', the results of the Pb-isotope analyses, and a thorough going investigation of the industrial ceramics, we would have a much larger data base upon which to ground our arguments about the nature of the pyrotechnological processes used at Malyan in the Banesh Period. This data, in concert with comparable information from the study of the materials from the Kaftari Period excavations (also currently underway at MASCA and to be published elsewhere), will then position the Malyan metallurgical assemblages as important technological markers in the continuing effort to understand metallurgical developments on the Iranian Plateau, one of the Asian continent's preeminent 'heartlands' of metallurgical technology.

BANESH SHELLS, SHARK/RAY VERTEBRAE, AND EGGSHELLS FROM ABC AND TUV

David S. Reese

Shells From Banesh Levels

This study is based on the shells in the collection of the University of Pennsylvania Museum recovered from the Banesh Period (ca. 3400-2800 B.C.) levels in Operations ABC and TUV at Tal-e Malyan. The shell counts discussed here, which are not exactly the same as the counts presented in Table 18, are based on information available at the time of this study. Shells from ABC are listed in the register (Appendix A. I.), which provides provenance and other information. Additional measurements and descriptive details resulting from this study are presented separately in Section IIB of Appendix A. The provenance of shells from TUV is presented by Nicholas (1990).

Operation ABC Shell

The Banesh levels of Operation ABC yielded 1,115 marine shells, with most (1036, 93%) from Building Level 2. The vast majority of the ABC Banesh marine shells are found in Stratum 8B (937 shells or 84%). This is followed by Stratum 8D, which yielded 93 marine shells (8.3%). Corridor 118 (Strata 8B and 8D) produced a total of 906 marine shells, of which 886 are nacre inlays. Also to be noted are the large number of *Dentalium* from Stratum 8B, Room 130 (86 examples; with 71 in one lot) which must be part of the split sample of 110 *Dentalium* originally noted as coming from this room (published as Room 11 in Sumner 1974:164).

The majority of the shells are nacre (mother-of-pearl) inlays, including *Pinctada margaritifera L.* (pearl oyster) shells, there are 985 pieces of nacre, or 88.4% of the collection. *Dentalium* is the second most common shell, 115, or 10.3% of the collection. The rarer forms include six *Engina mendicaria* (striped whelk), five *Conus* (cone shell), two *Ancilla*, one *Monodonta/Gibbula* (topshell), one *Turritella*, and one shell ring fragment. Operation ABC also produced about 30 fresh-water shells (25 *Unio tigridis*, four *Melanopsis praemorsa* [one holed], several small gastropods), and 14 land snails.

Operation TUV Shell

Banesh levels in Operation TUV yielded about 160 marine shells (about 45 *Pinctada* or nacre, 36 *Ancilla*, nine *Dentalium*, two cowries with holes in them, one *Oliva*) (Table A2a), about 22 fresh-water shells (19 *Unio* [one worked], three *Melanopsis*) (Table A2b), and about four land snails (Table A2c). All *Ancilla* were found together in BL II, Area 379, lot 31, the northwest end of V166 (Nicholas 1990, Fig. 23), and probably come from one ornament.

Malyan is located about 190 km, as-the crow-flies, from the Persian Gulf and more than 300 km by caravan route. The marine shells are one of the non-local items found at the site, along with calcite, chlorite, zeolite, and obsidian.

Comparanda to the Marine Shells

The forms exploited at Malyan have a long history of use in Iran. The comparanda given here are simply to indicate that these same species were used as ornaments (and inlay) over a very long period of time both before and after the Banesh period.

Worked and unworked *Pinctada* are known from a number of sites. Cut *Pinctada* are known from Tal-i-Iblis (Caldwell 1967:408). Shahr-i Sokhta produced unworked *Pinctada* (Durante 1979:338; Tosi and Biscione 1981:44, fig. 50). Worked and unworked *Pinctada* are known from Tepe Yahya (Lamberg-Karlovsky 1970, pl. 27R-S; Durante 1979:338, figs. 13-14; Tosi and Biscione 1981:44, figs. 21-22, 25-32; Beale 1986b:176, 178, 314-15, 318-25, figs. 7.9e, g, 7.19e). *Pinctada* are known from Uruk, Jemdet Nasr, and Early Dynastic layers at Farukhabad (Talbot 1981). Worked *Pinctada* are known from Susa (Tosi and Biscione 1981:44, figs. 9, 15). *Pinctada* inlay of various shapes are known from Parthian and later Qasr-i Abu Nasr (Old Shiraz)(Whitcomb 1985:fig. 74e, pls. 53-54) and *Pinctada* ornaments and containers are also present (Ibid., figs. 70f 74e). *Pinctada* inlay of various shapes are known from Ctesiphon (Upton 1932:192).

Dentalium shells are known from: Tepe Ali Kosh (Hole et al. 1969: 244); Chagha Sefid (Hole 1977:242); Tal-i-Iblis (Caldwell 1967: 217, 408, fig. 7:6); Tepe Yahya (Lamberg-Karlovsky 1970: pls. 27P, 37J; Durante 1979:338; Tosi and Biscione 1981:44; Beale 1986b:176, 314-15, 320-21); Susa (Le Brun 1978b:91. fig. 41:2, 9, pl. XX; Tosi and Biscione 1981:44, fig. 14); Tepe Sialk (Tosi and Biscione 1981:fig. 20); Iron Age Hasanlu (Reese 1989:81, fig. 6); Iron Age Surkh Dum-i-Luri (Curvers 1989b:389, 396-8, 410, pl. 230m). *Dentalium* shells are known from Uruk, Jemdet Nasr, and Early Dynastic layers at Farukhabad (Talbot 1981).

Holed *Engina* are known from: Ali Kosh (Hole et al. 1969:243-44); Shahr-i Sokhta (Tosi and Biscione 1981:43, 75, fig. 54); Tepe Yahya (Tosi and Biscione 1981:43, 75, fig. 83; Beale 1986b: 320-25); Susa (Durante 1979:332, 338; Tosi and Biscione 1981:43, 75, fig. 16); Tepe Sialk (Tosi and Biscione 1981:75, fig. 20); Tepe Hissar (Durante 1979:332, 338, fig. 18; Tosi and Biscione 1981:43); Hasanlu (Reese 1989:80, figs. 2, 19); Surkh Dum-i-Luri (Curvers 1989b:389, 396-99, 410, pl. 230g-h); Qasr-i Abu Nasr (Old Shiraz)(Whitcomb 1985, fig. 70u, w). *Engina* are known from Uruk, Jemdet Nasr, and Early Dynastic layers at Farukhabad (Talbot 1981).

Apically holed *Conus* are known from Tal-i-Iblis (Caldwell 1967:408, figs. 34:13, 36:14); Shahr-i Sokhta (Durante 1979:338; Tosi and Biscione 1981:43, figs. 46-48, 53); Tepe Yahya (Lamberg-Karlovsky 1970:pl. 37D; Durante 1979:338; Tosi and Biscione 1981: 43-44, figs. 37-39; Beale 1986b:320-23); Susa (Tosi and Biscione 1981:43, figs. 12, 15-6); Tall-i-Bakun A (Langsdorff and McCown 1942:75, pl. 8:19); Hasanlu (Reese 1989:81, fig. 11). *Conus* shells are known from Uruk, Jemdet Nasr, and Early Dynastic layers at Farukhabad (Talbot 1981).

Apically holed *Oliva* are known from: Late Chalcolithic Kamtarlan I (van Loon 1989:116, 119, pl. 76i); Tal-i-Iblis (Caldwell 1967:217, 408, fig. 7:4); Shahr-i Sokhta (Durante 1979: 332; Tosi and Biscione 1981:43); Tepe Yahya (worked and unworked; Lamberg-Karlovsky 1970:pl. 27P; Durante 1979:332, 338; Tosi and Biscione 1981:43, figs. 81, 91; Beale 1986b:316-17, 320-25); Susa (Tosi and Biscione 1981:figs. 15-16); Tall-i-Bakun A Level III (Langsdorff and McCown 1942:75, pl. 8:18); Surkh Dum-i-Luri (Curvers 1989b:397-99, 401, pl. 230i). *Oliva* are known from Uruk, Jemdet Nasr, and Early Dynastic layers at Farukhabad (Talbot 1981).

Shark/Ray Vertebrae

There are three examples of shark or ray vertebrae from the Banesh levels at ABC:

•mf 6795, pierced hole in center, incised line on exterior, D 15.25, T 7.5, hole 2.5, (Fig. 38c).

•mf 6793, pierced hole in center, said to be traces of yellow pigment in the central carved band and traces of black in the upper and lower bands, eroded, chipped, D 15.25, T 7.5, hole 3, (Fig. 38d).

•mf 6664, pierced hole in center, incised line on exterior, traces of yellow pigment on upper and lower surfaces, L 8, T 3.5, hole 1, (Fig 38e)

The fish remains from Malyan have not yet been identified (Zeder 1991:86) so it is unclear if other shark/ray remains are present at the site. Several other Iranian sites have holed shark/ray vertebrae. Djaffarabad produced a shark vertebra measuring 18 x 9 mm with a hole in the center (Dollfus 1971, fig. 29:12). The Acropole at Susa produced a shark vertebra from Late Period I with a hole in the center (Le Brun 1971, fig. 42:3) while the Ville Royale produced another with a hole in the center dated to about 2700 B.C. (Carter 1980:19, 70, fig. 18:12). Tall-i-Bakun A Level III produced a holed shark (?) vertebra (Langsdorff and McCown 1942:75, pl. 84:10).

Unmodified shark vertebrae are also known from Ur and Tell el'Queili (Larsa) in Iraq (Reese 1984:192) and 56 unmodified shark and ray vertebrae are known from 2150-1900 B.C. Qala'at al-Bahrain (Van Neer and Uerpmann 1994: 445-46, fig. 2087).

At least three species of shark ascend the Tigris River as far as Baghdad (Khalaf 1961).

Ostrich Eggshell Fragments

Although no ostrich bones have been reported (Zeder 1991), several ostrich eggshell fragments were recovered from Banesh levels:

•mf 2071, 2 fragments (Fig 38a)
•mf 9868, 2 joining pieces, 43.25 x 23.75, T 2 (Fig. 38b)

The last ostrich in Iran was sighted near Kerman at the end of the 19th century. The last ostriches in Arabia were killed around 1948. A wild ostrich was seen near Petra in 1966 (Stone 1982). Ostrich eggshells have a wide archaeological distribution including China, India, the Near East, and most of the Mediterranean basin. The egg could have been eaten and the eggshell could be used as a container or to make beads.

Ostrich eggshells are known from various sites in Iran: in Luristan (Finet 1982:74; Curvers 1989b:368)

and from Parthian and later Qasr-i Abu Nasr (Old Shiraz) (Whitcomb 1995, fig. 74i; complete, with a carefully made opening).

In Iraq they are known from: Kish (Laufer 1926:2-3, pls. II-III; Mackay 1925:19, 1929: 136; Moorey 1970); Nineveh (Beck 1931: 432-34); Ur (Woolley 1934, pl. 156); Nuzi (Starr 1937-9:488, 492); Aqar Quf (Baqir 1945:14); Nippur (Torelli 1965:333 n. 2); Babylon (Torelli 1965:333 n. 2); Abu Salabikh (Postgate 1980:73); Tell Kannas (Finet 1982:72); Khirbet ed Diniye (Caubet 1985:88 n. 31);and Tell Haddad in the Hamrin basin (displayed in Iraq Museum, Baghdad). They are also known from Bahrein (Torelli 1965:333, 334; Ibrahim 1982:35, pl. 44:7-8) and eastern Syria: Tell Asherah/ Terqa (Thureau-Dangin and Dhorme 1924:290; Mount-Williams 1980:2-4) and Mari (Parrot 1937:83, fig. 16, 1953:2).

ARCHAEOLOGICAL INDICATORS OF CRAFT PRODUCTION

Massimo Vidale

A brief examination of a small selected collection of artifacts recovered from the excavation of the Banesh architectural levels in Operation ABC made it evident that the assemblage included a series of finds doubtless demonstrating the performance of a variety of craft activities, mainly the production of beads in semiprecious stones, stone vases, and some form of metalworking. These finds were recovered from a variety of different contexts, including both secondary and tertiary deposits as defined in Chapter 1. Therefore the relationship between this assemblage and the ABC buildings is, for the most part, an indirect one. Nonetheless, it seems reasonable to assume that the deposits used to infill and level the destroyed architectural units to form a foundation for further rebuilding came form an area relatively close to the ABC buildings and could well have been procured without major excavations by mixing architectural debris from the reconstruction activity with materials taken from dumps that accumulated in the surrounding area during previous phases.

If this assumption is reasonable, we may consider this collection as a series of inclusions originally belonging to domestic and industrial trash piles, discarded (in broad sense) in the neighborhood of these buildings. It is highly probable that some social and economic relationship existed between people living in the ABC buildings and people moving and working in the immediately surrounding spaces and buildings. In this light, the minimal hypothesis we presently accept is that the assemblage is an indirect, scanty archaeological reflection of a series of activities somehow "attracted to", if not controlled, by the major buildings in the ABC area.

The limited size of the assemblage and the varied typology of the finds make any form of quantitative evaluation impossible. The objects are taken as simple evidence of consumption and production of goods in the various base materials present. It is evident even from this preliminary examination that a rich repertory of base materials were shipped across long-distance and within local exchange networks for consumption or transformation at Malyan. The diversity of finds within such a small assemblage also precludes any detailed analysis of manufacturing techniques. The discussion is presented in form of a catalogue of drawings and photographs with brief descriptions of individual items whenever needed. This brief contribution to the report on the excavation of the Banesh ABC complex is intended to integrate archaeological analysis with the limited but specific information provided by the assemblage, in the hope of contributing to our general understanding of the Banesh settlement of Tal-e Malyan.

In the following description, if not otherwise stated, the three consecutive measurements are in cm, and refer respectively to length, width, thickness of each find. In the case of beads and a few other finds, length refers to the length of the object as measured along the perforation axis, and the second measured dimension is the diameter. Color values, whenever possible, are given according the Munsell coding system. The mineralogical identification of the stone specimens in general is as described in Appendix A although the identification noted here departs from the original identification in several cases.

Bead Production

Rock Crystal and Rose Quartz

The specimens of rock crystal and rose quartz in the ABC assemblage are quite variable. Some crystal pieces (Fig. 37a, b) are unweathered fragments, probably "mined" and extracted from cavities in the mother rock, or coming from quartz geodes. Among the needle-like crystals some were previously reported to have

a rounded, worn point, suggesting they had been used as tools for some form of piercing or scraping (M. J. Blackman, personal communication). Examination of the present assemblage failed in revealing this type of feature. Other pieces were obviously collected in forms of stream pebbles. Some of these finds are chipped defective items (Fig. 37f) and one is a complete pebble-like lump still retaining its original crystal shape (Fig. 37l). Others are crystals that underwent a strong wind deflation process before being collected and shipped to Malyan (Fig. 37d, e).

This evidence shows that rock crystal and rose quartz were collected from at least three different types of geological settings, suggesting some form of unsystematic, expedient source exploitation. A single broken, possibly unfinished rock crystal bead (Fig. 37g) shows one of the possible end products manufactured from rock crystal for the Banesh settlement of Malyan. To shape such a hard stone into the thin bicone preforms needed for disk beads is not an easy task, and the investigation of this peculiar beadmaking technology would be a very interesting topic for future research.

Various Semi-precious Stones

This small group of lithics may be referred to the production of ornaments in various types of stone: calcite Fig 37n, w; clinoptilolite Fig. 37h, i, k; perhaps turquoise Fig. 37m, q; greyish agate Fig.37o; carnelian Fig. 37p, t and possibly some type of white, fine grained marble-like stone Fig. 37r, s. Needless to say, this evidence is so scanty that it hardly can be taken as a positive indication of craft production being carried out in situ at an appreciable scale. The chipping of an agate nodule usually results in a total loss of 85-90% of its weight, producing hundreds and hundreds of flakes in the same spot. Nonetheless, a defective unexhausted lump, a flake, and an unfinished ground bead blank suggest that some agate and carnelian beads were manufactured, perhaps episodically, not too far from the ABC buildings. This notion is supported by the presence of a chert drill (Fig. 35j) identical to those discovered at Shahdad in a specialized carnelian bead making context (Salvatori and Vidale 1982). An alternative explanation could be that small amounts of agate manufacturing debitage and unfinished items were stored in this area for further processing or recycling. Clinoptilolite disk beads were intensively produced within the TUV compound (Nicholas 1990; Blackman and Vidale n. d.), while in the ABC collection this type of manufacturing activity is documented by two unfinished cylindrical beads and two pieces of raw material (Fig. 37h, i, k). In terms of consumption and discard of small stone artifacts, the assemblages also includes limestone balls and spindle whorls (Fig. 43d).

Faience Beads

One micro-bead (mf 1287) from ABC is morphologically and technologically identical to "paste" specimens produced in Baluchistan (Mehrgarh) as early as ancient Chalcolithic times (Vidale 1990). Other beads, classified as "frit" (mf 598, 1306, 9952) may be made of similar material.

Beads Made of Organic Materials

The fragments of ostrich shell from Malyan appear unworked, and most probably originally belonged to eggs used as containers or curiosities (Fig. 38a, b). Fish vertebra beads are very peculiar ornaments, produced with a careful carving and painting technique; their original yellow and black color should have been very attractive (Fig 38c-e).

Bitumen seems to have been a widely exploited and processed material at Malyan. Among the finds on record are lumps with vegetal imprints from roofings or insulation plastering on walls. Other lumps in the assemblage show flat surfaces with sharp edges and represent perhaps small pre-forms imported for further processing. We might presume that the finest qualities of bitumen were employed for the production of the collection of beautiful black beads (Fig. 38f, i, l-q). Semi-finished bitumen objects and manufacturing debitage are not present in the collection, indicating that debitage was immediately recycled by remelting or that manufacturing was carried out somewhere else. The location and the role of pyrotechnology in the production of bitumen ornaments would reward further research.

Banded Travertine Vessels: Production and Recycling

The attractive, soft translucent stone used for the production of small vessels (Fig. 40e; 41a-c) is identified (personal communication, M. J. Blackman) as a variety of banded travertine, whose possible sources were located in rocky outcrops relatively close to the settlement. This type of industry seems to be similar to the alabaster industry so widespread at Shahr-i Sokhta, extensively studies by Ciarla (1979, 1985, 1990). The flakes represented in the assemblage doubtless refer to the preliminary stages of reduction, when the cortex surfaces had to be removed for a first, rough shaping of the preforms. Even in this case, we should take into account the considerations expressed for agate manufacturing—the amount of debitage is definitely too low to support the hypothesis of a meaningful local production. The collection also includes fragments of finished vessels; while some pieces could have been simply discarded in dumps and later incorporated in architectural filings, some pieces (usually thicker) have a regular squared contour that could suggest some form of reworking. Recycling of vessel walls for the manufacture of beads and a wide range of different objects has been well documented by Ciarla for the Shahr-i Sokhta alabaster industry (1979:330-331; 1985) as well as for the chlorite containers of Failaika (1990). In the ABC assemblage, the discovery of a travertine rim fragment with clear traces of grinding on a fracture surfaces shows the result of a failed attempt to shape the piece into a squared pre-form, possibly for a bead(Fig. 40c).

Specialized Stone Tools

The ABC assemblage produced one unusual tool (Fig. 42i) that is made of a very fine grained light brownish gray stone (2.5 Y 6/2). The tool has a triangular section with convex sides, and three major functional surfaces, all characterized by regular, convex contour. One of the faces shows a central depression, with a surface that is covered by an intentional pecking, to grant a better adherence of the tool in the hand of the craftsman. This tool was evidently intended to effect a fine smoothing on some material, most probably over curved (interior?) surfaces. Observation of the surfaces of the tool shows patterns of short, thin parallel wear marks, with an oblique orientation towards the main axis of the object. Possibly, tools of this type were used to smooth the interior of stone containers—but at present this observation is only conjecture. At any rate, this is a highly specialized tool, originally meant for a well defined use.

The slate tool (Fig. 42h) could have been used to pierce any type of soft material, and remains an isolated find of indeterminate function.

Proto-Elamite Glyptic Art from Operation ABC

Holly Pittman

One of the most important categories of finds from operation ABC is the glyptic art. In combination with other evidence, the glyptic allows consideration of such questions as the function of the ABC buildings, their chronological position relative to the sites of Susa, Tepe Yahya and Shahr-i Sokhta, and their function relative to the contemporary building in operation TUV. The ABC glyptic assemblage, including both cylinder seals and impressions, is worthy of study in its own right because of its extremely high quality, which expands our understanding of Proto-Elamite style, iconography, and sealing practice.

Description

Building Levels 5 and 4

Building Level 5 and the construction stratum between BL 5 and BL 4 (Stratum 12) yielded one conical jar stopper and more than 17 fragments of mud sealings, all without seal impressions. This represents the earliest evidence of sealing practice at Malyan. Jar stoppers continue to be found in Building Level 4 (Fig, 42b). It is significant to note that such conical jar stoppers do not occur in later levels. This is consistent with the change of sealing practice as it is known at Susa in the Acropole sounding and it correlates, as we will see, with a change in glyptic style.

Two seals (Fig. 44a, b) were found in the bricky construction fill (DC 35) of Building Level 4 together with a small number of fragmentary impressions of different seals. It is assumed that finds recovered from these tertiary deposits belong to a time that predates the construction of BL 4 although it is possible that some of these finds were incorporated in the bricky fill at the time the building was razed and may relate to activities contemporary with the occupation of BL 4. The imagery of the glyptic from BL 4 is entirely consistent with a dating equivalent to the period of the gap in the Acropole sounding at Susa, which has been designated as Level 17X (Dittmann 1986b) or Level 17A (Le Brun 1971).

Building Level 3 and Stratum 9

Stratum 9, between ABC Building Levels 2 and 3, was composed of bricky material and Building Level 3 wall painting fragments. It derives from the destruction of BL 3 to provide the level surface on which BL 2 was built. Within this jumble of building debris, but always below the earliest BL 2 floors, were two closely related concentrations of detritus (Str. 9, and 10A, DC 23) from administrative operations including six clay tablet fragments and more than 170 clay sealing fragments. Virtually all of the clay sealing fragments found in these clusters were large pieces of sealings used to secure large-mouthed storage jars. Most of them had been covered over with a rough fabric or with animal skin tied under the rim with rope, the knot of which was sealed with a clay seal-impressed sealing. The excavated rooms in BL 3 produced very few storage jar sherds, and no storage installations such as those in Room 71 of BL 2, with the implication that the sealings in these clusters were the result of storage activities nearby, but not in the excavated BL 3 rooms. On the floors of BL 3 were found twelve tablet fragments including one with a seal impression (Fig. 44c) and one clay sealing without impressions (mf 1973).

The assemblage from BL 3 and Stratum 9 includes a total of twenty-four individual images, of which eight can be fully reconstructed. Stylistically and iconographically they are closely related to glyptic images from levels 16 through 14B in the Acropole sounding at Susa and can be securely dated to that chronological range.

Building Level 2

The upper floor and the surface of Platform 27 (Stratum 8B, DC 21, 28, 37) of Building Level 2 produced an assemblage that includes eight sealing fragments impressed with four different designs (mf 637.3, Cat. 33; mf 637.2, Cat. 34; mf 637.1, Cat. 35; mf 636, Cat. 36; Cat. numbers are listed in the Stp column of the Register, Appendix A). In addition, eight tablet fragments were found, two of which bear seal impressions (mf 623, Cat. 37, Fig. 44g; mf 633, Cat. 38). The lower floor of BL 2 (Stratum 8D, DC 29) produced 36 sealings (mf 1969, Cat. 9; mf 1949, Cat. 10).

The presence of tablets and sealings supports the interpretation of BL 2 as a warehouse in which goods were stored under some form of administrative authority. The exact nature of this authority—whether personal, kinship based, secular, or religious—is not known.

Iconographically and stylistically the glyptic images from BL 2 are closely related to those from BL 3 and Stratum 9. They belong to the same time range, equivalent to Susa, Acropole 16-14B. Nothing in the glyptic suggests that the occupation at ABC continued into the late Proto-Elamite phase, contemporary with levels 14A and 13 in the Acropole sounding and to levels 18-13 in Ville Royale at Susa. The glyptic evidence suggests that ABC Building Levels 3 and 2 are essentially contemporary with Building Level 3 in operation TUV. Such a correlation is, of course approximate, but judging from the glyptic, the occupation at TUV continued into a period somewhat later than ABC, equivalent to the late Proto-Elamite phase known at Susa in the Ville Royale and level 14a and 13 of the Acropole sounding.

Stylistic and Iconographic Discussion

Our understanding of the Proto-Elamite style has been established through the assemblage of more than 400 images retrieved by the French through excavations at Susa. The chronological development of that large group was confirmed by the controlled excavations in the Acropole (Le Brun 1971). There are three basic phases in the Proto-Elamite development, which Dittmann (1986a; 1986b) has termed early, middle and late, a periodization that works well for the glyptic. The early and middle phases are represented at Malyan in operation ABC.

The images from Building Level 4 are typical of the early phase of the Proto-Elamite glyptic style. (Fig. 44a, b). Characteristic is the narrow iconographic range consisting almost exclusively of rows of horned animals, usually caprids, either alone or with certain symbols. As at Godin and Susa, these early images have stylistic features that become more pronounced in the middle Proto-Elamite phase such as the emphasis on landscape elements, the compact proportions of the animal bodies, and the "lively" appearance of the animals in comparison with the contemporary ones in southern Mesopotamia.

The assemblage of glyptic art from Building Levels 3 and 2, belongs to the middle phase. As known from Susa, there are four different style types in this phase: the glazed steatite or piedmont style; the wheelcut style; the incised style; and the classic style. At other installations where the glyptic art of the Proto-Elamite period has been found—TUV at Malyan, the Susa Acropole, at Tepe Yahya, and at Shahr-i Sokhta—

the entire range of style types is always represented. However, at ABC the assemblage is unusually coherent stylistically. This is a feature that is certainly a reflection of the special character of the installation. All of the glyptic images from ABC, with one exception, are fine examples of the "classic" style type. The one exception is a wheelcut rendering of a file of scorpions (Fig. 44 d). Such a homogeneous assemblage reinforces the idea that seals with certain types of imagery, defined through both iconographic and stylistic traits, were used in the proto-literate period under certain circumstances. We see this functional differentiation when we examine the other style groups and it is particularly true of the glazed steatite style, which is only used for storage.

The term "classic" was first applied to a certain style of glyptic from Susa by Pierre Amiet (1972:133). Unlike the other style types which consist predominantly of abstract design elements, the classic style uses figural imagery. Although there is a range, the three most commonly used images are lions, bulls and caprids. The basic stylistic feature is the use of flat planes for body masses that are articulated through linear rather than modeled differentiation.

The theme of animals acting as humans is the most distinctive theme in Proto-Elamite art. Among the ABC glyptic six examples of this theme were found. One shows a caprid acting as a scribe (Fig. 44f) a role that at Susa is assumed by a bull. In Building Level II, a theme well known at Susa was found impressed on a fragment of a large tablet. It shows a lion and the bull standing with limbs together in positions of power or reverence (Fig. 44g).

Among the classic Proto-Elamite images from ABC are examples identical to ones known from Susa such as the bull rampant away from a plant (Fig. 44e) and ones such as the whorl of lion heads that is without parallel at Susa (Fig. 44h). There is a considerable range both within the style and the iconography of the classic style. Analysis of the Malyan glyptic has shown that although there are features unique to Malyan, we cannot be confident that they define a regional variant. It is certainly possible that they are inherent in the range of the classic style and there is nothing in the Malyan glyptic assemblage that one might argue could not occur at Susa.

The function of the glyptic at ABC is predominantly sealings for large jars that were covered with coarse fabric. One complete and four fragments of tablets were seal impressed and a few door and small jar sealings can be identified among the sealing types. There is no functional or stylistic indication that any of the seals or sealings found at ABC were brought in from the outside.

V

Anshan in the Proto-Elamite Era

Two great cycles of sedentary population growth and decline are apparent in the archaeological record of Fars (Sumner 1990a, 1990b, de Miroschedji 2003, and Wilkinson 2003). Proto-Elamite civilization appeared at the end of the first cycle (Abdi 2003) and the Achaemenid Empire was founded at the end of the second (Sumner 1994b).

The first cycle began with the establishment of small agricultural villages early in the sixth millennium B.C., followed by a long period of population growth and settlement expansion culminating in the Bakun cultural florescence. Bakun ceramics, found throughout the southern Zagros as far east as Iblis (Caldwell 1968) and as far south as Yahya (Beale 1986a), define a coherent stylistic province within the larger Ubaid *oikoumene* proposed by Braidwood and Howe (1962; see also Dyson 1965), and later refined by Caldwell (1968). Bakun stylistic unity is evidence for an intensity of communications within the region that implies an unprecedented level of economic, social, and perhaps political integration. Evidence for productive specialization, a two level settlement hierarchy, and the development of a simple system of administrative control using stamp seals, all coincide with the apex of Bakun population late in the fifth millennium (Alizadeh 1988a, 1988b, 1994). Bakun prosperity, based in large part on irrigation agriculture, could not be sustained. After a thousand years of expansion and intensive exploitation the fields irrigated by Kur River system perhaps lost fertility due to excessive irrigation and ineffective drainage, which raised the water table and produced soil salinity (Sumner 1994a).

Bakun painted ceramics disappeared around the turn of the fifth millennium and were replaced by a plain red pottery designated Lapui ware. Shifts in the location of some Lapui settlements away from the irrigated heartland of the valley (Sumner 1988b) imply that the initial response to decreasing productivity of field crops was a shift to greater reliance on animal husbandry. We have no excavated evidence pertaining to topics such as Lapui social differentiation, administrative control, or productive specialization, but survey data demonstrate a precipitous decline in sedentary population. This population collapse began after the Middle Bakun Stage when there were 85 settlements (99 ha) in the valley (Sumner 1994a). By the end of the Bakun period, represented by sites with both Bakun and Lapui components, there were still 65 settlements (62 ha) in the valley. Late in the Lapui period, represented by sites with both Lapui and Banesh components, only 18 villages (19 ha) were left on the plain and all evidence of a settlement hierarchy had disappeared. These settlements were clustered around natural marshy pastures or along the spring-watered margins of the valley (Sumner 1988b), while the formerly fertile central district, irrigated by the Kur River during Bakun times, was virtually deserted.

The explanation outlined here for this sedentary population collapse, discussed in more detail elsewhere (Sumner 1988b and 1994a), addresses only a narrow range of proximate economic causes in what must have been a complex evolutionary and historical process involving many interrelated factors. The virtually simultaneous population decline in Luristan (Henrickson, E. 1985 and 1994), Deh Luran, Susiana (Hole 1987:85; Neely and Wright 1994:211-214, Figure VI.1, Kouchoukos and Hole 2003), the Susiana hinterlands (Wright 1987), the Bakhtiari highlands (Zagarell

1982:65), Fasa and Darab, (de Miroschedji 1973), and in districts around Tepe Yahya (Prickett 1986:237), suggests the importance of general processes that must transcend local environmental and cultural variation across these regions. Although it is probable that underlying systemic problems associated with agricultural production during the first cycle of population expansion in western Iran will be identified eventually in all of these regions, it is also probable that climatic change played a role in the evolving economic and demographic patterns (Henrickson, E. 1985:40-41). At present the unresolved difficulties of correlating the sequence of climatic change with the archaeological sequence make the role of climatic variation in Fars problematic (Hole 1994).

As sedentary population in the KRB approached its lowest ebb in late Lapui times, between 3500 and 3400 B.C., the scene was set for the appearance of Early Banesh culture, the first stage of Proto-Elamite civilization in Fars.

Banesh Culture and Proto-Elamite Civilization in the KRB

The transition from Lapui to Initial and then Early Banesh ceramics evident in the sounding at Tal-e Kureh (Alden, Appendix D) carries the implication that cultural continuity, so characteristic of earlier times in the valley, continued right up to the threshold of Proto-Elamite civilization in the Early Banesh Period. There is great stylistic unity between ceramic and other finds of the Early Banesh Period and those of the Middle Period, when the earliest known tablets in the KRB appeared. These texts have both numerical and ideographic signs. However, the presence of an earlier phase with sealed numerical tablets, but without ideographic signs, cannot be ruled out. This unified Banesh culture was the economic and political context in which Proto-Elamite administrative technology, including writing, either evolved locally or was introduced from outside. If the presence of this administrative technology, and all that it implies, over a great territory extending from Susa in the west to Shahr-e Sokhte (Amiet and Tosi 1978) in the east and from Hissar (Dyson 1987) in the north to Yahya (Lamberg-Kalovsky 1971) in the south justifies the appellation "Proto-Elamite Civilization," then at least in Fars one must seek the seeds of this civilization no later than the early Banesh Period and perhaps much earlier.

Early Banesh Settlement, Population, and Economy

The most notable characteristic of the Early Banesh Phase is the small number and unusual location of settlements. Only 36 sites with a total area of 52.6 ha (Appendix E, Table E1) are assigned to this phase, including Tal-e Qarib as discussed below. The estimated sedentary population of the valley would have been between 5,300 and 10,600 using 100 and 200 people/ha as lower and upper conversion factors (see Appendix E for details). The decline in sedentary population, beginning in late Bakun times accelerated in the Lapui Phase, and continued in the Early Banesh Phase.

Some of the Early Phase sites, scattered around the edges of the valley or located near rocky ridges rising from the valley floor, had ready access to spring water flowing from the foot of the mountains. These villages most likely subsisted on the produce of irrigated and dry farmed fields as well as animal husbandry. There is also evidence for pastoral nomads, specialized centers of craft production, including ceramics (Appendix E, Table E 2), and distribution centers.

A cluster of sites extending for more than 10 km along the southern slope of Kuh-i Kuruni (Fig. 2, centered in grid square 63N-84E), includes a number of unmounded or very low sites situated on the rocky talus slope, shielded from the winter north winds and warmed by the winter sun. This is the region of the valley most commonly used in recent times as the site of winter camps, including rectangular stone tentstands occupied by pastoral nomads. The presence of similar rectangular stone alignments of undetermined date and the presence of Banesh sherds as the major surface component on some of these sites raises the possibility that the region was also used by nomadic peoples engaged in specialized animal husbandry in Banesh times.

There is also a cluster of 6 sites, collectively referred to here as Tal-e Qarib (Appendix E; Fig. 2, grid square 62N-84E), situated almost exactly in the center of the northwest quadrant of the valley, not far from the geographical center of the Early Banesh population (Alden 1982a:98). The population of Qarib is estimated to have been between 700 and 1,400. Although bounded on the west by a marshy area, no ready source of irrigation water was available closer than several springs about 10 km to the north. It is probable that these villages engaged in dry farming and animal husbandry but survey evidence (Alden 1979, Sumner

1972a) also indicates that craft production and distribution were important activities.

Alden discovered evidence of stone and plaster vessel production or distribution at Tal-e Qarib. Three materials were represented: banded travertine, grainy limestone, and a fine white material originally classified as soft limestone. Vessels made of a similar soft white material excavated at Malyan and analyzed by James Blackman (1982) proved to be made of burnt lime plaster; subsequent examination of samples from the Tal-e Qarib surface collection shows that they were made of the same material. The interpretation of these plaster vessels as indicative of a production site is supported both by the fragility of the plaster, indicating import from a distance was unlikely, and by the fact that many examples were broken during production, as shown by the presence of chisel marks on the surface of some fragments. These plaster vessels, quite striking in profile, were often decorated with colored paste or inlay (Alden 1979, Fig. 55). It is important to note, however, that the plaster vessels from Middle Banesh levels at Malyan (Figs. 40i, j, k; 41d-f) are different from the Qarib vessels in both profile and decorative technique.

There is no evidence that the banded travertine and grainy limestone vessels were produced at Qarib, but the very high frequency of finds from Qarib (383 total, 280 from a single collection unit), as compared to the sum (20) from all other Banesh surface collections at sites visited by Alden (1979:114), indicates the presence of a stone bowl market or trans-shipment point. In reaching this conclusion Alden (1979:115) noted the absence of raw materials and partly finished vessels that might indicate a workshop and the absence of restorable vessels that might suggest a ploughed up burial. The Qarib surface collection also includes a grooved hammerstone, a well-made pestle, a stone spindle whorl, a whetstone, and a frit (?) 6 hole spacer bead (Alden 1979, Fig. 57). No other Banesh site produced such a diverse surface collection, which may be a further indication of the status of Qarib as a distribution center. However, Alden (1979:199) observed that the site had been plowed for the first time in many years just before his visit and he attributes the richness of the surface assemblage at least in part to this circumstance.

Another mound in the Tal-e Qarib cluster produced a huge ceramic dump—7000 m^2—with an extraordinarily high density of straw tempered sherds—17 kg/m^2 (Alden 1979). This dump is clearly associated with the production of straight sided straw tempered goblets (Fig. 22r, u, y; Pl. 15), one variant of the most characteristic Banesh vessel form. The goblets are wheel thrown, as indicated by interior markings and string cut bases, and were no doubt produced by professional potters.

Finally, there are 6 sites with evidence of grit tempered pottery production and 3 with evidence of straw tempered pottery production that were occupied in the Early Banesh period, although they may not all have been engaged in production at that time. Alden (1982a) has demonstrated that Tal-e Qarib was a distribution center for grit tempered pinched rim bowls (Fig. D5:28, 29) produced at Tal-e Kureh. He argues further that the frequency pattern justifies the identification of Qarib as a market, a conclusion that is best summarized in his words:

> The normal distribution (lack of multimodality) of pinch length and pinch thickness indicates that the pinched-rim bowls were made at a single site by a single school of potters. The difference in means between exported bowls and those found on the production site implies that the bowls were selected for export on stylistic and functional criteria by a small group of distributors. The frequency of the bowls in the 100% surface collection units implies that consumers acquired their bowls from the cluster of sites around 8G38. Covariation of surface frequency with distance from this group of sites indicates that the distance component of distribution cost was significant, and it hints at a market rather than a managed allocation system for the distribution of grit-tempered ceramics. Although ceramics were certainly manufactured on a small scale at many of the Early Banesh sites in the region, the indirect distribution system clearly filled an important portion of most sites' demand for pottery. (Alden 1982a:100) (*note*: site 8G38 is the main mound in the cluster referred to here as "Tal-e Qarib")

Blackman (1981) has demonstrated that the Middle Banesh grit tempered wares excavated at Malyan were usually produced using low carbonate clay sources, clearly distinct from the alluvial clays available from the valley floor, which were only suitable for the low fired straw tempered wares. He suggests that grit tempered production sites, which were located near the mountains, were so located to take advantage of clay deposits in shale beds above the talus slopes and fuel from the wooded hillsides. The same reasoning explains the location of Early

Banesh grit tempered production sites such as Tal-e Kureh.

In summary, the Early Banesh settlement system was composed of at least 29 small villages engaged in mixed farming, probably with some emphasis on sheep and goat herding. This rural sedentary population, and probably a much larger population of nomadic herdsmen, was served by a small distribution center, possibly a market town, located at Tal-e Qarib. The Qarib craftsmen produced utilitarian vessels in clay and fine decorated plaster vessels. Qarib was a center or market for the distribution of these products as well as pottery produced by craftsmen elsewhere in the valley and stone vessels imported from an unknown source. It is not unreasonable to speculate that metal objects and stone or shell beads may have been produced or stocked and distributed from Qarib although no direct evidence of this possibility is available at present.

The Early Banesh political system may have been quite small in scale, based on a segmentary kinship system. However, if Fars was already inhabited by a large nomadic population engaged in animal husbandry (Sumner 1988b, 1994a), a more complex system would have been necessary to mediate competition between the sedentary and nomadic elements of the population, each with its own distinctive mode of subsistence production. Such a system could have evolved locally out of economic and political competition among different sections of a segmentary system. If the preceding Lapui polity was composed of loosely allied simple chiefdoms supported by surplus production of staple commodities—grain and animals or animal products—then Early Banesh may represent the shift from staple finance to wealth finance (Stein, G. 1994:40, with references). Thus the appearance of specialized craft production and a central distribution center at Qarib, economically rationalized in terms of savings in production and transport costs (Alden 1982a), creates increased economic interdependence and hence the need for greater political integration, the first steps toward the foundation of a Proto-Elamite polity.

Middle Banesh Settlement and Population

The Middle Banesh settlement system consists of Malyan, with an estimated population between 4,000 and 16,000, Qarib with an estimated population between 700 and 1,400 and 26 villages with an estimated aggregate population between 3,400 and 6,800 (for discussion of these estimates see Appendix E). The total population of the valley might have fallen anywhere within the range between 8,000 and 24,000, but probably was not much greater than 14,000. At this time the long decline in sedentary population that began late in the Bakun period, nearly a thousand years earlier, is finally reversed.

This demographic recovery was manifested in the urban population of Malyan, which sheltered approximately half of the sedentary population of the valley. Although the rural village population, including Qarib, declined between Early and Middle Banesh, this decline in village population was not enough to explain the growth of Malyan as entirely the result of village population migrating into the city. The estimated area of rural settlements in Middle Banesh, including Qarib, is 12.1 ha less than the estimate for Early Banesh, representing a population of only some 1,200 to 2,400 countrymen who could have moved to Malyan. The remaining 2,800 to 13,600 souls required to populate Malyan are still to be accounted for. They could come from natural population growth within the valley, they could be prosperous nomads settling down to convert wealth into land or other property (Barth 1961:101-111), or they could be immigrants from another region.

It has been assumed that average population growth rates in ancient societies would not have exceeded 0.1% per year (Carneiro and Hulse 1966; Hassan 1981), but estimated growth rates in prehistoric Fars suggest periods of relatively rapid growth—as great as 0.4% per year—with population doubling every 175 years (Sumner 1990b). If we assume that the estimated minimum Early Banesh population—5,300—was established by 3550 B.C. and doubled to 10,600 by 3200 B.C., the annual rate of growth would have been 0.2%, which is within reason for a few generations. A more radical assumption would be that the minimal Early Banesh population doubled twice, to 21,200, which is somewhat less than the maximum estimate of 24,000 for Middle Banesh. For this increase to take place in 350 years would require a growth rate of 0.4%. This is rapid growth by prehistoric standards, but still possible without immigration for a limited time under favorable local circumstances. These estimated demographic parameters neither require nor eliminate the possibility of nomads becoming sedentary or immigrants arriving from outside the valley.

The theory that a substantial nomadic population engaged in animal husbandry existed in Fars at this time is not inherently unlikely, but rests entirely on circumstantial evidence (Sumner 1986). It has been argued that the prehistory of pastoral nomadic life in Fars began as early as the Bakun period (Alizadeh 1988a, 1988b, 1994; Sumner 1988b, 1994a) and continued to be a factor in the economic and political life of the region up until the present. The notion that some of these nomads settled in the valley, possibly at Malyan, in Middle Banesh times is certainly a plausible conjecture.

Immigration of small groups of people from Susiana to Fars in the Banesh period has been suggested by Alden (1982b:620, 1987:161). Lamberg-Karlovsky (1986:197; see also 1978:116; 1989; 1996:112-113) puts it this way: "within a century of 3000 B.C the sites of Tepe Sialk, (Period IV), Tal-I Malian (Banesh Period), and Tepe Yahya (Period IVC), all in distant regions of the Iranian Plateau, are colonized by Proto-Elamites from Susiana."

Whether or not immigration or colonization, as opposed to the diffusion of ideas and techniques, was a significant factor in the arrival of Proto-Elamite administrative technology—tokens, Proto-Elamite writing, and sealing practices—in Fars and beyond is still an open question. However, present evidence suggests that these administrative tools may have originated at Susa, where it is claimed earlier developments can be traced (Amiet 1979a, 1979b, 1986, 1993; Le Brun and Vallat 1978; Pittman 1997; T. Potts 1994:74; Stolper 1985; Vallat 1986). However the critical transition—if indeed "transition" is the correct concept—from the numerical tablets found in Susa II (Acropole I, 18, 17) and the fully evolved Proto-Elamite texts from Susa III (Acropole I, 16-14A) is not known from any stratigraphic context. The nature and duration of the stratigraphic break between Acropole I, level 17 and level 16 is not known, so we can only speculate on the changes that might have occurred between Susa II and III. This statement is not inconsistent with the notion, expressed by various scholars, that the center of Proto-Elamite power and its associated purely Iranian culture was located in Fars. A telling statement of this view comes from Amiet (1993:25): "Above all Susa was annexed by a new cultural and probably historical entity which grew up around the city of Anshan, which was founded at this time (Susa III) in present Fars. This entity, certainly highland in origin, expressed itself in an original writing system used for a non-Sumerian language that we describe as Proto-Elamite."

Middle Banesh Economy and Society

Although we have more information on social and economic conditions during the Middle Banesh Phase at Malyan than for either the Early or the Late Banesh Phase, it must be emphasized that the excavated sample is extremely small and certainly biased. Seven building levels were excavated in two operations—TUV (Nicholas 1990: 22, 29, 34) and ABC—with an aggregate area of less than 2,000 square meters, excluding TUV BL 1, which is assigned to Late Banesh. These excavations represent considerably less than 0.5% of 40 ha, the minimal estimated area of the Middle Banesh city. Furthermore, these buildings, located in only two quarters of the city, do not represent five different contemporaneous locations. The following description is presented without further expression of reservations raised by the minimal nature of the excavated sample.

Food preparation and consumption is clearly the major activity conducted in the northwest rooms of TUV BL 2. These rooms contained several hearths, built-in storage jars, milling stones, low storage bins, and a high concentration of animal bones. A number of other rooms in both TUV and ABC are equipped with hearths or domed ovens, possibly used for food preparation, but none of these rooms have a complete range of kitchen equipment. One oven in ABC BL 4 may have been a commercial or communal bread oven.

Sheep and goats dominate the faunal assemblage at both TUV and ABC (Zeder 1984, 1988, 1991). The TUV assemblage, as compared to ABC, has a broader range in the age of butchering and a slightly greater proportion of low meat-bearing body parts. This pattern suggests that animals were sometimes procured directly from herders at TUV and that decisions on the age of butchering were closely related to optimal herd management rather than maximum energy return. However, the secular trend at TUV is toward a narrower range of species, increased proportion of sheep, and a more restricted range in butchering age. Thus the trend at TUV and the characteristic pattern at ABC suggest the introduction of an indirect meat procurement system, and perhaps a shift in herd management toward maximum energy return strategies. Cattle and domestic ass (Zeder 1986) are minor elements in both faunal assemblages, but pigs are found only at TUV and gazelle are found only at ABC.

Carbonized seeds were, for the most part, introduced into the archaeological record as the result of using animal dung for fuel (Miller 1982, 1984a, 1984b; Miller and Smart 1984). The herds grazed in pastures characterized by sedges, grasses, and weedy legumes and on wheat and barley stubble fields.

There is considerable evidence in Middle Banesh deposits for a variety of craft activities. The raw materials used in craft production were procured in the immediate vicinity, from other regions in Fars (bitumen), and from sources as distant as the peripheries of the Iranian desert (native copper or ore), the Persian Gulf (shell), Afghanistan (lapis lazuli), eastern Anatolia, and Caucasia (obsidian)(Fig. 1). The most striking pattern to emerge from analysis of this data is the observation that nearly every secondary excavated context, a reliable indicator of local activities, at TUV and ABC produced evidence for a variety of production activities in the form of unworked or partially worked raw materials, production debris, and tools. The expectation that specialized craft production would be spatially localized and that different crafts would be segregated is not confirmed by the data, suggesting that craft production was not highly organized or centrally administered.

The strongest evidence for metallurgy comes from TUV, Levels 2 and 3, in the form of slag, furnace wall fragments, and copper prills, but similar finds are recorded from many contexts at ABC. Although evidence of coppersmithing is less likely to occur in archaeological deposits because copper can be recycled easily, small fragments of copper bar stock and sheet metal were found at TUV and ABC. It is probable that the Malyan smiths used arsenical copper ores or partially refined copper from deposits at Anarak (Talmessi-Meskani) near Tepe Sialk on the edge of the Iranian desert (Fig. 1).

Shell work is also widespread in Middle Banesh levels at both TUV and ABC. The ABC BL 2 warehouse yielded hundreds of pieces of geometric shell inlay. There is no evidence that these finds represent an inlay-decorated artifact, rather, they appear to be pieces of inlay produced and stored for future work. The same building also produced a cache of *Dentalium* shells, no doubt intended for bead production. At TUV there is considerable evidence for small scale shell working to produce both beads and inlay.

The production of beads from a variety of materials is indicated for several contexts at ABC. Isolated finds of gold, steatite, *Dentalium*, marble, bitumen, bone, and stone beads, together with unworked bitumen, *Dentalium*, cone shell, and partially worked carnelian do not prove production but are strongly sug-

gestive. The production of clinoptilolite (MAT 127 V 2; a variety of zeolite) beads is unequivocally established for TUV BL 3 by the recovery of both raw material and partially drilled beads (Blackman and Vidale, n.d.). Even more tantalizing is the presence of a few lapis lazuli and turquoise beads and unworked specimens of both minerals.

The most ubiquitous of all craft activities, flint knapping, is not considered to be a specialized craft. Evidence in the form of cores, debitage, finished blades, and tools is found throughout Banesh deposits. The reduction sequence study conducted by Kardulias (Chapter 4) suggests that early stages of core preparation were not often executed at ABC. This may be interpreted as an indication of some level of specialization in the procurement and distribution of lithic raw materials. However, it may just as easily be the result of unspecialized individuals on periodic flint gathering expeditions checking the quality and reducing the weight of flint before it is carried back to Malyan for later tool production.

The TUV flint assemblage has not been studied intensively, but the proportion of finds assigned to flint production (Class 1) and cutting tools (Class 13) is practically identical to the proportions at ABC. At TUV miscellaneous tools (Class 14) are more common than at ABC and piercing or boring tools (Class 15) are less common (Table 14). This comparison suggests that flint knapping activities were similar at TUV and ABC.

In addition to local cherts and jaspers from stream beds and outcrops in the valley, a fine translucent tan chert was also used and must have come from outcrop deposits probably located south of the valley (Blackman, p. c.). Long range trade in obsidian is also attested in Middle Banesh levels. Blackman's (1984) analysis of Banesh obsidian demonstrates that Nemrut Dağ I supplied 83% of all analyzed obsidian found in Banesh contexts (ABC, TUV). Two Banesh samples came from an unidentified source (Blackman Group E or Zarnaki Tepe which is the same as Renfrew's Group 3a; Blackman p.c.) that is probably north of Lake Van. One Banesh sample found at TUV came from a source some 100 km NW of Nemrut Dağ that is now identified as Bidgol B (Blackman Group D which is the same as Renfrew's Group 1g; Blackman p.c.). Bidgol B is the only source identified for obsidian from Yahya VA-IVB.

These observed patterns lead Blackman (1984: 36-38) to argue that Middle Banesh Malyan received most of its obsidian along a route essentially the same as the "Zagros Interaction Zone" running west of the

Zagros as proposed by Renfrew and Dixon (1976) for earlier Deh Luran sites. Yahya, on the other hand, would have been supplied with obsidian from the Bidgol B source along a route passing through the region of Lake Urmia, where obsidian from this source is common (Renfrew and Dixon 1976), and then along the eastern foothills and through the valley systems of the southern Zagros to Malyan and Yahya.

Little or no evidence was recovered from Malyan Banesh levels indicating local pottery production. The production of straw tempered ware may have continued at Tal-e Qarib but such production may also have taken place outside the excavated limits at Malyan. Blackman's (1981) analysis of the clays used for grit tempered wares shows that at least two clay sources were in use throughout the Middle Banesh Phase. It is unlikely that grit-tempered ware was produced at Malyan because suitable clays were not available. Six of the known grit tempered ceramic production villages (Appendix E, Table E2) were still occupied in Middle Banesh times; they probably produced grit-tempered pottery that was distributed throughout the valley. Present evidence does not allow us to determine if the distribution center for this pottery remained at Qarib, was shared with Malyan, or shifted to Malyan. Furthermore, we cannot determine if the same kind of marketplace continued to function after the Early Banesh Phase.

There is no evidence that plaster vessels were produced at Malyan and this too may have continued to be a craft activity centered at Tal-e Qarib although no examples of the incised and painted Malyan Middle Banesh plaster vessels were found at Qarib. Blackman (1982) has demonstrated that burned lime was also used in wall plaster, both for ordinary walls and for decorated walls, best represented by ABC BL 3, but also known in other levels at ABC and TUV. Lime burning was a seasonal activity conducted near the source of limestone in the summer, probably by part time specialists. Normally small-scale production would meet the demand for wall plaster and plaster vessels. However, a major project such as the construction of ABC BL 3 would require some four to eight thousand kilograms of lime, according to Blackman's calculations. Since lime deteriorates and cannot be stockpiled over several seasons, an unusually high demand could very well disrupt the normal patterns of production and distribution. Blackman suggests that such unusual demand might require administrative authority to shift the effort of potters, or other craftsmen with the requisite technical knowledge, away from their normal activities to lime burning. Simple market forces might also accomplish the necessary adjustment in production without administrative intervention.

There are a number of artifacts in the Middle Banesh assemblage that do not appear to have been produced within the excavated limits at Malyan, or at other production sites in the valley. Beyond a few stone cylinders that may have been seal blanks, there is no evidence of seal cutting. Although there may be a local style produced at Malyan, it appears possible that some of the seals were imported from Susa. Stone bowls made of banded travertine, marble, calcite, limestone, and chlorite, are relatively rare but nevertheless occur in practically all contexts. Unworked or partly worked pieces of calcite and limestone are also found but they were not necessarily used in stone bowl production; it is assumed at least some, and perhaps the bulk, of these vessels were imported.

Scattered evidence of spinning, weaving, basketry, and reed mat production is present in Middle Banesh levels but no production centers were located. There are also quantities of mineral raw materials such as specular hematite and bitumen, not specifically identified with any of the production activities just described, but no doubt used in production or trade.

Middle Banesh levels at Malyan have produced a significant corpus of Proto-Elamite tablets (Stolper 1976, 1984) and sealings, and a smaller collection of seal stones, bullae, small geometric objects (counters or sling missiles?), and potters marks. Proto-Elamite tablets were recovered from ABC BLs 4, 3, and 2 and from TUV BLs 3, and 2. The tablets occur in three size categories with either one inscribed line, 2 or 3 lines, or 5 to 10 lines. All of the tablets appear to have both numerical and ideographic signs although some of the smallest tablets appear to have only a single vertical stroke in addition to the numerical signs. The legible signs are comparable to signs in the Proto-Elamite A script from Susa and Yahya, confirming their identity as Proto-Elamite (Stolper 1976 and Damerow and Englund 1989).

The tablets often begin with one or two signs that function as a heading and may designate the administrative unit or corporate body controlling the recorded transaction (Damerow and Englund 1989:13–17, 61). One such sign is the "hairy triangle" found in the first or second position at Susa, Malyan, and Yahya. A variety of diacritical signs inserted inside the hairy triangle may be interpreted as indicative of smaller sub-units within a larger entity, suggesting a hierarchical administrative structure.

The heading is followed by one or more entries that may be only numerical notations or may be more complex entries that have signs to designate persons involved and commodities or objects counted, followed by numerical notations (Damerow and Englund 1989:13–17). One such sign, found at Susa, Malyan and Yahya, is a triangular grouping of impressions interpreted by Damerow and Englund (1989:61) as signifying a male slave or low ranked worker. Texts at Yahya are interpreted as recording the receipt of grain rations. Other examples may record the number of animals in the charge of individuals (Damerow and Englund 1989:54-57).

The Proto-Elamite numerical systems appear to be specialized for the different types of objects or commodities enumerated, much like the Archaic numbering systems in Mesopotamia (Damerow and Englund 1989:21-30). The summation of individual entries is the final entry on many tablets and the magnitude of these totals has been taken as an indication of the size and scope of the Proto-Elamite administrative system. At Yahya the texts are interpreted as recording agricultural transactions: lists of animals, tabulations of grain rations issued, and distribution of seed grain. "The level of these administrative notations, the size of the recorded numbers of animals and humans and the measures of grain, are without exception entirely within the range of expected *local* activity." (Damerow and Englund 1989:62). The preliminary study of Malyan texts finds totals somewhat greater then the totals from Yahya, but also certainly within the range expected for local agricultural or other administrative records. However it is interesting that the numbers on texts from ABC may be as large as 700 and even 1400 while the texts from TUV have much smaller numbers, up to no more than 153. In contrast to the small numbers recorded at Yahya and Malyan, the numbers from Susa range up to perhaps 20,000 animals and over 30,000 grain measures (Damerow and Englund 1989:63, note 171).

Proto-Elamite glyptic art from Malyan has been divided into four stylistic groups by Pittman (1997:7, 8). These groups, comparable to groups established by Amiet (1972) for glyptic art from Susa, include an early P-E style, represented by several examples from ABC BL 4A and BL 3B; a classic P-E style well represented at ABC BLs 2 and BL 3A, as well as TUV BLs 2 and 3. There is also a diverse group of schematic styles characterized by abstract patterns and several seal cutting techniques. All of the stylistic groups are usually represented in any context producing P-E sealings. Thus, the ABC buildings represent an unusual, if not unique context in which the classic Proto-Elamite style occurs in abundance with few examples of the other styles. The Malyan corpus finds close parallels in Susa Acropole I:16-14. Neither the earlier "craft activity" seals (Acropole I:17-18) nor the later "interlocking style" (Ville Royale 18B) are present in the Malyan corpus.

The Malyan seals were impressed on tablets, bullae, jar covers, door locks, and tags. Many of these items are not transportable, indicating that sealings were both affixed and broken open in most of the contexts in which they were found. This conclusion is reinforced by Blackman's (Zeder and Blackman 2003) demonstration that all sealing clays analyzed were from local alluvial sources. The sealing contexts include an elaborate building (ABC BL 3), a large warehouse (ABC BL 2), and buildings with evidence of both craft production and domestic activities (ABC BL 4, TUV BLs 2 and 3). Sealings from the first two contexts may represent record keeping and material processing on a non-domestic institutional level, whereas seals from the latter contexts should represent activities organized on a smaller domestic scale. None of these contexts necessarily imply administrative activities of such great complexity or large scale that they would be beyond the capacity of a lineage based tribal polity (Pittman 1994b).

To summarize, the evidence from Middle Banesh deposits indicates that Malyan was a small city inhabited by craftsmen, many of whom may have been part-time farmers or herdsmen. The storage and distribution of agricultural products, raw materials, and craft products was controlled and recorded using seals and Proto-Elamite tablets. Trade and craft production may have occurred in either household or more formal institutional contexts, possibly both, and the administrative control mentioned above would have been in the hands of representatives of kin based units or institutions organized on other principles, temples for example.

Production involved materials imported from both distant and regional sources and products were probably distributed (marketed?) at Malyan and Qarib. The level of craft production appears to have exceeded the needs of the small local sedentary population, which suggests that these products may have been distributed to a pastoral nomadic population for consumption or trade. The nomadic population could have acted as middlemen or simply as carriers in a trading network that may have extended to Mesopotamia in the west and the Indus valley in the east.

The role of trade in the Proto-Elamite world has been the subject of much debate (Alden 1982a, 1982b, 1987; Amiet 1979a, 1979b, 1986, 1993; Beale 1973:142-143; Lamberg-Karlovsky 1977, 1978; Pittman 1994b, 1997:17-18; D. Potts 1977; T. Potts 1994:80-85; Weiss and Young 1975). Beyond the sure knowledge that Proto-Elamite communities *imported* a variety of raw materials and perhaps some finished products from distances of well over 1000 kilometers, we have little knowledge of the nature, extent, or management of this trade.

It is generally agreed that the Proto-Elamite texts from Yahya deal with local agricultural production (Damerow and Englund 1989:62-64) and it seems likely that the Malyan texts serve much the same purpose. However, in texts from Susa we encounter records of animals and grain measures in the thousands in addition to work crews in the hundreds (Damerow and Englund 1989, note 171; Nissen, Damerow, and Englund 1993:75-79). It is difficult to reconcile these numbers with the exceptionally small sedentary population documented for Susiana at this time (Susa III) (Alden1982b: 618; 1987). The notion that some of these transactions are related to trade between Mesopotamia and Proto-Elamite pastoral nomadic tribesman is an interesting possibility. The addition of agricultural products, particularly animals, to discussions of trade between the highland Iran and Mesopotamia may answer some of the objections to Alden's description of Susa as a "port-of-trade" (Alden 1982b:624).

The Late Banesh Phase

The Malyan city wall, enclosing 200 hectares, was constructed during the Late Banesh Phase (Sumner 1985). The design of the wall, as revealed in operation BY8 and several non-archaeological cuts (Fig. 4) consists of an outer wall founded on large stone footers and at least two parallel inner walls. The innermost wall is reinforced by a solid brick packing 5 meters thick. The estimated volume of bricks to construct the wall would have required a labor force of some 1000 men working for about 140 days (Sumner 1985:159). There is also evidence that buildings were constructed along the inside of the wall. Very little additional excavated evidence is available on Late Banesh Malyan. There is no evidence of a Late Banesh Building at ABC. However, a small test excavation in operation H5, just north-west of ABC, produced Late Banesh deposits. In addition, TUV BL 1 may have also been occupied in Late Banesh times. Surface collections from the city wall are dominated by Late Banesh sherds and some late Banesh sherds appear in other surface collection units as well.

Despite the lack of excavated evidence, the great extent of the city wall, implying a large labor investment, strongly suggests that Malyan was a populous city for at least some time during the Late Banesh period and continued to be the center of administration and production in the valley. The rural population, located at Tal-e Qarib, by then reduced to a population of only 450 to 900, and 15 small villages, is estimated to have been between 3,200 and 6,400, down slightly from the Middle Banesh Phase.

The end of Proto-Elamite civilization, sudden and without warning, has been the subject of theoretical discussion (Alden 1982b; Amiet 1993:26; Lamberg-Karlovsky 1989:xi-xii; T. Potts 1994:85-86), but no detailed explanation, supported by archaeological data has been advanced.

The evolution of civilization in Central Fars during the succeeding centuries of the third millennium is obscure. There is some evidence that Malyan may have been inhabited by a small population but intensive survey has revealed no other sites for the time between the Late Banesh Phase and the appearance of the Kaftari culture at about 2200 B. C. We may assume that tribal polities, including both sedentary and nomadic elements, participated in developments leading to the foundation of the Simaski Dynasty as described by Stolper (1982; see also Henrickson, R. 1984). No doubt the powerful role played by Anshan (Tal-e Malyan) in subsequent Elamite history was based, at least in part, on the military strength of a large pastoral nomadic population.

Appendix A

Part I. Register of Finds

The register presents coded data on 1133 registration entries recording 2537 finds that were recovered during the excavation of the Operation ABC Banesh levels. Some of these items, found on the surface (DC 31), in backdirt (DC 39), or during cleaning operations (DC 41) have been assigned to the Banesh period on stylistic grounds (Lot Indicator B) and are included in the analysis. Other finds found out of context or in mixed lots that include both Kaftari and Banesh deposits are coded to indicate this status (Lot Indicator M). A number of flints from problematic contexts were analyzed by Kardulias before the stratigraphic analysis was completed for the Banesh levels reported here. These flints are listed in Table 25, but are not listed in this register. The abbreviated column headings used in the Register are as indicated in parentheses after the heading in the following sections.

Find (mf #)

This column records the Malyan five digit find number, abbreviated "mf," as assigned in the master register. This is a single series for all operations and all seasons; thus, each mf number was only used once. In some instances multiple finds from the same lot were originally registered in groups. In many cases these groups were later split and new mf numbers were assigned to the second, third, and fourth item in a group originally registered together. In other instances, particularly in the case of flints and lumps of clay with seal impressions, the distinctiveness of finds originally registered together was only recognized during analysis. In those instances the individual finds

were identified by adding a decimal number to the original registration number. The initial zeros in mf numbers are omitted in this monograph; thus mf 00025 is written here as mf 25.

Object (M #)

This column records the four digit Malyan object number, abbreviated "M," as assigned in the master register. Object numbers were only assigned to museum quality objects following criteria established by the representative of the Iranian Centre for Archaeological Research. Many finds assigned an mf number do not have an object number. Finds illustrated in the preliminary reports (Sumner 1792b, 1973, 1974, 1976) were identified by the object number (M #).

Operation (OP)

This column records the Operation designation: A, A1, B, B1, C, C1, ABCN, ABCS, or ABC, as described in Chapter I (Fig. 5).

Lot (LOT)

This column records the lot number, beginning with 000 (surface finds) and continuing in a separate series for each operation. Additional information on ceramic finds and animal bones recorded by lot number but not registered, is reported in the Lot Inventory (Appendix B).

Lot Indicator (LI)

This column records the Lot Indicator codes: M = vertically mixed; material in this lot may include material from more that one stratum. H = horizontally

Table A1
TYPE CODES

TYPE CODE		SUM	TYPE CODE		SUM
001	awl	2	046	stamp seal	0
002	ball	52	047	tablet	29
003	bead	138	048	tile	7
004	blade, flint	56	049	tool	24
005	boss	0	050	tube	2
006	bowl	2	051	vessel	38
008	brick	1	053	wheel	2
010	button	0	054	wire	0
011	cone	9	057	mineral sample	129
012	core, flint	10	058	plaster, wall/floor	2
013	cylinder	1	059	relief	13
014	cylinder seal	2	060	woven mat./textile	2
015	disc	5	061	needle	1
016	disc, perforated	3	062	sheet metal	4
017	door socket	1*	063	bar metal	17
018	figurine, animal	2	065	clay squeeze	1
019	figurine, human	3	069	knob	1
020	flakes & debitage	137	070	vessel leg	0
022	hand tool	8	071	potter's mark	2
024	hook	1	073	celt	1
025	inlay	983	074	misc. sample	83
031	loop	14	076	seeds	3
033	nail	1	077	charcoal	22
037	pin	4	079	carbonized sample	41
039	point	6	083	fossil	2
040	pot	3	088	shells	248
042	ring, small	7	091	pigment sample	15
043	sealing	364	094	soil sample	7
044	slag	15	095	botanical sample	2
045	spindle whorl	2	096	brick-phytolith sample	8

* = not registered

mixed; material in this lot comes from a single stratum but may be from more than one cultural feature (i.e., from different rooms). G = good context; material from this lot came from a single stratum in a single feature. In many cases specific finds from mixed lots (M or H) were assigned to the proper stratum and feature on the basis of information in the field notes, photographs, or sketch plans; in such cases those specific finds are assigned Lot Indicator G. B = stylistically Banesh; used for Banesh style finds from stratigraphically later contexts, from Kaftari-Banesh mixed lots, from the mound surface (DC 31), the excavation dump (DC 39), or found while cleaning an area previously excavated, usually at the beginning of a season or in preparation for record photographs (DC 41). K = intrusive Kaftari find, identified on stylistic criteria.

Feature Number (FT #)

This column records Feature Numbers, which constitute a single series used to record features in all ABC operations. Each Feature Number is used only once within the ABC operations reported here. The single series was first established in 1976. At that time each previously recorded feature that had been excavated in more than one operation and had been assigned several feature numbers, one for each operation in which the feature was excavated, was assigned a single number. The Lot Index (Appendix B) lists the Feature number for each Lot. Additional information on features is reported in Appendix C.

Feature (FEAT)

This column records a four letter designation for types of features: AREA (open space, character not identified), BNCH (bench), COUR (courtyard), CRDX (corridor), DBLK (blocked doorway), DOOR (door), HRTH (hearth), OVEN (oven), PITX (pit), PLAT (platform), PYTH (pythos), ROOM (room), WALL (wall). Features are described in Chapter I and listed in the Feature Inventory (Appendix C).

Building Level (BL)

This column records the Building Level as described in Chapter I.

Stratum (STR)

This column records the Stratum as described in Chapter I.

Deposit Code (DC)

This column records the Deposit Code as described in Chapter I (Table 1).

Class (CL)

This column records the following codes: Class—0 = finished artifacts, 1 = materials that show evidence of human workmanship, 2 = raw material, 3 = production by-products, 4 = carbonized botanical material, 5 = miscellaneous samples. These codes were assigned in the field by registrars as described in Chapter IV.

Type (TYP)

This column records Type codes as shown in Table A1.

Sub-Type (SBT)

This column records the sub-type for certain types of finds as follows:

The reduction sequence sub-types for flints or type of blade segment, as assigned by Kardulias in Chapter IV:

PDF = primary decortication flake
2DF = secondary decortication flake
2NCF = secondary non-decortication flake
3NCF = tertiary non-decortication flake
PBS = proximal blade segment
MBS = medial blade segment
DBS = distal blade segment

The motif and functional classification of cylinder seals Type 14, impressed sealings Type 43, or seal impressed tablets Type 47 are as assigned by Pittman (see Chapter IV) in her catalog of ABC glyptic. Some of these types are illustrated and discussed in Chapter IV and a full description of each type will be published in a separate monograph by Pittman. The letter following each catalog number is a preliminary classification of glyptic by function as follows: C = cylinder seal, D = door sealing, J = jar sealing, T = sealed tablet, W = wall sealing.

Material (MAT)

This column records the material for each find as shown in Table A-2.

Variety (V)

This column records the material variety as shown in Table A-2.

The material and variety coding system was designed by M. James Blackman. Material codes were first assigned by the Registrar in the field, often in consultation with Blackman or John Nickerson. Finds in the University of Pennsylvania collection were later checked for accuracy by Blackman. Other specialists have also contributed to the identification of materials, including E. Ehlers (minerals), Massimo Vidale (minerals), John Nickerson (minerals), David Reese (shells), and Vincent Pigott (metals, slag). Variety codes were assigned by Blackman or Nickerson or by the field registrars in consultation with Blackman. The variety codes for shell, which partly duplicate the original field MAT codes, were assigned by David Reese for all shells in the University of Pennsylvania collection.

Length (LN)

Width (WD)

Thickness (TK)

MAT	V		SUM
000	unknown or miscellaneous		2
100	known stone or mineral		55
101	quartz		3
	1	rock crystal	12
	2	amethyst	0
	3	rose quartz	0
	4	milky quartz	0
102	cryptocrystalline quartz		11
	1	flint	6
	2	chert	145
	3	jasper	44
	4	agate	0
	5	prase	10
	6	quartzite	0
	7	chalcedony	3
	8	sard (brown chalcedony)	0
	9	opal (opaline quartz)	0
103	carbonate rock		1
	1	travertine-banded marble	4
	2	green marble	1
	3	white marble	5
	4	calcite	18
	5	limestone (all types)	20
	6	dolomite	1
	7	red/pink marble	1
	8	magnesite	0
	9	aragonite	0
104	hematite		
	1	crystal (specular)	32
	2	earthy (red ochre)	3
	3	compact (red)	1
105	obsidian		13
106	turquoise		2
107	lapis lazuli		4
108	carnelian		4
109	malachite		0
110	talc rock		2
	1	talcose schist	0
	2	steatite	5
	3	hematic talc (red)	0
	4	grey talc	0
	5	pale green, pure talc	1
111	chlorite rock		1
	1	chlorite schist	0
	2	chlorite	0
112	serpentine		0
113	actinolite		0
114	gypsum		0
	1	selenite	0
	2	alabaster	0
115	pyrite		2
116	bitumen/asphalt		80

MAT	V		SUM
117	sandstone		1
	1	jasper sandstone	0
	2	hematitic sandstone	0
	3	limestone (sand-size particles)	0
118	conglomerate		0
	1	jasper conglomerate	0
	2	limestone conglomerate	0
	3	siliceous conglomerate	1
119	slate		2
120	siltstone		0
121	shale		0
122	claystone		0
	1	clay-ironstone concretion	0
123	igneous rocks		0
	1	acid igneous	0
	2	intermediate	0
	3	basic igneous	0
	4	basalt	0
124	limonite		1
	1	earthy limonite (yellow ochre)	0
125	azurite		2
126	native elements		0
	1	sulfur	0
127	zeolite/zeolite beating rock		1
	1	heulanite	0
	2	clinoptilolite	4
	3	mordenite	0
128	natrojarosite		0
129	sulfate minerals		0
	1	barite	1
	2	anydrite	1
130	metamorphic rocks		1
	1	cordierite/cordierite schist	0
131	magnetite		0
132	vivianite		0
133	pyrophyllite		1
200	unidentified metal		0
201	copper base metal		52
	1	arsenical	5
202	gold		3
203	lead		32
204	iron		1
205	silver		0
300	bone, antler, horn, wood		11
301	ivory, tooth		1
400	unidentified silica-based material		2
401	baked clay		68
402	glass		0
403	frit		6
404	unbaked clay		453
405	glazed ceramic		0
500	unidentified shell		37
501	bi-valve shell, mother-of-pearl		1075
502	*Dentalium* shell		130
503	*Cowrie* shell		0
504	cone-shaped shell		23
505	olive shell		0

(Continued on next page)

Table A2 (continued)

MAT	V		SUM
506	scallop shell		0
50x	crustacean variety codes assigned by Reese		
		1 *Ancilla*	
		2 *Conus*	
		3 *Dentalium*	
		4 *Engina*	
		5 gastropod (fresh water)	
		6 land snail	
		7 *Melanopsis* (fresh water)	
		8 *Monodonta*	
		9 nacre	
		10 *Pinctada*	
		11 *Unio* (fresh water)	
600	botanical material/leaf impressions		10
601	charcoal		62
602	wood (not carbonized)		2
701	plaster		50
		1 mud/clay plaster	0
		2 gypsum plaster	0
		3 lime plaster	0
800	slag		16

Weight (WT)

These columns record the Length, Width, Thickness in cm, and Weight in grams. Incomplete dimensions or partial weights are indicated by *.

Functional Class, (FA, FB, FC)

These three columns record Functional Classes 1 through 22. Three columns are used only because some TYPES are assigned to as many as three different functional classes. The Functional Classes are defined and described in Chapter IV.

Status (STAT)

This column records the Status in the production/consumption/discard model. The codes are defined in Chapter IV (Fig. 29).

Quantity (QTY)

In some cases several items were registered under the same mf number. This column allows for these items to be counted. Since the number of fragments of some items (i.e. broken sealings and tablets) varies as the items are mended or, in other cases (mineral and other samples) is not considered a useful measure of frequency, these quantities should be used with caution.

Illustrations (FG/PL)

This column records Figure number and Plate number, in that order separated by a slash, for finds illustrated in this monograph.

Notes (NOTES)

This column includes citations for previous publication of finds and additional information that varies with type of find or material:

MAT 100, 701

MAL-numbers identify samples analyzed by Blackman (1982) in his study of plaster.

MAT 105:

MAO-numbers identify samples subjected to neutron activation trace elemental analysis by Blackman (1984). Identified obsidian sources are abbreviated: NMRD is Nemrut Dag.

MAT 404:

MAC-numbers identify samples of small clay objects, not sealings or tablets, subjected to neutron activation trace elemental analysis by (Zeder and Blackman 2003).

MAS-numbers identify clay samples from sealings and tablets subjected to neutron activation trace elemental analysis by Blackman (Zeder and Blackman 2003).

MAT 601

P or TUNC = Pennsylvania or Tehran University C14 laboratory sample numbers, followed by a source citation.

MAT 601

F numbers identify flotation samples processed by Miller (1982)

Citation abbreviations:

Carriveau	Carriveau 1978
Iran 12	Sumner 1974
Iran 14	Sumner 1976
Kadmos	Stolper 1985
RC 15	Bovington et. al, 1973

RC 20	Fishman and Lawn 1978
Renfrew	Renfrew and Dixon 1976
4th Symposium	Stolper 1976
Kadmos 24	Stolper 1985

Location (L)

This column records the location of finds as follows:

I—Iran Bastan, Tehran;
M—Malyan,
P—Pennsylvania (may be on loan),
L—lost,
D—destroyed in analysis.

Two locations are recorded for some finds or samples that were divided into two parts.

Appendix A, Register

mf #	M #	OP	LOT	LI	FT#	FEAT	EL	STR	DC	CL	TYP	SBT	MAT	V	LN	WD	TK	WT	FA	FB	FC	STAT	QTY	FIG/PL	NOTES	L
174	174	B	44	M	71	ROOM	2	8A	35	0	51		103	1	5.6*	9	0.5	24		12		C5.0	1	41/-	rim, green-brown bands	P
177	177	B	40	M	71	ROOM	2	8A	35	0	2		100			2.2			21			C6.1	1		stone	I
189	189	A	41	G	34	ROOM	3A	10A	21	0	51		701		7.1*	30		79		12	20	C5.0	1	41/21	Iran 12, Fig. 5 k	P
194	194	B	50	M	28	WALL	2	8D	36	0	2		100			2.6			21			C6.1	1		polished black stone	I
199	199	B	50	M	28	WALL	2	8D	36	0	42		201		2		0.4	3	16			C6.0	1	36/-	oval section	P
205	205	B	54	G				12	34	0	42		500	2		3.3*	0.4	1	16			C5.0	1		medium sized gastropod	I
207	207	B	54	G				12	34	0	2		404			2.2		12	21			C6.0	1		black	I
209	209	B	57	G	66	ROOM	4A	13A	37	0	3		502	3	2.6	0.5		1	16			C6.0	1		ribbed	P
218	218	A	0	G			2	8A	35	0	48		401		41	19.9	2.4		17				1		six holes, bitumen on edges	I
219	219	A	44	M				9	34	0	51		401						23			C5.0	1	28/-	pithos sherd, house motif	I
220	220	B	63	G	64	ROOM	4A	13A	21	0	3		100		1	0.6			16			C6.0	3		weathered orange stone, oval	I
222	222	B	60	G	65	ROOM	4B	14B	29	0	3		502						16			C6.0	1			I
223	223	B	63	G	64	ROOM	4A	13A	21	0	3		103	3	0.2	0.3		1	16			C6.0	1		cylindrical	P
224	224	A	46	G	34	ROOM	3A	10A	37	0	3		500			1.1			16			C6.0	1		pierced disk	I
226	226	A	44	G				9	34	0	58		701						17				1		red, yellow, black	I
228	228	A	41	G	34	ROOM	3A	10A	37	0	74		300						23			C6.0	1		knob	I
530	530	C	60	M	117	CRDX	2	8A	35	0	53		401		5.7		3		23			C6.0	1	42/-	Iran 12, Fig. 10 f	I
531	531	C	62	G	71	ROOM	2	8A	35	0	40		401		4	3.3			23	12		C6.0	1		miniature pot, Kaftari?	I
575	575	C	60	B	117	CRDX	2	8A	35	0	31		401		3.8	1.9	0.9		23			C5.0	1		all ribbed	P
576	576	B 1	39	G	154	ROOM	2	8A	35	0	49		119		10.2	5.2	1.3	70	15			C6.1	1	42/-	punch or drill	I
577	577	C	64	G	118	CRDX	2	8A	35	0	39	2NCF	102		4.3	2.1	0.5		22			C6.0	1	-/20	stemmed point	I
579	579	B 1	39	G	154	ROOM	2	8A	35	0	39	2NCF	102	2	4.9	1.9	0.6	4	22			C6.0	1	35/20	stemmed point, no use wear	P
590	590	B 1	39	G	131	ROOM	2	8B	21	0	3		502		3.3	0.5			16			C6.0	1	43/	carved spiral and bands	I
598.1	598	B 1	39	G	131	ROOM	2	8A	35	0	3		403		0.7	0.7	0.2		16			C6.0	1		frit	I
598.2	598	B 1	39	G	131	ROOM	2	8A	35	0	3		403		1*	1	0.3		16			C5.0	1		frit	I
599	599	C 1	33	G	131	ROOM	2	8B	29	0	3		301		2.3	1.5	0.5	3	16			C6.0	1		four hole spacer	P
600.1	600	C 1	34	G	130	ROOM	2	8B	37	0	3		502	3					16			C6.0	13		all ribbed	P
600.2	600	C 1	34	G	130	ROOM	2	8B	37	0	3		502		2.5	0.5		5	16			C6.0	1		polished	I
601	601	C 1	39	G	128	ROOM	2	8B	21	0	11		404		2.0*	3.3*	2.5		16		10	C5.1	1	43/-	jar stopper, not impressed	I
604	604	C 1	62	G	71	ROOM	2	8A	35	0	50		201		7.2	2.1		25	14			C6.0	1	36/20	bronze tube, flange at one end	P
607	607	C 1	39	G	128	ROOM	2	8B	37	0	43	37-	404		5.7*	4.2*	2.5		21	10		C5.1	1	44/22	Iran 12, Fig. 12 r, Pl. III A,	P
623	623	C 1	39	G	128	ROOM	2	8B	37	0	43		404		2.4*	1.6*	1.1		21			C5.2	1		no signs	I
624	624	C 1	66	G	71	ROOM	2	8B	21	0	47		404		4.4*	2.7*	1.8		21			C5.1	1		number and pictographic signs	I
625	625	C 1	66	G	71	ROOM	2	8B	21	0	47		404		2.9*	1.9*	1.1*		21			C5.1	1		number and pictographic signs	I
626	626	C 1	66	G	71	ROOM	2	8B	21	0	47		404		3.3*	2.1*	1.2*		21			C5.1	1		number and pictographic signs	I
627	627	C 1	66	G	71	ROOM	2	8B	21	0	47		404		3.6	2.5	1.5		21			C6.0	1		Kadmos 24, Fig. 2	P
628	628	C 1	67	G	118	CRDX	2	8B	21	0	47		404		9	7	3		16			C6.0	4		apical holes	I
629	629	C 1	34	G	130	ROOM	2	8B	37	0	3		504		9	7	3		16			C6.0	4		apical holes	I
632	632	C 1	41	G	128	ROOM	2	8B	29	0	47	38T	404		2.5*	1.9*	1.2		21	10		C5.1	1		Iran12, Kadmos 24, Fig. 2	I
633	633	C	66	G	71	ROOM	2	8B	21	0	43		404		2.8*	2.1*	1.3*		21			C5.1	1		tablet?	P
634	634	C	66	G	71	ROOM	2	8B	21	0	47		404						21			C5.1	1		number signs	I
635	635	C	66	G	71	ROOM	2	8B	21	0	47		404						21			C5.2	3		no signs	I
636	636	C	66	G	71	ROOM	2	8B	21	0	43	36-	404		5.0*	4.0*	2.9		21	10		C5.1	1		number and pictographic signs	I
637.1	637	C	66	G	71	ROOM	2	8B	21	0	43	35-	404		3.8*	3.2	2.3		21	10		C5.1	1		MAS-108, ABC clay group	P
637.2	637	C	66	G	71	ROOM	2	8B	21	0	43	34-	404		3.8*	3.2	2.3		21	10		C5.1	1		MAC-042, ABC clay group	P
637.3	637	C	66	G	71	ROOM	2	8B	21	0	43	33-	404		3.8*	3.2	2.3		21	10		C5.1	1		MAS-110, TUV clay group	P
639	639	C 1	33	G	128	ROOM	2	8B	29	0	4		102		7	1.8	1			13		C6.1	1		backed, nibble	I
643	643	A 1	32	G	186	ROOM	2	8B	37	0	48		401		40.5	21	2.6		17				1	-/14	six holes	I
644	644	C 1	37	G	130	ROOM	2	8B	21	0	3		602		0.7	0.6		3	16			C6.3	1		charred	P
645	645	C 1	37	G	130	ROOM	2	8B	21	0	3		504	2	3.4	2.4		14	16			C6.0	1		apical hole, 0.5x0.4	P

Appendix A, Register (*continued*)

mf #	M #	OP	LOT	LI	FT#	FEAT	EL	STR	DC	CL	TYP	SBT	MAT	V	LN	WD	TK	WT	FA	FB	FC	STAT	QTY	FIG/PL	NOTES	L
654	654	C 1	36	G	128	ROOM	2	8B	37	0	40		401		15.0*	10	3.8*		7			C3.0	1		possible join with mf1730	P
655	655	B 1	0	G	165	PYTH	2	8B	28	0	18		404		8.2	3.8*	3.8*			20	20	C6.0	1	42/21	bull, Iran 12, Fig. 12 q	P
656	656	B 1	0	G	165	PYTH	2	8B	28	0	19		404		7.2	5.5	1.9			20	20	C6.0	1	42/21	male, Iran 12, Fig. 12 p	I
741		B 1	39	G	154	ROOM	2	8A	35	0	25		501	9	1.7	0.6	0.2	1		4		P3.1	1	39/-	zigzag	P
742		B 1	39	G	154	ROOM	2	8B	37	0	45		404		2.2	2.2	1.4		14			C6.0	1		biconical	I
743		B 1	39	K	154	ROOM	2	8A	35	0	19		401		4.6*	1.8*	2.9								intrusive Kaftari	I
745.1		B 1	39	G	154	ROOM	2	8B	37	0	25		501			1.8	0.2			4		P3.1	1	39/-	0.3 cm hole, incised	I
745.2		B 1	39	G	154	ROOM	2	8B	37	0	25		501		3.5	0.7	0.1			4		P3.1	1		slightly tapered	I
746		B 1	39	G	131	ROOM	2	8B	37	0	51		401		6.4*	5.7*	1.4			12		C5.0	1	27/-	crenellated tray?	I
748		B 1	37	G	71	ROOM	2	8B	37	0	1		300		6.3*	1.5	1		15			C5.1	1		bone awl	I
749.1		B 1	39	G	131	ROOM	2	8B	21	0	25		501		2.6	1.5	0.1			4		P3.1	4		round, with 0.3 cm hole	I
749.2		B 1	39	G	131	ROOM	2	8B	21	0	25		501		2	1				4		P3.1	1	39/-	arched or straight	I
749.3		B 1	39	G	131	ROOM	2	8B	21	0	25		501		2	0.5	0.5			4		P3.1	1	39/-	incised around edge	I
749.4		B 1	39	G	131	ROOM	2	8B	21	0	25		501		1	0.5	0.5			4		P3.1	1	39/-	incised along length	I
751.1		C 1	34	G	130	ROOM	2	8B	37	0	25		501	9	3.5	0.9	0.1			4		P3.1	1	39/-	rectangular, 2 incised lines	P
751.2		C 1	34	G	130	ROOM	2	8B	37	0	25		501	9	3.3	0.6	0.1			4		P3.1	1	39/-	rectangular, incised lines	P
751.3		C 1	34	G	130	ROOM	2	8B	37	0	25		501	9	1.9	1.5				4		P3.1	1	39/-	rectangular, broken, 3 pieces	P
752		B 1	39	G	154	ROOM	2	8B	37	0	31		401		3.7*	2.2	0.8	5	23	4		C5.0	1		knob or sealing?	P
753		B 1	39	G	131	ROOM	2	8B	37	0	69		404		3.8	3.8	1.6		23			C5.0	1			I
754		C	60	B	117	CRDX	2	8A	35	0	31		401		2.5*	2.3	1.1		23			C5.0	1			I
755		B 1	39	H	131	ROOM	2	8A	35	0	2		100			1.7			21			C6.0	1		green stone	P
756.1		B 1	41	G	130	ROOM	2	8C	37	0	25		501	9	3.2	0.8	0.2			4		P3.1	1	39/-	1.7 inside dia., plaster on edge	P
756.2		B 1	41	G	130	ROOM	2	8C	37	0	25		501	9	1.5	0.7	0.2			4		P3.1	1	39/-	rectangular	P
758.1		B 1	39	G	154	ROOM	2	8B	37	0	3		100		0.5	0.5	0.2		16			C6.0	1		white stone disk	I
758.2		B 1	39	G	154	ROOM	2	8B	37	0	3		100		0.3	0.3	0.1		16			C6.0	2		black disk	I
760		B 1	39	G	154	ROOM	2	8B	37	0	74		201		2.1*	0.8	0.3		14			C5.1	1	36/-	chisel?	P
761		C 1	39	G	128	ROOM	2	8B	37	0	47		404						9			P2.0	1		no signs, tablet clay?	I
763.1	763	C 1	33	G	128	ROOM	2	8B	29	1	63		201		4.3	0.2			2	4		R2.2	1		wire hook, 1.6 cm wide	I
763.2	763	C 1	33	G	128	ROOM	2	8B	29	1	63		201		3.9	0.2			2			R2.2	1		wire	I
764		C	67	G	118	CRDX	2	8B	21	0	16		602	3	2.3	0.8	0.8	3	16	13		C5.0	1	38/-	charred, center hole 0.4	P
850		A	37	M	71	ROOM	2	8A	35	0	4		102	3	3.9*	2.4*	1.1	9		13		C6.0	1			P
851		A	37	M	71	ROOM	2	8A	35	5	88		501					12		4		P2.2	1			P
852		A	37	M	71	ROOM	2	8A	35	3	74		201	2					2			P2.1	3			P
853		A	37	M	71	ROOM	2	8A	35	1	57		110	4							3	P2.2	1			P
854		A	37	M	71	ROOM	2	8A	35	2	57		103	4				1			3	P2.1	1		tiny chip	P
855		A	37	M	71	ROOM	2	8A	35	0	51		103	4	1.1*		0.4	4		12		C5.0	1			P
856		A	37	M	71	ROOM	2	8A	35	3	20		102	2					1			P2.1	1			I
857		A	37	M	71	ROOM	2	8A	35	5	88		501	4				15		4		P2.2	1			P
865		A	37	M	71	ROOM	2	8A	35	0	51		103					0.8		12		C5.0	1			P
866		A	37	M	71	ROOM	2	8A	35	5	88		501					15		4		P2.2	1			P
867		A	37	M	71	ROOM	2	8A	35	0	57		701					12	17			C6.0	1		white	P
868		A	38	M	186	ROOM	2	8A	35	3	51		701		5.4*	4.9*	0.9	52	17	12	20	C5.0	1		relief bands	P
871		A	41	G	34	ROOM	3A	10A	37	5	74		0					21	2			P1.0	1			P
872		A	41	G	34	ROOM	3A	10A	34	0	58		701					17	17				1		red	P
873		A	44	G		ROOM	3A	9	34	1	91		701					1000*	17				1		white, grey, red, orange, black	P
874		A	46	G	34	ROOM	3A		9	34	63		201	1	2	0.2	0.2	1	2	3	3	R2.2	1	-/25	see Section II A	P
875		A	44	G				9	34	3	91		701					125	17				1		black	P
930		A 1	33	G	187	ROOM	2	8B	37	3	20		105		2.2*	1.5		3	17			P3.1	1		MAO-008, NMRD 1, green	P
931		A 1	29	H	185	ROOM	2	8B	37	1	57		701					34	17				1		white	P
932		A 1	29	H	185	ROOM	2	8B	37	2	57		115	3	1.6	1.3	1.2	7	7			C6.0	1		strike-a-light?	P

Appendix A, Register (continued)

mf#	M#	OP	LOT	LI	FT#	FEAT	EL	STR	DC	CL	TYP	SBT	MAT	V	LN	WD	TK	WT	FA	EB	FCl	STAT	QTY	FIG/PL	NOTES	L
933		A 1	29	H	185	ROOM	2	8B	37	3	74		203		2	1	0.4	6	2			R2.2	2		fragments, isotope analysis	P
934		A 1	29	H	185	ROOM	2	8B	37	2	57		104	1	2	1		36	9			P2.2	1			P
1002	668	ABCN	1	B					41	0	25		501	10	1.2	0.6	0.1			4		P3.1	1	39/-	rectangular	P
1003		ABCN	1	B					41	0	59		501	10	8.2*	5.4*	1.7			12	20	C5.0	1	27/17	bull, Iran 14. Fig. 3 d	I
1019		B 1	39	G	71	ROOM	2	8B	37	0	3		400		0.9	0.5			16			C5.0	1	37/-	MAL-0111	I
1020		B 1	37	K	71	ROOM	2	8A	35	0	19		401		4.2*	2.7	2.8						1	37/-	intrusive Kaftari	P
1023		ABCN	9	M	118	CRDX	2	8A	35	1	91		701						17				1		MAC-005, orange, black	P
1026		ABCS	3	G	160	WALL	2	8C	36	2	57		101	1	3.1	1.7	1.1	13			3	P2.2	1	37/-	rolled, abraded	P
1029		ABCS	7	M	156	WALL	2	8D	36	0	51		103	1	2.6*	4.0*	1.1	29		12		C5.0	1	41/-	translucent white base	P
1030	676	ABCS	0	B					40	0	25		202		2.5	2	0.1		16	20		C6.0	1	43/21	Iran 14, Fig. 5 n, Pl. III I	I
1043	689	ABCS	13	M				9	34	0	59		401		19.3*	45.0*	1.3		16	12	20	C5.0	1	27/17	Iran 14, Fig. 3 c, Pl. IV C	I
1044	690	ABCS	7	M	156	WALL		8D	36	0	59		401		10.6*	8.6*			12	20		C5.0	1	27/16	crenellation	I
1047	694	ABCS	0	G				9	34	0	51		100		6.1*	12	0.6		12	20		C5.0	1	41/-	MAT 701 OR 1025	I
1049	691	ABCS	14	G	268	ROOM	3A	10A	37	0	59		401		21.9*	23.1*	1.1		12	20		C5.0	1	27/17	Iran 14, Fig. 3 b, Pl. IV B	I
1065		ABCN	23	M	207	ROOM	2	8A	35	1	49	2NCF	102	2	2.9*	2.1*	0.4	3	14			C5.0	1	35/-	pointed, no use wear	P
1069		ABCN	30	G	207	ROOM	2	8B	37	0	12		102	3	3	3.3*	3.2	30	1			P2.1	1		flake core	P
1075		ABCS	6	G	189	PLAT	2	8C	36	3	20	2NCF	102	3	2.2*	1.6	0.4	1	1			P2.1	1			P
1081		ABCN	47	M	28	WALL	2	8D	36	0	20	2NCF	102	3	1.9	1.9*	0.5	2	1			P2.1	1			P
1082		ABCS	9	M	106	WALL	2	8D	36	0	49	2NCF	102	2	2.1	1.2	0.3	1	15			C6.0	1	35/-	drill	P
1083.1		ABCN	47	G	28	WALL	2	8D	36	3	20	2NCF	102	2	1.5	1.6	0.1	1	1			P2.1	1			P
1083.2		ABCN	47	G	28	WALL	2	8D	36	3	20	2NCF	102	2	1.5*	1.7	0.3	1	1			P2.1	1			P
1087		ABCN	1	B					41	0	25		501	9				6		4		P3.1	15		square, rectangular	P
1088.1		ABCN	1	B					41	0	25		501	10	1.2	0.9	0.1	1		4		P3.1	1		rectangular, scored & incised	P
1088.2		ABCN	1	B					41	0	25		501	10	1.3	1	0.1	1		4		P3.1	1		v notch, scored & incised	P
1089		ABCN	30	G	207	ROOM	2	8B	37	0	25		501	9	3.2	0.9	0.1	1		4		P3.1	2		Pinctada crescent	P
1090		ABCN	1	B					41	0	25		501	9				8		4		P3.1	14		crescents, squares, rectangles	P
1092		ABCN	50	H	71	ROOM	2	8D	29	5	60		404						11			C5.0	1		mat impression	P
1093		ABCN	17	G	118	CRDX	2	8B	37	0	25		501	9				26		4		P3.1	75		geometric shapes, split sample	IP
1094		ABCN	1	B					41	0	15		401			1	0.2		21			C6.0	1			P
1095		ABCS	10	G	125	WALL	2	8D	36	5	88		501	11				4		4		P2.1	8		chips, right	P
1096		ABCS	9	G	106	WALL	2	8D	36	5	88		501	11				1		4		P2.1	2		fragments	P
1098		ABCN	31	G	371	DBLK	2	8C	36	1	88		501	10	2.2	1.5	0.3	1		4		P2.2	2		brown exterior, 1 cut edge	P
1101.1		ABCS	7	M	156	WALL	2	8D	36	5	88		501	11				4		4		P2.1	6		fragments	P
1101.2		ABCS	7	M	156	WALL	2	8D	36	5	88		501	10				2		4		P2.1	6		fragments	P
1106.1		ABCN	19	M	265	ROOM	2	8A	35	5	88		501	11				1		4		P2.1	6		fragments	P
1106.2		ABCN	19	M	265	ROOM	2	8A	35	5	83		100					1				P2.1	2		fragments	P
1107		ABCN	19	M	265	ROOM	2	8A	35	0	25		504	4	1.2*	0.8	0.6	1		4		P2.2	1		fossil bivalve (cf. Gryphaea)	P
1109		ABCN	15	G	118	CRDX	2	8B	37	5	88		504	5	2.5*	1.2	0.8	1	16			P3.1	1		blue and white bands	P
1111		ABCN	1	B					41	1	88		504					1		4		P2.2	2		distal break, hole d. 0.2	P
1112		ABCN	14	G	117	CRDX	2	8B	37	1	88		504	2	1.4	1	0.3	1	16	4		C6.0	1		hole at apex, d. 0.1, red, white	P
1113		ABCN	14	G	117	CRDX	2	8B	37	5	88		501	10				1		4		P2.1	1		hinge fragment	P
1114		ABCS	12	G	117	CRDX	2	8A	35	5	88		502	3	2.8	0.4		1	16			C6.0	1		has tip	P
1116		ABCN	23	M	207	ROOM	2	8A	35	5	88		502	3	2.8	0.5		1	16			C6.0	1		ribbed	P
1117		ABCN	30	G	207	ROOM	2	8B	37	5	88		502	3	2	0.4		1	16			C6.0	1		ribbed, has tip	P
1119.1		ABCN	23	M	207	ROOM	2	8A	35	0	25		501	9	1.6	1.1	0.1	1		4		P3.1	1		rounded, pointed end, scored	P
1119.2		ABCN	23	M	207	ROOM	2	8A	35	0	3		500	1					16			C6.0	1		open apex	P
1119.3		ABCN	23	M	207	ROOM	2	8A	35	0	88		500	7				1		4		P1.0	1		costate	P
1119.4		ABCN	23	M	207	ROOM	2	8A	35	0	25		501	9	2*	1.3	1	0.1		4		P3.1	1		rounded, pointed end, scored	P
1122	697	ABCN	1	B					41	0	51		110		2.0*	3.8*	0.7		12	20		C5.0	1	40/-	incised chevron design	I
1126		ABCN	10	M	117	CRDX	2	8A	35	0	51		701		2.9*	3.0*	0.4		12	12		C5.0	1		MAL-1010, soft white rim	P

Appendix A, Register (*continued*)

mf #	M #	OP	LOT	LI	FT#	FEAT	EL	STR	DC	CL	TYP	SBT	MAT	V	IN	WD	TK	WT	FA	FB	FC	STAT	QTY	FIG/PL	NOTES	L
1127	699	ABCS	9	M	106	WALL	2	8D	36	0	51		100		10.4*	40.1	1.2			12		C5.0	1	41/-	MAT 701 or 103-5, spotted	I
1130		ABCN	49	G	211	ROOM	3A	10A	35	0	51		100		2.2*	1.5*	0.2			12		C5.0	1		MAL-0134, green-grey	P
1131.1		ABCN	50	H	71	ROOM	2	8D	29	3	42		201		1.5		0.2		2			R2.2	1		ring fragment	P
1131.2		ABCN	50	H	71	ROOM	2	8D	29	3	74		201						2			R2.2	1		fragment	P
1132	700	ABCS	0	B					40	0	61		201		10.3	0.3			14			C5.0	1	36/-		x
1133		ABCS	22	G	191	DBLK	2	8C	36	3	74		203		8.5	1.7	0.5		2			R2.2	2		fragments, isotopic analysis	P
1134	701	ABCN	31	G	371	DBLK	2	8C	36	0	24		201		2.3*	0.2			14			C5.0	1	36/20	square section	I
1135	702	ABCN	30	G	207	ROOM	2	8B	37	0	42		201		1.4		0.2		16			C6.0	1	36/-		I
1136		ABCS	13	M				9	34	1	63		203		3.1	0.4		3	2			R2.2	1	36/-		P
1137		ABCS	13	M				9	34	1	63		201		3.2	0.3		1	2			R2.2	1	-/25	see Section II A	I
1142	703	ABCS	18	M					41	0	42		201		2.1		0.2		16			C6.0	1	36/-		I
1143		ABCN	47	G	28	WALL	2	8D	36	1	62		201		3.3	2.4	0.2	6	2			R2.2	1	-/26	see Section II A	P
1145.1		ABCN	9	M	118	CRDX	2	8A	35	3	74		201					9	2			P2.1	1		prill	P
1145.2		ABCN	9	M	118	CRDX	2	8A	35	3	63		201	1	2	1	0.5	9	2			R2.2	1	-/26	see Section II A	I
1147		ABCS	3	G	160	WALL	2	8C	36	3	44		800					2	2			P2.1	1		lump of cu slag and ceramic	I
1148		ABCN	1	M					41	0	42		201			2.2		2	2			R2.2	1	36/-		x
1149		ABCN	38	G	127	WALL	2	8D	36	2	57		103	5				92	9			P2.2	1			P
1161		ABCS	58	G	260	AREA	3A	10A	29	5	77		601					5	7			P2.1	1			I
1165		ABCN	14	M	268	ROOM	3A	10A	35	5	77		601						7			P2.1	1			I
1166		ABCS	14	M	268	ROOM	3A	10A	35	5	77		601						7			P2.1	1			I
1186	710	ABCN	58	G	260	AREA	3A	10A	29	0	59		401		4.0*	4.2*	1.1			12	20	C5.0	1	27/17	bovine hooves	I
1187	711	ABCS	25	M	269	ROOM	3A	10A	37	0	59		401		7.1*	17.2*	1			12	20	C5.0	1	27/17	horn, rope, white paste	I
1192	716	ABCN	59	M	220	ROOM	3A	10A	35	0	59		401		8.1*	6.0*	1.1			12	20	R2.2	1	27/16	lid, leaf, white paste	I
1193	717	ABCS	58	G	260	AREA	3A	10A	29	0	59		401		5.0*	4.5*	0.6			12	20	P2.1	1	27/16	rectangle	I
1204		ABCS	14	G	268	ROOM	3A	10A	37	0	2		103	5	3.7			59	21			R2.2	1			P
1210		ABCN	59	M	220	ROOM	3A	10A	35	0	49	PBS	102	2	2	0.9	0.3	1	15			P2.2	1		backed drill	P
1217		ABCS	26	G	269	ROOM	3A	10A	37	3	20		119					3	9			P2.1	1			P
1219		ABCS	7	M	156	WALL	2	8D	36	3	20	2NCF	102	5	1.5*	1.7*	0.2	1	1			P2.1	1			P
1221		ABCN	57	G	211	ROOM	3A	10A	37	0	4	MBS	102	3	2	1.4	0.6	2			13	C6.1	1	34/-		P
1224		ABCN	50	H	71	ROOM	2	8D	29	3	49	2NCF	102	2	2.1*	2.8	0.4	4	14			C5.0	1		pointed	P
1225		ABCS	2	G	14	WALL	2	8C	36	3	20	2DF	102	2	4.4	1.8	0.7	4	1			P3.1	1	30/-	heat treated	P
1226		ABCS	6	G	189	PLAT	2	8C	36	0	20	2DF	102	2	2.4*	1.6	1.2	2	1			P2.1	1			P
1231		ABCN	61	G	260	AREA	3A	10B	29	0	49	2NCF	102	3	3.2	3.1	0.8	9	14			C6.1	1	31/-	retouched	P
1236	725	ABCN	49	G	211	ROOM	3A	10A	35	0	4	DBS	102	2	4.1	2.3	0.7				13	C6.3	1	33/20	denticulated, gloss, bitumen	I
1237		ABCN	49	G	211	ROOM	3A	10A	35	0	20	2NCF	102	2	3.2	2.8	0.8	9			13	C6.1	1	32/-	used to cut meat	P
1238		ABCN	48	G				9	34	0	4		102	2	4.6	1.2	0.2	2			13	C6.2	1	33/-		P
1260		ABCN	59	M	220	ROOM	3A	10A	35	5	88		501	11				1	4			P2.1	1			P
1262.1		ABCS	25	G	269	ROOM	3A	10A	21	0	25		501	10	2.6	1.7		1	4			P3.1	1		hole d. 0.2; 2 worked edges	P
1262.2		ABCS	25	G	269	ROOM	3A	10A	21	0	25		501	10	2.7	1		1	4			P3.1	1			P
1264		ABCS	18	M					41	5	88		501	11				3	4			P2.1	4		right fragments	P
1265		ABCS	0	B					40	1	25		501	9	0.8	0.7	0.1	4	4			P3.1	4		one is cut	P
1266.1		ABCS	3	G	160	WALL	2	8C	36	1	25		501	10	1.4	1	0.2	2	4			P3.1	1		rectangular with beveled edge	P
1266.2		ABCS	3	G	160	WALL	2	8C	36	1	88		501	10				10	4			P2.1	7		fragments	P
1267		ABCS	5	G	155	PLAT	2	8C	36	5	88		501	10	2.7	2.2	0.4	5	4			P2.1	1		fragment	P
1268.1		ABCN	1	B					41	5	88		502	3	3.4	0.5		1	16			C6.0	1		ribbed	P
1268.2		ABCN	1	B					41	5	88		502	3	2.7	0.5		1	16			C6.0	1		ribbed	P
1269.1		ABCS	7	M	156	WALL	2	8D	36	1	25		501	11				4	4			P3.1	4		distal fragments	P
1269.2		ABCS	7	M	156	WALL	2	8D	36	1	25		501	11				1	4			P3.1	1		fragment	P
1272		ABCN	50	H	71	ROOM	2	8D	29	0	25		501	9				3	4			P3.1	7		4 rect, 1 Y, 2 irregular, hole	P
1273		ABCN	48	G				9	34	5	88		500	6				1	4			P1.0	2		small	P

Appendix A, Register (continued)

mf #	M #	OP	LOT	LI	FT#	FEAT	BL	STR	DC	CL	TYP	SBT	MAT	V	LN	WD	TK	WT	FA	FB	FC	STAT	QTY	FIG/PL	NOTES	L
1274		ABCN	49	G	211	ROOM	3A	10A	35	5	88		501	10	1.5	1.4	0.3	1		4		P2.1	2		joining fragments	P
1275.1		ABCS	17	G				9	34	5	25		501	10	0.9	0.6	0.1	3		4		P2.1	1		rectangular; 1 cut edge	P
1275.2		ABCS	17	G				9	34	5	88		501	10				3		4		P2.1	2		fragments; 1 cut edge	P
1276		C	67	G	118	CRDX	2	8B	21	0	25		501	9				28		4		P3.1	64		rectangles, disks, curved	P
1277		ABCS	40	G	190	WALL	2	8D	36	5	88		501	9				2		4		P2.1	1			P
1279		ABCN	71	M	222	ROOM	3A	10A	35	5	88		501	10	1.7	1.5	0.4	2		4		P2.1	1		fragment	P
1285		ABCS	39	G	270	ROOM	3A	10A	35	0	3		101	1	0.3	0.9*		2			3	P3.2	1	37/-	unfinished?	P
1287		ABCN	74	G	33	WALL	3B	11B	36	0	3		403		0.6	0.3		1	16			C6.0	1		white frit cylinder	P
1288		ABCN	71	M	222	ROOM	3A	10A	35	0	3		103	3	0.2	0.6		1	16			C6.0	1	37/-	white	P
1289		ABCN	76	G	260	AREA	3A	10B	37	1	45		103	7	2.5		1.3	11	14			C6.0	1	43/-	reddish brown	P
1294		ABCN	30	G	207	ROOM	2	8B	37	1	3		100		0.1	1.2		1			3	P3.2	1	38/-	hole 0.2, edge not smoothed	P
1300		ABCS	28	G	267	ROOM	2	10A	35	1	3		108		0.2	0.5		1			3	P3.2	1	37/-	incompletely polished	P
1303		ABCN	50	H	71	ROOM	2	8D	29	0	4		105		1.1	0.8	0.3	2		13		C6.0	1		MAO-018, Renfrew 3A, grey	P
1305		ABCN	17	G	118	CRDX	2	8B	37	0	3		116		1	0.9	0.3	1	16			C6.0	1	38/-	sub-rect. 2 hole spacer	P
1306		ABCN	0	B	118	CRDX	2	8B	29	0	3		403		0.2		0.2	1	16			C6.0	1			P
1307		ABCN	47	G	28	WALL	2	8D	36	0	3		100		0.5	0.6			16			C6.0	1		MAL-0164, dark green	P
1308		ABCN	8	M	155	PLAT	2	8C	36	0	3		103	3	0.3	0.5		1	16			C6.0	1	37/-	white	P
1388		ABCN	90	G	118	CRDX	2	8D	29	4	79		601						7			P2.1	1		P-2335, RC 20(2)	P
1436		ABCN	50	H	71	ROOM	2	8D	29	0	51		701		3.1*	3.8*	1			12	20	C5.0	1		MAL-1004, relief bands	P
1439		ABCS	14	M	268	ROOM	3A	10A	35	0	51		100		4.3*	1.6*	0.9			12		C5.0	1		MAH-134, black	P
1441		ABCN	83	M				9	34	0	51		701		3.2*	4.8*	0.7			12	20	C5.0	1		MAL-1005, relief bands	P
1446		ABCN	115	M					41	0	51		103	3	2.6*	3.2*	0.7	12		12	3	R2.2	1	40/-	translucent white, chipped	P
1462	849	ABCS	36	G	271	ROOM	3A	10A	23	0	43	11J	404		4.4*	3.8*	1.5	21	21	10		C5.1	1	44/22	Iran 14, Fig. 4 h, PL. III C	I
1463	850	ABCS	36	G	271	ROOM	3A	10A	23	0	43	23J	404		2.2*	3.9*	0.7		21	10		C5.1	1			I
1464	851	ABCS	36	G	271	ROOM	3A	10A	23	0	43	12J	404		2.2*	2.6*	1		21	10		C5.1	1			I
1465	852	ABCS	36	G	271	ROOM	3A	10A	23	0	43	21J	404		2.7*	3.2*	1.5		21	10		C5.1	1			I
1466	853	ABCS	36	G	271	ROOM	3A	10A	23	0	43	16J	404		2.0*	2.2*	1.2		21	10		C5.1	1			I
1467	854	ABCS	36	G	271	ROOM	3A	10A	23	0	43	14J	404		2.4*	2	1.5		21	10		C5.1	1			I
1468	855	ABCS	36	G	271	ROOM	3A	10A	23	0	43	11J	404		3.0*	2.0*	1.1		21	10		C5.1	1			I
1469	856	ABCS	36	G	271	ROOM	3A	10A	23	0	43	11J	404		2.4*	1.7*	0.9		21	10		C5.1	1			I
1470	857	ABCS	36	G	271	ROOM	3A	10A	23	0	43	13J	404		4.5*	3.9*	1.5		21	10		C5.1	1			I
1471	958	ABCS	32	B				10A	40	0	43	21J	404		5.1*	5	2.7		21	10		C5.1	1			I
1472	859	ABCS	36	G	271	ROOM	3A	10A	23	0	43	14J	404		4.0*	2.5*	1.6		21	10		C5.1	1	-/22		I
1473	860	ABCS	36	G	271	ROOM	3A	10A	23	0	43	21J	404		2.7*	2.0*	2.1		21	10		C5.1	1	44/-		I
1474	861	ABCS	36	G	271	ROOM	3A	10A	23	0	43	21J	404		3.2*	2.0*	1.6		21	10		C5.1	1			I
1475	862	ABCS	36	G	271	ROOM	3A	10A	23	0	43	21J	404		2.9*	2.8*	1.5		21	10		C5.1	1			I
1476	863	ABCS	36	G	271	ROOM	3A	10A	23	0	43	14J	404		2.3*	1.4*	0.6*		21	10		C5.1	1			I
1477		ABCS	36	G	271	ROOM	3A	10A	23	0	43		404						21	10		C5.1	3		possibly impressed	I
1478	867	ABCS	36	G	271	ROOM	3A	10A	23	1	65		404		6.9	2.6			9			P2.0	1		MAC-026, twist. clay squeeze	I
1496		ABCS	65	G	304	ROOM	3B	11B	29	0	37		201		9.4	0.2		16	16			C6.0	1	36/20		I
1498		ABCS	18	M					41	1	63		201		3	0.5	0.5	3	2			R2.2	6	-/27	see Section II A	P
1499		ABCS	25	M	269	ROOM	3A	10A	37	3	44		800					8	8			P2.1	1		ceramic slag?	P
1500		ABCS	36	G	271	ROOM	3A	10A	23	3	44		800					6	8			P2.1	1		ceramic slag?	P
1504		ABCS	72	G	260	AREA	3A	10B	37	0	37		201		3.3*	0.3		2	16			C5.1	1		see Section II A	P
1508		ABCN	106	H	229	ROOM	3B	11B	29	3	74		201					1	2			P2.1	1		prill	P
1509		ABCN	117	M					41	3	74		201					2	2			P2.1	1		prill	P
1510		ABCN	95	G	118	CRDX	2	8D	29	3	74		203					3	2			R2.2	1		Pb isotope, NBS2431	P
1512		ABCN	90	G	118	CRDX	2	8D	29	3	74		201					1	2			P2.1	1		prill	P
1514		ABCN	100	M	211	ROOM	3A	10A	41	1	1	1	201	1	2.4	0.3	0.3	3	15			C6.0	1	-/27	awl, see Section II A	P
1515		ABCN	99	H	211	ROOM	3A	10A	37	3	74		201					1	2			P2.1	1	-/28	see Section II A	P

Appendix A, Register (*continued*)

mf #	M #	OP	LOT	LI	FT#	FEAT	BL	STR	DC	CL	TYP	SBT	MAT	V	LN	WD	TK	WT	FA	BB	FC	STAT	QTY	FIG/PL	NOTES	L
1516.1		ABCN	65	M				9	34	3	74	2II	201					1	2			P2.1	1		drill	P
1516.2		ABCN	65	M				9	34	3	42		201					1	2			R2.2	1		fragment	P
1555	872	ABCS	36	G	271	ROOM	3A	10A	23	0	43	2II	404		6.9	2.9*	2.2		21	10		C5.1	1			I
1556	873	ABCS	36	G	271	ROOM	3A	10A	23	0	43	14I	404		4.0*	3.7*	1.9		21	10		C5.1	1			I
1557.1	874	ABCS	36	G	271	ROOM	3A	10A	23	0	43	12I	404						21	10		C5.1	1			I
1557.2	874	ABCS	36	G	271	ROOM	3A	10A	23	0	43	12I	404						21	10		C5.1	1			I
1557.3	874	ABCS	36	G	271	ROOM	3A	10A	23	0	43	12I	404						21	10		C5.1	1			I
1557.4	874	ABCS	36	G	271	ROOM	3A	10A	23	0	43	15I	404		3.1*	4.2*	2.2		21	10		C5.1	1		Iran 14, Fig. 4 a	I
1558	875	ABCS	46	G				9	23	0	43	18I	404		6.2*	2.7*	1.4		21	10		C5.1	1	44/-	Iran 14, Fig. 4 d, Pl. III L	I
1559	876	ABCS	36	G	271	ROOM	3A	10A	23	0	43	2II	404		8.0*	3.3*	2.4*		21	10		C5.1	1			I
1560	877	ABCS	36	G	271	ROOM	3A	10A	23	0	43	13I	404		6.7*	4.2*	2		21	10		C5.1	1			I
1561	878	ABCS	46	G				9	23	0	43	14I	404		3.4*	3.4*	1		21	10		C5.1	1		MAS-164, ABC clay group	IP
1563	880	ABCS	46	G				9	23	0	43	14I	404		8.6*	5.0*	2.1		21	10		C5.1	1			I
1564	881	ABCS	46	G				9	23	0	43	14I	404		2.3*	3.0*	2.2		21	10		C5.1	1			I
1565	882	ABCS	46	G				9	23	0	43	14I	404		9.1*	4.1*	2		21	10		C5.1	1		MAS-166, ABC clay group	I
1566	883	ABCS	46	G				9	23	0	43	14I	404		6.0*	4.4*	2.3		21	10		C5.1	1			I
1567	884	ABCS	46	G				9	23	0	43	14I	404		4.0*	4.3*	2.2		21	10		C5.1	1			I
1568	885	ABCS	46	G				9	23	0	43	14I	404		3.6*	4.6*	1.7		21	10		C5.1	1		MAS-153, ABC clay group	I
1569	886	ABCS	46	G				9	23	0	43	14I	404		690*	3.6	1.4		21	10		C5.1	1		MAS-160, ABC clay group	IP
1570	887	ABCS	46	G				9	23	0	43	14I	404		3.8*	2.7*	1.2		21	10		C5.1	1			I
1571	888	ABCS	46	G				9	23	0	43	14I	404		4.5*	3.2*	1.4		21	10		C5.1	1		MAS-160, ABC clay group	IP
1572	889	ABCS	46	G				9	23	0	43	2II	404		6.5*	4.5*	2		21	10		C5.1	1	-/22	Iran 14, Fig. 4 I, Pl. III A	I
1573	890	ABCS	46	G				9	23	0	43	2II	404		13.2*	5.5	1.9		21	10		C5.1	1			I
1574	891	ABCS	46	G				9	23	0	43	2II	404		9.7*	5.7	2.5		21	10		C5.1	1			I
1575	892	ABCS	46	G				9	23	0	43	2II	404		7.0*	6.0*	3.1		21	10		C5.1	1		MAS-173, ABC clay group	IP
1576	893	ABCS	46	G				9	23	0	43	2II	404		6.6*	4.6*	2.6		21	10		C5.1	1			I
1577	894	ABCS	46	G				9	23	0	43	2II	404		5.1*	2.8	0.9		21	10		C5.1	1			I
1578	895	ABCS	46	G				9	23	0	43	2II	404		6.0*	5.3	2.4		21	10		C5.1	1			I
1579	896	ABCS	46	G				9	23	0	43	2II	404		3.5*	3.5	1.7		21	10		C5.1	1			I
1580	897	ABCS	46	G				9	23	0	43	2II	404		4.3*	3.5*	2.2		21	10		C5.1	1			I
1581	898	ABCS	46	G				9	23	0	43	2II	404		4.5*	3.9*	1.9		21	10		C5.1	1			I
1582	899	ABCS	46	G				9	23	0	43	2II	404		2.1*	2.1*	1.4		21	10		C5.1	1			I
1613	932	ABCS	46	G				9	23	0	43	2II	404		12.0*	5.4*	2		21	10		C5.1	1		MAS-178, ABC clay group	IP
1614	933	ABCS	46	G				9	23	0	43	2II	404		7.5*	5.0*	2.5		21	10		C5.1	1			I
1615	934	ABCS	46	G				9	23	0	43	2II	404		2.1*	2.6*	1.4*		21	10		C5.1	1			I
1616	935	ABCS	46	G				9	23	0	43	2II	404		2.2*	1.6*	1		21	10		C5.1	1			I
1617	936	ABCS	46	G				9	23	0	43	2II	404		2.1*	1.6*	1.1		21	10		C5.1	1			I
1618	937	ABCS	46	G				9	23	0	43	2II	404		2.8*	2.1*	1.8		21	10		C5.1	1			I
1619	938	ABCS	46	G				9	23	0	43	14I	404		3.5*	4.6*	1.7		21	10		C5.1	1			I
1620	939	ABCS	46	G				9	23	0	43	14I	404		2.1*	2.4*	1.4		21	10		C5.1	1			I
1621	940	ABCS	46	G				9	23	0	43	14I	404		2.7*	2.0*	1.9*		21	10		C5.1	1			I
1622	941	ABCS	46	G				9	23	0	43	24-	404		2.8*	1.7	0.5		21	10		C5.1	1		Iran 14, Fig. 4 k	I
1623	942	ABCS	46	G				9	23	0	43	13I	404		6.5*	4	1.8		21	10		C5.1	1			I
1624	943	ABCS	46	G				9	23	0	43	19I	404		6.8*	4.2	1.1		21	10		C5.1	1		Iran 14, Fig. 4 c	I
1625	944	ABCS	46	G				9	23	0	43	27I	404		3.0*	2.7	1.7		21	10		C5.1	1			I
1626	945	ABCS	46	G				9	23	0	43	17I	404		3.2*	3.0*	1.2		21	10		C5.1	1		Iran 14, Fig. 4 e	I
1627	946	ABCS	46	G				9	23	0	43	14I	404		5.5*	3.9*	1.9		21	10		C5.1	1			I
1628	947	ABCS	46	G				9	23	0	43	25I	404		3.7*	3.3*	1.2		21	10		C5.1	1		Iran 14, Fig. 4 f	I
1629	948	ABCS	46	G				9	23	0	43	13I	404		11.7*	5.0*	2		21	10		C5.1	1		MAS-162, ABC clay group	IP
1630	949	ABCS	46	G				9	23	0	43	13I	404		6.0*	4.7	2		21	10		C5.1	1			I

Appendix A, Register (*continued*)

mf #	M #	OP	LOT	LI	FT#	FEAT	BL	STR	DC	CL	TYP	SBT	MAT	V	LN	WD	TK	WT	FA	FB	FC	STAT	QTY	FIG/PL	NOTES	L
1631	950	ABCS	46	G				9	23	0	43	23J	404		4.5*	4.5	2.1		21	10		C5.1	1			I
1632	951	ABCS	46	G				9	23	0	43	13J	404		6.0*	4.4	2.2		21	10		C5.1	1			I
1633	952	ABCS	46	G				9	23	0	43	13J	404		5.1*	4.0*	1.9		21	10		C5.1	1			I
1634	953	ABCS	46	G				9	23	0	43	13J	404		9.0*	5.2	2.4		21	10		C5.1	1			I
1635	954	ABCS	46	G				9	23	0	43	21J	404		3.2*	3.5*	0.8		21	10		C5.1	1			I
1636	955	ABCS	46	G				9	23	0	43	23J	404		3.0*	2.0*	0.6*		21	10		C5.1	1			I
1637	956	ABCS	46	G				9	23	0	43	20J	404		4.7*	4.0*	2.1		21	10		C5.1	1		MAS-165, ABC clay group	IP
1638	957	ABCS	46	G				9	23	0	43	21J	404		2.9*	1.7*	1.3*		21	10		C5.1	1			I
1639.1		ABCS	46	G				9	23	1	43		404						21	10		C5.1	3		MAS-136, ABC group, impres+Z53?	IP
1639.2		ABCS	46	G				9	23	0	43		404							10		C5.1	13		not impressed	IP
1640	958	ABCS	46	G				9	23	0	43	14J	404		2.4*	1.9*	0.8		21	10		C5.1	2		impressed	I
1641	959	ABCS	46	G				9	23	0	43	14J	404		2.7*	4.0*	1.7		21	10		C5.1	1			I
1642	960	ABCS	46	G				9	23	0	43	14J	404		4.2*	4.0*	1.9		21	10		C5.1	1		MAS-152, ABC clay group	IP
1643	961	ABCS	46	G				9	23	1	43		404		15.5*	7.0*	3.8			10		C5.1	1		not impressed, trial sealing?	I
1644	962	ABCS	46	G				9	23	0	43	23J	404		3.7	2.3	1.3		21			C5.1	1		Iran 14, Fig. 4 j	I
1645.1	963	ABCS	46	G				9	23	0	43		404							10		C5.1	10		not impressed	I
1645.2	963	ABCS	46	G				9	23	0	43	21J	404		2.5*	2.2*	1.5		21	10		C5.1	2		impressed	I
1646	964	ABCS	46	G				9	23	0	43	26-	404		2	1.7*	0.8		21	10		C5.1	1			I
1647	965	ABCS	46	G				9	23	0	43	23J	404		2.2*	1.5	0.9*		21	10		C5.1	1			I
1648	966	ABCS	46	G				9	23	0	43	23J	404		1.5*	1.4*	1.0*		21	10		C5.1	1			I
1649	967	ABCS	46	G				9	23	1	43	14J	404						21	10		C5.1	1			I
1650		ABCS	46	G				9	23	1	43	14J	404						21	10		C5.1	1			I
1651	968	ABCS	46	G				9	23	0	43	14J	404		4.9*	4.1*	1.5		21	10		C5.1	1			I
1652	969	ABCS	46	G				9	23	0	43	14J	404		4.0*	2.1*	1.7*		21	10		C5.1	1			I
1653	970	ABCS	46	G				9	23	0	43	14J	404		7.0*	6.3	2.4		21	10		C5.1	1			I
1654	971	ABCS	46	G				9	23	0	43		404		4.3*	3.0*	1.8*		21	10		C5.1	1	44/-	impressed	I
1655	972	ABCS	46	G				9	23	0	43	14J	404		3.2*	3.3*	1.7		21	10		C5.1	1			I
1656	973	ABCS	46	G				9	23	0	43	14J	404		3.9*	4.5	1.7		21	10		C5.1	1			I
1657	974	ABCS	46	G				9	23	0	43	14J	404		3.8*	4.1*	1.8		21	10		C5.1	1		MAS-157, ABC clay group	I
1658	975	ABCS	46	G				9	23	0	43	14J	404		4.3*	2.4*	1.5		21	10		C5.1	1			I
1659	900	ABCS	46	G				9	23	0	43	21J	404		3.0*	3.1*	1.5*		21	10		C5.1	1			I
1685	1000	ABCN	90	G	118	CRDX	2	8D	29	0	47		404		5.6	4.1	1.4		21			C6.0	1	/21	Iran14, Pl. III H	I
1686	1001	ABCS	46	G				9	23	0	47		404		4.2	3	1.2		21			C6.0	1		Kadmos 24, Fig. 2, 4th Symp.	I
1687	1002	ABCS	46	G				9	23	0	47		404		4.2	3.1	1.2		21			C6.0	1		4th Symposium, p.108	I
1688	1003	ABCS	46	G				9	23	0	47		404		4.2	3	1.2		21			C6.0	1		4th Symposium, p.108	I
1689	1004	ABCS	36	G	271	ROOM	3A	10A	23	0	47		404		4.6	2.8*	1.5		21			C5.1	1		4th Symposium, p.108	I
1690	1005	ABCS	82	G	307	AREA	4A	13A	21	0	47		404		5.2*	3.4	1.9		21			C5.1	1		4th Symposium, p.108	I
1692	1007	ABCN	125	G	222	ROOM	3B	11B	29	0	47	7T	404		5.0*	3.2*	1.6*		21			C5.1	1	44/-	4th Symposium, p.108	I
1693	1008	ABCN	125	M	211	ROOM	3B	11B	29	0	47	22L	404						21			C5.1	11		fragments	I
1712	1027	ABCS	46	G				9	23	0	43	14J	404		3.6*	4.8*	2.1		21	10		C5.1	1			I
1713	1028	ABCS	46	G				9	23	0	43	14J	404		2.4*	1.5*	0.9*		21	10		C5.1	1			I
1714	1029	ABCN	90	G	118	CRDX	2	8D	23	0	43	8J	404		4.9*	3.5*	2.0*		21	10		C5.1	1		MAS-156, ABC clay group	IP
1715.1	1030	ABCS	46	G				9	23	0	43	28J	404						21	10		C5.1	1			I
1715.2	1030	ABCS	46	G				9	23	0	43	22L	404						21	10		C5.1	1			I
1716	1031	ABCS	46	G				9	23	0	43		404						21			C5.1	1			I
1726	1041	ABCN	50	H	71	ROOM	2	8D	29	0	71		401		9.2*				21			C5.0	1	28/18	pithos rim, incised PE sign	I
1730	1045	ABCN	38	G	127	WALL	2	8D	36	0	51		401		18.0*	12.0*	0.9		7			C3.0	1		possible join with mf 654	I
1731	1046	ABCN	90	G	118	CRDX	2	8D	29	0	59		401							12	20	C5.0	1	27/16	rope, leaf, Iran 14, Fig. 3 a	I
1732	1047	ABCS	91	B						40	0	59		401		5*	4.2*	1.02			12	20	C5.0	1	27/-	rope, leaf	I
1733	1048	ABCS	58	G	34	ROOM	3B	11B	29	0	59		401		4.0*	3.4*	0.7			12	20	C5.0	1	27/-	rope, leaf	I

Appendix A, Register (*continued*)

mf #	M #	OP	LOT	LI	FT#	FEAT	BL	STR	DC	CL	TYP	SBT	MAT	V	LN	WD	TK	WT	FA	FB	FC	STAT	QTY	FIG/PL	NOTES	L
1737	1050	ABCN	0						31	0	18		401		8.0*	6.0*	7.2*			12	20	C5.0	1	42/-	humped bull spout	I
1901	1188	ABCS	84	B	307	AREA	4A	13A	35	0	14	1C	100		2	1			21			C6.0	1	44/22	Iran 14, Fig. 5, Plate 11	I
1903	1190	ABCN	131	G	241	CRDX	4A	13A	35	0	14	3C	701		2.3*	1.4			21			C5.1	1	44/-	Iran 14, Fig. 5 1	I
1906	1193	ABCS	14	M	268	ROOM	3A	10A	35	0	73		100		3.2	2.7	1.5		14			C6.1	1	43/-	tool for stone bowl production?	I
1907	1194	ABCN	81	G	129	ROOM	2	8D	29	0	74		100		4	2.2	0.3		23			P3.0	1	43/-	black, soft, angular	I
1908	1195	ABCS	18	M					41	0	39	2NCF	102		3.8	2.1	0.7		22			C6.0	1		stemmed point	I
1913	1200	ABCN	30	G	207	ROOM	2	8B	37	0	53		401		8.1		4.1		23			C6.0	1	42/-		I
1916	1203	ABCN	158	G	247	ROOM	5	15A	37	0	37		201		12.5	0.7			16			C6.0	1	36/20		I
1918	1205	ABCN	156	H	66	ROOM	4B	14B	29	0	37		201		7.9	0.3			16			C6.0	1	36/20		I
1921.1	1208	ABCN	81	G	129	ROOM	2	8D	29	0	15		100		2.6	0.5			16			C6.0	1	38/-	MAT116 ?, hole 0.4 cm dia.	I
1921.2	1208	ABCN	81	G	129	ROOM	2	8D	29	0	3		100		0.3	0.3			16			C6.0	1	38/-	found in the hole of mf1921.1	I
1925	1212	ABCS	153	G	236	PITX	4A	13A	22	0	40	6I	401		27.5	21.5			7			C3.0	1	-/15	straw tempered goblet	P
1932.1		ABCS	66	G	281	COUR	4A	13A	37	0	43		404						21	10		C5.1	1		MAS-175, ABC clay group	P
1932.2		ABCS	66	G	281	COUR	4A	13A	37	0	43	13J	404						21	10		C5.1	1			P
1934		ABCS	72	G	241	CRDX	4A	13A	37	1	43		404							10		C5.1	4		not impressed	I
1949	1220	A 1	90	G	118	CRDX	2	8D	29	0	43	10J	404		5.1*	3.6*	1.2		21	10		C5.1	1		Iran 14, Fig.4 g, Pl. III I	I
1956.1		A 1	29	H	185	ROOM	2	8B	37	1	43		404							10		C5.1	1		MAC-025, ABC clay group	P
1956.2		A 1	29	H	185	ROOM	2	8B	37	1	43		404							10		C5.1	1		MAC-041, ABC clay group	P
1969	1224	ABCN	90	G	118	CRDX	2	8D	29	0	43	9J	404		8.2*	5	1.3		21	10		C5.1	1		Iran 14, Fig. 4 i	I
1970.1		ABCN	90	G	118	CRDX	2	8D	29	0	43	9J	404						21	10		C5.1	1		MAS-101, ABC clay group	IP
1970.2		ABCN	90	G	118	CRDX	2	8D	29	0	43	9J	404						21	10		C5.1	1		MAS-169, ABC clay group	IP
1970.3		ABCN	90	G	118	CRDX	2	8D	29	0	43		404						21	10		C5.1	27			IP
1971		ABCN	148	G	236	PITX	4A	13A	22	0	43	2J	404						21	10		C5.1	1		MAS-133, ABC clay group	IP
1973		ABCN	125	M	211	ROOM	3B	11B	29	0	43		404						21	10		C5.1	1		MAS-135, ABC group., impress.	IP
1974		ABCN	90	G	118	CRDX	2	8D	29	0	43		404						21	10		C5.1	1		door sealing?, impressed?	I
1975		ABCN	90	G	118	CRDX	2	8D	29	0	43	13J	404						21	10		C5.1	1			I
1976		ABCN	143	M	64	ROOM	4A	13A	37	1	43		404							10		C5.1	4		not impressed	I
1978		ABCN	148	G	236	PITX	4A	13A	22	1	11		404							10		C5.1	1		MAS-132, unknown clay	IP
1979.1		ABCN	143	M	64	ROOM	4A	13A	37	0	43	4J	404						21	10		C5.1	1		MAS 134, ABC clay group	IP
1979.2		ABCN	143	M	64	ROOM	4A	13A	37	0	43		404						21	10		C5.1	1		MAS-106, ABC clay group	IP
1980		ABCN	90	G	118	CRDX	2	8D	29	1	43		404							10		C5.1	9		thin disks, mat impression	I
1981		B 1	0	G	163	PYTH	2	8B	28	1	43		404							10		C5.1	1		not impressed	I
2012.1		ABCN	149	G	236	PITX	4A	13A	22	0	2		404						21			C6.0	30			P
2012.2		ABCN	149	G	236	PITX	4A	13A	22	0	2		404						21			C6.0	1			P
2013.1		ABCN	90	G	118	CRDX	2	8D	29	0	2		404						21			C6.0	1		MAC-010, ABC clay, hollow	P
2013.2		ABCN	90	G	118	CRDX	2	8D	29	0	2		404		4	3.5			21			C6.0	1		MAC-029, TUV clay hollow?	P
2014		ABCN	152	G	236	PITX	4A	13A	22	0	2		404		4	3.5			21			C6.0	1		MAC-009, ABC clay source	P
2015.1		ABCS	36	G	271	ROOM	3A	10A	23	1	43	16J	404						21	10		C5.1	1			I
2015.2		ABCS	36	G	271	ROOM	3A	10A	23	1	43		404						21	10		C5.1	20		MAS 109, ABC clay group	IP
2016.1		ABCS	36	G	271	ROOM	3A	10A	23	0	43	16J	404						21	10		C5.1	1			I
2016.2		ABCS	36	G	271	ROOM	3A	10A	23	0	43	29J	404						21	10		C5.1	1			I
2016.3		ABCS	36	G	271	ROOM	3A	10A	23	0	43	30J	404						21	10		C5.1	6			I
2016.4		ABCS	36	G	271	ROOM	3A	10A	23	0	43	31-	404						21	10		C5.1	1			I
2017		ABCS	46	G				9	23	1	43		404							10		C5.1	9		not impressed	I
2018		ABCS	46	G				9	23	0	43	16J	404						21	10		C5.1	1		impressed	I
2019.1		ABCS	46	G				9	23	0	43		404						21	10		C5.1	1			I
2019.2		ABCS	46	G				9	23	0	43	19J	404						21	10		C5.1	1			I
2019.3		ABCS	46	G				9	23	0	43	32-	404						21	10		C5.1	1			I
2019.4		ABCS	46	G				9	23	0	43		404						21	10		C5.1	21		impressed	I
2020		ABCS	36	G	271	ROOM	3A	10A	23	0	43		404						21	10		C5.1	10		impressed	I

Appendix A, Register (*continued*)

mf #	M #	OP	LOT	LI	FT#	FEAT	EL	STR	DC	CL	TYP	SBT	MAT	v	LN	WD	TK	WT	FA	FB	FC	STAT	QTY	FIG/PL	NOTES	L
2021.1		ABCS	46	G				9	23	0	43	21J	404						21	10		C5.1	1			I
2021.2		ABCS	46	G				9	23	0	43	21J	404						21	10		C5.1	1			I
2021.3		ABCS	46	G				9	23	0	43	21J	404						21	10		C5.1	1			I
2021.4		ABCS	46	G				9	23	1	43		404							10		C5.1	5		not impressed	I
2022		ABCS	60	M				12	34	1	43		404							10		C5.1	2		not impressed	I
2023		ABCS	66	G	281	COUR	4A	13A	37	0	43	5J	404						21	10		C5.1	1			I
2024		ABCS	60	M				12	34	1	43		404							10		C5.1	1		not impressed	I
2025.1		ABCS	46	G				9	23	1	43	17J	404						21	10		C5.1	1			I
2025.2		ABCS	46	G				9	23	1	43		404							10		C5.1	11			I
2026		ABCS	46	G				9	23	1	43		404						21	10		C5.1	1		impressed	I
2027		ABCS	36	G	271	ROOM	3A	10A	23	1	43		404							10		C5.1	2		not impressed	I
2028		ABCS	36	G	271	ROOM	3A	10A	23	1	43		404						21	10		C5.1	2		MAS-105, ABC clay group	IP
2029		ABCS	36	G	271	ROOM	3A	10A	23	0	43		404						21	10		C5.1	1		possibly impressed	I
2071		B	0	B					31	5	74		300		4.4*	2.3*		7	9			P2.2	1	38/-	ostrich egg shell	I
2090		B	44	M	71	ROOM	2	8A	35	3	20	DEB	106						1			P2.1	1			P
2091		B	43	M	31	ROOM	2	8A	35	2	57		103					1			3	P2.2	1	37/-	green	P
2092		B	43	M	31	ROOM	2	8A	35	2	57		103	4				2			3	P2.2	1		translucent white CRYSTAL	P
2094		B	45	M	117	CRDX	2	8A	35	2	57		107								3	P2.2	1			P
2098		B	40	M	71	ROOM	2	8A	35	0	51		103	4	2.4*	1.5*	0.9	7	1	12		C5.0	1	40/-	rim	I
2101		B	40	M	71	ROOM	2	8A	35	3	20	DEB	102						1			P2.1	1			I
2102		B	40	M	71	ROOM	2	8A	35	3	57		100	2	2.7	2.1	2	21	2			P1.0	1		slag or ore, mineral unknown	P
2103		B	40	M	71	ROOM	2	8A	35	0	4		102	2						13		C6.0	1			I
2104		B	40	M	71	ROOM	2	8A	35	3	74		201					6	2			P2.1	1		prill	P
2105		B	40	M	71	ROOM	2	8A	35	2	57		103	5				27	9			P2.2	1		oolitic	P
2106.1		B	40	M	71	ROOM	2	8A	35	5	88		500	10				5		4		P2.1	1		distal fragment	P
2106.2		B	40	M	71	ROOM	2	8A	35	0	88		500	11						4		P2.1	2		fragments	P
2108		B	48	M	63	ROOM	3A	10A	37	5	39	2NCF	102	3	1.6	1.4	0.2	1	22			C6.0	1	35/-	tranchet point, no use wear	P
2113		B	48	M	63	ROOM	3A	10A	37	0	49		102		3.4	0.5		1		13		C6.0	1		microlithic crescent	I
2116		B	44	M	71	ROOM	2	8A	35	5	88		502	3				1	16			C6.0	1			P
2117		B	44	M	71	ROOM	2	8A	35	3	44		800	3				15	2			P2.1	1			P
2118		B	44	M	71	ROOM	2	8A	35	5	88	2NCF	501	10	2*	2.1	0.4	6		4		P2.1	1		hinge fragment., 2 drilled holes	P
2119.1		B	44	M	71	ROOM	2	8A	35	3	20	2NCF	102	2	1.9*	1.3	0.3	2	1			P2.1	1			P
2119.2		B	44	M	71	ROOM	2	8A	35	1	20	2NCF	102	2	2.2*	2.4*	0.5	1	1			P2.1	1			P
2119.3		B	44	M	71	ROOM	2	8A	35	3	49	2NCF	102	2					14			C5.1	1	35/-	pointed, used to scrape bone	P
2120		B	44	M	71	ROOM	2	8A	35	3	74		201	1	0.7	0.7	0.5	4	2			P2.1	1	-/28	see Section II A	P
2121		B	44	M	71	ROOM	2	8A	35	5	88		500	6				2		4		P1.0	2			P
2145		B	71	M	71	ROOM	2	8A	35	1	57		102	2					1		3	R2.2	1		banded, jasper?	P
2146		B	73	G	71	ROOM	2	8B	37	1	88		501	10				6		4		P2.1	2		distal frag., partly drilled hole	P
2147		B	49	G	63	ROOM	3B	11B	29	3	44		800						2			P2.1	1		Carriveau 1978, MASCA-20	P
2148		B	49	G	63	ROOM	3B	11B	29	1	51		701					22		12		C4.0	1		vessel?	P
2149		B	49	G	63	ROOM	3B	11B	29	2	57		115					7	7			C6.0	1		strike-a-light?	I
2150		B	49	G	63	ROOM	3B	11B	29	3	20		102						1			P2.1	2			P
2152		B	50	G	28	WALL	2	8D	36	0	91		701					103	17			C6.3	1		red	I
2153		B	50	M	28	WALL	2	8D	36	0	4	2DF	102	3	2.4	1.9	0.6	4	1	13		P2.1	1		denticulated, gloss, heavy wear	I
2154.1		B	50	M	28	WALL	2	8D	36	3	20	PDF	102	3	2.3	1.4	0.9	3	1			P2.1	1			P
2154.2		B	50	M	28	WALL	2	8D	36	3	20		102	3	2.1	1.1	1.1	1	1			P2.1	1			P
2154.3		B	50	M	28	WALL	2	8D	36	3	20	2NCF	102	3	2.3	1.8	0.4	2	1			P2.1	1			P
2154.4		B	50	M	28	WALL	2	8D	36	3	20	2NCF	102	3					1			P2.1	1			P
2155		B	50	M	28	WALL	2	8D	36	2	57		100					8	9			P1.0	1		pumice?	P
2156		B	50	M	28	WALL	2	8D	36	3	74		201					3	2			P2.1	1		corroded prill	P

Appendix A, Register (*continued*)

mf #	M #	OP	LOT	LI	FT#	FEAT	EL	STR	DC	CL	TYP	SBT	MAT	V	LN	WD	TK	WT	FA	FB	FC	STAT	QTY	FIG/PL	NOTES	L
2157		B	50	M	28	WALL	2	8D	36	5	88		501	11				14*		4		P2.1	2		burned fragments, left	P
2158		B	50	M	28	WALL	2	8D	36	0	4		102	2						13		C6.0	1		microblade	L
2159		B	51	H	63	ROOM	3A	10A	35	5	77		601						7			P2.1	1			I
2167		B	40	M	71	ROOM	2	8A	35	2	57		116					15	9		3	P2.2	1			P
2168		B	50	M	28	WALL	2	8D	36	2	57		116					39	9		3	P2.2	1			P
2169		B	50	M	28	WALL	2	8D	36	5	88		501	11				9		4		P2.1	1		fragment	P
2170		B	50	M	28	WALL	2	8D	36	3	44		800					61	8			P2.1	1		ceramic slag?	P
2174		B	43	M	31	ROOM	2	8A	35	2	57		116					42	9		3	P2.2	1			P
2175		B	43	M	31	ROOM	2	8A	35	2	20		102					1				P2.1	1			I
2176		B	54	G					12	35	0	39	2NCF	102	2	1.8	1.7	0.4	1	22			C6.0	1	35/-	tranchet point, no use wear	P
2182		B	54	G					12	34	2	57		100						9			P1.0	1		stone	I
2183		B	57	G	66	ROOM	4A	13A	37	5	88		501	11				1		4		P2.1	2		fragments	P
2184		B	56	G	65	ROOM	4A	13A	37	0	20	2DF	102	3	4.1	3.6	0.8	16	1		3	P3.1	1	30/-	no use wear	I
2185		B	57	G	66	ROOM	4A	13A	37	2	57		116						9		3	P2.2	1			I
2186		B	56	G	65	ROOM	4A	13A	37	2	57		116					5	9		3	P2.2	1		slightly costate, broken lip	P
2187		B	56	G	65	ROOM	4A	13A	37	5	88		504	7				1		4		P2.2	1		rim fracture ground smooth	P
2192		B	60	G	65	ROOM	4B	14B	29	0	51		103	4	1.9*	1.8*	0.6	5	12		3	R3.2	1	40/-		P
2193		B	62	G	70	DOOR	4A	13A	37	5	88		501	11				2	4			P2.1	2		distal fragments	P
2194		B	63	G	64	ROOM	4A	13A	21	1	88		504	4				2				P3.1	1		open apex, hole d. 0.2	P
2195.1		B	63	G	64	ROOM	4A	13A	21	4	77		601						7			P2.1	1		P2187, RC20(2)	I
2195.2		B	63	G	64	ROOM	4A	13A	21	5	77		601						7			P2.1	1		TUNC 31, RC15(4)	I
2196		B	65	G	64	ROOM	4A	13B	21	5	77		601					53	7			P2.1	1			P
2198		B	57	G	66	ROOM	4A	13A	37	5	88		501	11				1		4		P2.1	2		distal fragments	P
2200		B	64	M	66	ROOM	4A	13A	37	2	57		104	1				1	9			P2.2	1			P
2201		B	63	G	64	ROOM	4A	13A	21	3	74		127	2	1.5	1.5	0.4	1			3	P2.2	1	37/-	MAT identity uncertain	I
2202		B	63	G	64	ROOM	4A	13A	21	3	88		501	11				6		4		P2.1	1		half shell, left	P
2204.1		B	65	G	64	ROOM	4A	13B	21	3	20	3NCF	102	3	0.9	1.3	0.1	1	1			P2.1	1			P
2204.2		B	65	G	64	ROOM	4A	13B	21	3	20	3NCF	102	3	1	1	0.4	1	1			P2.2	1			I
2205		B	64	M	66	ROOM	4A	13A	37	5	88		500					1		4		P2.1	2			P
2206		B	65	G	64	ROOM	4A	13B	21	5	74		400					1				P2.2	1		animal tooth?	P
2207		B	64	M	66	ROOM	4A	13A	37	5	88		504	7				1	16			P3.1	1		irregular hole, gloss, intrusive?	P
2208		B	64	M	66	ROOM	4A	13A	37	3	20		102						1			P2.1	1			I
2282		B 1	37	H	131	ROOM	2	8A	35	5	88		502						16			C6.0	1			I
2283		B 1	39	H	131	ROOM	2	8A	35	3	74		201		1.4	0.4		1	2			P2.1	1		prill	P
2284		B 1	39	H	131	ROOM	2	8A	35	1	51		103	4			1.1	5	9			P3.0	1			P
2285.1		B 1	39	H	131	ROOM	2	8A	35	5	88		501	10				6	4			P2.1	1		fragment	P
2285.2		B 1	39	H	131	ROOM	2	8A	35	5	88		501	11				6	4			P2.1	1		distal hinge fragment	P
2286		B 1	39	H	131	ROOM	2	8A	35	2	57		104	1				2	9			P2.2	1			I
2287		B 1	37	G	71	ROOM	2	8A	35	1	74		300										1		boar tooth?	I
2288		B 1	39	H	131	ROOM	2	8A	35	3	74		201					4	2			P2.0	1		roasted iron-rich cu nodule	P
2289		B 1	39	H	131	ROOM	2	8A	35	0	91		701					113	17				1		yellow	P
2290		B 1	39	H	131	ROOM	2	8A	35	2	57		116					42	9		3	P2.2	1			P
2291		B 1	37	G	71	ROOM	2	8A	35	5	88		501	11				14		4		P2.1	2		fragments	P
2292.1		B 1	39	H	131	ROOM	2	8A	35	2	57		101	1	3.4	2.6	1.7	13			3	P2.2	1	37/-		P
2292.2		B 1	39	H	131	ROOM	2	8A	35	2	57		101	1	1.9	1.2	1.1	7			3	P2.2	1	37/-		P
2293		B 1	37	G	71	ROOM	2	8A	35	2	57		108					3			3	P2.2	1			P
2295		B 1	37	G	71	ROOM	2	8A	35	5	74		300						9			P2.2	1		ostrich eggshell	I
2296		B 1	37	G	71	ROOM	2	8A	35	3	44		800					9	8			P2.1	1		ceramic slag?	P
2298		B 1	39	H	131	ROOM	2	8A	35	1	57		701					14	17						white wall plaster	P
2299		B 1	37	G	71	ROOM	2	8A	35	5	76		600					83	17				1		intrusive seeds	P

Appendix A, Register (*continued*)

mf#	M#	OP	LOT	LI	FT#	FEAT	EL	STR	DC	CL	TYP	SBT	MAT	V	LN	WD	TK	WT	FA	FB	FC	STAT	QTY	FIG/PL	NOTES	L
2300		B 1	39	H	131	ROOM	2	8A	35	3	74		204					1	2			P2.2	1		iron-rich copper ore	P
2301		B 1	39	H	131	ROOM	2	8A	35	2	57		104	1				1	9			P2.2	1			P
2302		B 1	39	H	131	ROOM	2	8A	35	5	88		500							4		P2.2	1			I
2303		B 1	39	H	131	ROOM	2	8A	35	0	25		501							4		P3.1	1		incised	I
2304		B 1	39	H	131	ROOM	2	8A	35	1	63		201						2			R2.2	1			I
2305		B 1	39	H	131	ROOM	2	8A	35	3	20		105		1.2*	1.2		1	1			P3.1	1		MAO-011, NMRD 1, green	P
2306		B 1	39	H	131	ROOM	2	8A	35	1	91		100		3.4	3	3	20	5			P1.0	1		yellow iron oxide	P
2307		B 1	391	G	131	ROOM	2	8B	37	1	63		201						2			R2.2	1			I
2308		B 1	392	G	154	ROOM	2	8B	37	2	57		133					3	9			P2.2	1			P
2309		B 1	391	G	131	ROOM	2	8B	37	5	88		500	6				2		4		P1.0	3		small land snails	P
2310		B 1	391	G	131	ROOM	2	8B	37	2	57		104	1				1	9			P2.2	1			P
2311		B 1	39	H	131	ROOM	2	8A	35	5	77		601					4	7			P2.1	1			P
2312.1		B 1	392	G	154	ROOM	2	8B	37	5	88		501	9				3		4		P2.1	1		fragment	P
2312.2		B 1	392	G	154	ROOM	2	8B	37	5	88		501	11				3		4		P2.1	1		fragment	P
2313		B 1	392	G	154	ROOM	2	8B	37	2	12		102	2	4.9*	4	1.8	40	1		3	R2.2	1		flake core, like mf 7300	P
2314		B 1	392	G	154	ROOM	2	8B	37	1	62		200					1	2			R2.2	1	36/-	Pb or Ag?	P
2315		B 1	392	G	154	ROOM	2	8B	37	3	74		203					8	2			R2.2	3	36/-		P
2316		B 1	391	G	131	ROOM	2	8B	21	5	88		502	3				6	16			C6.0	10		all ribbed	P
2317		B 1	39	G	154	ROOM	2	8B	37	2	57		104	1				2	9			P2.2	1			P
2318		B 1	391	G	154	ROOM	2	8B	37	5	57		107								3	P2.2	1			P
2319		B 1	392	G	154	ROOM	2	8B	37	5	95		600					71				P2.2	1		brick, straw	I
2320		B 1	39	H	131	ROOM	2	8A	35	5	88		500							4		P2.2	1			I
2321		B 1	392	G	154	ROOM	2	8B	37	2	57		101						7			P2.1	1		weathered	I
2322		B 1	391	G	131	ROOM	2	8B	37	5	79		601									P2.1	1			I
2323		B 1	39	H	131	ROOM	2	8A	35	5	88		500							4		P2.2	1		small gastropod	P
2324		B 1	39	G	154	ROOM	2	8B	37	3	74		201						2			P2.0	1		roasted iron-rich cu nodule	P
2325		B 1	39	G	154	ROOM	2	8B	37	3	74		203					8	2			R2.2	1			L
2326		B 1	39	G	154	ROOM	2	8B	29	5	74		300						9			P2.2	1		ostrich eggshell	I
2327		B 1	39	H	131	ROOM	2	8A	35	5	88		500							4		P2.2	1			I
2328		B 1	39	H	131	ROOM	2	8A	35	5	88		500							4		P2.2	2			I
2329		B 1	39	H	131	ROOM	2	8A	35	5	88		502						16			C6.0	2			I
2330		B 1	37	G	71	ROOM	2	8A	35	5	74		300						9			P2.2	1		fish vertebra	I
2331		B 1	37	G	71	ROOM	2	8A	35	2	57		116					22	9		3	P2.2	1			P
2332		B 1	41	G	155	PLAT	2	8C	36	5	74		0		2.6	0.3		2	23			R2.2	1		circular impressions in clay	I
2333.1		B 1	37	G	71	ROOM	2	8B	21	3	74		203		2.3	0.6		2	2			R2.2	1		Pb isotope analysis	P
2333.2		B 1	37	G	71	ROOM	2	8B	21	3	74		203					2	2			P2.0	1			P
2334		B 1	41	G	155	PLAT	2	8C	36	2	57		103	4				143	9			P3.2	1	40/-	vessel preform, bands	P
2335		B 1	39	H	131	ROOM	2	8B	35	5	88		502					8	16			C6.0	1			I
2336		B 1	41	G	155	PLAT	2	8C	36	2	88		501	10				4		4		P2.2	2		blue, Pithos 164 painted band	P
2337		B 1	43	G	71	ROOM	2	8B	37	1	91		100					4	5	4		P2.2	1		2 cut lines; hole d. 0.1	P
2339.1		B 1	0	B					39	0	25		501	9	1.5	1.2	0.2	4	5	4		P3.1	1		circular, hole d. 0.3; eroded	P
2339.2		B 1	0	B					39	0	25		501	9		1.4	0.1	4		4		P3.1	1			P
2342		B 1	0	G	125	WALL	2	8D	36	5	88		501	10				80		4		P2.2	1		hinge and distal fragments, left	P
2343		B 1	0	G	165	PYTH	2	8B	28	4	79		601						7			P2.1	1		P-2186, RC 20(2)	P
2344		B 1	0	G	71	ROOM	2	8B	29	4	79		601						11			C5.1	1		P-2059, RC 20(2) bitumen	P
2430		C	60	M	117	CRDX	2	8A	35	5	83		103	5				55					1		fossil cone shell	P
2432		C	60	M	117	CRDX	2	8A	35	5	76		600					20					1		intrusive seeds	P
2438		C	65	G	128	ROOM	2	8A	35	2	57		101	1	3.9	3.7	2.1	36			3	P2.2	1	37/-	flaked at one end	P
2441		C	65	G	128	ROOM	2	8A	35	2	57		116					15	9		3	P2.2	1			P
2442		C	64	G	118	CRDX	2	8A	35	2	57		104	1				3	9		3	P2.2	1			P

Appendix A, Register (*continued*)

mf #	M #	OP	LOT	LI	FT#	FEAT	EL	STR	DC	CL	TYP	SBT	MAT	V	LN	WD	TK	WT	FA	FB	FC	STAT	QTY	FIG/PL	NOTES	L
2443		C	60	M	117	CRDX	2	8A	35	3	74		203		5.9	2	0.8	18	2			R2.2	1		Pb isotope, NBS2429	P
2447		C	67	M	118	CRDX	2	8B	21	0	57		104	1				24	9			P2.2	1		many platelets	P
2448		C	67	G	118	CRDX	2	8B	21	0	25		501	9				200		4		P3.1	669	39/-	geometric, holed, bitumen	IP
2449		C	67	G	118	CRDX	2	8B	21	5	88		502						16			C6.0	1			I
2450		C	67	G	118	CRDX	2	8B	21	2	57		103						9		3	P2.2	1		vessel production	I
2451		C	67	G	118	CRDX	2	8B	21	2	57		101								3	P2.2	1			I
2452		C	66	G	71	ROOM	2	8B	21	5	76		600					30					1		intrusive seeds	P
2453		C	67	G	118	CRDX	2	8B	21	5	77		601						7			P2.1	1			I
2454.1		C	67	G	118	CRDX	2	8B	21	5	88		502	3	2.2	0.5		2	16			C6.0	1		ribbed	P
2454.2		C	67	G	118	CRDX	2	8B	21	5	88		502	3	2.6	0.5		2	16			C6.0	1		ribbed	P
2455		C	67	G	118	CRDX	2	8B	21	3	74		203					14	2			R2.2	2	36/-		P
2456		C	67	G	118	CRDX	2	8B	21	5	88		500							4		P2.2	2			I
2458		C	67	G	118	CRDX	2	8B	21	0	91		701					27	17			P3.1	1		red	P
2554.1		C 1	34	G	130	ROOM	2	8B	37	5	88		501	10				4		4		P2.2	1		1 has 2 cut edges	P
2554.2		C 1	34	G	130	ROOM	2	8B	37	5	88		501	11				4		4		P2.2	1		left	P
2555		C 1	35	G	131	ROOM	2	8A	35	5	88		500		3	1.7	0.7			4		P2.2	1			I
2557		C 1	33	G	130	ROOM	2	8B	29	3	20		105	1	1.5	1.9	0.3		1			P3.1	1		MAO-016, Renfrew 3A	P
2563		B 1	39	H	131	CRDX	2	8A	35	2	57		104	1				3	9			P2.2	1		many platelets	P
2564		C	67	G	118	CRDX	2	8B	21	2	57		104	1				27	9			P2.2	1			I
2566		C 1	33	G	131	ROOM	2	8A	29	5	77		601						7			P2.1	1			I
2567		C 1	35	G	131	ROOM	2	8A	35	5	77		601						7			P2.1	1			I
2568		C 1	37	G	130	ROOM	2	8B	21	5	88		502						16			C6.0	1			I
2569		C 1	37	G	130	ROOM	2	8B	21	5	88		502	3				32	16			C6.0	70		9 crystals	P
2570		C 1	37	G	130	ROOM	2	8B	21	2	57		101	1				10			3	P2.2	1			P
2571		C 1	37	G	130	ROOM	2	8B	21	2	57		101	1	0.8*	0.5*					3	P2.2	1			I
2572		C 1	37	G	130	ROOM	2	8B	21	3	20		105	2	2.2	1.1	0.3	1	1			P3.1	1		MAO-017, NMRD 1, green	P
2573		C 1	39	G	128	ROOM	2	8B	37	3	4	MBS	102					1		13		C6.1	1	34/23	denticulated, gloss, cut grass	P
2574		C 1	40	G	129	ROOM	2	8B	37	5	88		500							4		P2.2	1			I
2575		C 1	34	G	130	ROOM	2	8B	37	5	88		500							4		P2.2	1			I
2576.1		C 1	38	G	129	ROOM	2	8A	35	1	25		501	10	1.5	0.6	0.1	4		4		P3.1	1		rectangle, broken end	P
2576.2		C 1	38	G	129	ROOM	2	8A	35	1	25		501	10	1.11	1	0.1	4		4		P3.1	1		2 cut edges	P
2577		C 1	36	G	128	ROOM	2	8A	35	1	57		101	1				4			3	P2.2	1			P
2578.1		C 1	36	G	128	ROOM	2	8A	35	5	88		501	11				12		4		P2.2	1		left	P
2578.2		C 1	36	G	128	ROOM	2	8A	35	5	88		501	10				12		4		P2.2	1		3 fragments, each with cut edge	P
2580		B 1	39	G	154	ROOM	2	8B	37	0	2		103	4		1.5		6	21			P2.2	1			P
2583		B	43	M	31	ROOM	2	8A	35	2	57		101	1	2.1	1.4	0.8	4			3	P2.2	1	37/-	rolled smooth	P
2584		B 1	39	H	131	ROOM	2	8A	35	2	57		101	1	4.6	2.3	1.7	19			3	P3.2	1	37/-	rolled smooth	P
2588		B 1	39	H	118	ROOM	2	8A	35	2	57		102	2	1.7	0.9		7			3		1		bead rough-out	P
2590		C	64	G	118	CRDX	2	8A	35	0	4		105		3.5*	2.5*	1.2	1		13		C6.0	1		MAO-005, NMRD 1, green	P
2592		A	38	M	186	ROOM	2	8A	35	3	20		105		2.4*	2.1*	1.6	9	1			P3.1	1		MAO-002, NMRD 1, green	P
2593		ABCS	46	G				9	23	1	43		404						21	10		C5.1	1		not impressed	I
2594		ABCS	46	G				9	23	0	43		404						21	10		C5.1	1		impressed	I
2595.1		ABCS	46	G				9	23	0	43		404						21	10		C5.1	6		impressed	I
2595.2		ABCS	46	G				9	23	0	43		404		2.5*	2.0*				10		C5.1	10		not impressed	I
2596		ABCS	46	G				9	23	1	43		404							10		C5.1	3		not impressed	I
2597		ABCS	46	G				9	23	0	43		404		5.7	5.6	0.7		21	10		C5.1	1		stamped or incised "X"	I
2598		ABCS	38	M	38	DOOR	3A	10A	35	0	43	8J	404		6.6*	5	1.4		21	10		C5.1	1			I
2599		ABCS	46	G				9	23	1	43		404		2.6*	2.4*	1.8*			10		C5.1	1		not impressed	I
2600		ABCS	46	G				9	23	1	43		404		5.2*	1.9*	0.9			10		C5.1	1		not impressed	I
2601		ABCS	46	G				9	23	1	43		404		5.6*	2.4*	1.5			10		C5.1	2		not impressed	I

Appendix A, Register (*continued*)

mf #	M #	OP	LOT	LI	FT#	FEAT	EL	STR	DC	CL	TYP	SBT	MAT	V	LN	WD	TK	WT	FA	FB	FC	STAT	QTY	FIG/PL	NOTES	L
2602		ABCS	10	G	125	WALL	2	8D	36	1	43		404		4.3*	3.8*	1.2					C5.1	1		not impressed	I
2603		ABCS	46	G				9	23	1	43		404		3.5*	3.7	2.2			10		C5.1	1		not impressed	I
2604		ABCS	46	G				9	23	1	43		401		1.9	2.4	0.9*			10		C5.1	1		not impressed	I
2605		ABCS	46	G				9	23	1	43		404		6.7*	5.1	1.3			10		C5.1	1		not impressed	I
2606		ABCS	46	G				9	23	1	43		401		2.9*	2.2	1.1			10		C5.1	6		not impressed	I
2607		ABCS	46	G				9	23	1	43		404							10		C5.1	8		not impressed	I
2608		ABCS	46	G				9	23	1	43		404		3.4*	3.0*	1.8			10		C5.1	1		not impressed	I
2609		ABCS	46	G				9	23	0	43		404		3.6	3.4	1.1		21	10		C5.1	1		impressed, motif ?	I
2610		ABCS	46	G				9	23	1	43		404		2.5*	3.7*	1			10		C5.1	1		not impressed	I
2611		ABCS	46	G				9	23	1	43	13J	404							10		C5.1	1			I
2612		ABCS	46	G				9	23	1	43		404		2.1*	2.5*	0.7		21	10		C5.1	1		not impressed	I
2613		ABCS	46	G				9	23	0	43		404		4.7	4	2.5	1		10		C5.1	1		not impressed	I
2614		ABCS	46	G				9	23	1	43	14J	404		4.1*	3.4*	1.7		21	10		C5.1	1		MAS-150, clay group ?	IP
2615		ABCS	46	G				9	23	1	43		404		5.6*	4.2*	1.5					C5.1	1		not impressed	I
2616	1226	ABCN	141	G	241	CRDX	4A	13A	37	0	6		401		21.3	20			18			C3.0	1	22/15		I
2633	1606	ABCN	148	G	236	PITX	4A	13A	22	0	22		117		18.6	14.5	2.1	415	7			C6.1	1		small ground stone tool	I
2634	1627	ABCN	148	G	236	PITX	4A	13A	22	5	22		103	5	10.7	7.2	4.1	485	7			C6.1	1		rubbing or pounding stone	I
2635	1628	ABCN	148	G	236	PITX	4A	13A	22	0	22		103	5	9.9*		3.7		14			C5.1	1		grinding or polishing stone	I
3730		ABC	25	G	281	COUR	4B	14B	29	0	91		701					1	17				1		yellow	M
3731		ABC	4	G	334	MISC	4A	13C	49	0	74		401		6.1	4.9	1.1	33	23			C6.0	1		triangular clay cake	M
3733		ABC	8	G	334	MISC	4A	13C	49	5	88		501					1		4		P2.2	2		fragments	M
3734		ABC	5	G	240	WALL	4A	13C	36	5	57		103	5				59	17				1		gravel used in foundation	M
3735		ABC	17	G	251	ROOM	5	15A	35	2	57		125					1	2			P2.2	1			P
3736		ABC	34	G	353	COUR	5	15B	21	2	57		104	1				1	9		3	P2.2	1			M
3737		ABC	4	G	353	COUR	5	15A	35	0	91		701					1	17				1		black, white	M
3738		ABC	11	G	247	ROOM	5	15A	37	0	91		701					1	17				1		red	M
3739		ABC	3	G	241	CRDX	4A	13B	29	0	91		701					1	17				1		yellow	M
3741		ABC	3	G	241	CRDX	4A	13B	29	3	74		201					1	2			P2.1	1		prill	P
3742		ABC	19	G	331	AREA	4B	14A	37	3	74		201		1.4	0.5	0.5	3	2			P2.1	1	-/28	see Section II A	P
3743		ABC	12	G	331	AREA	4B	14A	37	3	74		201			1.1		1	2			P2.1	2		prills	P
3745		ABC	2	M			5		41	0	51		103	5	3.5*	3.5*		17	12			C5.0	1			M
3746		ABC	34	G	353	COUR	5	15B	21	0	51		103	1	3.6*	4.7*	0.5	33	12	12		C5.0	1	41/-	painted rim	M
3748		ABC	4	G	239	WALL	4B	14B	36	3	20		102	2	2.4	1.9		3	1			P2.1	1			M
3749		ABC	8	G	334	MISC	4A	13C	49	3	20		102	2	3.6	3		20	1			P3.1	1		decortication flake	M
3750		ABC	3	G	241	CRDX	4A	13B	29	2	57		103	5				13	9			P2.2	1		vessel production	M
3751		ABC	8	G	334	MISC	4A	13C	49	0	4		102	2	2.8	1.4		2	1	13		C6.1	1	-/19	nibbled on both edges	M
3752	1353	ABC	8	G	334	MISC	4A	13C	49	0	12		105		2.4	1.7		3	1			P2.1	1		exhausted blade core	I
3753		ABC	14	G	332	AREA	4B	14A	37	0	4		105		1.3	0.7		1				C6.0	1	-/19	MAO-022, NMRD 1, green	P
3754		ABC	8	G	334	MISC	4A	13C	49	0	4		102	2	2	1		1		13		C6.2	1	-/19		M
3755		ABC	14	G	332	AREA	4B	14A	37	3	20		102	3	1	0.9		1		13		P2.1	1	-/19	MAO-021, NMRD 1, green	M
3756		ABC	8	G	334	MISC	4A	13C	49	0	4		105		2.5	1.5		1		13		C6.0	1	-/19		M
3757		ABC	5	G	240	WALL	4B	14B	36	0	4		102	2	1.9	1.8		2		13		C6.0	1	-/19		M
3758		ABC	8	G	334	MISC	4A	13C	49	0	4		102	2	3.6	1.3		2		13		C6.1	1	-/19	nibbled, gloss	M
3759		ABC	8	G	334	MISC	4A	13C	49	0	4		102	2	3.3	1.2		1		13		C6.1	1	-/19	nibbled, gloss	M
3760	1354	ABC	7	G	323	WALL	4B	14B	36	0	4		102	2	5.7	1.1		2		13		C6.1	1	-/19	nibbled	I
3761		ABC	4	G	334	MISC	4A	13C	49	3	44		102	2	2.3	0.7		1		13		C6.1	1	-/19	nibbled, gloss	M
3762		ABC	25	G	281	COUR	4B	14B	37	5	79		800					32	2			P2.1	1			P
3765		ABC	28	G	336	AREA	5	15A	37	5	79		601						7			P2.1	1			P
3766		ABC	28	G					37	5	79		601					13	7			P2.1	1			P
3767		ABC	29	G	346	ROOM	5	15A	37	5	79		601					3	7			P2.1	1			P

Appendix A, Register (continued)

mf #	M #	OP	LOT	LI	FT#	FEAT	BL	STR	DC	CL	TYP	SBT	MAT	V	LN	WD	TK	WT	FA	FB	FC	STAT	QTY	FIG/PL	NOTES	L
3768		ABC	32	G	359	AREA	5	15B	37	1	43		404		3.4*	2.2*						C5.1	1		not impressed	I
3769		ABC	32	G	359	AREA	5	15B	37	1	11		404							10		C5.1	1		jar stopper, no impression	I
3770		ABC	20	G	339	HRTH	4B	14A	28	0	6		401		14.5	25			21			C5.0	1		incised + on bottom	M
3772		ABC	34	G	353	COUR	5	15B	21	5	79		601					6	7			P2.1	1			P
3773		ABC	7	G	323	WALL	4B	14B	36	5	79		601					13	7			P2.1	1		P-3060 comb. w/ mf 4055	P
3774		ABC	40	G	363	OVEN	5	15B	28	4	79		601					17	7			P2.1	1			P
3775		ABC	3	G	241	CRDX	4A	13B	29	5	79		601					2	7			P2.1	1			P
3776		ABC	10	G	241	CRDX	4A	13B	29	5	79		601					2	7			P2.1	1			P
3777		ABC	12	G	331	AREA	4B	14A	37	5	79		601					1	7			P2.1	1			P
3778		ABC	14	G	332	AREA	4B	14A	37	5	79		601					2	7			P2.1	1			P
3779		ABC	15	G	331	AREA	4B	14A	37	5	79		601					2	7			P2.1	1			P
3916		ABC	47	G	369	AREA		18A	50	3	20		102	2	1.2	0.9		1	1			P2.1	1	-/19		M
3918		ABC	32	G	359	AREA	5	15B	37	0	4		102	2	3.4	1.1		4		13		C6.0	2			M
3919		ABC	45	G	367	AREA		16	50	3	20		102	2	1.9	1.2		1	1			P2.1	1			M
3920		ABC	47	G	369	AREA		18A	50	0	49	2NCF	102	2	3.2	1.7	1.1	3	14			C6.0	1	-/19	pointed	M
3921		ABC	45	G	367	AREA		16	50	3	20		102	3	1.3*	1.3		1	1			P2.1	1			M
3922		ABC	47	G	369	AREA		18A	50	0	12		102	3	2.3	1.6		4	1			P2.1	1	30/19	exhausted blade core	M
3923		ABC	45	G	367	AREA		16	50	0	20		102	2	3.4	2.9		3	1			P3.1	1			M
3924		ABC	47	G	369	AREA		18A	50	3	20		102	2	3.1	1.8		3	1			P3.1	1			M
3926		ABC	34	G	353	COUR	5	15B	21	0	4		102	3	2.5	1.4		2		13		C6.0	1			M
3927		ABC	47	G	369	AREA		18A	50	3	20		102	2	3.8	2.2		6	1			P3.1	1			M
3928		ABC	47	G	369	AREA		18A	50	3	20		102	2	1.7	0.9		1	1			P2.1	1			M
3929		ABC	47	G	369	AREA		18A	50	3	4		102	2	0.4	0.4		1		13		C6.2	1		microblade	M
3930		ABC	47	G	369	AREA		18A	50	0	49		102	2	3.6	1.7		4	14			C6.0	1	-/19	scraper	M
3931		ABC	47	G	369	AREA		18A	50	3	20		102	2	1.9	1.5		1	1			P2.1	1			M
3932		ABC	47	G	369	AREA		18A	50	3	20		102	3	1.1	0.5		1	1			P2.1	1			M
3933		ABC	47	G	369	AREA		18A	50	3	20		102	2	3.6	2.8		7	1			P3.1	1			M
3934		ABC	47	G	369	AREA		18A	50	3	20		102	2	1.2	1		1	1			P2.1	1			M
3939		ABC	47	G	369	AREA		18A	50	3	49		102	2	0.9	0.4		1	15			C5.0	1	-/19	broken drill point?	M
3940		ABC	35	G	360	HRTH	5	15B	37	2	57		104	2				51	5			P2.2	1		red	M
3941		ABC	31	M	348	AREA	5	15A	37	2	91		124	5				11	5			P2.2	1		yellow	M
3946		ABC	47	G	369	AREA	5	18A	50	0	22		103		9.7	5.2			14			C6.0	1		grinding or polishing stone	M
3947		ABC	40	G	363	OVEN	5	15B	28	0	74		404		4.4	2.8	2.2		9			P2.2	1		sealing clay, no impression	I
3948		ABC	40	G	363	OVEN	5	15B	28	1	43		404							10		C5.1	13		not impressed	M
4007		ABC	13	G	331	AREA	4B	14A	37	5	77		601						7			P2.1	1		F207	P
4015		ABC	20	G	339	HRTH	4B	14A	28	5	77		601						7			P2.1	1		F215	P
4016		ABC	23	G	343	HRTH	4B	14A	28	5	77		601						7			P2.1	1		F216	P
4020		ABC	24	G	342	ROOM	5	15A	37	5	77		601						7			P2.1	1		F220	P
4025		ABC	29	G	346	ROOM	5	15A	37	5	77		601						7			P2.1	1		F225	P
4030		ABC	27	G	345	HRTH	4B	14B	28	5	77		601						7			P2.1	1		F230	P
4055		ABC	40	G	363	OVEN	5	15B	28	4	77		601						7			P2.1	1		F255: P-3060, w/ mf 3774	P
4098		ABC	48	G	369	AREA		18A	50	5	94		600										1		phytolith sample	P
4099		ABC	49	G	369	AREA		18A	50	5	94		600										1		phytolith sample	P
4112		ABC	48	G	369	AREA		18A	50	5	77		601						7			P2.1	1		F278	P
4115		ABC	49	G	369	AREA		18A	50	1	43		601						7			P2.1	1		F281	P
4295		ABC	0	G	104	WALL	2	8D	36	5	96		600						17				1		brick	P
4296		ABC	0	G	210	WALL	3B	11B	36	5	96		600						17				1		brick	P
4297		ABC	0	G	290	BNCH	4A	13B	36	5	96		600						17				1		brick	P
4298		ABC	0	G		WALL	5	15B	36	5	96		600						17				1		brick	P
4306		ABC	0	G	104	WALL	2	8D	36	5	96		404						17				1		brick, seed impression	P

Appendix A, Register (*continued*)

mf#	M#	OP	LOT	LI	FT#	FEAT	BL	STR	DC	CL	TYP	SBT	MAT	V	LN	WD	TK	WT	FA	FB	FC	STAT	QTY	FIG/PL	NOTES	L
4307		ABC	0	G	210	WALL	3B	11B	36	5	96		404						17				1		brick	P
4308		ABC	0	G	290	BNCH	4A	13B	36	5	96		404						17				1		brick	P
4309		ABC	0	G		WALL	5	15B	36	5	96		404						17				1		brick	P
5081		ABC	37	G	353	COUR	5	15B	21	2	57		104	3				3	5			P2.2	1		red	P
5082.1	1431	ABC	21	G	281	COUR	4A	13A	21	0	3		202		0.2	0.3			16			C5.0	2	43/-	gold foil beads	I
5082.2	1431	ABC	21	G	281	COUR	4A	13A	21	0	3		403						16			C5.0	1		blue and white frit	I
5979		ABCN	79	G	222	ROOM	3A	10A	37	5	74		100					6	23				1			M
5981		ABC	1	M					41	0	22		100		6.4	5.1	2.7	164	14			C6.0	1		grinding or polishing stone	M
6055		ABCN	91	G	260	AREA	3A	10B	37	1	51		103	5	2.0*	1.8*	0.1	6	9			P3.2	1	40/-	rounded bevel rim, tool marks	M
6056		ABCS	10	G	125	WALL	2	8D	36	1	51		103	5	2.8*	3.3*			9			P3.2	1		flat square rim, tool marks	M
6057		ABCS	49	M					41	0	71		401						21			C5.0	1		potter's mark; Kaftari?	M
6421.1		B 1	39	G	154	ROOM	2	8B	37	0	25		501		2.7	1	0.1			4		P3.1	2	39/-	rectangular	I
6421.2		B 1	39	G	154	ROOM	2	8B	37	0	25		501		2.4	1	0.1			4		P3.1	1	39/-	rectangular	I
6427	534	C 1	33	G	130	ROOM	2	8B	29	0	3		502						16			C6.0	1			P
6428	580	C	64	G	118	CRDX	2	8A	35	0	31		401		3.8*	2.5	1	8	23			C5.0	1			I
6429	597	B 1	39	G	130	ROOM	2	8B	37	0	3		101		0.6	0.3			16			C6.0	1			I
6435		B 1	39	G	154	ROOM	2	8B	37	1	63		201		4.4	0.5			2		R2.2	1	36/-		I
6454		C 1	35	G	131	ROOM	2	8A	35	0	25		100		2.6	2.3	0.3	2		4		P3.1	1	39/-	equilateral Δ, concave base	P
6455.1		C 1	35	G	131	ROOM	2	8A	35	0	25	.	501	9	2.2	0.7	0.1	1		4		P3.1	1		curved	P
6455.2		C 1	35	G	131	ROOM	2	8A	35	0	25		501	9	2.1	0.6	0.1	1		4		P3.1	1		purple rectangle	P
6456		C 1	33	G	129	ROOM	2	8B	29	0	25		501					2		4		P3.1	1		irregular cut-out	P
6457		C 1	35	G	131	ROOM	2	8A	35	0	31		401						23			C5.0	1			I
6540		B	44	M	71	ROOM	2	8A	35	0	4	MBS	102	2	2.2	1.8	0.5	3		13		C6.2	1		no wear	P
6541		B	48	M	63	ROOM	3A	10A	37	0	4	DBS	102	2	2.8	1.3	0.3	1		13		C6.2	1	34/-		P
6542.1		B	50	M	28	WALL	2	8D	36	3	49	2DF	102	2	2.2*	1.9	0.6	1	14			C5.0	1		pointed	P
6542.2		B	50	M	28	WALL	2	8D	36	3	20	2NCF	102	2	2.8	1.7*	0.7	3	1			P3.1	1			P
6542.3		B	50	M	28	WALL	2	8D	36	3	20	2NCF	102	2	1.6*	2.6	0.6	1	1			P3.1	1			P
6542.4		B	50	M	28	WALL	2	8D	36	3	20	2NCF	102	2	1*	0.9*	0.4	1	1			P2.1	1			P
6542.5		B	50	M	28	WALL	2	8D	36	0	20	2DF	102	2	2.4*	1.9	0.8	4	1			P2.1	1	35/-		P
6543		B	50	M	28	WALL	2	8D	36	0	4	MBS	102	2	2.2	1.9	0.6	3		13		C6.0	1			P
6544		B	50	M	28	ROOM	4A	13A	37	3	12		102	5	4.1	2.3	2.3	27	1			P2.1	1		pebble flake core	P
6555		B	56	G	65	ROOM	4A	13A	37	0	20	DEB	102	3	0.7	0.8	0.4	1	1			P2.1	1			P
6556		B	56	G	65	ROOM	4A	13B	21	3	4	3NCF	102	5	1.2	0.8	0.2	1		13		C6.0	1	32/-		P
6560		B	65	G	64	ROOM	4A	13B	21	3	20		102	7				4	1		3	R2.2	2			P
6561.1		B	65	G	64	ROOM	4A	13B	21	3	20	2NCF	102	2	1.9	3.3	1.1	6	1			P3.1	1			P
6561.2		B	65	G	64	ROOM	4A	13B	21	3	20	PDF	102	2	1.2	1	0.2	1	1			P2.1	1			P
6564		B	50	M	28	WALL	2	8D	36	0	20	PDF	102	3	2.7	1.3	0.8	3	1			C6.1	1	30/-	used to cut meat	P
6565		B	50	M	28	WALL	2	8D	36	0	20	2DF	102	2	2.5*	1.8	0.4	3	14			C6.1	1		retouched	P
6574		C	64	G	118	CRDX	2	8A	35	0	51		103	4	5.6*	15	0.6	38	1			C5.0	1	40/-	rim	P
6595.1		ABCS	6	G	189	PLAT	2	8C	36	3	49	2NCF	102	2	3.3*	2.1	0.9	6	15			C5.0	1		drill	P
6595.2		ABCS	6	G	189	PLAT	2	8C	36	3	20	2NCF	102	2	1.2	2.2	0.3	1	1			P2.1	1			P
6596		ABCS	9	M	106	WALL	2	8D	36	3	20	2DF	102	2	1.8	1.6	0.3	1	1			P2.1	1			P
6597.1		ABCS	18	M					41	3	20	2DF	102	2	2.5*	2.0*	0.4	2	1			P3.1	1			P
6597.2		ABCS	18	M					41	3	20	2DF	102	2	1.9	1.5	0.2	1	1			P2.1	1			P
6597.3		ABCS	18	M					41	3	20	2DF	102	2	2.2	1.1*	0.7	1	1			P2.1	1			P
6597.4		ABCS	18	M					41	3	20	2DF	102	2	4.8	1.8	0.6	6	1			P3.1	1			P
6598		ABCS	18	M					41	3	20	2DF	102	3	3.8	2.9	0.5	6	1			P3.1	1	30/-	no use wear	P
6600		ABCN	23	M	207	ROOM	2	8A	35	3	20	2DF	102	2	2.2	1.9	0.3	2	1			P2.1	1		no use wear	P
6601		ABCN	30	G	207	ROOM	2	8B	37	3	20	2DF	102	1	3.7	4.2	1.4	24	1		3	R2.2	1		banded	P
6602		ABCN	30	G	207	ROOM	2	8B	37	0	20	2DF	102	2	2.1*	1.2	0.5	2	1			P2.1	1	30/-		P

mf #	M #	OP	LOT	LI	FT#	FEAT	EL	STR	DC	CL	TYP	SBT	MAT	V	IN	WD	TK	WT	FA	FB	FC	STAT	QTY	FIG/PL	NOTES	L
6603		ABCN	47	G	28	WALL	2	8D	36	0	20	2DF	102	2	1.6*	1.7	0.6	2	1			P2.1	1			P
6604		ABCN	47	G	28	WALL	2	8D	36	3	20	2DF	102	2	1.3	1.3	0.3	1	1			P2.1	1			P
6605		ABCN	50	H	71	ROOM	2	8D	29	3	20	2NCF	102	2	2.6	1.8	1.2	5	1			P3.1	1		used to incise hard material	P
6606		ABCN	50	H	71	ROOM	2	8D	29	0	20	2NCF	102	2	2.4*	1.6	0.4	2	1	13		C6.1	1			P
6607		ABCN	50	H	71	ROOM	2	8D	29	0	39	2NCF	102	1	1.3	1.3	0.1	1	22			C6.0	1	35/-	tranchet point, no use wear	P
6608		ABCN	50	M	71	ROOM	2	8D	29	3	20	2NCF	102	1	2.1*	1.2	0.4	1	1			P2.1	1			P
6609		ABCN	59	M	220	ROOM	3A	10A	35	0	20	2DF	102	2	1.8*	1.5	0.5	1	1			P2.1	1	30/-	no use wear	P
6611		ABCN	65	M			9	34	3	20	3NCF	102	7	1.5*	1	0.2	1	1		3	R2.2	1			P
6612		ABCN	69	G	220	ROOM	3A	10A	37	0	4	MBS	102	2	2.5	1.3	0.4	2	1	13		C6.1	1	34/-	backed, gloss, used to cut grass	P
6613		ABCN	76	G	260	AREA	3A	10B	37	3	20	2NCF	102	3	1.4*	2.1*	0.4	1	1			P2.1	1			P
6614		ABCN	83	M			9	34	3	20	2DF	102	3	3.3	3.2	0.6	8	1			P3.1	1			P
6615		ABCN	86	M	63	ROOM	3A	10A	37	3	20	2NCF	102	2	2.4*	3.9	0.5	7	1			P3.1	1	31/-		P
6616		ABCN	90	G	118	CRDX	2	8D	29	0	20	2NCF	102	3	3.5	1.7	0.3	2	1			P3.1	1			P
6617.1		ABCN	90	G	118	CRDX	2	8D	29	3	20	PDF	102	3	1.3	1.7	0.5	1	1			P2.1	1			P
6617.2		ABCN	90	G	118	CRDX	2	8D	29	3	20	DEB	102	3	2.4	1.5	0.9	3	1			P2.1	1			P
6618		ABCN	90	G	118	CRDX	2	8D	29	3	20	3NCF	102	5	1.1	1.4	0.3	1	1			P2.1	1		no use wear	P
6619		ABCN	92	M	260	AREA	3A	10A	35	0	4	PBS	102	2	3.1	1.3	0.3	2	1	13		C6.1	1	33/-	weak gloss, used to cut grass	P
6621		ABCN	95	G	118	CRDX	2	8D	29	3	20	2DF	102	5	4.4	2.6	0.5	8	1			P3.1	1		calcium carbonate encrusted	P
6622		ABCN	92	M	260	AREA	3A	10A	35	0	4	MBS	102	5	2.4	1	0.2	1	1	13		C6.0	1	34/-	gloss, used to cut grass	P
6624		ABCN	99	H	211	ROOM	3A	10A	37	0	4	MBS	102	2	2	1.4	0.4	1	1	13		C6.1	1	34/-		P
6625		ABCN	99	H	211	ROOM	3A	10A	37	3	20	2NCF	102	1	1.9	0.9	0.4	1	1			P2.1	1	32/-		P
6628		ABCN	106	H	229	ROOM	3B	11B	29	3	49	2NCF	102	2	2.7	2.1	0.6	4	14			C6.1	1	35/23	end scraper, used on hide	P
6629		ABCN	106	H	229	ROOM	3B	11B	29	0	4	PBS	102	1	1.9	0.8	0.2	1	1	13		C6.0	1	33/-		P
6630		ABCN	106	H	229	ROOM	3B	11B	29	0	4	DBS	102	3	3.6	2.2	0.5	4	1	13		C6.1	1	34/-	cortex	P
6638		ABCN	115	M				41	0	20	PDF	102	2	2.1	1.3	0.3	1	1			P2.1	1			P
6639		ABCN	115	M				41	3	20	2NCF	102	2	1.1	2.5	0.5	2	1			P3.1	1			P
6640		ABCN	119	G	63	ROOM	3B	11B	29	0	20	2NCF	102	2	3.7*	2.2	1	6	1			P3.1	1	31/-		P
6641		ABCN	120	G			12	34	3	49	2NCF	102	2	2.9*	1.8	0.6	3	14			C5.0	1		notched	P
6642		ABCN	124	M	67	ROOM	4A	13A	37	3	20	2DF	102	2	2.6*	0.9	0.4	1	1			P3.1	1			P
6643		ABCN	125	M	211	ROOM	3B	11B	29	0	4	MBS	102	2	1.5	1.4	0.4	1	1	13		C6.1	1	34/-	retouched	P
6644.1		ABCN	126	G			12	34	3	20	2NCF	102	2	1.5	2.6	0.5	4	1			P3.1	1			P
6644.2		ABCN	126	G			12	34	3	20	2NCF	102	2	2.6*	1.6	0.4	2	1			P2.1	1			P
6647		ABCN	128	G	66	ROOM	4A	13A	35	0	4	DBS	102	2	4	1.3	0.3	2	1	13		C6.2	1			P
6648		ABCN	128	G	66	ROOM	4A	13A	35	0	4	DBS	102	5	1.6	0.8	0.2	1	1	13		C6.1	1	34/-	gloss, used to cut grass	P
6649		ABCN	137	G	66	ROOM	4A	13A	37	0	3		110	2					16			C6.0	1			P
6656		ABCN	143	M	64	ROOM	4A	13A	37	0	4	PBS	102	3	4.2	1.4	0.4	3	1	13		C6.1	1	33/-		P
6657		ABCN	146	G	64	ROOM	4A	13A	37	0	4	MBS	102	2	2.4	1.5*	0.4	2	1	13		C6.1	1	34/-		P
6659		ABCN	157	G	246	ROOM	5	15A	35	0	4	MBS	102	2	2.7	1.3	0.2	1	1	13		C6.1	1			P
6660		ABCN	90	G	118	CRDX	2	8D	29	0	4	MBS	102	2	1.1	1.1	0.4	6	13			C6.1	1		truncated	P
6661		ABCN	90	G	118	CRDX	2	8D	29	0	4	MBS	102	5	2	1.2	0.4	2	1	13		C6.1	1	34/-	heat treated	P
6662		ABCN	90	G	118	CRDX	2	8D	29	0	4	PBS	102	2	3.2	1.2	0.4	1	1	13		C6.1	1	33/-	backed, gloss	P
6663		ABCN	90	G	118	CRDX	2	8D	29	0	49	2NCF	102	2	4.2*	2.1	0.7	6	14			C5.2	1	31/-	retouched, notched, no wear	P
6664		ABCN	30	G	207	ROOM	2	8B	37	0	3		300		0.7	0.3		1	16			C6.0	1	38/-	shark or ray, yellow pigment	P
6670		ABCN	10	M	117	CRDX	2	8A	35	0	20	3NCF	102	2	1.6*	0.6	0.3	1	1			P2.1	1			P
6681		B	71	M	71	ROOM	2	8A	35	3	20	2NCF	102	5	2.2*	1.4	0.5	2	1			P2.1	1			P
6682.1		B	71	M	71	ROOM	2	8A	35	3	20	DEB	102	2	2.4*	2.1	1.7	7	1			P2.1	1			P
6682.2		B	71	M	71	ROOM	2	8A	35	3	20	DEB	102	2	2.1*	1.1	1.1	2	1			P2.1	1			P
6682.3		B	71	M	71	ROOM	2	8A	35	3	20	PDF	102	2	2.4*	1.8*	0.6	2	1			P2.1	1			P
6682.4		B	71	M	71	ROOM	2	8A	35	3	20	2NCF	102	2	2.2*	1.7	0.4	1	1			P2.1	1			P
6683		B	71	M	71	ROOM	2	8A	35	0	4	MBS	102	2	1.4	1.2	0.3	1	13			C6.1	1			P

Appendix A, Register (*continued*)

mf#	M#	OP	LOT	LI	FT#	FEAT	EL	STR	DC	CL	TYP	SBT	MAT	V	IN	WD	TK	WT	FA	FB	FC	STAT	QTY	FIG/PL	NOTES	L
6684		B	71	M	71	ROOM	2	8A	35	0	4	MBS	102	2	1.4	1	0.3	1	14	13		C6.1	1		gloss	P
6685		B	71	M	71	ROOM	2	8A	35	0	49	MBS	102	2	1.6*	1.8	0.4	2	9			C5.0	1		pointed	P
6686		ABCN	14	G	117	CRDX	2	8B	37	2	57		104	1				1	9			P2.2	1			P
6688		ABCN	129	M	66	ROOM	4A	13A	37	2	57		104	2	4.6	2.2	2.1	25	5			P2.2	1		red	P
6689		ABCN	133	G	241	CRDX	4A	13A	37	2	57		104	1				1	9			P2.2	1			P
6690		ABCS	14	M	268	ROOM	3A	10A	35	2	57		104	1				1	9			P2.2	1			P
6695		ABCS	67	G	282	ROOM	4A	13A	35	2	57		116					5	9		3	P2.2	1			P
6696		ABCN	0	G		WALL	2	8D	36	2	57		116					2	17			C5.1	1		from edge of fired clay tile	P
6697		ABCN	117	M					41	2	57		116					31	9		3	P2.2	1			I
6698		ABCN	123	G	53	HRTH	3B	11B	36	0	3		116					2	16			C6.0	60	38/-		I
6700		ABCN	128	G	66	ROOM	4A	13A	35	2	57		116					2	9		3	P2.2	1			I
6702		ABCS	24	M	315	DOOR	3A	10A	35	2	57		116					35	9		3	P2.2	1			I
6703		ABCN	57	G	211	ROOM	3A	10A	37	2	57		104	1				2	9			P2.2	1			I
6704		ABCN	17	G	118	CRDX	2	8B	37	2	57		104	1				1	9			P2.2	1			I
6705		ABCN	47	G	28	WALL	2	8D	36	2	57		104	1				1	9			P2.2	1			I
6706		ABCN	50	H	71	ROOM	2	8D	29	2	57		104	1				2	9			P2.2	1			I
6707		ABCS	41	G	268	ROOM	3A	10A	35	2	57		104	1				1	9			P2.2	1			I
6709		ABCN	100	M					41	2	57		104	1				1	9			P2.2	1			I
6710		ABCN	80	G	260	AREA	3A	10A	35	2	57		104	1				1	9			P2.2	1			I
6711		ABCN	120	G				12	34	2	57		104	1				1	9			P2.2	1			I
6712		ABCN	86	M	63	ROOM	3A	10A	37	2	57		104	1				1	9			P2.2	1			I
6713		ABCS	46	G				9	23	2	57		104	1				1	9			P2.2	1			I
6714		ABCN	30	G	207	ROOM	2	8B	37	2	57		104	1				1	9			P2.2	1			P
6715		ABCN	90	G	118	CRDX	2	8D	29	2	57		104	1				30	9			P2.2	1			I
6716		ABCN	10	M	117	CRDX	2	8A	35	2	57		104	1				1	9			P2.2	1			P
6717		ABCN	9	M	118	CRDX	2	8A	35	2	57		101	1	2.5	1.6	1.2	2			3	P2.2	1	37/-		P
6718		ABCN	86	M	63	ROOM	3A	10A	37	2	57		101	1	4.3	3.4	2.4	33			3	P2.2	1	37/-		P
6736		C	60	B	117	CRDX	2	8A	35	0	31		401						23			C5.0	1			I
6737		ABCN	99	H	211	ROOM	3A	10A	37	0	16		116			2	0.7	2	16			C5.0	1	38/-	worn	P
6738		ABCN	134	G	210	WALL	3B	11B	36	0	3		116			0.9	0.6	1	16			C6.1	1	38/-		P
6739		ABCN	143	M	64	ROOM	4A	13A	37	0	3		116			1	0.8	1	16			C6.0	1	38/-	broken, biconical	P
6740		ABCN	146	G	64	ROOM	4A	13A	37	0	3		116			0.9	0.9	1	16			C5.0	1	38/-	flattened white stone	P
6741		ABCS	73	G	288	CRDX	4A	13A	37	0	2		100			0.9	0.7	1			3	P3.2	1		green, broken, worn	P
6743		ABCS	58	M	34	ROOM	3B	11B	29	0	3		106			0.9	0.6	1	16			C5.1	1	37/-		P
6749		B	50	M	28	WALL	2	8D	36	1	62		201	1	2	0.3	0.1	1	2			R2.2	1	-/29	see Section II A	P
6772		ABCN	133	G	241	CRDX	4A	13A	37	0	33		201		2.2	1	0.8	19	19			C6.0	1	-/29	see Section II A	P
6774		ABCN	0	M					39	1	63		201										1	-/30	see Section II A	P
6779		ABCS	41	G	268	ROOM	3A	10A	35	1	57		701					66	17			P2.1	1		pure white lump	P
6784		B 1	39	H	131	ROOM	2	8A	35	3	44		800					15	2			P2.1	1			P
6786		ABCS	71	G	288	CRDX	4A	13A	35	3	44		800					2	2			P2.1	1			P
6787		ABCN	71	M	222	ROOM	3A	10A	35	3	44		800					10	2			P2.1	1			P
6788		ABCN	81	G	129	ROOM	2	8D	29	3	74		800					6	2			P2.1	1		corroded	P
6789		ABCN	139	G	307	AREA	4A	13A	21	3	44		800					22	2			P2.1	1			P
6790		ABCN	157	G	246	ROOM	5	15A	35	3	44		800					7	2			P2.1	1			P
6793		ABCN	30	G	207	ROOM	2	8B	37	0	3		300	1	1.5	0.8		1	16			C6.0	1	38/-	shark/ray, yellow, black pgmt	P
6795		ABCN	146	G	64	ROOM	4A	13A	37	0	3		300		1.5	0.8		1	16			C6.0	1	38/-	carved fish vertebra	P
6801		ABCS	66	G	281	COUR	4A	13A	37	0	91		701					54	17				1		yellow	P
6802		ABCN	129	M	66	ROOM	4A	13A	37	0	91		701					2	17				1		dark red	P
6808		ABCN	100	B					41	0	31		401						23			C5.0	2			I
6810		ABCN	153	G	236	PTTX	4A	13A	22	0	50		401	1	15.4*	4.6		14	14			C5.0	1	42/-	tuyère?, fired >800°C	P

Appendix A, Register (*continued*)

mf #	M #	OP	LOT	LI	FT#	FEAT	BL	STR	DC	CL	TYP	SBT	MAT	V	LN	WD	TK	WT	FA	FB	FC	STAT	QTY	FIG/PL	NOTES	L
6811		ABCN	156	H	66	ROOM	4B	14B	29	0	16		401		2.4		1.4	5		12	20	C5.0	1		pierced button base grit-tem	P
6812		ABCS	7	M	156	WALL	2	8D	36	0	59		401					3		4		P3.1	12		miniature rosette, red ware	P
6813		ABCN	81	G	129	ROOM	2	8D	29	0	25		501	9				4		4		P3.1	1		fragment	P
6815.1		ABCN	86	M	63	ROOM	3A	10A	37	3	25		501	10	3.3	1.7	0.3	1		4		P3.1	1		fragment	P
6815.2		ABCN	86	M	63	ROOM	3A	10A	37	3	25		501	10	1.1	0.5	0.2	1		4		P3.1	1		distal fragment	P
6815.3		ABCN	86	M	63	ROOM	3A	10A	37	0	88		501	11				1		4		P2.1	1			P
6816		ABCN	90	G	118	CRDX	2	8D	29	0	25		501	9				31		4		P3.1	69			P
6817.1		ABCN	90	G	118	CRDX	2	8D	29	0	3		504	2	3.1	2.2		15	16			C6.0	1		holed apex, worn, d. 0.2	P
6817.2		ABCN	90	G	118	CRDX	2	8D	29	0	3		504	2	2.5	1.7		15	16			C6.0	1		holed apex, broken lip	P
6818.1		ABCN	92	M	260	AREA	3A	10A	35	5	88		502	3	1.6	0.3		2	16			C6.0	1		ribbed	P
6818.2		ABCN	92	M	260	AREA	3A	10A	35	5	88		502	3	2.5	0.4		2	16			C6.0	1		ribbed	P
6818.3		ABCN	92	M	260	AREA	3A	10A	35	5	88		502	3	2.1	0.4		2	16			C6.0	1		ribbed	P
6818.4		ABCN	92	M	260	AREA	3A	10A	35	5	88		502	3	1.3	0.3		2	16			C6.0	1		smoothed	P
6820		ABCN	99	H	211	ROOM	3A	10A	37	0	25		501	10	1.3	0.8	0.2	1		4		P3.1	1			P
6822		ABCN	106	H	229	ROOM	3B	11B	29	5	88		501	11				1		4		P2.1	1		distal fragment	P
6823		ABCN	115	M					41	5	88		501	10	1.6			4		4		P2.1	1		distal fragment, cut edge?	P
6824		ABCN	116	G	228	ROOM	3B	11B	29	1	88		502	3		0.4			16			C6.0	1		polished, ribbed	P
6825		ABCN	122	M	260	AREA	3A	10A	35	5	88		501	10				35		4		P2.2	2		left hinge and body fragments	P
6826.1		ABCN	123	G	53	HRTH	3B	11B	36	5	25		501	10	2.4	0.7	0.3	2		4		P3.1	2		curved rectangle; scratches	P
6826.2		ABCN	123	G	53	HRTH	3B	11B	36	5	25		501	10				2		4		P3.1	1		distal fragment	P
6828		ABCN	133	G	241	CRDX	4A	13A	37	5	88		504	5				1		4		P2.2	1		apex fragment	P
6829		ABCN	136	G	64	ROOM	4A	13A	35	5	88		501	11				2		4		P2.1	1		fragment, left	P
6830		ABCN	146	G	64	ROOM	4A	13A	37	5	88		504	4	1.3			1	16			P3.1	1		open apex, hole d. 0.2	P
6831		ABCN	152	G	236	PITX	4A	13A	22	5	88		501	11				1		4		P2.1	2		hinge fragments	P
6832		ABCN	154	G	59	WALL	4B	14B	37	5	25		501	10	2.3		0.1	1		4		P3.1	1		broken, 1 side scored	P
6835		ABCS	73	G	288	CRDX	4A	13A	37	5	88		504	5				1		4		P2.2	2		tiny gastropods	P
6836		ABCS	75	G	210	WALL	3B	11B	36	5	88		501					1		4		P2.1	1		fragment	P
6837		ABCS	85	G	307	AREA	4A	13A	35	5	88		500	6				1		4		P1.0	3		small land snails	P
6838.1		ABCN	0	B					41	0	25		501	10	4.5	1.5	0.2	1		4		P3.1	1		rectangle, incised & scored	P
6838.2		ABCN	0	B					41	0	25		501	10						4		P3.1	1		fragment	P
7001.1		ABCS	25	G	269	ROOM	3A	10A	37	3	20	2NCF	102	2	2*	2.2	0.3	2	1			P2.1	1		no use wear	P
7001.2		ABCS	25	M	269	ROOM	3A	10A	37	3	49	3NCF	102	2	1.4*	0.6	0.5	1	15	13		C5.1	1	35/-	bitumen, used on hard material.	P
7002		ABCS	25	M	269	ROOM	3A	10A	37	0	4	2DF	102	2	2.4	0.7	0.3	1				C6.2	1	33/-		P
7003		ABCS	26	G	269	ROOM	3A	10A	37	3	20	2DF	102	2	1.8*	1.4	0.5	1	1			P2.1	1			P
7004		ABCS	29	G	267	ROOM	3A	10A	37	3	20	2NCF	102	2	1.4*	1.6	0.8	2	1			P2.1	1			P
7005		ABCS	29	G	267	ROOM	3A	10A	37	3	20	3NCF	102	2	1.1*	1.2*	0.21	1	1			P2.1	1			P
7006		ABCS	37	G				9	34	0	20	2NCF	102	3	1.0*	1.5	0.4	1	1			P2.1	1	32/-	no use wear	P
7007		ABCS	37	G				9	34	3	49	2NCF	102	3	4.2	4.9	1.8	29	14			C6.0	1		pointed	P
7008.1		ABCS	38	M	38	DOOR	3A	10A	35	3	20	2DF	102	2	2.3*	2.3	1	6	1			P2.1	1			P
7008.2		ABCS	38	M	38	DOOR	3A	10A	35	3	49	2NCF	102	2	3.4*	1.4	0.3	1	15			C5.0	1		drill	P
7009		ABCS	41	G	268	ROOM	3A	10A	35	3	20	2NCF	102	3	2.6*	2.3	0.5	4	1			P3.1	1			P
7010		ABCS	46	G				9	23	3	20	2DF	102	3	3.2	1.7	0.8	5	1			P3.1	1			P
7011		ABCS	51	G	130	ROOM	2	8C	29	3	20	2NCF	102	2	2	2.1*	0.5	2	1			P2.1	1			P
7012		ABCS	53	G	310	HRTH	2	8B	28	1	20	2NCF	102	2	4.2	3.2	1.3	20	14			P3.1	1	32/-	heat treated, no use wear	P
7013		ABCS	59	G	35	ROOM	3B	11B	29	0	49	2NCF	102	3	2	1.8	0.3	1	15			C6.0	1		drill	P
7014		ABCS	60	M				12	34	3	12		102	3	2.6	2.4	1.6	9	1			P2.1	1		flake core	P
7017		ABCS	66	G	281	COUR	4A	13A	37	3	20	2DF	102	3	1.5*	1.8	0.4	1	1			P3.1	1			P
7018		ABCS	68	G	283	AREA	4A	13A	35	3	20	3NCF	102	5	1.4*	0.9	0.2	1	1			P3.1	1			P
7019		ABCS	68	G	283	AREA	4A	13A	35	3	20	2NCF	102	2	4.5*	1.9	0.5	5	1			P3.1	1	31/-	no use wear	P
7020		ABCS	68	G	283	AREA	4A	13A	35	3	20	2NCF	102	3	2	1.3*	0.6	1	1			P2.1	1			P

Appendix A, Register (*continued*)

mf#	M#	OP	LOT	LI	FT#	FEAT	BL	STR	DC	CL	TYP	SBT	MAT	V	IN	WD	TK	WT	FA	FB	FC	STAT	QTY	FIG/PL	NOTES	L
7021		ABCS	69	G	268	ROOM	3B	11B	29	0	4	MBS	102	3	3.8	1.6	0.4	3		13		C6.2	1	34/-	backed, no use wear	P
7022		ABCS	71	G	288	CRDX	4B	13A	35	3	20	PDF	102	3	3.3*	1.8	0.8	5	1			P3.1	1			P
7023		ABCS	71	G	288	CRDX	4A	13A	35	3	20		102	2	2.4*	2	0.6	3	1			P2.1	1			P
7024		ABCS	75	G	210	WALL	3B	11B	36	0	4	DBS	102	2	3.1	1.5	0.3	2		13		C6.2	1			P
7025		ABCS	78	G	33	WALL	3B	11B	36	0	3		110	2					16			C6.0	1			P
7026		ABCS	79	M				12	34	0	4	PBS	102	2	3.3	1.3	0.3	2		13		C6.1	1	33/23	used to shave soft stone	P
7027		ABCS	82	G	307	AREA	4A	13A	21	0	4		102	2	1.6	1.2	0.3	1		13		C6.0	1	33/-		P
7028		ABCS	86	M	241	CRDX	4A	13A	35	3	20	2NCF	102	2	2.1	1.4	0.5	1	1			P2.1	1		no use wear	P
7029		ABCS	87	G	307	AREA	4A	13A	21	3	20	DEB	102	2	2	2	0.9	4	1			P2.1	1			P
7234		ABCS	78	M	215	DOOR	3A	10A	35	5	60		404	4					11			C5.0	1		reed impression	P
7236		ABCN	100	M					41	0	49		401		4.1	2.2	0.5	7	14			C6.0	1		grit-temp brick red scraper	P
7249		ABCN	100	B					41	0	31		401		3.2*	2.4	1	11	23			C5.0	2		buff ware w/ white paste	P
7254		ABCN	139	G	307	AREA	4A	13A	21	5	74		100					109	23				1		thermoluminescence sample	P
7255		ABCN	119	G	63	ROOM	3B	11B	29	5	74		100					1000					1		lump	P
7256		ABCN	162	G	236	PTTX	4A	13A	22	2	57		701					187	17			P2.0	1		grey stone chip	P
7260		ABCN	99	H	211	ROOM	3A	10A	37	2	57		100					1	9			P1.0	1		flake core	P
7263.1		ABCN	50	H	71	ROOM	2	8D	29	3	12		102	2	3.5*	4.6	2.7	41	1			P2.1	1			P
7263.2		ABCN	50	H	71	ROOM	2	8D	29	3	20	DEB	102	2	3.3	2	1.2	7	1		3	R2.2	1			P
7264		ABCN	47	G	28	WALL	2	8D	36	0	4	PBS	102	2	2	1.1	0.3	1		13		C6.2	1			P
7266		ABCN	17	G	118	CRDX	2	8B	37	2	57		104	1				1	9			P2.2	1			P
7267		ABCN	31	M	371	DBLK	2	8C	36	1	88		502	3	1.7*	0.3		1	16			C6.0	1		smoothed	P
7268		ABCN	14	G	117	CRDX	2	8B	37	1	88		504	4	1.2	0.8	0.2	1	16			C6.0	1		S005, open apex, has color	P
7269		ABCN	14	G	117	CRDX	2	8B	37	5	88		500	6				1		4		P1.0	1		S005	P
7270.1		ABCN	1	B					41	5	88		502	3	2.9	0.5		1	16			C6.0	1			P
7270.2		ABCN	1	B					41	5	88		502	3	1.6	0.4		1	16			C6.0	1			P
7271		ABCN	23	M	207	ROOM	2	8A	35	5	88		501	11				1		4		P2.1	1		distal fragment	P
7272		ABCN	146	G	64	ROOM	4A	13A	37	5	88		502	3	1.6	0.3		1	16			C6.0	1		ribbed, has tip	P
7273		ABCN	154	G	59	WALL	4B	14B	36	5	88		502	3	1.6	0.4		1	16			C6.0	1		ribbed	P
7274		ABCN	136	G	64	ROOM	4A	13A	35	5	88		502	3	1.9	0.5		1	16			C6.0	1		ribbed, has tip	P
7275		ABCN	90	G	118	CRDX	2	8D	29	5	88		501	11				7		4		P2.1	3		fragments: 2 left, 1 right	P
7276		ABCN	90	G	118	CRDX	2	8D	29	5	88		502	3	2.6	0.6		1	16			C6.0	1		ribbed	P
7277		ABCN	90	G	118	CRDX	2	8D	29	5	88		502	3	1.9	0.4		1	16			C6.0	1		ribbed	P
7278		ABCN	86	M	63	ROOM	3A	10A	37	0	3		500	1	0.9			1	16			C6.0	1		open apex, hole d. 0.1	P
7279		ABCN	122	M	260	AREA	3A	10A	35	2	57		104	1				1	9			P2.2	1			P
7280		ABCN	50	H	71	ROOM	2	8D	29	5	88		501	10				1		4		P2.1	2		distal frags., 2 poss. cut edges	P
7281		ABCN	152	G	236	PTTX	4A	13A	22	0	11		404		5.8		3	82		10		C5.1	1	42/-	conical jar stopper	P
7282		ABCN	152	G	236	PTTX	4A	13A	22	0	2		404			3.6		37	21			C6.0	1			P
7283		ABCN	152	G	236	PTTX	4A	13A	22	0	2		404			3.2		26	21			C6.0	1			P
7284		ABCN	152	G	236	PTTX	4A	13A	22	0	2		404			3.8		39	21			C6.0	1			P
7285		ABCN	152	G	236	PTTX	4A	13A	22	0	2		404			3.3		20	21			C6.0	1			P
7286		ABCN	152	G	236	PTTX	4A	13A	22	0	2		404			3		16	21			C6.0	1			P
7287		ABCN	152	G	236	PTTX	4A	13A	22	0	2		404			2.7		8	21			C6.0	1			P
7288		ABCN	152	G	236	PTTX	4A	13A	22	0	2		404			3.2		28	21			C6.0	1			P
7289		ABCN	152	G	236	PTTX	4A	13A	22	0	2		404			3		16	21			C6.0	1			P
7290		ABCN	152	G	236	PTTX	4A	13A	22	0	2		404			3.1		20	21			C6.0	1			P
7291		ABCN	152	G	236	PTTX	4A	13A	22	0	2		404			2.9		22	21			C6.0	1			P
7292		ABCN	149	G	236	PTTX	4A	13A	22	1	11		404							10		C5.1	1		conical jar stopper	I
7293		ABCN	149	G	236	PTTX	4A	13A	22	1	11		404							10		C5.1	1		jar stopper, no impression	I
7294		ABCN	154	G	59	WALL	4B	14B	36	0	51		103	3				3		12		C5.0	1		white body	P
7296		ABCN	10	M	117	CRDX	2	8A	35	0	51		103	2				2		12		C5.0	1		green body	P

Appendix A, Register (*continued*)

mf#	M#	OP	LOT	LI	FT#	FEAT	BL	STR	DC	CL	TYP	SBT	MAT	V	LN	WD	TK	WT	FA	FB	FC	STAT	QTY	FIG/PL	NOTES	L
7299		ABCN	9	M	118	CRDX	2	8A	35	2	57		103	5				53	9			P1.0	1		grey, limestone of ore?	P
7300		ABCN	50	H	71	ROOM	2	8D	29	2	12		102	2	6.7	3.8	3	86	1		3	R2.2	1		flake core, grey, banded	P
7301		ABCN	154	G	59	WALL	4B	14B	36	1	57		104	2				1	5			P2.2	1		red	P
7302		ABCN	154	G	59	WALL	4B	14B	36	1	57		108		0.8	0.8	0.6	1			3	P3.2	1	37/-	blank, smoothed, not drilled	P
7304		ABCN	129	M	66	ROOM	4A	13A	37	0	22		103	5	8.9	3.5	3.3	126	14			C6.1	1	42/-	grinding or polishing stone	P
7305		ABCN	0	B					39	0	51		103	5	2.9*	4.8*	1	13		12	20	C5.0	1	40/-	incised, red paint	P
7306		ABCN	146	G	64	ROOM	4A	13A	37	0	22		103	5	9.7*	7.0*	3.7	344	14			C6.1	1		grinding or polishing stone	P
7307		ABCN	90	G	118	CRDX	2	8D	29	3	20		105		1.2*	0.9		2	1			P3.1	1		MAO-032, NMRD 1	D
7308		ABCN	117	M					41	3	20		105		1.0*	0.8		1	1			P3.1	1		MAO-020, NMRD 1	P
7310.1		ABCN	16	G	117	CRDX	2	8B	37	5	79		601						7			P2.1	1		F2	P
7310.2		ABCN	16	G	117	CRDX	2	8B	37	5	88		502	3					16			C6.0	1		F2, small land snail	P
7310.3		ABCN	16	G	117	CRDX	2	8B	37	5	88		500	6						4		P1.0	1		F2, small land snail	P
7311		ABCN	15	G	118	CRDX	2	8B	37	5	79		601						7			P2.1	1		F3, shell	P
7315		ABCN	42	G	207	ROOM	4A	8B	37	5	79		601						7			P2.1	1		F7, shell	P
7321		ABCN	61	G	260	AREA	3A	10B	29	5	79		601						7			P2.1	1		F13, shell	P
7326		ABCN	68	G	220	ROOM	3A	10A	21	5	79		601						7			P2.1	1		F18, bone, shell	P
7329		ABCN	79	G	222	ROOM	3A	10A	37	5	79		601						7			P2.1	1		F21	P
7330.1		ABCS	77	G	290	BNCH	4A	13A	21	5	88		500	11						4		P2.2	2		F22; distal ends	P
7330.2		ABCS	77	G	290	BNCH	4A	13A	21	5	79		601						7			P2.1	1		F22, shell, sherds	P
7331		ABCN	76	H	269	ROOM	3B	11B	29	5	79		601						7			P2.1	1		F23, shell, sherds	P
7334		ABCS	48	G	268	ROOM	3B	11B	29	5	79		601						7			P2.1	1		F26	P
7362		ABCS	51	G	130	ROOM	2	8C	29	5	79		601						7			P2.1	1		F54, flint, slag, shell, limonite.	P
7366		ABCS	54	G	270	ROOM	3A	10A	37	5	79		601						7			P2.1	1		F58, shell	P
7367		ABCS	53	G	310	HRTH	2	8B	28	5	79		601						7			P2.1	1		F59, shell	P
7395		ABCS	77	G	290	BNCH	4A	13A	21	5	79		601						7			P2.1	1		F89, bead, shell	P
7402		ABCN	82	G	222	ROOM	3A	10A	37	5	79		601						7			P2.1	1		F96, shell	P
7403		ABCN	137	G	66	ROOM	4A	13A	37	5	79		601						7			P2.1	1		F97, bead	P
7409		ABCN	148	G	236	PTTX	4A	13A	22	5	79		601						23			P2.1	1		F103, shell	P
7410		ABCS	80	G	308	HRTH	4A	13A	28	5	79		601						7						F104	P
7422		ABCN	153	G	236	PTTX	4A	13A	22	5	79		601						23			P2.1	1		F116, shell	P
7423		ABCN	87	G	307	AREA	4A	13A	21	5	79		601						7						F117	P
7425.1		ABCN	153	G	236	PTTX	4A	13A	22	0	3		110	2	0.2	0.4			16			C6.0	1	37/-	F119	P
7425.2		ABCN	153	G	236	PTTX	4A	13A	22	0	3		110	2	0.2	0.4			16			C6.0	1	37/-	F119	P
7425.3		ABCN	153	G	236	PTTX	4A	13A	22	0	3		502	2	0.1	0.2			16			C6.0	1	38/-	F119	P
7425.4		ABCN	153	G	236	PTTX	4A	13A	22	5	79		601						23						F119	P
7432		ABCN	0	G		WALL	2	8D	36	5	95		100										1		MS5, brick w/seed impress.	P
7467		ABCN	152	G	236	PTTX	4A	13A	22	5	79		601										1		MS59, dissolved s-t sherds	P
7468		ABCN	152	G	236	PTTX	4A	13A	22	5	79		601										1		MS60, dirt in pot, mf 7467	P
7469		ABCN	153	G	236	PTTX	4A	13A	22	5	79		116						9			P2.1	1		MS61, dissol. s-t sherd, bitum.	P
7477		ABCN	149	G	236	PTTX	4A	13A	22	5	79		601						23			P2.2	1	37/-	MS73	P
7499		ABCS	2	G	14	WALL	2	8C	36	2	57		103	4	2.3	1.3	1.1	7			3	P2.2	1			M
7977		ABC	50	G		AREA		18B	50	0	4		102	2	3.5	1.1	0.3	2		13		C6.1	1		nibbled	M
8725		ABCN	53	G				9	34	2	44	800						24	8			P2.1	1		ceramic slag?	L
8733		ABCN	60	G	260	AREA	3A	10B	29	2	57		100					1	9			P1.0	1		iridescent blue-green	P
8851		ABCN	30	G	207	ROOM	2	8B	37	0	4		102	2	1.4	0.9	0.2	3		13		C6.0	1			M
9264		ABC	50	G	370	AREA		18B	50	3	20		102	2	3.8	1.8		3	1			P3.1	1			M
9265	1765	ABC	50	G	370	AREA		18B	50	0	4		102	2	6	1.7	0.3	4		13		C6.1	1		nibbled, notched?	I
9266		ABC	50	G	370	AREA		18B	50	0	4		102	2	3.6	1.1	0.2	1		13		C6.1	1		nibbled	M
9267		ABC	50	G	370	AREA		18B	50	0	20		102	2	1.2	0.7	0.2	1	1			P2.1	1			L
9268		ABC	50	G	370	AREA		18B	50	3	20	DEB	102	2	0.8	0.5		1	1			P2.1	1			M

Appendix A, Register (*continued*)

mf #	M #	OP	LOT	LI	FT#	FEAT	EL	STR	DC	CL	TYP	SBT	MAT	V	LN	WD	TK	WT	FA	FB	FC	STAT	QTY	FIG/PL	NOTES	L
9269		ABC	50	G	370	AREA		18B	50	3	20		102	2	1.2*	0.9		1	1			P2.1	1			M
9270		ABC	50	G	370	AREA		18B	50	0	8		404	2	4.9*	4.7*	2.6	43	17				1		s-t brick fragment	MP
9271		ABC	50	G	370	AREA		18B	50	3	20	DEB	102	2	2.3*	1.6		3	1			P2.1	4			M
9272		ABC	50	G	370	AREA		18B	50	0	20		102	2	1.7	1.1		2		13		C6.1	1		nibbled	M
9273		ABC	50	G	370	AREA		18B	50	0	20		102	2	2*	1.3		3		13		C6.1	1		nibbled	M
9274		ABC	51	G	370	AREA		18B	50	5	94		100					86					1		soil sample	M
9275		ABC	51	G	370	AREA		18B	50	1	57		701					15	17			P2.0	1		lump	M
9276		ABC	52	G	370	AREA		18B	50	5	74		100					55	9			P1.0	1		rock	M
9277		ABC	52	G	370	AREA		18B	50	0	74		401					2					1		g-t Banesh ceramic	P
9278	1806	ABC	54	G	372	AREA		19	50	5	4		102	2	3.1	0.8	0.2	2		13		C6.1	1		nibbled	I
9628		ABC	50	G	372	AREA		18B	50	5	94		100					125					1		phytolith sample	P
9629		ABC	56	G	372	AREA		19	50	5	94		100					215					1		virgin soil sample	P
9686		ABC	50	G	370	AREA		18B	50	3	20		102	3				1	1			P2.1	1			M
9687		ABC	55	G	372	AREA		19	50	5	94		100					94					1		virgin soil sample	P
9688		ABC	56	G	372	AREA		19	50	5	94		100										1		virgin soil sample	P
9759		ABC	56	G	370	AREA		18B	50	5	77		601										1		F468, no charcoal	P
9786		ABCN	95	G	118	CRDX	2	8D	29	0	51		100							12		C5.0	1			P
9787		ABCN	17	G	118	CRDX	2	8B	29	2	57		100						9			P1.0	1	37/-		P
9788		ABCN	123	G	53	HRTH	3B	11B	36	2	57		127	2							3	P2.2	1	37/-		P
9789		ABCN	143	M	64	ROOM	4A	13A	37	1	3		127	2							3	P3.2	2			P
9790		ABCN	99	H	211	ROOM	3A	10A	37	0	51		701							12		C5.0	1		MAL-1006, 1010, flat rim	P
9791		ABCN	134	G	210	WALL	3B	11B	36	0	51		701							12		C5.0	1		MAL-1007, round rim	P
9792		ABCN	139	G	307	AREA	4A	13A	21	2	57		103	6					9		3	P2.2	1		MAL-1008	P
9793		ABCN	119	G	63	ROOM	3B	11B	29	2	57		103	4					9			P2.2	1		MAL-1009	P
9795		ABCN	53	G				9	34	2	57		100						9			P1.0	1			P
9796		ABCN	100	M					41	1	74		100		4.4*	0.6										P
9797		ABCN	16	G	117	CRDX	2	8B	37	0	3		108		0.2	0.4			16			C6.0	1		F2	P
9798.1		ABCN	16	G	117	CRDX	2	8B	37	1	3		107								3	P3.0	1		F2	P
9798.2		ABCN	16	G	117	CRDX	2	8B	37	1	3		107								3	P3.0	1		F2	P
9800		ABCN	59	M	220	ROOM	3A	10A	35	2	57		118	3					9			P2.2	1			P
9805		ABCN	112	G	136	DBLK	2	8C	36	5	74		404									R2.2	14		MAC-028	P
9807		ABCN	90	G	118	CRDX	2	8D	29	3	74		203						2		3	R2.2	1		Pb isotope analysis	I
9808		ABCN	123	G	53	HRTH	3B	11B	36	2	57		116						9			R2.2	1			I
9814		ABCN	152	G	236	PITX	4A	13A	22	1	63		201					14	2			R2.2	1			I
9816		ABCN	120	G				12	34	1	57		701					19	17			P2.0	1			I
9817		ABCN	124	M	67	ROOM	4A	13A	37	1	57		701					55	17			P2.0	1			I
9818		ABCN	146	G	64	ROOM	4A	13A	37	1	57		701					740	17			P2.0	1			I
9819		ABCN	61	G	260	AREA	3A	10B	29	2	57		100					2	9			P1.0	1		red stone	I
9820		ABCN	71	M	222	ROOM	3A	10A	35	2	57		100					12	9			P1.0	1		red stone	I
9822		ABCN	143	M	64	ROOM	3A	13A	37	2	57		100					42	9			P1.0	1		yellow clay	I
9823		ABCN	59	M	220	ROOM	3A	10A	35	1	57		701					35	17			P2.0	1			I
9824		ABCN	93	G	63	ROOM	3A	10A	35	2	57		100					3	9			P1.0	1		black stone	I
9825		ABCN	92	M	260	AREA	3A	10A	35	2	57		100					32	9			P1.0	1		yellow, concoidal fracture	I
9827		ABCN	113	G	260	AREA	3A	10B	29	2	57		100					70	9			P1.0	1		flintlike stone	I
9828		ABCN	30	G	207	ROOM	2	8B	37	3	57		127					1			3	P2.2	1			P
9829		ABCN	10	M	117	CRDX	2	8A	35	3	74		201					3	2			R2.2	1			I
9830		ABCS	25	M	269	ROOM	3A	10A	37	2	57		104	1				1	9			P2.2	1			P
9831		ABCS	17	G				9	34	2	57		104	1				1	9			P2.2	1			P
9832		ABCS	2	G	14	WALL	2	8C	36	3	20	2DF	102	2	1.8*	1.9*	0.8	4	1			P2.1	1		heat treated	P
9833		ABCS	26	G	269	ROOM	3A	10A	37	3	49	2NCF	102	3	2.3	2.2	0.8	4	14			C6.0	1		pointed, heat treated	P

Appendix A, Register (continued)

mf #	M #	OP	LOT	LI	FT#	FEAT	HL	STR	DC	CL	TYP	SBT	MAT	V	LN	WD	TK	WT	FA	FB	FC	STAT	QTY	FIG/PL	NOTES	L
9834		ABCS	6	G	189	PLAT	2	8C	36	3	74		201		1.9	1.7	1.7	15	2			P2.2	1		copper ore	P
9835		ABCS	6	G	189	PLAT	2	8C	36	1	12		102	3	2*	3.1	2	12	1			P2.1	1		flake core, heat treated	P
9836		ABCS	9	M	106	WALL	2	8D	36	2	57		129	1	1.9	1.5	0.9	3			3	P2.2	1	37/-		P
9837		ABCS	10	G	125	WALL	2	8D	36	2	57		125						2		3	P2.2	1			P
9839		ABCS	15	G	268	ROOM	3A	10A	35	2	57		110	5							3	P2.2	1			P
9840		ABCS	26	G	269	ROOM	3A	10A	37	1	57		103	4				9	9		3	R2.2	1		vessel production	P
9841		ABCS	37	G				9	34	1	74		203					12	2			P2.2	1	36/-		P
9842		ABCS	46	G				9	23	2	57		103	5				21	9			C6.1	1		vessel production	P
9843		ABCS	60	M				12	34	0	2		103	5					14			C5.0	1		hammer	P
9844		ABCS	65	G	304	ROOM	3B	11B	29	0	51		103	5	2.9*	3.4*	1.1	9	1	12		P2.1	1		rim	P
9845		ABCS	71	G	288	CRDX	4A	13A	35	3	20		102	1	1.2	1.9	0.7	1	1			P2.1	1		facetted platform prep. flake	P
9846		ABCS	78	G	33	WALL	3B	11B	36	0	51		103	1			0.4	3		12		C5.0	1		body, banded	P
9847		ABCS	51	G	130	ROOM	2	8C	29	2	57		103	4				3	9		3	P2.1	1		flake, vessel production	P
9849		ABCS	79	M				12	34	0	51		103	5	3.1*	5.4*	1.2	19	12		20	C5.0	1	40/-	incised, red pant	P
9850		ABCS	78	G	33	WALL	3B	11B	36	3	44		800		3.5	2.2	1.7	2	2			P2.1	1		iron rich copper slag	I
9852		ABCS	66	G	281	COUR	4A	13A	37	1	57		701					9	17			P2.0	1			I
9853		ABCS	5	G	155	PLAT	2	8C	36	1	57		701					250	17			P2.0	1			I
9855		B	52	G				12	34	5	88		504	4	1.3			1	16			P3.1	1		open apex d. 0.2; bright color	P
9859		B	43	B	31	ROOM	2	8A	35	1	25		501	9	0.7	0.5	0.1	1	4			P3.1	1		rectangular	P
9860		B	44	M	71	ROOM	2	8A	35	5	88		501	11				2	4			P2.1	1		distal fragment	P
9861		B	50	M	28	WALL	2	8D	36	1	15		501	10	3.4	3.2	0.8	9	4			P3.1	1		roughly chipped disk	P
9863		B 1	39	H	131	ROOM	2	8A	35	5	88		500	6				1	4			P1.0	2		land snail	P
9864		B	40	M	71	ROOM	2	8A	35	2	25		501	9	2.9	0.6	0.1	1	4			P3.1	1		Pinctatada, rectangular	P
9867		C 1	38	G	129	ROOM	2	8A	35	5	88		504	7				2	4			P2.2	1		slightly costate	P
9868		A 1	0	B					31	5	74		100		3.0*	2.8*		2	9			P2.2	1	38/-	ostrich eggshell	P
9888	218	A	0	G					35	0	48		401	4	40.4	21	2.1	1	17				1		four holes, bitumen on edges	I
9889	218	A	0	G					35	1	48		401	10	41.4	20.2	2		17						six holes	I
9890	218	A	0	G					35	0	48		401	2	22.0*	22	2.9	2	17						four holes	I
9891	218	A	0	G					35	0	48		401	5	22.0*	21.5	2.8	9	17						four holes	I
9892	218	A	0	G				8A	35	0	48		401	2	20.3*	20.3	3.5	1	17						two holes	I
9897		B	40	M	71	ROOM	2	8A	35	2	57		103	4				13	9		3	P2.1	1	32/-	flake, vessel production	P
9898		B	49	G	63	ROOM	3B	11B	29	5	88		501	10				1		4		P2.1	1		small fragment	P
9899		B	49	G	63	ROOM	3B	11B	29	3	20		102	2				2	1			P2.1	1			P
9907		B	48	M	63	ROOM	3A	10A	37	0	12		102	5	2.1	2.3	1.1	6	1			P2.1	1		flake core	P
9908		B	49	G	63	ROOM	3B	11B	29	0	20	2NCF	102	2	1.8*	1.6	0.3	1	1			P2.1	1			P
9913		B	50	M	28	WALL	2	8D	36	2	57		103	4				2			3	P2.2	1			P
9919		B	50	M	28	WALL	2	8D	36	3	20	2NCF	102	2	4.7	3.8	1.1	16	1			P3.1	1			P
9924		C	67	G	118	CRDX	2	8B	21	1	57		104	1				1	9			P2.2	1			P
9929		ABCN	163	G	236	PITX	4A	13A	22	4	79		601						7			P2.1	1		P-2336, RC 20(2)	P
9930		ABCN	143	M	64	ROOM	4A	13A	37	4	79		601						7			P2.1	1		P-2334, RC 20(2)	P
9941		B 1	39	H	131	ROOM	2	8A	35	0	31		401	2	2.8*	2	0.9	4	23			C5.0	1		white paste on surface	P
9942		B 1	39	H	131	ROOM	2	8A	35	0	31		401	2	2.6*	2.2	1	5	23			C5.0	1		white paste on surface	P
9943		B 1	39	H	131	ROOM	2	8A	35	0	31		401					5	23			C5.0	1		white paste on surface	P
9944		B 1	39	H	131	ROOM	2	8A	35	0	31		401		1.5*	2.4	1.1	3	23			C5.0	1		white paste on surface	P
9951		B 1	39	H	131	ROOM	2	8A	35	0	51		103	4			0.5	1				C5.0	1		body	P
9952	597	B 1	39	H	131	ROOM	2	8A	35	0	3		403						12			C6.0	1		see Section II A	I
9956		A	44	M				9	34	3	62		201					9	2			R2.2	1	-/30	MAH-120, rim	P
9961		B 1	39	H	131	ROOM	2	8A	35	0	51		111							12		C5.0	1	40/-	polished, apical hole, d. 0.2	P
9963		C 1	37	G	130	ROOM	2	8B	21	0	3		504	2	1.3	1		1	16			C6.0	1			P
9964	645	C 1	37	G	130	ROOM	2	8B	21	0	3		500	8	2	1.9		3	16			C6.0	1		hole below apex, d. 0.3	P

Appendix A, Register (*continued*)

mf #	M #	OP	LOT	LI	FT#	FEAT	BL	STR	DC	CL	TYP	SBT	MAT	V	LN	WD	TK	WT	FA	FB	FC	STAT	QTY	FIG/PL	NOTES	L
9967		C 1	41	G	128	ROOM	2	8B	29	3	74		203					7	2			R2.2	2		Pb isotope analysis	P
9986.1		C 1	36	G	128	ROOM	2	8A	35	3	20	DEB	102	2	3	2.6	1.7	12	1			P3.1	1			P
9986.2		C 1	36	G	128	ROOM	2	8A	35	3	49	DEB	102	2	3.1	1.7	1.3	5	14			C6.0	1		pointed	P
9986.3		C 1	36	G	128	ROOM	2	8A	35	3	20	3NCF	102	2	1.1*	0.9*	0.2	1	1			P2.1	1			P
10204		B	50	M	28	WALL	2	8D	36	0	3		110						16			C6.1	1		MAL-0142	P
10215		B 1	39	H	131	ROOM	2	8A	35	0	74		701										1		MAL-1024	P
10217		B 1	39	H	131	ROOM	2	8A	35	1	57		701						17			P2.0	1			P
10220		ABCN	81	G	129	ROOM	2	8D	29	0	22		100		1.5*	3.3	0.9		14			C6.1	1		grinding or polishing stone	P
10222		ABCS	8	M	155	PLAT	2	8C	36	0	13		100						9			P3.2	1		calcite cylinder seal blank	P
10224		ABCN	149	G	236	PITX	4A	13A	22	1	57		100						9		3	P2.0	1		worked white stone	D
10239		ABCN	90	G	118	CRDX	2	8D	29	3	20		105		1.7*	1.2		2	1			P3.1	1		MAO-019, NMRD 1, green	P
10241		B	50	M	28	WALL	2	8D	36	2	57		100						9			P1.0	1			P
10244		ABCN	16	G	117	CRDX	2	8B	37	0	3		100						16			C6.0	1		MAT 300?	P
11224		ABCN	148	G	236	PITX	4A	13A	22	5	74		404										1		MS-62	P
11225		ABCN	149	G	236	PITX	4A	13A	22	5	74		404										1		MS-63	P
11226		ABCN	162	G	236	PITX	4A	13A	22	5	74		404										1		MS-67	P
11229		ABCS	28	G	267	ROOM	3A	10A	35	3	20	3NCF	102	2	1.6*	0.9	0.2	1	1			P2.1	1		no use wear	P
11230		ABCN	99	H	211	ROOM	3A	10A	37	3	20	3NCF	102	2	1.7	1.5	0.5	1	1			P2.1	1			P
11231		ABCN	99	H	211	ROOM	3A	10A	37	2	57		103	4				2			3	P2.2	1			P
11232		ABCN	99	H	211	ROOM	3A	10A	37	0	74		401		2.5*	3.0*	0.9	5	7			C5.1	1		strainer sherd	P
11233		ABCN	149	G	236	PITX	4A	13A	22	2	57		701					2	17			P2.0	1		lump	P
11234		ABCN	90	G	118	CRDX	2	8D	29	0	11		401		3.3*	0.8*		3	23			C5.0	1		thin tapering rod	P
11235		ABCN	139	G	307	AREA	4A	13A	21	2	57		701					16	17			P2.0	1		lumps	P
11246		ABCN	149	G	236	PITX	4A	13A	22	5	74		301					1					1		human deciduous molar	P
11262		ABCS	77	G	290	BNCH	2	13A	21	0	3		300						16			C5.0	1		F89, broken, charred	P
11264		ABCN	153	G	236	PITX	4A	13A	22	5	77		601						7			P2.1	1		MS-68	P
11283		B	50	M	28	WALL	2	8D	36	0	20		102	2		3.8	1		1			P2.1	1			P
11284		A	44	M				9	34	0	20		102	2					1			P3.1	1			P
11285		A	38	M	186	ROOM	2	8A	35	0	15		401						14			C6.0	1			P
11287		A	44	M				9	34	0	15		401			4	0.9		14			C6.0	1			P
11288		C 1	37	G	130	ROOM	2	8B	21	0	59		401		5.3*	5.1*	1.2			12	20	C5.0	1		burnished red ware	P
11291		A	37	M	71	ROOM	2	8A	35	0	11		401		7.9*	3.2*			17			C5.1	1		grey ware	P
11293		C 1	33	H		ROOM	2	8A	35	0	11		401		6.3*	6.0*			17			C5.1	1			P

PART II A. COPPER BASE METAL FINDS

FROM ABC AND TUV

*Vincent C. Pigott, Harry C. Rogers, &
Samuel K. Nash*

Analysis of Finds from ABC and TUV

The results of PIXE and metallographic analysis of each find is presented, first for the ABC collection, followed by the TUV collection. These results are presented in find number order (mf) and summarized for the entire Banesh collection in Table 27, For the ABC collection in Table A3, and for the TUV collection in Table A4. The full registration data for ABC finds is provided in Appendix A and the discussion of context is found in Chapters I and IV. The discussion of context for TUV finds has been published by Nicholas (1990).

Analysis of Finds From ABC

mf 0874, (Pl. 25a), BL 3A, Room 34, DC 37
Form: Bar stock-quadrangular section
PIXE Analysis:

Cu	97.000	As	1.600
Pb	0.042	Ni	0.100
Sb	0.120	Ag	0.048
S	≤0.010	Cl	≤0.002
Sn	≤0.070	Zn	≤0.570

Metallography: (Pl. 25b) Voids due to gas porosity are of a moderate size and extensive. The microstructure is heavily deformed. Thermal treatment, if any, was insufficient to homogenize the composition gradients in the cast structure. Inclusions are present, moderate sized and show some fragmentation as a result of a relatively low deformation temperature.

mf 1137, STR 9, DC 34
Form: Rod—with pointed, hooked end
PIXE Analysis:

Cu	95.100	As	1.770
Pb	0.610	Ni	⁻≤0.022
Sb	0.200	Ag	0.720
S	0.083	Cl	0.380
Sn	≤0.055	Zn	≤0.570
Fe	0.059		

Metallography:(Pl. 25c) The rod is approximately circular in cross-section and has a huge irregular wide-open crack or hole in the center, partially filled with corro-

sion product. Inclusions are moderately sized and numerous. Inclusions themselves are approximately equiaxed, but the associated porosity extends generally in the flow direction. The microstructure is fine-grained (ASTM G.S. No. 8), equiaxed, with a small degree of cold work present. There is only faint evidence present of the original cast structure. The fiber pattern indicates that this bar may have been shaped by some crude forming operations.

mf 1143, (Pl. 26a), BL 2, Wall 28, DC 36
Form: Sheet stock
PIXE Analysis:

Cu	95.800	As	0.960
Pb	0.610	Ni	⁻≤0.022
Sb	0.200	Ag	0.720
S	0.083	Cl	0.380
Sn	≤0.025	Zn	≤0.570
Fe	0.059		

Metallography: (Pl. 26b) Sample is heavily corroded with very little metal remaining. Microstructure is that of a fully-annealed sheet with a large grain size (ASTM G.S. No. 2). Many annealing twins are present. Grains are approximately equiaxed with extensive grain boundary porosity, the pores being large and disconnected.

mf 1145.2, (Pl. 26c), BL 2. Corridor 118, DC 35
Form: Bar stock with irregular, rectangular cross-section
PIXE Analysis:

Cu	92.200	As	3.060
Pb	3.34	Ni	0.120
Sb	≤0.030	Ag	0.047
Fe	0.29	S	0.041
Cl	≤0.012	Sn	≤0.070
Zn	≤0.57		

Metallography: Microstructure is heavily deformed with a significant fiber texture. Extensive moderate-sized porosity exists; some pores are associated with the relatively large non-metallic inclusions. From their color and the established high lead content of the sample, these are undoubtedly lead particles. Since they tend to be globular despite the evidence of extensive deformation, the temperature of deformation was probably in the warm working region, but above the melting point of lead; hence the globurization of the lead caused by surface tension when working ceased. A slight evidence of subgrain formation supports a low temperature recovery during warm processing.

mf 1498, (Pl. 27a), ABCS, DC 41
Form: Bar stock—quadrangular section
PIXE Analysis:

Cu	96.900	As	0.140
Pb	0.044	Ni	0.64
Sb	0.026	Ag	0.014
Fe	0.110	S	0.19
Cl	0.350	Sn	≤0.070
Zn	≤0.570		

Metallography: (Pl. 27b) Sample is very heavily corroded with extensive coarse porosity in outer regions. Cross section shows general wide cracks filled or partially filled with corrosion product. Nearby metal has considerable porosity. Microstructure has been worked then annealed and shows fine equiaxed grains (ASTM G.S. No. 6) with numerous annealing twins. There is also an extensive array of very fine inclusions approximately equiaxed in cross section. No fiber pattern is evident, but the inclusions are arranged in a pattern indicating they formed intergranularly on a prior grain structure.

Comments: The context for this artifact is not ideal. It was excavated during work on the edge of the 1971-74 operations. It was classified as Banesh because the excavator was working in Building Level 3; however, the artifact could have been washed down from Kaftari levels above.

mf 1504, BL 3A, Area 260, DC 37
Form: Bar Stock—quadrangular section with flattened end
PIXE Analysis:

Cu	96.700	As	1.550
Pb	≤0.044	Ni	0.55
Sb	0.075	Ag	0.037
Fe	0.052	S	≤0.008
Cl	0.071	Sn	≤0.027
Zn	≤0.570		

Metallography: The artifact is in the shape of a bar with one end approximately doubled in width by further flattening. The bar cross-section is roughly in the form of a parallelogram with the two smaller sides non-planar. In general, the inclusions are approximately equiaxed in cross-section. The bar cross-sectional shape and the fiber pattern of the inclusion distribution indicate that the preform for shaping this artifact was probably a round rod. This rod was flattened hot by side pressing in a temperature range for this composition that led to hot cracking at the center of the bar. This leads to a small central split parallel to the pressing direction. Because of the inherent instability of this

geometry and the lack of rigidity of the tooling used, further flattening causes the direction containing the split to rotate significantly. This asymmetry in deformation forced all the flow that produces side surface roll-up on the tooling flats to take place along one diagonal only. Thus, instead of approximating a rectangle, the bar cross-section approximates a parallelogram.

mf 1514—(Pl. 27c) ABCN, DC 41
Form: Awl with quadrangular section
PIXE Analysis:

Cu	97.100	As	1.140
Pb	0.047	Ni	0.360
Sb	≤0.032	Ag	0.160
Fe	0.150	S	0.103
Cl	≤0.012	Sn	≤0.070
Zn	≤0.570		

Metallography: (Pl. 27d) Microstructure is heavily deformed. Irregular flow pattern in longitudinal sample suggests incremental working. Thermal treatment, if any, was insufficient to homogenize the composition gradients in the cast structure. Extensive fine inclusions form a fiber texture following the metal flow. In the longitudinal section, inclusions are broken and strung out in the flow direction with significant amounts of associated strain-induced porosity. The cross section of the body of the artifact shows a nearly diagonal crack across the body now wide and filled with corrosion product, primarily cuprite. Fiber shows flow outward at the four corners, as though an originally round bar was hot flattened on four sides to make a square and cracked during deformation. Grain size is approximately ASTM G.S. No. 6-7. The cross section of the tapered portion of the artifact is kidney-shaped with the fiber running parallel with the curved surface.

Comments: See comments on mf 1498. They apply here. The only difference here is that Building Level 4 was being opened up. However, in the case of this artifact the elemental profile matches closely those from other Banesh artifacts from solid contexts.

mf 1515, BL 3A, Probably Room 211, DC 37
Form: Metal processing debris
PIXE Analysis:

Cu	97.800	As	0.220
Pb	≤0.044	Ni	≤0.022
Sb	0.140	Ag	0.067
Fe	0.180	S	0.026
Cl	0.410	Sn	<0.028
Zn	≤0.570		

Metallography: (Pl. 28a) Three prills are present

trapped in what may be slag or a corroded metal matrix. The structures of all three prills are similar: a cast cellular structure with intercellular material which is at times continuous, sometimes in globules. Cells are roughly equiaxed with a size equivalent to an ASTM G.S. No. 2. The interdendritic material contains frequent irregular inclusions and porosity, located particularly at triple points.

mf 2120, BL 2, Room 71, DC 35
Form: Metal processing debris
PIXE Analysis:

Cu	96.800	As	1.000
Pb	0.51	Ni	0.082
Sb	≤0.036	Ag	0.450
Fe	0.34	S	0.10
Cl	≤0.003	Sn	≤0.070
Zn	≤0.57		

Metallography: (Pl. 28b) Prill is entrapped in slag and has a fine dendritic structure typical of metal cooled from molten state. Interdendritic component contains a moderate amount of fine circular pores.

mf 3742, BL 4B, Area 331, DC 37
Form: Amorphous prill
PIXE Analysis:

Cu	96.000	As	1.780
Pb	0.240	Ni	0.220
Sb	≤0.730	Ag	0.051
Fe	0.130	S	0.079
Cl	0.390	Sn	≤0.034
Zn	≤0.570		

Metallography: (Pl. 28c) Prill is of variable thickness. It has a dendritic structure, the dendrites staining darker during etching. The inter-dendritic regions are lighter colored and contain the bulk of the small-to-medium-sized pores. This highly porous structure also contains a small number of very large pores. Most of the dendrites are moderately small and uniform in size. A few, however, are extremely large; these are located in the thicker portion of the prill.

mf 6749, (Pl. 29a), BL 2, Wall 28, DC 36
Form: Sheet stock
PIXE Analysis:

Cu	97.600	As	1.050
Pb	0.039	Ni	0.096
Sb	≤0.025	Ag	0.013
Fe	0.180	S	0.069
Cl	≤0.009	Sn	≤0.070
Zn	≤0.570		

Metallography: (Pl. 29b) Sample from the midplane of sheet has a microstructure that is mainly annealed after extensive cold work. Intermediate grain size (ASTM G.S. No. 2-3) with numerous annealing twins. Grains are approximately equiaxed. Moderate size inclusions, irregularly shaped and randomly oriented. No fiber texture is evident in this plane. Minor amount of deformation marking indicates a possible limited amount of post-annealing deformation. Sheet cross-section shows extensive corrosion which has penetrated inward from flat surfaces. Inclusions are elongated in width (not thickness) direction forming a moderately strong fiber texture, although the grains are roughly equiaxed.

mf 6772, (Pl. 29c), BL 4A, Corridor 241, DC 37
Form: Shaped Artifact
PIXE Analysis:

Cu	96.900	As	1.000
Pb	0.530	Ni	≤0.020
Sb	≤0.033	Ag	0.360
Fe	0.061	S	0.150
Cl	0.033	Sn	≤0.043
Zn	≤0.570		

Metallography: Pl. 29d) This artifact is a pointed, tapered object with a mushroomed head at the end opposite the point. It is probably an intermediate stage in the fabrication of an arrowhead or a spear point from a rod that was subsequently tapered then pounded hot into a die of some sort to improve the cross sectional shape and/or the taper. The mushroomed head would be removed to produce the finished product. The body of the artifact is annealed with an ASTM Grain Size No. 7, while the microstructure of the head shows considerable retained deformation. The cross section is rhombohedral but nearly square. There is a strong axial fiber texture with the inclusions markedly elongated. In the cross section, the inclusions are small and nearly equiaxed. The cast dendritic structure has not been obliterated but has been deformed considerably. The dendrites etch darker; the interdendritic material contains a significant number of small pores. The fiber flow pattern in the cross section supports the thesis that the preform shape was not sufficiently filled out at the corners, thus requiring the artifact to be pounded into a cavity with sharp corners in an attempt to force the metal into the corner region.

mf 6774, (Pl. 30a), context unknown (DC39)
Form: Rod—strongly tapered and irregularly curved
PIXE Analysis:

Cu	96.500	As	0.770

Table A3
COMPOSITION OF COPPER-BASE FINDS FROM ABC

mf #	Cu	As	Sn	Pb	Fe	Ni	Sb	Ag	Zn	Cl	S
0874	97.0	1.60	≤0.070	0.042	0.006	0.10	0.12	0.048	≤0.57	≤0.002	≤0.010
1137	95.1	1.77	≤0.055	0.61	0.059	≤0.022	0.20	0.72	≤0.57	0.38	0.083
1143	95.8	0.96	≤0.025	≤0.058	0.077	≤0.022	0.24	≤0.018	≤0.57	0.97	0.048
1145.2	92.2	3.06	≤0.070	3.34	0.29	0.12	≤0.030	0.047	≤0.57	≤0.012	0.041
1498	96.9	0.14	≤0.070	0.044	0.11	0.64	0.026	0.014	≤0.57	0.35	0.19
1504	96.7	1.55	≤0.027	≤0.044	0.052	0.55	0.075	0.037	≤0.57	0.071	≤0.008
1514	97.1	1.14	≤0.070	0.047	0.15	0.36	≤0.032	0.16	≤0.57	≤0.012	0.103
1515	97.8	0.22	≤0.028	≤0.044	0.18	≤0.022	0.14	0.067	≤0.57	0.41	0.026
2120	96.8	1.00	≤0.070	0.51	0.34	0.082	≤0.036	0.45	≤0.57	≤0.003	0.10
3742	96.0	1.78	≤0.034	0.24	0.13	0.22	≤0.73	0.051	≤0.57	0.39	0.079
6749	97.6	1.05	≤0.070	0.039	0.18	0.096	≤0.025	0.013	≤0.57	≤0.009	0.069
6772	96.9	1.00	≤0.043	0.53	0.061	≤0.020	≤0.033	0.36	≤0.57	0.033	0.15
6774	96.5	0.77	≤0.036	1.11	0.036	0.21	≤0.034	0.26	≤0.57	0.018	0.21
9956	97.1	0.37	≤0.024	≤0.049	0.18	0.29	≤0.033	0.043	≤0.57	0.53	0.13

Pb	1.110	Ni	0.21
Sb	≤0.034	Ag	0.260
Fe	0.036	S	0.21
Cl	0.018	Sn	≤0.036
Zn	≤0.570		

Metallography: The cross-section is nearly round. The inclusions are mildly elongated, less so in the central region. The inclusions in the latter region appear somewhat coarser and there is also mild porosity there. The fiber pattern indicates that metal flow was normal to the surface at locations approximately 180 degrees apart. At locations 90 degrees from these, metal flow is less and fiber patterns tend to parallel the outer surface.

Comments: The context for this artifact is not ideal. It was found on the dump during excavations in Banesh levels which had some Kaftari period wells cut down through them that were also being excavated. The elemental profile suggests a Banesh period attribution.

mf 9956, (Pl. 30b), Str 9, DC 34
Form: Sheet stock
PIXE Analysis:

Cu	97.100	As	0.370
Pb	0.049	Ni	0.29

Sb	≤0.033	Ag	0.043
Fe	0.180 S 0.13	Cl	0.530
Sn	≤0.024	Zn	≤0.570

Metallography: (Pl. 30c) This fully annealed sheet metal strip has a thickness which is mainly uniform but tapers down to a much smaller thickness at one end. Portion of uniform thickness is very coarse grained (ASTM G.S. No. 0-1). Grain size in the reduced section is much smaller (ASTM G.S. No. 4). This is an indication that the thickness variation is not the result of differential corrosion, but rather that the sheet was hammered at one edge perhaps in an attempt to form a cutting tool, the finer grain size resulting from the additional deformation at the tapered edge.

Analysis of Finds From Operation TUV

The context of TUV finds is presented in Nicholas (1990). In those cases below where PIXE analysis is not presented, it has not been performed.

mf 1141.1, Str 1, DC 34
Form: sheet stock
Metallography: Sample consists of a thin irregularly shaped sheet with a heavy corrosion crust, particularly

on one side. The metal is in the annealed condition with undeformed annealing twins. The ASTM G.S. No. is approximately 3–4. A uniformly scattered small to medium porosity, not on current grain boundaries is present. Some small inclusions are broken up and strung out in the width (length ?) direction as a result of prior working.

mf 1144.1, Str 1, DC 34
Form: amorphous lump
Metallography: 1144.1.1 (Pl. 31a) Sample consists of a thin, irregularly shaped lump with a heavy corrosion crust, particularly on one side. In the annealed condition with undeformed annealing twins the ASTM Grain Size No. is approximately 3–4. A uniformly scattered small to medium porosity, not on current grain boundaries is present. Some small inclusions are broken up and strung out in the width (length ?) direction as a result of prior working. The artifact is in the deformed state but has had limited thermal exposure as the original cast composition gradients are still clearly evident although modified in shape by the deformation. A fine grained microstructure with extensive strain markings is apparent.
Metallography: 1144.1.2 (Pl. 31b) is in the same condition as 1144.1.1. In the deformed lump the composition gradients appear as bands through the thickness of the lump.

mf 1144.2, Str 1, DC 34
Form: amorphous lump
Metallography: (Pl. 31c) Sample consists of a cross section of an irregularly shaped lump. The cross section is mostly non-metallic. The metallic portion consists of the corroded remains of a dendritic as-cast structure.

mf 1144.3, Str 1, DC 34
Form: amorphous lump
Metallography: (Pl. 31d) Sample consists of a cross section of an amorphous lump. It has an as-cast cellular dendritic structure; however, there are many annealing twins observable. Cell size varies between ASTM G.S. No. 0–1. There is a distribution of very large pores throughout the sample, many filled or partially filled with product. Numerous irregularly shaped inclusions are located in the interdendritic regions.

mf 1144.4, Str 1, DC 34
Form: amorphous lump
Metallography: (Pl. 32a) This sample is a pancake shaped lump. An as-cast structure is present with no evidence of deformation prior or current. The appearance of microstructure is cellular or granular with cell size approximately equal to ASTM G.S. No. 0. Etching in potassium dichromate followed by ferric chloride reveals a fairly thick interdendritic region between all the cells. The cells etch darker than the inter dendritic region. Of major interest is inclusion skeleton which nearly fills all the interdendritic regions. This inclusion is continuous with irregular angular edges.

mf 1480, Str 1, DC 40
Form: amorphous prill
Metallography: (Pl. 32b) Sample consists of a cross section of an amorphous lump. There are two extremely large pores present both filled with corrosion products. There are numerous other coarse and medium size pores. Chunks of corrosion are scattered about the matrix. Microstructure varies from region to region. Some areas are fully dendritic. Size is moderate. Other regions have a high content of fine inclusions and limited dendritic appearance (similar to mf 5165). Corrosion crust is generally thin, but is extremely thick in one location.

mf 1483, BL 2, Str 7, DC 35
Form: amorphous prill
Metallography: (Pl. 32c) Cross section of a very irregularly shaped as-cast lump. One region has a fine dendritic cast structure. There are a few large pores. One region has extensive porosity and associated corrosion product. The remainder of sample has a granular appearance with associated boundary pores and inclusions. Size is approximately ASTM G.S. No. 4.

mf 1488, (Pl. 33a), BL 1, Str 5, DC 36
Form: bar stock, quadrangular section
Metallography: (Pl. 33b) This sample clearly has a cast structure. The sharpness of boundaries between dendritic structures makes it appear to be two-phased. The dendrites etch darker. The interdendritic material is light. Considerable fine porosity exists mostly in the interdendritic material.

mf 1490, BL 2, Str 7, DC 35
Form: quadrangular bar
PIXE Analysis:

Cu	96.6	As	2.06
Sn	<0.070	Pb	0.32
Ni	0.092	Ag	0.12
Sb	0.12	Fe	0.045
Cl	<0.009	Zn	<0.57
S	0.044		

Metallography: Sample consists of a roughly square cross-section of bar. The metal appears to have been cut from a plate as the inclusions are flattened, running parallel to the top and bottom surfaces and normal to the side surfaces. This indicates a attempt to flatten rough side surfaces. There is moderate-size scattered porosity. Grain size is fine (ASTM G.S. No 7-8) and is lightly deformed after annealing i.e. the grains have considerable strain markings, but there is little shape change.

mf 3540, Str 9, DC 34
Form: amorphous prill
Metallography: (PL. 33c) Sample consists of a cross section of a large lump having the shape of a slice of bread. A moderately coarse, fully dendritic, as-cast microstructure is present. Inclusions are found in the interdendritic regions. Extensive moderate sized porosity is partially filled with inclusion material. These appear to be generally at triple points between dendrite arms. There is also a thin corrosion crust.

mf 3569, BL 3A, Str 10, DC35
Form: shaped metal
PIXE Analysis:

Cu	94.7	As	3.73
Pb	0.16	Ni	0.095
Sb	0.12	Ag	0.28
Fe	0.33	S	0.037
Cl	<0.007	Sn	<0.070
Zn	<0.57		

Metallography: (Pl. 33d) Sample appears to be the discarded impacted head of an object forced into a die by pounding. The artifact was removed and kept; the deformed head was discarded. The specimen is close to the as-cast condition showing a pattern of cast concentration gradients. The dendrites themselves etch light and there are fine inclusions distributed throughout the structure. The impacted portion obviously exhibits extensive metal flow. The body portion also shows considerable deformation in terms of strain markings. There is no evidence of grain boundaries or annealing twins. This and the clarity of the deformed cast structure shows this artifact was undoubtedly hot deformed directly following casting.

mf 3678, BL 3A, Str 10, DC 23
Form: triangular lump
PIXE Analysis:

Cu	65.4	As	1.50
Pb	0.33	Ni	0.070
Sb	28.2	Ag	2.8
Fe	0.11	S	0.86
Cl	<0.013	Sn	<0.070
Zn	<0.57		

Metallography: (Pl. 34a) The overall appearance of this metal is silvery. The microstructure is in the as-cast condition. There is a moderate amount of large globular porosity with a higher concentration toward the middle. The matrix consists of two intermixed metals one with a slight coppery tint the other pale silvery. Superimposed on the matrix is a large number of fleurettes of medium grey precipitate concentrated but not exclusively in the silvery part of the matrix. Pixe results indicate that the sample is a binary alloy of copper and antimony with substantial amounts of silver and arsenic present. Such metal could result from the smelting of a grey copper ore or *fahlerz*.

mf 3858, BL 3A, Str 10, DC 35
Form: amorphous prill
PIXE Analysis:

Cu	87.7	As	7.15
Pb	0.11	Ni	0.095
Sb	1.00	Ag	2.4
Fe	0.30	S	0.054
Cl	0.47	Sn	<0.070
Zn	<0.57		

Metallography: Sample exhibits a highly porous cast structure with some of the pores filled with corrosion product.

mf 3956, (Pl. 34b), Str 1, DC 13
Form: sheet stock
Metallography: (Pl. 34c) Sample consists of a cross section of thin sheet tapered strongly in the width direction. The thickness is relatively uniform except at the lee side where the thickness tapers down almost to an edge. The metal is in annealed state plus some final working. On etching, migrational banding through the thickness of the strip shows the remains of the original cast concentration gradients not removed by thermal processing. Strip had undergone considerable deformation prior to the final ordeal as evidenced by the tendency of the inclusions to be broken up and strung out in the width direction producing inclusion particle packets with aspect ratios in the range of 6/1 to 10/1. The tapering at the one side was produced by mechanical deformation which caused the banding to taper down along with tapering down of the strip thickness.

mf 3973.1, BL 3A, Str 10, DC 51
Form: amorphous prill
PIXE Analysis:

Cu	96.3	As	2.52
Pb	0.16	Ni	0.13
Sb	< 0.024	Ag	0.15
Fe	0.054	S	0.072
Cl	<0.011	Sn	<0.070
Zn	<0.57		

Metallography: Microstructure appears to be as-cast with a high degree of porosity. One region is principally metal with moderate-size porosity both transgranular and intergranular. Grain size is non-uniform varying between ASTM G.S. No. 1 and 5. Grains are roughly equiaxed. A second region is porous to the point of being spongy with the large holes filled with corrosion product—some look like geodes. There appears to be a fine precipitate in grains.

mf 3973.2, BL 3A, Str 10, DC 51
Form: amorphous prill
PIXE Analysis:

Cu	93.6	As	3.33
Pb	0.88	Ni	0.14
Sb	<0.035	Ag	0.34
Fe	0.82	S	0.15
Cl	0.10	Sn	<0.070
Zn	<0.57		

Metallography: (Pl. 34d) This sample consists of a cross section which is nearly round. A faint coarse as-cast dendritic pattern shows clearly. There is a fine transgranular precipitate. Extensive coarse porosity is irregular in shape.

mf 3973.3, BL 3A, Str 10, DC 51
Form: amorphous prill
Metallography: (Pl. 35a) Sample consists of a cross section of an amorphous lump with shape of an isosceles triangle. Its coarse as-cast structure appears cellular with equivalent ASTM G.S. No. 1-2. No evidence of current or prior deformation exists. Outer boundary region contains coarse porosity with moderately coarse porosity scattered throughout the body. Inclusions are of two types. Etching with potassium dichromate reveals there is extensive fine precipitation throughout. Within the cells (or dendrite bodies) the precipitate is extremely fine and equalized. In the interdendritic regions there are substantially fewer precipitates; these, however, are elongated with the long axis oriented along some specific family of crystallographic directions. Further staining with ferric chloride etch shows these cells to be part of a group of "superstructures", each containing a number of cells but having different orientations.

mf 5041, BL 2, Str 8C, DC 36
Form: amorphous prill
PIXE Analysis:

Cu	85.5	As	5.60
Pb	5.8	Ni	0.081
Sb	0.80	Ag	1.0
Fe	0.27	S	<0.010
Cl	0.19	Sn	<0.070
Zn	<0.57		

Metallography: Sample exhibits an as-cast structure with considerable moderately large size porosity. The cast structure shows a classical dendritic pattern. Inclusions appear to be of two types. Grey inclusions are concentrated in a region at one end, while large globular inclusions are concentrated in the central region. They are few in number. Many of the small and moderate-size inclusions are duplex in structure.

mf 5042, BL 2, Str 8C, DC 29
Form: amorphous prill
Metallography: (Pl. 35b) Sample consists of a kidney-shaped cross section of an amorphous lump. Roughly one-third of the sample is heavily non-metallic, filled with strangely shaped duplex inclusions. The primarily metallic portion has a cellular cast structure. There are also numerous large irregularly shaped pores, some lined with inclusion material. Etching with potassium dichromate reveals a cast dendritic or cellular structure. The cells are relatively small (ASTM G.S. No. approx. 3-5) and are filled with a fine spherical precipitate. The interdendritic regions are precipitate free but contain coarse inclusions. Distributed throughout the cross section are a few cells or dendrite arms significantly larger than the majority. The central position of each of these is free of the fine precipitate. The latter are confined to the border region of these cells.

mf 5044, Str 9, DC 34
Form: amorphous prill
Metallography: (Pl. 35c) Sample consists of a cross section of an amorphous lump. It has a cellular cast microstructure. Cell size is approximately equal to ASTM G.S. No. 2. There are numerous pores, a few of which are extremely large. Many pores are large and there are very many medium size pores. Many pores are filled or partly filled with non-metallic corrosion

products. There is a heavy corrosion crust all around the sample.

mf 5163, BL 3A, Str 10, DC 35
Form: amorphous prill
Metallography: (Pl. 35d) Sample consists of a cross section of an amorphous lump. A significant corrosion crust of variable thickness is present. The microstructure is fully dendritic, as-cast and moderately coarse. There appear to be inclusions both in the interdendritic regions and in the dendrites themselves.

mf 5165, BL 3A, Str 10, DC 35
Form: amorphous prill
Metallography: Sample consists of a cross section of an amorphous lump with heavy corrosion crust. There is significant corrosion penetration into the metal. The microstructure of cross section is as-cast, but is non-uniform. Some regions are clearly dendritic with inclusions in the interdendritic regions, while other regions have a network of fine inclusions surrounding a cellular structure finer than that in the dendritic regions.

mf 5319, BL 3A, Str 10, DC 35
Form: amorphous prill
Metallography: (Pl. 36a) Sample consists of a cross section of a nearly round artifact with a relatively fine fully dendritic cast structure. There is a very high inclusion content in the interdendritic regions.

mf 5434, (Pl. 36b), BL 2, Str 8C, DC 36
Form: bar stock, quadrangular section
Metallography: (Pl. 36c) Sample consists of a cross section of a nearly rectangular slightly tapered bar. The metal is in the annealed condition (ASTM G.S. No. 3-4). The outer region all around shows intergranular corrosion layers of great thickness, partially filled with a corrosion product. There is also a large internal width-wise split, not at mid-thickness however. With the bulk of the sample there are both inclusions and porosity. The distribution of the inclusions produces a fiber pattern in the width direction although the inclusion themselves are not elongated. There are pores containing strung out smaller inclusions, however. Of major interest, at one edge, the fiber at both corners turns the corner and starts to flow toward the midplane. The precipitates and pores in the midplane region at this edge are fine and equiaxed. It appears that an attempt has been made to shape this with more complex tooling than a hammer. The use of a 'die' of some sort is possible.

mf 5438, BL 3A, Str 10, DC 51
Form: rod
PIXE Analysis:

Cu	94.4	As	1.70
Pb	1.8	Ni	0.15
Sb	0.57	Ag	0.58
Fe	0.052	S	0.15
Cl	0.12	Sn	<0.070
Zn	<0.57		

Metallography: (Pl. 36d) Sample has a relatively circular cross-section and exhibits a cast structure—a cellular growth pattern viewed on end. Cells are irregular in cross-section and vary considerably in size. Intercellular material is thick and has extensive porosity and/or inclusions. ASTM G.S. No. 2—5.

mf 5439.1, BL 3A, Str 10, DC 51
Form: amorphous prill
PIXE Analysis:

Cu	94.2	As	0.98
Pb	3.3	Ni	0.12
Sb	0.41	Ag	0.10
Fe	0.25	S	<0.012
Cl	<0.011	Sn	<0.070
Zn	<0.57		

Metallography: (Pl. 37a) Sample exhibits a cast structure which appears to be cellular (partly dendritic.) There is a big cell size variation with thick intercellular material present. The latter contains extensive fine to medium porosity.

mf 5440, Str 9, DC 34
Form: amorphous prill
PIXE Analysis:

Cu	95.5	As	2.26
Pb	0.13	Ni	0.078
Sb	0.064	Ag	0.034
Fe	1.1	S	0.044
Cl	0.092	Sn	<0.070
Zn	<0.57		

Metallography: Sample exhibits a dendritic as-cast structure with a moderate amount of fine porosity. There are also a few random large pores filled with corrosion product. Inclusions of two different compositions are found generally in separate locations in the metal. The first type are moderate-sized light grey in color and seem to form along boundaries. The second type of inclusions are small equiaxed and darker grey.

mf 5441, BL 3A, Str 10, DC 51
Form: sheet stock
PIXE Analysis:

Cu	96.2	As	1.57
Pb	0.46	Ni	0.10
Sb	0.51	Ag	0.20
Fe	0.14	S	<0.017
Cl	0.017	Sn	<0.070
Zn	<0.57		

Metallography: (Pl. 37b) Sample consists of a cross section of sheet stock with irregular thickness. It was clearly previously worked. Working producing extensive fibering in the transverse direction. Thermal effects were insufficient to homogenize the casting composition gradients which remain as alternating bands parallel to the broad surfaces. Scattered porosity with some holes moderately large. Metal was left in the annealed condition. Grains with ASTM G.S. No. 5 also showed large undeformed annealing twins.

mf 6086.1, Str 9, DC 34
Form: slag
PIXE Analysis:

Cu	92.9	As	4.74
Pb	0.34	Ni	0.081
Sb	<0.026	Ag	0.10
Fe	0.51	S	0.10
Cl	0.45	Sn	<0.070
Zn	<0.57		

Metallography: Sample contains minimal uncorroded metal. What survives has a coarse dendritic structure. Extensive irregular porosity generally filled with corrosion products.

mf 6086.2, Str 9, DC 34
Form: amorphous lump
PIXE Analysis:

Cu	94.0	As	4.38
Pb	0.11	Ni	0.092
Sb	0.091	Ag	0.27
Fe	0.26	S	0.066
Cl	0.052	Sn	<0.070
Zn	<0.57		

Metallography: (Pl. 37c) In this sample the little metal which has survived is in the as cast condition. It shows a coarse dendritic structure. There is extensive irregular porosity present along with a large amount of corrosion product which has a fine grained duplex structure.

mf 6932, Str 1, DC 32
Form: flat fragment
Metallography: (Pl. 37d) Sample consists of a cross section of a piece of sheet stock, roughly square with two opposite sides slightly bent up. Metallurgically, the sample is in the annealed condition. Certain grains are equiaxed with a size equivalent to ASTM G.S. No. 2-3. They contain undeformed annealing twins. The sample is heavily corroded with intergranular corrosion penetration, particularly from the surface. The walls of the penetrating corrodent are very thick compared to normally observed corrosion penetration. There is no evidence of either inclusion or pore elongation in the length (width ?) direction. In fact, inclusions are virtually nonexistent.

mf 6936.1, BL 3B, Str 12, DC 22
Form: prill
PIXE Analysis:

Cu	94.1	As	2.04
Pb	0.29	Ni	0.050
Sb	0.13	Ag	0.21
Fe	1.2	S	0.17
Cl	1.00	Sn	<0.070
Zn	<0.57		

Metallography: (Pl. 38a) Sample exhibits a highly porous as-cast structure with a pronounced dendritic pattern.

mf 6937, (Pl. 38b), BL 2, Str 7, DC 21
Form: "pin" with hooked end
PIXE Analysis:

Cu	95.0	As	1.92
Pb	0.070	Ni	0.089
Sb	<0.017	Ag	0.39
Fe	0.054	S	0.98
Cl	0.20	Sn	<0.070
Zn	<0.57		

Metallography: (Pl. 38c) Sample consists of a cross section of a circular rod which is covered with intermediate-sized porosity (not quite as large as grains). Pores in the central area are larger and more numerous. The metal is relatively free of inclusions. The metal has been worked, annealed and worked again. The grain size is approximately ASTM G.S. No. 7.

mf 6943, Str 1 DC 34
Form: spheroidal prill
Metallography: (Pl. 38d) Sample consists of a cross sec-

Table A4
COMPOSITION OF COPPER-BASE FINDS FROM TUV

mf #	Cu	As	Sn	Pb	Fe	Ni	Sb	Ag	Zn	Cl	S
1490	96.6	2.06	≤0.070	0.32	0.045	0.092	0.12	0.12	≤0.57	≤0.009	0.044
3569	94.7	3.73	≤0.070	0.16	0.33	0.095	0.12	0.28	≤0.57	≤0.007	0.037
3678	65.4	1.50	≤0.070	0.33	0.11	0.070	28.2	2.8	≤0.57	≤0.013	0.86
3858	87.7	7.15	≤0.070	0.11	0.30	0.095	1.00	2.4	≤0.57	0.47	0.054
3973.1	96.3	2.52	≤0.070	0.16	0.054	0.13	≤0.024	0.15	≤0.57	≤0.011	0.072
3973.2	93.6	3.33	≤0.070	0.88	0.82	0.14	≤0.035	0.34	≤0.57	0.10	0.15
5041	85.5	5.60	≤0.070	5.8	0.27	0.081	0.80	1.0	≤0.57	0.19	≤0.010
5438	94.4	1.70	≤0.070	1.8	0.052	0.15	0.57	0.58	≤0.57	0.12	0.15
5439.1	94.2	0.98	≤0.070	3.3	0.25	0.12	0.41	0.10	≤0.57	≤0.011	≤0.012
5440	95.5	2.26	≤0.070	0.13	1.1	0.078	0.064	0.034	≤0.57	0.092	0.044
5441	96.2	1.57	≤0.070	0.46	0.14	0.10	0.51	0.20	≤0.57	0.017	≤0.017
6086.1	92.9	4.74	≤0.070	0.34	0.51	0.081	≤0.026	0.10	≤0.57	0.45	0.10
6086.2	94.0	4.38	≤0.070	0.11	0.26	0.092	0.091	0.27	≤0.57	0.052	0.066
6936.1	94.1	2.04	≤0.070	0.29	1.2	0.050	0.13	0.21	≤0.57	1.00	0.17
6937	95.0	1.92	≤0.070	0.070	0.054	0.089	≤0.017	0.39	≤0.57	0.20	0.98
7109	95.7	1.29	≤0.070	0.061	0.18	0.47	0.035	0.047	≤0.57	0.14	0.33

tion of an amorphous lump. The microstructure exhibits a very coarse dendritic cast structure but with extensive deformation markings at certain locations, particularly in the surface zone. Extrusive porosity is present in the interdendritic regions. Pore sizes vary over a wide range and most pores are free of filler material.

mf 7097, (Pl. 39a), Str 1, DC 34
Form: sheet stock
Metallography: (Pl. 39b) Cross section of bent irregularly shaped sheet with a heavy corrosion crust on one side. Metallurgically the sample has been lightly deformed following annealing as there are numerous strain markings as well as annealing twins. There is a considerable variation in grain size from one side to the other (not in the thickness direction. At one end the ASTM G.S. No. is approximately 1 and the middle region, 5-6 and at the other end 3. Grains are roughly equiaxed there are numerous coarse pores, some partially filled with inclusions, distributed throughout the sheet these are probably not cuprite. There is no evidence of fiber flow.

mf 7109—(Pl. 39c), Str 1, DC 34
Form:"tongue" shaped sheet metal artifact

PIXE Analysis:

Cu	95.7	As	1.29
Pb	0.061	Ni	0.47
Sb	0.035	Ag	0.047
Fe	0.18	S	0.33
Cl	0.14	Sn	<0.070
Zn	<0.57		

Metallography: (Pl. 39d) Sample consists of a cross-section of a tongue shaped piece of sheet metal of variable thickness. Considerable extended porosity parallel to the strip surfaces. Of greater significance are large elliptical cavities whose major axes run parallel to the artifact's surfaces. These are probably not opened cracks but result from the flattening of prior spherical cavities during the manufacture of the sheet. The grain size is ASTM G.S. No. 6. In the bulk of the sheet the metal has been lightly cold-worked after annealing but is more heavily deformed at the thinner end.

mf 11243, BL 2, Str 8B, DC 22
Form: amorphous lump
Metallography: (Pl. 40) Cross section of an odd shaped artifact in the as-cast condition. There is a very heavy corrosion crust on one side and there is an extensive corrosion penetration, mainly along interdendritic

boundary regions. Many large holes are evident, filled with corrosion products. In terms of microstructure, different regions fall into one of two general categories. In one type there are coarse dendrite arms with a relatively low number of small inclusions. In the other, there are numerous small inclusions. There is extensive precipitation of a spherical precipitate in the dendrites. Also, there can be seen a large number of short cracks in the dendrite arms. Their cause is unknown.

Part II B. Shells from ABC and TUV

David Reese

All shells recovered from Banesh levels at ABC are included in the Register of Finds, Part I of Appendix A, following the contextual and descriptive coding conventions of the register, including measurements expressed in centimeters. Only those shells studied by the author have a variety (V) code in the Register of Finds. Additional descriptive details for the shells from Banesh levels at ABC and TUV are presented here in Tables A5 (ABC) and A6 (TUV). All of the shells listed in Table A5 (ABC) were studied by the author, but only those shells in Table A6 (TUV) coded with an * were available for this study. However, other TUV shells are listed by type to supplement data published by Nicholas (1990); in some cases descriptive details are added on the basis of published photographs or figures.

Measurement conventions used in these tables are: L = length, D = diameter, T = thickness, and W = width, recorded in millimeters. "Cone" shells include *Conus, Engina, Melanopsis* and other gastropods. "Olive" shells may be *Oliva, Ancilla,* or some other gastropod. Unspecified nacre (mother-of-pearl) is probably from the marine *Pinctada* but could also be from the fresh-water *Unio*.

A. ABC Marine shells

      1) *Ancilla*
mf 1119.3, open apex, L 9
mf 7278, *A. acuminata*, open apex, L 9, hole 1.25
      2) *Conus*
mf 645, irreg. hole at apex, L 33.75, W 24.25, hole 4.75 x 4
mf 1112, ground-down hole at apex, L 14.25, W 10, hole 1
mf 6817, 2 *C. taeniatus*, 2 holed apex, 31.25 x 22, ground-down hole 1.5; 25 x 16.75, ground-down hole
      1, broken lip
mf 9963, ground-down apex hole, L 13, W 9.5, hole 2
      3) *Dentalium*
mf 209, ribbed, L 26, W 4.5
mf 600, 13, all ribbed, one shell contained a small bead:
      has tip, worn, L 37.25, W 4.25
      has tip, small shell in mouth, L 29, W 4.25
      has tip, not stringable, L 24, W 4
      has tip, L 20.75, W 3.75
      no tip, water-worn, L 14.75, W 4
      no tip, worn, L 19, W 3.75
      no tip, L 18, W 4
      no tip, L 21.75, W 4.25
      no tip, L 21, W 4.25
      broken tip, L 23, W 4 upper center, L 9.75, W 3.5 center, L 15.5, W 3.75 L 28.75, W 4.75
mf 1114, ribbed, L 28, W 4.25, has tip
mf 1116, ribbed, L 28.25, W
mf 1117, ribbed, has tip, L 19.75, W 4
mf 1268, 2 ribbed, L 33.5, W 5; L 26.25, W 5
mf1277, nacre fragment, probably *Pinctada*, small piece
mf 2116, L 33.75, W 5.25
mf 2316, 10, all ribbed:
      has tip, L 23.75, W 4
      has tip, L 29.5, W 4.5
      has tip, bit worn, small shell in mouth, L 26, W 4.25
      water-worn, center, L 18, W 4
      L 35, W 5.25
      no tip, L 18, W 4.75
      no tip, small shell in mouth, L 21, W 4.5 L 27, W 4
      small shell in mouth, L 25.5, W 4.25
      center, L 9.75, W 3.75
mf 2569, 70
mf 6427,
mf 6818, 4, 3 ribbed, L 15.75, W 3; L 25, W 4; L 20.75, W 3.75; L 13, W 3.25
mf 6824, ribbed, L 16, W 4
mf 7270, 2 ribbed, L 29, W 5; L 16.25
mf 7272, ribbed, has tip, L 16.25, W 3
mf 7273, ribbed, L 15.75, W 4
mf 7274, ribbed, has tip, L 18.5, W 3.5
mf 7276, ribbed, L 25.75, W 5.5
mf 7310, small
      4) *Engina*
mf 1107, broken, has color, L c11.75
mf 2194, open apex, has color, L 10, hole 2
mf 6830, open apex, bright color, L 13, hole 1.75
mf 6833, ground-down hole on lower body, L 12, hole 3.25
mf 7268, open apex, has color, L 12.25, W 8, hole 2.25
mf 9855, open apex, bright color, L 13, hole 2.25
      5) *Monodonta*

mf 9964, *Monodonta/Gibbula* holed below apex, H 18, hole 2.75 (lot 37)

      6) Nacre (not specified as *Pinctada*)

mf 751.1, one end has 2 incised lines, L 35.25, W 9, T 1.25 (Fig. 39g)

mf 751.2, several lines incised along length on one side, L 33.25, W 6, T 1 (Fig. 39h)

mf 751.3, rectangle, L 19, W 15, now broken into 3 pieces (Fig. 39d)

mf 1087, 15 nacre inlay

mf 1090, 14 nacre inlay

mf 1093, 75 nacre inlay (?originally 120)

mf 1265, 3 nacre—1 cut, L 7.75, W 7.25, T 1

mf 1276, 84 nacre inlay (?originally 89)

mf 2339, 2 nacre inlay—1 fragment with 2 cut parallel lines, L 15.25, W 12, T 1.8 and holed, D 1.25;
      1 circle, D 13.75, hole D 3, T 1, one-half eroded

mf 2448, 669 nacre inlay (This is approximately half of the inlays found in this cluster; the other half is in
      Iran Bastan)

a) mf 2448, Smaller width rectangles:

  L 18.25, W 6.75, T 1—2 sides scored

  L 18.5, W 6, T 1.5—1 L beveled, 2 sides scored

  L 15.75, W 5.75, T 1—1 side scored

  L 22.75, W 6.25, T 1.25 —2 L beveled, 1 side scored

  L 12.75+, W 5, T 1.75—2 W beveled

  L 14.5, W 3.75, T 0.75—1 side incised lines

  L 29, W 5, T 0.75—1 side scored

  L 16.75, W 4, T 1.5—1 incised line

  L 15, W 4.75, T 1.1—2 sides scored

  L 20.75, W 4, T 1—2 L beveled

  L 14.25, W 4, T 2

  L 14.75, W 3.75, T 0.75—1 side scored

  L 15.75, W 3.75, T 1—1 L beveled, incised line, both sides

  L 10, W 5.25, T 1.5—1 L beveled, 1 side several incised lines, other side scored

  L 16.25, W 4, T 1

  L 14+, W 5.5, T 1.25—1 L beveled, 1 side scored

  L 14, W 4.9, T 1.2—1 L beveled, 1 side scored

  L 13.75, W 5, T 2—2 sides scored, 1 side deep incised line down L

  L 15, W 4.75, T 1—incised lines on 2 sides, 2 sides scored

  L 15.75, W 4.9, T 0.9—2 sides scored

  L 20.5, W 5.1, T 1—1 edge beveled, 2 sides scored

  L 26.25, W 4, T 1—1 deep incised line down L

  L 14.25, W 5.75, T 1—1 W beveled, 1 side scored

  L 19.25, W 4, T 1.2—2 sides scored

  L 11, W 5, T 1.2—4 sides beveled, 1 side scored

  L 11.75, W 4.9, T 0.75—2 L beveled, 1 side scored

  L 18.5, W 4.5, T 1.4—1 L beveled, 2 sides scored

  L 15.75, W 4.5, T 1.1

  L 14.75+, W 5, T 1.25—3 edges beveled, 1 incised line

  L 11.25, W 5.75, T 1—1 incised line on 2 sides, 1 side scored

  L 17.2, W 3.75, T 1.25—1 side scored

  L 21, W 4.5, T 1—1 side scored

  L 9.5, W 6, T 1.2—1 L beveled

  L 13.2+, W 4.2, T 1

  L 17.25, W 4, T 1.5—1 L + 1 W beveled

  L 11.25, W 5.75, T 1.7—2 L beveled

  L 13, W 4.75, T 0.7—1 side scored

  L 12.25, W 4, T 1.2—1 W beveled, 1 incised line

  L 13.75, W 5, T 1—1 side scored

  L 17, W 6.5, T 1—1 W beveled, 1 incised line

  L 12.5, W 4.75, T 1.2—1 W beveled

  L 17, W 5.25, T 1—1 W beveled

  L 10, W 4.25, T 1.2

  L 10.25, W 6.2, T 1.25—1 L beveled, 1 side scored

  L 13.25+, W 6, T 1.1—3 edges beveled, 1 incised line

  L 11, W 5, T 1—1 side scored

(continued on next page)

L 11.25, W 5, T 1.25—3 edges beveled
L 11, W 4.9, T 0.75
L 11.8, W 4, T 1.25—2 W + 1 L beveled
L 10, W 5.1, T 1—1 side scored
L 19.5+, W 5, T 1—2 sides scored
L 19, W 4, T 1—1 side scored
L 15.5, W 3.2, T 1—1 side 2 incised lines
L 12, W 4.75, T 1.75—1 side scored
L 13.5, W 4, T 1.25—2 L + 1 W beveled
L 16.5, W 4.25, T 1—1 L beveled, 1 side scored
L 10, W 4, T 1.25—1 L beveled. 1 incised line
L 8.5, W 3.75, T 1—1 L beveled, 1 incised line
L 13.5, W 3.75, T 0.8—1 side scored
L 14, W 4.25, T 1—1 L partly beveled, 1 side scored
L 12, W 4.2, T 0.8—1 L beveled
L 11.5+, W 5.5, T 0.8—1 L beveled
L 13+, W 4, T 0.8—1 side scored
L 14, W 4, T 1.3—1 L beveled, incised line, scored
L 9.8, W 3.3, T 1.1—2 W beveled
L 10+, W 5.2, T 1—1 side scored
L 8.8, W 3.5, T 1—1 W beveled
L 8, W 3.5, T 0.75—1 L beveled, 1 incised line
L 7, W 5, T 1.5—2 L, 1 W beveled
L 15, W 4, T 1—1 incised line
L 12.5, W 1.5, T 0.7—2 sides scored
L 14, W 4.25, T 1.2—4 edges beveled
L 14.75, W 4, T 1.75—1 W beveled, 1 side scored
L 15.75, W 4.2, T 1.3
b) mf 2448, Larger width rectangles:
   L 14, W 7.5, T 1.5—2 L + 1 W (not straight) beveled, 1 side scored
   L 22+, W 10, T 1.2—1 L beveled, 1 side scored
   L 15, W 8.25, T 1.25—1 side scored
   L 15+, W 7.75, T 1.2—1 L beveled, 1 incised line
   L 14.5, W 7.8, T 1.1
   L 13.75+, W 8.75, T 1—1 side scored
   L 13, W 10.75, T 1.25—1 L + 1 W beveled
   L 13.2, W 9.5, T 1.7—2 W + 1 L beveled, 1 incised line
   L 15+, W 9.25, T 1.2—1 L beveled
   L 19, W 8, T 1.25—1 L beveled
   L 19.5+, W 10, T 1—2 L beveled, 2 incised parallel lines on 1 side
   L 20.25, W 8.25, T 1.25—1 L beveled, 1 side scored
   L 17.5, W 8.75, T 1.25—1 L beveled
   L 20.5, W 10, T 1.77—2 L + 1 W beveled
   L 18.25, W 8, T 1.2—1 L + 1 W beveled
   L 19+, W 8.8, T 1.5—1 L beveled, 2 incised lines
   L 18, W 7.8, T 1.75
   L 19.5, W 7, T 1.2
   L 15.75, W 9.25, T 1.3—1 L + 1 W beveled
   L 14, W 8.75, T 1.5—1 L + 1 W beveled, 1 side scored
   L 16.2, W 8, T 1.2
   L 17.5, W 7.75, T 1.1—1 L + 1 W beveled, 1 side scored
   L 18, W 8.75, T 1.2—1 L + 1 W beveled
   L 14, W 8.1, T 1.5—1 L + 1 W beveled
mf 6455.1, curved, L 22, W 7, T 1
mf 6455.2, rectangular, dark purple, L 21, W 6, T 1
mf 6813, 12 nacre
mf 6816, 68 nacre inlay
mf 9859, L 7, W 5, T 1.2
   7) *Pinctada* (includes inlays and fragsments)
mf 741, inlay, zigzag, L 17, T 1.75 (Fig. 39n)
mf 756.1, inlay, curved, once had plaster residue on it, L 32.25, W 8, T 2 (Fig. 39s)

mf 756.2, inlay, rectangle, L 15, W 6.75, T 1.75 (Fig. 39c)

mf 935, 2 hinge fragments (1 right), both have one cut edge

mf 1002, inlay, rectangular, L 12.25, W 6, T 1.2

mf 1088, 2 inlay, rectangle, one side scored, incised line, L 12, W 8.75, T 1.25; chevron, L 13, W 10, T 1.1, triangular notch in long edge 3 x 3, both sides have scoring, one side has incised line

mf 1089, inlay, crescent, L 31.75, W 8.5, T 1

mf 1098, fragment with brown exterior and one cut edge, 22 x 14.74, T 3.25

mf 1101, 2 fragments

mf 1113, hinge fragment, unmodified

mf 1119.1, inlay, rounded exterior, opposite end pointed, one end broken, one side scored, L 20+, W 13, T 1

mf 1119.2, inlay, rounded exterior, opposite end pointed, one end broken, L 15.75, W 10.75, T 1

mf 1262, 2 fragments, one with exterior possibly ground off and part of circular hole, L 26, W 17, D hole 2.25; second fragment has at least two worked edges and scoring on exterior, L 26.75, W 9.5, T 1.2

mf 1266, fragments and 1 inlay, rectangular, L 13.5, W 10, T 1.5, long sides have beveled edges

mf 1267, fragment, 27 x 22, T 4.25

mf 1269, 4 fragments, distal

mf 1272, 7 inlay, 4 rectangular, 1 Y, 2 irregular, holed

mf 1274, 2 joining fragments, L 14.5, W 14.25, T 2.5

mf 1275, 1 rectangular inlay, L 9, W 5.5, T 1.2; 1 fragment with 1 cut edge

mf 1279, fragment, 17 x 14.5, T 4

mf 1294, inlay or bead, burnt, D 1.15 (DC 37) (Fig. 38j)

mf 2106.1, distal fragment

mf 2118, hinge fragment with 2 drilled holes next to each other, hole D 1.5

mf 2146, 2 fragments, 1 distal, 1 thick fragment with partly drilled hole, D 3

mf 2285.1, 2 fragments

mf 2291, 3 unmodified fragments

mf 2312.1, small fragment

mf 2336, fragments, unmodified

mf 2342, fragments, hinge and distal, left

mf 2554.1, 2 fragments, 1 worked piece, broken, 2 cut edges; 1 unmodified

mf 2576, 2 inlay, one rectangle, 15 x 6, one end broken, T 1; one with 2 cut edges, L 11, W 9.75, T 1; and 1 unworked distal end with exterior

mf 2578.2, 3 fragments, all have one cut edge

mf 6815, 2 fragments: 32.75 x 16.5, T 3; 10.5 x 5, T 1.5

mf 6820, inlay, rectangular, L 13, W 8, T 2

mf 6823, distal fragment, possibly 1 cut edge

mf 6825, hinge fragment (left) and body fragment

mf 6826, 2 fragments, 1 worked, curving rectangle, scratches on one side, L 24, W 6.75, T 2.5 and 1 distal end

mf 6832, inlay, broken, one side scored, L 23, T 1

mf 6838, 2 inlay, thin rectangle, with irregular large piece at one end, 2 incised lines and scoring, L 45, W 14.5, T 1.75; fragment

mf 7280, fragments, distal end, two possibly have one cut edge

mf 9861, chipped roughly circular, 34 x 32, T 7.5, bored exterior by marine organisms

mf 9864, inlay, rectangular, L 29.25, W 6, T 1

mf 9898, fragment

       8) Shell Ring

 mf 205, one-half preserved, made from medium-sized gastropod, polished, D 20.5, T 4

       9) *Turritella* cf. *terebra*

mf 1109, distal end, broken lip, preserved L 24, W 12, hole opposite mouth 1.5

mf 6828, apex fragment, preserved L 20

B. ABC Fresh-water shells

       1) *Melanopsis*

mf 1119.4, costate

mf 2187, slightly costate, has color, broken lip

mf 2207, smooth, has gloss, irregular hole, probably recent

mf 9867, slightly costate

       2) *Unio*

mf 1095, fragments, right

(continued on next page)

mf 1096, 2 small fragments
mf 1101, right
mf 1106, fragments
mf 1118, fragments, left
mf 1260, distal fragment
mf 1264, fragments, right
mf 1269, fragment
mf 1271, fragments, left
mf 2106.2, distal fragment
mf 2157, 13 fragments, 1 left, 2 burnt
mf 2169, 13 fragments (2-3 valves), 3 may have one cut edge
mf 2183, fragment
mf 2193, distal fragment
mf 2198, distal fragment
mf 2202, left
mf 2285.2, fragments (hinge, distal)
mf 2291, fragment, right
mf 2312.2, fragments
mf 2554.2, left
mf 2578.1, left
mf 6815, distal fragment
mf 6822, distal fragment
mf 6829, left
mf 6831, hinge fragment
mf 7271, distal fragment
mf 7275, 2 left, 1 right
mf 7330, 2 fragments, distal ends (from Flotation 022)
mf 9860, distal fragment

C. ABC Land Snails

mf 1273, 2 small land snails
mf 2121, 2 small land snails
mf 2309, 3 small land snails
mf 6835, tiny gastropods in dirt
mf 6837, 3 small land snails
mf 7269, small land snail
mf 7310, 1 small and 1 tiny land snail
mf 9863, 2 small land snails

D. Misc.

mf 1106, small fossil bivalve (cf. *Gryphaea*)
mf 6454, stone inlay, triangle, concave base, broken, L 26, W 23, T 3, (Fig. 39r)

A. TUV Marine shells

1) *Ancilla*

*mf 6877, 36 shells, all with irregularly holed apex or body and broken lip

2) *Conus*

mf 3546 a-c, 3 cone shell beads

mf 3556

mf 3696, *Conus/Strombus* apex bead, open apex, L ca. 18 (Nicholas 1990:136, pl. 30B)

mf 3697, L ca. 17 (Nicholas 1990:fig. 23)

mf 3700; mf 3728

mf 3871 (Nicholas 1990:fig. 23)

mf 3990; mf 5051; mf 5088; mf 5089

mf 5090 (Nicholas 1990:fig. 23)

mf 5380

mf 6030, bead, L 17, W 32

*mf 6879, broken lip, holed at apex, L 11.75, W 7.75, ground-down area 4.25, hole 1
    (Nicholas 1990:136, as bead)

*mf 6882, unholed, fresh, some color, L 33.5

*mf 6905, apex whorl bead, nicely worked distal end L 26.25, W 24, T 6.75, irregular central hole 9 x 7.75

3) *Cowrie*

mf 3555, 2 *Cowries*, holed on dorsum (Nicholas 1990: pl. 30A)

4) *Dentalium*

mf 1914, carved bead, L 17, W 5 (Nicholas 1990:136, pl. 26x)

mf 3701, L 17 (Nicholas 1990:fig. 23, pl. 30C)

mf 3701, L 17 (Nicholas 1990:fig. 23, pl. 30C)

mf 3703 (Nicholas 1990:fig. 23)

mf 3703 (Nicholas 1990:fig. 23)

*mf 6865, ribbed, L 19, D 4.25 (Nicholas 1990:134, as worked)

*mf 6880, ribbed, L 21, D 4.5

*mf 6886, ribbed, near tip, L 9, D 2.25 (Nicholas 1990:134, fig. 23)

*mf 6889, L 12.75, D 4.5 (Nicholas 1990: 134, fig. 23)

*mf 7098a-c, 3 ribbed, L 10.5, D 3, tip; L 11.25, D 3.25; L 8.5, D 3 (Nicholas 1990:134, fig. 23)

5) *Engina*

*mf 6887, much worn, smoothed sides, open apex, irregular hole on body, L 12, W 9
    (Nicholas 1990:134, as worked)

6) Nacre

mf 3549; mf 3550; mf 3603

mf 3604, inlay, L 14, W 10, T 1 (Nicholas 1990: fig. 23)

mf 3695, L ca. 17

mf 3699; mf 3814; mf 3815; mf 3816

mf 3988 (Nicholas 1990:fig. 23)

mf 3989, L ca. 63, W ca. 49

mf 3991; mf 5052

mf 5150, (Nicholas 1990:fig. 23)

mf 5151; mf 5162; mf 5177; mf 5178; mf 5204; mf 5221; mf 5294

mf 5381; mf 5382; mf 5383; mf 5442; mf 5444; mf 6045; mf 6090

mf 6091; mf 6092

*mf 6868, U-shaped inlay, 5 x 3, T 1.25

*mf 6891, probably *Pinctada*, L 14.75, W 11.5, T 2.75, carefully made hole 2, one edge worked, eroded

mf 7134

mf 7973 (Nicholas 1990:fig. 23)

7) Olive

mf 352, bead (Nicholas 1990:136; U168, lot 70)

mf 3547, bead

mf 3548, bead

mf 3553, bead (Nicholas 1990:fig. 23)

mf 3557, probably holed apex, L 24 (Nicholas 1990:136, pl. 30D)

mf 6088; mf 6089

(continued on next page)

        8) Pinctada (including nacre inlays)

*mf 1091.1, inlay, rectangular, L 8.75, W 6, T1.25

*mf 1100.1, rectangle, L 13.25, W 5.25, T 1.5

mf 3605, hinge fragment, unworked (Nicholas 1990:pl. 30E)

*mf 6398, fragment, 19 x 13.75, T 3

*mf 6862.1, fragment, L 26.25, W 19, T 2.25 (Nicholas 1990:134, fig. 23, as bivalve)

mf 6866.1 (Nicholas 1990:fig. 23; as worked, but actually not modified)

*mf 6873, rectangle, L 27.25, W 11.5, T 1, has one incised line; hinge fragment, eroded

*mf 6875, fragment, part of circular object with exterior edge rounded and interior edge cut, L 30.5, W 25,
    T 5

*mf 6883, hinge fragment, bored by marine

*mf 6884, fragment, L 16.5, W 8.5, T 2

        9) Misc.

mf 1099, worked bivalve

mf 1258.1

mf 3551, worked ?bivalve

mf 3554, worked ?bivalve

mf 3698, worked shell (Nicholas 1990:fig. 23)

mf 3702, shell

mf 3869, shell

mf 3870, shell

mf 5317, shell

mf 5422, shell

mf 5443, shell

mf 6890, *Venus sp.* fragment (Nicholas 1990:fig. 23)

B. TUV Fresh-water shells

        1) *Melanopsis*

*mf 6397, smooth, broken lip

*mf 6399, slightly costate, burnt (Nicholas 1990:134, fig. 23)

*mf 6869, slightly costate, broken lip

        2) *Unio*

*mf 1091.2, fragment

*mf 1097, right valve

*mf 1100.2, distal fragment

*mf 1104, fragments

mf 1105, fragments

*mf 6396, 2 distal fragments, one (L 11.5, W 12.5, T 2) possibly cut along one edge

*mf 6862.2, fragment, left

*mf 6863, fragments, right valve

*mf 6864, hinge fragment (Nicholas 1990:134, fig. 23)

*mf 6866.2, fragments, left (Nicholas 1990:fig. 23)

*mf 6867, distal fragment (Nicholas 1990:134, fig. 23)

*mf 6870, fragment

*mf 6871, 2 fragments

*mf 6872, distal fragment, possibly cut on two sides, L 15, W 13, T 2.75, length of cut edge 12

*mf 6874, 2 fragments (Nicholas 1990:134, fig. 23, as bivalve)

*mf 6876, fragments

*mf 6878, small distal fragments

*mf 6888fragments (Nicholas 1990:134, fig. 23, as bivalve)

*mf 6963, distal fragment, burnt, L 18.25, W 9.75. T 2 (Nicholas 1990:134, fig. 23, as worked shell;
    possibly two cut edges)

C. TUV Land snails

*mf 1257, small land snail

*mf 1258.2, 2 small land snails with slight color and gloss

*mf 6885, land snail (Nicholas 1990:134, fig. 23, listed as olive shell)

Appendix B

Lot Inventory

The Lot Inventory, presented here in two parts, provides information about all Banesh lots excavated in the levels reported in this monograph. The first eight columns, which present the same data in Part I and Part II are as follows: Operations (OP) are as shown in Fig. 5 and described in the Introduction. Lot numbers (LOT) as assigned sequentially for each operation. The Lot Indicator, as described in Appendix A and discussed in Chapter I. Where a particular lot has more than one Lot Indicator the distinction, which applies to specific finds or groups of finds as indicated in Appendix A, is based on field notes, plans, photographs or other information that clarifies the status of particular finds. Features (FT# and FEAT) are those within which lots were excavated (DC 21-29, 35, 37, 50) or are the lots used to actually remove the bricks and mortar of a feature (DC 36). Features are inventoried in Appendix C and discussed in Chapter I. Building Level (BL) Stratum (STR) and Deposit Code (DC) are as described in Chapter I.

Part I reports the number of registered finds from each lot or part of a lot, as detailed in Appendix A.

The number of Banesh and Kaftari sherds is based on summary counts completed in the field or later in the laboratory at Ohio State University. The weight and number of animal bones are taken from data reported by Zeder (1985, 1991). None of these numbers can be considered definitive. The number of finds is the best indicator of the productivity of a particular lot because greater care was exercised in collecting and recording finds. Although an effort was made to keep track of all sherd and bone lots, parts or all of some lots may be missing from this inventory. The volume in cubic meters (M^3) is listed for all lots for which measurements are available as discussed in Chapter I.

Part II reports the counts and weights of straw tempered forms and other sherds where this data is available. The columns are: R# for number of straw tempered rims, RWT for their weight in grams, T# and TWT for the count and weight of straw tempered trays, and P# and PWT for the count and weight of straw tempered goblet pedestal bases. Part II also reports the count of beveled rim bowl sherds (column headed BRB), miscellaneous straw tempered forms (column headed MSCL).

OP	LOT	LI	FT #	FEAT	BL	STR	DC	FINDS	BAN	KAF	WT BNS	BONES	M3
A	0	G			2	8A	35	6					
A	37	M	71	ROOM	2	8A	35	14	41	57			5.40
A	38	M	186	ROOM	2	8A	35	3	33	25			
A	40	M	28	WALL	2	8D	36	0	38				4.10
A	41	G	34	ROOM	3A	10A	21	1					
A	41	G	34	ROOM	3A	10A	37	3					2.00
A	43	G	27	PLAT	2	8C	36	0					
A	44	G			9		34	3	31	1			
A	44	M			9		34	4	31	1			
A	45	M	28	WALL	2	8D	36	0	17	3			
A	46	G	34	ROOM	3A	10A	37	2	12				2.00
A	47	G	35	ROOM	3A	10A	37	0					4.50
A	48	G			12		34	0					
A 1	0	B					31	1					
A 1	29	H	185	ROOM	2	8B	37	7					7.50
A 1	32	G	186	ROOM	2	8B	37	1					
A 1	33	G	187	ROOM	2	8B	37	1	19				
ABC	0	G	104	WALL	2	8D	36	2					
ABC	0	G		WALL	5	15B	36	2					
ABC	0	G	210	WALL	3B	11B	36	2					
ABC	0	G	290	BNCH	4A	13B	36	2					
ABC	1	M					41	1					
ABC	2	M					41	1					
ABC	3	G	241	CRDX	4A	13B	29	4	7				2.00
ABC	4	G	353	COUR	5	15A	35	1					
ABC	4	G	334	MISC	4A	13C	49	2					
ABC	4	G	239	WALL	4B	14B	36	2	25				
ABC	5	G	240	WALL	4A	13C	36	2	38				4.30
ABC	6	G	249	ROOM	5	15A	35	0	0				0.20
ABC	7	G	323	WALL	4B	14B	36	2	39				1.90
ABC	8	G	334	MISC	4A	13C	49	9	73				9.40
ABC	9	G	247	ROOM	5	15A	35	0	0				0.80
ABC	10	G	241	CRDX	4A	13B	29	1	60				
ABC	11	G	247	ROOM	5	15A	37	1	2				0.70
ABC	12	G	331	AREA	4B	14A	37	3	17				3.04
ABC	13	G	331	AREA	4B	14A	37	1	7				0.06
ABC	14	G	332	AREA	4B	14A	37	3	41				3.00
ABC	15	G	331	AREA	4B	14A	37	1	15				0.30
ABC	16	H	336	AREA	5	15A	35	0	1				
ABC	17	G	251	ROOM	5	15A	35	1	2				0.80
ABC	18	G	333	AREA	4B	14A	37	0	4				0.90
ABC	19	G	331	AREA	4B	14A	37	1	7				0.30
ABC	20	G	339	HRTH	4B	14A	28	2	0				
ABC	21	G	281	COUR	4A	13A	21	3	63	7			0.10
ABC	22	G	342	ROOM	5	15A	37	0	2				0.10
ABC	23	G	343	HRTH	4B	14A	28	1	0				
ABC	24	G	342	ROOM	5	15A	37	1	1				0.10
ABC	25	G	281	COUR	4B	14B	29	2	5				0.10
ABC	26	G	346	ROOM	5	15A	35	0	8				0.54

OP	LOT	LI	FT #	FEAT	BL	STR	DC	FINDS	BAN	KAF	WT BNS	BONES	M3
ABC	27	G	345	HRTH	4B	14B	28	1	0				
ABC	28	G	336	AREA	5	15A	37	1	15				
ABC	29	G	346	ROOM	5	15A	37	2	4				1.07
ABC	30	H	336	AREA	5	15A	37	0	9				
ABC	31	M	348	AREA	5	15A	37	1	14				0.30
ABC	32	G	359	AREA	5	15B	37	4	3				0.90
ABC	33	G	347	ROOM	5	15A	35	0	6				1.20
ABC	34	G	353	COUR	5	15B	21	4	13				1.84
ABC	35	G	360	HRTH	5	15B	37	1	18				
ABC	37	G	353	COUR	5	15B	21	1	6				
ABC	39	G	358	AREA	5	15B	37	0	1				0.70
ABC	40	G	363	OVEN	5	15B	28	16	5				
ABC	42	G	367	AREA	5	15B	29	0	0				
ABC	45	G	367	AREA		16	50	3	0				
ABC	47	G	369	AREA		18A	50	14	0				
ABC	48	G	369	AREA		18A	50	2	0				
ABC	49	G	369	AREA		18A	50	2	0				
ABC	50	G	370	AREA		18B	50	17	0				
ABC	51	G	370	AREA		18B	50	2	0				
ABC	52	G	370	AREA		18B	50	2	1				
ABC	53	G	371	AREA		19	50	0	0				
ABC	54	G	372	AREA		19	50	1	0				
ABC	55	G	372	AREA		19	50	1	0				
ABC	56	G	372	AREA		19	50	2	0				
ABCN	0	B	118	CRDX	2	8B	29	1					
ABCN	0	G		WALL	2	8D	36	2					
ABCN	0	B					31	1					
ABCN	0	B					39	2					
ABCN	0	B					41	2					
ABCN	1	B					41	41					
ABCN	9	M	118	CRDX	2	8A	35	5	23	4			1.94
ABCN	10	M	117	CRDX	2	8A	35	5	21	10	46	82	0.53
ABCN	11	G	117	CRDX	2	8A	35	0	0				0.19
ABCN	12	G	117	CRDX	2	8A	35	1	0				0.16
ABCN	13	G	117	CRDX	2	8B	35	0	51				0.16
ABCN	14	G	117	CRDX	2	8B	37	5	31				0.23
ABCN	15	G	118	CRDX	2	8B	37	2	0				0.42
ABCN	16	G	117	CRDX	2	8B	37	7	0				
ABCN	17	G	118	CRDX	2	8B	37	79	15				0.42
ABCN	18	G	117	CRDX	2	8B	29	0	8				0.42
ABCN	19	M	265	ROOM	2	8A	35	3	18	7			0.21
ABCN	20	G	265	ROOM	2	8B	37	0	8		113	41	0.48
ABCN	21	G	207	ROOM	2	8A	35	0	0				0.14
ABCN	22	G	136	DBLK	2	8C	36	0	12				1.05
ABCN	23	M	207	ROOM	2	8A	35	8	3	7			1.80
ABCN	24	M	264	DBLK	2	8C	36	0	9	3			0.86
ABCN	29	G	207	ROOM	2	8B	35	0	0				0.10
ABCN	30	G	207	ROOM	2	8B	37	14	19		94	108	0.50
ABCN	31	G	371	DBLK	2	8C	36	3	0				

OP	LOT	LI	FT #	FEAT	BL	STR	DC	FINDS	BAN	KAF	WT BNS	BONES	M3
ABCN	37	M				9	34	0	10				
ABCN	38	G	127	WALL	2	8D	36	2	16				1.60
ABCN	42	G	207	ROOM	2	8B	37	1	0				0.10
ABCN	43	G	106	WALL	2	8D	36	0	10				
ABCN	44	G	207	ROOM	2	8A	35	0	4				
ABCN	47	G	28	WALL	2	8D	36	11					
ABCN	48	G				9	34	3	10				
ABCN	49	G	211	ROOM	3A	10A	35	5	0				3.00
ABCN	50	H	71	ROOM	2	8D	29	24	60				
ABCN	53	G				9	34	2	51		101	101	
ABCN	56	G	211	ROOM	3A	10A	37	0	3				0.10
ABCN	57	G	211	ROOM	3A	10A	37	2	5		10	6	
ABCN	58	G	260	AREA	3A	10A	29	3	42				0.35
ABCN	59	M	220	ROOM	3A	10A	35	6	83	1			2.70
ABCN	60	G	260	AREA	3A	10B	29	1	23		43	94	0.02
ABCN	61	G	260	AREA	3A	10B	29	3					0.02
ABCN	65	M				9	34	3	34	3	166	177	4.34
ABCN	66	G	220	ROOM	3A	10A	37	0			18	13	0.60
ABCN	68	G	220	ROOM	3A	10A	21	1	30				0.04
ABCN	69	G	220	ROOM	3A	10A	37	1			28	4	0.07
ABCN	70	G	220	ROOM	3A	10A	29	0	3				0.40
ABCN	71	M	222	ROOM	3A	10A	35	4	23	7			2.88
ABCN	72	G	260	AREA	3A	10B	37	1	57		257	198	0.77
ABCN	73	G	222	ROOM	3A	10A	37	0	1		28	30	0.49
ABCN	74	G	33	WALL	3B	11B	36	1	14				
ABCN	75	G	224	DOOR	3A	10A	35	0	5				0.32
ABCN	76	G	260	AREA	3A	10B	37	2					0.06
ABCN	77	G	260	AREA	3A	10B	37	0					0.10
ABCN	78	M	215	DOOR	3A	10A	35	1					
ABCN	79	G	222	ROOM	3A	10A	37	2	1		13	23	0.19
ABCN	80	G	260	AREA	3A	10A	35	1	13				
ABCN	81	G	129	ROOM	2	8D	29	17	12				1.05
ABCN	82	G	222	ROOM	3A	10A	37	1					0.10
ABCN	83	M				9	34	2	15	3			
ABCN	84	M	63	ROOM	3A	10A	35	0	8	3			1.00
ABCN	85	G	222	ROOM	3B	11B	29	0					0.10
ABCN	86	M	63	ROOM	3A	10A	37	7	46	9			5.76
ABCN	90	G	118	CRDX	2	8D	29	150	92		690	397	1.36
ABCN	91	G	260	AREA	3A	10B	37	1	32				0.25
ABCN	92	M	260	AREA	3A	10A	35	7	18	3			
ABCN	93	G	63	ROOM	3A	10A	35	1	15				1.33
ABCN	95	G	118	CRDX	2	8D	29	3	10		56	31	1.01
ABCN	99	H	211	ROOM	3A	10A	37	10	90		409	446	2.88
ABCN	100	B					41	4					
ABCN	100	M					41	4					
ABCN	106	H	229	ROOM	3B	11B	29	5	73		190	277	1.25
ABCN	112	G	136	DBLK	2	8C	36	1	13				0.03
ABCN	113	G	260	AREA	3A	10B	29	1	28				
ABCN	114	G	260	AREA	3A	10B	29	0					

OP	LOT	LI	FT #	FEAT	BL	STR	DC	FINDS	BAN	KAF	WT BNS	BONES	M3
ABCN	115	M					41	4	9	11	71	18	
ABCN	116	G	228	ROOM	3B	11B	29	1					1.20
ABCN	117	M					41	3			315	89	
ABCN	118	G	260	AREA	3A	10B	37	0	6				
ABCN	119	G	63	ROOM	3B	11B	29	3	25				4.90
ABCN	120	G				12	34	3					
ABCN	121	G	261	WALL	3B	11B	36	0	56				3.40
ABCN	122	M	260	AREA	3A	10A	35	3					
ABCN	123	G	53	HRTH	3B	11B	36	64					
ABCN	124	M	67	ROOM	4A	13A	37	2	14	7	62	23	2.37
ABCN	125	M	211	ROOM	3B	11B	29	13	24	2			
ABCN	125	G	222	ROOM	3B	11B	29	1					
ABCN	126	G				12	34	2	17				17.20
ABCN	128	G	66	ROOM	4A	13A	35	3	19				8.12
ABCN	129	M	66	ROOM	4A	13A	37	3	12	1	121	97	1.40
ABCN	131	G	241	CRDX	4A	13A	35	1	37		46	22	5.00
ABCN	133	G	241	CRDX	4A	13A	37	3	29		298	229	1.22
ABCN	134	G	210	WALL	3B	11B	36	2	22				
ABCN	136	G	64	ROOM	4A	13A	35	2	8				2.25
ABCN	137	G	66	ROOM	4A	13A	37	2					0.01
ABCN	139	G	307	AREA	4A	13A	21	4	831		5934	3632	0.18
ABCN	141	G	241	CRDX	4A	13A	37	1	13		37	49	1.80
ABCN	142	G	67	ROOM	4A	13A	29	0	11				1.16
ABCN	143	M	64	ROOM	4A	13A	37	12	76	1	69	45	0.13
ABCN	146	G	64	ROOM	4A	13A	37	7	26		170	145	0.34
ABCN	148	G	236	PITX	4A	13A	22	7	15		321	208	0.06
ABCN	149	G	236	PITX	4A	13A	22	38	29		614	422	0.04
ABCN	152	G	236	PITX	4A	13A	22	17	11		273	141	0.04
ABCN	153	G	236	PITX	4A	13A	22	9	25		939	280	0.06
ABCN	154	G	59	WALL	4B	14B	36	5	12				
ABCN	155	G				12	34	0	5				
ABCN	156	H	66	ROOM	4B	14B	29	2					
ABCN	157	G	246	ROOM	5	15A	35	2			68	20	2.90
ABCN	158	G	247	ROOM	5	15A	37	1	2		29	21	0.60
ABCN	159	G	64	ROOM	4A	13A	37	0	10		171	80	0.20
ABCN	160	G	249	ROOM	5	15A	37	0			58	51	0.30
ABCN	161	G	251	ROOM	5	15A	37	0			15	9	0.30
ABCN	162	G	236	PITX	4A	13A	22	2	18		829	282	0.04
ABCN	163	G	236	PITX	4A	13A	22	1	1				0.00
ABCS	0	G				9	34	1					
ABCS	0	B					40	6					
ABCS	1	G	193	DBLK	2	8C	36	0	5				0.77
ABCS	2	G	14	WALL	2	8C	36	3	20				
ABCS	3	G	160	WALL	2	8C	36	10	120				
ABCS	4	G	157	DBLK	2	8C	36	0	17				1.12
ABCS	5	G	155	PLAT	2	8C	36	2	2				
ABCS	6	G	189	PLAT	2	8C	36	6	4				
ABCS	7	M	156	WALL	2	8D	36	21	22	3			2.93
ABCS	8	M	155	PLAT	2	8C	36	2	3				

OP	LOT	LI	FT #	FEAT	BL	STR	DC	FINDS	BAN	KAF	WT BNS	BONES	M3
ABCS	9	G	106	WALL	2	8D	36	2					
ABCS	9	M	106	WALL	2	8D	36	4	17	13			
ABCS	10	G	125	WALL	2	8D	36	11	23				3.17
ABCS	12	G	155	PLAT	2	8C	36	0					
ABCS	13	M				9	34	3	20	10			
ABCS	14	M	268	ROOM	3A	10A	35	5	50	8			
ABCS	14	G	268	ROOM	3A	10A	37	2					2.40
ABCS	15	G	268	ROOM	3A	10A	35	1					1.20
ABCS	16	G	268	ROOM	3A	10A	37	0					
ABCS	17	G				9	34	4	14				
ABCS	18	M					41	17					
ABCS	21	G	190	WALL	2	8D	36	0	10				0.62
ABCS	22	G	191	DBLK	2	8C	36	2	6				0.16
ABCS	23	G				9	34	0					
ABCS	24	M	315	DOOR	3A	10A	35	1	37				0.32
ABCS	25	M	269	ROOM	3A	10A	37	6	19	1	82	42	1.10
ABCS	25	G	269	ROOM	3A	10A	21	2					
ABCS	26	G	269	ROOM	3A	10A	37	4	5				
ABCS	27	M	71	ROOM	2	8D	29	0	23	2			
ABCS	28	G	267	ROOM	3A	10A	35	2			119	148	1.50
ABCS	29	G	267	ROOM	3A	10A	37	2			9	3	1.00
ABCS	32	B					40	1					
ABCS	35	G	154	ROOM	2	8D	29	0	27				1.84
ABCS	36	G	271	ROOM	3A	10A	23	73	14				1.40
ABCS	37	G				9	34	3					
ABCS	38	M	38	DOOR	3A	10A	35	3	11	14			
ABCS	39	G	270	ROOM	3A	10A	35	1	27				0.88
ABCS	40	G	190	WALL	2	8D	36	1	6				0.62
ABCS	41	G	268	ROOM	3A	10A	35	3	9				1.23
ABCS	46	G				9	23	214	6				
ABCS	47	G	271	ROOM	3A	10A	37	0	6				0.50
ABCS	48	G	268	ROOM	3B	11B	29	1					0.10
ABCS	49	M					41	1	3	4			
ABCS	50	G	155	PLAT	2	8C	36	0	24				10.50
ABCS	51	G	130	ROOM	2	8C	29	3	3		65	42	0.03
ABCS	53	G	310	HRTH	2	8B	28	2					
ABCS	54	G	270	ROOM	3A	10A	37	1	11				0.11
ABCS	55	G	260	AREA	3A	10A	35	0	10				0.90
ABCS	57	M	16	WALL	3B	11B	36	0	20	1			2.32
ABCS	58	G	34	ROOM	3B	11B	29	2	7				0.92
ABCS	59	G	35	ROOM	3B	11B	29	1	5				
ABCS	60	M				12	34	5	62	1			
ABCS	65	G	304	ROOM	3B	11B	29	2	62				0.35
ABCS	66	G	281	COUR	4A	13A	37	6	19				2.31
ABCS	67	G	282	ROOM	4A	13A	35	1	5				1.00
ABCS	68	G	283	AREA	4A	13A	35	3	10				1.62
ABCS	69	G	268	ROOM	3B	11B	29	1	7				
ABCS	70	G	267	ROOM	3B	11B	29	0	8				1.05
ABCS	71	G	288	CRDX	4A	13A	35	4	23				1.60

OP	LOT	LI	FT #	FEAT	BL	STR	DC	FINDS	BAN	KAF	WT BNS	BONES	M3
ABCS	72	G	241	CRDX	4A	13A	37	4	19				0.92
ABCS	73	G	288	CRDX	4A	13A	37	3	6				1.00
ABCS	74	G	241	CRDX	4A	13A	37	0	20				1.10
ABCS	75	G	210	WALL	3B	11B	36	2	6				
ABCS	76	H	269	ROOM	3B	11B	29	1	9				
ABCS	77	G	290	BNCH	4A	13A	21	5	13		291	66	0.40
ABCS	78	G	33	WALL	3B	11B	36	3	13				0.90
ABCS	79	M				12	34	2	30				
ABCS	80	G	308	HRTH	4A	13A	28	1	1				
ABCS	81	G	307	AREA	4A	13A	35	0	30				2.60
ABCS	82	G	307	AREA	4A	13A	21	2	29		113	36	0.95
ABCS	83	G	210	WALL	3B	11B	36	0	19				0.79
ABCS	84	B	307	AREA	4A	13A	35	1	37				0.40
ABCS	85	G	307	AREA	4A	13A	35	3	76				0.60
ABCS	86	M	241	CRDX	4A	13A	35	1	21	1			
ABCS	87	G	307	AREA	4A	13A	21	2	20		103	14	0.10
ABCS	88	G	297	ROOM	4A	13A	35	0	12				0.30
ABCS	91	B					40	1					
ABCS	101	G	269	ROOM	3A	10A	37	0	0		150	71	
B	0	B					31	1					
B	40	M	71	ROOM	2	8A	35	13	2	80			5.40
B	43	B	31	ROOM	2	8A	35	1					
B	43	M	31	ROOM	2	8A	35	5	33	5			2.10
B	44	M	71	ROOM	2	8A	35	13	29	27			5.40
B	45	M	117	CRDX	2	8A	35	1	9	9			4.10
B	46	M	63	ROOM	3A	10A	35	0	10	2			9.20
B	47	M	57	WALL	2	8C	36	0	73	9			1.70
B	48	M	63	ROOM	3A	10A	37	4	11	1			2.80
B	49	G	63	ROOM	3B	11B	29	8	18				3.80
B	50	G	28	WALL	2	8D	36	1					
B	50	M	28	WALL	2	8D	36	31	18				12.60
B	51	H	63	ROOM	3A	10A	35	1	4				7.70
B	52	G				12	34	1	8				1.40
B	53	G	63	ROOM	3A	10A	37	0					1.90
B	54	G				12	34	4	19				0.50
B	55	G	67	ROOM	4A	13A	37	0					1.00
B	56	G	65	ROOM	4A	13A	37	5					1.10
B	57	G	66	ROOM	4A	13A	37	6	5				0.50
B	60	G	65	ROOM	4B	14B	29	4					2.20
B	62	G	70	DOOR	4A	13A	37	2					0.10
B	63	G	64	ROOM	4A	13A	21	7	36				0.39
B	64	M	66	ROOM	4A	13A	37	4					0.90
B	65	G	64	ROOM	4A	13B	21	8	1				0.80
B	66	G	252	ROOM	5	15A	35	0	50				3.70
B	67	G	72	DOOR	4A	13A	37	0					0.20
B	71	M	71	ROOM	2	8A	35	9					
B	72	H	71	ROOM	2	8A	35	0					1.60
B	73	G	71	ROOM	2	8B	37	2					
B	74	G	376	DBLK	2	8D	36	0					0.90

OP	LOT	LI	FT #	FEAT	BL	STR	DC	FINDS	BAN	KAF	WT BNS	BONES	M3
B 1	0	G	163	PYTH	2	8B	28	1					
B 1	0	G	165	PYTH	2	8B	28	3					
B 1	0	G	71	ROOM	2	8B	29	1					
B 1	0	G	125	WALL	2	8D	36	1					
B 1	0	B					39	2					
B 1	37	G	71	ROOM	2	8B	21	2					
B 1	37	G	71	ROOM	2	8A	35	9	11				2.70
B 1	37	K	71	ROOM	2	8A	35	1					
B 1	37	G	71	ROOM	2	8B	37	1					
B 1	39	G	131	ROOM	2	8B	21	8	15				
B 1	39	G	131	ROOM	2	8A	35	2					
B 1	39	G	154	ROOM	2	8A	35	3					
B 1	39	H	131	ROOM	2	8A	35	44					
B 1	39	K	154	ROOM	2	8A	35	1					
B 1	39	G	71	ROOM	2	8B	37	1					
B 1	39	G	131	ROOM	2	8B	37	2					
B 1	39	G	130	ROOM	2	8B	37	1					
B 1	39	G	154	ROOM	2	8B	37	17					
B 1	40	G	131	ROOM	2	8B	37	0					1.40
B 1	41	G	155	PLAT	2	8C	36	4	8				17.85
B 1	41	G	130	ROOM	2	8C	37	2					
B 1	43	G	71	ROOM	2	8B	37	1	7				
B 1	44	G	186	ROOM	2	8A	35	0					
B 1	45	G	131	ROOM	2	8B	37	0					1.90
B 1	48	G	71	ROOM	2	8B	37	0	42				
B 1	51	G	154	ROOM	2	8A	35	0					
B 1	52	G	131	ROOM	2	8A	35	0					
B 1	391	G	131	ROOM	2	8B	21	10					
B 1	391	G	131	ROOM	2	8B	37	7					7.20
B 1	392	G	154	ROOM	2	8B	37	10					0.30
C	60	B	117	CRDX	2	8A	35	3					
C	60	M	117	CRDX	2	8A	35	4	81	9			
C	62	G	71	ROOM	2	8A	35	2	40				11.70
C	64	G	118	CRDX	2	8A	35	5	102				9.60
C	65	G	128	ROOM	2	8A	35	2					
C	66	G	71	ROOM	2	8B	21	14	16				0.13
C	67	G	118	CRDX	2	8B	21	749					1.90
C	70	M	63	ROOM	3A	10A	35	0	18	1			
C	72	G	71	ROOM	2	8B	37	0					1.60
C 1	33	G	128	ROOM	2	8B	29	3					
C 1	33	G	129	ROOM	2	8B	29	1					
C 1	33	G	130	ROOM	2	8B	29	2					
C 1	33	G	131	ROOM	2	8B	29	2					
C 1	33	H			2	8A	35	1	136				
C 1	34	G	130	ROOM	2	8B	37	25	33				6.38
C 1	35	G	131	ROOM	2	8A	35	6	29				4.30
C 1	36	G	128	ROOM	2	8A	35	6	3				
C 1	36	G	128	ROOM	2	8B	37	1	3				1.48
C 1	37	G	130	ROOM	2	8B	21	79	19				2.10

OP	LOT	LI	FT #	FEAT	BL	STR	DC	FINDS	BAN	KAF	WT BNS	BONES	M3
C 1	38	G	129	ROOM	2	8A	35	3					3.10
C 1	39	G	128	ROOM	2	8B	37	4					1.50
C 1	40	G	129	ROOM	2	8B	37	1					0.50
C 1	41	G	128	ROOM	2	8B	29	3					0.60
								2537	5317	377	13634	8313	363.11

OP	LOT	LI	FT #	FEAT	BL	STR	DC	R#	RWT	T#	TWT	P#	PWT	BRB	MSCL
A	46	G	34	ROOM	3A	10A	37	5		1				2	
ABC	3	G	241	CRDX	4A	13B	29	3				1			
ABC	4	G	239	WALL	4B	14B	36	21				4			
ABC	5	G	240	WALL	4A	13C	36	23		6		2		1	1
ABC	7	G	323	WALL	4B	14B	36	26		1		5		1	
ABC	8	G	334	MISC	4A	13C	49	46		10		4		2	2
ABC	10	G	241	CRDX	4A	13B	29	30		7		1			2
ABC	12	G	331	AREA	4B	14A	37	9		7				1	
ABC	13	G	331	AREA	4B	14A	37	7							
ABC	15	G	331	AREA	4B	14A	37	7		1					1
ABC	16	H	336	AREA	5	15A	35	1							
ABC	17	G	251	ROOM	5	15A	35	2							
ABC	18	G	333	AREA	4B	14A	37	2		1				1	
ABC	25	G	281	COUR	4B	14B	29	4							
ABC	26	G	346	ROOM	5	15A	35	3		4					
ABC	28	G	336	AREA	5	15A	37	9				1			2
ABC	29	G	346	ROOM	5	15A	37	2		1					
ABC	30	H	336	AREA	5	15A	37	1							
ABC	32	G	359	AREA	5	15B	37	3							
ABC	33	G	347	ROOM	5	15A	35	6							
ABC	34	G	353	COUR	5	15B	21	6				3			1
ABC	35	G	360	HRTH	5	15B	37	5		7		1		1	4
ABC	37	G	353	COUR	5	15B	21	2				4			
ABC	39	G	358	AREA	5	15B	37	1							
ABC	40	G	363	OVEN	5	15B	28			4					
ABCN	9	M	118	CRDX	2	8A	35	11		5		1			
ABCN	13	G	117	CRDX	2	8B	35	25		7		2		1	
ABCN	14	G	117	CRDX	2	8B	37	17		3		3			
ABCN	17	G	118	CRDX	2	8B	37	9		1					
ABCN	18	G	117	CRDX	2	8B	29	3		2					
ABCN	20	G	265	ROOM	2	8B	37	3		2					
ABCN	22	G	136	DBLK	2	8C	36	7		2					
ABCN	24	M	264	DBLK	2	8C	36	7		3					
ABCN	30	G	207	ROOM	2	8B	37	13		1					
ABCN	38	G	127	WALL	2	8D	36	8		4		1			
ABCN	43	G	106	WALL	2	8D	36	6		1					
ABCN	44	G	207	ROOM	2	8A	35	4							
ABCN	48	G				9	34	4		1		1			
ABCN	50	H	71	ROOM	2	8D	29	33		5		2			
ABCN	53	G				9	34	34		13		1			
ABCN	57	G	211	ROOM	3A	10A	37	4				1			
ABCN	58	G	260	AREA	3A	10A	29	25		6				2	
ABCN	59	M	220	ROOM	3A	10A	35	68		7		2			
ABCN	60	G	260	AREA	3A	10B	29	20		3					
ABCN	65	M				9	34	24		6		2		1	
ABCN	68	G	220	ROOM	3A	10A	21	21		7					
ABCN	71	M	222	ROOM	3A	10A	35	19		1		2			1
ABCN	72	G	260	AREA	3A	10B	37	46		3		3			
ABCN	74	G	33	WALL	3B	11B	36	8		2		1			

OP	LOT	LI	FT #	FEAT	BL	STR	DC	R#	RWT	T#	TWT	P#	PWT	BRB	MSCL
ABCN	75	G	224	DOOR	3A	10A	35	2						1	
ABCN	80	G	260	AREA	3A	10A	35	11		1		1			
ABCN	81	G	129	ROOM	2	8D	29	8				1			
ABCN	83	M				9	34	12				1			
ABCN	90	G	118	CRDX	2	8D	29	62		11		3			
ABCN	91	G	260	AREA	3A	10B	37	22		5				1	
ABCN	92	M	260	AREA	3A	10A	35	9		1		1			
ABCN	93	G	63	ROOM	3A	10A	35	9		1		1			1
ABCN	95	G	118	CRDX	2	8D	29	7		1				1	
ABCN	99	H	211	ROOM	3A	10A	37	78	443	5	85	1	38		
ABCN	106	H	229	ROOM	3B	11B	29	58		10		1			
ABCN	112	G	136	DBLK	2	8C	36	8							
ABCN	113	G	260	AREA	3A	10B	29	27							
ABCN	118	G	260	AREA	3A	10B	37	4				1			
ABCN	119	G	63	ROOM	3B	11B	29	19		1		2		2	
ABCN	121	G	261	WALL	3B	11B	36	24		3		3		1	
ABCN	125	M	211	ROOM	3B	11B	29	20		2					
ABCN	126	G				12	34	12				3			
ABCN	128	G	66	ROOM	4A	13A	35	12						2	
ABCN	129	M	66	ROOM	4A	13A	37	8				2		2	
ABCN	131	G	241	CRDX	4A	13A	35	23		5		2			
ABCN	133	G	241	CRDX	4A	13A	37	17		2		1		1	
ABCN	136	G	64	ROOM	4A	13A	35	5				1		1	
ABCN	139	G	307	AREA	4A	13A	21	450	4249	159	6930	102	10800	1	3
ABCN	141	G	241	CRDX	4A	13A	37	8		1		1			
ABCN	142	G	67	ROOM	4A	13A	29	5		1				1	
ABCN	143	M	64	ROOM	4A	13A	37	32		25		1			7
ABCN	146	G	64	ROOM	4A	13A	37	14	123	2	55				5
ABCN	148	G	236	PITX	4A	13A	22	9	224			2	625		4
ABCN	149	G	236	PITX	4A	13A	22	17	177	3	36	5	622		4
ABCN	152	G	236	PITX	4A	13A	22	5	47	3	96	1	116		2
ABCN	153	G	236	PITX	4A	13A	22	23	240			2	212		
ABCN	154	G	59	WALL	4B	14B	36	10	103					1	
ABCN	155	G				12	34	3	39	2	20				
ABCN	158	G	247	ROOM	5	15A	37								1
ABCN	159	G	64	ROOM	4A	13A	37	4	46	5	195				
ABCN	162	G	236	PITX	4A	13A	22	8	131	8	433	1	296		
ABCS	1	G	193	DBLK	2	8C	36			2					
ABCS	2	G	14	WALL	2	8C	36	11		4					
ABCS	4	G	157	DBLK	2	8C	36	4		3		1			1
ABCS	7	M	156	WALL	2	8D	36	8		5		1			
ABCS	8	M	155	PLAT	2	8C	36	1						1	
ABCS	10	G	125	WALL	2	8D	36	11		2		1		2	
ABCS	17	G				9	34	11		2		1			
ABCS	21	G	190	WALL	2	8D	36	5				1			
ABCS	22	G	191	DBLK	2	8C	36	4							
ABCS	24	M	315	DOOR	3A	10A	35	28		2					
ABCS	25	M	269	ROOM	3A	10A	37	17							1
ABCS	26	G	269	ROOM	3A	10A	37	3				1			

OP	LOT	LI	FT #	FEAT	BL	STR	DC	R#	RWT	T#	TWT	P#	PWT	BRB	MSCL
ABCS	27	M	71	ROOM	2	8D	29	11						2	
ABCS	35	G	154	ROOM	2	8D	29	10		5		2		1	1
ABCS	36	G	271	ROOM	3A	10A	23	6		2		1			
ABCS	39	G	270	ROOM	3A	10A	35	14						2	
ABCS	40	G	190	WALL	2	8D	36	4		1					
ABCS	47	G	271	ROOM	3A	10A	37	3							
ABCS	50	G	155	PLAT	2	8C	36	9	86	2	135	2	208		1
ABCS	51	G	130	ROOM	2	8C	29	2	13						
ABCS	55	G	260	AREA	3A	10A	35	7							
ABCS	57	M	16	WALL	3B	11B	36	10		1					
ABCS	58	G	34	ROOM	3B	11B	29	4	46						
ABCS	59	G	35	ROOM	3B	11B	29	2	16						
ABCS	60	M				12	34	42	421			3	199		2
ABCS	65	G	304	ROOM	3B	11B	29	28	193						
ABCS	66	G	281	COUR	4A	13A	37	12		2		1			
ABCS	70	G	267	ROOM	3B	11B	29	3	35			1	7		
ABCS	72	G	241	CRDX	4A	13A	37	12						1	
ABCS	73	G	288	CRDX	4A	13A	37	1	8						
ABCS	74	G	241	CRDX	4A	13A	37	2	15	1	20	1	38		
ABCS	76	H	269	ROOM	3B	11B	29	4	84						
ABCS	77	G	290	BNCH	4A	13A	21	2	35						
ABCS	78	G	33	WALL	3B	11B	36	9		2					
ABCS	79	M				12	34	8	63			2	218		
ABCS	80	G	308	HRTH	4A	13A	28			1					
ABCS	81	G	307	AREA	4A	13A	35	18		4					
ABCS	82	G	307	AREA	4A	13A	21	15		7	632	3	84		
ABCS	83	G	210	WALL	3B	11B	36	10		1		2			
ABCS	86	M	241	CRDX	4A	13A	35	8		4		2		2	
ABCS	88	G	297	ROOM	4A	13A	35	3		3					
B	43	M	31	ROOM	2	8A	35	16	200	5	186	2	253		
B	49	G	63	ROOM	3B	11B	29	7	116					2	
B	52	G				12	34	6	75	2	99				
B	54	G				12	34	18	198	1	50				
B	57	G	66	ROOM	4A	13A	37	5	73						
B	63	G	64	ROOM	4A	13A	21	13	130	8	200	1	62		
B	66	G	252	ROOM	5	15A	35	19		14		3		1	2
B 1	41	G	130	ROOM	2	8C	37	4		1				1	1
C	66	G	71	ROOM	2	8B	21	6	51	4	100	2	144		
C	70	M	63	ROOM	3A	10A	35	2		2		1			
C 1	34	G	130	ROOM	2	8B	37	6		7		4		1	1
C 1	36	G	128	ROOM	2	8A	35					2			
						SUM		2152		492		229		44	51

Appendix C

Feature Inventory

The Feature Inventory provides information about all features excavated in the levels reported in this monograph. The first 2 columns (FT #, FEAT) list all ABC Banesh features in numerical order. In 1971, 1972, and 1974 features were assigned numbers sequentially within each operation (Fig. 5). In 1974 it became apparent that this system was not working well for adjacent operations in which the same feature would be assigned different numbers. At the end of the 1974 season a single number was assigned to each feature from a new feature number series. New features excavated in 1976 and 1978 were assigned numbers in the same series. A concordance of new and old feature numbers is bound into each site supervisor's notebook and in the register of finds to be deposited in the University of Pennsylvania Museum of Anthropology and Archaeology archives.

Different types of features are abbreviated: AREA (open space, character not identified), BNCH (bench), COUR (courtyard), CRDX (corridor), DBLK (blocked doorway), DOOR (door), HRTH (hearth), OVEN (oven), PITX (pit), PLAT (platform), PYTH (pythos), ROOM (room), WALL (wall).

The second two columns (BL, STR) show the building level and stratum assigned to the feature. Constructed features are assigned the stratum number of the surface on which they were constructed (walls, platforms, doorblockings, hearths, ovens), on which they rest (pithoi), or from which they were excavated (pits, foundation trenches). For example: Wall 28 was built on Stratum (surface) 8D and is assigned to that stratum (Fig. 6); Pit 236 was excavated in antiquity from Stratum (floor) 13A in Room 64 and is assigned to that stratum. Open features (rooms, areas, corridors, doors) are assigned the stratum number of the strata within the feature. For example, Room 30 contained Strata 8A through 8D and is assigned to Stratum 8.

The next two columns list the context of features to facilitate the location of features. For example: Wall 12, in BL 2, is the north wall of Room 30 and Platform 13 is in Room 30 (Fig. 20); Room 30, in turn, is in the southeast part of BL 2 (Fig. 20). Door-blocking 26 is in Wall 106 (Fig. 20). Room 66 is in the central north part of BL 4 (Fig. 9).

The next four columns list the number of finds, Banesh and Kaftari sherds, and bones as described in Appendix B, and with the same reservations.

Appendix C, Feature Inventory

FT #	FEAT	BL	STR	CONTEXT FEAT		FIND	BAN	KAF	BONE
12	WALL	2	8C	30	ROOM-N	0			
13	PLAT	2	8C	30	ROOM	0			
14	WALL	2	8C	186	ROOM-N	3	20		
15	WALL	3	11B	34	ROOM-E	0			
16	WALL	3	11B	34	ROOM-N	0	20	1	
17	WALL	3	11B	268	ROOM-E	0			
18	WALL	3	11B	35	ROOM-N	0			
26	DBLK	2	8C	106	WALL	0			
27	PLAT	2	8D	71	ROOM	0			
28	WALL	2	8D	71	ROOM-E	43	73	3	
29	DBLK	2	8C	28	WALL	0			
30	ROOM	2	8		SE	0			
31	ROOM	2	8		SE	6	33	5	
32	PLAT	2	8C	30	ROOM	0			
33	WALL	3	11B	211	ROOM-E	4	27		
34	ROOM	3	10		SE	8	19		
35	ROOM	3	10		SE	1	5		
36	HRTH	3	11B	35	ROOM	0			
37	DOOR	3	10	17	WALL	0			
38	DOOR	3	10	33	WALL	3	11	14	
39	DOOR	3	10	15	WALL	0			
53	HRTH	3	11B	63	ROOM	64			
56	WALL	2	8C	31	ROOM-N	0			
57	WALL	2	8D	31	ROOM-N	0	73	9	
59	WALL	4	14B	66	ROOM-E	5	12		
60	WALL	4	14B	65	ROOM-N	0			
61	PLAT	4	14B	64	ROOM	0			
62	WALL	4	14B	64	ROOM-N	0			
63	ROOM	3	10		NE	22	155	16	
64	ROOM	4	13		C	35	157	1	270
65	ROOM	4	13		NE	9			
66	ROOM	4	13		C-N	20	36	1	97
67	ROOM	4	13		NE	2	25	7	23
69	DOOR	4	14B	60	WALL	0			
70	DOOR	4	14B	59	WALL	2			
71	ROOM	2	8		C-N	102	271	166	
72	DOOR	4	14B	59	WALL	0			
103	WALL	2	8D	117	CRDX-E	0			
104	WALL	2	8D	128	ROOM-N	2			
105	WALL	2	8D	118	CRDX-N	0			
106	WALL	2	8D	131	ROOM-E	6	27	13	
113	PYTH	2	8B	71	ROOM	0			
114	PYTH	2	8B	71	ROOM	0			
115	PYTH	2	8B	71	ROOM	0			
116	PYTH	2	8B	71	ROOM	0			
117	CRDX	2	8		NE	26	201	28	82
118	CRDX	2	8		N	993	242	4	428
125	WALL	2	8D	130	ROOM-E	12	23		
126	WALL	2	8D	130	ROOM-N	0			

FT #	FEAT	BL	STR	CONTEXT FEAT		FIND	BAN	KAF	BONE
127	WALL	2	8D	131	ROOM-N	2	16		
128	ROOM	2	8		C-N	16	6		
129	ROOM	2	8		NW	20	12		
130	ROOM	2	8		W	109	55		42
131	ROOM	2	8		C-N	89	44		
132	WALL	2	8D	118	CRDX-N	0			
136	DBLK	2	8C	125	WALL	1	25		
146	BINX	2	8B	154	ROOM	0			
147	HRTH	2	8B	154	ROOM	0			
154	ROOM	2	8		C-S	31	27		
155	PLAT	2	8C	130	ROOM	8	37		
156	WALL	2	8D	154	ROOM-E	15	22	3	
157	DBLK	2	8C	156	WALL	0	17		
159	WALL	2	8D	185	ROOM-N	0			
160	WALL	2	8C	154	ROOM-N	10	120		
161	PYTH	2	8B	71	ROOM	0			
162	PYTH	2	8B	71	ROOM	0			
163	PYTH	2	8B	71	ROOM	1			
164	PYTH	2	8B	71	ROOM	0			
165	PYTH	2	8B	71	ROOM	3			
166	PYTH	2	8B	71	ROOM	0			
167	PYTH	2	8B	71	ROOM-N	0			
168	PYTH	2	8B	71	ROOM	0			
169	PYTH	2	8B	71	ROOM	0			
170	DOOR	2	8D	156	WALL	0			
185	ROOM	2	8		SW	6			
186	ROOM	2	8		C-S	4	33	25	
187	AREA	2	8		SW	0			
188	ROOM	2	8		SW	1	19		
189	PLAT	2	8C	185	ROOM	6	4		
190	WALL	2	8D	185	ROOM-E	1	16		
191	DBLK	2	8C	190	WALL	2	6		
192	WALL	2	8D	187	AREA-E	0			
193	DBLK	2	8C	156	WALL	0			
197	PYTH	2	8B	186	ROOM	0			
198	PYTH	2	8B	185	ROOM	0			
207	ROOM	2	8		NE	23	26	7	108
210	WALL	3	11B	230	ROOM-E	6	47		
211	ROOM	3	10		C-N	31	122	4	452
212	DOOR	3	10	33	WALL	0			
213	HRTH	3	11B	211	ROOM	0			
214	WALL	3	11B	63	ROOM-N	0			
215	DOOR	3	10	33	WALL	1			
216	DOOR	3	10	33	WALL	0			
217	DOOR	3	10	261	WALL	0			
219	WALL	3	11B	220	ROOM	0			
220	ROOM	3	10		C-N	8	116	1	17
221	DOOR	3	10	223	WALL	0			
222	ROOM	3	10		C	7	25	7	53

FT #	FEAT	BL	STR	CONTEXT	FEAT	FIND	BAN	KAF	BONE
223	WALL	3	11B	222	ROOM-N	0			
224	DOOR	3	10	272	WALL	0	5		
225	WALL	3B	11A	230	ROOM-N	0			
226	WALL	3B	11A	229	ROOM-N	0			
227	WALL	3B	11A	228	ROOM-N	0			
228	ROOM	3B	11A		SW	1			
229	ROOM	3B	11A		NW	5	73		277
230	ROOM	3B	11A		NW	0			
231	DOOR	3B	11A	226	WALL	0			
232	ROOM	3B	11A		NW	0			
233	WALL	4	14B	67	ROOM-N	0			
234	DOOR	4	14B	233	WALL	0			
236	PITX	4A	13A	64	ROOM	74	99		1333
238	HRTH	4	14B	67	ROOM	0			
239	WALL	4	14B	66	ROOM-E	2	25		
240	WALL	4A	13B	241	CRDX	2	38		
241	CRDX	4A	13		NW	15	206	1	300
242	WALL	4A	13B	241	CRDX-W	0			
244	WALL	5	15B	251	ROOM-E	0			
245	DOOR	5	15A	244	WALL	0			
246	ROOM	5	15		NE	2			20
247	ROOM	5	15		C-N	2	4		21
248	WALL	5	15B	247	ROOM-N	0			
249	ROOM	5	15B		C-N	0			51
250	WALL	5	15B	246	ROOM-E	0			
251	ROOM	5	15		C-S	1	2		9
252	ROOM	5	15		SE	0	50		
253	ROOM	5	15		NE	0			
254	WALL	5	15B	251	ROOM-N	0			
255	WALL	5	15B	346	ROOM-N	0			
256	WALL	5	15B	348	AREA-N	0			
257	WALL	5	15B	246	ROOM-N	0			
258	WALL	5	15B	252	ROOM-N	0			
259	HRTH	5	15B	252	ROOM	0			
260	AREA	3A	10		NW	23	229	3	292
261	WALL	3	11B	220	ROOM-N	0	56		
264	DBLK	2	8C		WHERE?	0	9	3	
265	ROOM	2	8		NE	3	26	7	41
267	ROOM	3	10		C-S	4	8		151
268	ROOM	3	10		C-S	13	66	8	
269	ROOM	3	10		SW	13	33	1	113
270	ROOM	3	10		SW	2	38		
271	ROOM	3	10		SW	71	20		
272	WALL	3	11B	267	ROOM-N	0			
273	WALL	3	11B	270	ROOM-N	0			
274	WALL	3	11B	269	ROOM-N	0			
275	WALL	3	11B	271	ROOM-N	0			
276	WALL	3	11B	304	ROOM-E	0			
277	HRTH	3	11B	268	ROOM	0			

FT #	FEAT	BL	STR	CONTEXT FEAT		FIND	BAN	KAF	BONE
278	HRTH	3	11B	269	ROOM	0			
279	WALL	3	11B	268	ROOM-N	0			
281	COUR	4A	13		SE	11	87	7	
282	ROOM	4A	13		SE	1	5		
283	AREA	4A	13		SE	3	10		
284	WALL	4A	13B	281	COUR-E	0			
285	WALL	4A	13B	282	ROOM-E	0			
286	WALL	4A	13B	283	AREA-N	0			
287	WALL	4A	13B	283	AREA-E	0			
288	CRDX	4A	13		S	7	29		
289	WALL	4A	13B	283	AREA-W	0			
290	BNCH	4A	13B	288	CRDX	7	13		66
291	WALL	4A	13B	288	CRDX-N	0			
292	WALL	4A	13	307	AREA-E	0			
293	ROOM	4A	13		SE	0			
294	WALL	4A	13B	293	ROOM-N	0			
295	WALL	4A	13	288	CRDX-SE	0			
296	WALL	4A	13B	293	ROOM-S	0			
297	ROOM	4A	13		SE	0	12		
298	WALL	4A	13B	297	ROOM-N	0			
299	HRTH	4A	13B	281	COUR	0			
300	OVEN	4A	13B	297	ROOM	0			
301	AREA	4A	13		SE	0			
304	ROOM	3B	11A		SW	2	62		
306	WALL	4A	13A	282	ROOM-N	0			
307	AREA	4A	13A		SW	12	1023		3682
308	HRTH	4A	13B	307	AREA	1	1		
310	HRTH	2	8D	130	ROOM	2			
311	HRTH	3B	11B	228	ROOM	0			
315	DOOR	3	10	279	WALL	1	37		
316	DOOR	3	10	210	WALL	0			
317	DOOR	3	10	276	WALL	0			
318	DOOR	3B	11A	275	WALL	0			
319	DOOR	3	10	273	WALL	0			
320	DOOR	3	10	274	WALL	0			
321	DOOR	4A	13B	296	WALL	0			
322	DOOR	4	14B	323	WALL	0			
323	WALL	4	14B	281	COUR-N	2	39		
324	DOOR	5	15A	257	WALL	0			
325	DOOR	5	15B	248	WALL	0			
326	WALL	5	15B	358	AREA-E	0			
327	HRTH	5	15B	247	ROOM	0			
328	HRTH	4B	14B	332	AREA	0			
329	WALL	4B	14B	333	AREA-N	0			
330	WALL	4B	14B	332	AREA-N	0			
331	AREA	4B	14A		NW	6	46		
332	AREA	4B	14A		NW	3	41		
333	AREA	4B	14A		SW	0	4		
334	MISC	4A	13B	240	WALL	11	73		

FT #	FEAT	BL	STR	CONTEXT FEAT		FIND	BAN	KAF	BONE
336	AREA	5	15A	ABOVE	358-59	1	25		
337	DOOR	5	15B	254	WALL	0			
338	DOOR	5	15B	255	WALL	0			
339	HRTH	4B	14B	331	AREA	2			
340	WALL	5	15B	342	ROOM-N	0			
341	DOOR	5	15B	340	WALL	0			
342	ROOM	5	15		SW	1	3		
343	HRTH	4B	14B	331	AREA	1			
344	HRTH	5	15B	353	COUR	0			
345	HRTH	4B	14B	333	AREA	1			
346	ROOM	5	15		C-S	2	12		
347	ROOM	5	15		C-S	0	6		
348	COUR	5	15		SE	1	14		
350	DOOR	5	15B	244	WALL	0			
351	DBLK	5	15B	244	WALL	0			
353	COUR	5	15		SW	6	19		
355	HRTH	5	15B	353	COUR	0			
356	WALL	5	15B	359	ROOM-N	0			
357	HRTH	5	15B	359	ROOM	0			
358	AREA	5	15		NW	0			
359	AREA	5	15		W	4	3		
360	HRTH	5	15B	348	AREA	1	18		
361	HRTH	5	15B	358	AREA	0			
362	HRTH	5	15B	358	AREA	0			
363	OVEN	5	15B	358	AREA	16	5		
364	WALL	5	15B	349	DOOR	0			
365	HRTH	5	15B	348	AREA	0			
366	HRTH		16	370	AREA	0			
367	AREA		16	370	AREA	3			
368	WALL	5	15B	342	ROOM-E	0			
369	AREA		18A	370	AREA	18			
370	AREA		18B	BELOW	246-47	21	1		
371	DBLK	2	8C	106	WALL	3			
372	AREA		19	370	AREA	4			
373	ROOM	3	10		NE	0			
374	DOOR	3	10	17	WALL	0			
375	DOOR	3	10	381	WALL	0			
376	DBLK	2	8C	28	WALL	0			
377	NICH	3	11B	63	ROOM	0			
378	NICH	3	11B	35	ROOM	0			
379	NICH	3	11B	268	ROOM	0			
380	PLAT	3B	11A	228	ROOM	0			
381	WALL	3	11B	269	ROOM-S	0			
382	MISC	3	11B	268	ROOM	0			
383	DBLK	4A	13B	284	WALL	0			
384	DOOR	4A	13C	242	WALL	0			
385	NICH	3B	11A	225	WALL	0			
386	MISC	2	8B	118	CRDX	0			
387	WALL	3B	11A	220	ROOM	0			

Appendix C, Feature Inventory

FT #	FEAT	BL	STR	CONTEXT FEAT	FIND	BAN	KAF	BONE
	WALL	5			2			
	WALL	2			2			

Appendix D

Excavations at Tal-e Kureh

Between the fourth and fifth seasons of excavation at Malyan, a test excavation was made in a Banesh period site called Tal-e Kureh ("Kiln Mound"). This site, originally reported by Sumner as the type site for the Banesh Period (1972; infra., Appendix E site S-5R4 = A-7F1), is located near the village of Banesh in the northernmost corner of the Baiza district of the Marv Dasht plain 13 km north of Tal-e Malyan (Fig. 2, grid 63N-83E). Although small in extent, the excavation yielded a good sample of stratified material spanning the end of the Lapui and beginning of the Banesh periods. In addition, it produced evidence of Banesh period ceramic manufacturing technology and a small sample of faunal material and charcoal relating to the occupation of the site.

Tal-e Kureh was chosen for testing because a systematic surface survey of Banesh period settlements in the Marv Dasht plain indicated that this site had been occupied during the period of transition from Lapui to Banesh style ceramics. Thus, an excavation had the potential to yield a stratigraphic record of the changes in ceramic styles that occurred during this poorly known era. In addition, surface finds of ceramic slag, kiln debris, overfired pottery, and ceramic manufacturing tools indicated that Tal-e Kureh was a site where Banesh grit-tempered pottery was manufactured. Excavation would help define the chronological extent of this activity and might also provide useful information on the technology and organization of ceramic manufacturing during this era. Because the site had so much surface evidence of ceramic manufac-

turing, it also appeared likely that an excavation would yield enough charcoal for C-14 dating of the excavated materials. Finally, a significant portion of the site had recently been bulldozed during construction of a nearby road. A test excavation would ensure that at least some evidence from the site was preserved if this destruction continued. It appeared that even a small excavation would provide data relevant to a number of chronological, functional, and processual problems.

The Excavation

The excavation at Tal-e Kureh was carried out between January 10 and January 20, 1977.[*] Four days were spent excavating a 1 x 2 m unit to a depth of 2.15 m and an additional day was spent drawing the sections and backfilling the test pit. During the rest of the time snow and mud prevented any access to the site. In fact, the bad weather was responsible for the decision to limit excavation to a single unit—the original plan had been to clear a second 1 x 2 m unit to the west of the first, excavating by natural depositional levels, but conditions made this impossible.

[*] I am indebted to Dr. Firouz Bagherzadeh, director of the Center, for his help in obtaining a test permit and for his interest in this research. Ms. Anne Saurat, Assistant to the Director and Mr. Allahqoli Islami, ICAR representative in Fars, also deserve thanks for their assistance in facilitating this excavation. The work was funded through National Science Foundation grant BNS-76-81955 as part of the author's dissertation research and enabled by a permit from the Iranian Center for Archaeological Research.

Tal-e Kureh is a small site. The mounded area, approximately 150 m. by 110 m., stands a maximum of 1.5 m above plain level and the total area of sherd scatter is about 2.7 ha. (Fig. D1, Pl. 41). Sometime prior to the fall of 1976 about 15% of the mound had been bulldozed to provide fill for a nearby road. This destruction revealed three ashy areas, large quantities of ceramics, and frequent examples of what appear to have been kiln debris; it also left a section that allowed the test excavation to be located in an area of the site that had not been disturbed in antiquity.

Digging was done by a single workman using a large pick, small pick, and shovel. Sherds, bones, and charcoal were collected in the excavation by this man and outside of the unit by the author and one other workman. Excavated soil was examined by hand using a trowel and a portion of each excavation unit (Lot) was sifted through a 3 mm mesh screen, both to insure that no relatively common small artifact was being systematically missed and to aid in the recovery of bone and charcoal. Regrettably, soil and weather conditions made complete screening of each lot impractical.

Stratigraphy

The stratigraphy of the sounding (Fig. D2) is not complex and in most cases the excavation units, Lots 2-13, corresponded reasonably well with the natural strata (Fig. D2, I-VII). Only Strata II and IIIa were badly mixed during the excavation. In brief, there are three major breaks in the depositional sequence: a burned surface in Stratum VI, a prepared floor at the top of Stratum V, and the ashy Stratum II. These divide the excavation into four possibly significant units.

Stratum I

This stratum, composed of unmixed Lots 2-4 and mixed Lot 5, is about 65 cm thick and shows no distinct subdivisions. The uppermost 15 to 20 cm (Stratum Ia) had been thoroughly weathered and contain little bone. Lower frequencies of soft, friable chaff-tempered body sherds in this lot may also be due to this weathering. Below the weathered layer lies a stratum of similar material distinguished only by being more compact. It is composed of small lumps of yellow/buff clay scattered through a matrix of friable light brown clay. Lot 3 is unmixed material from this layer,

Stratum Ib. The lowest part of Stratum I, layer Ic, is like Ib except that it lacks the small clay lumps.

Stratum II

Stratum II, composed of mixed Lots 5 and 6, is a layer of fine dark gray clay containing ash and bits of charcoal. It is about 10 cm thick and slopes downward to the north. It may represent material cleaned from a kiln or large fire and dumped in a low pile, although in such an event a higher concentration of slag or burned clay might be expected. Possibly this layer was washed or blown in from a nearby deposit of such debris.

Stratum III

This stratum, composed of unmixed Lots 7, 8, 9, and mixed Lot 6, is 50 to 60 cm thick and composed of several distinct subunits. Stratum IIIa consists of friable light brown clay with many sherds and bones; the material from this layer was excavated as Lots 6 and 7. The soil of IIIa is readily distinguishable from the soil of IIIb but the line dividing the subunits is not sharp. These layers appear to represent incidents of trash dumping, with perhaps only brief intervals separating the episodes. Stratum IIIb, excavated in Lots 7 and 8, is a sticky yellowish brown clay containing frequent flakes and lumps of charcoal. Layers IIIc to IIIe also seem to represent single incidents of dumping centered to the south of the excavation unit. IIIc is a layer of fine yellow/buff clay containing a lens of darker yellow/brown clay. It probably represents in situ burning, and it grades into layer IIIb in the north end of the section. Below lies a layer (IIId, Lot 9) of light brown clay with charcoal which is similar to stratum IIIa but lacks the higher layer's concentration of sherds and bone. Finally, in the southwest corner of the excavation there is a thin deposit, IIIe, of yellow/buff clay lumps in an ashy gray matrix.

Stratum IV

Stratum IV, composed of mixed Lot 10, is a very thin layer of powdered charcoal and fine clay. Although the soil contained a great deal of carbonized material there were no pieces large enough to collect for carbon dating. The most noteworthy features of this layer are its regular thickness and the smooth horizontal surface that it rests on. This stratum may represent a deposit of burned straw or ashy material that was dumped or blown onto a floor from elsewhere on the site.

LOT	2	3	4	5	6	7	8	9	10	11	12	13	SUM
LAPUI FINE WARE COUNT	0	1	3	1	0	1	2	11	35	4	4	0	62
PERCENT	0	1	3	1	0	1	7	32	54	31	29	0	
ROUGH SLIPPED WARE: COUNT	0	8	8	10	7	12	9	15	13	4	1	0	87
PERCENT	0	8	8	11	13	17	31	44	20	31	7	0	
BANESH GT: RIMS, BASES: COUNT	21	63	61	57	29	35	13	5	8	1	9	2	304
PERCENT	66	61	63	63	52	49	45	15	12	8	64	100	
BANESH CT: RIMS, BASES: COUNT	11	32	25	22	20	24	5	3	9	4	0	0	155
PERCENT	34	31	26	24	36	33	17	9	14	31	0	0	
SUM: ALL WARES	32	104	97	90	56	72	29	34	65	13	14	2	608
BANESH GRIT-TEMPERED RIMS:													
BOWLS: CARINATED	0	0	3	1	2	0	0	1	1	0	0	0	8
PINCHED RIM	0	0	5	7	4	1	0	0	1	0	2	0	20
IMPRESSED RIM	0	0	0	0	1	1	0	0	0	0	0	0	2
ROUND RIM	4	14	11	2	0	1	1	0	0	1	0	0	34
JARS: HOLE MOUTH	0	2	4	4	0	2	3	2	1	1	0	0	19
COLLARED NECK	0	1	4	3	2	2	1	0	0	0	0	0	13
FOLDED RIM	0	10	0	0	0	1	0	0	0	0	0	0	11
BOWLS, JARS: CLUB RIM	3	4	7	4	4	6	1	2	0	0	0	0	31
RIM FORMS: HORIZONTAL LEDGE	0	2	3	5	1	5	2	1	1	0	1	0	21
EXT BEV LEDGE	1	1	4	4	2	2	2	1	0	0	0	0	17
WH GT WARE	1	4	0	0	1	0	2	0	0	0	0	0	8
OTHER: NOSE LUGS	1	1	0	0	0	0	0	0	0	0	0	0	2
WALL CONES	1	1	1	0	0	0	0	0	0	0	0	0	3
SUM: BANESH GT CLASSIFIED	11	40	42	30	17	21	12	7	4	2	3	0	189
COMPARE	10	38	47	33	19	26	13	11	10	3	3	0	213
BANESH CHAFF-TEMPERED FORMS:													
BRB RIMS	7	25	22	14	18	21	5	1	9	3	0	0	125
BRB BODIES	7	39	50	33	15	30	1	1	20	5	0	0	201
BR TRAYS	0	0	0	0	0	1	0	2	0	0	0	0	3
BANESH TRAYS	0	0	1	3	2	0	0	0	0	0	0	0	6
ST GOBLET BASE	1	0	0	0	0	0	0	0	0	0	0	0	1
ROUND RIMS	3	4	1	3	0	1	0	0	0	0	0	0	12
THICKENED RIMS	0	1	0	0	0	0	0	0	0	0	0	0	1
OTHER RIMS	0	2	1	2	0	1	0	0	0	1	0	0	7
SUM: BANESH CT CLASSIFIED	18	71	75	55	35	54	6	4	29	9	0	0	356
CERAMIC PRODUCTION FINDS:													
CERAMIC SLAG	3	8	6	25	2	10	2	0	0	0	0	0	56
PIERCED BOWLS	5	16	3	8	3	2	1	0	0	0	0	0	38
WASTERS	0	7	2	1	0	2	0	0	0	0	0	0	12
RING SCRAPERS	0	0	0	1	0	0	0	0	0	0	0	0	1
SUM: CERAMIC PRODUCTION FINDS	8	31	11	35	5	14	3	0	0	0	0	0	107
STONE FINDS:													
VESSEL FRAG: TRAVERTINE	0	0	1	0	0	0	0	0	0	0	0	0	1
WHITE LIMESTONE	1	0	0	0	0	0	0	0	0	0	0	0	1
FLINT: FLAKES	1	0	0	0	0	0	0	0	2	1	3	0	7
BLADE	0	0	0	0	0	0	0	0	1	0	0	0	1
SUM: STONE FINDS	2	0	1	0	0	0	0	0	3	1	3	0	10

Stratum V

The 30 cm thick Stratum V, composed of mixed Lots 10 and 11, is divided into two depositional units which were not separated during excavation. The uppermost Stratum Va is a compact yellow/brown clay with some horizontal lamination. It contains straw temper and lumps of harder bricky material and was almost certainly a prepared interior floor made from brick and mud plaster rubble. This layer was quite clean, but the few sherds in it are from a different depositional context and may be of quite different date than the materials from strata Vb and Vc. Vb is a layer of gray ashy clay in the north of the excavation unit that grades into Vc after being clearly distinguishable for only about 30 cm Stratum Vc is brown fairly loose clay containing midden-type debris, and most of the material recovered from Lot 10 came from this layer.

Stratum VI

Stratum VI is composed of mixed Lot 11. Stratum VIa is a deposit of black ashy clay 2 cm to 4 cm thick. VIb is a very thin layer of clay burned red that underlies the southern third of layer VIa. This stratum appears to represent the in situ remains of a fire but there is no evidence to indicate whether this fire was controlled or accidental.

Stratum VII

Stratum VII , composed of unmixed Lots 12, 13, and mixed lot 11, is a layer of undifferentiated friable brown clay that is at least 50 cm thick. It is quite compact, but contains holes made by roots, insects, and small rodents. There is no sign of straw temper in the clay. Cultural remains become less and less common deeper in this layer, and in the lowest 10 cm of the stratum almost nothing was recovered. Excavation was stopped at this point.

Excavated Materials

Ceramics

All ceramic materials from the excavation were washed, counted, and weighed. Then rims, bases, and decorated body sherds were separated from plain body sherds and divided into five ware categories distinguished by paste, temper, and surface treatment: Lapui Fine Ware, Banesh Rough Slipped Ware, Banesh Grit-

Tempered Ware, Banesh Chaff Tempered Ware, and White Grit Tempered Ware. Finally the rim, base, and decorated body sherds of the three most common Banesh wares were divided into types of vessel form and counted (Table D1; Figs. D4-D8).

Lapui Fine Ware

Lapui Fine Ware was first identified in the uppermost level of excavation at Tal-e Bakun A (Langsdorff and McCown 1942:32-33), and it was named Bakun A-V Ware soon thereafter (McCown 1942:48). This ware was described in more detail by Sumner (1972:40-42; 1988b), who gave it the name used here. It is readily distinguishable from all other wares found in the Kur Basin, primarily because of its fine paste, although it has occasionally been confused with the later Kaftari Red Ware because of its color.[*] Lapui Fine Ware is compact, well-knit, and breaks with a sharp, even edge. The paste is either red or buff, with very fine or no visible temper; the surface varies from smoothed to lightly burnished. Sherds with red paste are often unslipped, but when buff paste is used it has a red (5R 4/8) to almost black (7.5R 2.5/2) slip. Vessels of the red paste and buff paste varieties thus have superficially similar appearances even though the results were achieved by very different methods.

Lapui Fine Ware is well-fired and fire clouding is unusual. Lime pops in the paste are not uncommon. A Lapui Period ceramic production site on the western edge of the Kur River basin, site 10F1 (Sumner 1972), was covered with melted and vitrified sherds, which would seem to indicate that the manufacture of this ware required extended firing at high temperatures.

The most common shapes of this ware are open bowls (Sumner 1972: Plate XII:F-I; Plate XIV:A-D and J-Q) hole-mouth jars (Sumner 1972: Plate XIII:B, D; Plate XV:B, C), and pots with straight or everted simple rims (Sumner 1972: Plate XII:J-N; Plate XIII:F-T). Bases are generally flat, although ring and pedestal bases are also found. Decoration is rare, though sherds with pierced round lugs, horizontal bands of fugitive white paint, black painted patterns, and incised decoration have all been found (Sumner 1972: Plate XV:I, M-N; Plate XVI:I, O-P). Forms with carinations are rare, and when they

---

[*]See, for example, Chakrabarti and Moghadam (1977:166-168), where Gotch's (1971) incorrect identification of Kaftari Red Ware sherds as Bakun A-V Ware causes the authors to mistakenly suggest contacts between Fars and the Indus Valley during the 4th millennium B.C. According to Sumner (1988b) the red ware from Tall-i Nokhodi is also Kaftari Red Ware and not, as Goff (1963) suggests, similar to the earlier Lapui Fine Ware.

are found they seem to mark a terminal phase of the Lapui period. Lapui Fine Ware may become slightly more porous in the late part of the period, and the sorts of surface decoration described above may also distinguish a later part of the Lapui period.

Banesh Grit-tempered Ware

This ware is well-fired with medium to heavy coarse grit temper.[*] Both paste and temper in this ware are quite variable. The temper is generally either rounded black mineral grit of coarse to very coarse angular grit or grog fired to the color of the clay body. Other sorts of mineral temper are often found, but they are so variable they resist easy categorization. Some sherds show a crumbly fracture while others are nearly vitrified, but most fracture cleanly. Typical pastes vary from very pale brown (10YR 8/4) to red (7.5R 5/8), are slightly porous, and sherds of this ware often have darker (less oxidized) cores. Banesh Grit-Tempered Ware could certainly be divided into regionally or chronologically meaningful subtypes but for the time being a single broad category seems most useful.

Banesh Grit-Tempered Ware sherds usually have a fugitive, slightly fugitive, or flaky slip that ranges in color from light pinkish white through red to gray. On one red-slipped variety, pinched-rim bowls (Fig. D5:28, 29; Fig. D6:23, 28; see also Alden 1982a:91-95) the interior and exterior surface is decorated with streak-burnishing, but in most cases there are no signs of smoothing or burnishing on the vessel surfaces. Two types of surface treatment seem to have chronological and/or regional significance. Streak burnishing (found primarily on pinched-rim bowls but also on some medium-sized storage jars) is common only in the Early Phase of the Banesh period, when it is found on more than 5% of all red-slipped sherds (Alden 1979:50). Mottled light gray slip, most commonly on medium to very large storage jars and at Tal-e Kureh found only on the surface, represents the Late Middle Phase of the Banesh (Alden 1979:51).

Painting is common on this ware, especially on the shoulders of jars. Black horizontal bands, often painted over bands or areas of thick white slip, are the most frequent design element (Fig. D5:17, 23; Fig. D6:16, 20; Fig. D7:4, 6, 33); white or red bands and black-on-white or polychrome geometric patterns (Fig.

D5:16, 26, 27; Fig. D7: 13, 14, 35) are rarer. The lips and carinations of carinated bowls are frequently painted with black bands (Alden 1979, Fig. 39). This paint, however, is often flaky or fugitive and typically was applied over only limited portions of any vessel. As a result, the percentage of Banesh Grit-Tempered Ware vessels with painted decoration is presently unclear.

The range of Banesh Grit-Tempered Ware forms found in the test excavation at Tal-e Kureh is limited chronologically, functionally, and in terms of sample size. A more complete picture is given by data from regional surveys and the extensive excavations at Tal-e Malyan, which indicate that the most common forms of Grit-Tempered Ware are straight-sided and carinated bowls, bowls with impressed or tic-painted rims, deep club-rim bowls or wide-mouth jars, and jars with a wide variety of neck and rim forms. Pierced nose lugs and finger or stick-impressed decorative bands are common in this ware and very large storage jars over a meter high are often encountered. The range of shapes, rim forms, and decoration found on Banesh Grit-Tempered Ware has been published for surface collections (Sumner 1972, Pls. XIX-XXIII and Alden 1979, Figs. 36-46) and excavated collections (Nicholas 1990, Pls. 14-24; also Figs. 24-28 and D4-D7 of this volume).

Banesh Chaff-tempered Ware

As its name implies, the distinguishing feature of this ware is its temper, which consists of large quantities of coarsely chopped grass, straw, or chaff. Grains of barley have been found in several examples of this pottery from Malyan (Miller 1982), indicating that the tempering material may have been a by-product of threshing. Surface colors of Chaff-Tempered Ware sherds typically range from reddish yellow (7.5YR 7/6) to light red (2.5YR 6/6), but lighter pink (5YR 8/3) and darker reddish brown (5YR 5/4) examples are not uncommon.

Chaff-Tempered Ware vessels are generally poorly fired. Sherds are porous, their surfaces are chalky with neither slip nor burnishing, and they usually show finger marks from casual forming and smoothing. Thicker sherds, particularly goblet bases, often have incompletely oxidized cores and examples of these bases have even dissolved during washing. The lack of ceramic slag or kiln debris on three sites with very high concentrations of Chaff-Tempered Ware sherds— interpreted as production sites for Chaff-Tempered Ware vessels (Alden 1979:102-104), and the soft, incompletely fired character of many examples of this

---

[*] In temper descriptions the first adjective (light/medium/heavy) are used to refer to the density of tempering agents, while the second adjective (fine/medium/coarse) specifies the relative coarseness of the temper.

ware imply that these ceramics were fired in the open, probably beneath piles of reeds or straw. If this is true, then Banesh Chaff-Tempered Ware may have been only seasonally produced, perhaps during the driest part of the year after the summer harvest but before the onset of winter rains.

Chaff-Tempered Ware vessels come in three common forms: low-sided trays, large goblets, and beveled-rim bowls, and in several other forms that are far less common: troughs, low-sided basins, folded-rim jars with flat bases and sometimes drooping spouts, flaring squared jar or plate rims, and pierced bowls. Examples of these forms from surface collections in the Kur River Basin are described in more detail in Alden (1979:213-216 and Figs. 31-35).

Banesh Rough-slipped ware

The Tal-e Kureh excavation yielded a previously undefined ware having similarities to both Lapui Fine and Banesh Grit-Tempered wares but with a distinctly rougher surface. This ware is named after that characteristic surface treatment.

Banesh Rough-Slipped Ware has a slightly porous to well-knit paste and is tempered with medium-fine to coarse mineral grit. It is well-fired and lime pops are common, though not as common as in Lapui Fine Ware. The most distinctive feature of this ware is its surface treatment. Typical sherds have a thin slip or wash varying from red through brown or black in color and adhering tightly to the body of the vessel. Off-white to white sherds occasionally appear as well. Unlike Lapui Fine Ware, however, much of this variability in color appears to be the result of poorly regulated firing conditions rather than deliberate. Finally, in contrast to other Lapui and Banesh period wares, the surface of Rough-Slipped Ware sherds is neither smoothed nor burnished but noticeably grainy and rough.

Rough-Slipped Ware vessel and rim forms (Figs. D4-D7) share a number of similarities with both Lapui Fine and Banesh Grit-Tempered Ware vessels. Hole-mouth jars (a common Lapui Fine Ware form) and club rim and carinated bowls (typical Banesh Grit-Tempered Ware shapes) are found in Rough-Slipped Ware. The specific rim forms of the Rough-Slipped Ware vessels, however, tend to be different; more complex than most Lapui rims but not as strongly bent as many Banesh examples. Banesh Rough-Slipped Ware vessels appear to be hand-built rather than wheel thrown, and no examples of very large vessels were found.

Sherds of Rough-Slipped Ware were identified in surface collections from several sites in the Kur Basin, but because the paste of this ware is very similar to the paste of Banesh Grit-Tempered Ware specific identifica-tion of body sherds, particularly when weathered, is not always possible.

White Grit-tempered Ware

This ware is readily distinguished from other wares of the Lapui and Banesh periods because of the way it was fired and its distinctive white temper. Sherds of this ware are typically fully reduced or have an oxidized (reddish brown) core and reduced (gray to black) surface. Examples of this ware vary in color from reddish yellow (5YR 6/6) or red (10R 4/6) to dark black and often show fire clouding. They are tempered with coarse white angular grit, perhaps feldspar or quartzite, and the paste is dense and soft. The ware fractures unevenly and edges of the sherds tend to crumble. This ware is used exclusively for short-necked jars with everted rims and simple rounded lips (Fig. D8:35-38; also Alden 1979, Figure 53:1-10). Variations in body thickness within even small sherds indicate that these vessels were made by hand rather than thrown on a wheel. In size and shape these vessels look like cooking pots, and several sherds from the excavation even had a layer of soot on their exterior surface. It seems plausible, therefore, to suggest that the presence of this ware reflects domestic activities involving food preparation.

Ceramic Production Debris

A series of distinctive ceramic types associated with ceramic production (ring scrapers, Pierced Chaff-Tempered Bowls, and ceramic "spoons") and several sorts of pyrotechnic debris (ashy slag, fragments of some kind of installation, and ceramic wasters) were found on the surface and in the sounding at Tal-e Kureh. Examples of the objects and materials listed above were recovered from the surface of the entire site and from Lots 2 through 8 in the test excavation. No lower lot contained any material associated with ceramic production, tentatively indicating that ceramic production at the site only began in the middle stages of its occupation.

Three surface concentrations of ash, slag, and fragments from kilns or furnaces were found in the bulldozed area of the site; if such installations were scattered in similar density over the entire mound then there may be the remains of 15 to 20 kilns at Tal-e Kureh. In addition, three different potter's marks were identified in surface collections from the site (Alden 1979, Fig. 53). Taken as a whole, these data imply that during at least the middle phase of its occupation Tal-e Kureh was a location where grit tempered ceramics were being produced. More speculatively, the concentrations of specialized ceramic production tools and debris on the site seems to indicate that during the time it was being so used, ceramic production at Tal-e Kureh was being carried out by a group of artisans who were either full or part-time specialists.

Ceramic Slag

Ceramic slag is a greenish or bluish gray glassy material, typically full of bubbles and very porous. A common by-product of wood-fired pyrotechnic production processes, it is formed when ashes and clay in the combustion chamber of a kiln or furnace are fused and then harden into glassy masses. Examples of this material often have bits of kiln or furnace lining attached to one side, but even when such evidence is absent ceramic slag is readily distinguished from the denser and less porous slag produced by metallurgical activities. At Tal-e Kureh the fragments of ceramic slag recovered in surface collections were relatively large and dense, but the test excavation yielded smaller and more porous bits. This slag was presumably cleaned out of kilns or furnaces when they were being relined, then dumped outside the immediate area being used for craft production.

Ceramic Wasters

Many overfired or warped sherds were found in the surface collections from Tal-e Kureh and a few similarly defective sherds were recovered in the test excavation. All such sherds were of grit-tempered wares or pieces of Pierced Chaff-Tempered Bowls. The most common firing defect encountered at Tal-e Kureh was a blistered, melted, or cracked surface; warped sherds and sherds with bubbles or delaminations were less common. Some of these sherds may have been damaged after being incorporated into the lining or fuel of a kiln, but in such cases the broken edges of the sherd would also be melted. In order to minimize the potential for confusion created by such non-production processes, only sherds with firing defects and sharply broken edges are counted as wasters.

Kiln Debris

All fragments of chaff-tempered burned clay that could not be distinguished as pieces of vessels were classified as kiln debris. Most larger pieces of such material were identifiable as pieces of kiln floors or wall linings. These fragments were either flat or slightly curved, with a paste both more lumpy and containing less chaff than normal Banesh Trays, Goblets, and Beveled Rim Bowls and also lacking the distinctive surface textures of these vessel types. They were also more highly fired than any chaff-tempered vessels except the pierced bowls. The material classified as kiln debris might well include fragments of hearths or debris from burned structures. However, because the

stratigraphic distribution of these remains parallels the distribution of ceramic slag, errors of classification within this category of material are probably not significant.

Ceramic Ring Scrapers

Ceramic ring scrapers are a specialized tool used in the production of grit-tempered ceramics, a function inferred from the distribution of these objects and from the wear patterns observed on the working edges of fragments of these objects (Alden 1988). A subsequent study by Japanese scholar, who made a series of ceramic ring scrapers and examined the wear patterns produced by their use, confirmed those conclusions experimentally. Twelve fragments of ceramic ring scrapers were found on the surface of Tal-e Kureh and one fragment was recovered in the test excavation, from Lot 5 (Alden 1979:88 and Fig. 54; Alden 1988, Table 1 and Fig. 2). Four of these fragments, including one with a potter's mark, are illustrated here (Fig. D8:31-34).

Ceramic "Spoons"

Six of these curious objects (Alden 1979, Fig. 54, 25-30) were found in the surface collections from Tal-e Kureh. To my knowledge such objects have not previously been identified on any other site, although it should be noted that the profiles of these items are similar enough to the profiles of shallow dishes or plates that they might easily be missed or misidentified, especially in collections where the ceramics were badly broken up. It seems likely that these 'spoons' were used in connection with the manufacture of grit-tempered ceramics—they appear uniquely on a site where ceramic manufacturing was taking place, they are common enough to indicate they were being used at Tal-e Kureh with some frequency, and one of the 'spoons' is marked with the same potter's mark that appears on a ceramic ring scraper and several vessel fragments.

When unbroken, these objects would be perhaps 8 to 12 cm long, with a lenticular outline and a slightly concave surface. They appear to have been made by throwing a shallow dish or plate and then cutting a piece off of that vessel when it was leather-hard. The resulting object is roughly scoop-shaped; both ends are pointed with one edge more curved and the other straighter. The cut edge was smoothed and both ends rounded off while the clay was still soft and the resulting object was subsequently fired. No evidence of wear or work-related damage was visible on the examples I examined.

Although I have called these objects 'spoons,' it seems unlikely that they functioned as stirrers, servers, or scoops. There were no traces of handles or handle attachments on any of the six examples recovered at Tal-e Kureh, and they are not concave enough to have served as effective scoops or serving utensils. If they were tools used in ceramic manufacture, however, they might have been used as 'ribs' or 'pressers.' A rib is a tool, now usually made of hard rubber, that modern-day potters use to shape and smooth the surface of large vessels thrown on a wheel. 'pressers' (I don't know any technical term for such tools) are objects used to support the interior of a hand-built pot while coils or plates of clay are being pushed together by exterior finger pressure. Such 'pressers' can be made from almost anything (I saw a potter at Acoma pueblo using one such tool made of a well-worn piece of dried gourd, and she told me the same piece of gourd had been used by her mother), and although I know of no ethnographic instances where such tools are made of ceramic they certainly could be. While ceramic ribs would presumably show signs of erosive wear, ceramic pressers, because they are not rubbed back and forth, might very well not. For the time being, however, the function of these curious objects remains unknown. Two of these objects are illustrated here (Fig. D8:29, 30).

Pierced Chaff-tempered Bowls

In many ways Pierced Chaff-Tempered Bowls (Alden 1979, Fig. 34) look like thicker versions of the well-known Uruk Beveled Rim Bowls. In particular, the interior (carelessly smoothed) and exterior (rough and pebbly) surfaces of the two vessel types are identical. The wares of the two types, however, are distinctly different. Pierced Chaff-Tempered Bowls have heavier quantities of coarser chaff temper and a grayish color and brittle, friable texture indicating that they were fired at higher temperatures. The Pierced Chaff-Tempered Bowls are also about twice as thick as normal Beveled Rim Bowls, and their rim shapes range from rounded to beveled rather than displaying the consistently beveled lip of normal Beveled Rim Bowls. The most unusual feature of these vessels, however, is that most large fragments have one or more deep finger-made holes in their side or base. In some cases these holes pierce the vessel, but just as frequently they do not go entirely through the bowl's wall (Alden 1979, Table 27).

Pierced Chaff-Tempered Bowls are strongly associated with evidence of grit-tempered ceramic production during the Banesh period in the Kur River basin. They are found in significant numbers—from tens to hundreds of fragments—on four of the five Banesh sites where surface collections yielded ceramic slag or ceramic ring scrapers, while only one fragment of a Pierced Chaff-Tempered Bowl was found on any of the other Banesh period occupations in the region (Alden 1979:87). A contextual association does not demonstrate a functional one, and I have no idea how the pierced bowls might have been used in the process of making grit-tempered ceramics. Nevertheless, the association between these distinctive vessels and other indications of grit-tempered ceramic production is strong enough that it seems probable that they played some kind of a role in the ceramic manufacturing process. Four of these bowls are illustrated here (Fig. D8:4-7).

Stone, Bone, and Charcoal

Stone

The test excavation produced very little stone (Table D1). There were, however, two fragments of stone vessels: one of banded travertine and the other of fine-grained white limestone or plaster. Vessels made from both types of stone are very common at Tal-e Qarib (site 8G38), a site that appears to have served as a distribution center for pinched-rim bowls manufactured at Tal-e Kureh (Alden 1982a:97-98), and it is possible that stone vessels like the ones recovered here were distributed through the same local exchange system. The travertine fragment comes from Lot 4 (Stratum I) and the fine white limestone fragment from Lot 7 (Stratum III). Eight fragments of flint were also recovered from the test excavation; seven of these were chunks or flakes and one was a blade. These fragments reveal little except that there is no evidence for any activity taking place at Tal-e Kureh that required large quantities of stone or stone tools.

Animal Bone

The animal bone recovered from the excavation was badly broken up. In general, the low bone frequencies in the uppermost excavation units probably reflect the effects of weathering while the pattern of breakage implies that all of the excavated deposits represent or include midden debris. Because of the condition and limited quantity of bone little more than a list of species present will be available.

Charcoal

Three charcoal samples were submitted to the University of Pennsylvania laboratory for Carbon-14 dating (Chapter 3, Table 13). Stratum III is dated by the samples from Lots 8 and 9, while the date from Lot 10 dates Stratum V. All of the samples were too small to be cleaned for contamination by organic acids and all have large standard deviations because they had to be

Table D2
PROPOPTIONS OF LAPUI FINE WARE FROM THE EXCAVATION

Lots	11–13	10	9	8	7	6
% Lapui, weight	24.5	28.3	13.8	5.0	0.7	0.2
% Lapui, count	38.2	40.5	19.9	11.0	3.7	1.7

counted on a small sample counter.

The stratigraphically earlier charcoal sample from Lot 9 gives a later date than the sample taken from the overlying Lot 8. Given the large standard deviations of these dates, however, this reversal is not disturbing. Taken together, the three carbon dates indicate that the Banesh occupation in the region began somewhere around 3400 B.C., a figure that agrees well with the chronological connections indicated by ceramic parallels between early Banesh materials and ceramics from other regions of Iran.

Definition of Ceramic Phases

One of the primary goals of this test excavation was to recover data that would allow a stratigraphic definition of the later Lapui and earlier Banesh ceramic periods. In light of this goal, the excavation was successful. Stratigraphy, ware proportions, and the presence of ceramic production debris were used to define and distinguish Terminal Lapui, Initial Banesh, and Early Banesh phases. Since vessel shapes, rim forms, and decorative attributes are not used in defining these phases, ceramic phase markers can be isolated from the excavation data and used without circularity to define the phases during which other sites in the region were occupied. Phases and their derived ceramic markers are discussed below.

The stratigraphy of the test excavation (Fig. D2) suggests three breaks in the depositional sequence exposed at Tal-e Kureh. The earliest break is the evidence of burning implied by Stratum VI. The second break occurs at the prepared floor (Stratum IV) separating Stratum V deposits from those of Stratum III. The third break is defined by the ashy Stratum II. Proportions by count (Table D1) of the various ceramic wares, however, imply that only the break represented by the floor of Stratum IV (between Lots 10 and 9) is of major cultural significance. Table D2 shows that the percentage of Lapui wares above Stratum IV (Lots 6-9) is only half that of the layers below the Stratum IV break (Lots 10-13), and Lapui wares quickly decrease to

an insignificant part of the corpus above Lot 9. Therefore, Lot 10 will be defined as the last Lapui level and Lot 9 as the earliest Banesh unit. Strata V-VII are Lapui, Stratum IV is empty, and Strata III-I are Banesh.

The Early phase of the Banesh period is arbitrarily defined as the time when Tal-e Kureh was a production site for Banesh Grit-Tempered ceramics. Table D1 shows that ceramic manufacturing debris first appears in Lot 8 and only appears in quantity in Lot 7; an examination of the excavation sections shows that this pattern is explained if Stratum IIIa represents deposits from the beginning of the time of ceramic production at this site. The absence of wasters and decrease in the counts of other types of debris in Lot 2 hint that ceramic production may have ceased during the deposition of Stratum I, but extensive disturbance of the uppermost layers by plowing seems very probable and it is difficult to say when ceramic production ceased on the basis of the small sounding made. Tentatively, however, the Early phase of the Banesh will be identified with Strata Ib-IIIa. This automatically defines the Initial Banesh phase as Strata IIIb-IIIe (i.e. the strata between the last Lapui and first Early Banesh deposits) and the Middle Banesh phase as beginning with Stratum Ia (Fig. D3).

Phase Markers

At this point it is possible to examine the ceramics from the test excavation and identify phase markers—distinctive shapes or sorts of decoration that are found only in a single phase or in two phases but not in a third. Such phase markers can be used to specify periods during which other sites were occupied; the markers identified here were among those used to specify periods of occupation for Banesh sites surveyed in the author's dissertation research. The three Banesh and one Lapui phases defined above are discussed below.

Terminal Lapui Phase

No distinctive Lapui shapes or decorative motifs were recorded from the Tal-e Kureh test excavation.

The sherds were universally small and only rim shape and approximate orientation could be distinguished. Since this period was not of immediate interest no effort was made to devise a typology of Lapui rim shape, and at present it is not possible to gain access to the Tal-e Kureh collections. However, there was one sherd from Lot l0 (Fig. D4:5) with red painted designs on a ware with a fine buff paste—apparently Asupas ware (Sumner 1972:42). Several similar sherds were found in the surface collections from Tal-e Kureh and a series of Lapui Fine Ware sherds with distinctive rim forms and shapes were also collected.

The unusual characteristics of the Lapui sherds from surface collections can at least tentatively be used to define a Terminal phase of the Lapui Period. This step is justified by the observations that 1) the pre-Banesh occupation of Tal-e Kureh appears to be relatively short (only 0.8 meters of accumulation) and to directly precede the Banesh occupation, and 2) the assemblage of Lapui Fine Ware from the site is quite different from the broader Lapui assemblage illustrated by Sumner (1972:Pl. XII-XVI). Tentatively, phase markers for the Terminal Lapui are:

1. Asupas ware, sherds of a fine buff paste with designs in red, brown, or black paint on vessels with shapes similar to those of Lapui Fine Ware. Painting with both wide and fine line decoration is illustrated by Sumner (1972:Pl. XVII:A-F and O-R). Sherds of Asupas Ware from Tal-e Kureh are illustrated in Alden 1979, Fig. 52:32, 33 and here in Fig. D4:5.
2 Carinated Bowls of Lapui Fine Ware (Alden 1979, Fig. 52:13, 15, 16).
3 Collared Neck Jars of Lapui Fine Ware (Alden 1979, Fig. 52:18, 19).
4 Lapui Fine Ware Bowls with flattened everted rims (Alden 1979, Fig. 52:2, 13, 16).
Other possible Terminal Lapui phase markers include Lapui Fine Ware sherds with a) fugitive white painted bands (Alden 1979, Fig. 52:3), b) rolled or flattened lips (Alden 1979, Fig. 52:8-11, 14, 17, 20), c) pierced round lugs (Sumner 1972:Pl. XV:I; XVI:O,P), and d) spouts (Alden 1979, Fig. 52:9).

Initial Banesh Phase

Distinctive markers for the Initial Banesh phase (Tal-e Kureh strata IIIb-IIIe, Lots 8 and 9 unmixed and Lot 7, mixed) include:

1. Beveled Rim Trays, which are made of Chaff-Tempered Ware in a shape similar to Banesh Trays but with beveled rims and the appearance of being more carefully manufactured (Alden 1979, Fig. 35:1-9 and p.

220). They are easily distinguished from Beveled Rim Bowls because both the outside and inside are smoothed, but they must be distinguished from trough spouts with beveled lips (Alden 1979, Fig. 35:12), which have straight sides.

Ceramic types and features which are found in but are not limited to the Initial Banesh Phase include:

1. Beveled Rim Bowls without associated Banesh Trays occur in both the Terminal Lapui and Initial Banesh phases. This feature can only be used with confidence in dating excavated samples, but surface assemblages with more Beveled Rim Bowls than Banesh Trays probably have either Initial or Early Banesh components.
2. Painted Lapui fine ware, with red or gray slip and simple painted bands (Alden 1979, Fig. 52:27, 28) indicates either a Terminal Lapui or Initial Banesh occupation.
3. Rough Slipped Ware is found in the Terminal Lapui, Initial Banesh, and Early Banesh phases. Rough Slipped Ware is found in greatest frequency during the Initial Banesh, but because it can be difficult to distinguish from Lapui Common Ware, and on the other end of the continuum from Banesh Grit Tempered ware, it is less reliable as a phase indicator.
4. Horizontal white painted bands are also found from the Terminal Lapui through the Early Banesh phases, but like Rough Slipped Ware this characteristic is most frequent in the Initial Banesh phase. Fig. D4:17 illustrates an example on Rough Slipped Ware from Lot 9; counts are given in Table 52.

Certain forms of vessels in Rough Slipped Ware are undoubtedly good indicators of Initial Banesh occupations but the excavated sample is too small to allow any such types to be distinguished. Pedestal bases with horizontal painted bands may also be possible markers for the Initial Banesh.

Early Banesh Phase

The test excavation revealed several excellent Early Banesh ceramic markers, and several types found in Early Banesh contexts plus one additional phase. These markers are:

1. Red slip is found on over 5% of the body sherds in Lots 4-6, and it is less common in all other lots. Thus, the use of a red slip appears related, chronologically, to production of grit-tempered pottery at Tal-e Kureh. This measure is difficult to apply to surface collections, but it would seem a useful criterion in evaluating excavation samples.

2. Pinched Rim Bowls with streak burnished red slip are found in Lots 7-4, where they are rather common (14 of 17 Pinched Rim Bowl rims are streak burnished, and those 17 bowl rims constitute 13.6% of all rims classified). Three examples are found in Lots 10 and 12, but because these pieces are very small and because no red slip was found in the body sherds from those lots I believe those three examples represent either prehistoric mixing or mixing during excavation. The presence of this type of bowl is thus taken as a definite indication of an Early Banesh occupation.

Ceramic types and features which are found in but not limited to the Early Banesh Phase include:

1. Pinched Rim Bowls with any other sort of surface treatment are taken to indicate either Initial or Early phase occupation, because examples of this shape with different slips were found on an Initial phase ceramic production site, 8G42.

2. In Chaff Tempered Ware, Straight Sided Goblets (which are associated with round rim shapes) and Banesh Trays initially appear in the Early Banesh levels. Both types appear to continue through the entire Banesh sequence, but their absence from a site may indicate that it was an earlier occupation.

3. Folded and Collared Neck Jar rims on vessels of Banesh Grit Tempered Ware appear in Lot 7 and continue through the rest of the sequence at Tal-e Kureh. Folded rims (Figure D5:21; Figure D7:29) are relatively rare, but the collared type (Figure D5:12, 24, 27; Figure D6:24, 26, 35; Figure D7:8, 10, 17, 26) is common. Their terminal date, however, remains to be identified from other sites or through surface associations. Black horizontal bands painted over broad white bands show a parallel distribution and are common on the shoulders of medium and large-sized storage jars. Nose lugs (Figure D6:31), rare in the excavation, are also associated with this type of jar.

Early Middle Banesh Phase

Lot 2, the uppermost excavation unit in the test pit, belongs by definition to the Early Middle phase of the Banesh Period because it represents a time when grit-tempered ceramics are no longer being manufactured at this site. There is only a single decorative feature that seems to appear for the first time in this layer, mottled gray slip. However, surface associations at other sites indicate that this is a Late Middle or Late phase marker, and sherds with this slip were found in low proportions over most of the surface of Tal-e

Kureh. Therefore, I assume that the two sherds of this type that were found in Stratum I were incorporated into the soil by mixing from material that had originally been deposited in now-eroded layers of the site.

The Origins of Banesh Ceramics

One problem that this test excavation was aimed at clarifying was the origin of Banesh style ceramics. A 1 x 2 meter test excavation is clearly insufficient to support much in the way of a solution, but as there are no other data available from excavations that pertain to this problem, some speculation would seem justifiable

There are two general processes by which Banesh ceramics may have appeared in the Kur River Basin—local evolution or introduction from outside the region by either diffusion or immigration. Previous surface survey (Sumner 1972) indicated a sharp distinction between both the ceramic style and the settlement pattern of the earlier Lapui and later Banesh periods, at least implying an introduction of Banesh style ceramics from outside of the region. My own resurvey and the Tal-e Kureh test excavation both indicate that the situation is less straightforward. The following discussion is limited to the ceramic evidence from the test excavation described here, surface collections from the rest of the Kur Basin, and comparanda from Susa.

First, it has been observed (Sumner 1988b:28) that Lapui fine ware is strongly paralleled in Susa Acropole I:24-25 and in Acropole II:8. This observation, based on examination of the relevant materials from Susa in 1977, implies that there were rather close connections between the lowland Susiana and highland Kur Basin during Lapui times, i.e. during the first half of the fourth millennium B.C. Thus, the appearance of ceramic types from the lowlands during the final stage of the Lapui period would not be surprising. Such an occurrence is evidenced by the discovery of Beveled Rim Bowl rims in Lots 11 and 10 (Terminal Lapui) in the Tal-e Kureh excavation.

However, during neither the Lapui nor the Banesh periods are highland ceramics identical to ceramics of the Susiana, as might be expected in a replacement or large-scale movement of population. The highland and lowland ceramic corpuses seem to become most similar during the Late Middle phase of the Banesh (Alden 1979:60-61), when ties between the Kur Basin and Susa Acropole I:16-14B (Le Brun 1971; 1978a) in ceramics and features such as tablets and seal styles become quite close. But the lack of such strong parallels during the Initial and Early Middle phases of the Banesh should probably not be given too much importance, for Acropole I:23-19 (which produced almost no ceramics) and the gap between Acropole I:17 and I:16 take up much of the time when parallels should be found at Susa with these phases of the Banesh. There are numerous clear ties between Early Banesh ceramics and the material from Susa Acropole I:18-17 (Le Brun 1978b), and those levels at Susa also show much similarity to Uruk materials from Mesopotamia.

In summation, there are good parallels between Lapui materials from the Kur River Basin and excavated ceramics from Susa Acropole I:24-25. The Terminal Lapui and Initial Banesh are not readily paralleled at Susa, though this may only reflect the dearth of material from the relevant levels 23-19 of the Acropole I sounding. There are many parallels between Early Banesh ceramics and the materials from Susa I:18-17, a time during which the ceramics at Susa are essentially identical to the Mesopotamian Uruk assemblage. It is important to note, however, that several features commonly found in Uruk ceramics (both in Mesopotamia proper and at Susa), specifically cross-hatched incising and reserve slip decoration, are not found in the Early Banesh. The Early Middle Banesh is only poorly defined and there is a stratigraphic gap in the Susa Acropole I sounding between 17 and 16; hence little of significance can be said about that time period. There are, however, close parallels between the ceramics from Susa and the Kur River Basin during Late Middle Banesh/Susa I:16-14B times. Indeed, the similarities between these assemblages are almost as close as those between Susa and Mesopotamia during the Early Banesh. This is the pattern that must be interpreted in trying to understand the relationship between highland and lowland Iran during Banesh times.

Shared ceramic features during Lapui times suggest regular movement of individuals and ideas between the two regions, and a ready acceptance of both. This pattern of interaction changes in the Initial Banesh, when settlement patterns in the Kur River Basin seem to reflect the immigration of small groups into the region and the establishment of a complex of settlements in the western half of the valley (Alden 1979:155-162). It is extremely interesting, however, to see in the parallels between Early Banesh and Susa 18-17 a continuing acceptance of lowland ceramic features in the highlands during a time when Susa was apparently dominated by Mesopotamian influence. Of particular significance is the discovery that specific technological features of ceramic manufacture (i.e. the use of ring scrapers and the presence of Pierced Chaff-Tempered Bowls) are shared between the two regions. During the Late Middle Banesh, however, the situation seems to be different—Susa's ceramics share many characteristics with highland Banesh material, but these assemblages are quite distinct from the ceramics of Jemdet Nasr style found in southern Mesopotamia.

Perhaps the highland Kur River Basin can be seen as inhabited during the Lapui period by a society less politically complex than contemporaneous lowland societies. These highland residents readily accept ideas (and perhaps people) from the lowland societies, as indicated by the appearance during Terminal Lapui/Initial Banesh times of Beveled Rim Bowls, chaff-tempered ceramic ware, and vessel shapes with good Uruk parallels (although such features appear primarily in the westernmost portion of the Kur River Basin). When the Susiana falls under the dominance of the Uruk polities of Lower Mesopotamia during the Late Uruk (Susa Acropole 1:18-17), the settlements in the Kur River Basin adopt a number of lowland ceramic styles but by no means to the degree that Uruk ceramics appear in and actually displace indigenous ceramics in northern Mesopotamia (Algaze 1993:19-60). The time of conflict postulated by Johnson (1987:124-125) for Late Uruk Period Susiana, like the introduction of Uruk-like settlements in Syro-Mesopotamia described by Algaze, may represent the actual conquest of those regions by some Lower Mesopotamian polity, but the ceramic sequence no compelling evidence of such a conquest in the Kur River Basin.

The pattern of borrowing ceramic styles alters again in Late Middle Banesh/Susa 16-14B times, when highland styles reappear at Susa (Alden 1987, Fig. 42). The Jemdet Nasr period polities of Lower Mesopotamia seem to have lost control over the Susiana, and the ceramics of Susa are once again most closely related to those found in the Iranian highlands. This has been interpreted as a time when an independent Proto-Elamite political entity controlled much of southern and southwestern Iran, using their control over highland resources and trade routes as a basis for political power vis-a-vis the Jemdet Nasr/E. D. I polities of southern Mesopotamia (Alden 1982b). The cyclical pattern of highland-lowland interaction which was a long-standing feature of relations between Khuzistan and Fars during historic times (Amiet 1979a, 1979b) appears to have emerged as early as the 4th millennium B.C.

Appendix E

Inventory of Banesh Sites

The Banesh period was first defined (Sumner 1972) on the basis of ceramics that did not belong to any of the Marv Dasht ceramic cultures defined by Vanden Berghe (1952, 1954). This new ceramic assemblage was found in surface collections from 25 sites. Alden's survey added another 14 sites with Banesh components and additional surveys around Malyan added several sites to the inventory. A comparison of Alden's survey data with large scale maps (1:5,000) and aerial photographs not available to Alden in the field resulted in some changes in the area measurements, changes in some grid numbers, and the identification of some of Alden's sites with previously recorded sites. The current inventory of Banesh sites includes 42 sites with Banesh components and 18 with doubtful Banesh components. Sites are classified as having doubtful components if there are unclassified ceramics in the surface assemblage that have some Banesh attributes, but cannot be classified as Banesh with assurance. These sites are not counted in the following analysis. There are also 2 sites that produced very small numbers of Banesh and Kaftari sherds representing final non-habitation special function components. These sites are omitted from the analysis.

Inventory of Sites

The inventory of sites, presented in Table E2, uses the following conventions and abbreviations, listed here for each column.

Grid Number

The first two digits define the south boundary of the grid square in which the site is located; the second 2 digits define the west boundary of the grid square (Fig. 2). The third and fourth digits define the distance of the site from the south boundary and the west boundary respectively. For example, the first site in the inventory is in the grid square north of 60N and east of 85E; the site is 1.9 km north of 60N and 4.9 km east of 85E.

Field Number

The first field number column lists the field numbers assigned to sites in my initial survey (Sumner 1972, Appendix A, Part I, Column B). The prefixes identify sites first surveyed by Vanden Berghe (V) (1952, 1954), Sumner (S), including resurvey of Vanden Berghe's sites (VS), and sites surveyed by Andrew Williamson (W). This number identifies sherd bags and sherds from the survey in the collection of the University of Pennsylvania Museum of Archaeology and Anthropology, the Oriental Institute, and Iran Bastan in Tehran. The second field number column lists field numbers assigned during subsequent survey by Alden (1979) (prefix A), Jacobs (1980) (Prefix J) and Joseph Kole (personal communication) (prefix K). In some cases I have modified the correlation between sites originally recorded during my survey and sites later surveyed by Alden (1979, Table 19) and Jacobs (1980, Table 11). The group of sites in grid square 6284 with a Q suffix are the sites collectively designated Tal-e Qarib.

Type of Site (Type)

The morphological classification of sites as shown in the Type column uses the following codes; combinations indicate several morphological types are present:

C—complex site composed of numerous small mounds

F—fort or citadel, on mountain ridge or spur

G—*ghare*, cave or shelter site

H—horizontal, unmounded site

K—*kharabi*, recently abandoned village; wall stubs still standing

Q—*qale*, hollow mounded site, often the next stage after *kharabi*

S—stone foundations or tent stands

T—*tepe*, *tal*, mounded site

Hectares (Ha.)

The measured or estimated total area of each site is indicated in hectares.

Height (Ht.)

The measured or estimated height of each site above local plain level is indicated in meters.

Lapui (Lap.)

The Lapui (Lap.) column lists the area in hectares assigned to Lapui component of sites which produced Lapui sherds in the surface assemblage. The following column, labeled X, indicates sites with special non-habitation Lapui components (S), or doubtful Lapui components (D).

Banesh (Ban.)

The Banesh (Ban.) column lists the area in hectares assigned to the Banesh component of sites which produced Banesh sherds in the surface assemblage. The following column, labeled Y, indicates sites with special non-habitation Banesh components (S), or doubtful Banesh components (D).

Early, Middle, and Late Banesh

The Early (EBN), Middle (MBN) and Late (LBN) Banesh columns list the area assigned to each Banesh sub-phase.

Kaftari (Kaf.)

The Kaftari (Kaf.) column indicates the presence of a Kaftari habitation component (P) or doubtful component (D).

Notes

The following abbreviations are used in the Notes column:

ASP—an Asupas component; for Asupas see Sumner 1972

BRB—bevel rim bowl

ED—Early Dynastic

GTP—grit tempered ceramic production site

STP—straw tempered ceramic production site

Settlement Patterns

Rural Settlements

On the basis of excavations at Malyan, his sounding at Tal-e Kureh (Appendix D), and his survey of Banesh sites, Alden (1979) divided the Banesh sequence into 5 sub-phases: Initial, Early, Early Middle, Late Middle, and Late Banesh. Using a set of 29 ceramic criteria he (1979, Appendix E, Table 48) was able to assign 20 sites to one or more of his Banesh chronological sub-phases. In the present analysis Alden's Initial Phase is included in the Early Banesh Phase and his Early Middle and Late Middle Phases are combined to form a Middle Banesh Phase. The result of combining these sub phases, using some of Alden's doubtful assignments (indicated by a ? in his Figure 48), and using a slightly broader set of chronological criteria, is to increase the number of sites that can be assigned to sub-phases to 33. The results of different assignments to chronological sub-phases are compared in Table E1. Malyan is counted as a small village (estimated area 1.2 ha) in the early Banesh Phase and is omitted from Table E1 in the Middle and Late Phases. The site area figures listed in the table are based on the revised site inventory (Table E2) and differ in some cases from the areas assigned by Alden (1979, Appendix E).

The general trend, a decrease in rural sedentary population, is similar in the sub-phase assignments shown in columns A and B, but is exaggerated in column B where there are proportionally more Early Banesh

Table E1
BANESH SUB-PHASE ASSIGNMENTS:
TOWN (QARIB) AND VILLAGE SITES ONLY

	A		B		Unassigned		Sum	
	N	HA	N	HA	N	HA	N	HA
Early Banesh								
Qarib			6	6.8	–	–	6	6.8
Villages			22	37.0	8	8.8	30	45.8
Sub-total	14	18.9	28	43.8	8	8.8	36	52.6
Proportion %			39	42				
Middle Banesh								
Qarib			6	6.8	–	–	6	6.8
Villages			19	27.0	7	6.7	26	33.7
Sub-total	14	17.3	25	33.8	7	6.7	32	40.5
Proportion %			35	32				
Late Banesh:								
Qarib			3	4.5			3	4.5
Villages			16	22.1	5	5.5	21	27.6
Sub-total	12	15.4	19	26.6	5	5.5	24	32.1
Proportion %			26	26				
Summation								
Sites	20	23.1	32	38.7	9	7.8	40	46.4
Aggregation, Components			72	104.2	20	21.0	92	125.2

NOTE: Column A is based on Alden 1979, Table 48. Column B is based on my reanalysis of Alden's data and my own data. Sites in the "unassigned" column were not counted in earlier presentations of this data (Sumner 1986, 1990b).

components and fewer Late Banesh components. The proportions in column B are used to assign the sites in the unassigned column, which did not produce enough sherds for assignment by either Alden's or Sumner's criteria. This process is accomplished in two steps: 1) the 72 components with 104.2 ha classified in column B came from 32 sites with 38.7 ha, which implies that the 9 unassigned sites with 7.8 ha should produce 20 components with 21 ha; 2) these 20 components and 21 ha are assigned to Early, Middle, and Late Banesh in the proportions (%) shown in the proportions row of column B. The result of this exercise is that all 40 Banesh sites appear in the Sum column of Table E1. It is assumed that the Sum column represents a reasonable minimum estimate of the number and aggregate area of settlements and a fair estimate of population trends, but not absolute population, during the Banesh Period.

It is clear that Table E1 represents an underestimate of Banesh settlements because some of the doubtful sites are probably Banesh and because there are no doubt undiscovered Banesh sites in the valley. Analysis of large scale maps and aerial photographs suggests that approximately than 70% of the mounded sites in the central region of the valley (North 61-64; East 83-89), where Banesh sites are concentrated, were recorded. From this figure we can estimate that some 12 Banesh mounded sites and an indeterminate number of surface camp sites remain unrecorded within these central grid squares, in addition to unrecorded sites outside the central region.

Even without applying similar hypothetical additions to the Shamsabad, Bakun, and Lapui, site inventories, it is evident that the Early Banesh sedentary rural population was at the lowest ebb it had been since the Shamsabad Phase two millennia earlier (Sumner 1986, 1988b, 1990a, 1990b). Similarly, the Kaftari rural sedentary population only 6 centuries later was more than 4 times the Late Banesh rural sedentary population (Sumner 1989a). Some implications of these demographic patterns are discussed above in Chapter V.

Table E2
INVENTORY OF SITES

Grid No.	Field #	Field #	Type	Ha	Ht	Lap	X	Ban	Y	EBN	MBN	LBN	Kaf	Notes
60851949	S-564C	A-10G14	T	1.1	3	1.1	•	•	D	•	•	•		
60852211		A-10G16	H	0.1		•	•	•	D	•	•	•		
60852752	S-5V9	A-10H7	T	1	1.5	1	•	0.8	•	0.8	0.8	0.8		stone bowl
60861280	S-5P6	A-10I3	T	1.2	1	1.2	•	1.2	•	1.2	1.2	1.2		ASP; ED II/III seal; stone bowl
60895308	S-		SGG	•		•	S	•	D	•	•	•		
61840181	S-5W4	A-9G14	T	0.4	1	0.4	•	•	D	•	•	•		
61855427	S-5G5		TT	0.3	1	•	•	0.3	•	•	•	0.3		burials
61859732	S-5H8		T	0.3		•	•	•	D	•	•	•	D	
61867101	S-5E5		T	0.2	1	0.2	•	•	S	•	•	•		BRB
61868707	VS-502		TL	8		0.8	•	0.8	•	0.8	0.8	•	P	
61869005	S-502A	A-9H5	T	1.4	2.5	•	•	•	S	•	•	•	P	stone bowl
61872078	VS-603	J-9J10?	T	2.2	3	•	•	0.8	•	•	•	•	P	BRB
61887295	VS-629	J-9K1	T	15		1.2	•	1.2	•	•	•	1.2	P	STP
62830650	S-BA11		TH	0.5		•	D	0.5	•	•	•	•	P	
62831259	S-5R8	A-8F8	T	130		1.2	•	40	•	1.2	40	40	P	Tal-e Malyan; wall cone
62831333	S-BZA		T	0.2		•	•	•	D	•	•	•	P	
62840656	S-5M3	A-8G24	T	1.5	2	•	•	•	D	•	•	•	P	Bakun ceramic production
62842165	S-5L9	A-8G21	T	0.7		•	D	•	D	•	•	•		wall cone
62842172	S-5L6	A-8G36Q	T	1.2	2	•	•	0.8	•	0.8	0.8	0.8		
62842556	S-5M1	A-8G23	T	1.2	2	•	•	1.2	•	1.2	1.2	1.2		wall cone
62842572	S-5M0	A-8G38Q	T	3		•	•	3	•	3	3	3	D	A-8G35; STP; cone; stone bowl
62842768		A-8G40Q	T	2	1	•	•	2	•	2	2	•		
62842778	S-5L4	A-8G34Q	T	0.7	1	•	•	0.7	•	0.7	0.7	0.7		A-8G39
62842973		A-8G19Q	T	0.2	2	•	•	0.2	•	0.2	0.2	•		storage jars
62843174		A-8G37Q	T	0.1	0.3	•	•	0.1	•	0.1	0.1	•		STP goblet; wall cone
62847926	S-5T9		F	10		•	D	•	D	•	•	•	D	
62848687	S-552	A-8G5	QT	1.2	1	•	•	1.2	•	1.2	1.2	•	P	
62849090	S-551	A-8G2	KH	1		0.8	•	1	•	1	1	1		
62849365	S-556	A-8G1	SH	1		0.8	•	1	•	1	1	1		ASP
62849865		A-8G42	TT	0.8	1.5	0.8	•	0.8	•	0.8	0.8	•		GTP
62850463	S-5F5	A-9H1	T	0.4	0.3	•	•	0.4	•	0.4	•	•		grinding stones
62850832	S-5I0	A-8G33	T	1.9	4	1.2	•	1.9	•	1.9	•	•		BRB
62851729	VS-5C6		C	4.7	1	•	•	0.8	•	•	•	•	P	
62853116	S-5K3		T	0.8	3	•	•	•	D	•	•	•	D	
62853764	S-523	A-8H11	KT	2.8	2	0.8	•	1.2	•	1.2	1.2	•		stone bowl
62855116	S-5I8	A-8G12	T	1.4	2	•	•	0.8	•	0.8	0.8	0.8		
62856155		A-8H21	SH	0.8		•	•	•	D	•	•	•		
62857071	S-541		H	0.8		0.8	•	•	D	•	•	•		
62872351	VS-628	J-8J4	T	9.6	7	1.2	•	1.2	•	1.2	•	•	P	
62875861	S-686	A-8J2	H	1.2		1.2	•	1.2	•	1.2	1.2	1.2		GTP; wall cone
63830703	S-5U5	K-	T	2.3	6	•	•	•	D	•	•	•		
63832896		A-7F9	SH	1		•	D	•	D	•	•	•		
63833489		A-7F8	SH	1		•	•	1	•	1	1	1		GTP; wall cone; stone bowl
63833586	S-5R4	A-7F1	T	2.8	1.5	1.2	•	2.8	•	2.8	2.8	2.8		ASP; GTP; wall cone; stone bowl
63840166		A-7G15	T	0.4	0.3	•	•	0.4	•	0.4	0.4	0.4		GTP; wall cone
63840369	S-5R5	A-7G7	SH	2.9		•	•	2.9	•	2.9	2.9	2.9		GTP; wall cone; stone bowl
63841049		A-7G12	SH	0.6		•	•	0.6	•	•	0.6	0.6		
63841263		A-7G14	SH	1.2		•	•	0.8	•	•	•	•		
63841454		A-7G13	SH	1		0.8	•	0.8	•	•	•	•		
63841633		A-7G9	H	0.1		0.1	•	•	D	•	•	•		
63841638		A-7G8	SH	0.1		•	•	•	D	•	•	•		
63842207		A-7G16	T	0.4		•	•	0.4	•	•	0.4	0.4		ST tray production
63842403	S-5R2	A-7F2	SH	4.5		1.2	•	1.2	•	•	•	•	P	
63843986	S-597	A-7G4	TH	1.2	2	•	•	•	D	•	•	•		
63852917	S-592	A-7G6	C	1.9	1.5	•	•	0.8	•	•	0.8	0.8	P	
64824794	W-7M1		TT	1.1	3	1.1	•	1.1	•	•	•	•		
64833225	W-7M7		T	2	3	•	•	2	•	2	•	•		stone bowl
64833723	W-7M6		T	1	3	•	•	1	•	•	•	•		
64833728	S-704		C	3.6	6	•	•	3.6	•	3.6	•	•		
64833822	W-7M5		T	0.8	2	•	•	0.8	•	•	•	•		
64835735	S-737		G	•		•	•	•	D	•	•	•		
64851881	S-733	A-6H1	TH	1.4	6	1.4	•	1.2	•	1.2	1.2	•		ASP; stone bowl
	Actual Count							10.5		36.6	68.1	62		
	Assigned									7.2	5.7	4.5		
	Sum									43.8	73.8	67		

Town and City

Qarib

There is a cluster of Banesh sites in grid square 62N84E, named Qarib after the largest site in the cluster. Depending on how sites are defined there are 6 to 8 sites in this cluster, all within a square area slightly less than 1 km on a side. Qarib has been interpreted as a market town engaged in the distribution of ceramics and stone or plaster vessels and perhaps other products or commodities (Alden 1979, 1982a; Sumner 1986). The following description of the Qarib cluster is based on Alden's dissertation (1979), his unpublished field notes, my own field notes, and the Dorudzan Irrigation Project Map (1:5,000).

The Qarib cluster takes its name from Tal-e Qarib (S-5M0; A-8G38), which is a low habitation mound composed of a relatively dispersed pattern of sherd clusters suggesting a low density occupation (Alden 1979, Fig. 27). Other sites in the Qarib cluster also appear to be unmounded or low (ca. 1 m) sites composed of dispersed sherd scatters representing low density occupations.

Evidence for production of straw tempered wares is found at a triangular mound (A-8G35) located 200 m to the SSW of Qarib (S-5M0). This site is a straw tempered pottery dump filled solid with broken goblets and trays in an area of over 0.5 ha to an estimated depth of 0.6 m. Just to the west of the pottery dump is a half hectare shallow hollow that may have been the source of clay to produce the goblets. A second, smaller (0.1 ha), straw tempered pottery production dump (A-8G37) containing mostly goblets, but also some trays, is located some 500 m north of Qarib.

In addition to the evidence for straw tempered pottery production there is evidence for distribution of plaster and stone vessels in the form of a dense concentration of fragments along the eastern edge of Qarib (S-5M0). The presence of tool marks suggests the white plaster vessels with elaborate inlay (Alden 1979, Fig. 55) were made at Qarib. Although there is no evidence that the limestone and travertine vessels (Alden 1979, Figs. 56-58) were made at the site, the large number and concentration of these finds implies that they were distributed from Qarib. Other finds at Qarib include a biconical spindle whorl, a facetted rubbing stone, and a grooved hammer stone or mace (Alden 1979, Fig. 57). No other unusual finds are recorded for the Qarib cluster except for a cluster of large storage vessel rims and a concentration of grinding stones from a small habitation site (A-8G19) located about 300 m north of Qarib (S-5M0). Alden suggests that this site may be the habitation site for the potters who produced the A-8G37 pottery dump, located just 200 m to the NNE. The presence of the grinding stones and storage jars might also indicate something more than processing grain for local consumption.

Malyan

Although there is no direct evidence for an Early Banesh component at Malyan it is assumed that at least one of the Middle Banesh mounds buried below later Kaftari deposits had an Early Banesh component.

Alden (1979:195; Fig. 26) first suggested that Middle Banesh Malyan was a cluster of 4 or 5 settlements, very much like Qarib. He estimated the minimum aggregate area of these settlements at ca. 27 ha and the maximum area at ca. 73 ha based on archaeological excavations, observation of Banesh deposits in qanats and canals, and surface collections. Additional observations in qanats, made after Alden's study, suggest that the estimate of minimum area should be increased to ca. 40 ha and the maximum to ca. 80 ha.

The double wall along the western slope of ABC BL 4, large foundation stones observed in a collapsed qanat north of Operation Z46, and the stone foundations observed by Alden along the north slope of the TUV mound all suggest the possibility that individual settlements in the Middle Banesh cluster were fortified (Fig. 4).

Average settlement population densities (people per ha) can be used with some confidence to estimate regional population from aggregate site area, with the understanding that variation in population density among settlements is accounted for by the averaging process (Kramer 1982; Sumner 1979, 1989b). However, population estimates for individual settlements are far more problematic, especially urban places, and are best expressed by a range of values. For Middle Banesh Malyan the minimum acceptable estimate (low area estimate of 40 ha multiplied by a low conversion factor of 100 people/ha) is 4,000 and the maximum acceptable estimate (high area estimate 80 ha x high conversion factor 200 people/ha) is 16,000.

The extent of occupation at Late Banesh Malyan is more difficult to estimate. Excavated Late Banesh levels are known only at TUV, BL 1; the upper Banesh strata in the deep sounding at Operation H5 (Fig. 4, NE corner of Operation GHI); and the lower strata in the trench across the city wall at Operation BY8. Other evidence of the presence of Late Banesh levels is rare. Late Banesh painted grit tempered ceramics, which are quite distinctive, are well known from Operation BY8 (Sumner 1985), but were rarely found in surface collections except along the north stretch of the city wall, where late Banesh painted sherds are common. Although Banesh coarse straw tempered sherds are common in qanat backdirt piles and in deposits observed in collapsed qanats and canals crossing the site (Fig. 4, symbol ⊗), Late Banesh painted sherds are rare in these contexts.

We are left with the extent of the Banesh city wall as the only basis for estimating the area of Late Banesh Malyan. The city wall is well defined topographically along the northern edge of the unoccupied open space west of Operation TUV. From the NE corner the wall can be traced south, through the modern village, then curving to the west and ending at Operation BY8. Intermittent traces of the wall are also visible west and north of Operation EDD. It is assumed that the wall around the southwest quarter of the site, where it cannot be traced, was either destroyed in antiquity or by more recent agricultural activity.

More than three dozen large foundation stones have been recorded in association with the city wall. These stones appear in 2 parallel rows at an elevation 1 or 2 m above the modern plain level in the low saddles between segments of the north wall mound. Foundation stones are also present at this elevation in a cut made by villagers in the city wall mound just north of the modern village.[*] Likewise a foundation

---

[*]The term "modern village" designates the walled village located on the mound beside a walled garden where the landlords house is located (Fig. 4). Visitors to the site in 1999 inform me this village has been abandoned and the inhabitants have built new houses to the west (Kamyar Abdi, p.c.)

stone feature, probably a gate, just above modern plain level is located in a gap in the city wall mound 450 m south of the south wall of the modern village. A second group of stones is found at a higher level embedded in the surface of the wall mound just south of the modern village and in the Kaftari levels excavated at Operation BY8 (Sumner 1985). These stones are roughly finished and generally measure about 1 x 0.5 x 0.5 m.

The clear evidence of a Late Banesh city wall found at BY8, together with the predominance of Late Banesh sherds in surface collections along the north segments of the wall mound suggest that the wall surrounding the site, which encloses some 200 ha, was first built in Late Banesh times; it was later rebuilt in the Kaftari Period (Sumner 1985). It is possible that the Late Banesh city wall enclosed a smaller area, perhaps following the 18 or 19 m contour line around the main mound between ABC and Z46. However, this would leave the wall at BY8 disconnected and out of alignment and there is no topographic indication of such a wall.

A number of large stones similar to the foundation stones observed in the north wall are visible on the surface around Operation Z46 and in undisturbed Middle Banesh—but not Late Banesh—deposits revealed in a collapsed qanat about 150 m north of Z46. The Late Banesh surface assemblage on the north wall is difficult to explain if the wall was built in Kaftari times because the adjacent flat area produced no evidence of a Banesh deposit that could have been excavated to make bricks for the wall.

Although the evidence is not conclusive, it is likely that the late Banesh city wall enclosed some 200 ha. Within this circumvallation the built-up area of the city may have been as large as 40 ha, but was probably much smaller in view of the rarity of late Banesh sherds in the Malyan assemblage from all contexts.

References

Abdi, Kamyar
2003   From Ériture to Civilization: Changing Paradigms on Proto-Elamite Archaeology. In *Yeki bud, yeki nabud, Essays on the Archaeology of Iran in Honor of William M. Sumner*. Naomi F. Miller and Kamyar Abdi, eds. Los Angeles: Cotsen Institute of Archaeology, University of California.

Alden, John R.
1979   Regional Economic Organization in Banesh Period Iran. Ph.D. dissertation, Department of Anthropology, University of Michigan. Ann Arbor: University Microfilms.
1982a   Marketplace Exchange as Indirect Distribution: An Iranian Example. In *Contexts for Prehistoric Exchange*. Jonathon E. Ericson and Timothy K. Earle, eds. Pp. 83–101. New York: Academic Press.
1982b   Trade and Politics in Proto-Elamite Iran. *Current Anthropology* 23(6):613–40.
1987   The Susa III Period. In *The Archaeology of Western Iran*. Frank Hole, ed. Pp. 157–70. Washington: Smithsonian Institution Press.
1988   Ceramic Ring Scrapers: An Uruk Period Pottery Production Tool. *Paléorient* 14(1):143–50.
2003   Sherd Size and the Banesh occupation in the ABC Operation at Malyan, Iran. In *Yeki bud, yeki nabud, Essays on the Archaeology of Iran in Honor of William M. Sumner.* Miller, Naomi F. and Kamyar Abdi, eds. Los Angeles: Cotsen Institute of Archaeology, University of California.

Algaze, Guillermo
1993   *The Uruk World System: The Dynamics of Expansion of Early Mesopotamian Civilization*. Chicago and London: University of Chicago Press.

Alizadeh, Abbas
1988a   Mobile Pastoralism and the Development of Complex Societies in Highlands of Iran: The Evidence from Tall-i Bakun A. Ph.D. dissertation, Department of Near Eastern Languages and Civilizations, University of Chicago.
1988b   Socio-Economic Complexity in Southwestern Iran during the Fifth and Fourth Millennia B.C.: The Evidence from Tall-I-Bakun A. *Iran* 26:17–34.
1994   Social and Economic Complexity and Administrative Technology in a Late Prehistoric Context. In *Archives before Writing: Proceedings of the International Colloquium Oriola Romano, October 23–25, 1991*. Piera Ferioli, Enrica Fiandra, Gian Giacomo Fissore, and Marcella Frangipane, eds. Pp. 35–54. (with Response by Pierre Amiet. Pp. 55–57).
n.d.   *The Origins of State Organizations in Prehistoric Highland Fars, Southern Iran*. Chicago: Oriental Institute, University of Chicago.

Amiet, Pierre
1966   *Elam*. Auvers-sur-Oise: Archée Editeur.
1972   *Glyptique susienne des origines à l'époque des perses achéménides*. MDP 43, 2 vols. Paris: Geuthner.

1979a   Archaeological Discontinuity and Ethnic
         Duality in Elam. *Antiquity* 53(209):195-204.
1979b   Alternance et dualité. Essai d'Interprétation
         de l'Histoire Élamite. *Akkadica* 15:2-24.
1986   *L'âge des échanges inter-iraniens 3500-1700
         avant J.-C.* Notes et documents des musées de
         France 11. Paris: Éditions de la Réunion des
         Musées Nationaux.
1993   The Period of Irano-Mesopotamian Contacts
         3500-1600 BC. In *Early Mesopotamia and
         Iran: Contact and Conflict 3500-1600 BC.*
         John E. Curtis, ed. Pp. 23-30. London: British
         Museum Press.

Amiet, Pierre and Maurizio Tosi
1978   Phase 10 at Shahr-i Sokhta: Excavations in
         Square XDV and the Late 4th Millennium B.C.
         Assemblage of Sistan. *East and West* 28:9-31.

Bamforth, Douglas B., George Burns, and Craig
         Woodman
1990   Ambiguous Use Traces and Blind Test Results:
         New Data. *Journal of Archaeological Science*
         17(4):413-430.

Baqir, Taha
1945   Iraq Government Excavations at 'Aqar Quf.
         Second Preliminary Report, 1943-44. *Iraq
         Supplement*.

Barth, Fredrik
1961   *Nomads of South Persia: The Basseri Tribe of
         the Khamseh Confederacy*. London: George
         Allen and Unwin.

Bazin, D., and H. Hübner
1969   *Copper Deposits in Iran. Geological Survey
         of Iran.* Report 13, Tehran.

Beale, Thomas W.
1973   Early Trade in Highland Iran: A View from a
         Source Area. *World Archaeology* 5(2):133-48.
1978   Bevel Rim Bowls and their implications for
         change and economic organization in the
         later Fourth Millennium B.C. *JNES*
         37(4):289-313.
1986a   The Ceramics. In *Excavations at Tepe Yahya,
         Iran 1967-1975: The Early Periods*. Thomas
         W. Beale, ed. Pp. 39-89. American Schools of
         Prehistoric Research, Bulletin 38. Cambridge,
         MA: Harvard University Press.

1986b   The Small Finds. In *Excavations at Tepe
         Yahya, Iran 1967-1975: The Early Periods*.
         Thomas W. Beale, ed. Pp. 168-206. American
         Schools of Prehistoric Research, Bulletin 38.
         Cambridge, MA: Harvard University Press.

Beale, Thomas W. (ed.)
1986   *Excavations at Tepe Yahya, Iran 1967-1975:
         The Early Periods*. American Schools of
         Prehistoric Research, Bulletin 38. Cambridge,
         MA: Harvard University Press.

Beale, Thomas W. and C. C. Lamberg-Karlovsky
1986   Summary of Change and Development in the
         Early Periods at Tepe Yahya, 4900-3300 B.C. In
         *Excavations at Tepe Yahya, Iran 1967-1975:
         The Early Periods*. Thomas W. Beale, ed.
         American Schools of Prehistoric Research,
         Bulletin 38. Cambridge, MA: Harvard
         University Press.

Beale, Thomas W., and S. M. Carter
1983   On the Track of the Yahya Large Kuš :
         Evidence for Architectural Planning in the
         Period IVC Complex at Tepe Yahya.
         Paléorient 9(1):81-88.

Beck, Horace C.
1931   Beads from Nineveh. *Antiquity* 5:427-37.

Berthoud, T.
1979   Étude par l'analyse de traces et la modélisa-
         tion de la filiation entre minérai de cuivre et
         objets archéologiques du Moyen-Orient
         (IVème et IIIème millénaires avant notre ère),
         Doctoral Thesis, Paris: Université Pierre et
         Marie Curie.

Berthoud, T., and S. Cleuziou
1983   Farming Communities of the Oman Peninsula
         and the Copper of Makkan. *Journal of Oman
         Studies* 6:239-46.

Berthoud, T. and J. Françaix
1980   *Contribution à l'étude de la métallurgie de
         Suse aux IVe et IIIe millénaires. Analyse des
         éléments-traces par spectrométrie d'émission
         dans l'ultra-violet et spectrométrie de masse
         à étincelles*, Rappaort CEA-4-5033. Gif-sur-
         Yvette.

Blackman, M. James

1981 The Mineralogical and Chemical Analysis of Banesh Period Ceramics from Tal-e Malyan, Iran. In *Scientific Studies in Ancient Ceramics*. M. J. Hughes, ed. Pp. 7–20. British Museum Occasional Studies 19.

1982 The Manufacture and Use of Burned Lime Plaster at Proto-Elamite Anshan (Iran). In *Early Pyrotechnology: The Evolution of the First Fire-Using Industries*. Theodore Wertime and Steven Wertime, eds. Pp. 107–115. Washington: Smithsonian Institution Press.

1984 Provenance Studies of Middle Eastern Obsidian from Sites in Highland Iran. In *American Chemical Society Advances in Chemistry Series*, No. 205.. Joseph B. Lambert, ed. Pp. 19–50. Archaeological Chemistry III.

Blackman, M. James and Massimo Vidale

n.d. *Cinoptilolite Bead-making in Banesh Malyan*. Malyan Archive.

Bordaz, Jacques

1969 Flint Flaking in Turkey. *Natural History* 78:73–7.

1970 *Tools of the Old and New Stone Age*. Garden City, New York: Natural History Press.

Bovington, Charles, Azizeh Mahdavi, and Roghiyeh Masoumi

1973 Tehran University Nuclear Centre Radiocarbon Date List II. *Radiocarbon* 15(3):595–98.

Braidwood, Robert J. and Bruce Howe

1962 Southwestern Asia Beyond the Lands of the Mediterranean Littoral. In *Courses Toward Urban Life*. Robert J. Braidwood and Gordon R. Willey, eds. Pp.132–146. Chicago: Aldine.

Brézillon, Michel N.

1968 La Dénomination des objectes de pierre taillée: matériaux pour un vocabulaire des préhistoriens de langue française. *Gallia Préhistorique*. Supplément 4. Paris: CNRS.

Brice, William C.

1962-3 The Writing System of the Proto-Elamite Account Tablets of Susa. *Bulletin of the John Rylands Library* 45:15–39.

Bronk Ramsey, C.

1995 Radiocarbon Calibration and the Analysis of Stratigraphy: The OxCal Program. *Radiocarbon* 32(2) 425–430.

Budd, Paul

1993 Recasting the Bronze Age. *New Scientist Oct.* 23:33–37.

Budd, Paul, D. Gale, A. M. Pollard, R. G. Thomas, and P. A. Williams

1992 The Early Development of Metallurgy in the British Isles. *Antiquity* 66(252):677–86.

Bulgarelli, Grazia Maria

1977 Stone-working Techniques and Bone Industry. In *La Citta' Bruciata del Deserto Salato*. Pp. 263–76. Venice: Erizzo.

1979 The Lithic Industry of Tepe Hissar at the Light of Recent Excavation. In *South Asian Archaeology 1977*. M. Taddei, ed. Pp. 39–54. Istituto Universitario Orientale, Series Minor VI.

Busse, Heribert

1972 *History of Persia Under Qājār Rule*. Translated from the Persian of Hasan-e Fasā'i's Fārsnāma-ye Nāṣeri. New York: Columbia University Press.

Caldwell, Joseph R., ed.

1967 *Investigations at Tal-i-Iblis*. Illinois State Museum Preliminary Reports No. 9. Springfield: Illinois State Museum.

Caldwell, Joseph R.

1968 Pottery and Cultural History on the Iranian Plateau. *JNES* 28:178–83.

Carneiro, Robert L. and Daisy H. Hilse

1966 On Determining the Probable Rate of Population Growth During the Neolithic. *American Anthropologist* 68:177–81.

Carriveau, Gary W.

1978 Application of Thermoluminescence Dating Techniques to Prehistoric Metallurgy. In *Application of Science to the Dating of Works of Art*. William J. Young, ed. Pp. 59–67. Boston: Museum of Fine Arts.

Carter, Elizabeth

1980 Excavations in Ville Royale I at Susa: The Third Millennium B.C. Occupation. *Cahiers de la D.A.F.I.* 11:11-134.

1984 Archaeology. In *Elam: Surveys of Political History and Archaeology*. Berkeley: University of California Press. Pp. 103-313.

1996 *Malyan Excavation Reports*, Vol. II: *Excavations at Anshan (Tal-e Malyan): The Middle Elamite Period*. Philadelphia: The University of Pennsylvania Museum of Archaeology and Anthropology.

Carter, Elizabeth, and Matthew W. Stolper

1984 *Elam: Surveys of Political History and Archaeology*. Berkeley: University of California Press.

Caubet, Annie

1983 *Oeufs d'autruche au Proche Orient Ancien*. Report of the Department of Antiquities, Cyprus. Pp. 193-98. Nicosia.

Chakrabarti, Dilip K., and Parveen Moghadam

1977 Some Unpublished Indus Beads from Iran. *Iran* 15:166-68.

Charles, J. A.

1980 The Coming of Copper and Copper-Base Alloys and Iron: A Metallurgical Sequence. In *The Coming of the Age of Iron*. T. A. Wertime and J. D. Muhly, eds. Pp. 151-81. New Haven: Yale University Press.

1985 Determinative Mineralogy and the Origins of Metallurgy. In *Furnaces and Smelting Technology in Antiquity*. P.T. Craddock and M. J. Hughes, eds. Pp. 21-28. London: British Museum Press.

Chazan, M., and M. Lehner

1990 An Ancient Analogy: Pot Baked Bread in Ancient Egypt and Mesopotamia. *Paléorient* 16(2):21-36.

Chernykh, Evgenii N.

1980 Metallurgical Provinces of the 5th-2nd Millennia in Eastern Europe in Relation to the Process of Indo-Europeanization. *Journal of Indo-European Studies* 8, (3/4): 317-36.

Childe, V. Gordon

1950 The Urban Revolution. *Town Planning Review* 21:3-17.

Ciarla, Roberto

1979 The Manufacture of Alabaster Vessels at Shahr-i Sokhta and Mundigak in the 3rd Millennium B.C.: A Problem of Cultural Identity. In *Iranica*. G. Gnoli and A. V. Rossi, eds. Pp. 319-35. Naopli: Istituto Universitario Orientale.

1985 New Materials in the Study of the Manufacture of Stone Vases at Shah-i Sokhta. *East and West* 35(4):418-25.

1990 Fragments of Stone Vessels as a Base Material. Two Case Studies: Failaka and Shahr-i Sokhta. In *South Asian Archaeology 1987*. M. Taddei, ed. Pp. 475-91. Rome: IsMEO.

Cook, Scott

1982 *Zapotec Stoneworkers: The Dynamics of Rural Simple Commodity Production in Modern Mexican Capitalism*. Washington: University Press of America.

Crabtree, Don

1972 *An Introduction to Flintworking*. Pocatello: Idaho State University Museum.

Craddock, P.T., and N. D. Meeks

1987 Iron in Ancient Copper. *Archaeometry* 29(Pt. 2):187-204.

Curvers, H.H.

1989a Iron Age Bone and Shell Objects. In *The Holmes Expeditions to Luristan*. E. F. Schmidt et al., eds. Pp. 363-80. Chicago: The Oriental Institute, University of Chicago.

1989b Iron Age Beads. In *The Holmes Expeditions to Luristan*. E. F. Schmidt et al., eds. Pp. 381-411. Chicago: The Oriental Institute, University of Chicago.

Damerow, P., and R. K. Englund

1989 *The Proto-Elamite Texts from Tepe Yahya*. Cambridge: Peabody Museum of Archaeology and Ethnography.

Deaver, K.

1996 Appendix B. Lithic Clusters from the Middle Elamite Building (EDD). In *Malyan Excavation Reports*. Vol. II: *Excavations at Anshan (Tal-e Malyan): The Middle Elamite Period*. Elizabeth Carter, ed. Pp. 93-97. Philadelphia: The University of Pennsylvania Museum of Archaeology and Anthropology.

Dittmann, R.

1986a   Seals, Sealings and Tablets: Thoughts on the Changing Pattern of Administrative Control from the Late Uruk to the Proto-Elamite Period at Susa. In *Gamdat Naṣr: Period or Regional Style?* Uwe Finkbeiner and Wolfgang Röllig, eds. Pp. 171-98.

1986b   Susa in the Proto-Elamite Period and Annotations on the Painted Pottery of Proto-Elamite Khuzistan. In *Gamdat Naṣr: Period or Regional Style?* Uwe Finkbeiner and Wolfgang Röllig, eds. Pp. 332-66.

1987   Bemerkungen zum protoelamische Horizont. *AMI* 20:31-63.

Dollfus, G.

1971   Les Fouilles à Djaffarabad de 1969 à 1971. *Cahiers de la DAFI* 1: 17-86.

Durante, S.

1979   Marine Shells from Balakot, Shahr-i Sokhta and Tepe Yahya: Their Significance for Trade and Technology in Ancient Indo-Iran. In *South Asian Archaeology 1977*. M. Taddei, ed. Pp. 317-44. Naples: Istituto Universitario Orientale.

Dyson, R. H., Jr.

1965   Problems in the Relative Chronology of Iran, 6000-2000 B.C. In *Chronologies in Old World Archaeology*. Robert W. Ehrich, ed. Pp. 215-56. Chicago: University of Chicago Press.

1987   The Relative and Absolute Chronology of Hissar II and the Proto-Elamite Horizon of Northern Iran. In *Chronologies du Proche Orient*. Olivier Aurenche, Jacques Evin, and Francis Hours, eds. Pp. 647-78. Oxford: BAR International Series.

Dyson, R. H., Jr., and S. M. Howard, eds.

1989   *Tappeh Hesār: Reports of the Restudy Project, 1976*. Monographie di Mesopotamia II. Firenze: Casa Editrice Le Lettere.

Farshad, M., and D. Isfahanian

1977   Iran—The Homeland of Original Truss Structures. *Iran* 15:164-66.

Fasa'i, H.

1896   *Fārsnāma-ye Nāṣeri*. Tehran.

Finet, A.

1982   L'oeuf d'autruche. Studia Paula Naster Oblata II. *Orientalia Antiqua, Orientalia Lovaniensia Analecta* 13:66-77.

Fishman, B., and B. Lawn

1978   University of Pennsylvania Radiocarbon Dates XX. *Radiocarbon* 20(2):210-33.

Fox, W. A.

1984   Dhoukani Flake Blade Production in Cyprus. *Lithic Technology* 13(2):62-67.

Fox, W. A. and David Pearlman

1987   Threshing Sledge Production in the Paphos District in Western Cyprus. In *Connections: An Archaeological Symposium*. D.W. Rupp, ed. Pp. 227-34. Goteborg: Paul Astroms Forlag.

Fullagar, R. L. K.

1991   The Role of Silica in Polish Formation. *Journal of Archaeological Science* 18(1):1-24.

Gale, N. H., A. Papastamaki, Z. A. Stos-Gale, and K. Leonis

1985   Copper Sources and Copper Metallurgy in the Aegean Bronze Age. In *Furnaces and Smelting Technology in Antiquity*. P.T. Craddock and M.J. Hughes, eds. Pp. 81-102. London: British Museum Press.

Garthwaite, G. R.

1983   *Khans and Shahs: A Documentary Analysis of the Bakhtiyari in Iran*. New York: Cambridge University Press.

Gilman, Antonio

1981   The Development of Social Stratification in Bronze Age Europe. *Current Anthropology* 22:1-23.

Goff, Clare L.

1963   Excavations at Tall-i-Nokhodi. *Iran* 1:43-70.

Gotch, Paul

1971   Bakun A 5 Pottery—A History and Statement of Possibilities. *Bulletin of the Asia Institute of Pahlavi University* 2:73-90.

Hakemi, Ali
1992   The Copper Smelting Furnaces of the Bronze
        Age in Shahdad. In *South Asian Archaeology
        1989*. Catherine Jarrige, ed. Pp. 119-32.
        Madison, WI: Prehistory Press.

Hansman, John
1972   Elamites, Achaemenians, and Anshan. *Iran*
        10:101-24.

Hassan, Fekri A.
1981   *Demographic Archaeology*.   New York:
        Academic Press.

Hauptmann, Andreas
1980   Zur frühbronzezeitlichen Metallurgie von
        Shahr-i Sokhta (Iran).   *Der Anschnitt*
        32(2-3):55-61.

Helmig, D.
1986   Versuche zur analytisch-chemischen Charakteris-
        ierung frübronzezeitlicher Techniken der
        Kupferverhüttung In Shahr-i-Sokhta/Iran.
        Diplomarbeit, Faculty of Chemistry, Ruhr-
        University, Bochum, Germany.

Henrickson, Elizabeth F.
1985   The Early Development of Pastoralism in the
        Central Zagros Highlands (Luristan). *Iranica
        Antiqua* 20: 1-42.
1994   The Outer Limits: Settlement and Economic
        Strategies in the Central Zagros Highlands
        During the Uruk Era. In *Chiefdoms and
        Early States in the Near East: The
        Organizational Dynamics of Complexity*.
        Gil Stein and Mitchell S. Rothman, eds. Pp.
        85-102.   Madison, WI: Prehistory Press.

Henrickson, Robert C.
1984   Šimaški and Central Western Iran: The
        Archaeological Evidence. *ZA* 74:98-122
1986   A Regional Perspective on Godin III Cultural
        Development in Central Western Iran. *Iran*
        24:1-55.

Heskel, Dennis
1982   The Development of Pyrotechnology in Iran
        during the Fourth and Third Millennia B.C.
        Ph.D. dissertation, Dept. of Anthropology,
        Harvard University.   Ann Arbor: University
        Microfilms International.

Heskel, Dennis, and Carl C. Lamberg-Karlovsky
1980   An Alternative Sequence for the Development
        of Metallurgy: Tepe Yahya, Iran. In *The
        Coming of the Age of Iron*. Theodore A.
        Wertime and James D. Muhly, eds. Pp. 229-66.
        New Haven: Yale University Press.

Hinz, Walter
1972   *The Lost World of Elam: Re-creation of a Vanished
        Civilization*. New York: New York University Press.

Hole, Frank
1977   *Studies in the Archaeological History of the Deh
        Luran Plain: The Excavation of Chagha Sefid*.
        Museum of Anthropology, Memoires No. 9. Ann
        Arbor: University of Michigan.
1987   Settlement and Society in the Village Period.
        In *The Archaeology of Western Iran*. Frank
        Hole, ed. Pp. 79-106. Washington: Smithsonian
        Institution Press.
1994   Environmental Instabilities and Urban
        Origins. In *Chiefdoms and Early States in the
        Near East: The Organizational Dynamics of
        Complexity*.   Gil Stein and Mitchell S.
        Rothman, eds. Pp. 121-51. Madison, WI:
        Prehistory Press.

Hole, F., K. V. Flannery, and J. A. Neely
1969   *Prehistory and Human Ecology of the Deh
        Luran Plain: An Early Village Sequence from
        Khuzistan, Iran*. Museum of Anthropology,
        Memoirs No. 1. Ann Arbor: University of Michigan.

Ibrahim, M.
1982   *Excavations of the Arab Expedition at Sar el-
        Jisr, Bahrain*. Bahrain: Ministry of Information.

Jacobs, L. K.
1979   Tell-i Nun: Archaeological Implications of a
        Village in Transition. In *Ethnoarchaeology*.
        Carol Kramer, ed. Pp. 175-91. New York:
        Columbia University Press.
1980   Darvazeh Tepe and the Iranian Highlands in
        the Second Millenium B.C. Ph.D. dissertation,
        Department of Anthropology, University of
        Oregon. Ann Arbor: University Microfilms.

Jacobsen, T.
1987   *The Harps that Once-Sumerian Poetry in
        Translation*.   New Haven: Yale University
        Press.

Johnson, G.A.

1973 *Local Exchange and Early State Development in Southwestern Iran*. Museum of Anthropology, Anthropological Papers No 51. Ann Arbor: University of Michigan.

1987 The Changing Organization of Uruk Administration on the Susiana Plain. In *The Archaeology of Western Iran: Settlement and Society from Prehistory to the Islamic Conquest*. Frank Hole, ed. Pp. 107–39. Washington, D.C: Smithsonian Institution Press.

Keeley, L. H.

1980 *Experimental Determination of Stone Tool Uses: A Microwear Analysis*. Chicago: University of Chicago Press.

Keirns, A. J.

n.d. *Banesh Sherd Typology*. manuscript dated 1976 in the Malyan Archive.

Khalaf, Kamal T.

1961 *The Marine and Freshwater Fishes of Iraq*. Baghdad: Al-Rabitta Press.

Koucky, Frank L., and Arthur Steinberg

1982 Ancient Mining and Mineral Dressing on Cyprus. In *Early Pyrotechnology: The Evolution of the First Fire-Using Industries*. Theodore Wertime and Steven Wertime, eds. Pp. 149–80. Washington: Smithsonian Institution Press.

Kouchoukos, Nicholas, and Frank Hole

2003 Changing Estimates of Susiana's Prehistoric Settlement. In *Yeki bud, yeki nabud: Essays on the Archaeology of Iran in Honor of William M. Sumner*. Naomi F. Miller and Kamyar Abdi, eds. Pp. 53–60. Los Angeles: Cotsen Institute of Archaeology, University of California.

Kramer, Carol

1982 *Village Ethnoarchaeology: Rural Iran in Archaeological Perspective*. New York: Academic Press.

Lamberg-Karlovsky, Carl C.

1970 *Excavations at Tepe Yahya, Iran, 1967–1969: Progress Report No. 1*. American School of Prehistoric Research, Bulletin 27. Cambridge:

Peabody Museum, Harvard University; Shiraz: Asia Institute, Iran.

1971 The Proto-Elamite Settlement at Tepe Yahya. *Iran* 9:87–96.

1973 Urban Interaction on the Iranian Plateau: Excavations at Tepe Yahya, 1967–1973. Albert Reckitt Archaeological Lecture. Proceedings of the British Academy 59. London: Oxford University Press.

1977 Foreign Relations in the Third Millennium at Tepe Yahya. In *Le Plateau Iranien et l'Asie Centrale des Origines à la Conquête Islamique*. Pp. 33–43. Paris: Centre National de la Recherche Scientifique.

1978 The Proto-Elamites on the Iranian Plateau. *Antiquity* 52:114–20.

1986 Third Millennium Structure and Process: From the Euphrates to the Indus and the Oxus to the Indian Ocean. *Oriens Antiquus* 25(3–4):189–219.

1989 Introduction. In *The Proto-Elamite Texts from Tepe Yahya*. Peter Damerow and Robert K. Englund. Pp. v–xiv. American School of Prehistoric Research, Bulletin 39. Cambridge: Peabody Museum, Harvard University.

1996 *Beyond the Tigris and Euphrates: Bronze Age Civilizations*. Beer-Sheva, Studies by the Department of Bible and Ancient Near East 9. Ben-Gurian University of the Negev.

Lambert, Maurice

1972 Hutéludush-Insushnak et le pays d'Anzan. *Revue d'Assyriologie* 66:61–76.

Langsdorff, Alexander, and Donald E. McCown

1942 *Tall-i-Bakun A. Season of 1932*. Chicago: University of Chicago Press.

Laufer, Berthold

1926 *Ostrich Egg-shell Cups of Mesopotamia and the Ostrich in Ancient and Modern Times*. Field Museum of Natural History, Anthropology Leaflet 23. Chicago: Field Museum.

Le Brun, Alain

1971 Recherches stratigraphiques à l'Acropole de Suse (1969–1971). *Cahiers de la D.A.F.I.* 1:163–216.

1978a Suse, chantier "Acropole 1." *Paléorient* 4:177–92.

1978b Le niveau 17B de l'Acropole de Suse (campagne de 1972). *Cahiers de la D.A.F.I.* 9:57–154.

Le Brun, Alain, and Françoise Vallat
1978   L'origine de l'écriture à Suse. *Cahiers de la D.A.F.I.* 8:11-59.

Lechtman, Heather
1980   The Central Andes: Metallurgy without Iron. In *The Coming of the Age of Iron*. Teodore A. Wertime and James D. Muhly, eds. Pp. 267-334. New Haven: Yale University Press.

Loon, Maurits N. van
1989   Chalcolithic Bone and Shell Objects. In *The Holmes Expeditions to Luristan*. E. F. Schmidt et al., eds. Pp. 115-116. Chicago: The Oriental Institute, University of Chicago.

Mackay, Ernest
1925   *Report on the Excavation of the "A" Cemetery at Kish, Mesopotamia, Part I*. Chicago: Field Museum of Natural History.
1929   *A Sumerian Palace and the "A" Cemetery at Kish, Mesopotamia, Part II*. Chicago: Field Museum of Natural History.

Maczek, M. von, E. Preuschen, and R. Pittioni
1952   Beiträge zum Problem des Ursprunges der Kupfererzverwertung in der Alten Welt. *Archaeologia Austriaca* 10:61-70.

Majidzadeh, Yousef
1979   An Early Prehistoric Coppersmith Workshop at Tepe Ghabristan. In *Akten des VII Internationalen Kongresses für Iranische Kunst und Archäologie, Munich, 1976*. Pp. 82-92. Berlin: Dietrich Reimer.

Malfoy, J.-M., and M. Menu
1987   La métallurgie du cuivre à Suse aux IVe et IIIe millénaires: analyses en laboratoire. In *Métallurgie susienne I*, Vol. 1. F. Tallon, ed. Pp. 355-73. Paris: Éditions de la Réunion des musées nationaux.

McCown, D. E.
1942   *The Comparative Stratigraphy of Early Iran*. The Oriental Institute. Chicago: University of Chicago Press.

McKerrel, Hugh, and Ronald F. Tylecote
1972   The Working of Copper-Arsenic Alloys in the Early Bronze Age and the Effect on the Determination of Provenance. *Proceedings of the Prehistoric Society n.s.* 38:209-18.

Meeks, Nigel D., G. de Sieveking, M. S. Tite, and J. Cook
1982   Gloss and Use-Wear Traces on Flint Sickles and Similar Phenomena. *Journal of Archaeological Science* 9(4):317-40.

Meulengracht, Anne, Patrick McGovern, and Barbara Lawn
1981   University of Pennsylvania Radiocarbon Dates XXI. *Radiocarbon* 23(4):227-240.

Miller, Naomi F.
1982   Economy and Environment of Malyan, a Third Millennium B.C. Urban Center in Southern Iran. Ph.D. dissertation, Department of Anthropology, University of Michigan. Ann Arbor: University Microfilms.
1984a   The Use of Dung as Fuel: An Ethnographic Example and an Archaeological Application. *Paléorient* 10(2):71-79.
1984b   The Interpretation of Some Carbonized Cereal Remains as Remnants of Dung Cake Fuel. *Bulletin on Sumerian Agriculture* 1:45-47.
1985   Paleoethnobotanical Evidence for Deforestation in Ancient Iran: A Case Study of Urban Malyan. *Journal of Ethnobiology* 5(1):1-19.
1990a   Clearning Land for Farmland and Fuel: Archaeobotanical Studies of the Ancient Near East. In *Economy and Settlement in the Near East: Analysis of Ancient Sites and Materials. MASCA Research Papers in Science and Archaeology*. Supplement to Vol. 7. Naomi Miller, ed. Pp. 71-78. Philadelphia: University of Pennsylvania Museum of Archaeology and Anthropology.
1990b   Archaeobotanical Perspectives on the Rural-Urban Connection. In *Economy and Settlement in the Near East: Analysis of Ancient Sites and Materials*. Naomi Miller, ed. Pp. 79-83. Philadelphia: University of Pennsylvania Museum of Archaeology and Anthropology.

Miller, Naomi F., and Tristine L. Smart
1984   Intentional Burning of Dung as Fuel: A Mechanism for the Incorporation of Charred Seeds Into the Archaeological Record. *Journal of Ethnobiology* 4(1):15-28.

Miroschedji, Pierre de
1971   *Poteries élamites du Fars Oriental*. Tehran: Ministry of Culture and Art.
1972   Prospections archéologique dans les vallées de Fasa et de Darab. In *Proceedings of the*

First Annual Symposium on Archaeological Research in Iran, 1972. Firuz Bagherzadeh, ed. Pp. 1–7. Tehran: Iranian Centre for Archaeological Research.

1974 Tépé Jalyan, une nécropole du IIIe millénaire av. J.-C. au Fars Oriental (Iran). *Arts Asiatiques* 30:19–64.

1976 Un four de potier du IVe millénaire sur le tell de l'Apadana. *Cahiers de la D.A.F.I.* 6:13–45.

2003 Susa and the Highlands: Major Trends in the History of Elamite Civilization. In *Yeki bud, yeki nabud: Essays on the Archaeology of Iran in Honor of William M. Sumner*. Naomi F. Miller and Kamyar Abdi, eds. Pp. 17-38. Cotsen Institute of Archaeology. Los Angeles: University of California.

Moorey, Peter R. S.

1970 Cemetery A at Kish: Grave Groups and Chronology. *Iraq* 32(Pt. 2):86–128.

1982 Archaeology and Pre-Achaemenid Metalworking in Iran: A Fifteen Year Retrospective. *Iran* 20:81–101.

Mount-Williams, Linda

1980 Terqa Preliminary Reports. *Object Typology of the Third Season: The Third and Second Millennia*. Syro-Mesopotamian Studies. Malibu, Ca: Undina Publications.

Movius, Hallam L., Nicholas David, H. Bricker, and R.B. Clay

1968 *The Analysis of Certain Major Classes of Upper Palaeolithic Tools*. Cambridge: Peabody Museum.

Neely, James A. and Henry T. Wright

1994 *Early Settlement and Irrigation on the Deh Luran Plain: Village and Early State Societies in Southwestern Iran*. Ann Arbor: University of Michigan.

Nicholas, Ilene M.

1980 A Spatial/Functional Analysis of Late Fourth Millennium Occupation at the TUV Mound, Tal-e Malyan, Iran. Ph.D. disseration, Department of Anthropology, University of Pennsylvania. Ann Arbor: University Microfilms.

1981 Investigating an Ancient Suburb: Excavations at the TUV Mound, Tal-e Malyan, Iran. *Expedition* 23(3):39–47.

1987 The Function of Bevelled-rim Bowls: A Case Study at the TUV Mound, Tal-e Malyan. *Paléorient* 13(2):61–72.

1990 *Malyan Excavation Reports*, Vol. I: *The Proto-Elamite Settlement at TUV*. Philadelphia: The University of Pennsylvania Museum of Archaeology and Anthropology.

Nickerson, Janet W.

1977 Malyan Wall Paintings. *Expedition* 19(3):2–6.

1979 The Study, Analysis and Interpretation of the Human and Animal Figurines from Tal-e Malyan (Anshan), Iran. Honors A.B. Thesis, Ohio State University.

Nickerson, John L.

1983 Intrasite Variability During the Kaftari Period at Tal-e Malyan (Anshan), Iran. Ph.D. dissertation, Department of Anthropology, The Ohio State University. Ann Arbor: University Microfilms.

1991 Investigating Intrasite Variability at Tal-e Malyan (Anshan), Iran. *Iranica Antiqua* 26:1–38.

Nissen, Hans J.

1970 Grabung in den Quadraten K/L XII in Uruk-Warka. *Baghdader Mitteilungen* 5:101–191.

Nissen, Hans J., Peter Damerow, and Robert K. Englund

1993 *Archaic Bookkeeping: Early Writing and Techniques of Economic Administration in the Ancient Near East*. Chicago: University of Chicago Press.

Odell, G. H. and F. Odell-Vereecken

1980 Verifying the Reliability of Lithic Use-Wear Assessments by Blind Tests: The Low Power Approach. *Journal of Field Archaeology* 7:87–120.

Palache, C., H. Berman and C. Frondel

1944 *The System of Mineralogy 1*. New York: Wiley and Sons.

Parrot, André

1937 Les fouilles de Mari, troisième campagne (hiver 1935–36). *Syria* 18:53–84.

1953 Acquisitions et inédits du Musée du Louvre. *Syria* 30:1–4.

Pigott, Vincent C.

1989a Archaeo-metallurgical Investigations at Bronze Age Tappeh Hesār, 1976. In *Tappeh Hesār, Reports of the Restudy Project, 1976*. Robert H. Dyson, Jr. and Susan M. Howard, eds. Pp. 25–33. Firenze: Casa Editrice Le Lettere.

1989b   Bronze. In *Encyclopaedia Iranica*, Volume IV, Fascicle 5. Pp. 457-71. New York: Routledge and Kegan Paul.

1999a   A Heartland of Metallurgy: Neolithic/Chalcolithic metallurgical origins on the Iranian Plateau. In *The Beginnings of Metallurgy: Proceedings of the International Conference, Bochum 1995*. Hauptmann, Andreas, et al. eds. Pp. 107-121. Der Anschnitt: Zeitschrift für Kunst und Kultur im Bergbau; Veroffentlichungen aus dem Deutschen Bergbau-Museum.

1999b   The Development of Metalworking on the Iranian Plateau: An Archaeometallurgical Perspective. In *The Archaeometallurgy of the Asian Old World*. Vincent C Pigott, ed. Philadelphia: University of Pennsylvania Museum of Archaeology and Anthropolgy Publications.

Pigott, Vincent C., Susan M. Howard and Stephen M. Epstein
1982   Pyrotechnology and Culture Change at Bronze Age Tepe Hissar. In *Early Pyrotechnology: The Evolution of the First Fire-Using Industries*. Theodore Wertime and Steven Wertime, eds. Pp. 215-236. Washington: Smithsonian Institution Press.

Pittman, Holly
1994a   *The Glazed Steatite Glyptic Style: The Structure and Function of an Image System*. Berlin: Dietrich Reimer Verlag.

1994b   Towards an Understanding of the Role of Glyptic Imagery in the Administrative Systems of Proto-Literate Greater Mesopotamia. In *Archives before Writing: Proceedings of the International Colloquium Oriola Romano, 1991*. Piera Ferioli, Enrica Fiandra, Gian Giacomo Fissori, and Marcella Frangipane, eds. Pp. 177-203. Rome: Centro Internazionale di Ricerche Archeologiche Antropologiche e Storiche.

1997   The Administrative Function of Glyptic Art in Proto-Elamite Iran: A Survey of the Evidence. Sceaux d'Orient et leur emploi. *Res Orientales* 10:1-31.

n.d.   *Seals and Sealings from Tall-i Malyan*. Malyan Excavation Reports. Philadelphia: University of Pennsylvania Museum of Archaeology and Anthropology.

Postgate, J. Nicholas
1980   Early Dynastic Burial Customs at Abu Salabikh. *Sumer* 36(1-2):65-82.

Potts, Daniel T.
1977   Tepe Yahya and the End of the 4th Millennium on the Iranian Plateau. In *Le Plateau Iranien et l'Asie Centrale des Origines à la Conquête Islamique*. Pp. 24-31. Paris: Centre National de la Recherche Scientifique.

Potts, Timothy F.
1994   *Mesopotamia and the East: An Archaeological and Historical Study of Foreign Relations ca. 3400-2000 B.C.* Oxford: Oxford University Committee for Archaeology.

Prickett, Martha
1986   Settlement during the Early Periods. In *Excavations at Tepe Yahya, Iran 1967-1975: The Early Periods*. Thomas W. Beale, ed. Pp. 215-46. American Schools of Prehistoric Research, Bulletin 38. Cambridge: Harvard University Press.

Prinz, M., G. Harlow, and J. Peters (eds.)
1978   *Simon and Schuster's Guide to Rock's and Minerals*. Translation of A. Mottana, A. Crespi and G. Liborio. New York: Simon and Schuster.

Rapp, George, Jr.
1988   On the Origins of Copper and Bronze Alloying. In *The Beginning of the Use of Metals and Alloys*. R. Maddin, ed. Pp. 21-27. Cambridge, MA: MIT Press.

Reese, David S.
1984   Shark and Ray Remains in Aegean and Cypriote Archaeology. *Opuscula Atheniensia* 15:188-192.
1989   Treasures from the Sea: Shells and Shell Ornaments from Hasanlu IVB. *Expedition* 31(2-3):80-86.

Reiner, Erica
1973   The Location of Anšan. *Revue d'Assyriologie* 67:57-62.

Renfrew, Colin and J. E. Dixon
1976   Obsidian in Western Asia-A Review. In *Problems in Economic and Social Archaeology*. G. de G. Sieveking, I. H. Longworth, and K. E. Wilson, eds. Pp. 137-52. London: Duckworth.

Rosenberg, Michael

1989   The Evidence for Craft Specialization in the Production of Chipped Stone Blades at Tappeh Hesār. In *Tappeh Hesār: Reports of the Restudy Project, 1976*. Robert H. Dyson, Jr. and Susan M. Howard, eds. Pp. 111-118. Florence: Casa Editrice Le Lettere.

Rostoker, William and James R. Dvorak

1991   Some Experiments with Co-smelting to Copper Alloys. *Archeomaterials* 5(1):5-20.

Rostoker William; Vincent C. Pigott and James R. Dvorak

1989   Direct Reduction to Copper Metal by Oxide-Sulfide Mineral Interaction. *Archeomaterials* 3(1):69-87.

Runnels, Curtis N.

1982   Flaked-Stone Artifacts in Greece during the Historical Period. *Journal of Field Archaeology* 9(3):363-73.

Salvatori, Sandro and Massimo Vidale

1982   A Brief Surface Survey of the Proto-historic Site of Shahdad (Kerman) Iran. *Rivista di Archeologia* (Rome) 6:5-10.

Schiffer, Michael B.

1972   Archaeological Context and Systemic Context. *American Antiquity* 37(2):156-165

1976   *Behavioral Archaeology*. New York: Academic Press.

Schmandt-Besserat, Denise

1986   Tokens at Susa. *Oriens Antiquus* 25(1-2):93-125.

1992   *Before Writing*. Austin: University of Texas Press.

1996   *How Writing Came About*. Austin: University of Texas Press

Schmidt, Erich F.

1937   *Excavations at Tepe Hissar, Damghan*. Philadelphia: University of Pennsylvania Museum of Archaeology and Anthropology.

Schmidt, Erich F., Maurits N. van Loon, H. H. Curvers

1989   *The Holmes Expeditions to Luristan*. Chicago: The Oriental Institute, University of Chicago.

Schürenberg, H.

1963   Über iranische Kupfererzvorkommen mit komplexen Kobalt-Nickelerzen. *Neues Jahrbuch für Mineralogie Abhandlungen* 99(2):200-30.

Semenov, S.A.

1964   *Prehistoric Technology*. London: Cory, Adams, and Mackay.

Sheets, Payson D. and G. Muto

1972   Pressure Blades and Total Cutting Edge: An Experiment in Lithic Technology. *Science* 175:632-634.

South, Stanley

1977   *Method and Theory in Historical Archaeology*. New York: Academic Press.

Starr, R. F. S.

1937-9   *Nuzi, Excavations at Yorgan Tepe near Kirkuk, Iraq (1927-1931) I*. Cambridge: Harvard University Press.

Stech, Tamara

1990   Neolithic Copper Metallurgy in Southwest Asia. *Archeomaterials* 4(1):55-61.

Stech, Tamara and Vincent C. Pigott

1986   The Metals Trade in Southwest Asia in the Third Millennium B.C. *Iraq* 48:39-64.

Stein, Sir Aurel

1936   An Archaeological Tour in the Ancient Persis. *Iraq* 3:111-230.

Stein, Gil

1994   Economy, Ritual, and Power in 'Ubaid Mesopotamia. In *Chiefdoms and Early States in the Near East: The Organizational Dynamics of Complexity*. Gil Stein and Mitchell S. Rothman, eds. Pp. 35-46. Madison, WI: Prehistory Press.

Steinkeller, Piotr

1982   The Question of Marhaši: A Contribution to the Historical Geography of Iran in the Third Millennium B.C. *Zeitschrift für Assyriologie und Vorderasiatische Archäologie* 72 (II):237-265.

Steve, Marie-Joseph and Henri Gasche

1971   *L'Acropole de Suse*.   Mémoires de la Délégation archéologique Française en Iran 46. Paris: Paul Geuthner.

Stolper Matthew W.

1976   Preliminary Report on Texts from Tal-e Malyan 1971-1974. In *Proceedings of the 4th Annual Symposium on Archaeological Research in Iran*. Firuz Bagherzadeh, ed. Pp. 89-100. Tehran: Iranian Centre for Archaeological Research.

1982   On the Dynasty of Šimaški and the Early Sukkalmahs. *Zeitschrift für Assyriologie und Vorderasiatische Archäologie* 72:42-67.

1984   *Texts from Tall-i Malyan, I: Elamite Administrative Texts (1972-1974)*. Philadelphia: University of Pennsylvania Museum of Archaeology and Anthropology.

1985   Proto-Elamite Texts from Tal-i Malyan. *Kadmos* 24(1):1-12.

Stone, E.

1982   The Camel Bird of Arabia. *Aramco World Magazine* 33/2: 10-11.

Sumner, William M.

n.d.   *Instructions for Excavation and Recording, Malyan*. (First issued in 1971 with revised and enlarged versions through 1978). Malyan Archives.

1972a   Cultural Development in the Kur River Basin, Iran: An Archaeological Analysis of Settlement Patterns. Ph.D. dissertation, Department of Anthropology, University of Pennsylvania. Ann Arbor: University Microfilms.

1972b   Tall-i Malyan. *Iran* 10:176.

1973   Malyan. *Iran* 11:199-200.

1974   Excavations at Tall-i Malyan, 1971-72. *Iran* 12:155-80.

1976   Excavations at Tall-i Malyan (Anshan) 1974. *Iran* 14:103-15.

1979   Estimating Population by Analogy: An Example. In *Ethnoarchaeology*. Carol Kramer, ed. Pp. 164-174. New York: Columbia University Press.

1985   The Proto-Elamite City Wall at Tal-e Malyan. *Iran* 23:153-61.

1986   Proto-Elamite Civilization in Fars. In *Ğamdat Nasr: Period or Regional Style?* Uwe Finkbeiner and Wolfgang Röllig, eds. Pp.

199-211. Beihefte zum Tübinger Atlas des Vorderern Orients vol. 62. Wiesbaden: Ludwig Reichert.

1988a   Maljān, Tall-e (Anšan). In *Reallexikon der Assyriologie und Vorderasiatischen Archäologie*. Band 7.(3/4). Pp. 306-20. Berlin: Walter de Gruyter.

1988b   Prelude to Proto-Elamite Anshan: The Lapui Phase. P. Amiet Festscrift. *Iranica Antiqua* 23:23-43.

1989a   Anshan in the Kaftari Phase: Patterns of Settlement and Land Use. In *Archaeologia Iranica et Orientalis: Miscellanea in Honorem Louis Vanden Berghe*. L. de Meyer and E. Haerinck, eds. Pp. 135-61. Gent: Peeters Presse.

1989b   Population and Settlement Area: An Example from Iran. *American Anthropologist* 91(3):631-41.

1990a   Full Coverage Regional Archaeological Survey in the Near East: An Example from Iran. In *The Archaeology of Regions: A Case for Full-Coverage Survey*. S. K. Fish and S. Kowalewski, eds. Pp. 87-115. Washington: Smithsonian Institution Press.

1990b   An Archaeological Estimate of Population Trends Since 6000 B.C. in the Kur River Basin, Fars Province, Iran. In *South Asian Archaeology 1987*. M. Taddei, ed. Pp. 3-16. Rome: IsMEO.

1994a   The Evolution of Tribal Society in the Southern Zagros Mountains, Iran. In *Chiefdoms and Early States in the Near East: The Organizational Dynamics of Complexity*. Gil Stein and Mitchell S. Rothman, eds. Pp. 47-65. Madison, WI: Prehistory Press.

1994b   Archaeological Measures of Cultural Continuity and the Arrival of the Persians in Fars. In *Achaemenid History VIII: Continuity and Change*. Heleen Sancisi-Weerdenburg, Amélie Kuhrt, and Margaret C. Root, eds. Pp. 97-105. Leiden: Nederlands Instituut voor het Nabije Oosten.

1999   The Birds of Anshan. In *The Iranian World: Essays on Iranian Art and Archaeology Presented to Ezat O. Negahban*. Abbas Alizadeh, Yousef Majidzadeh and Shapur Malek-Shahmirzadeh, eds. Pp. 85-100. Tehran: Iran University Press.

Talbot, Nancy
1981   Shell Artifacts. In *An Early Town on the Deh Luran Plain: Excavations at Tepe Farukhabad*. Henry T. Wright, ed. Pp. 162-63. Museum of Anthropology, Memoirs No. 13. Ann Arbor: University of Michigan.

Tallon, Françoise
1987   *Métallurgie Susienne*, 2 Vols. Paris: Editions de la Réunion des musées nationaux.

Thureau-Dangin, F. and R. P. Dhorme
1924   Cinq jours de fouilles à 'Asharâh 7-11 Septembre 1923. *Syria* 5:265-93.

Torelli, M.
1965   Un uovo di struzzo dipinto conservato nel Museo di Tarquinia. *Studi Etruschi* 33: 329-65.

Tosi, Maurizio and Rafaello Biscione
1981   *Conchiglie, Il commercio e la lavorazione delle conchiglie marine nel medio oriente dal IV al II millennio A.C.* Rome: De Luca Editore.

Tringham, Ruth, G. Cooper, G. Odell, Barbara Voytek, and Anne Whitman
1974   Experimentation in the Formation of Edge Damage: A New Approach to Lithic Analysis. *Journal of Field Archaeology* 1(1-2):171-96.

Tylecote, Ronald F. and Hugh McKerrell
1971   Examination of Copper Alloy Tools from Tal y Yahya, Iran. *Bulletin of the Historical Metallurgy Group* 5 (1):37-38.
1986   Note: Examination of Copper Alloy Tools from Tepe Yahya. In *Excavations at Tepe Yahya, Iran 1967-1975: The Early Periods*. Thomas W. Beale, ed. Pp. 213-14. American Schools of Prehistoric Research, Bulletin 38.

Unger-Hamilton, Romano
1984   The Formation of Use-Wear Polish on Flint: Beyond the "Deposit versus Abrasion" Controversy. *Journal of Archaeological Science* 11(1):91-98.
1985   Microscopic Striations on Flint Sickle-Blades as an Indication of Plant Cultivation: Preliminary Results. *World Archaeology* 17(1):121-6.

Upton, J. M
1932   The Expedition to Ctesiphon. 1930-1932. *Bulletin of the Metropolitan Museum of Art* 27:188-97.

Vallat, François
1980   *Suse et l'Elam*. Recherche sur le grandes civilisations, Mémoire No. 1. Paris: Éditions ADPF.
1986   The Most Ancient Scripts of Iran: The Current Situation. *World Archaeology* 17(3):335-47.

Vanden Berghe, Louis
1952   Archaeologische Opzoekingen in de Marv Dasht Vlakte (Irān). *Jaarbericht Ex Oriente Lux* 12:211-20.
1954   Archaeologische Navorsingen in de Omstreken van Persepolis. *Jaarbericht Ex Oriente Lux* 13:394-408.
1959   *Archéologie de L'Irān Ancien*. Leiden: E. J. Brill.

Van Neer, Wim and M. Uerpmann.
1994   Fish Remains from Excavation 520 at Qala'at al-Bahrain. In *Qala'at al-Bahrain I The Northern City Wall and the Islamic Fortress*. F. Højlund and H. H. Andersen, eds. Pp. 445-54. Moesgaard, Aarhus: Jutland Archaeological Society Publications 30(1).

Vatandoost-Haghighi, A. R.
1978   Aspects of Prehistoric Iranian Copper and Bronze Technology. Ph.D. Dissertation, Institute of Archaeology, London.

Vaughan, Patrick C.
1985   *Use-Wear Analysis of Flaked Stone Tools*. Tucson: University of Arizona Press.

Vidali, M. L.
1995   Stoneware Industries of the Indus Civilization. In *Ceramics and Civilization*, Vol. 5. D. Kingery, ed. Pp. 231-56. Westerville OH: American Chemical Society.

Voigt, Mary M.
1983   *Haji Firuz Tepe, Iran: The Neolithic Settlement*. Philadelphia: University of Pennsylvania Museum of Archaeology and Anthropology.

Voigt, Mary M., and Robert H. Dyson, Jr.
1992   The Chronology of Iran, ca. 8000-2000 B.C. In *Chronologies in Old World Archaeology* (Third Edition). Robert W. Ehrich, ed. Vol. I, Pp. 122-78; Vol. II, Pp. 125-53. Chicago: University of Chicago Press.

Wasilewska, A.
1991   To Be or Not To Be a Temple? Possible Identification of a Banesh Period Temple at Tall-i Malyan, Iran. *Mesopotamie et Elam, Mesopotamian History and Environment.* Pp. 143-52. Actes de la XXXVIème RAI, Gand, 10-14 juillet 1989. University of Ghent.

Watson, Patty Jo
1979   *Archaeological Ethnography in Western Iran.* Tucson: University of Arizona Press.

Weiss, Harvey, and T. Cuyler Young, Jr.
1975   The Merchants of Susa: Godin V and Plateau-Lowland Relations in the Late Fourth Millennium B.C. *Iran* 13:1-17.

Whitcomb, Donald S.
1985   *Before the Roses and Nightingales: Excavations at Qasr-i Abu Nasr, Old Shiraz.* New York: Metropolitan Museum of Art.

Wilkinson, T. J.
2003   Archaeological Survey and Long-term Population Trends in Upper Mesopotamia and Iran. In *Yeki bud, yeki nabud: Essays on the Archaeology of Iran in Honor of William M. Sumner.* Naomi F. Miller, and Kamyar Abdi, eds. Pp. 39-52. Monograph 48. Cotsen Institute of Archaeology. Los Angeles: University of California.

Woolley, Sir Leonard
1934   *Ur Excavations II. The Royal Cemetery.* London: Oxford University Press.

Wright, Henry T.
1987   The Susiana Hinterlands During the Era of Primary State Formation. In *The Archaeology of Western Iran.* Frank Hole, ed. Pp. 141-55. Washington, DC: Smithsonian Institution Press.

Wright, Henry T. and Gregory Johnson
1975   Population, Exchange, and Early State Formation in Southwestern Iran. *American Anthropologist* 77:267-89.

Wright, Henry T. and Eric A. Rupley
2001   Calibrated Radiocarbon Age Determinations of Uruk-related Assemblages. In *Uruk Mesopotamia and Its Neighbors: Cross-cultural Interactions in the Era of State Formation.* M.S. Rothman, ed. Pp. 85-122. School of American Research Seminar Series. Santa Fe: SAR Press.

Yerkes, Richard
1987   *Prehistoric Life on the Mississippi Floodplain.* Chicago: University of Chicago Press.

Young, Donald and Douglas B. Bamforth
1990   On the Macroscopic Identification of Used Flakes. *American Antiquity* 55(2):403-9.

Young, T. Cuyler, Jr.
1969   *Excavations at Godin Tepe: First Progress Report.* Ontario: Royal Ontario Museum, Art and Archaeology.
1986   Godin Tepe Period VI/V and Central Western Iran at the End of the Fourth Millennium. In *Ğamdat Naṣr: Period or Regional Style?* Uwe Finkbeiner and Wolfgang Röllig, eds. Pp. 212-28. Beihefte zum Tübinger Atlas des Vorderern Orients vol. 62. Wiesbaden: Ludwig Reichert.

Zagarell, Allen
1982   *The Prehistory of the Northeast Bahtiyari Mountains, Iran: The Rise of a Highland Way of Life.* Weisbaden: Ludwig Reichert.

Zeder, Melinda A.
1984   Meat Distribution at the Highland Iranian Urban Center of Tal-e Malyan. In *Animals and Archaeology: 3. Early Herders and their Flocks.* Juliet Clutton-Brock and Caroline Grigson, eds. Pp. 279-307. Oxford: BAR International Series.
1985   Urbanism and Animal Exploitation in Southwest Highland Iran, 3400-1500 B.C. Ph.D. dissertation, Department of Anthropology, University of Michigan. Ann Arbor: University Microfilms.
1986   The Equid Remains from Tal-e Malyan, Southern Iran. In *Equids in the Ancient World.* R. H. Meadow and Hans-Peter Uerpmann, eds. Pp. 366-412. TAVO, Reihe A, 19(1). Wiesbaden: Dr. Ludwig Reichert Verlag.

1988   Understanding Urban Process through the Study of Specialized Subsistence Economy in the Near East. *Journal of Anthropological Archaeology* 7:1-55.

1991   *Feeding Cities: Specialized Animal Economy in the Ancient Near East*. Washington: Smithsonian Institution Press.

Zeder, Melinda A. and M. James Blackman

2003   Economy and Administration at Banesh Malyan: Exploring the Potential of Faunal and Chemical Data for Understanding State Process. In *Yeki bud, yeki nabud, Essays on the Archaeology of Iran in Honor of William M. Sumner*. Naomi F. Miller, and Kamyar Abdi, eds. Los Angeles: Cotsen Institute of Archaeology, University of California.

Zwicker, Ulrich

1980   Investigations on the Extractive Metallurgy of Cu/Sb/As Ore and the Excavated Smelting Products from Norsun-Tepe (Keban) on the Upper Euphrates (3500-2800 B.C.). In *Aspects of Early Metallurgy*. W.A. Oddy, ed. Pp. 13-26. British Museum Occasional Paper 17. London: British Museum.

Figures

FIGURE 1

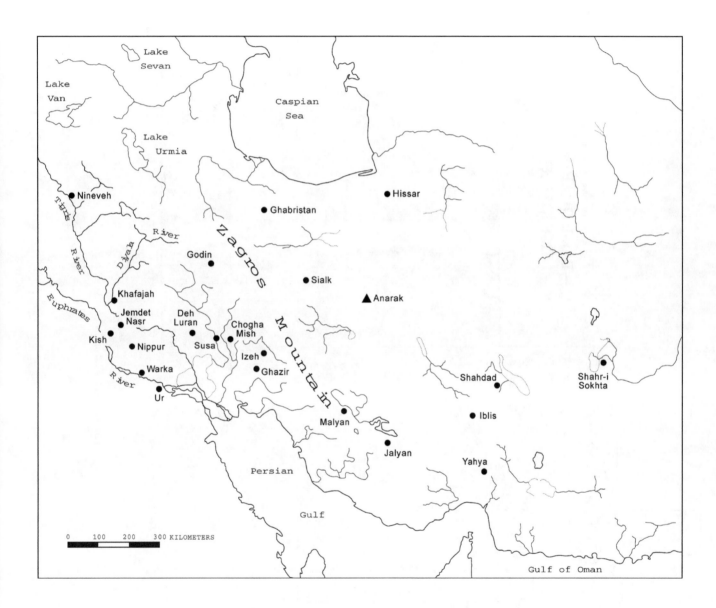

Iran.

FIGURE 2

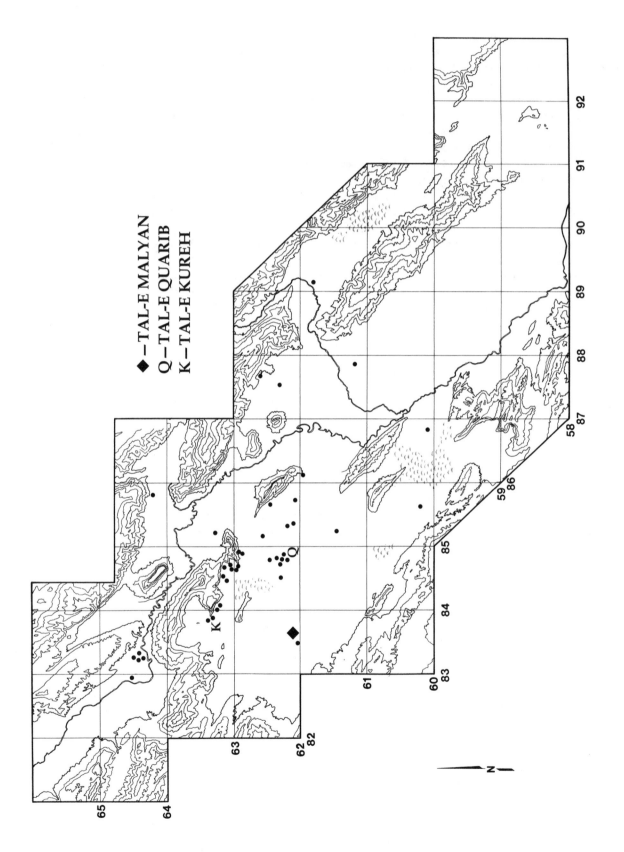

The Kur River Basin in the Banesh Period.

FIGURE 3

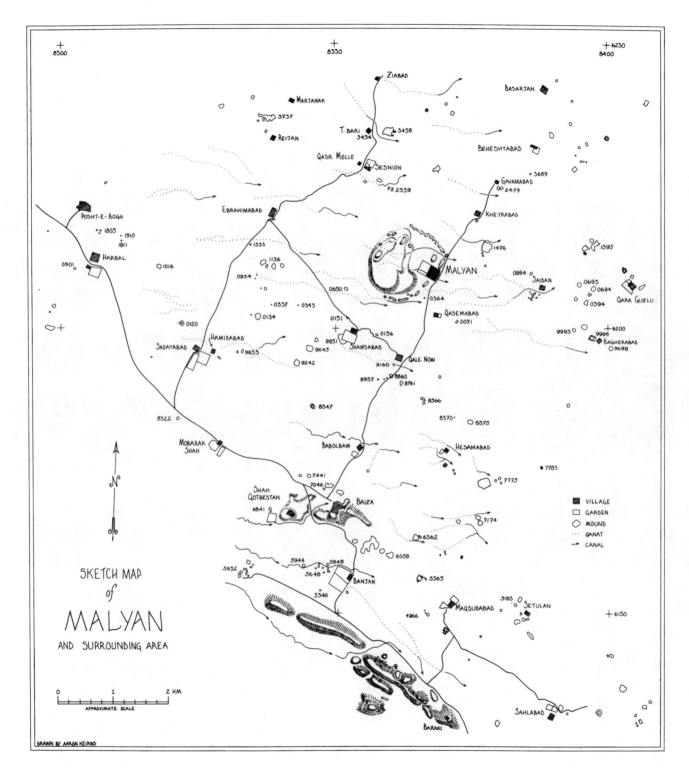

Sketch map of the Baiza District.

FIGURE 4

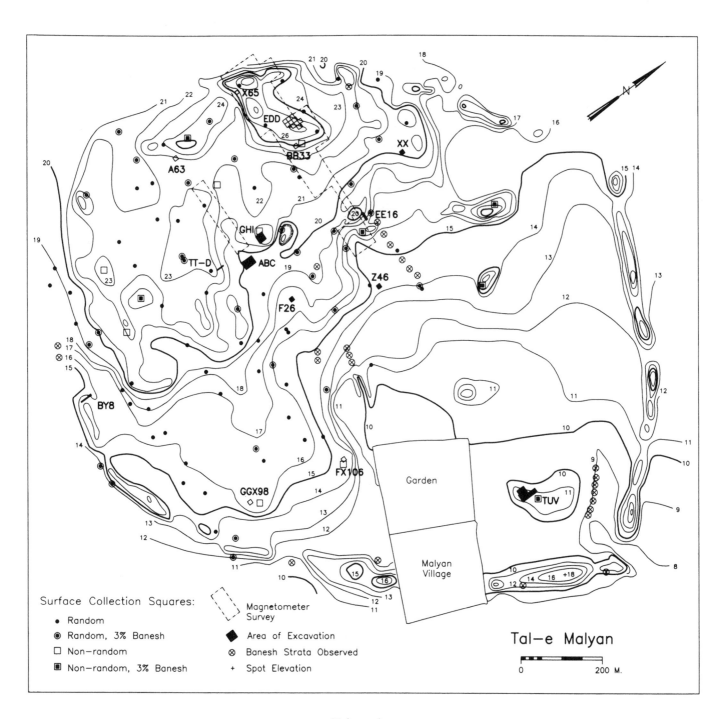

Malyan plan.

FIGURE 5

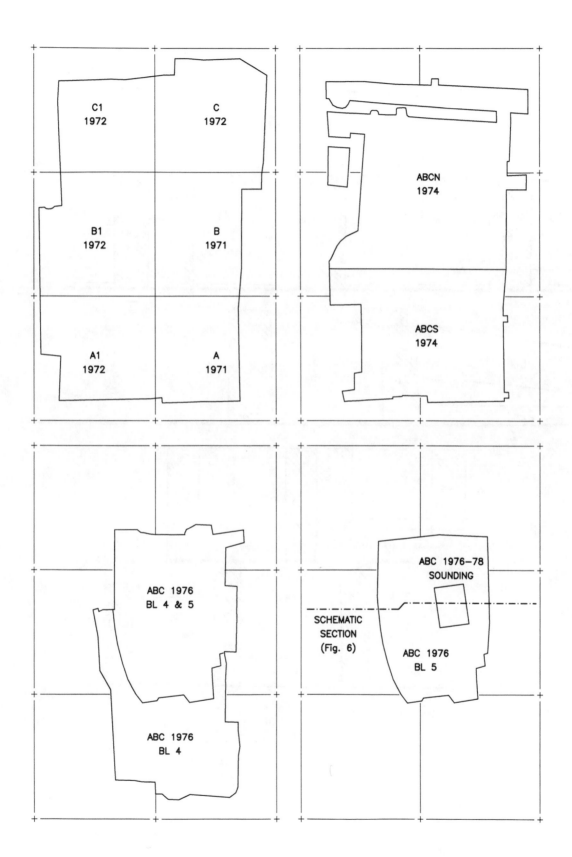

Limits of excavations at Operation ABC, 1971-1978.

FIGURE 6

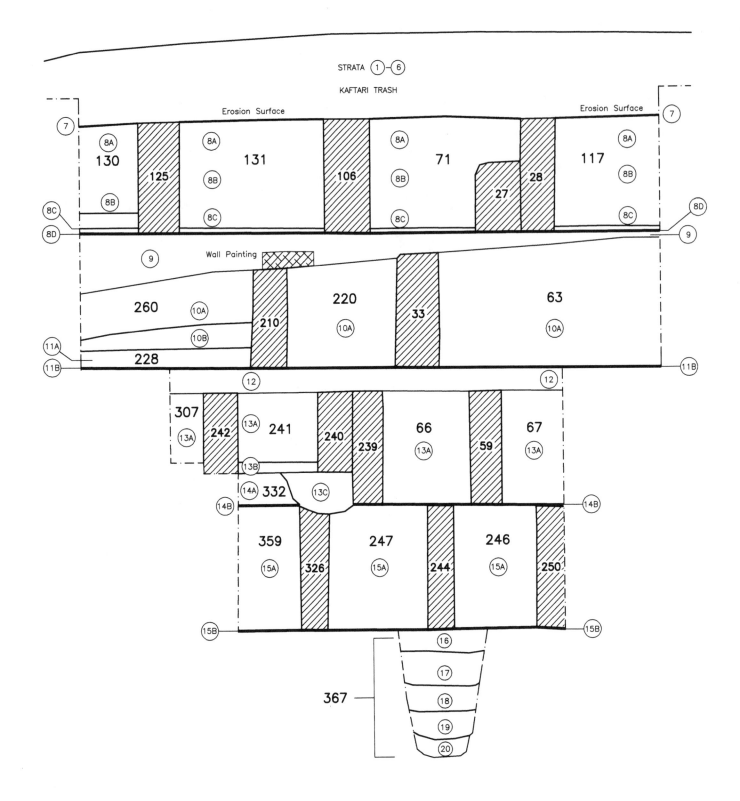

Schematic stratigraphic diagram.

FIGURE 7

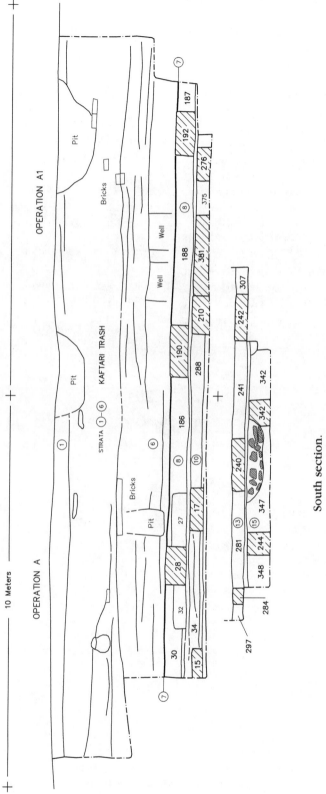

South section.

FIGURE 8

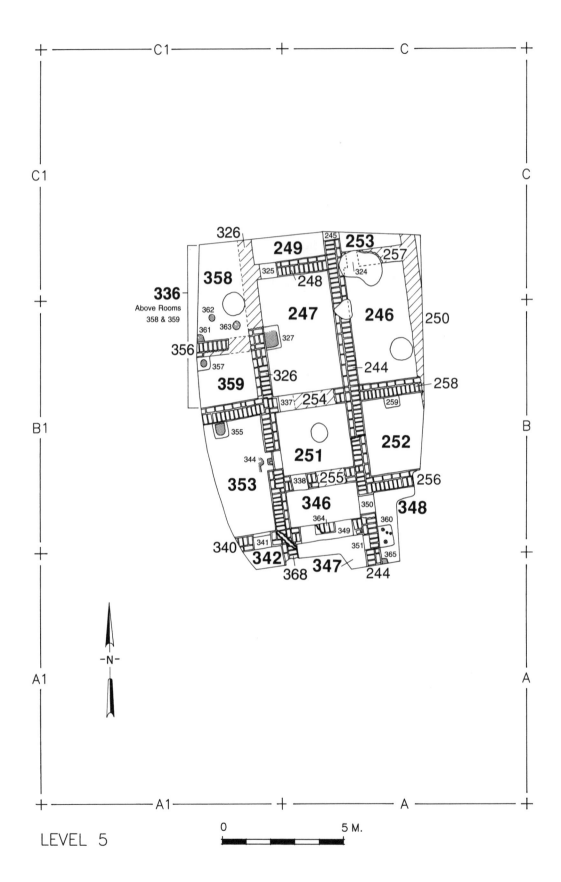

LEVEL 5

0   5 M.

Plan of Building Level 5.

FIGURE 9

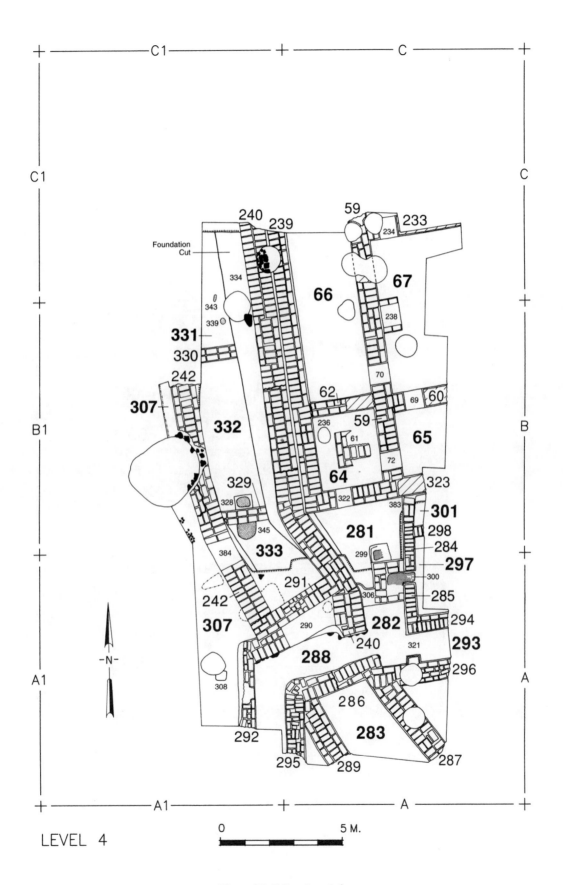

LEVEL 4

0   5 M.

Plan of Building Level 4.

FIGURE 10

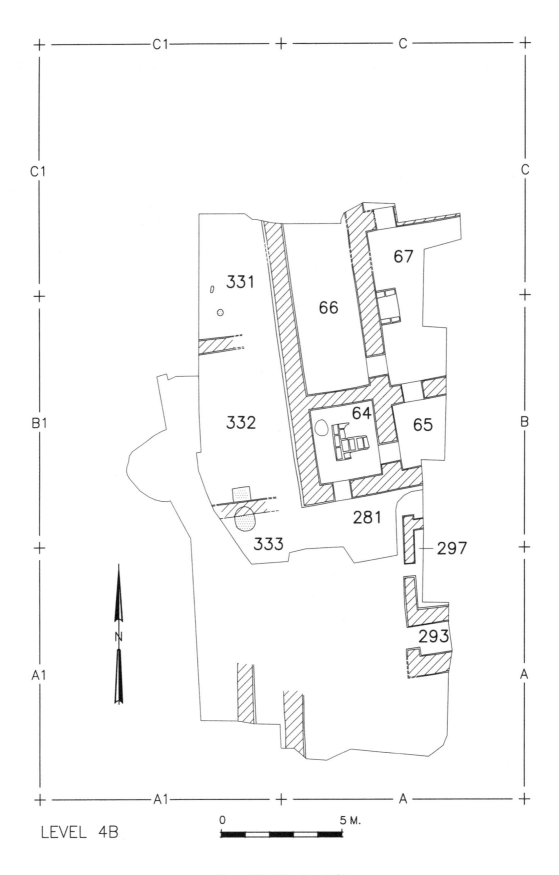

LEVEL 4B

Plan of Building Level 4B.

FIGURE 11

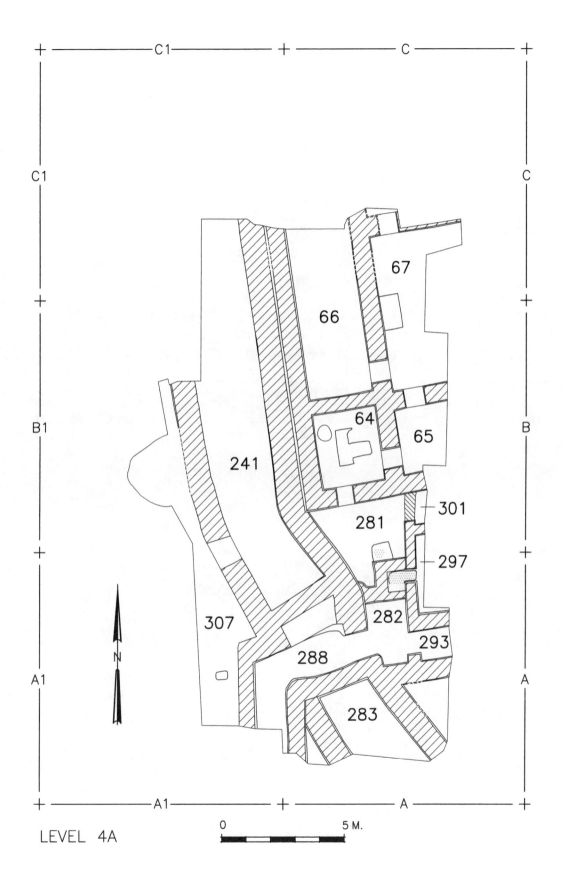

LEVEL 4A

0   5 M.

Plan of Building Level 4A.

FIGURE 12

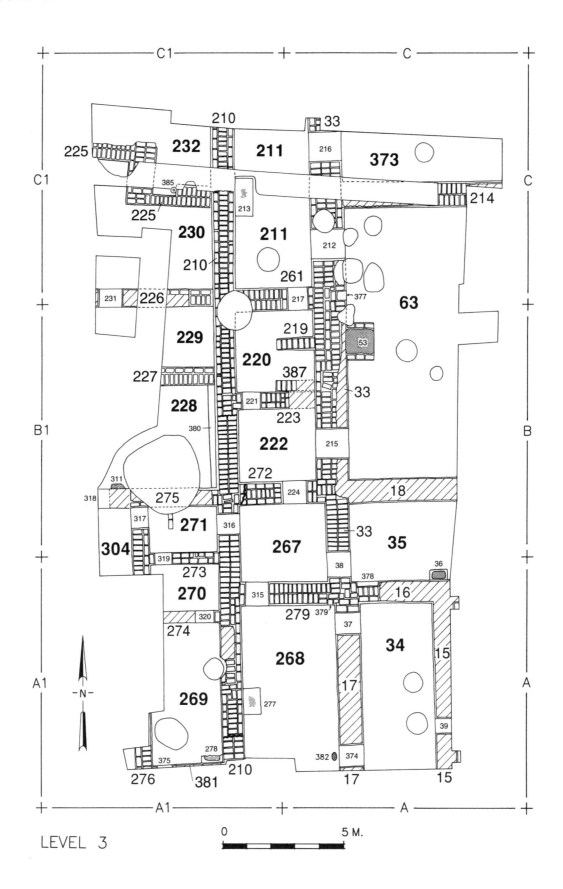

LEVEL 3

0   5 M.

Plan of Building Level 3.

FIGURE 13

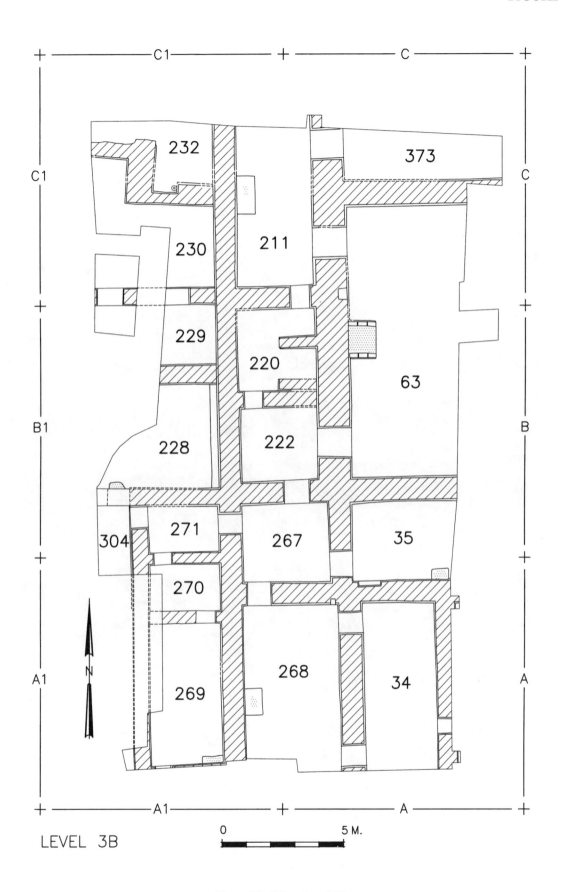

LEVEL 3B

0   5 M.

Plan of Building Level 3B.

FIGURE 14

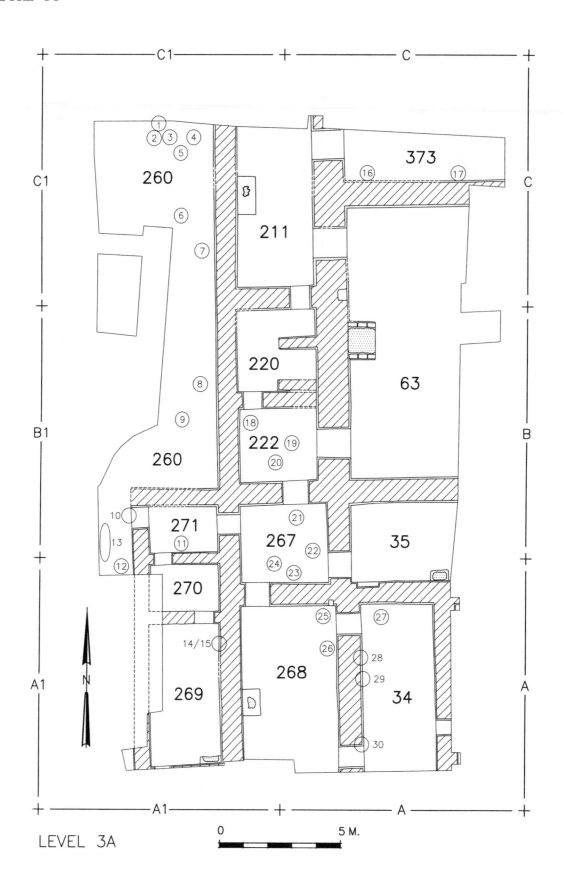

LEVEL 3A

0   5 M.

Plan of Building Level 3A.

FIGURE 15

Wall Paintings, Step Patterns

	Location	Field No.	Strat.
a.	3	ABCN-229	10A
b.	4	ABCN-228	10A
c.	13A	ABCS-154	11A
d.	13C	ABCS-152	11A
e.	11	ABCS-144	10A
f.	2	ABCN-230	10A
g.	21	ABCS-40	10A
h.	13D	ABCS-151	11A
i.	7	ABCN-83	10A
j.	8	ABCN-123	10A

Note: Location is as shown on the Plan of BL 3A (Fig. 14).

FIGURE 15

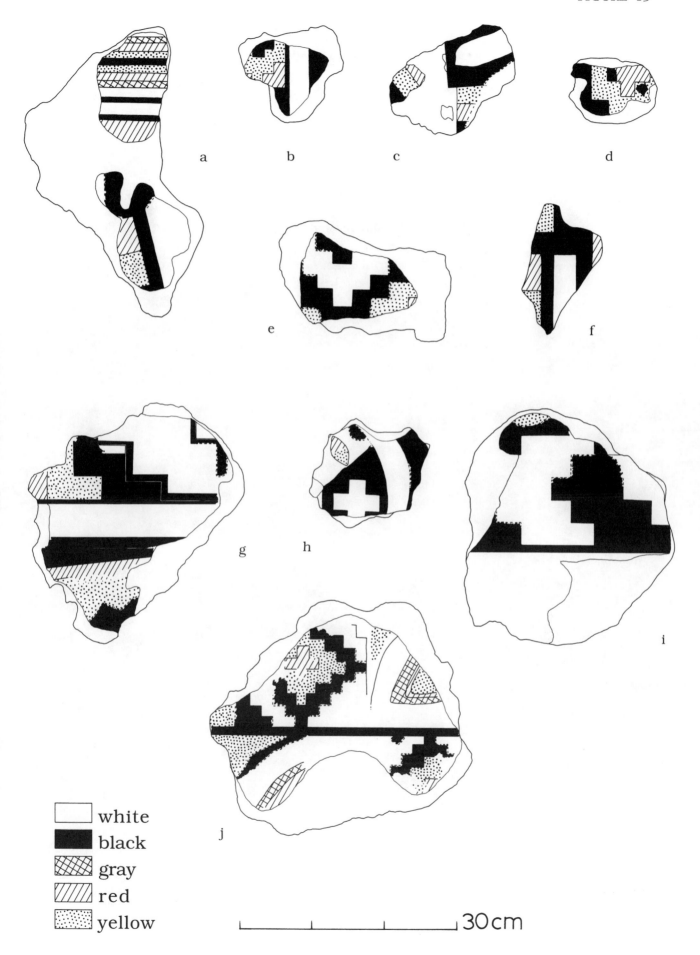

a b c d

e f

g h i

j

white
black
gray
red
yellow

30cm

FIGURE 16

Wall Paintings, Step Patterns

	Location	Field No.	Strat.
a.	20	ABCN-146	10A
b.	18	ABCN-144	10A
c.	5	ABCN-188	10A
d.	26	ABCS-37	10A
e.	15	ABCS-156	10A
f.	28	A-110	10A

Note: Location is as shown on the Plan of BL 3A (Fig. 14).

FIGURE 16

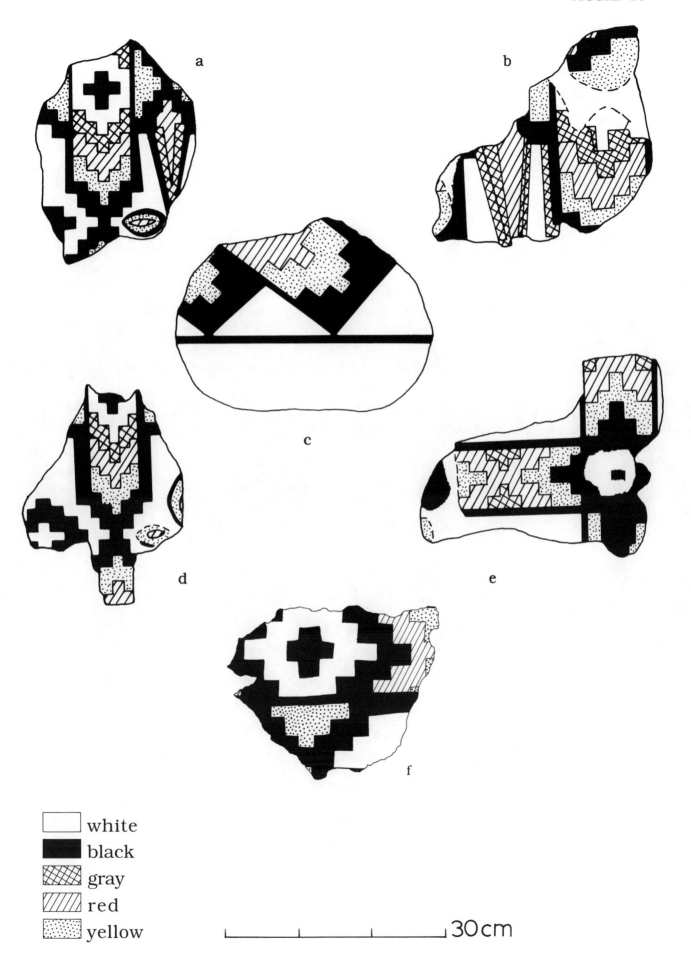

white
black
gray
red
yellow

30cm

FIGURE 17

Wall Paintings, Rosettes

	Location	Field No.	Strat.
a.	29	mf 226	10A
b.	25	ABCS-15	10A

Note: Location is as shown on the Plan of BL 3A (Fig. 14).

FIGURE 17

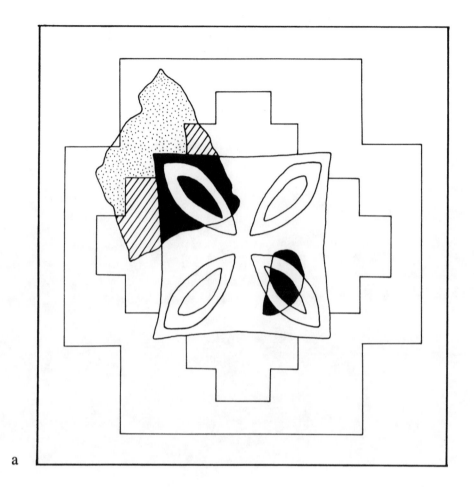

a

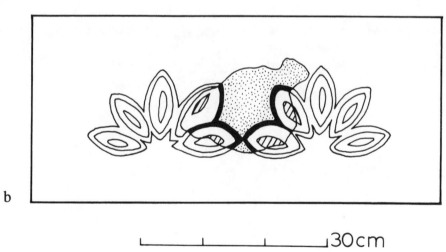

b

30cm

FIGURE 18

Wall Paintings, Step and Rosette

	Location	Field No.	Strat.
a.	10	ABCS-119	10A
b.	16	ABCN-227	10A
c.	12	ABCS-145	10A

Note: Location is as shown on the Plan of BL 3A (Fig. 14).

FIGURE 18

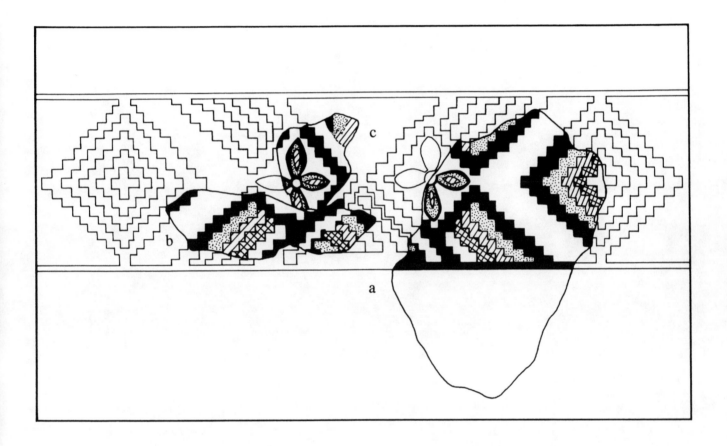

30cm

FIGURE 19

Wall Paintings, Swirl

	Location	Field No.	Strat.
a.	19	ABCN-145	10A
b.	27	A-none	10A
c.	27	A-none	10A
d.	30	A-none	10A
e.	30	A-none	10A

Note: Location is as shown on the Plan of BL 3A
(Fig. 14).

FIGURE 19

30cm

FIGURE 20

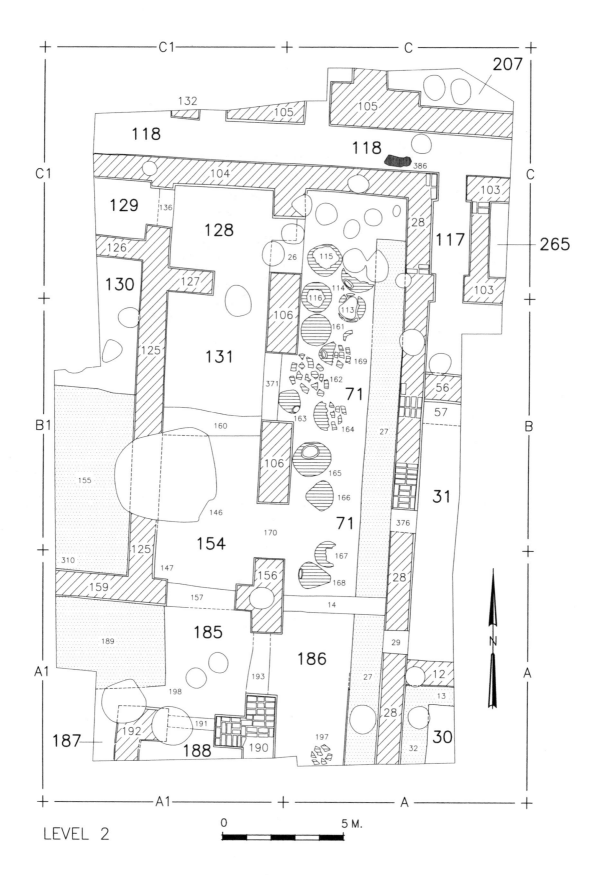

LEVEL 2

0   5 M.

Plan of Building Level 2.

FIGURE 21

Straw Tempered Goblet Rims

	Operation	Lot	BL	DC	Feat.		Operation	Lot	BL	DC	Feat.
a.	ABCN	139	4	23	307	ac.	ABCS	60	12	34	
b.	ABCN	139	4	23	307	ad.	B	44	2	35	71
c.	B	54	12	34		ae.	B	43	2	35	31
d.	ABCN	139	4	23	307	af.	ABCN	149	4	22	236
e.	ABCN	139	4	23	307	ag.	A	44	9	34	
f.	B	54	12	34		ah.	B	66	5	35	253
g.	B	63	4	21	64	ai.	B	49	3	29	63
h.	B	40	K			aj.	B	43	2	35	31
i.	B	49	3	29	63	ak.	B	43	2	35	31
j.	ABCN	139	4	23	307	al	B	54	12	34	
k.	ABCN	139	4	23	307	am.	B	66	5	35	252
l.	ABCN	139	4	23	307	an.	ABCN	146	4	37	64
m.	ABCN	139	4	23	307	ao.	ABCN	146	4	37	64
n.	B	49	3	29	63	ap.	ABCS	26	3	37	269
o.	ABCN	139	4	23	307	aq.	ABCN	125	3	29	211
p.	ABCN	139	4	23	307	ar.	ABCS	76	3	29	269
q.	ABCN	139	4	23	307	as.	ABCS	76	3	29	269
r.	ABCN	139	4	23	307	at.	B	40	K		
s.	ABCN	148	4	22	236	au.	B	44	2	35	71
t.	ABCN	162	4	22	236	av.	ABCN	163	5	41	252
u.	ABCS	55	3	35	260	aw.	ABCN	83	9	34	
v.	ABCN	153	4	22	236	ax.	B	43	2	35	31
w.	ABCS	76	3	29	369	ay.	B	66	5	35	252
x.	ABCS	77	4	21	290	az.	B	44	2	35	71
y.	ABCS	74	4	37	241	ba.	ABCN	139	4	23	307
z.	ABCN	154	4	36	59	bb.	ABCS	72	4	35	241
aa.	ABCN	148	4	22	236	bc.	ABCN	139	4	23	307
ab.	ABCN	162	4	22	236	bd.	ABCS	77	4	21	290

Note: 9 and 12 in the BL column are Strata; K indicates a Kaftari context. Abbreviations used in Figures 22–29: D.A.F.I. 1 is Le Brun 1971, D.A.F.I. 6 is de Miroschedji 1976, D.A.F.I. 9 is Le Brun 1978a, and TUV is Nicholas 1990.

Goblet rim parallels: Acropole I:15B, D.A.F.I. 1, Fig. 60:7-11; Acropole I:17B, D.A.F.I. 9, Fig. 20:9-15; TUV, Plate 13.

Rim types illustrated as follows: Type A = a–k; intermediate A/B = l-r; Type B = s–ac; Type C = ad–ai; Type D = aj–aq; Type E = ar–aw; variants = ax–bd

FIGURE 21

5 cm

FIGURE 22

Straw Tempered Goblet Bases and Other Forms

	Oper.	Lot	BL	DC	Feat.	Notes
a.	B	44	2	35	71	
b.	ABCN	139	4	21	307	
c.	B	44	2	35	71	
d.	ABCN	99	3	37	211	spout Acropole I:17B, D.A.F.I. 9, Fig. 31:6
e.	B	44	2	35	71	spout, Apadana 1038, D.A.F.I. 6, Fig. 7:6
f.	ABCN	142	4	29	67	
g.	ABCN	24	2	36	264	Iran 14, Fig. 8:k
h.	ABC	1	—	41	—	
i.	B	44	2	35	71	
j.	B	47	2	36	57	
k.	B	49	3	29	63	
l.	B	50	2	36	28	
m.	B	50	2	36	28	
n.	ABCS	54	3	37	270	
o.	ABCS	60	12	34	—	
p.	ABCN	146	4	37	64	
q.	B	57	4	37	66	Acropole I:16, D.A.F.I. 1, Fig. 61:6
r.	ABCN	141	4	37	241	mf 2616, Pl.15a, b. Acrop. I:17B, D.A.F.I. 9, Fig. 20:9; Acropole I:17, D.A.F.I. 1, Fig. 47:6, 7; TUV, Pl. 13:u
s.	C1	33	2	35	—	
t.	C1	34	2	37	130	Acropole I:16-15, D.A.F.I. 1, Fig. 60:1-4; TUV, Pl. 13:w-bb
u.	ABCN	139	4	21	307	
v.	ABCN	139	4	21	307	
w.	ABCN	139	4	21	307	
x.	A1	26		Kaftari lot		
y.	ABCS	60	12	34	—	
z.	ABCN	139	4	21	307	
aa.	ABCN	139	4	21	307	
ab.	A1	33	2	37	88	
ac.	ABCS	46	9	23	—	

Note: 9 and 12 in the BL column are Strata.

FIGURE 22

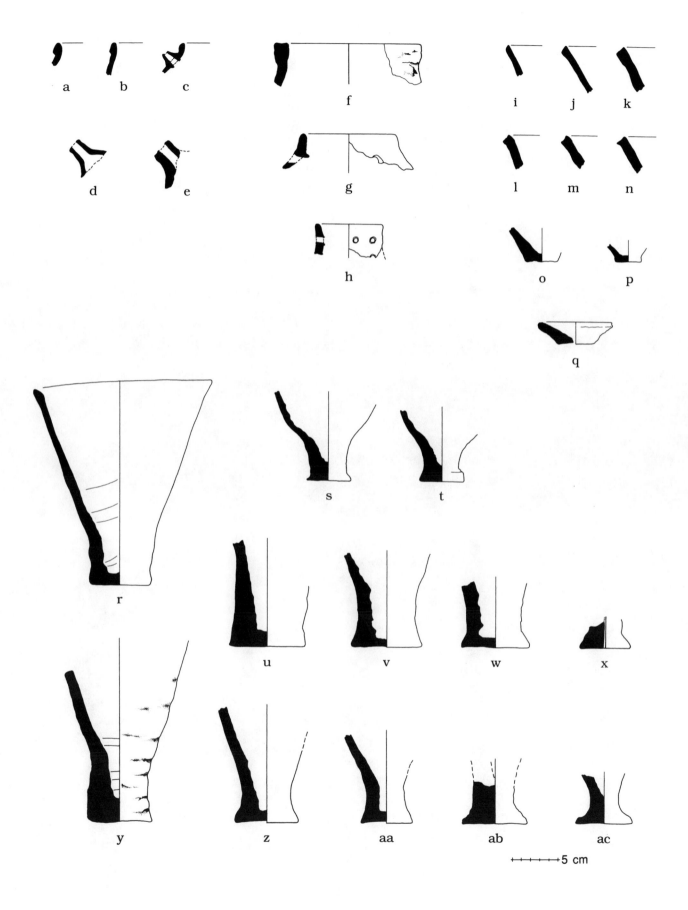

a b c f i j k

d e g l m n

h o p

q

r s t

u v w x

y z aa ab ac

5 cm

FIGURE 23

Straw Tempered Trays

	Oper.	Lot	BL	DC	Feat.
a.	A1	32	2	37	186
b.	B	44	2	35	71
c.	ABCN	139	4	21	307
d.	ABCN	159	4	37	64
e.	ABCN	139	4	21	307

Parallels are found in Acropole I:14,15, D.A.F.I. 1,
Fig. 60:14-17; TUV, Plate 13:a-j, Plate 14:c, d

FIGURE 23

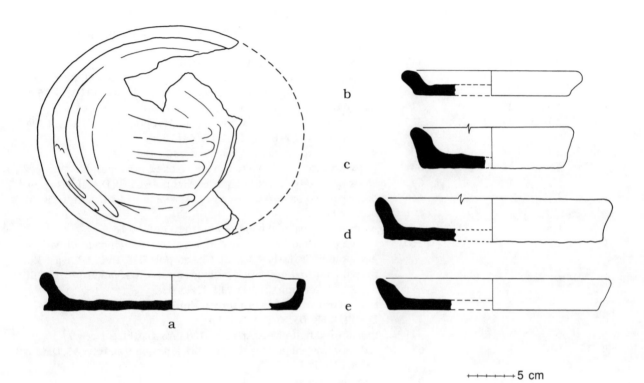

a

b

c

d

e

⊢┼┼┼┼→5 cm

FIGURE 24

Grit Tempered Bowls

	Oper.	Lot	BL	DC	Feat.	Description
a.	ABCS	35	2	29	154	buff slip/brick brown paste. Acropole I:14A, D.A.F.I. 1, Fig. 65:11
b.	B	44	2	35	71	dark brown painted band/buff/brown paste
c.	ABCS	75	3	36	210	dark brown painted band/abrasive red buff/brown paste. TUV, Pl. 20:j
d.	ABCS	9	2	36	106	dark grey painted band burn. rim/buff/orange buff
e.	C	44		Kaftari lot		brown paint/buff slip/st brick paste
f.	ABCN	125	3	29	211	worn brown painted bands/buff slip/grey paste. Acropole I:17B, D.A.F.I. 9, Fig. 34:4
g.	ABCN	14	2	37	117	brown slip above carination/buff paste
h.	ABCN	126	12	34		red slip/brick paste brown core. Acropole I:14A, D.A.F.I. 1, Fig. 65:12
i.	ABCN	90	2	29	118	dark red burnished surface/white gt dark brick paste. TUV, Pl. 15:c
j.	C	66	2	21	71	dark red scraped surface/white gt dark brown paste
k.	ABCN	139	4	21	307	abrasive grey surface/dark grey paste. Acropole I:17B, D.A.F.I. 1, Fig. 45:1;Acropole I:14B, D.A.F.I. 1, Fig. 61:2
l.	ABCN	143	4	37	64	worn dark brown painted band/red buff/brick paste
m.	ABCN	146	4	37	64	brown painted band/white slip above band/brick paste
n.	B	63	4	21	64	black painted band/red/red paste. Acropole I:17B, D.A.F.I. 9, Fig. 34:5
o.	B	63	4	21	64	black painted band/red /red paste. Acropole I:14B, D.A.F.I. 1, Fig. 61:3. Iran 12 Fig.5j
p.	B	63	4	21	64	worn brown painted band/red buff/red buff paste
q.	C	64	2	35	118	brown paint/tan/brick paste dark grey core brown paint BRW. Acropole I:17B, DAFI 9, Fig. 22:12;Acropole I:13, D.A.F.I. 1, Fig. 65:6
r.	C	21		Kaftari lot		brown paint/red buff/brick paste grey core. Acropole I:17B, D.A.F.I. 9, Fig. 22:12;Acropole I:13, D.A.F.I. 1, Fig. 65:6
s.	C1	33	2	35	131	streaky brown paint/worn brown slip/brick paste. Acropole I:13, D.A.F.I. 1, Fig. 65:16;TUV, Pl. 20:n
t.	B	63	4	21	64	red slip/red buff paste. Apadana 1083:A6, D.A.F.I. 6, Fig. 4:9
u.	B	63	4	21	64	red slip/crushed pottery temper? brick paste. Apa. 1083:A5, D.A.F.I. 6, Fig. 4:12;TUV, Pl. 20:d
v.	B	63	4	21	64	grey slip/grey paste
w.	ABCN	14	2	37	117	worn buff slip/brick paste
x.	B	63	4	21	64	worn grey slip/grey buff paste
y.	ABCS	70	3	29	267	black painted band/red slip/no visible temper crumbly tan paste. Acropole I:17B, D.A.F.I. 9, Fig. 22:4;Apadana 1038:A3, D.A.F.I. 6, Fig. 4:1
z.	ABCN	37	9	34		burnished grey/grey paste brown core.
aa.	A	44	9	35		grey/grey paste. TUV, Pl. 21:g
ab.	C1	34	2	37	130	grey slip/grey paste. Acropole I:17B, D.A.F.I. 9, Fig. 22:17;Acropole I:15, D.A.F.I. 1, Fig. 61:12;TUV, Pl. 20:m, 21:h
ac.	ABCS	59	3	29	35	buff/tan paste. Acro. I:15, D.A.F.I. 1, Fig. 61:13

Note: 9 and 12 in the BL column are Strata.

FIGURE 24

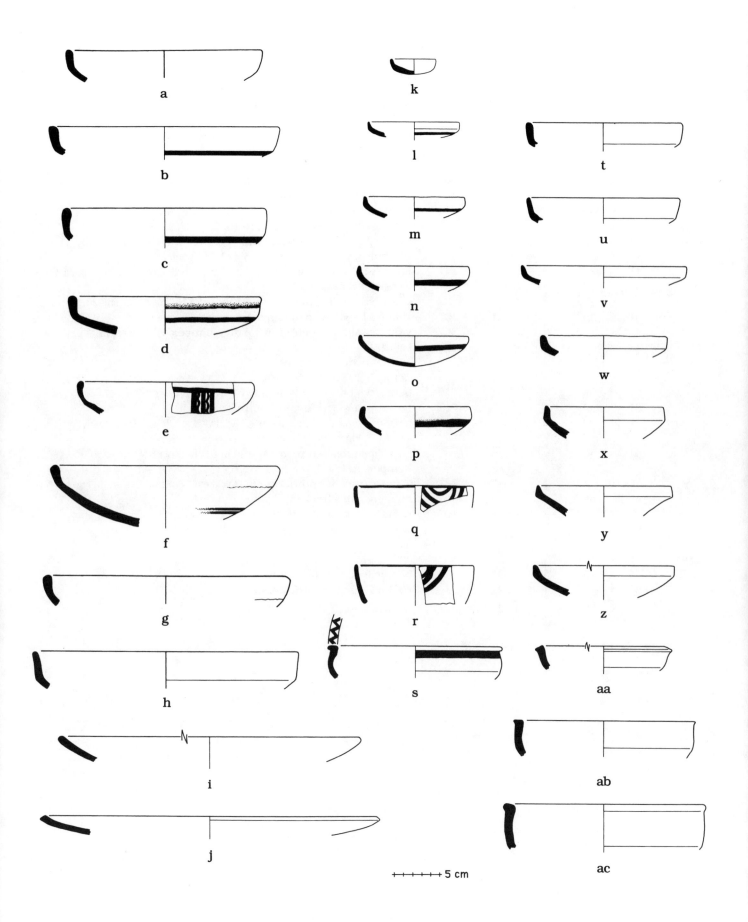

+++++→ 5 cm

FIGURE 25

Grit Tempered Closed Forms

	Oper.	Lot	BL	DC	Feat.	Description
a.	ABCN		2	37	128	black painted bands/red/red paste; general form, black bands, Acropole I:15, D.A.F.I. 1, Fig. 63:1; rim form Acropole I:1??, D.A.F.I. 1, Fig. 66;TUV, Pls. 17:g and 19:j
b.	ABCN	139	4	21	307	buff/buff paste.Acropole I:17B, D.A.F.I. 9, Fig. 27:7
c.	ABCS	35	2	29	154	crackled brown slip/brown paste. Apadana 1038:A1, 2, D.A.F.I.6, Fig. 6:15, 16. TUV, Pl. 19:e
d.	ABCN	139	4	21	307	brown slip/buff. Acrop. I:17B, D.A.F.I. 9, Fig. 24:5, 7
e.	ABCN	139	4	21	307	abrasive buff/brown paste dark core
f.	ABCS	55	3	35	260	tan/dark brick
g.	ABCN	139	4	21	307	Apadana 1038:B, D.A.F.I. 6, Fig. 6:10;TUV, Pl. 19:t
h.	C1	33	2	35		brown painted bands white wash between shoulder bands/tan slip/brown paste. Acropole I:15, D.A.F.I. 1, Fig. 63:1, 2
i.	ABCN	125	3	29	211	impressed band worn black painted band/red slip/brick brown paste
j.	B	57	4	37	66	abrasive red buss/brick paste
k.	ABCN	139	4	21	307	white wash/red tan/tan paste.Acropole I:17B, D.A.F.I. 9, Fig. 26:3
l.	ABCN	139	4	21	307	abrasive grey/grey paste brown core
m.	ABCN	139	4	21	307	worn red slip/red buff/brown paste. Acropole I:17B, D.A.F.I. 9, Fig. 29:1
n.	A	44	9	35		red buff/white gt grey paste. Acropole I:17B, D.A.F.I. 9, Fig. 24:3
o.	C	66	2	21	71	buff/green buff paste.Acropole I:15, D.A.F.I. 1, Fig. 63:9
p.	B1	37	2	35	71	brown painted band/buff/buff paste
q.	ABCN	90	2	29	118	red/brown paste. Apadana 1038:A5, D.A.F.I. 6, Fig. 6:4;Acropole I:15, D.A.F.I. 1, Fig. 63:3;TUV, Pl. 18:i
r.	ABCS	46	9	23	-	grey slip/st red buff paste. Acropole I:17B, D.A.F.I. 9, Fig. 26:6; Acropole I:116, 15, D.A.F.I. 1, Fig. 63:13. 14
s.	ABCN	141	4	37	241	abrasive brown slip/brick paste. Apadana 1038:A4, D.A.F.I. 6, Fig. 6:8
t.	ABCS	85	4	35	307	buff lime pops/brick buff paste.
u.	ABCN	139	4	21	307	red tan/brick paste dark core
y.	C	64	2	35	118	worn brown painted rim impressed rope/red buff/dark red paste dark core
w.	ABCN	139	4	21	307	
x.	ABCN	158	5	37	247	buff lime pops/st buff paste
y.	B	63	4	21	64	red buff lime pops/brick paste
z.	ABCN	99	3	37	211	tan/tan paste

Note: 9 in the BL column is Stratum.

FIGURE 25

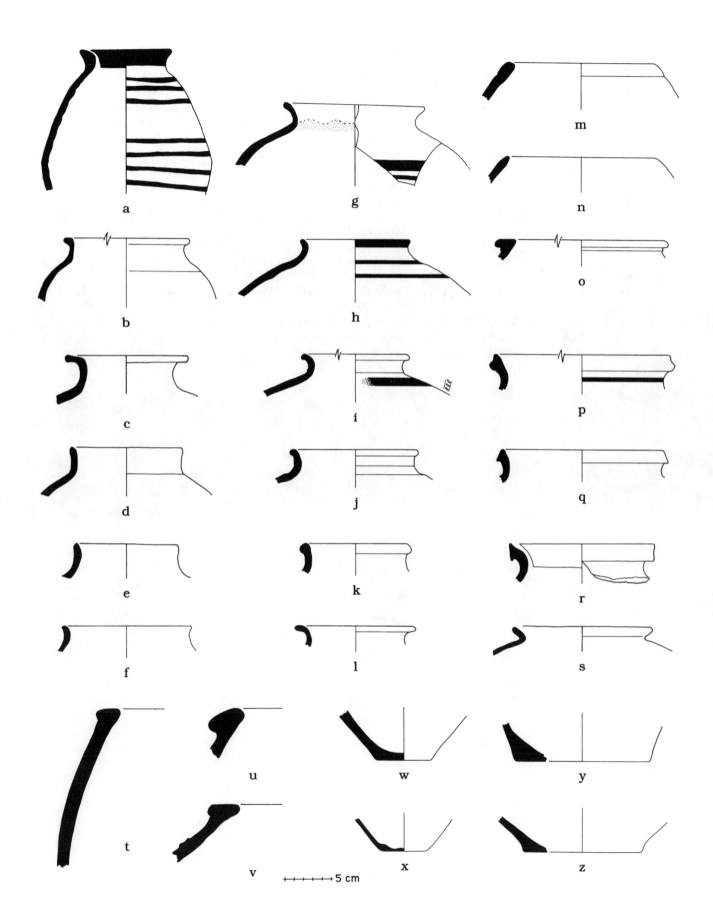

FIGURE 26

Special Grit Tempered Forms

	Oper.	Lot	BL	DC	Feat.	Description
a.	ABCN	74	3	36	33	buff slip/red brown. Acropole I:17, D.A.F.I. 1, Fig. 45:11
b.	B	66	5	35	252	black painted bands/white slip between bands/red slip/tan paste
c.	ABC	20	4	28	331	burnished grey/grey paste. mf 3770. Acropole I:17, D.A.F.I. 1, Fig. 45:4
d.	ABCN	139	4	21	307	red slip/brick paste dark core
e.	ABCS	60	12	34	-	brown painted band/tan slip over rim to line/brown paste. Acropole I:17, D.A.F.I. 1, Fig. 46:16, 17
f.	ABCN	126	12	34	-	streaky red bands or worn slip lime pops/brick buff paste
g.	A	4	Kaftari lot			maroon paint/white slip above carination/red buff paste dark core. Acropole I:15B, D.A.F.I. 1, Fig. 64:8
h.	B	63	4	21	6	brown painted bands/brown slip/brown paste grey core. Iran 12 Fig. 5h. Acropole I:14B, D.A.F.I. 1, Fig. 64:6
i.	ABCS	88	4	35	297	black paint/white slip/brick buff paste
j.	ABCS	35	2	29	154	worn black painted band/brick buff paste. Acropole I:17B, D.A.F.I. 9, Fig. 24:9, 10
k.	ABCN	86	3	37	63	black paint/red slip/orange buff paste
l.	ABCS	50	2	51	155	abrasive buff/brick paste

Note: 12 in the BL column is Stratum.

FIGURE 26

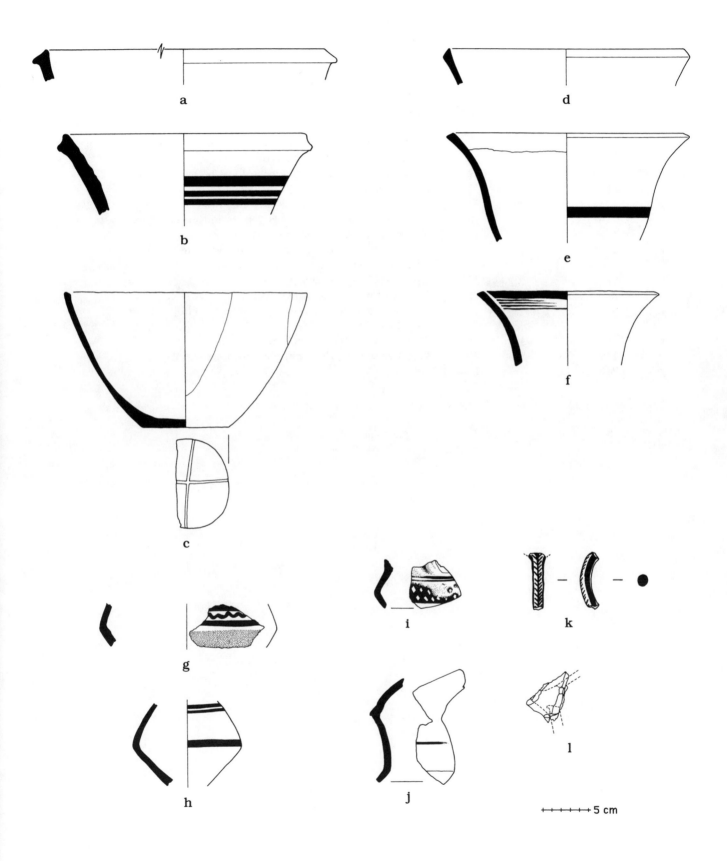

FIGURE 27

Relief Decorated Pottery

	mf	BL	DC	Feat	Description
a.	1731	2	29	118	Pl. 16a, white chalky paste on leaves and rope /brick/no visible temper orange red paste. Iran 14 Fig 3a , Pl. IVe
b.	1732		Kaftari lot		white paste missing/brick/no visible temper orange red paste
c.	1049	3A	37	268	Pl. 17a, applied cow relief slightly separated from surface at edge/exterior brown slip interior red slip/brown paste. Iran 14 Fig. 3b Pl. IVg
d.	1043	9	34	—	Pl. 17d, relief bovine carved? worn black paint?/white paste on surface/interior burnished/st red paste
e.	1192	3A	35	220	Pl. 16b, lid, white paste/relief incised leaf/buff slip/red paste
f.	nr		Kaftari lot		brick/brick paste
g.	1733	3B	29	34	grey buff interior red interior/dark grey paste
h.	1187	3A	37	269	Pl. 17g, white paste on rope/black paint in rope cracks/red paste
i.	1186	3B	29	260	Pl. 17e, white past/red buff/st red grey core.
j.	1003	—	41	—	Pl. 17c, possible rider's leg tan slip on buff paste background/brick paste. Iran 14 Fig 3d
k.	nr	2	35	71	appliquéd grey/grey paste
l.	nr	2	37	71	dark grey/bricky paste brown core
m.	nr		Kaftari lot		red/red paste grey core possibly from inside Pithos 114 or 115. Iran 12 Fig. 7d
n.	1044	2	36	156	Pl. 16d, fugitive black paint/buff slip/st buff paste
o.	1193	3A	29	260	Pl. 16c, light orange lime pops/st buff paste
p.	746	2	37	131	tile?

Note: Items f and k-m listed as "nr" were not registered. 9 in BL column is stratum.

FIGURE 27

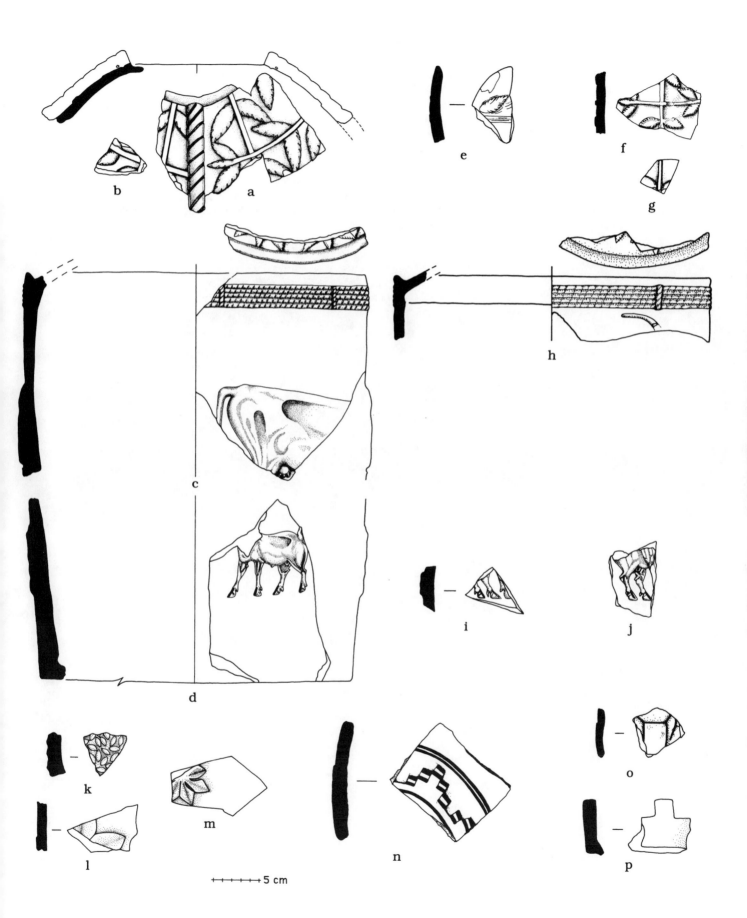

+++++→5 cm

FIGURE 28

Pithoi From BL 2

a.   From Room 71, the form illustrated is Pythos 168. The painted design is from Pithos 115, which is more sharply carinated than the form shown.

b.   This sherd (mf 219) was recorded in a mixed Stratum 9 lot, but is probably from BL 2 Room 186, possibly from Pythos 187.

c.   From Room 71, design from an unidentified pithos.

d.   From Room 71; compare Yahya IVC, Lamberg-Karlovsky 1973, Fig. 4:A.

e.   From Room 71, Pythos 162, black paint/smooth orange-red/fine black grit, brick red paste.

f.   From Room 71, painted design from Pithos 168, form as illustrated in Fig. 27:a.

g.   From Room 71, pithos rim (mf 1726, Pl. 18a), buff red surface with brown firing bloom/red paste. Outside rim dia. ca. 58 cm; inside dia. ca. 34 cm. The incised potters mark is a common Proto-Elamite sign, # 1 in Brice's sign list (Brice 1962, Fig. 1).

FIGURE 28

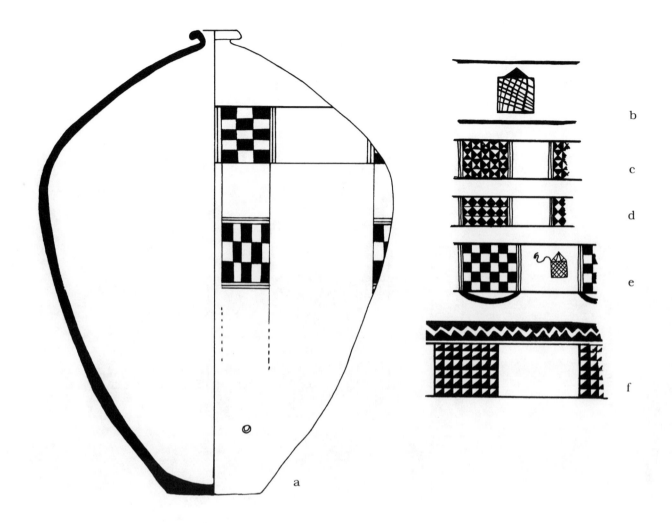

b

c

d

e

f

├──┼──┼──┼──┤ 25 cm

a

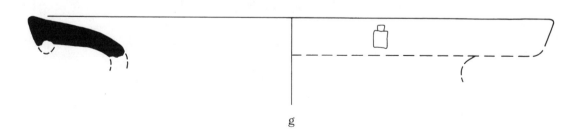

g

├──┼──┤ 5 cm

FIGURE 29

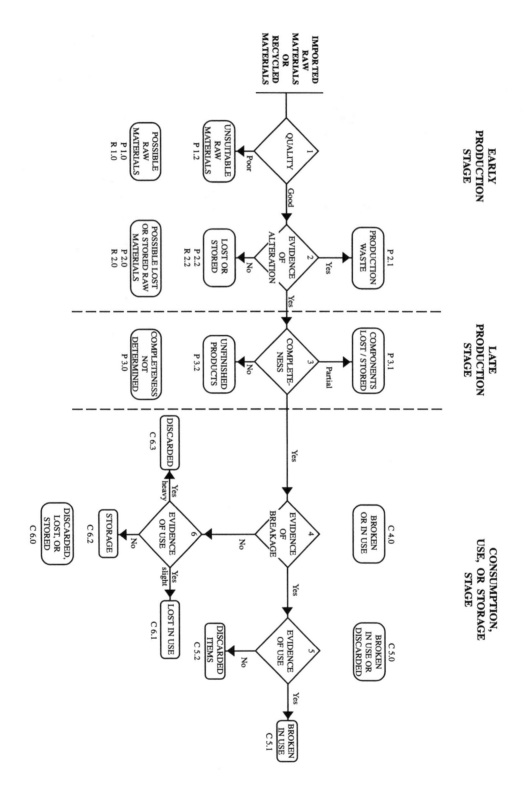

The production, use, and discard cycle of finds.

FIGURE 30

Flint Core and Flakes

	mf	BL	DC	Feat.	Description
a.	3922	—	50	369	Pl.19, core
b.	6564	2	36	28	PDF, retouch, cut meat
c.	1225	2	36	14	2DF, heat treated
d.	6598	3A	41	267	2DF, retouch, no wear
e.	6609	3A	35	220	2DF, no wear
f.	6602	2	37	207	2DF
g.	2184	4A	37	65	2DF, no wear

Note: In Figures 30-35 the edges that showed microscopic traces of wear are indicated by a line parallel to the worn edge and the direction of movement in tool use is indicated by arrows.

FIGURE 30

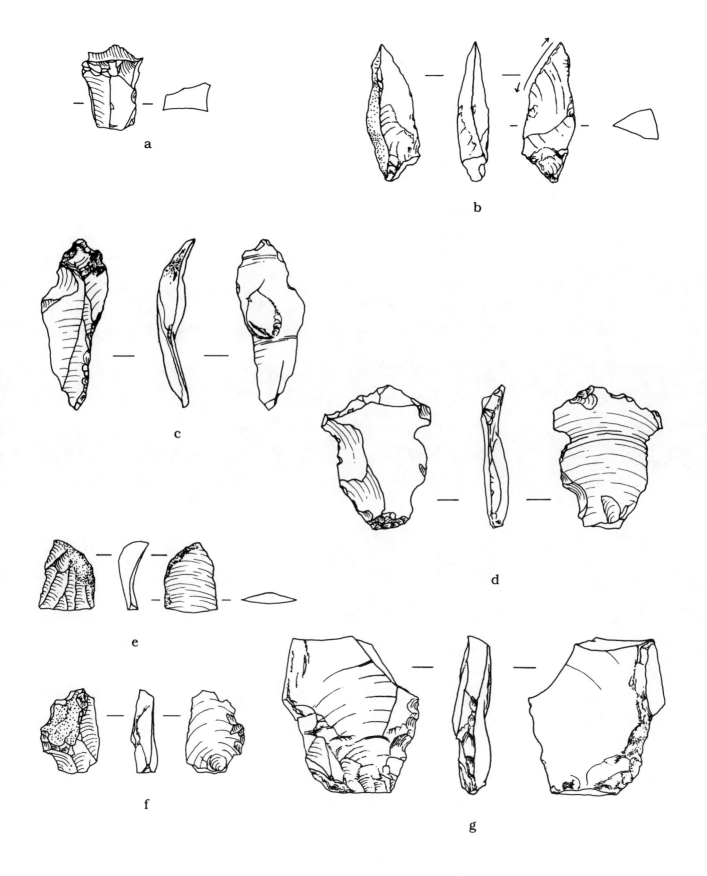

FIGURE 31

Flint Flakes

	mf	BL	DC	Feat.	Description
a.	1231	3A	29	260	2NCF, retouch, calcium carbonate on ventral face
b.	7019	4A	35	283	2NCF, no wear
c.	6663	2	29	118	2NCF, retouch, notch, no wear
d.	6616	2	29	118	2NCF
e.	6640	3B	29	63	2NCF

FIGURE 31

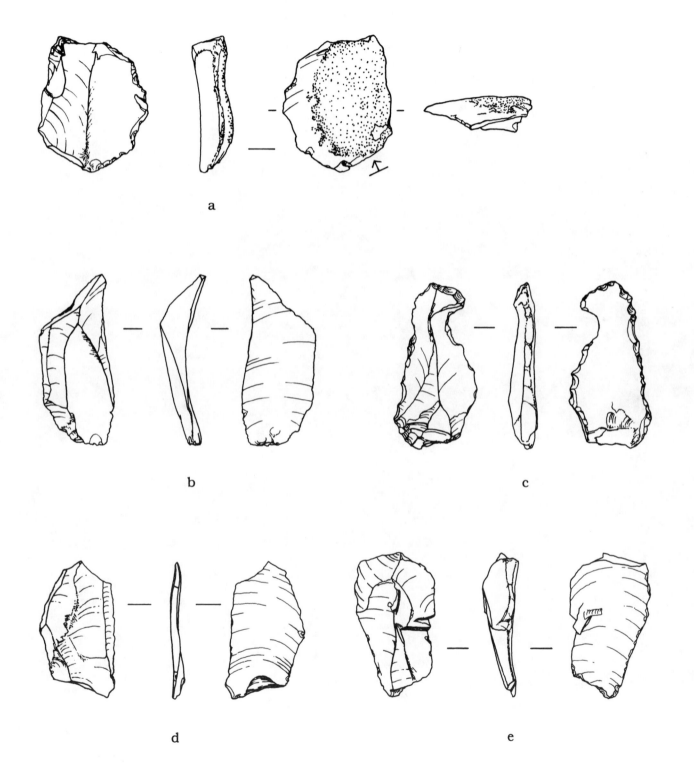

a

b

c

d

e

FIGURE 32

Flint Flakes

	mf	BL	DC	Feat.	Description
a.	1237	3A	35	211	2NCF, cut meat?
b.	6625	3A	37	211	2NCF
c.	7006	—	34	—	2NCF, no wear
d.	7012	2	28	310	2NCF, heat treated, no wear
e.	9908	3A	29	63	2NCF
f.	6556	4A	37	65	3NCF

FIGURE 32

a

b

c

e

d

f

FIGURE 33

Flint Blades and Blade Segments

	mf	BL	DC	Feat.	Description
a.	7002	3A	37	269	Blade
b.	1238		34		Blade
c.	1236	3A	35	211	Pl. 20b, Denticulated, gloss, bitumen hafting
d.	6656	4A	37	64	PBS
e.	7026		34		Pl. 24, PBS, shaving soft stone?
f.	6619	3A	35	260	PBS, weak gloss,
g.	6662	2	29	118	PBS, backed, gloss
h.	7027	4A	21	307	PBS
i.	6629	3B	29	229	PBS

FIGURE 33

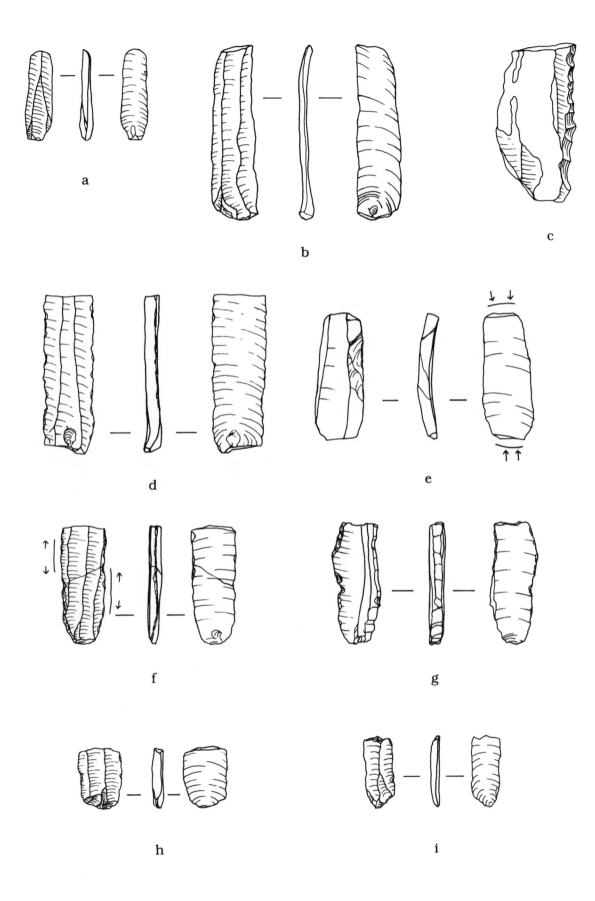

a

b

c

d

e

f

g

h

i

FIGURE 34

Flint Blades and Blade Segments

	mf	BL	DC	Feat.	Description
a.	2573	2	37	128	pl. 23b, c; MBS, denticulated, gloss, grass
b.	6661	2	29	118	MBS, heat treated
c.	1221	3A	37	211	MBS
d.	6657	4A	37	64	MBS
e.	6612	3A	37	220	MBS, gloss, grass
f.	7021	3B	29	268	MBS, backed, no wear
g.	6643	3B	29	211	MBS, retouch
h.	6648	4A	35	66	DBS, gloss, grass
i.	6624	3A	37	211	MBS, gloss, grass
j.	6541	3A	37	63	DBS, no wear
k.	6630	3B	29	229	DBS, cortical

FIGURE 34

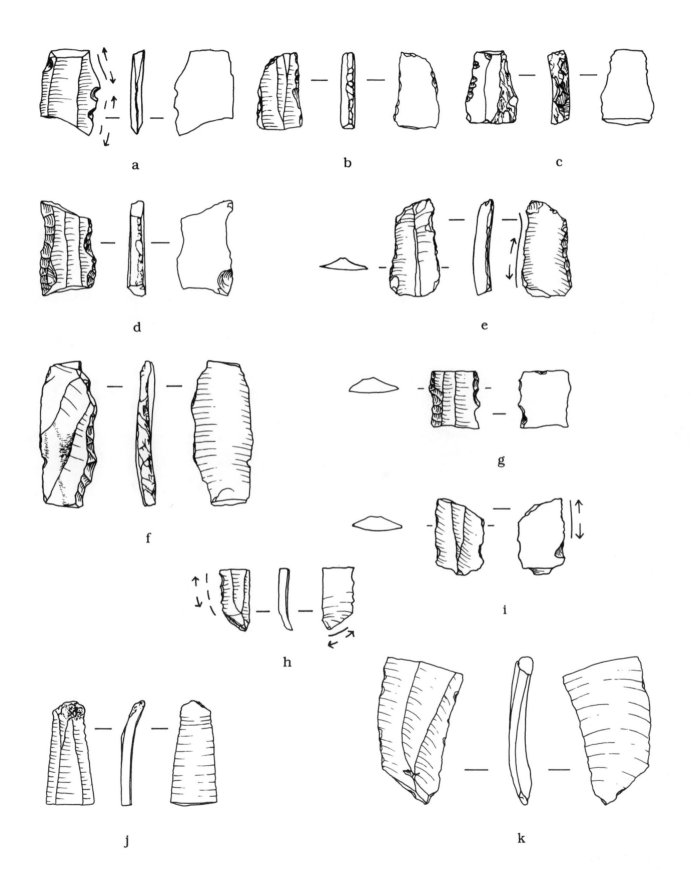

a

b

c

d

e

f

g

h

i

j

k

FIGURE 35

Flint Pointed Tools, Points, Scraper, and Drills

	mf	BL	DC	Feat.	Description
a.	1065	2	35	207	2NCF, pointed
b.	2119.3	2	35	71	2NCF, pointed/scrape bone
c.	579	2	35	131	Pl. 20a, 2NCF, stemmed point/no wear
d.	6628	3B	29	229	Pl. 23d, 2NCF, end scraper/scrape hide
e.	6607	2	29	71	2NCF, tranchet/no wear
f.	2108	3A	37	63	2NCF, tranchet/no wear
g.	2176		34		2NCF, tranchet/no wear
h.	6542.5	2	36	28	2DF, pointed, drill?
i.	1082	2	36	106	2NCF, drill?
j.	7001.2	3A	37	269	3NCF, drill, bitumen/hard material

FIGURE 35

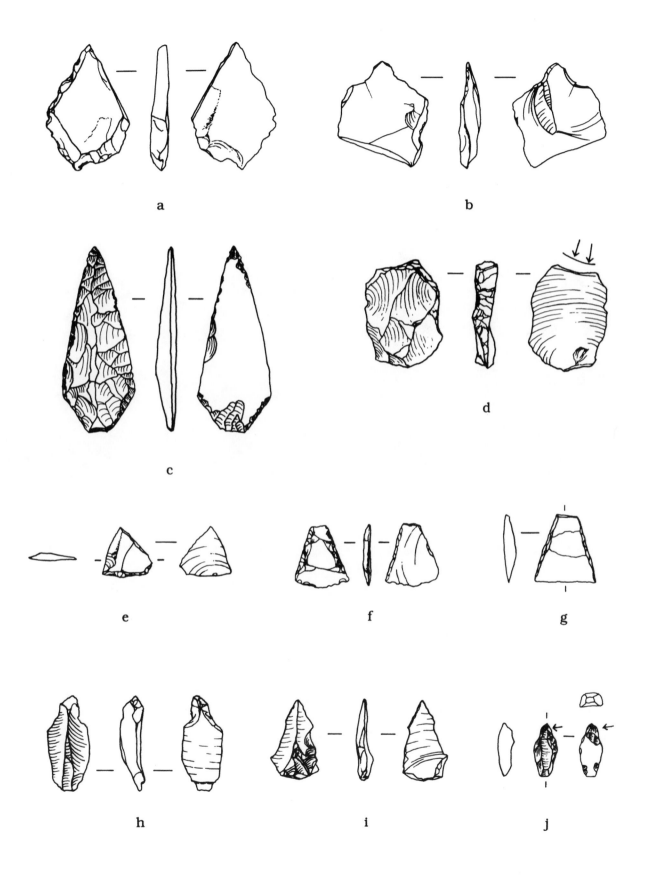

a

b

c

d

e

f

g

h

i

j

FIGURE 36

Metal Objects

	mf	BL	DC	Feat.	Description
a.	1134	2	36	371	Pl. 20e, cu/br hook
b.	1135	2	37	207	cu/br ring
c.	1148	—	41	—	cu/br ring
d.	1142	—	41	—	cu/br ring
e.	199	2	36	28	cu/br ring
f.	607	2	35	71	Pl. 20d, cu/br tube (reconstruction)
g	1918	4B	29	66	Pl. 20c, cu/br pin
h.	1916	5	37	247	Pl. 20c, cu/br pin
i.	1132	—	40	—	cu/br needle
j.	1496	3A	23	304	Pl. 20c, cu/br pin
k.	2455	2	21	118	lead
l.	9841	9	34	—	lead
m.	2315	2	37	154	lead
n.	1136	9	34	—	lead
o.	2314	2	37	154	lead or silver
p.	760	2	37	154	cu/br chisel ?
q.	6435	2	37	154	cu/br bar

Note: 9 in the BL column is stratum.

FIGURE 36

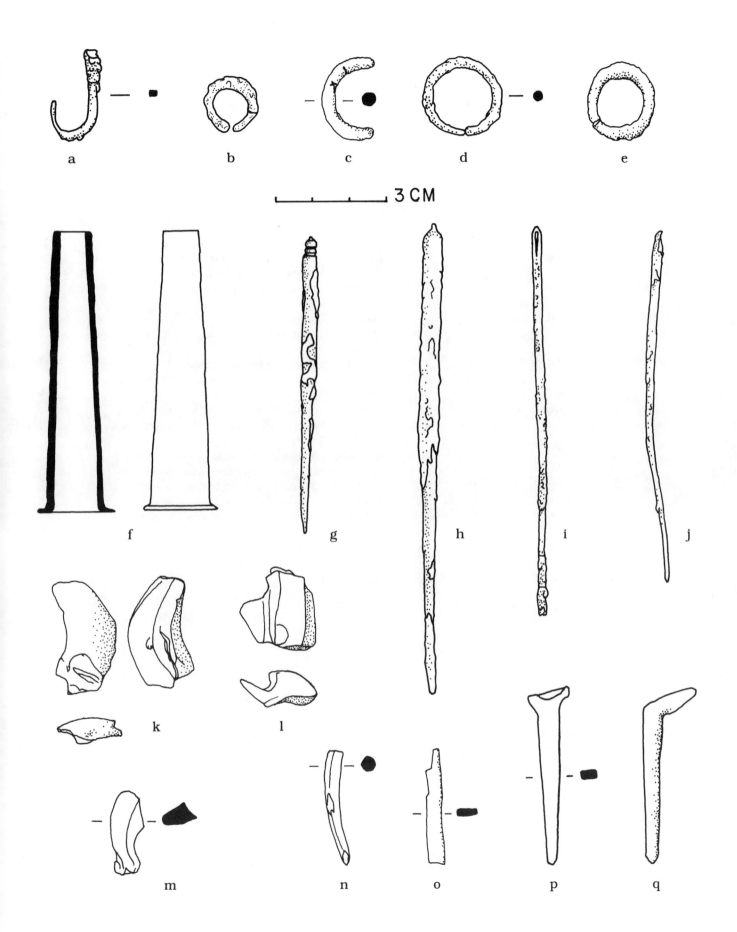

a   b   c   d   e

3 CM

f   g   h   i   j

k   l

m   n   o   p   q

FIGURE 37

Stone Beads and Bead Production

	mf	BL	DC	Feat.	Description
a.	2292.1	2	35	131	broken crystal
b.	2292.2	2	35	131	broken crystal, hexagonal section
c.	2583	2	35	131	wind-deflated, crystal fragment, flattened section, pinkish shadow
d.	2584	2	35	131	wind-deflated, crystal fragment
e.	6718	3A	37	63	rose quartz, parallel wind deflation striations on 3 sides, and a fracture on a 4th
f.	2438	2	35	128	rock crystal rolled pebble, opaque cortex, chipped apex, possibly cracked along an inner cleavage plane
g.	1285	3A	35	270	broken, unfinished crystal bead, diameter > 0.83.
h.	9788	3B	36	53	defective blocklet of clinoptilolite, traces of preliminary stages of forming by grinding
i.	9789	4A	37	64	unfinished broken clinoptilolite bead
j.	1019	2	37	71	clay bead
k.	2201	4A	21	64	flake of clinoptilolite
l.	1026	2	36	160	crystal, hexagonal section rolled into a pebble, opaque cortex
m.	2091	2	35	31	turquoise (?), weathered, some cortex
n.	9836	2	36	106	flake, calcite or travertine, light brown (7.5 YR 6/4)
o.	6717	2	35	118	agate
p.	7302	4B	36	59	carnelian barrel-shaped bead blank, weathered, lost or discarded after grinding, retains chipping traces, color (2.5 YR 6/8)
q.	6743	3B	29	34	broken bead in light-green, turquoise-like stone or possibly faience, porous, powdery, badly weathered
r.	1288	3A	35	222	sub-cylindrical disk bead in white stone or shell
s.	1308	2	36	155	sub-cylindrical disk bead, white stone or shell
t.	1300	3A	35	267	carnelian biconical disk bead, yellowish brown (10 YR 5/8)
u.	7425.2	4A	22	236	red steatite biconical disk bead
v.	7425.1	4A	22	236	red steatite biconical disk bead
w.	7499	2	36	14	calcite crystal

FIGURE 37

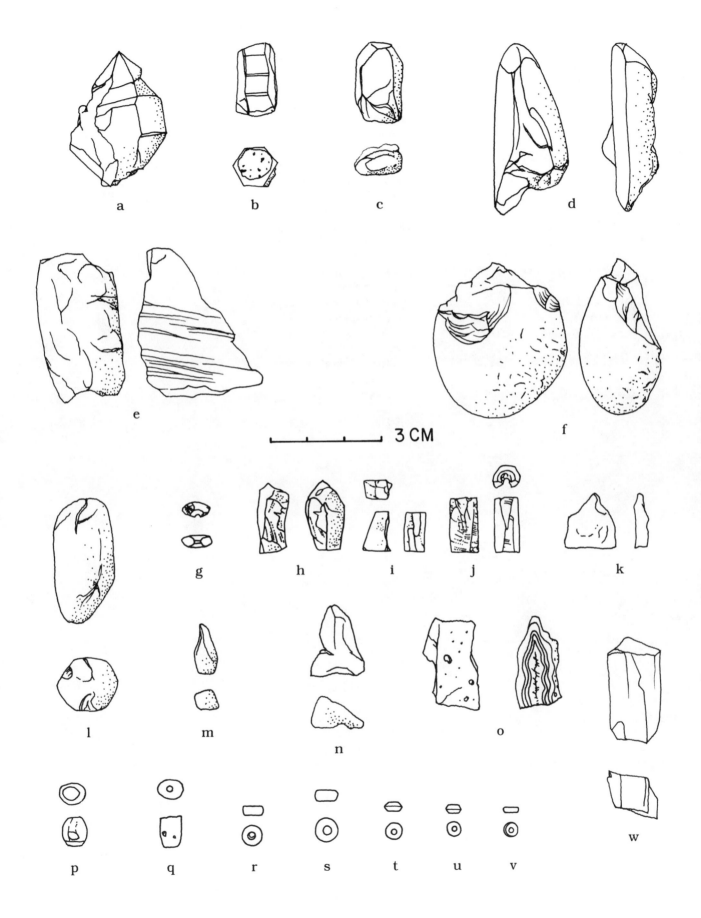

3 CM

FIGURE 38

Organic Beads and Ostrich Shell

	mf	BL	DC	Feat.	Description
a.	2071	—	31	—	ostrich egg shell
b.	9868	—	31	—	ostrich egg shell
c.	6795	4A	37	64	fish vertebra, outer surface carved
d.	6793	2	37	207	fish vertebra, traces of yellow pigment in central carved band, traces of black on the upper and lower bands
e.	6664	2	37	207	fish vertebra, outer surface carved, traces of yellow pigment (2.5 Y 8/6) on the upper and lower surfaces; central perforation in all 3 fish vertebra beads seem to have been pierced rather than drilled
f.	1921.1	2	29	129	bitumen (?) disk bead
g.	764	2	21	118	charred wooden disk
h.	6737	3A	37	211	short cylindrical bead
i.	1305	2	37	118	square bitumen 2 hole spacer
j.	1294	2	37	207	shell (?), edge not smoothed
k.	7425.3	4A	22	236	dentalium, flotation
l.	1921.2	2	29	129	bitumen (?), from hole in mf 1921.1
m.	6740	4A	37	64	biconical bitumen
n.	6739	4A	37	64	biconical bitumen bead
o.	6738	3B	36	210	worn bitumen
p.	6698	3B	36	53	rounded biconical bitumen
q.	6698	3B	36	53	short cylindrical bitumen

FIGURE 38

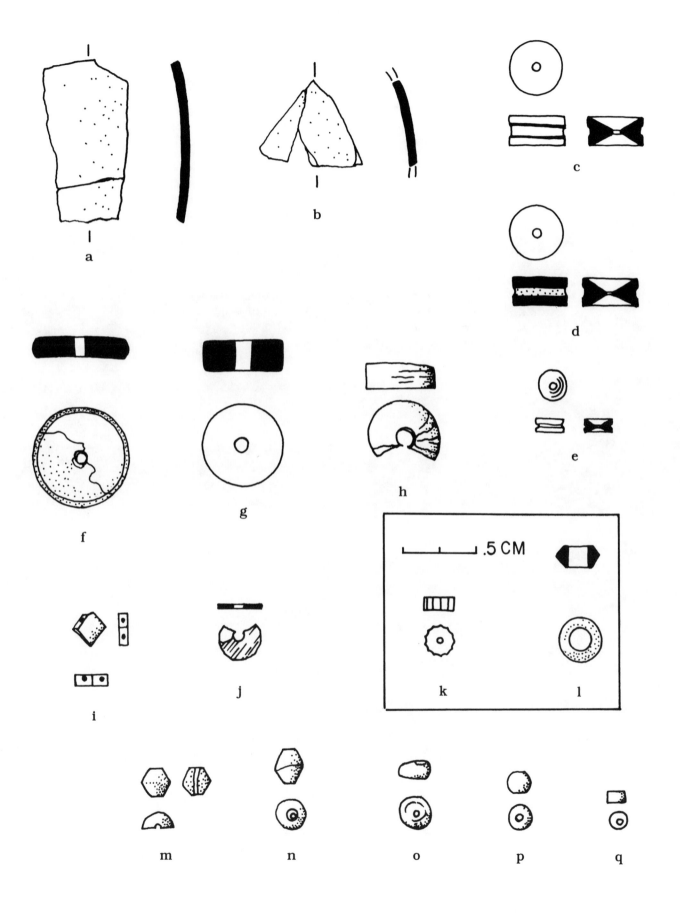

FIGURE 39

Mother of Pearl Inlay

	mf	BL	DC	Feat.	Description
a.	2448	2	37	118	
b.	1002	2	41	130	
c.	756.2	2	37	130	
d.	751.3	2	37	130	now broken into 3 pieces
e.	6421.1	2	37	154	
f.	6421.2	2	37	154	
g.	751.1	2	37	130	incised
h.	751.2	2	37	130	incised
i.	749.3	2	21	131	incised
j.	749.4	2	21	131	incised
k-m.	2448	2	37	118	
n.	741	2	35	154	
o.	2448	2	37	118	
p.	2448	2	37	118	
q.	745.1	2	37	154	central hole and incision
r.	6454	2	35	131	white stone inlay
s.	756.1	2	35	131	
t.	745.2	2	37	154	
u-dd.	2448	2	37	118	

FIGURE 39

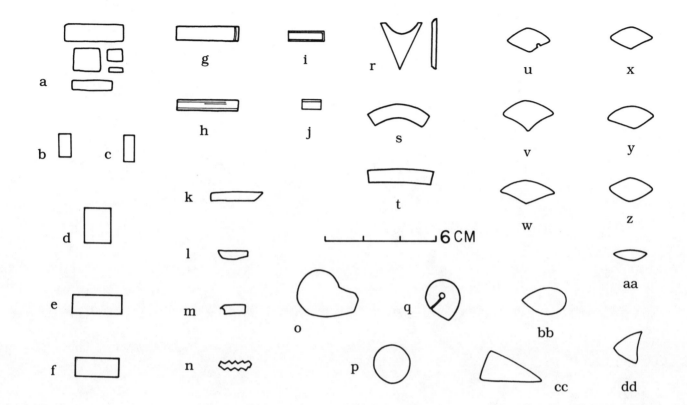

FIGURE 40

Stone Vessels and Vessel Production

	mf	BL	DC	Feat.	Description
a.	1446	—	41	—	white marble
b.	2098	2	35	71	calcite
c.	2192	4B	29	65	calcite
d.	6574	2	35	118	calcite
e.	2334	2	36	155	calcite
f.	1122	—	41	—	incised talc rock
g.	9961	2	35	131	chlorite
h.	—	2	29	—	schist
i.	6055	3A	37	260	limestone (?), tool marks
j.	7305	—	39	—	incised, crosshatched area is painted red
k.	9849	9	34	—	incised, crosshatched area is painted red

Note: 9 in the BL column is stratum.

FIGURE 40

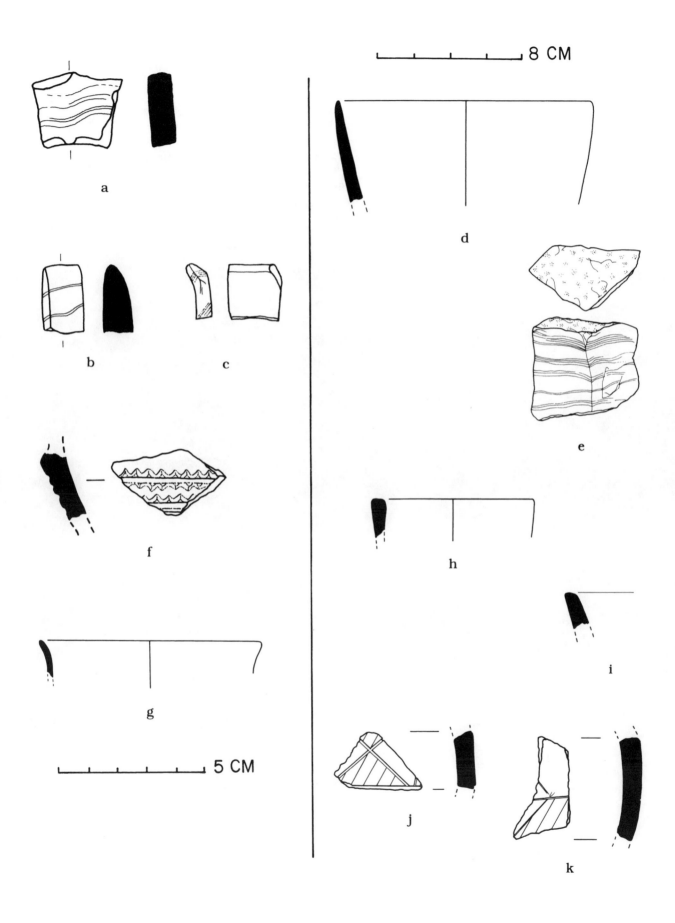

FIGURE 41

Stone and Plaster Vessels

	mf	BL	DC	Feat.	Description
a.	3746	5	21	353	travertine, paint on rim
b.	174	2	35	71	green and brown banded marble (travertine)
c.	1029	2	36	156	banded marble (travertine)
d.	1047	9	34	—	plaster or limestone
e.	189	3A	21	34	Pl. 21d, plaster, incised, hatched area painted red, black area painted black
f.	1127	2	36	106	plaster or limestone grey-black spots inside and outside

Note: 9 in the BL column is Stratum.

FIGURE 41

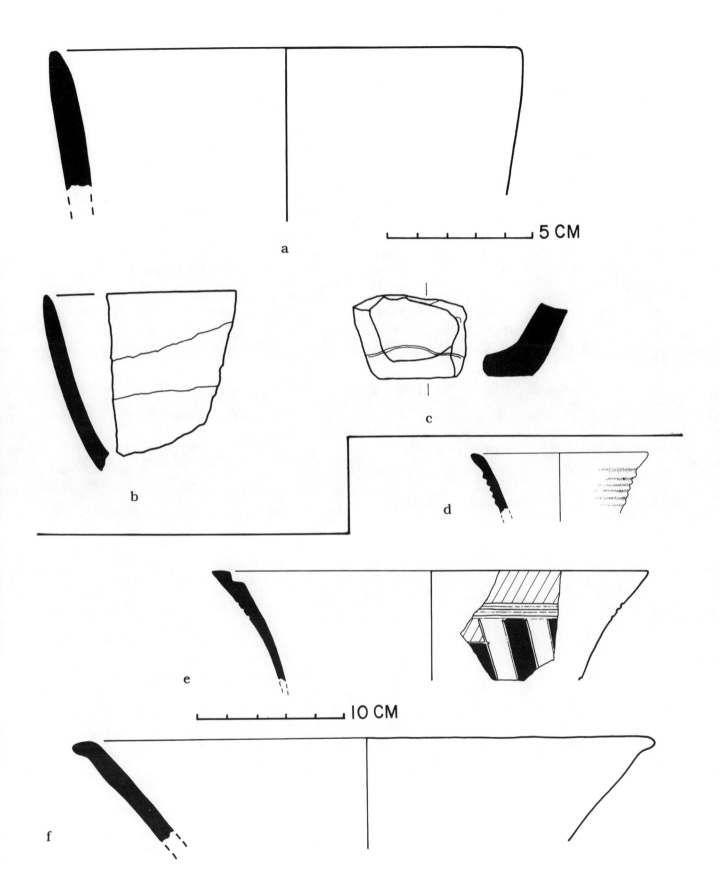

FIGURE 42

Miscellaneous Objects

	mf	BL	DC	Feature	Description
a.	1913	2	37	207	fired ceramic wheel, straw tempered buff ware with grey core. From an unmixed lot, wheels like this are common in Kaftari, but very rare in Banesh
b.	7281	4A	22	236	conical clay jar stopper
c.	530	2	35	118	fired grit tempered ceramic wheel; black paint on buff surface; from a mixed lot, possibly Kaftari
d.	6810	4A	22	236	fired grit tempered ceramic tube, possibly a tuyère
e.	1737	—	31	—	baked clay humped bull spout, red matte surface, possibly slipped; assigned to Banesh on stylistic grounds
f.	655	2	28	165	Pl. 21b, unfired clay bull figurine
g.	656	2	28	165	Pl. 21a, unfired clay human figurine
h.	576	2	35	154	chipped slate boring tool, signs of wear
i.	7304	4A	37	66	fine grey stone rubbing tool, pecked, has thin striations on convex surface

FIGURE 42

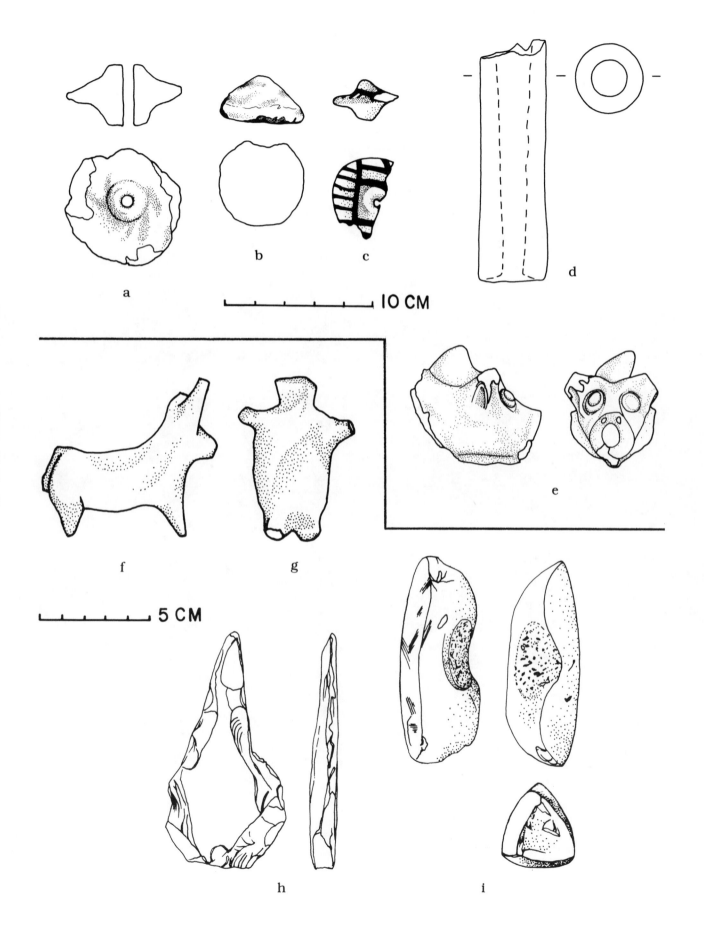

a

b

c

d

10 CM

f

g

e

5 CM

h

i

FIGURE 43

Miscellaneous Objects

	mf	BL	DC	Feat.	Description
a.	590	2	21	131	carved dentalium; spiral bands
b.	1030	—	39	—	Pl. 21c, gold foil leopard with impressed or incised decoration, ln. 2.5 cm; found on dump while excavating BL 3A
c.	5082.1	4A	21	281	2 gold foil beads; found with a white and blue frit bead (mf 5082.2)
d.	1289	3A	37	260	dark red whorl or bead
e.	1907	2	29	129	black soapstone (?) angular object; inside smooth, carving marks on outside
f.	1906	3A	35	268	stone celt (?), carving marks visible
g.	604	2	37	128	oval shaped unfired clay plug

FIGURE 43

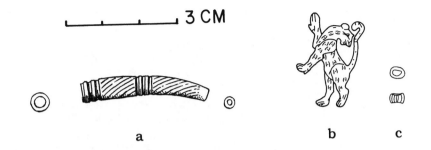

a   b   c

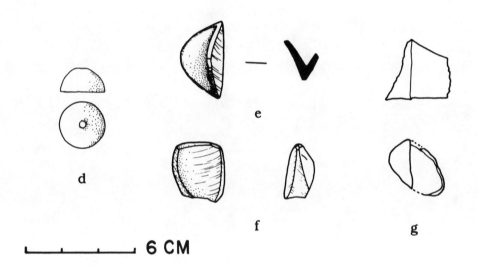

d   e   f   g

FIGURE 44

Seals and Sealings

	mf	BL	DC	Feat.	Description
a.	1901	4A	35	307	Pl. 22b, design 1, early P-E figural, white stone or plaster (?), 1:1.2
b.	1903	4A	35	241	design 3, early P-E figural, white plaster, 1:1.2
c.	1692	3B	29	222	design 7, early P-E figural, 1 sealed tablet (?)
d.	1462	3A	23	271	Pl. 22d, design 11, wheelcut figural, 3 jar sealings (mf 1468, 1469) from the same context
e.	1558	9	23	-	design 18, classic P-E figural, 1 jar sealing
f.	1654	9	23	-	design 19, classic P-E figural, 2 jar sealings from the same context
g.	623	2	37	128	Pl. 22a, design 37, 1 sealing, function unknown
h.	1473	3A	23	271	design 21, classic P-E figural, 43 jar sealings, 6 from this context and 37 from Stratum 9, DC 23

Note: 9 in BL column is stratum.

FIGURE 44

a

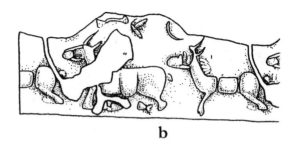

b

c

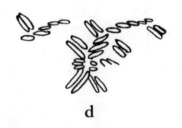

d

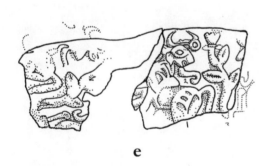

e

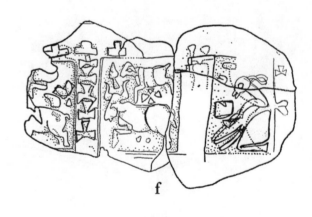

f

g

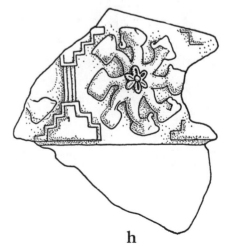

h

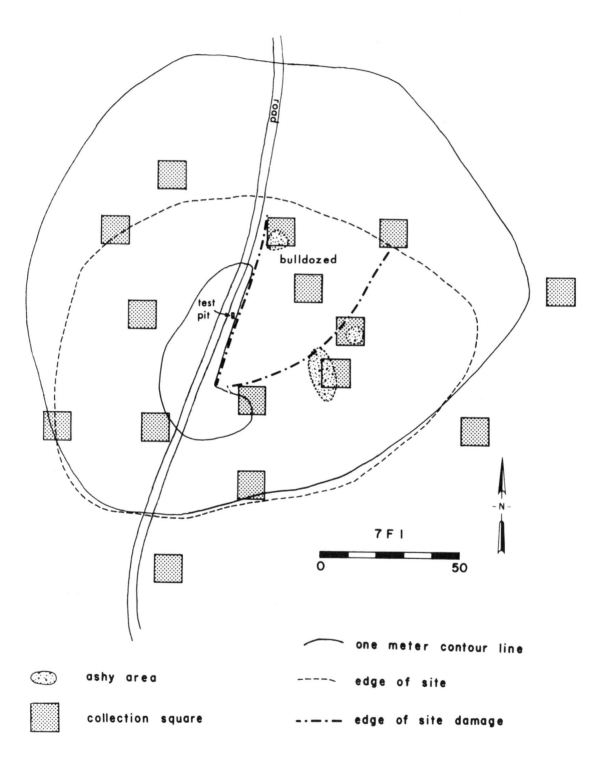

road

bulldozed

test
pit

7 F I

0   50

- N -

one meter contour line

ashy area

edge of site

collection square

edge of site damage

Plan of Tal-e Kureh.

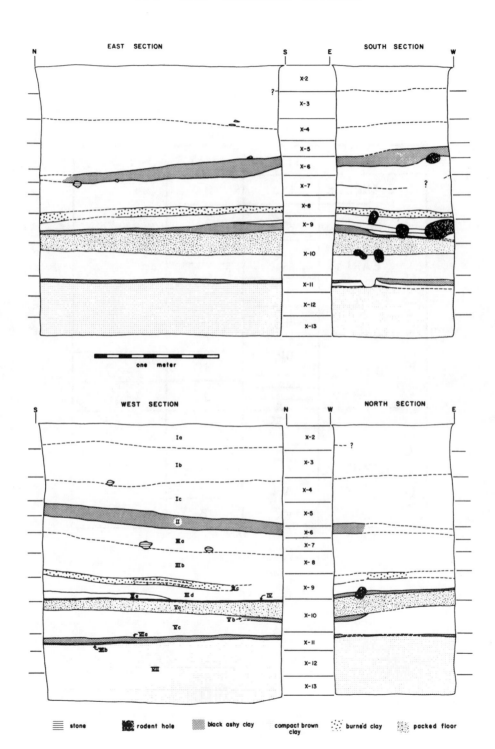

7FI TEST EXCAVATION SECTIONS

one meter

stone   rodent hole   black ashy clay   compact brown clay   burned clay   packed floor

Sections: Test Excavation.

	PHASE	STRATUM	LOT	C-14 DATE
B	E. MIDDLE	I-a	2	
A		I-b	3	
N	EARLY	I-c	4	
E			5	
S		II	6	
H		III-a	7	
	INITIAL	III-b	8	3350-3370 ±280
		c d e	9	3150 ±240
L		V-a	10	3770 ±300
A		V-c		
P	TERMINAL	VI	11	
U		VII	12	
I			13	

Phase Structure.

1. L. 13 O.D. uncertain. Unclassified rim, rough slipped ware; red with red (2.5YR 4/4) interior and gray (10R 4/1) exterior slip, heavy coarse grit temper.
2. L. 12 O.D. uncertain. Pinched rim bowl, Banesh grit tempered ware; red with red (2.5YR 5/6) slip and interior and exterior streak burnishing, medium coarse grit temper.
3. L. 10 O.D. uncertain. Flaring neck jar, Banesh grit tempered ware, red with red (2.5YR 6/6) slip, medium grit temper with lime pops.
4. L. 10 O.D. 10 cm. Flaring neck jar, rough slipped ware; red with red (10R 4/4) slip, medium coarse grit temper.
5. L. 10 Vessel diameter uncertain. Painted 'X' pattern, Asupas ware(?); buff unslipped with thin red paint, medium coarse grit temper.
6. L. 10 B.D. 6.5 cm. Ring base, rough slipped ware; brown-orange body with gray core and brown-orange mot tled slip, heavy coarse grit temper. Ring is molded onto a flat string-cut base.
7. L. 10 O.D. 32 cm. Folded pinched jar rim, Banesh grit tempered ware; gray with gray (10R 5/1) slip, heavy medum grit temper.
8. L. 9 O.D. uncertain. Unclassified jar rim, rough slipped ware; brown with gray (N 4/0) slip, medium coarse grit temper.
9. L. 9 O.D. uncertain. Flaring neck jar, rough slipped ware; brown with brown (5YR 6/4) slip, heavy medium grit temper.
10. L. 10 O.D. 32 cm. Folded pinched jar rim, Banesh grit tempered ware; red with red (10R 6/6) slip, heavy medium grit temper with lime pops.
11. L. 9 O.D. 24 cm. Unclassified jar rim, Banesh grit tempered ware; gray with gray (10R 4/1) slip, medium coarse grit temper. Overfired.
12. L. 9 O.D. 16 cm. Unclassified bowl rim, rough slipped ware; brown with brown (5YR 5/3) slip, light fine grit temper.
13. L. 9 O.D. 22 cm. Exterior beveled bowl rim, rough slipped ware; red with red (2.5YR 5/6) slip, very light medium grit temper with lime pops.
14. L. 9 O.D. 9 cm. Horizontal ledge rim, ware uncertain; gray with uncertain slip, medium coarse grit temper. Overfired and possibly a waster.
15. L. 9 O.D. 22 cm. Club rim bowl/jar, rough slipped ware; brown with reddish brown (5R 5/4) slip, very heavy coarse grit temper.
16. L. 9 O.D. 46 cm. Square rim bowl/jar, rough slipped ware; light brown with brown to gray mottled slip, heavy coarse grit temper.
17. L. 9 O.D. 8.5 cm. Hole mouth jar, rough slipped ware; buff with dark gray (5YR 5/1) slip and two white painted bands, light medium grit temper.
18. L. 8 O.D. 12 cm. Unclassified bowl, rough slipped ware; reddish brown with reddish brown (2.5YR 6/4) slip, light medium grit temper.
19. L. 8 O.D. 10 cm. Unclassified bowl, ware uncertain; red without slip, medium coarse grit temper.
20. L. 8 O.D. 6 cm. Unclassified jar, ware uncertain; red without slip, medium grit temper.
21. L. 8 O.D. 12 cm. Hole mouth jar, rough slipped ware; buff with dark gray (10YR 4/1) slip, heavy coarse grit temper.
22. L. 8 O.D. 12 cm. Hole mouth jar, rough slipped ware; bicolor body (red exterior, gray interior) with reddish (5YR 6/4) slip, heavy coarse grit temper.
23. L. 8 O.D. 10 cm. Unclassified jar, ware uncertain; red without slip, medium grit temper.
24. L. 8 O.D. 26 cm. Club rim bowl/jar, rough slipped ware; light red with yellowish red (2.5YR 6/8) slip, light medium grit temper.

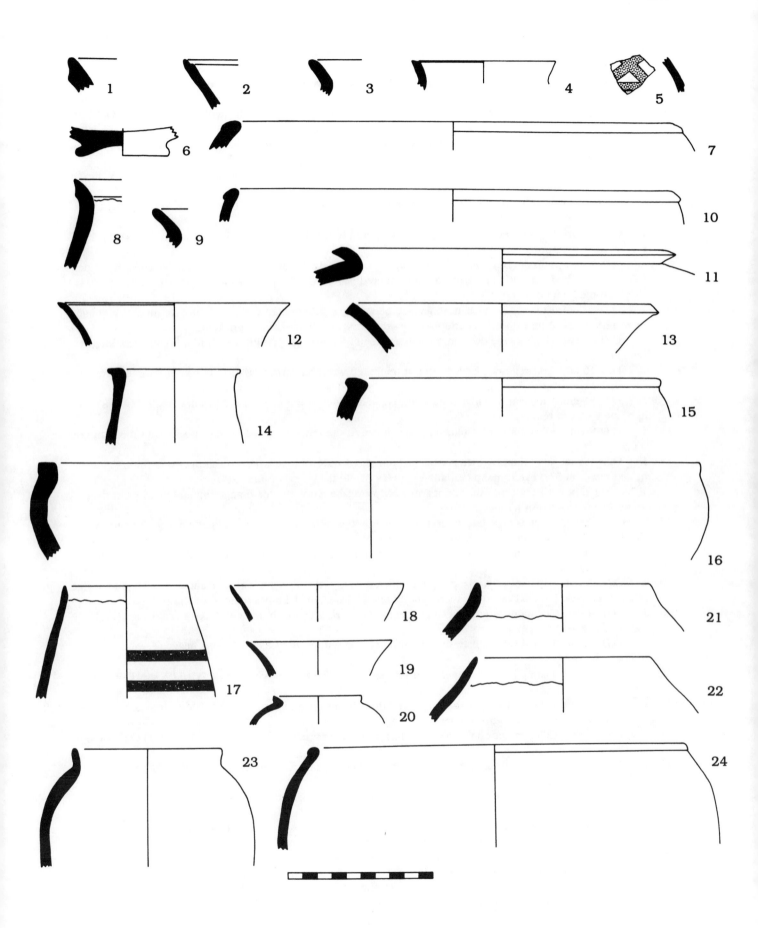

1. L. 8 O.D. 20 cm. Unclassified rim, Banesh grit tempered ware; red with red (10R 5/6) slip, light medium grit temper.
2. L. 8 O.D. 20 cm. Horizontal ledge rim, Banesh grit tempered ware; red with red (10R 6/7) slip, medium coarse grit temper.
3. L. 8 O.D. 28 cm. Exterior beveled bowl, Banesh grit tempered ware; reddish brown with red (10R 5/4) slip, medium coarse grit with some lime pops.
4. L. 8 O.D. 12 cm. Horizontal ledge rim, Banesh grit tempered ware; red with red (2.5YR 6/6) slip, light medium grit temper.
5. L. 8 O.D. 14 cm. Exterior beveled bowl or jar, rough slipped ware; red with reddish brown (10R 5/6) slip, medium grit temper with some lime pops.
6. L. 7 O.D. 22 cm. Unclassified bowl, rough slipped ware; brown with reddish brown (10R 5/3) slip, light fine grit temper.
7. L. 7 O.D. 28 cm. Unclassified bowl, Banesh grit tempered ware; brown with reddish brown (10R 5/4) slip, light medium grit temper.
8. L. 7 O.D. 36 cm. Club rim bowl, Banesh grit tempered ware; red with uncertain slip, medium coarse grit temper.
9. L. 7 O.D. 16 cm. Unclassified jar, Banesh grit tempered ware; reddish brown with reddish brown (2.5YR 5/4) slip, light medium grit temper.
10. L. 7 O.D. 32 cm. Club rim bowl, Banesh grit tempered ware; pale orange with red (10R 5/6) interior and light brown (5YR 6/4) exterior slip (variation appears due to firing), heavy coarse grit temper.
11. L. 7 O.D. 20 cm. Horizontal ledge rim, Banesh grit tempered ware; buff with red (10R 5/4) slip, medium grit temper.
12. L. 7 O.D. 16 cm. Collared neck jar, Banesh grit tempered ware; buff with red (2.5YR 5/2) interior and gray (2.5YR 4/1) exterior slip (variation appears due to firing), heavy medium grit temper.
13. L. 7 O.D. 36 cm. Club rim bowl/jar, rough slipped ware; reddish orange with reddish orange (2.5YR 6/8) slip, light medium grit temper.
14. L. 7 O.D. 9 cm. Hole mouth jar, rough slipped ware; reddish orange with red (10R 4/6) slip, light medium grit temper.
15. L. 7 O.D. 38 cm. Club rim bowl/jar, Banesh grit tempered ware; orange with reddish brown (2.5R 4/4) interior and red (10R 5/4) exterior slip (variation appears due to firing), medium coarse grit temper.
16. L. 7. Painted bow tie pattern, Banesh grit tempered ware; orange with pale orange slip and black paint over white, heavy coarse grit temper.
17. L. 7. Black painted bands on white, Banesh grit tempered ware; pale orange with lightly burnished dark red slip, light medium grit temper with some lime pops.
18. L. 7 O.D. 24 cm. Club rim bowl, rough slipped ware; red with mottled pinkish red (5YR 6/6) slip, medium coarse grit temper.
19. L. 7 O.D. 18 cm. Flaring neck jar, Banesh grit tempered ware; red body with gray core and red (10R 5/6) interior and gray exterior (10R 4/1) slip (variation appears due to firing), medium grit temper with lime pops.
20. L. 7 O.D. 30 cm. Flaring neck jar, Banesh grit tempered ware; greenish body with flaky gray (10YR 5/1) slip, medium coarse grit temper.
21. L. 7 O.D. 18 cm. Folded rim jar, Banesh grit tempered; red with pink (2.5YR 7/4) slip, heavy very coarse grit temper.
22. L. 7 O.D. 22 cm. Flaring neck jar, Banesh grit tempered; reddish brown with red (2.5YR 5/5) slip, light coarse grit temper.
23. L. 3 (shown with Lot 6). Black painted bands on white, Banesh grit tempered ware; reddish orange with thin dark red slip, heavy medium grit temper.
24. L. 6 O.D. 16 cm. Collared neck jar, Banesh grit tempered ware; greenish buff with gray (10R 3/1) exterior slip, light medium grit temper.
25. L. 7 O.D. 24 cm. Exterior beveled rim, Banesh grit tempered ware; red with red (7.5R 5/6) slip, heavy very coarse grit temper.
26. L. 6. Other painted pattern, Banesh grit tempered ware; thin red slip with black paint over white, heavy coarse grit temper.
27. L. 6 O.D. 14 cm. Collared neck jar with other painted pattern, Banesh grit tempered ware; red with red (10R 5/8) slip and black paint over white, medium grit temper. May be from same vessel as 65:15.
28. L. 6 O.D. 20 cm. Pinched rim bowl, Banesh grit tempered ware; red with red (2.5YR 4/2) streak burnished interior and lighter red (2.5YR 5/6) burnished exterior, heavy coarse grit temper with some lime pops.
29. L. 6 O.D. 18 cm. Pinched rim bowl, Banesh grit tempered ware; red with red (2.5YR 5/8) streak burnished interior and exterior, medium coarse grit temper with lime pops.

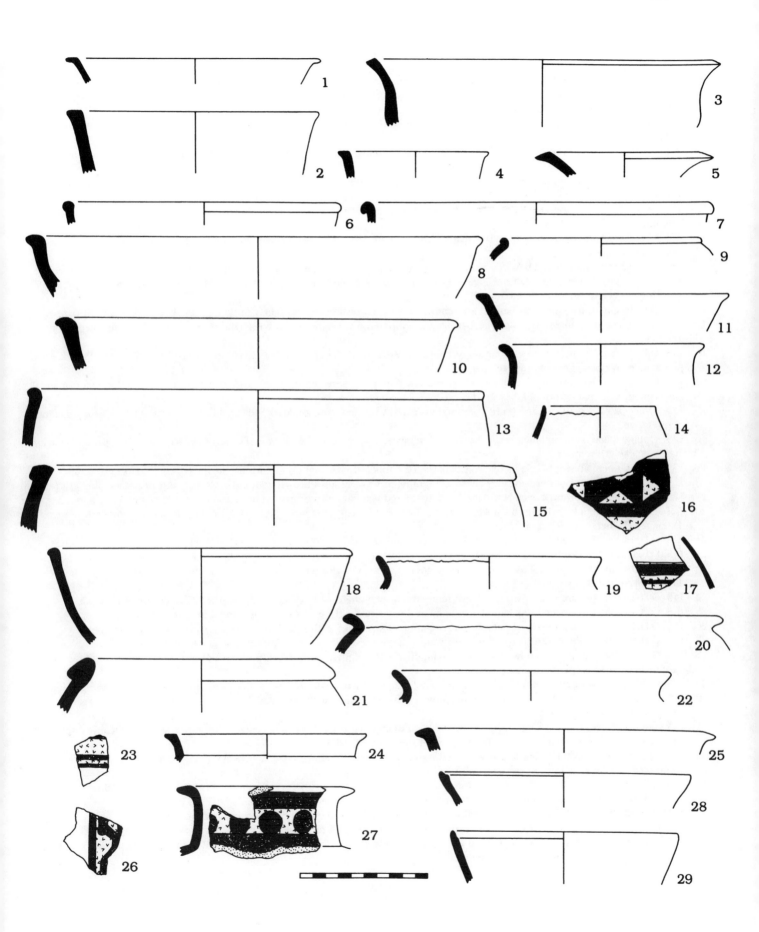

1. L. 6 O.D. 36 cm. Club rim bowl/jar, Banesh grit tempered ware; orangish red with red (10R 6/6) streak burnished interior and exterior slip, heavy coarse grit temper with lime pops.
2. L. 6 O.D. 8 cm. Unclassified (possibly a pedestal base) Asupas ware; buff with no slip and a painted black band, no visible temper.
3. L. 6 O.D. 24 cm. Club Rim bowl, Banesh grit tempered ware; light red with red (10R 4/6) slip and perpendicular black tics on a white painted rim, medium coarse grit temper.
4. L. 6 O.D. 18 cm. Exterior beveled rim, Banesh grit tempered ware; reddish orange with red (10R 5/6) slip) and black tics and band over white paint, heavy coarse grit temper.
5. L. 6 O.D. 7 cm. Exterior beveled rim, rough slipped ware; reddish brown with reddish brown (2.5YR 5/4) slip, heavy medium grit temper.
6. L. 6 O.D. 14 cm. Exterior beveled ledge rim, Banesh grit tempered ware; reddish brown with red (10R 5/4) slip, heavy medium grit temper.
7. L. 5 O.D. 18 cm. Horizontal ledge rim, Banesh grit tempered ware; red with red (10R 5/6) slip, medium coarse grit temper with a few lime pops.
8. L. 5 O.D. uncertain. Horizontal ledge rim, Banesh grit tempered ware; reddish brown with reddish brown (2.5YR 5/4) slip, heavy coarse grit temper.
9. L. 5 O.D. 12 cm. Unclassified bowl/jar, Banesh grit tempered ware; brown with brown (5YR 6/5) slip, light medium grit temper.
10. L. 5 O.D. 12 cm. Exterior beveled rim, Banesh grit tempered ware; reddish orange with gray (10R 4/1) interior and red (10R 4/4) exterior slip (variation appears due to firing), medium grit temper.
11. L. 6 O.D. 16 cm. Flaring neck jar, Banesh grit tempered ware; reddish brown with gray (10R 4/1) slip, heavy medium grit temper.
12. L. 6 O.D. uncertain. Horizontal ledge rim, Banesh grit tempered ware; light brown with light brown (2.5YR 7/4) slip, medium grit temper.
13. L. 5 O.D. 26 cm. Round rim bowl, Banesh grit tempered ware; reddish orange with reddish orange (2.5YR 6/6) slip and black tics on white painted rim, light coarse grit temper.
14. L. 5 O.D. 22 cm. Exterior beveled rim bowl, Banesh grit tempered ware; red with red (10R 5/8) slip and interior and exterior streak burnishing, black painted tics on beveled lip, medium coarse grit temper.
15. L. 5. Other painted pattern, Banesh grit tempered ware; red with gray core and dark red slip, black paint over white, heavy medium grit temper.
16. L. 5. Double black band outlining white, Banesh grit tempered ware; orange with brownish red flaky slip and black paint over white, heavy coarse grit temper.
17. L. 5 O.D. 36 cm. Exterior beveled ledge rim, Banesh grit tempered ware; light buff with no slip, heavy very coarse grit temper.
18. L. 5 O.D. 20 cm. Exterior beveled rim, Banesh grit tempered ware; reddish brown with red (10R 4/6) slip, heavy medium grit temper.
19. L. 5 O.D. 16 cm. Exterior beveled rim, Banesh grit tempered ware; reddish brown with traces of red slip, medium grit temper.
20. L. 5. Carinated shoulder with horizontal black bands, Banesh grit tempered ware; greenish buff with no slip, medium grit temper. Estimated diameter at carination 12 cm.
21. L. 5 O.D. 15 cm. Pinched folded rim jar, rough slipped ware; red with reddish brown (2.5YR 4/4) slip, heavy coarse grit temper.
22. L. 5 0.D. 20 cm. Interior beveled jar, Banesh grit tempered ware; red with red (2.5YR 5/6) slip, medium coarse grit temper.
23. L. 5 O.D. 16 cm. Pinched rim bowl, Banesh grit tempered ware; red with red (2.5YR 5/6) streak burnished interior and exterior slip, heavy coarse grit temper.
24. L. 5 O.D. 18 cm. Collared neck jar, Banesh grit tempered ware; orange with red (10R 5/6) slip, medium coarse grit temper.
25. L. 5 O.D. 14 cm. Unclassified rim, Banesh grit tempered ware; red with red (10R 5/6) slip, medium grit temper.
26. L. 5 O.D. 17 cm. Collared neck jar, Banesh grit tempered ware; orange with red (7.5R 5/6) slip, heavy coarse grit temper.
27. L. 5 O.D. 9.5 cm. Hole mouth jar, rough slipped ware; red with red (2.5YR 6/8) slip, light fine grit temper.
28. L. 5 O.D. 20 cm. Pinched rim bowl, Banesh grit tempered ware; red with red (2.5YR 5/6) streak burnished interior and exterior slip, heavy coarse grit temper with lime pops.
29. L. 5 O.D. 26 cm. Wide ledge rim, Banesh grit tempered ware; red with reddish gray (10R 4/2) mottled slip, heavy coarse grit temper.
30. L. 5. Impressed band on jar, Banesh grit tempered ware; reddish orange with red streak burnished slip, heavy coarse grit temper. Decoration is wedge impressed.
31. L. 5. Impressed band on jar, rough slipped ware; reddish orange with red slip, heavy coarse grit temper. Decoration above shallow groove is wedge impressed, and a scar from a pierced round lug is visible.
32. L. 5. Impressed band on jar, Banesh grit tempered ware; orange with reddish orange slip, heavy coarse grit temper. Decoration is impressed lines in a slightly impressed band.
33. L. 5 O.D. uncertain. Club rim bowl/jar, Banesh grit tempered ware; greenish with reddish gray (10R 5/3) interior and white (10YR 8/2) exterior slip (variation appears due to firing), heavy medium grit temper. Overfired.
34. L. 5 O.D. 22 cm. Wide ledge rim, Banesh grit tempered ware; red with red (10R 5/8) slip, heavy coarse grit temper.
35. L. 5 O.D. 22 cm. Collared neck jar, Banesh grit tempered ware; red with red (10R 6/6) slip, heavy coarse grit temper.
36. L. 5 O.D. 46 cm. Club rim bowl/jar, Banesh grit tempered ware; greenish with reddish gray (10R 4/1) slip and light interior and exterior burnishing, heavy medium grit temper.

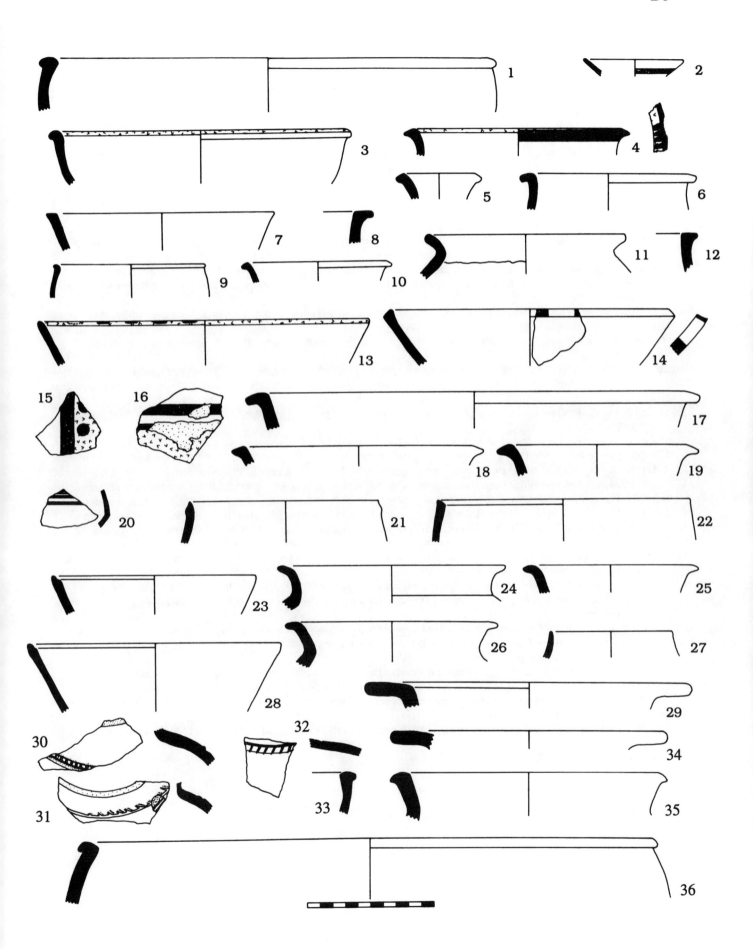

1. L. 4 O.D. 40 cm. Club rim bowl, Banesh grit tempered ware; red with red (10R 5/6) slip, medium grit temper.
2. L. 4. Impressed squiggle, rough slipped ware; orangish brown with no slip, heavy coarse grit temper.
3. L. 4 O.D. 38 cm. Club rim bowl/jar, rough slipped ware; orangish red with red (10R 5/6) slip, heavy coarse grit temper.
4. L. 4 O.D. uncertain. Hole mouth jar, Banesh grit tempered ware; buff with buff (7.5YR 7/4) slip and black painted bands, medium fine grit temper.
5. L. 4 O.D. 36 cm. Club rim bowl/jar, Banesh grit tempered ware; orange with reddish gray (10R 4.5/1.5) slip, heavy coarse grit temper.
6. L. 4. Black bands on white, Banesh grit tempered ware; reddish orange with burnished dark red slip, medium grit temper.
7. L. 4 O.D. 30 cm. Pinched folded rim bowl/jar, Banesh grit tempered ware; greenish with gray (N 4/0) slip, medium coarse grit temper.
8. L. 4 O.D. 14 cm. Collared neck jar, Banesh grit tempered ware; brown with reddish gray (10R 5/2) slip, heavy medium grit temper.
9. L. 4 O.D. 28 cm. Pinched rim bowl, Banesh grit tempered ware; brownish red with brownish red (2.5YR 5/4) streak burnished interior and exterior slip, medium coarse grit temper.
10. L. 4 O.D. 16 cm. Collared neck jar, Banesh grit tempered ware; orange with red (2.5YR 6/6) slip, heavy coarse grit temper.
11. L. 4 O.D. 22 cm. Exterior beveled rim, Banesh grit tempered ware; red with red (10R 5/6) slip, medium grit temper.
12. L. 4 O.D. 10 cm. Horizontal ledge rim, Banesh grit tempered ware; red with fugitive red (10R 6/6) slip, medium grit temper.
13. L. 4. Painted triangles pattern, Banesh grit tempered ware; orange with reddish orange slip and black paint over white, medium coarse grit temper.
14. L. 4. Other painted pattern, Banesh grit tempered ware; reddish brown with red slip and black paint over white, medium grit temper.
15. L. 4 O.D. 15 cm. Exterior beveled rim, Banesh grit tempered ware; reddish orange with reddish orange (2.5YR 5/4) slip, heavy coarse grit temper.
16. L. 4 O.D. 18 cm. Horizontal ledge rim, Banesh grit tempered ware; buff with white (10YR 7/2) slip, medium grit temper.
17. L. 4 O.D. 5 cm. Collared neck jar, Banesh grit tempered ware; orangish red with dark red (10R 4/2) slip, medium coarse grit temper.
18. L. 4 O.D. 32 cm. Pinched folded rim jar, Banesh grit tempered ware; greenish overfired body with gray (N 4/0) slip, heavy coarse grit temper.
19. L. 4 O.D. 14 cm. Round rim bowl, Asupas ware(?); buff with no slip, light fine grit temper.
20. L. 3 O.D. 34 cm. Unclassified jar rim, Banesh grit tempered ware; red with light gray (10R 8/2) slip, heavy medium grit temper.
21. L. 4 O.D. 10 cm. Pinched folded rim, Banesh grit tempered ware; buff with uncertain slip, light coarse grit temper.
22. L. 3 O.D. 24 cm. Pinched folded rim, rough slipped ware; red with brown (2.5YR 6/4) slip, heavy medium grit temper.
23. L. 3 O.D. 20 cm. Unclassified rim, Banesh grit tempered ware; reddish brown with dark red slip (10R 4/2), medium grit temper.
24. L. 3 O.D. 16 cm. Pinched folded rim, Banesh grit tempered ware; brown with uncertain slip, medium coarse grit temper.
25. L. 3 O.D. 18 cm. Flaring neck jar, Banesh grit tempered ware; overfired with uncertain slip, heavy coarse grit temper.
26. L. 3 O.D. 9 cm. Collared neck jar, Banesh grit tempered ware; brown with yellowish (5YR 6/6) slip, medium grit temper.
27. L. 3 O.D. 8 cm. Exterior beveled rim, ware uncertain; red with uncertain slip and rough surface, heavy medium grit temper.
28. L. 3 O.D. 16 cm. Flaring neck jar, Banesh grit tempered ware; red with red (10R 5/6) slip, heavy coarse grit temper.
29. L. 3 O.D. 18 cm. Folded rim jar, Banesh grit tempered ware; red with red (10R 5/6) slip, heavy medium grit temper.
30. L. 3. Perpendicular line painted pattern, Banesh grit tempered ware; orangish red with dark red slip and black paint over white, heavy coarse grit temper.
31. L. 2 O.D. 14 cm. Exterior beveled rim, Banesh grit tempered ware; reddish brown with no slip, medium very coarse grit temper.
32. L. 2 O.D. 16 cm. Horizontal ledge rim bowl, Banesh grit tempered ware; red with white (10YR 8/4) slip and traces of red paint on top of lip, medium coarse grit temper.
33. L. 3. Black bands on white, Banesh grit tempered ware; red with gray core and uncertain slip, heavy medium grit temper.
34. L. 2 O.D. 30 cm. Club rim bowl/jar, Banesh grit tempered ware; light orange with tan (10YR 6/4) slip, temper not noted.
35. L. 2. Perpendicular line and squiggle painted patterns, Banesh grit tempered ware; reddish orange with dark red slip and black paint over white, heavy coarse grit temper.
36. L. 3. Horizontal painted bands, ware uncertain; pinkish buff with yellow unslipped surface, light medium grit temper.

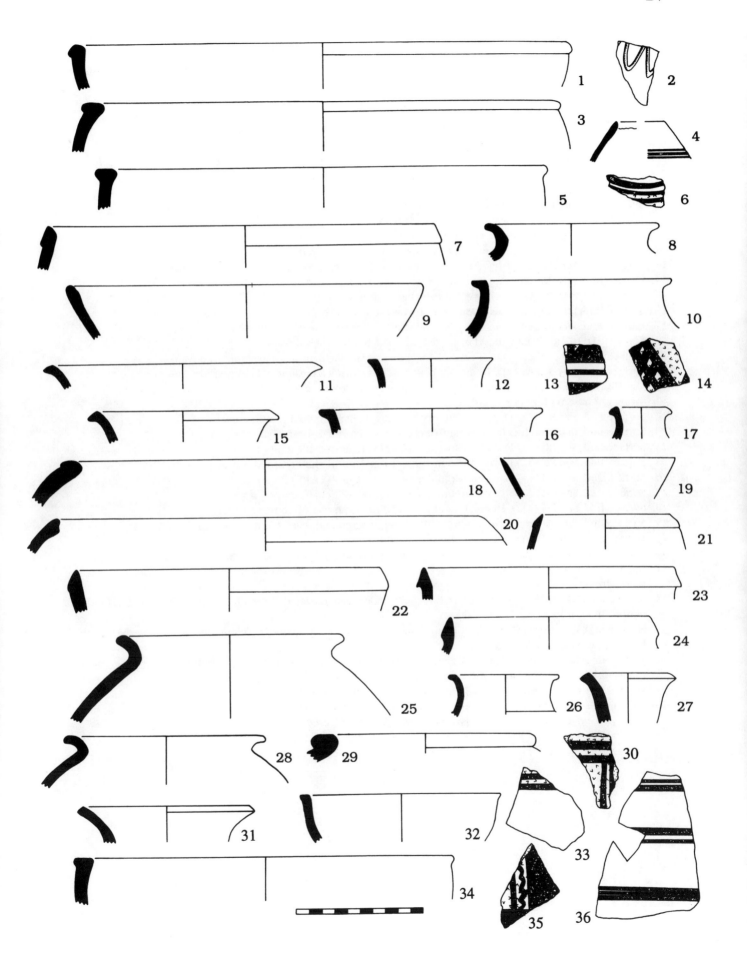

1. Lot 3 Straight short tubular spout, Banesh grit tempered ware.
2. Surface find, Tal-e Kureh Short trough spout, Banesh grit tempered ware; red with uncertain slip, light medium grit temper.
3. Surface find, Tal-e Kureh Short trough spout, Banesh grit tempered ware?; buff with no slip, light medium grit temper.
4. Surface find, Tal-e Kureh O.D. 14 cm. Pierced chaff tempered bowl, Banesh chaff tempered ware.
5. Surface find, Tal-e Kureh O.D. 14 cm. Pierced chaff tempered bowl, Banesh chaff tempered ware.
6. Surface find, Tal-e Kureh O.D. 16 cm. Pierced chaff tempered bowl, Banesh chaff tempered ware.
7. Surface find, Tal-e Kureh O.D. 14 cm. Pierced chaff tempered bowl, Banesh chaff tempered ware.
8. Surface find, Site 7G7 Straight sided goblet base, Banesh chaff tempered ware.
9. Surface find, Site 8G35 Straight sided goblet base, Banesh chaff tempered ware.
10. Lot 9 Beveled rim tray, Banesh chaff tempered ware.
11. Surface find, Tal-e Kureh Beveled rim tray, Banesh chaff tempered ware.
12. Surface find, Tal-e Kureh Beveled rim bowl, Banesh chaff tempered ware.
13. Surface find, Tal-e Kureh Beveled rim bowl, Banesh chaff tempered ware.
14. Surface find, Tal-e Kureh Drain spout (?), Banesh chaff tempered ware.
15. Surface find, Site 7G16 Banesh tray, Banesh chaff tempered ware.
16. Surface find, Tal-e Kureh Banesh tray, Banesh chaff tempered ware.
17. Surface find, Tal-e Kureh Banesh tray, Banesh chaff tempered ware.
18. Lot 11 O.D. 16 cm. Shallow bowl or jar rim, Banesh chaff tempered ware.
19. Surface find, Tal-e Kureh O.D. 18 cm. Shallow bowl or jar rim, Banesh chaff tempered ware.
20. Surface find, Tal-e Kureh O.D. 18 cm. Shallow bowl or jar rim, Banesh chaff tempered ware.
21. Lot 3 B.D. 6 cm. Flat base, Banesh grit tempered ware; buff with gray (5YR 5/1) slip, medium grit temper. String cut base with potter's mark.
22. Surface find, Site 8G37 O.D. 20 cm. Pinched goblet rim, Banesh chaff tempered ware.
23. Surface find, Tal-e Kureh O.D. uncertain Thickened goblet rim, Banesh chaff tempered ware.
24. Surface find, Site 8G37 O.D. 14 cm. Round goblet rim, Banesh chaff tempered ware.
25. Surface find, Site 8G35 O.D. 18 cm. Round goblet rim, Banesh chaff tempered ware.
26. Surface find, Site 8G35 O.D. 22 cm. Round goblet rim, Banesh chaff tempered ware.
27. Surface find, Site 7G7 O.D. 14 cm. Round goblet rim, Banesh chaff tempered ware.
28. Surface find, Site 7G7 O.D. 18 cm. Round goblet rim, Banesh chaff tempered ware.
29. Surface find, Tal-e Kureh Ceramic 'spoon,' Banesh grit tempered ware; brown with tan (7.5YR 7/4) slip, heavy coarse grit temper. Potter's mark on interior of object.
30. Surface find, Tal-e Kureh Ceramic 'spoon,' Banesh grit tempered ware; red with no slip, medium grit temper.
31. Lot 5 O.D. 8 cm. Ceramic ring scraper, ware unclassified; brown with no visible temper. Inner upper edge is worn sharp.
32. Surface find, Tal-e Kureh O.D. 9 cm. Ceramic ring scraper, ware unclassified; green (overfired) with no visible temper. Inner upper edge is worn sharp.
33. Surface find, Tal-e Kureh O.D. 9 cm. Ceramic ring scraper, ware unclassified; yellow buff with no visible temper. Inner upper edge is worn sharp.
34. Surface find, Tal-e Kureh O.D. 8 cm. Ceramic ring scraper, ware unclassified; yellow buff with no visible temper. Inner upper edge is unworn. Potter's mark on exterior of ring.
35. Lot 3 O.D. 14 cm. Flaring neck jar, Banesh white grit tempered ware.
36. Lot 3 O.D. 20 cm. Flaring neck jar, Banesh white grit tempered ware.
37. Lot 6 O.D. uncertain. Flaring neck jar, Banesh white grit tempered ware.
38. Lot 8 O.D. 18 cm. Flaring neck jar, Banesh white grit tempered ware.

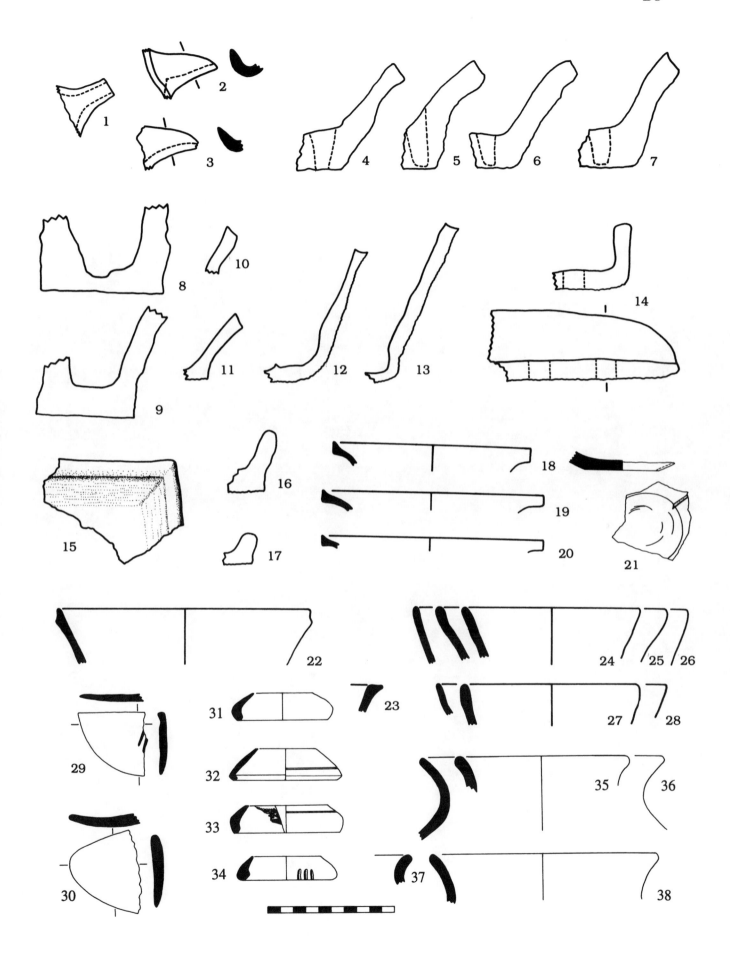

Plates

PLATE 1

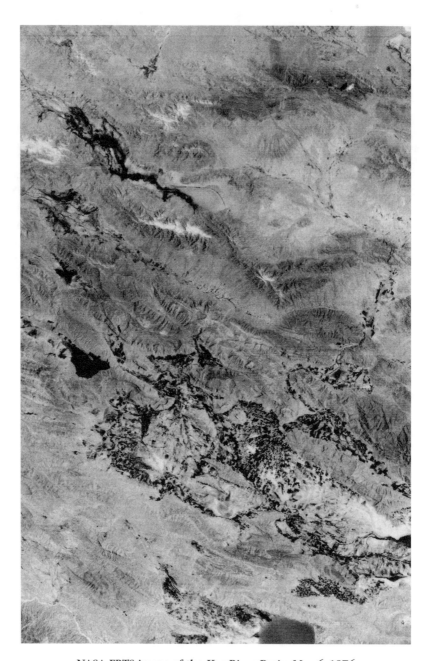

NASA ERTS image of the Kur River Basin, May 6, 1976.

PLATE 2

Aerial view of Operation ABC from the South with Operation GHI in the background.

PLATE 3

Operation ABC from the South (Building levels 2–5 indicated by roman numerals).

PLATE 4

Operations A and B from the North, 1971, Erosion Surface 7 in the background capping Wall 28 of BL 2; BL 3A walls outlined in lower right.

PLATE 5

a. BL 5 from the East.

b. BL 5 from the North.

PLATE 6

a. BL 4, South, from the West.

b. BL 4, North, from the West.

PLATE 7

a. BL 4, stone foundation of Wall 240.

b. BL 4, black and white wall paint in Door 321.

PLATE 8

BL 3 from the South showing wall paintings.

PLATE 9

BL 3 from the North showing wall paintings; BL 2 Walls 104 and 105 in the foreground.

PLATE 10

a. BL 3, Hearth in Room 35.

b. BL 3, Niche in Room 35.

PLATE 11

a. BL 3 wall painting, Figs. 15c, 14:5.

b. BL 3 wall painting, Figs. 18a, 14:19.

PLATE 12

a. BL 3 wall painting, Figs. 17b, 14:16.

b. BL 3 wall painting, Figs. 15a, 14:20.

PLATE 13

a. Building Level 2 from the North; left, Pythoi 167 and 168 in Room 71; right Door 170.

b. Building Level 2 from the East.

PLATE 14

a. BL 2 from the North, Wall 104, Rooms 128, 131.

b. BL 2 from the North, Wall 104, Rooms 129, 130.

c. BL 2 clay tile, mf 643.

d. BL 2 reed mat.

PLATE 15

a. Pedestal base goblet, mf 2616, Fig. 22r.

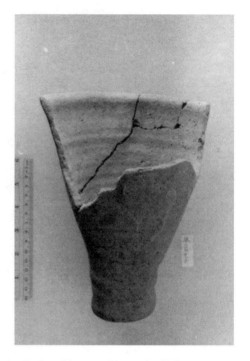

b. Pedestal base goblet, mf 2616, Fig. 22r.

c. Pedestal base goblet, mf 1925.

PLATE 16

a. Relief rope and leaf rim, mf 1731, Fig. 27a.

b. Relief leaf lid, mf 1192, Fig. 27e.

5 cm

d. Relief step motif, fugitive paint, mf 1044, Fig. 27n.

c. Relief sherd, mf 1193, Fig. 27o.

PLATE 17

a. Relief rope and cow, mf 1049, Fig. 27c.

b. Relief rope and horn, mf 1187, Fig. 27h.

c. Relief bovid, mf 1003, Fig. 27j.

d. Relief bovid, mf 1043, Fig. 27d.

e. Relief bovid, mf 1186, 27i.

PLATE 18

a. Incised sign on jar rim, mf 1726, Fig. 28g.

b. Incised sign on jar near base. BL 2, Room 71.

c. Storage jar, nose lug, BL3A, DC 37, Room 211.

d. and e. Storage jar, painted step patter, BL 3A, DC 37, Room 211.

PLATE 19

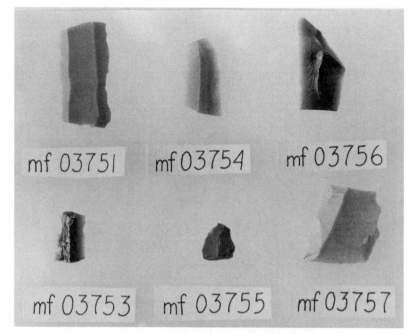

mf 03751 mf 03754 mf 03756

mf 03753 mf 03755 mf 03757

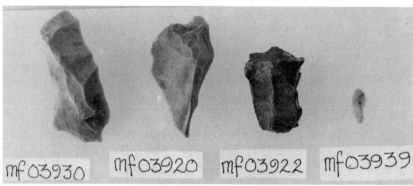

mf 03930 mf 03920 mf 03922 mf 03939

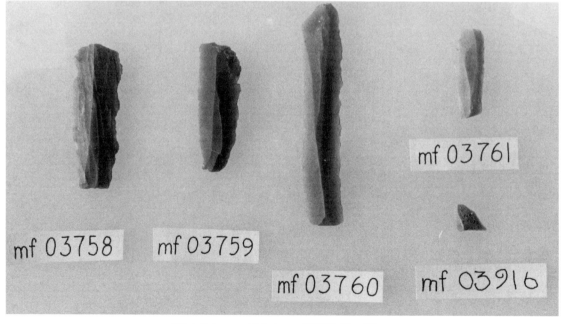

mf 03761

mf 03758 mf 03759

mf 03760 mf 03916

Flint flakes and blades; mf 3922, Fig. 30a.

PLATE 20

a. Stemmed points; mf 579, Fig. 35c and mf 577.

b. Blade with bitumen, mf 1236, Fig. 33c.

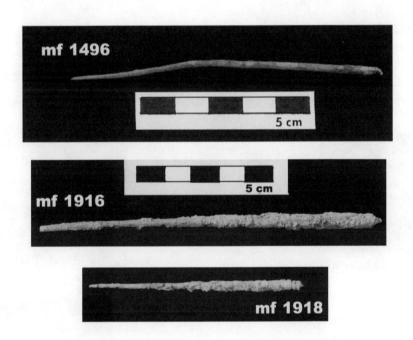

c. Copper pins, mf 1496, 1916, 1918, Fig. 36j, h, g.

d. Copper tube, mf 607, Fig. 36f.

e. Copper hook, mf 1134, Fig. 36a.

PLATE 21

a. Human figurine, mf 656, Fig. 42g.

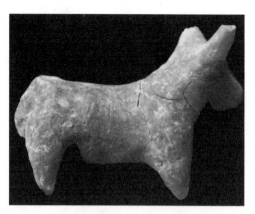

b. Bull figurine, mf 655, Fig. 42f.

c. Gold foil leopard,
mf 1030, Fig. 43b.

d. Incised and painted plaster vessel
fragment, mf 189, Fig. 41e.

e. Proto-Elamite tablet, mf 1685.

PLATE 22

b. Cylinder seal, mf 1901, Fig. 44:a.

a. Seal impression, mf 623, Fig. 44g.

d. Seal Impression, mf 1462, Fig. 44d.

c. Seal impression, mf 1572, compare mf 1473, Fig. 44h.

e. Seal impression, mf 1472.

PLATE 23

a. mf 1085, 200x magnification, right medial dorsal surface; used for cutting grass.

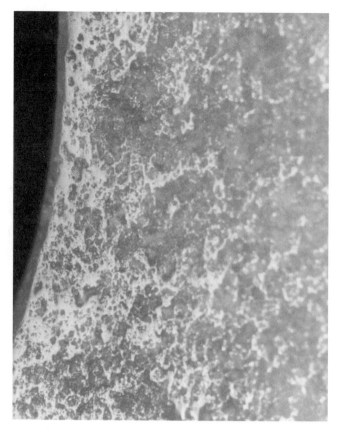

b. mf 2573, 100x magnification, left medial dorsal; used for cutting grass; Fig. 34a.

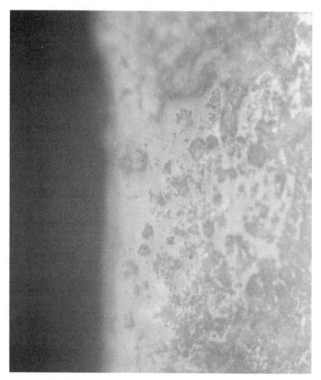

c. mf 2573, 200x magnification, left medial dorsal; used for cutting grass; Fig. 34a.

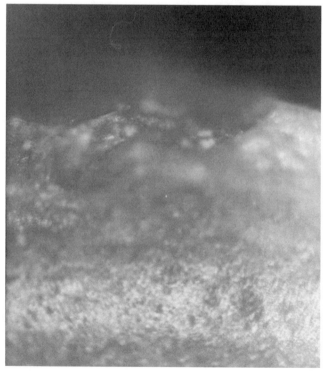

d. mf 6628, 200x magnification, distal edge ventral; used for hide scraping; Fig 35d.

PLATE 24

mf 7026, 200x magnification, distal edge ventral striation;
used for shaving soft stone; Fig. 33e.

PLATE 25

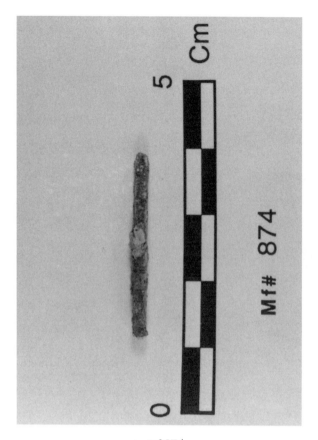

a. mf 874.

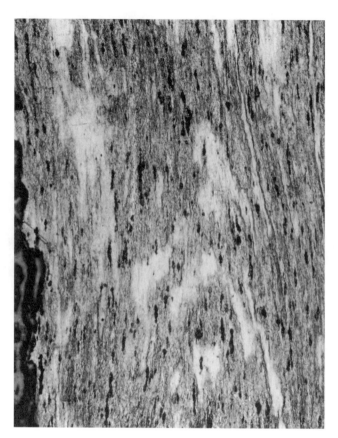

b. mf 874, 100x.

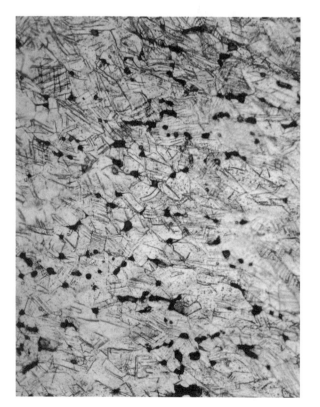

c. mf 1137, 400x.

PLATE 26

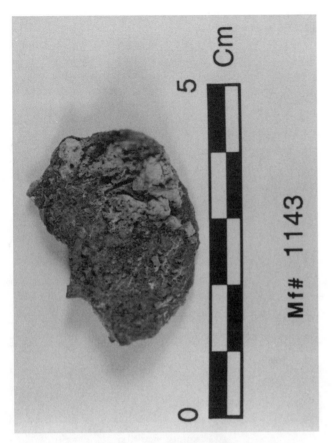

a. mf 1143.

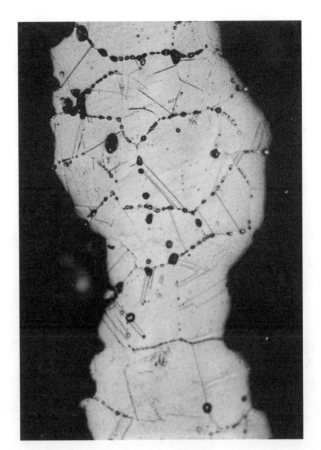

b. mf 1143, 200x.

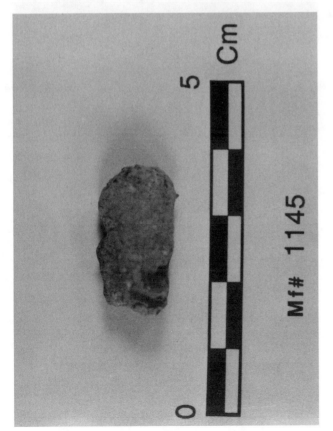

c. mf 1145.2.

PLATE 27

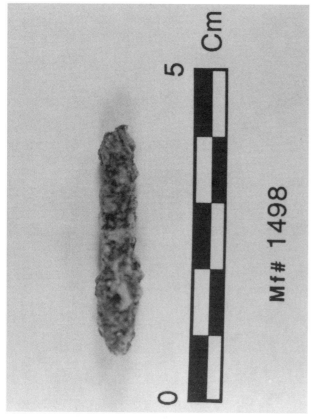

a. mf 1498.

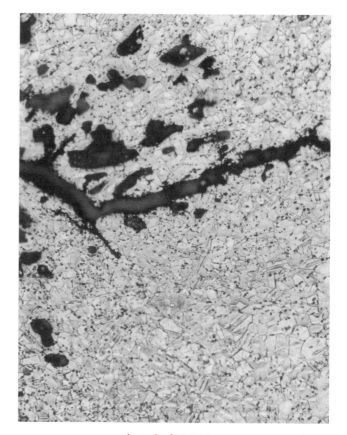

b. mf 1498, 200x.

c. mf 1514.

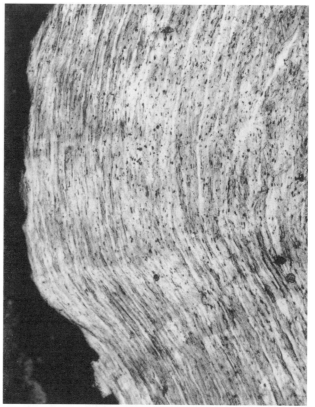

d. mf 1514, 100x.

PLATE 28

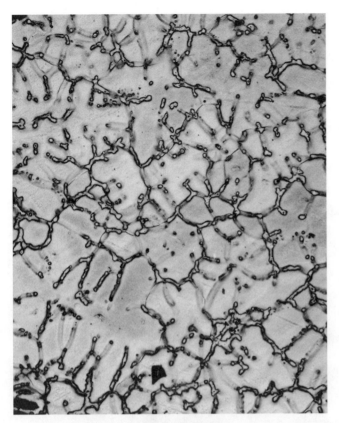

a. mf 1515, 100x.

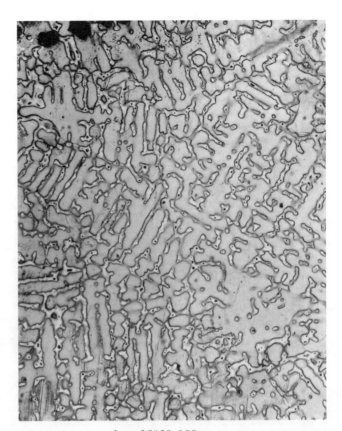

b. mf 2120, 100x.

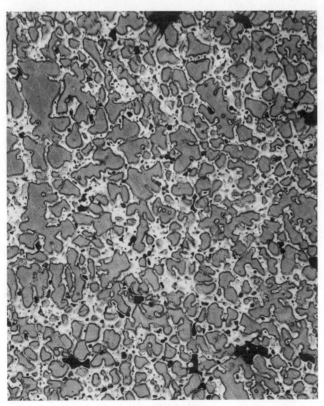

c. mf 3742, 100x.

PLATE 29

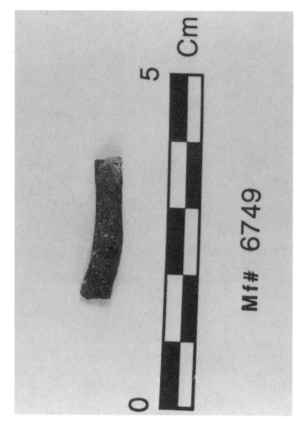

a. mf 6749.

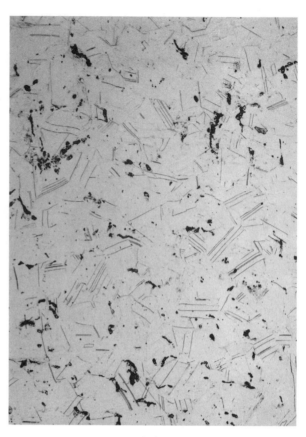

b. mf 6749, 100x.

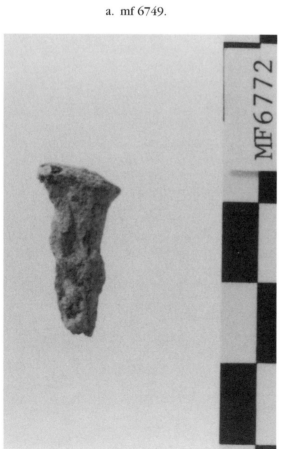

c. mf 6772.

d. mf 6772, 100x.

PLATE 30

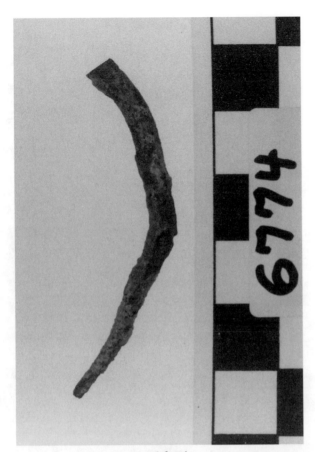

a. mf 6774.

b. mf 9956.

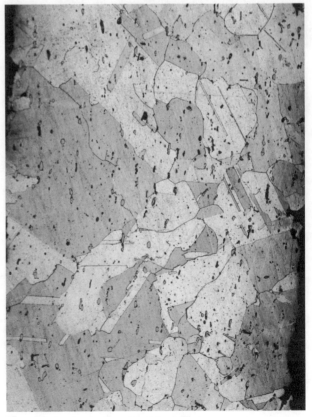

c. mf 9956, 100x.

PLATE 31

a. mf 1144.1.1, 55x.

b. mf 1144.1.2, 400x.

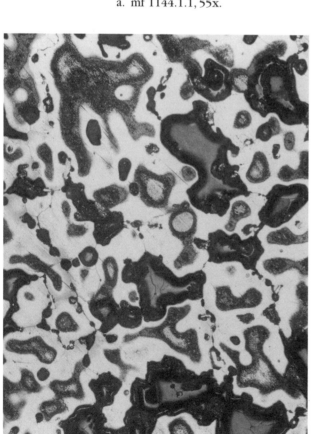

c. mf 1144.2, 100x.

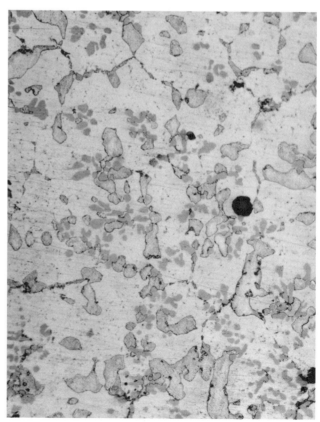

d. mf 1144.3, 400x.

PLATE 32

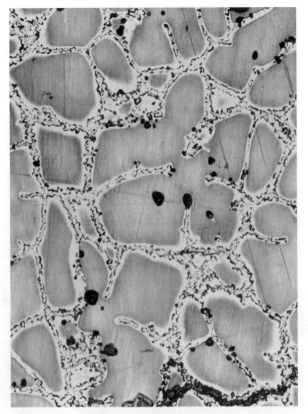

a. mf 1144.4, 100x.

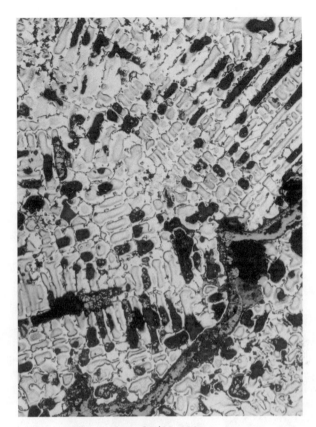

b. mf 1480, 100x.

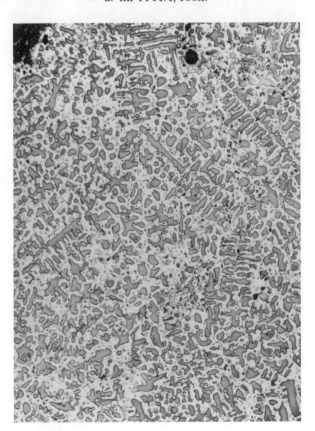

c. mf 1483, 100x.

PLATE 33

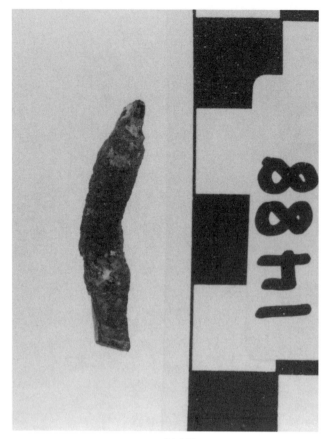

a. mf 1488.

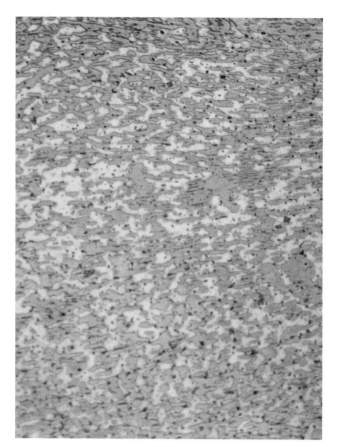

b. mf 1488, 100x.

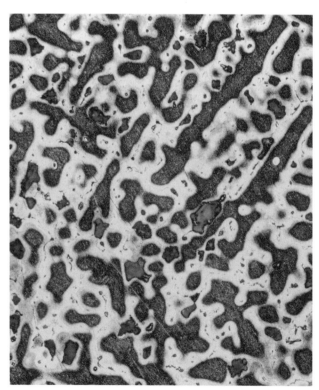

c. mf 3540, 100x.

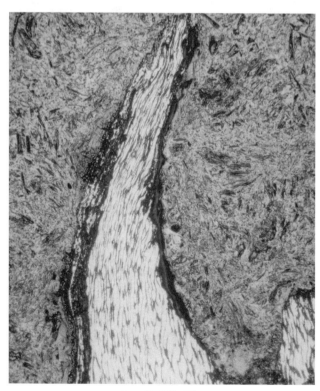

d. mf 3569, 55x.

PLATE 34

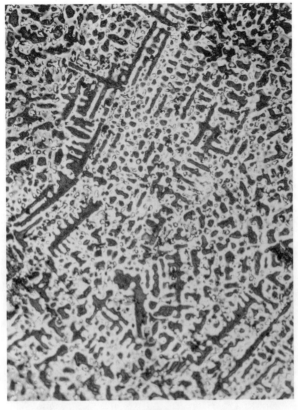

a. mf 3678, 200x.

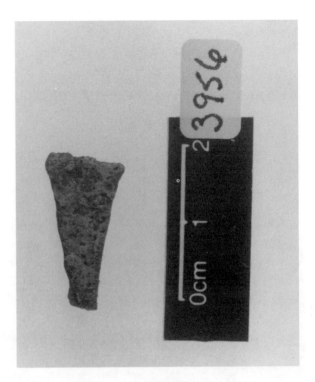

b. mf 3956.

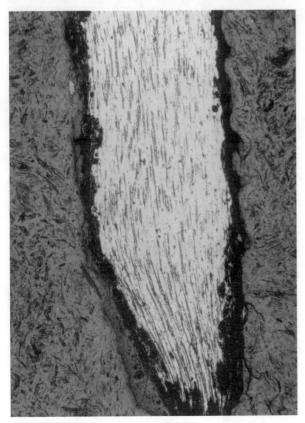

c. mf 3956, 55x.

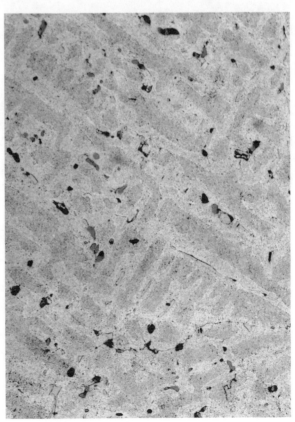

d. mf 3973.2, 100x.

PLATE 35

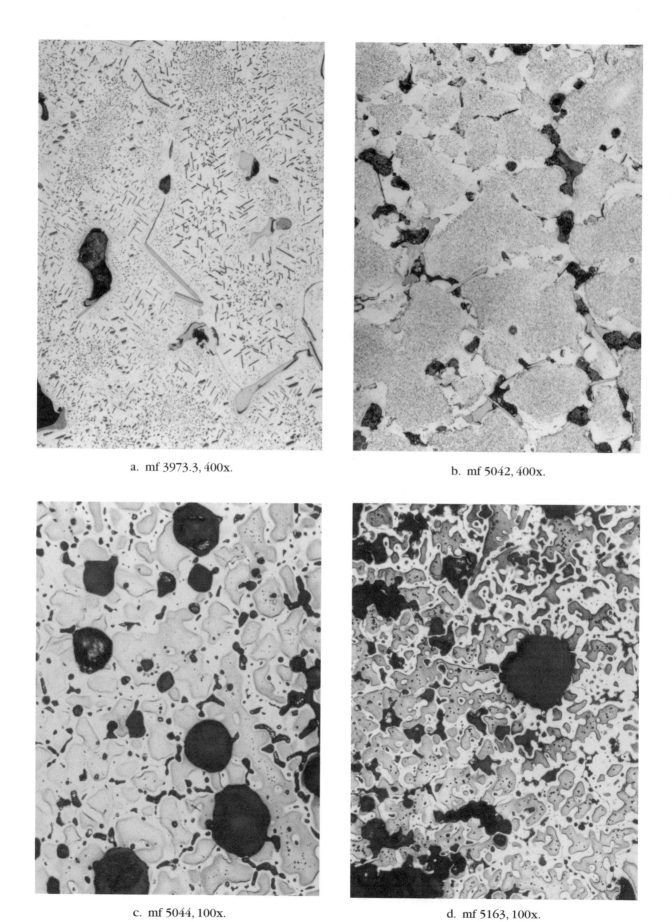

a. mf 3973.3, 400x.

b. mf 5042, 400x.

c. mf 5044, 100x.

d. mf 5163, 100x.

PLATE 36

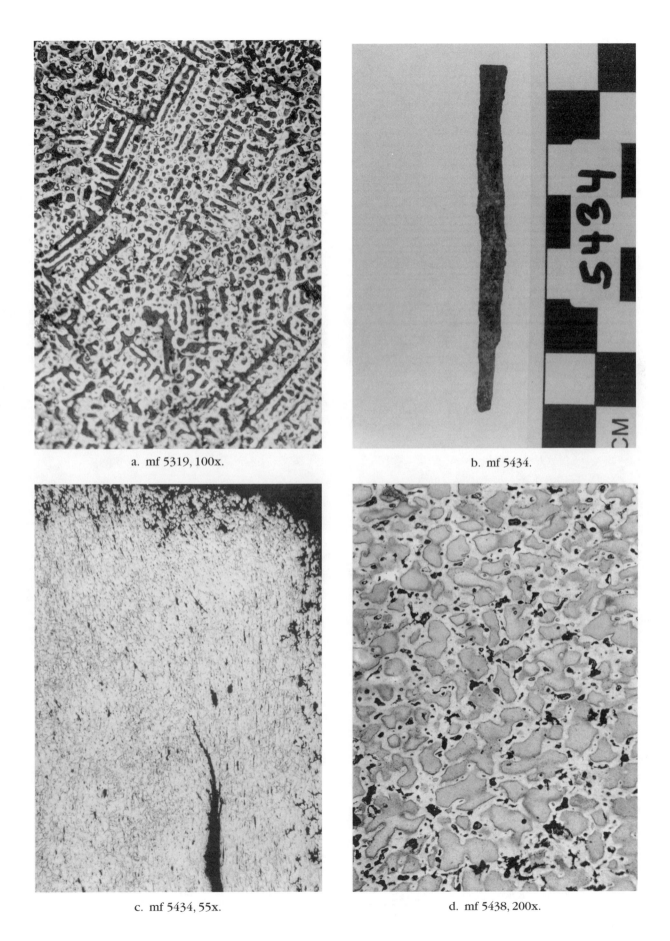

a. mf 5319, 100x.

b. mf 5434.

c. mf 5434, 55x.

d. mf 5438, 200x.

PLATE 37

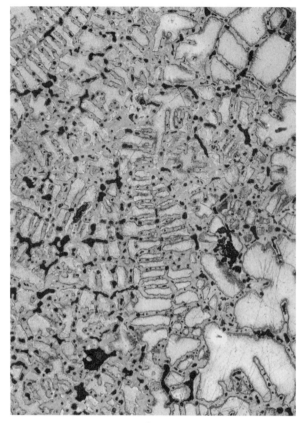

a. mf 5439.1, 100x.

b. mf 5441, 200x.

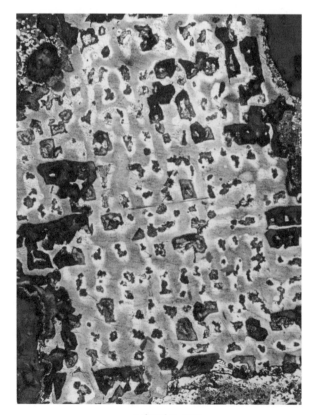

c. mf 6086.2, 100x.

d. mf 6932.

PLATE 38

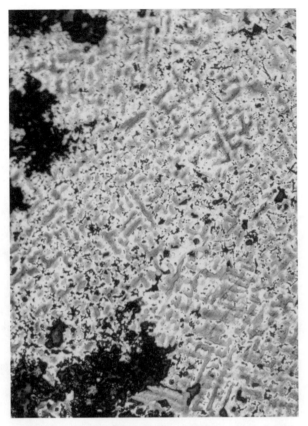

a. mf 6936.1, 100x.

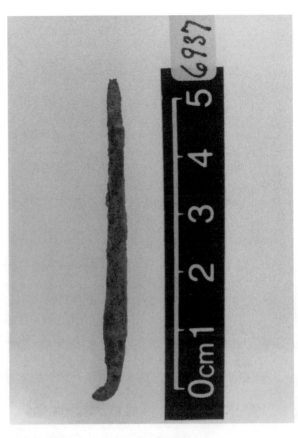

b. mf 6937.

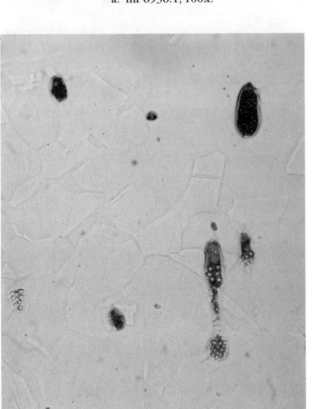

c. mf 6937, 600x.

d. mf 6943, 100x.

PLATE 39

a. mf 7097.

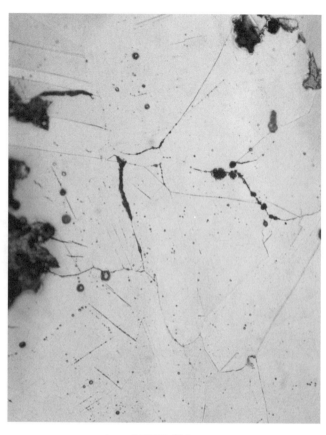

b. mf 7097, 400x.

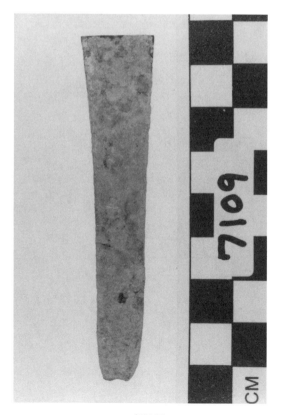

c. mf 7109.

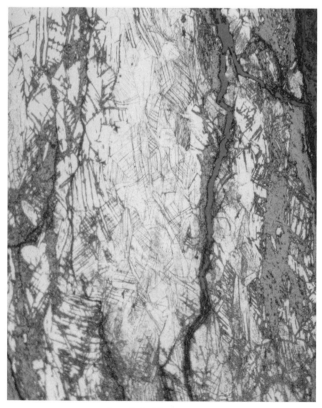

d. mf 7109, 200x.

PLATE 40

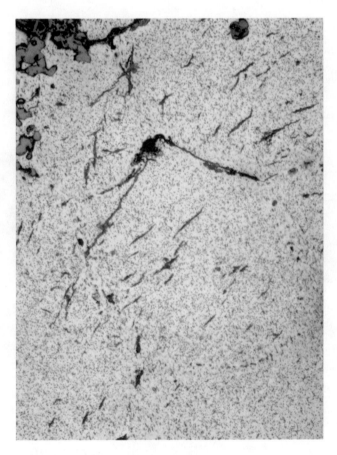

mf 11243, 600x.

PLATE 41

Tal-e Kureh seen from the west.

Index